This book has been prepared by
Laurence Urdang Associates Ltd, Aylesbury

Editor Jennifer Speake MA, B Phil
Assistant editor Sarah Mitchell BA

Series editor Alan Isaacs PhD, BSc

Contributors
Dr Simon Blackburn
Dr Alexander Broadie
Ogilvie M. C. Buchan MA, BA
T. E. Burke MA, PhD
Terrell Carver BA, BPhil, DPhil
John Cottingham MA, DPhil
Graham Curtis BA, MPhil
R. F. Dearden BA, PhD
Jennifer Drake-Brockman MA, BPhil
Antony Flew MA, DLitt
Mary Garay BA
Patrick Gardiner MA
Friedhelm E. Hardy MA, DPhil
Geoffrey Harrison BA, MLitt
Desmond Paul Henry BA, PhD
Alan Isaacs PhD, BSc
Dr Anthony Kenny

N. R. M. de Lange MA, DPhil
Peter Leech BA, MA, PhD
Colin Lyas MA
Ian McMorran MA, DPhil
David A. McNaughton BA, BPhil
Sarah Mitchell BA
Michael Moran BA
Ian R. Netton BA, PhD
G. H. R. Parkinson MA, DPhil
J. F. Procopé PhD
M. A. Proudfoot MA
Stephen Read BA, MSc
G. A. J. Rogers BA, PhD
Mary E. Tiles BPhil, PhD
J. E. Tiles MSc, DPhil
I. C. Tipton MA, B Litt

Preface

'My philosophy is . . .' When a leading figure in the eye of the media is
invited to adorn some ceremonial occasion by discoursing upon the
philosophy of whatever it may be or when we speak of someone taking
something philosophically, the word is being used in a perfectly reputable
and useful sense. In this sense philosophy is a matter of standing back a
little from the ephemeral urgencies to take an aphoristic overview that
usually embraces both value-commitments and beliefs about the general
nature of things.

But, although the two senses are not altogether unrelated, it is with
philosophy in a second sense that this *Dictionary* deals. For better or for
worse, we are concerned here with the very different activity pursued as an
academic discipline by departments of philosophy within institutions of
tertiary education. To the immediate question, 'What (in this sense) is
philosophy?' a good preliminary answer might be that given by a
distinguished and well-loved Cambridge professor. The story is told
that the preferred response of G. E. Moore was to gesture towards his
bookshelves: 'It is what all these are about.' So let us too start by saying
that philosophy is the main subject of most of the writings of Plato; of
Aristotle's *Metaphysics* and *Nicomachean Ethics*; of large parts of the
works of St Thomas Aquinas, Duns Scotus, and William of Ockham; of
the *Meditations* of Descartes; of the *Ethics* of Spinoza and the *Monadology*
of Leibniz; of Locke's *Essay concerning Human Understanding*; of
Berkeley's *Three Dialogues* and *Principles of Human Knowledge*; of
Hume's *Inquiry concerning Human Understanding* and Kant's *Critique of
Pure Reason*; and, finally, in the present century, of Moore's own
Principia Ethica, of Russell's *Our Knowledge of the External World* and
Mysticism and Logic, and of Wittgenstein's *Tractatus Logico-
Philosophicus*.

It is only after we have become acquainted with several specimen problems, and with some distinctively philosophical approaches to these problems, that it can begin to be illuminating to press the question, 'What is it that distinguishes all this as philosophical?' If this tactic strikes you as cowardly, even evasive, then ask yourself how you would set about answering the question 'What is mathematics?', put by someone who had not enjoyed so much as a primary school training in counting and calculation. 'Philosophy' is not a shorthand term; it refers to a kind of activity with which the questioner is most likely to be completely unfamiliar. So the best response to the uninitiate's question, 'What is philosophy?', is not to labour to formulate a neat dictionary definition but instead to offer a few typical philosophical problems as specimens and illustrations, adding whatever remarks may then be necessary to enable enquirers to identify further examples for themselves.

A. N. Whitehead once remarked, with no more exaggeration and distortion than is inevitable in any such epigram, that later philosophy has consisted in a series of footnotes to Plato. So let us use as a prime example, what many contemporaries prefer to call a paradigm case, the topic discussed in *Theaetetus*: 'What is knowledge?' Plato makes it very clear in this dialogue that he is concerned with logical and semantic issues. What does it mean to say – and what is logically presupposed and implied by saying – that something is known? To settle these issues would indeed, in one sense, be to show how knowledge is possible and when and under what conditions it can exist. But Plato is asking the philosopher's logical, conceptual, and semantic questions and these are altogether different from the factual questions asked by the psychologist or the physiologist; their concern would be to investigate the actual mechanisms either of perception or of the expression of assertions in speech or writing. Plato's questions are likewise altogether different from the equally factual questions asked by those whose subject is misleadingly and too narrowly described as the sociology of knowledge. For, in so far as this kind of sociologist really is concerned with knowledge in particular and not beliefs in general (regardless of whether these are or are not known to be true), he is not asking what knowledge essentially is. He is, rather, asking what social conditions promote or inhibit the acquisition of what sorts of knowledge.

As a second paradigm case, one might consider the much disputed issues of 'freewill or predestination' and 'freewill or determinism'. Both phrases are prejudicial and misleading. For the strictly philosophical questions ask what is logically presupposed and logically implied by various kinds of discourse and whether these presuppositions are or are not logically compatible with one another. In the one case it is not a matter of whether the essentials of theism are true or whether we are often (or ever) responsible agents in making our own choices. The relevant question is whether the idea of a creator God, not only all foreseeing but also the sustaining cause of our every action and our very existence, is compatible with the ideas of human responsibility and human choice. Again in the case of the second phrase it is not a matter of whether the Universe is in some sense deterministic nor whether there is in human conduct some reserved area of indeterminism. Here the question is whether the sciences, and in particular the human sciences, presuppose or reveal some form of determinism and whether this is or not logically compatible with whatever may be presupposed or implied by our everyday discourse about choice and human action. To describe these issues as those of freewill *or* determinism, or their theological predecessors as those of freewill *or* predestination, is to beg the central philosophical questions in an incompatibilist sense.

Because the present book sets out to be a dictionary of philosophy in the second of the two senses distinguished earlier, very little attention is given to anything that is philosophical only in the first and more popular interpretation. This, and not European parochialism, is why the classics of Chinese philosophy get such short shrift. The *Analects* of Confucius and the *Book of Mencius* are both splendid, of their kind. But neither sage shows much sign of interest in the sort of question thrashed out in *Theaetetus*. The truth is that these classics contain little argument of any sort. When, later in the same tradition, Mo Tzu speaks of the Will of Heaven and when he repudiates fatalism, he does not attempt to analyse these concepts. What he offers as support for his preferred doctrines is an appeal to either his own authority or that of the Sage Kings, or else he points to the unfortunate practical consequences of people holding alternative views to his own. 'If the gentlemen . . . really want the world to be rich and dislike it to be poor . . . they must condemn the doctrine of fatalism. It is a great harm to the world.'

This is a wholly different ball game from that being played by Aristotle in Chapter IX of his *De Interpretatione* in his discussion of the problem of the seafight. Here he first presents a philosophical argument for fatalism and then dismisses it on the basis of his own counter-argument to show (not that it is antisocial or damaging to the interests of the working class but) that it is invalid.

Because philosophy, as we understand it, is characteristically argumentative and essentially directed towards the determination of what logical relations do and do not obtain, a course in this discipline can be, can indeed scarcely fail to be, a fine mental training. However, once we are fully aware of how totally different the two senses of the word 'philosophy' are, we do need to notice that many of the issues of philosophy as an intellectual discipline are in some way relevant to philosophy as world-outlook. To glimpse this truth we need look no further than our two paradigm cases. If, for instance, either an analysis of the concept of knowledge or an examination of the presuppositions and implications of scientific practice should reveal that authentic objective knowledge is either generally or in some particular spheres impossible, then it must become preposterous to strive to subordinate private practice or public policy to what is thereby proved to be unobtainable. Again, if the findings of the psychological and social sciences really do show that there is no room for choice and for responsibility, then the rational man has somehow to jettison either these ideas or those of the human sciences.

So much for explaining what this *Dictionary* is a dictionary of. And, essentially, it is a dictionary, not an encyclopedia. The majority of items are accounts of the meanings of key words and phrases. We have nevertheless so far departed from true purity of Johnsonian purpose as to admit biographical entries; for the greatest philosophers these entries run to as much as three or four thousand words. We hope that the dictionary's users will find it of value to have both kinds of information in a single volume. A table of symbols and abbreviations has been added on pp. xii–xiii.

Except for this present Preface the whole is heavily cross-referenced. Asterisks preceding a text word or name indicate that the word or name itself constitutes a separate entry, where additional relevant information will be found. In addition there are also explicit verbal injunctions to refer to relevant material under other headings. Although the aim has been to make each individual entry comprehensible and self-sufficient we both hope and expect the normal unit of consultation will be two or three entries rather than one. We, as an editorial team, have encouraged contributors to make a special point of anticipating and correcting common mistakes and popular misconceptions; we hope that many users will detect, and welcome, a certain sense of pedagogic mission. We have not credited particular entries to particular contributors. This is partly because many entries are too short to bear the weight of initials and partly because – in some cases – drastic editing has been necessary in order to preserve uniformity and balance in the book as a whole.

We believe that we have produced a reference book both more comprehensive and in some other ways better than any of its predecessors and competitors. Yet it is obvious that we must have omitted some items that ought to have been included and admitted some interlopers that ought not to have been. So I conclude by inviting detailed criticism, which I shall keep on file until such time as it can be put to constructive use, either by me in the production of a revised edition of the present *Dictionary* or by someone else hoping to do better by learning from and correcting the mistakes that I have missed or made. For, although the other members of the editorial team and the many contributors have collectively and in some cases individually put in far more work than I, there is no escaping the fact that, in the words of Harry Truman: 'The buck stops here.'

Antony Flew

Department of Philosophy
University of Reading
England

Propositional (or sentential) logic

symbol	connective	example	read as
& (ampersand)		$P \& Q$	
$\wedge$	conjunction	$P \wedge Q$	
$\cdot$		$P \cdot Q$	P and Q
$\vee$ (vel)	disjunction	$P \vee Q$	P or Q
$\supset$ (hook)	conditional	$P \supset Q$	P materially implies Q or
$\rightarrow$		$P \rightarrow Q$	(informally) if P then Q
iff	biconditional	P iff Q	P if and and only if Q
$\leftrightarrow$		$P \leftrightarrow Q$	
$\equiv$		$P \equiv Q$	
$\neg$		$\neg P$	not P or it is not the case that P
$-$	negation	$- P$	
$\sim$ (tilde)		$\sim P$	

P, Q or p, q stand for sentences.

Predicate (or quantificational) logic

symbol	description	stand for
F, G	predicate constants	predicates (e.g. " . . . is tall", " . . . runs".)
$a, b, c,$	individual constants	individual names (and function like proper names of objects)
$x, y, z,$	variables	place holders (and function like pronouns)
$\forall$	universal quantifier	"for all . . ." or "for every . . ." $(\forall x)Fx =$ for all x, F is true of x
$\exists$	existential quantifier	"for some . . .", or "there is one . . ." $(\exists x)Gx =$ for some x, G is true of x
ι (iota)	definite description operator	"the unique . . ." $(\iota x)Fx =$ the one and only x that is F
E !	E shriek	"there is exactly one . . ." $(E!x)Fx =$ there is exactly one x that is F

Set theory

symbol		explanation
ϵ (epsilon)	membership	$x \in A$ = x is a member of A
$\subset$	proper inclusion	$A \subset B$ = A is a proper subset of B *or* A is properly included in B (N.B. it is not the case that $A \subset A$)
$\subseteq$	inclusion (subset)	$A \subseteq B$ = A is a subset of B *or* A is included in B (N.B. $A \subseteq A$. A is a subset of A)
$\cap$ (cap)	intersection	$A \cap B$ = the set of all things belonging to both A and B
$\cup$ (cup)	union	$A \cup B$ = the set of all things belonging to A or belonging to B
$\langle \ \rangle$	ordered relation	$\langle x, y \rangle$ = the pair x, y in that order
$\{\}$ (brace)	sets	sets are indicated either (1) extentionally: $\{1, 3, 5, 7\}$ = the set consisting of the numbers 1, 3, 5, and 7. or (2) by definition: $\{x: \phi x\}$ = the set consisting of all things that satisfy the condition ϕ. N.B. (2) is also written $\hat{x}(\phi x)$
$\emptyset$ or 0 or $\{\}$	the null set	the empty set
$\times$	Cartesian product (read as 'cross')	$A \times B = \{\langle x, y \rangle : x \in A, \ \& \ y \in B\}$

Formal languages and systems

symbol	stand for
L	language
S	system
wff	well-formed formula
ϕ, ψ	wffs
Γ, Δ	sets of wffs
$\vdash$ (turnstile)	". . . is provable from . . ."
$\vDash$	". . . is a valid consequence of . . ."
$\top$	the true
$\bot$	the false

Modal logic

symbol	stand for
$\square$	necessarily
$\lozenge$	possibly

A

Abailard, Peter. *See* Abelard.

abandonment. One of the central ideas of atheistic existentialists, such as *Sartre. Since God does not exist there can be no objective values or meaning to life; thus man is thrust out into the world, "abandoned". He must make decisions, distinguish right from wrong, but as there is no guiding hand he is thrown back entirely on himself.

Abbagnano, Nicola (1901-). Italian existentialist philosopher. He studied at Naples and lectured in Turin from 1936, becoming co-editor of the journal *Rivista di filosofia.*

Influenced by *Husserl's *phenomenology and by the works of *Kierkegaard, *Heidegger, and *Jaspers, Abbagnano presented his "philosophy of the possible" in the three-volume *Storia della filosofia* (1946-50). Human existence must be interpreted as the series of possibilities that follow the realization of being and every act of choice. Not enough attention is given in modern modal logic to the meaning either of 'possible' as distinct from 'potential' (here taken as implying predetermination and perhaps actualization) or of 'contingent' (here taken as implying the necessity of something else). Every possibility has its positive and negative aspects (*see* double aspect theory) and there is a logical relationship between possibility and freedom, for which Abbagnano argues in *Possibilità e libertà* (1956); the *normative 'ought-to-be' is the moral equivalent of the empirical 'may-be'.

abduction. 1. A *syllogism of which the *major premise is true but *minor premise is only probable. **2.** The name given by C. S. *Peirce to the creative formulation of new statistical hypotheses that explain a given set of facts.

Abelard (*or* **Abailard**), Peter (1079-1142). French philosopher, logician, and theologian. Details of his life and misad-

ventures are contained in his *Historia Calamitatum Mearum* (The Story of my Misfortunes). When still quite young he studied under the famous nominalist Roscelin. In Paris Abelard became first a pupil and later the opponent of the realist William of Champeaux (*see* nominalism; realism; universals and particulars). One of Abelard's many quarrels was with Fulbert, a canon of Paris, whose niece Heloïse was successively pupil, lover, and covert wife of Abelard. In 1118, Abelard, having been castrated by ruffians in Fulbert's employ, retired to a monastery. It is from this period onwards that his writings are usually dated.

On the logical side Abelard commented on the Neoplatonic Porphyry's *Isagoge* (*see* scholasticism), on Aristotle's *Categories*, as well as on the *De Divisionibus* (On Classification) attributed to Boethius. His *Dialectica*, a logical work in its own right, was repeatedly revised until a few years prior to his death. The *Scito te Ipsum* (Know Thyself) contains a well worked out ethics of intention. *Sic et Non* (For and Against) stimulates discussion by listing, for a total of 158 controverted questions, points on which authoritative theological texts appear to be discordant (for example, on whether faith should be supported by reason). Other works are his *Introduction to Theology*, and a treatise on the Trinity. St. *Bernard of Clairvaux was among his theological opponents.

Abelard played a major part in the universals controversy, a part that was shaped by the form in which that controversy presented itself to *scholasticism. His stance in general was anti-realist. The extreme form of one type of realism held, in effect, that in the end there are only ten objects, these being the ten Aristotelian *categories. Thus any diversities within the category of substance—even between, for example, a horse and a rock—are really cases of variations within a single object. One of Abelard's arguments against this theory relies on the fact that it absurdly makes the same thing have simultaneously contrary qualities. Another, and saner, form of realism which he also attacks is the collection theory, according to which the universal is the collection of all the objects in question. Thus the universal *man* is simply all men; the latter, that is, comprise a collective class. Some of Abelard's criticisms of this theory rely on his neglect of the distinction between a mere collection and a complete collection, or on the ordinary fact that the ways in which parts of a class relate to their whole are not identical in the two cases of collective classes and classes in the more usual (distributive) sense. Nevertheless, certain sections of his theory of collective classes deal interestingly with identity and continuity, and in particular with the nature of allegedly "principal parts" necessary for continued identity. (This discussion allowed Roscelin, with whom he quarrelled, to cast doubt on Abelard's post-1118 identity.)

Although thus opposed to these and other realist theories, Abelard is nevertheless critical of psychologistic or nominalistic theories of the universal. For him, talk involving universals is in a sense about things, since, for example, being a man is not being a horse. But this does not mean that universals as such are things. A similar attitude is evinced in his discussion of the way in which propositions have meaning.

Abrabanel, Judah. *See* Ebreo.

absolute idealism. *See* idealism.

absolute space. Space regarded as an entity within which bodies are placed, and which itself has real properties, such as shape or extension. This view was held by Newton, but opposed by Leibniz and most subsequent philosophers. *See also* relativity; space and time, philosophy of.

absolute, the. A term used by post-Kantian idealist metaphysicians to cover the totality of what really exists, a totality thought of as a unitary system somehow both generating and explaining all apparent diversity. For *Schelling and

Hegel reality is spiritual, and their absolute is a very unanthropomorphic philosophical God, rather than Nature. The more atheistical F. H. Bradley begins by arguing that all the fundamental categories of ordinary thought are corrupted by irremovable contradictions, and hence must be dismissed as mere appearance: quality and relation, substance and cause, subject and object, time and space, are all equally irredeemable. The absolute, which is reality, must have a nature which is above all these merely apparent categories. It must transcend all relational thinking, though all thinking is somehow or other relational. It must have a unity overcoming and passing beyond all relations and differences. No wonder, perhaps, that mischievous critics represented it as being, like our brave captain's map, "a perfect and absolute blank"; or as being like the night, in which all cows are black. The idea is anticipated by *Spinoza, in his notion that reality is one single substance, *Deus sive Natura*, God or Nature.

absolutism. 1. (in politics) The exercise of power unrestricted by any checks or balances. **2.** (in philosophy) The opposite of 'relativism', and hence infected with all the same ambiguity and indeterminacy. *Compare* relativism.

abstract ideas. A concept the peculiar nature of which has been a longstanding concern with philosophers. If words are employed meaningfully then, surely, the user must have an idea of what they mean; indeed perhaps that idea *is* the meaning? Granted this seductively obvious assumption, then a question arises about such general words as 'man', or 'animal', or 'triangle'. Since they cannot refer to anything individual and particular, maybe what is involved is abstract ideas conceived as special kinds of mental images. *Locke once suggested that such abstract general ideas must have all the diverse characteristics of all the individuals belonging to the class "yet all and none of these at once" (*Essay* IV (vii) 9). *Berkeley leapt upon this unhappy suggestion, excoriating it as contradictory and absurd. His own first proposal was later hailed by *Hume as "one of the greatest and most valuable discoveries that has been made of late years in the republic of letters" (*Treatise* I (i) 7). Offered in the *Principles*, it was that we employ a particular idea from the class, as representative of it. Later, and often unnoticed, in *Alciphron* (VII 14) Berkeley sketched but never developed an altogether different account, suggestive of the later *Wittgenstein: significant expressions may have meaning simply because they have a use; as, "for instance, the algebraic mark, which denotes the root of a negative square, hath its use in logistic operations, although it be impossible to form an idea of any such quantity." *See also* conceptualism; nominalism; realism; universals and particulars.

abstraction. In thought, leaving out, by not attending to, the apparently irrelevant distinguishing features (or even common features) of the several individuals falling within a class. All classification must involve some abstraction. In classifying a group of individuals as yellow, one is ignoring any other respects in which they either resemble or differ from one another. What is called abstract or non-objective art ought rather to be described as non-representational. Abstraction is found rather in the simplifications of represented objects, for instance in Picasso's cubist period. In opposing actuality to 'mere abstraction' philosophers contrast the world of existence with that of *subsistence.

absurdity. In the vulgar sense, obvious falsity or opposition to common sense or reason. The argument form called *reductio ad absurdum* consists in deriving a definite contradiction, that is, both a proposition and its negation, from a set of premises; whence it follows that at least one of the set must be false if the others are true. Philosophers and linguists have attempted to provide criteria for the kind or kinds of apparently non-self-contradictory absur-dity exemplified in sentences such as 'Colourless green ideas sleep furiously'. *See* category mistake.

Abunaser. *See* al-Fārābī.

Academy of Athens. In effect, the first university, established by *Plato about 385 BC. The 'Old Academy' of Plato and his immediate successors was sometimes distinguished from both the 'Middle Academy' of *Arcesilaus and the 'New Academy' of *Carneades with their sceptical tendencies (*see* Scepticism). An Athenian school of *Neoplatonism, calling itself the Academy, was closed down, as a bastion of paganism, in 529 AD.

Academy of Florence. The informal college established in 1462 at Careggi, near Florence, in imitation of Plato's *Academy of Athens. Under the guidance of *Ficino, it played a leading role in the Platonic revival in Renaissance Europe.

acceptance. One possible reaction to a theory or to evidence. A philosopher of science who believes that evidence never decisively proves or refutes a scientific theory may conclude that acceptance of a theory ought always to be provisional or partial. This seems, however, to conflict with the high confidence we all place in the technologies and predictions that are justified by a well tested theory. The conflict is particularly marked in statistics, where the provisional nature of the evidence is often very clear. *See also* Popper; science, philosophy of.

access. *See* privileged access.

accident 1. (in scholastic philosophy) That which in itself has no independent or self-sufficient existence, but only inheres in a *substance. This latter may remain in a more or less fixed form, while "its" accidents disappear or alter. **2.** (in Aristotelian logic) An inessential property, that which may be attributed to a substance without being essential to that substance. For instance, a girl may be blonde, but she must be female;

blondeness in this example is an accident, femaleness is not.

accident, fallacy of the. *See* converse fallacy of the accident.

Achilles and the tortoise (*or* **Achilles paradox**). *See* Zeno's paradoxes.

acquaintance *and* **description, knowledge by.** Where the word 'know' takes a direct object, as in 'Father knew Lloyd George' or 'Pan Am knows America', philosophers speak of *knowledge by acquaintance*; where it is followed by a that-clause, as in 'I know that *p*', they talk of *knowledge by description*. In the *Republic*—in developing the great images of the sun, the line, and the cave—*Plato starts from the idea that every cognitive faculty must and can only involve knowledge by acquaintance. Hence all such faculties must have, like varieties of perception, their own peculiar objects for us to be acquainted with. *See also* knowledge.

acrasia (*or* **akrasia**). (Greek for: weakness.) An alternative name for *weakness of the will. The term derives from the Aristotelian distinction between the *akrates*, the morally weak man, and the *enkrates*, the man who can resist temptation. *See also* Plato.

action. A word sometimes applied to things (for example, the action of acid on metal), but primarily relating to the doings of purposive *agents*. Aristotle distinguished an action—what a man does (*poiesis*)—from what merely happens to him (*pathos*: usually translated 'affection' or 'passion').

There are three main philosophical problems about action. (1) The first concerns how it is to be defined. The standard account, 'a bodily movement preceded by an act of will', runs into problems (*see* volition). (2) The second issue concerns the evaluation or appraisal of action (*see* responsibility).

(3) A source of much recent debate has been the *explanation* of action. The 'actions' of a drugged or hypnotized man are explicable in terms of special causal antecedents; but what of a normal rational action, such as putting on an overcoat to go out? Should we say that my *reason* for donning the coat (wanting to avoid the cold) is the *cause* of my action? A standard objection to this view depends on the Humean thesis that a cause is logically independent of its effects: it is alleged that the connection that such explanations would invoke ('whenever someone desires to avoid the cold, and a coat is the best way to do it, and nothing prevents him, then he puts on a coat') is a trivial logical connection—a mere explication of what desiring something *means*. However, it seems a mistake to suppose that desires can only be specified by reference to the acts in which they issue; so this type of objection appears unfounded.

Some philosophers are opposed in principle to the attempt to explain action causally, because they fear such an approach threatens human freedom. But such a threat would only arise if the mental antecedents of action turned out to be occurrences that were somehow beyond the agent's control.

action at a distance. The idea, in physics, that one body can affect another without any intervening mechanical link between them. The use of the term implies a remote and instantaneous influence by the body, without any apparent mechanism for transmitting the force produced.

This would seem to be the case in gravitational interactions, for example, where two masses mutually attract although they are separated by empty space. From Newton's time until the early 19th century such phenomena (including magnetic and electrostatic interactions) were explained by postulating hypothetical fluids, such as the luminiferous ether, to transmit a force.

In modern physics the idea of hypothetical fluids has been abandoned and action at a distance is described in terms of what Einstein himself characterized as "the rather artificial notion" of fields. This model allows the phenomena to be quantified and "explained" in terms of local interactions. Thus an electric charge is said to set up an electric field in the space around it; a second charge in this region experiences a force by interaction with this field. An alternative, but mathematically equivalent, description uses the idea of *virtual particles*, exchanged between the interacting bodies. Such interactions are not instantaneous but are transmitted at the velocity of light. According to the general theory of *relativity a gravitational field is the result of a "bending" of space-time caused by the presence of a mass. So far attempts to extend this idea to electrical and other interactions, thus producing a unified field theory, have been unsuccessful.

actuality *and* **potentiality.** **1.** Contrasting terms for that which has form, in Aristotle's sense, and that which has merely the possibility of having form. Actuality (Greek: *energeia*) is that mode of being in which a thing can bring other things about or be brought about by them—the realm of events and facts. By contrast, potentiality (Greek: *dynamis*) is not a mode in which a thing exists, but rather the power to effect change, the capacity of a thing to make transitions into different states. **2.** In the philosophy of *Husserl actuality (German: *Wirklichkeit*) means existence in space and time, as opposed to possibility.

Adelard of Bath (fl. 12th century). English writer on philosophy, important for transmitting Arabic scientific learning to the West. His main philosophical work, *De Eodem et Diverso* (On Identity and Difference), contains one of the medieval solutions to the difficulty of allowing an equally full degree of reality both to the existence of the individual and to that of the species and genus to which he or it belongs. Adelard argued that species and genus are unaffected by individuating characteristics (*see* genus; individuation, principle of).

ad hominem argument. (Latin for: argument directed at a man.) The name

stands for two kinds of argument. The first kind is a fallacious argument (*see* fallacy) whereby the premises merely attack a particular man (for example, for his unwholesome moral character) while the conclusion purports to establish the falsity of a thesis he holds. The argument may establish some interesting inconsistency between the man and his views, or lead one to find the grounds on which he holds them to be suspect. But it shows nothing about the truth or falsity of his thesis.

The second kind is an argument taking as its premise something that is accepted by the other party but not perhaps by the arguer and deducing a consequence unacceptable to that other party. This form of argument is sometimes dismissed as fallacious or otherwise improper. Such rejection is quite wrong. There is no fallacy in drawing from a premise a conclusion that does indeed follow. Nor is there anything improper about showing someone that they cannot consistently hold that and reject this.

For instance, it was discovered that close private associates of a political leader had been profiting generously from real estate deals of a kind that that politician had denounced as wicked. Opponents who pointed out that these practices were inconsistent with his stated principles were attacked as slanderers and hypocrites for no better reason than that they had never themselves lived by, nor even pretended to accept, those politically popular but contentious principles.

This second kind of argument *ad hominem* is not improper but quite specially appropriate where two disputants are in moral disagreement. For how could one be moved nearer to the other better or more rationally than by being shown that his own first stated principles would require conclusions that he himself would also find repugnant?

a dicto secundum quid ad dictum simpliciter. (Latin for: from the phrase qualified to the same phrase without qualification.) In traditional logic, a fallacy also known as the *converse fallacy of the accident.

a dicto simpliciter ad dictum secundum quid. (Latin for: from the phrase without qualification to the same phrase qualified.) In traditional logic, a fallacy also known as the fallacy of the accident. *See* converse fallacy of the accident.

Aenesidemus (1st century BC). Sceptical philosopher, active in Alexandria. His works, now lost, included *Pyrrhonian Discourses* and an *Outline of Pyrrhonism*. Originally an Academic, Aenesidemus broke away to revive an authentic Pyrrhonian philosophy. He systematically reduced the argument for "suspension of judgment" to ten "tropes" or modes. *See* Pyrrho; Scepticism.

aesthetics. The philosophical study of art. In its original Greek derivation, the term denoted the study of sense experience generally, and it was not until the mid-18th century, following a usage introduced by the German philosopher A.G.*Baumgarten, that a particular reference to the idea of *beauty in nature and art was established. The current meaning developed even later in the 18th and early 19th centuries, coinciding with the first clear articulation of the concept of fine art.

Although discussions of beauty have always figured in the history of philosophy, these discussions were, until the modern period, invariably linked to primary concerns with epistemology and ontology, or with moral and social value, or with logic. *Plato and *Aristotle, for example, were both concerned with the question whether art could embody and communicate knowledge and truth. And Plato's view that it could not—that art stood at several removes from reality—led him to proscribe most forms of art from his ideal Republic, lest its citizens be diverted from nobler pursuits. In the early 18th century, empiricist philosophers such as Francis *Hutcheson and David *Hume were primarily concerned with the standards and logic of our judgments of taste and beauty.

The real impetus to the idea of aesthetics as a distinctive branch of philosophy occurred in the work of Baumgarten and, especially, *Kant. For each came to regard aesthetic consciousness as a significant and unitary element of human experience generally. In Kant's view, aesthetic judgment is unlike either theoretical (that is, cognitive) judgment or practical (that is, moral) judgment, in that it is effected entirely subjectively, solely in reference to the subject himself (though the judgment nevertheless commands universal assent in virtue of the common ground of our subjectivity). At the same time, Kant argued in his *Critique of Judgment* (1790), aesthetic judgment provides the essential focus for connecting the theoretical and practical aspects of our nature. It can thus reconcile the worlds of nature and freedom which he had earlier, in the *Critique of Pure Reason* (1781) and the *Critique of Practical Reason* (1788), shown to be distinct.

Kant's aesthetic theories were to find extensive elaboration in the work of later German philosophers such as Friedrich *Schiller, *Schopenhauer, and *Hegel, where their special concern with the subjective conditions of aesthetic consciousness, and, particularly, the role of the *imagination, led to an increasingly intimate relation between aesthetics and the philosophy of mind.

The historical trends within aesthetics tend to be reflected in contemporary practice. Many Anglo-American philosophers, for instance, have followed the empiricist tendency and concerned themselves with the logic of aesthetic evaluation and critical judgment; on the other hand, in the wake of Tolstoy's classic *What is Art ?*, Marxist-orientated philosophers have given special prominence to the matter of the moral and social value of art. More recently, there has been a return to the Kantian and post-Kantian association of aesthetics and philosophy of mind—though this line of research has long found favour with the existential philosophers and phenomenologists—and particular attention has been paid to the import of Freud's explorations of the workings of the imagination and the unconscious mind.

Contemporary aesthetics, though, has a strong analytic flavour, and a great deal of its literature takes the form of closely focused essays and articles. Two concerns tend to predominate. First, the analysis of what are, technically, theories of art: for instance, the theories of art as form, or as expression, or as symbol, and the idealist theory propounded earlier this century by Benedetto *Croce and R.G. *Collingwood. Second, the analysis of certain concepts within art: for instance, the concept of the work of art itself, and the concepts of meaning, intention, representation, and illusion within the arts.

But it should be noted that, at least in modern British philosophy, aesthetics has not yet found a wholly assured place. What aesthetics is, or should be, about—for instance, how far it is distinct from the interests of art-criticism and theory on the one hand, or, on the other, of psychology—itself constitutes a familiar matter of philosophical debate.

affirming the antecedent. In a *hypothetical proposition, such as 'If the thief entered through the window, then there will be footprints in the flowerbed', the if part is called the antecedent and the then part the consequent. Four inferences can be drawn from propositions of this if *p* then *q* form, two valid and two invalid. To *affirm the antecedent* is to argue, validly, that because *p* therefore *q*. To *deny the consequent* is to argue, again validly, that since *q* is false, *p* must also be false. To *affirm the consequent* is to argue, invalidly, that because *q* therefore *p*. To *deny the antecedent* is to argue, again invalidly, that because *p* is false *q* must also be false.

The traditional Latin forms of the labels for the two valid modes are still found: *modus (ponendo) ponens* for affirming the antecedent; and *modus (tollendo) tollens* for denying the consequent.

affirming the consequent. *See* affirming the antecedent.

a fortiori. (Latin for: from the stronger.) A phrase used to signify 'all the more' or 'even more certain'. If all men are mortal, then *a fortiori* all Englishmen—who constitute a small sub-class of all men—must also be mortal. This might be labelled an *argumentum a fortiori*.

after-image. The visual version of what psychologists called 'after-sensation', wherein a visual image resembling an observed object persists after the external stimulus assumed to have caused it has been withdrawn. *See* critical realism; Gestalt; perception.

Age of Reason. *See* Enlightenment.

agnosticism. The thesis that, contrary to what atheists and theists alike assume, it is either in practice or in principle impossible to know whether or not God exists. In various forms, agnosticism recurs throughout the history of thought. It had some notable exponents in Victorian England, for example, T. H. Huxley, who coined the term. Their position was occasioned partly as a result of philosophical questioning, inspired by *Hume and *Kant, of the very possibility of human knowledge of realms transcending possible experience. But during the same period, uncritical acceptance of the Bible as divine self-revelation was also under pressure from scientific and historical research. Faith may, however, be possible where knowledge strictly so-called is not, and hence there is a sense in which it is logically possible, even if psychologically difficult, to be both a philosophical agnostic and a religious believer.

Traditional agnosticism, which regards the statement that God exists as unverifiable but nonetheless meaningful, was rejected by logical positivists, who held that if unverifiable it is *ipso facto* meaningless (*see* logical positivism). More recent philosophy of religion, much preoccupied with the unique character of the concept of God, and of religious belief and discourse in general, often agrees with agnostics that insoluble problems do indeed arise from treating religious doctrines as quasi-scientific theses about the nature of reality. But it takes this as an indication that the real function of such doctrines may be quite different. See religion, philosophy of.

agreement, method of. See Mill's methods.

ahiṃsā. (Sanskrit for: non-injury.) The doctrine, particularly supported by the Jains and Buddhists, that it is wrong to kill another living thing, however humble. The belief underlying this doctrine is that all living creatures possess souls of essentially the same kind, and because of transmigration (see metempsychosis) the soul of some revered ancestor may be temporarily inhabiting some lowly animal form.

Ājīvika. See Indian materialism.

akrasia. See acrasia.

Albertus Magnus (or **Albert the Great**) (c.1200–80). Scholastic philosopher and theologian, who worked in Germany and Paris. Famed for the extent of his knowledge (hence his nickname 'Doctor Universalis'), he wrote commentaries on all Aristotle's works. He is particularly important for transmitting to the Middle Ages Greek and Islamic work in the natural sciences. *Aquinas was among his pupils. See also Aristotelianism.

Albo, Joseph (c.1380–c.1444). Spanish-Jewish philosopher, and pupil of *Crescas. Albo was essentially an eclectic, drawing his ideas indifferently from Jewish, Islamic, and scholastic Christian sources. His Sefer ha-'Ikkarim (Book of Principles) is in purpose a work of apologetics, furnishing a rational justification of Judaism. It was very popular in Jewish circles, and was much admired by some later Christian theologians (for example, Grotius and Richard Simon).

alchemy. A medieval philosophy combining an occult cosmology with practical chemical experimentation. Origina-

ting independently in Hellenistic Egypt and ancient China, alchemy remained a legitimate and recognized branch of philosophy in Europe and the Islamic world for over 1500 years. In its practical aspects it became the precursor of modern chemistry. Basing their world view on Aristotelian physics, the alchemists sought to isolate the prima materia (first matter), out of which they believed all objects in the physical world could be created. Strong Neoplatonic and Kabbalistic influences pervade Renaissance alchemical tracts and a mystical approach based on occult correspondences and 'sympathies' became increasingly apparent (see Kabbalah; Neoplatonism).

The practical alchemist sought three things: the elixir of life, the universal panacea, and, most notoriously, the means of transmuting base metals into gold (see philosopher's stone). It was this gold-making aspect of alchemy that prompted Chaucer's punning quip in the Prologue to The Canterbury Tales about the penniless Oxford student: "But al be that he was a philosophre,/Yet hadde he but litel gold in cofre."

Alcmaeon of Croton. The only considerable follower of *Pythagoras from the same or the immediately following generation. Alcmaeon's interests were mainly medical. He contended that health is a matter of maintaining a balance between various opposing powers. Although apparently believing in the immortality of the soul, he certainly maintained that the brain is essential to the operations of all the senses. See Presocratics.

Alexander, Samuel (1859–1938). Australian-born philosopher who from 1877 studied mathematics, classics, and philosophy at Oxford, and later experimental psychology at Freiburg. He was subsequently professor of philosophy at Manchester (1893–1924). Main philosophical work: Space, Time and Deity (2 volumes, 1920).

Alexander was one of the most influential figures in the realist reaction against the idealism prevalent during his early career. He held that knowledge, generally, consists in the "compresence" of a mental act and an object, that is, it is essentially of a mind-independent world. His epistemology forms part of an all-embracing metaphysical system, tracing the evolution of the world from space-time, seen here as its primitive stuff, towards deity, its still unrealized ideal. *See* realism.

Alexandrian School. A centre of *Neoplatonism in 5th- and 6th-century Alexandria. Unlike its rival at Athens (*see* Academy of Athens), the Alexandrian School became Christian, concentrating on scholarly commentary, rather than theurgy and metaphysical speculation. It survived the capture of Alexandria by the Arabs (641 AD) and transmitted much Neoplatonist learning to the Middle Ages.

al-Fārābī, Abū Naṣr (*or* Abunaser) (*c.*870–950). Islamic philosopher. Main work: *al-Madīnat al-Fāḍilah* (The Virtuous City).

The history of Islamic *Neoplatonism may be said to start properly with al-Fārābī (*see* Islamic philosophy). He studied philosophy in Baghdād and became the leading logician of his day, producing a number of commentaries on Aristotle's *Organon* and *Porphyry's *Isagoge.* He was greatly influenced by Plato's *Republic*: his interest in ethics and the concept of justice led him to write a similar work, commonly known by the abbreviated title *The Virtuous City.* This virtuous city was one in which the good life was sought and all the virtues abounded. By contrast, al-Fārābī identified four types of corrupt city that fell far short of this ideal. However, his fundamental Neoplatonism caused him to open the work with a discussion of the Plotinian One rather than, as in Plato, with a consideration of justice. He believed, like Plato, that the rule of philosophy was utterly essential for the perfect state and that without it the state would perish. However, if the state lacked an individual paragon who possessed all the philosophical virtues, then rule could be shared among a group of people who did (*see* philosopher kings).

algebra. That part of mathematics concerned with the study of abstract structures containing (at least) operations that have the properties of addition and multiplication. Elementary algebra largely deals with the solving of polynomial equations and the introduction of various sorts of numbers required for this task. Higher algebra is the study of structures satisfying sets of axioms.

algebraic number. *See* number.

al-Ghazālī, Abū Ḥāmid Muḥammad (*or* Algazel) (1058–1111). Islamic philosopher and theologian. Main works: *Tahāfut al-Falāsifah* (The Incoherence of the Philosophers) (completed 1095), *Iḥyā' 'Ulūm al-Dīn* (The Revival of the Religious Sciences) (written *c.*1096-1100), *al-Munqidh min al-Ḍalāl* (Deliverance from Error) (written *c.*1108).

An Islamic tradition states that a renewer of the Islamic faith will arise every hundred years, and al-Ghazālī, called in medieval Europe Algazel, came to believe that he was one such renewer for the sixth Islamic century (12th century AD). After a period as a professor in Baghdād, he suffered a spiritual crisis in 1095 that resulted in a speech impediment and nervous breakdown. al-Ghazālī then abandoned academic life for the ascetic regime of a ṣūfī (Islamic mystic) though he later returned briefly for about three years. Throughout his life he tried to defuse the tensions between philosophy and theology, and it was his outstanding achievement to have made theology more philosophical: by using such methods as syllogistic logic to rebut Neoplatonism and bolster Islamic dogma, he ensured that future theologians would do likewise. *See also* Islamic philosophy.

algorithm. An explicit and finite step-by-step procedure for solving a problem or achieving a required end, for example, the truth table test for whether a propositional formula is a tautology. The set of instructions for doing simple multiplication is an algorithm.

alienans. A medieval term distinguishing certain adjectives that form peculiarly tight relations with the nouns to which they are applied. For example, whereas the phrase 'a red book' says of an object that it is both a book and red, the phrase 'alleged murderer', containing the alienans adjective 'alleged', does not imply that someone is both alleged and a murderer, but only that the term 'murderer' is said to be, but perhaps is not, truly applicable.

alienation. In English originally and for a long time a term only employed strictly with reference either to progressive insanity or to the transfer of property. But in recent decades it has also become a vogue word, suggesting estrangement from or powerlessness in society, and the depersonalization of the individual in large and bureaucratic organizations. The main influence here has been the discovery of the *Economic and Philosophical Manuscripts of 1844*, written by *Marx under the spell of *Hegel and of such rather older Young Hegelians as *Feuerbach. A lesser and separate influence has been that of Max *Weber and other sociological students of bureaucracy.

aliorelative. Irreflexive. *See* relation.

al-Kindī, Ya'qūb ibn Ishāq (d. after 866 AD). Islamic philosopher. Twenty-four of his main works are collected and edited by M. A. H. Abū Rīdah in *Rasā'il al-Kindī al-Falsafiyyah* (Philosophical Treatises of al-Kindī) (1950–53).

al-Kindī is unanimously hailed as the father of Islamic philosophy. His association with intellectual movements like the Mu'tazilah (*see* Islamic philosophy) led him to try to integrate the strands of Greek philosophy and Islamic doctrine that were current in the vital intellectual ferment of the 9th-century Islamic empire. The synthesis was not always successful and al-Kindī's groping

*Neoplatonism led to some philosophical difficulties being overlooked. Settling in Baghdād, he won the favour of three pro-Mu'tazilah caliphs who were themselves interested in philosophy. Though he handicapped himself by a complicated and often longwinded style of writing, al-Kindī made a lasting twofold contribution to the development of Islamic philosophy: he played a major role in the spread of Greek thought, and by his use, development, and even invention of new terms, he substantially enlarged Arabic philosophical terminology. He was probably the first Islamic philosopher to add a sixth term or voice (*al-Shakhs*: the individual) to Porphyry's fivefold classification of species, genus, differentia, property, and accident in the *Isagoge*.

altruism *and* **egoism.** As a philosophical term 'altruism' may most usefully be seen in opposition to (ethical) 'egoism'. Egoism rests on the hypothesis that morality can be explained ultimately in terms of self-interest, albeit so-called enlightened self-interest. For the egoist, the apparent conflicts between the demands of morality and of personal gain are merely conflicts between different aspects of our self-interest—indirect *v.* direct or long-term *v.* short-term. A general explanation of morality and interest might be stated thus: all our benefits come from the existence of a stable society; the observance of certain moral rules is a necessary condition of such a society; hence we have an interest in maintaining moral order.

The altruist will point to the obvious weakness of such arguments in that they only prove that we have an interest in other people abiding by the moral rules, not that it is in our interest to abide by them. The central claim of altruism then is negative: that the explanation of morality cannot be reduced to self-interest. This can be restated more positively: that an interest in other people *for their own sake* is a necessary condition of morality. While this is no doubt true, it does not support the stronger claim that a desire to help others is a sufficient condition of morality.

ambiguity. The existence of two or more clearly different senses in the meaning of a word or expression. Anyone claiming that a word or expression is ambiguous must, therefore, be ready to specify the senses that they wish to distinguish: the word 'funny' is thus ambiguous, having both the ha-ha and the peculiar senses (*compare* vagueness).

Another form of ambiguity is known as *systematic ambiguity*. This arises with words or expressions that may always have the same meaning when applied to one kind of thing, but have a different meaning when applied to another kind of thing. One example given by Aristotle, who was the first to draw attention to this phenomenon, concerns the word 'healthy'. Both places and people can be healthy. But though Boston may or may not be more healthy than Birmingham, and Mrs. Briggs than Mr. Briggs, it makes no sense at all to ask whether Boston is more or less healthy than Mr. Briggs.

Ambrose, St. (*c.*340-397). Bishop of Milan and influential writer on the philosophy of religion. He successfully opposed the Arian heresy, which held that Jesus and God were not of the same substance, that the divinity of Jesus was questionable, and hence that he might be subordinate to God. Ambrose's own affirmation of the independence of the Church from the secular state was attacked much later by *Hobbes, among others.

ampliative argument. *See* induction.

analogy. Likeness or similarity. The positive analogy between the two terms of a comparison—their likenesses—may be contrasted with the negative—their unlikenesses. Argument by analogy infers that, because this is like that in some respects, this and that must therefore be similar also in others. As deductions such conclusions, obviously, do not follow. Yet they may sometimes be usefully suggestive, because in fact true. Scholastics also elaborated doctrines of analogy trying to show how human language might be used to say something about a transcendent God: for example, in Cajetan's *The Analogy of Names.*

analytic *and* **synthetic.** A distinction between kinds of *proposition or statement based on the nature of the evidence required to establish their truth. There are several non-equivalent ways of drawing such a distinction.

1. A statement is an analytic truth if and only if the concept of the predicate is included in the concept of the subject; otherwise, if it is true, it is a synthetic truth. This is the distinction made by *Kant, who introduced the terms. Thus 'All bodies are extended in space' or 'All husbands are male' are analytic propositions because the ideas of extension and maleness are already contained in those of body and husband. On the other hand, 'Some bodies are heavy' or 'A green light indicates "Go"' are synthetic, since the ideas of heaviness and of 'Go' are not necessarily contained in the subject ideas.

Kant's distinction has been criticized: first, for being indeterminate—it is not at all clear what is or is not to be counted as thus contained; second, for being inappropriately psychological, and hence for possibly yielding different determinations for different individuals; and third, for assuming that all propositions must be of the subject-predicate form—the form to which the attention of the traditional formal logic was so largely confined.

Attempts to remedy these defects have usually produced, either quite explicitly psychological principles of division, or else logical and epistemological criteria tending to collapse the analytic/synthetic into the a priori/a posteriori or the logically necessary/contingent distinctions (*see* a priori and a posteriori; Hume's fork; necessary and contingent truth). In the former case the criterion may be whether the predicate is or is not consciously thought in the subject, and what the speaker would or would not say in response to immediate questions. In the latter it becomes, what can or cannot be deduced by a purely logical analysis, and what it would or would not be self-contradictory to assert.

2. A statement is an analytic truth or falsehood if it can be proved or disproved from definitions by means of only logical laws, and it is synthetic if its truth or falsity can be established by other means. This was the distinction postulated by Frege and followed by the logical positivists, who maintained that all the truths of mathematics and logic are both analytic and tautological. (As regards arithmetic this view had been anticipated by Leibniz.) As Wittgenstein said in the *Tractatus*: "The propositions of logic are tautologies. The propositions of logic therefore say nothing. (They are the analytical propositions.)... Mathematical propositions express no thoughts" (6.1,6.11, and 6.21).

3. A statement is an analytic truth if it is true in virtue of the meanings of the words it contains; a statement is a synthetic truth if it is true in virtue of the way the world is.

Others, most notably *Quine, have refused to accept or recognize any analytic/synthetic distinction, arguing that while something of this sort may have a limited usefulness as a model of the different ways in which we may come to know truths, it does not mark a clear division between types of knowledge, and it rests on unsound notions of sameness of meaning and definition.

anamnēsis. (Greek for: recollection.) *See* reminiscence, argument from.

Anaxagoras of Clazomenae (*c.*500/ 499-*c.*428/7 BC). An influential Greek Presocratic philosopher who spent much of his working life at Athens, where he suffered a politically motivated prosecution for impiety. His cosmology reacts sharply against the *monism of *Parmenides, and insists against *Zeno of Elea that matter must be infinitely divisible. The main philosophical interest is negative: even the mind, which plays

so large a part, is still—like everything else in the *Presocratics—corporeal.

Anaximander of Miletus (d. *c.*547/6 BC). The second of the Greek speculators about Nature as a whole (after *Thales of Miletus). Anaximander apparently suggested that the first principle must be something indeterminate rather than one particular kind of matter, such as water. He also seems to have believed in some fundamental tension in things, conceived in curiously legal terms. More certainly, he maintained that the earth is at the centre of the Universe, and not supported by anything, that all living things orginated from slime, and that mankind must have evolved from some other species reaching self-supporting adulthood more quickly. *See* Presocratics.

Anaximenes of Miletus. A younger compatriot of *Anaximander of Miletus. He held that air is the fundamental matter, which takes on other forms and appearances by condensation and rarefaction. These derivative substances, he may have thought, became in their turn the elements of compounds. His other cosmological notions, being closer to popular traditions, are less interesting, but there was some meteorological speculation, using the conception of rarefying and condensing air. *See* Presocratics.

and. A *connective that in colloquial English has several logically distinct uses. For example, (1) He took aim and fired; (2) She did not come and he was left waiting; (3) It was raining and blowing a gale; (4) John and Julia both have fair hair; (5) John and Julia are twins. In (1) 'and' has the force of 'and then' whereas in (2) it has the force of 'and so'. In neither of these cases can the order of the connected items be reversed without changing that sense of the sentence; 'He fired and took aim' and 'He was left waiting and she did not come' do not mean the same as (1) and (2) respectively. In (3) 'and' is used to join two simple statements 'It was raining', 'It was blowing a gale', so forming a compound statement having the force of the joint assertion of its component statements. In this case, reversal of the order of the statements makes no difference to what is said; 'It was blowing a gale and raining' says the same as (3). It is this use of 'and' on which logicians have concentrated and have represented in the following ways: if *p* and *q* stand for statements, then '*p* and *q*' is written '*pq*', '*p.q*', '*p & q*', or '*p* $\wedge$ *q*'. In this sense '*p* and *q*' is the joint assertion (or *conjunction* or *logical product*) of *p* and *q*. (4) can be treated as an example of this use by expanding it to 'John has fair hair and Julia has fair hair' but (5) cannot since 'John is a twin and Julia is a twin' might be said when John's twin is David and Julia's twin is Jane, in which case it would be misleading to say that John and Julia are twins. In the use of 'and' to form the conjunction of two statements, it is often claimed to be a *truth-functional connective or a truth-functional operator whose definition is given by the *truth-table

p	&	*q*
T	T	T
T	F	F
F	F	T
F	F	F

and '*p & q*' is said to be a truth-functional compound of *p* and *q*.

Angelic Doctor. The traditional scholastic nickname for St. Thomas *Aquinas.

Angst. (German for: anxiety, anguish.) In existentialist philosophy, the dread occasioned by man's realization that his existence is open towards an undetermined future, the emptiness of which must be filled by his freely chosen actions. Anxiety characterizes the human state, which entails constant confrontation with possibility and the need for decision, with the concomitant burden of responsibility. *See also* bad faith; existentialism.

anima. (Latin for: soul). **1.** *See* soul. **2.** (in Jungian psychology) The part of the *collective unconscious within an indi-vidual that represents the feminine aspect of man's nature.

animal soul. An analogue in animals of the human soul or mind. A reaction to the Cartesian view that man alone possessed a soul, the doctrine of animal soul claimed that animal behaviour was not physicalistically explicable, but implied mental functioning and the existence of soul. *See also* brutes; panpsychism; soul; world soul.

animism. The view that everything in the Universe, including even plants and inanimate objects, has some kind of psychological being more or less tenuously similar to that of human and non-human animals. Thus it is asserted that a stone is not only an aggregate of moving molecules but has 'awareness' of other bodies in, for example, attracting and repelling them or being affected along with them by gravity. When this theory is held by primitive peoples, it is called animism. Philosophical animists have often been described, more politely, as 'panpsychists' (*see* panpsychism). Doctrines of this sort have been held by numerous thinkers, including Empedocles, Plotinus, Leibniz, Schopenhauer, Peirce, Schiller, Whitehead, Alexander, de Chardin, and Waddington.

Anselm, St. (1033-1109). Scholastic philosopher, born at Aosta (Piedmont), who became Archbishop of Canterbury (1093-1109).

One of the first medievals to apply the Aristotelian logic inherited from *Boethius towards the clarification of his own theological tenets, Anselm is therefore sometimes said to be the father of scholasticism. Until recently he has been of most interest to philosophers of religion, on account of the Neoplatonism he displays in proofs of the existence of God. In the *Monologion* (Soliloquy) God is seen as that good through which all good things are good or as that existent through which all existents exist, and in the *De Veritate* (On Truth) as that truth through which all true things are true. His most famous argument is contained in his *Proslogion* (Discourse); it is the one that has been known since *Kant as the *ontological argument for the existence of God.

Of quite general philosophical interest are his early dialogues. Thus in *De Veritate* he investigates the multiple senses of 'truth'. *De Libertate Arbitrii* (On Freewill) deals with free choice and its necessary conditions. *De Casu Diaboli* (on the Devil's Fall) attempts to resolve the paradoxes inherent in the idea that moral evil originated in the fall from righteousness of a God-created Satan. These three early dialogues display to the full Anselm's brilliance in using linguistic analysis as a means for resolving conceptual puzzles. A further early dialogue, *De Grammatico* (Concerning the literate) applies such analysis in the purely logical field, and investigates the mode of meaning of adjectival terms such as 'white' and 'literate' ('*grammaticus*'). Must that meaning be elucidated only by reference to the qualities (whiteness, literacy) in question (as Aristotle had stated) or must some account of the denotation (such as human beings, in the case of literacy) also be included (as the grammarians had claimed)? Anselm replies that the grammarian's account, based on usage, cannot do justice to the adjective's capacity for constant redeployment in hitherto unencountered contexts; the purely logical account must have an openness that leaves room for such redeployment. To define 'literate' as '...having literacy' merely makes it plain that it no more signifies human beings than does 'white', and puts no restrictions on its possible future applications. A similar account must be extended to all such adjectival terms. His analyses also include investigations of the senses of 'to do' (*facere*), 'to give' (*dare*), 'to be obligated' (*debere*), 'to will' (*velle*), and of the puzzles concerning such apparent names as 'nothing' and 'nobody'. Thus "Nothing taught me to fly" is Anselm's analogue of the discussion in Lewis Carroll of Alice's claim that nobody passed her in the road; Anselm evolves

quantificational construals that avoid the odd consequences that ensue if 'nothing' is taken to be a name that names something. In dealing with 'doing' he moves into the foundations of an action theory that has recently been hailed as highly significant, and whose consequences are still the subject of controversy. He took some part in the early medieval controversy on universals, being an opponent of the nominalist Roscelin. *See* nominalism; scholasticism; universals and particulars.

antecedent. *See* conditional.

antecedent, affirming (or denying) the. *See* affirming the antecedent.

anthroposophy. An occult system claiming that the key to wisdom and to an understanding of the Universe lies in man himself. The original Greek coinage signified 'wisdom about man'. It is now applied to the philosophically eclectic teachings of Rudolf Steiner (1861-1925), who believed that cultivation of man's evolving spiritual perceptions was the most important task facing humanity. *Compare* theosophy.

antilogism. *See* inconsistent triad.

antinomianism. The view that ordinary moral laws are not applicable to Christians, whose lives, it is said, are governed solely by divine grace. Opponents of this position have always pointed, during its not infrequent recurrences, to its alarming ethical implications. By extension, it is also possible to speak of the antinomianism of other putative moral elites.

antinomy. An obsolescent synonym for paradox or contradiction.

Antiochus of Ascalon (*c*.130-68 BC). Academic philosopher. Abandoning the *Scepticism professed by the *Academy of Athens since *Arcesilaus, Antiochus claimed to be reviving the doctrines of the 'Old Academy', of which the Stoic and Peripatetic systems were mere adaptations. His own teaching was a blend of all three philosophies; it included a Stoic epistemology and the Peripatetic moral attitude that complete blessedness requires material and physical—in addition to mental—well-being. Antiochus' writings are now lost, but *Cicero made considerable use of them.

Antisthenes (*c*.445-*c*.360 BC). Athenian philosopher, disciple of *Socrates. He wrote numerous works that survive only in fragments. Principally a moralist, though also interested in literature and linguistic theory, Antisthenes advocated the austerely simple life. Because of his influence on *Diogenes of Sinope, he ranked as a founder of Cynicism. *See also* Cynics.

antisymmetric. *See* relation.

antithesis. *See* Hegel.

antonym. A word of contrary meaning: 'good' is an antonym of 'bad'. *Compare* homonym; synonym.

apodeictic (*or* **apodictic**). A term used in Aristotelian logic to indicate the mode or modality of a proposition. An apodeictic proposition is one that asserts that something is necessarily the case or that something is impossible, as for example 'Seven cannot be more than nine'.

apodosis. *See* conditional.

aporetic. Raising questions and objections, without necessarily providing answers. Such a procedure is characteristic of *Socrates in the early dialogues of *Plato. A difficulty of this sort is sometimes labelled, by Ryle and others, an aporia (Greek for: puzzle).

aporia. *See* aporetic.

a posteriori. *See* a priori and a posteriori.

apperception. Self-consciousness or inner awareness, in contrast with 'perception', denoting outer awareness. First used by *Leibniz in this sense, the term is now particularly associated with *Kant's distinction between empirical apperception or self-consciousness, and transcendental apperception, or the a priori unity of consciousness on which the coherence and meaning of experience is held to depend.

a priori *and* **a posteriori.** (Latin for: from what comes before *and* from what comes after.) A distinction between sorts of statement or *proposition based on how one may acquire knowledge of their truth. Hence it becomes also a distinction between kinds of *knowledge. The expressions were first introduced in the late scholastic period to translate two technical terms of Aristotle's theory of knowledge. This first usage is now obsolete.

What is still current stems from *Descartes, *Leibniz, and other writers of the 1600s. Both terms are applied to propositions, to arguments, and to ideas or concepts. An *a priori* proposition is one that can be known to be true, or false, without reference to experience, except in so far as experience is necessary for understanding its terms. An *a posteriori* proposition can be known to be true, or false, only by reference to how, as a matter of contingent fact, things have been, are, or will be (*see* necessary and contingent truth).

Arguments are a priori primarily in so far as they attempt to deduce conclusions from a priori propositions (*see* deduction). But there is a secondary usage in which the expression refers to any appeal to antecedent probabilities or to considerations of general theory, as opposed to data more or less directly concerned with the particular matter in question.

The application of the term to concepts is disputed between empiricists and rationalists (*see* empiricism; rationalism). *Locke and *Hume argued that all our ideas or concepts are derived from experience. Against this, others, such as *Plato and *Leibniz, have contended that there are some notions of great importance—for instance, substance, equality, cause, or likeness and difference—that could not have been so derived; these notions are on this account rated a priori concepts. It has also been argued, above all by *Kant, that some such a priori concepts are presupposed by the very possibility of experience, and indeed the existence of synthetic a priori knowledge is central to Kant's whole "Copernican revolution" in philosophy.

It should be recognized that the account just given of the a priori/a posteriori distinction, and the accounts given elsewhere of the adjacent distinctions between *analytic and synthetic and between necessary and contingent propositions, cannot but to some extent prejudice these great debates. The reason is that, like so many debates in philosophy, they are in large part about what distinctions and what concepts are appropriate.

aprioism. The philosophical position, opposed to *empiricism, held by those who characteristically consider that the mind is furnished with *innate ideas and that there exists the possibility of genuine knowledge independent of experience. *See* a priori and a posteriori; Kant; Locke.

Aquinas, St. Thomas (*c.*1225-74). Scholastic philosopher, born at Roccasecca near Aquino in Italy. He was schooled by the Benedictine monks of Monte Cassino and studied liberal arts at the University of Naples. Against the bitter hostility of his family he joined the Dominican Order of begging friars in 1244 and studied philosophy and theology at Paris and at Cologne under *Albertus Magnus. From 1254 to 1259 he lectured at Paris, becoming a full professor ('regent master') in 1256. During the decade 1259 to 1269 Aquinas was in Italy, occupying various posts in his order and in the service of the Popes at Orvieto, Rome, and Viterbo. From 1269 to 1272 he taught for a second period at Paris during a period of lively theological and philosophical controversies in the University. His teaching career ended due to ill health in 1273 after a year at the University of Naples where he had begun his career as an undergraduate. He died at Fossanova on 7 March 1274 while journeying to Lyons to take part in the Church Council there. Three years after his death a number of

propositions representing his views were condemned by ecclesiastical authorities in Paris and Oxford; but in 1323 he was canonized by Pope John XXII at Avignon and in 1879 Pope Leo XIII issued an encyclical commending his works to Catholic scholars.

Aquinas's works, though all written within twenty years are enormously voluminous. Best known are his two massive syntheses of philosophy and theology, the *Summa contra Gentiles* (Against the Errors of the Infidels), which by itself is sixty thousand words longer than the whole corpus of Berkeley's philosophy, and the *Summa Theologiae*, which expounds his mature thought at even greater length. These encyclopedic works, though theological in intent and largely in subject matter, contain much material that is philosophical in method and content. The earliest of Aquinas's theological syntheses, his commentary on the *Sentences* of Peter Lombard, then a century old, is the least philosophically rewarding to read. Most explicitly philosophical is the series of commentaries on Aristotle (on the *Analytics*, *De Anima*, *De Caelo*, *Ethics*, *De Interpretatione*, *Metaphysics*, and *Physics*, and parts of the *Politics*) and a number of pamphlets written during his Paris sojourns for teaching or polemical purposes. These last include the *De Ente et Essentia*, a juvenile work on being and essence, the *De Principiis Naturae* on the causes of change in nature, the *De Unitate Intellectus* attacking the Averroist view that the whole of mankind has only a single intellect, and the *De Aeternitate Mundi* arguing that philosophy cannot prove that the cosmos had a beginning in time. Among the most lively of Aquinas's remains are the *Quaestiones Disputatae*, records of live academic debates on a variety of theological and philosophical topics such as truth (the *De Veritate*), divine power (the *De Potentia*), the soul (the *De Anima*), and free choice (the *De Malo*). Matter of philosophical interest can be found even in Aquinas's commentaries on books of the Bible, such as his exposition of the Book of Job. Aquinas wrote a dense, lucid, and passionless Latin which, though condemned as barbaric by Renaissance taste, can serve as a model of philosophical discourse. The majority of his works are now available in English translation.

Aquinas's first service to philosophy was to make the works of Aristotle known and acceptable to the Christian West, against the lifelong opposition of conservative theologians who were suspicious of a pagan philosopher filtered through Muslim commentaries (see Aristotelianism). Aquinas's commentaries on the translations of his friend William of Moerbeke made students in western universities familiar with Aristotle's own ideas. In his theological writings Aquinas showed to what a considerable extent it was possible to combine Aristotelian positions in philosophy with Christian doctrines in theology. Although his principal philosophical themes and techniques are Aristotelian, Aquinas was no more a mere echo of Aristotle than Aristotle was of Plato. In addition to working out the relationship between Aristotelianism and Christianity Aquinas develops and modifies Aristotle's ideas within the area of philosophy itself. Thus, for instance, the part of the *Summa Theologiae* devoted to general ethical questions (the *Prima Secundae*) expounds and improves upon Aristotle's account of happiness, virtue, human action, and emotion before going on to relate these teachings to the specifically theological topics of divine law and divine grace.

Naturally Aquinas's philosophy of physics has been antiquated by the progress of natural science, and his philosophy of logic has been rendered archaic by the development of mathematical logic and the reflection of philosophers and mathematicians in the hundred years since Frege. But his contributions to metaphysics, philosophy of religion, philosophical psychology, and moral philosophy entitle him to an enduring place in the first rank of philosophers.

In metaphysics Aquinas applies the Aristotelian distinction between actuality and potentiality to a wide variety of topics and problems. If we consider any substance, such as a piece of wood, we find a number of things that are true of that substance at a given time, and a number of other things, that, though not true of it at that time, can become true of it at some other time. Thus, the wood, though it *is* cold, *can be* heated and turned into ash. Aristotelians called the things which a substance *is* its actualities, and the things which it *can be* its potentialities: thus the wood is actually cold but potentially hot, actually wood, but potentially ash. The change from being cold to being hot is an accidental change which the substance can undergo while remaining the substance that it is; the change from wood to ash is a substantial change, a change from being one kind of substance to another. The actualities involved in changes are called 'forms': accidental forms if involved in accidental change; substantial forms if involved in substantial change. 'Matter' is used as a technical term for what has the capacity for substantial change.

All terrestrial objects, Aquinas believed, consisted of matter and form. But in addition to these composite entities there were pure forms: angelic beings with no particle of matter in their composition. The principle of *individuation for terrestrial beings—what makes two things of a kind two and not one—is matter: two peas in a pod may resemble each other as much as you like, but they are two peas and not one because they are two different parcels of matter. Angels, having no matter, can never be two of a kind: one angel differs from another as a man differs from a dog; each angel is a species of its own.

Aquinas sometimes speaks, particularly in his juvenile works, as if the coming of something into existence were another case of the actualization of a potentiality, like a pint of milk turning into butter: a non-existent essence acquires the actuality of existence. In his more mature thinking on the topic, he insisted that the creation of beings could not be regarded as the actualization of shadowy essences in this way. But he continued to use the terminology of essence and existence to mark a distinction between God and creatures: in all creatures essence and existence were distinct (for the creatures might never have existed) while in God essence and existence were one (for God's existence is necessary in a unique sense). Aquinas's writing on *esse* or existence is a strange mixture of insight and confusion: the confusion has not prevented his theory of Being from becoming an object of great admiration among his followers.

The doctrine of matter and form spills over from Aquinas's metaphysics into his philosophy of mind in a number of ways. Forms can exist in two ways: with *esse naturale* (that is, as the form which makes a piece of matter the kind of thing it is) or with *esse intelligibile* (that is, as an idea in someone's mind). Moreover, the human soul is the form of the human body: it is the possession of human life and human powers that makes a particular parcel of matter the body it is. Against theological opposition Aquinas insisted that the rational soul is the *only* substantial form of the human body: for this he was condemned after his death by those who believed in a hierarchy of souls, intellectual, animal, and vegetable, plus a form of corporeity. This archaic dispute has its contemporary counterpart in the debate whether memory or bodily continuity is the criterion of *personal identity.

The two principal powers of the human soul, for Aquinas, are the intellect and the will. The intellect is the capacity to think: to form concepts and to possess beliefs. Concepts and beliefs are called by Aquinas 'species', an ambiguous term with the many senses of the English word 'idea'. The intellect is the power to acquire, possess, and exercise *species*: the power to acquire them, by operating upon sense experience, is called the active intellect (*intellectus agens*) and the power to store and exercise them is called the receptive intellect (*intellectus possibilis*). Against Muslim commentators on Aristotle, Aquinas maintained that every individual human being possessed both kinds of intellect; and against Platonizing theologians he insisted that for both the acquisition and exercise of intellectual ideas the cooperation of the imagination was necessary. The imagination he considered as a type of interior sense faculty, providing objects for the intellect to contemplate and modify.

Aquinas's theory of the will builds on the theory of voluntariness, choice, and human action familiar to readers of Aristotle's *Nicomachean Ethics*. Aquinas improves on Aristotle by developing a concept of intention (intermediate between Aristotle's concepts of voluntariness and choice) and by having a worked out theory of conscience. His detailed and subtle analysis of the elements of human free choice and action is one of the most easily comprehensible and permanently valuable features of his philosophy.

Aquinas's most famous contribution to the philosophy of religion is his *Five Ways or proofs of the existence of God. Motion in the world, Aquinas argues, is only explicable if there is a first unmoved Mover; the series of efficient causes in the world must lead to an uncaused Cause; contingent and corruptible beings must depend on an independent and incorruptible necessary Being; the varying degrees of reality and goodness in the world must be approximations to a subsistent maximum of reality and goodness; the orderly teleology of nonconscious agents in the Universe entails the existence of an intelligent universal Orderer. Several of the Five Ways seem to depend on antiquated physics, and none of them has yet been restated in a way clear of fallacy. The more valuable part of Aquinas's natural theology is his examination of the traditional attributes of God, such as eternity, omnipotence, omniscience, benevolence, and his exposition and resolution of many of the philosophical problems which they raise. In the wider area of philosophy of religion Aquinas's most influential contribution was his account of the relationship between faith and reason and the independence of philosophy from theology. Faith is a conviction as unshakeable as knowledge, but unlike knowledge not based on rational vision: the conclusions of faith cannot contradict those of philosophy but they are neither derived from philosophical reasoning nor are they the necessary basis of philosophical argument. Faith is, however, a reasonable and virtuous state of mind because reason can show the propriety of accepting divine revelation.

Even after his canonization Aquinas did not enjoy in the Middle Ages that official status in the Catholic Church which has been accorded to him in modern times. Most medieval Thomists were Dominicans, and it was only in the period between the First and the Second Vatican Councils that the study of Thomist doctrines was enjoined as a regular part of the education of all Catholic clergy. The official sanction given to Aquinas's work by Catholic authorities was in fact an obstacle to the serious critical study of his philosophy: many Catholics tended to study textbooks 'according to the mind of the Angelic Doctor' rather than to read his own writings, while non-Catholics shied away from him as being the spokesman for a party line. Textbook Thomism presented theories such as the analogy of Being, the doctrine of natural law, the real distinction between essence and existence, which represented hardenings of a fluid and nuanced position in Aquinas himself. But in recent decades the work of dedicated medievalists, secular as well as Christian, and the waning of official Catholic Thomism have begun to make room for a just appreciation of Aquinas's genius based upon purely philosophical criteria.

Arab philosophy. *See* Islamic philosophy.

Arcesilaus (*c.*316-242 BC). Sceptic and inaugurator of the 'Middle Academy'. Under Arcesilaus, its sixth head, the *Academy of Athens adopted the sceptical approach to philosophy, that characterized it for the next two centuries. A formidable dialectician, Arcesilaus concentrated his attacks on the Stoics. Apart from some verse, he wrote nothing. *See* Scepticism.

Archelaus of Athens. A pupil of *Anaxagoras and teacher of *Socrates. His small contribution, to cosmology rather than philosophy, seems to have consisted in amending the system of Anaxagoras, using elements drawn from other predecessors.

Arendt, Hannah (1906-75). German-born philosopher who came to the U.S. in 1941 as a refugee from the Nazis. *Origins of Totalitarianism* (1951), a study of the decline of 19th-century Europe's political systems and the expansionist and antisemitic tendencies that arose in its wake, established her reputation as a political scientist. Her Gifford Lectures (delivered 1972, 1974; published posthumously as *The Life of the Mind* (2 volumes, 1978)) express her profound unease at the powerlessness of philosophy, from Plato to the present day, to influence mankind's actions for good.

aretē. (Greek for: excellence.) *See* Plato.

argument. *See* function.

argument from (*or* to) design. By far the most popular and widely persuasive of all the traditional arguments for the existence of God, also called the teleological argument. It is usual to proceed not from admitted instances of design deductively (*see* deduction), but from observations of regularity and integration, by some sort of argument from experience, to the conclusion that these must be the work of a Designer. It is therefore better, and now becoming more usual, to say not argument *from* but argument *to* design.

Among the classic statements of this kind of argument are those found in Cicero's *De Natura Deorum*, the *Natural Theology* of William Paley, and the fifth of the *Five Ways of St. Thomas Aquinas. It was assailed by *Hume, first in Section XI of his *Inquiry concerning Human Understanding* and then in the posthumously published *Dialogues concerning Natural Religion.*

The first important distinction is between, on the one hand, appealing to divine intervention and contrivance in order to explain some phenomenon for which it is believed that a purely secular science will forever prove unable to account and, on the other, urging that even the most universal and fundamental regularities uncovered by scientists cannot be intrinsic to the Universe itself, but must be imposed and sustained by God (see creation; Universe and universe). Contentions of the former sort, which are not necessarily inconsistent with the latter, are at any time apt to be discredited by the latest news of successes on the science front; this is one reason why contemporary theologians sometimes speak disrespectfully of the idea of a *God of the gaps. A thesis of the latter kind, which some find in Aquinas, is not similarly exposed. It can, on the contrary, afford to hail the triumphs of science as enriching its own premises. *Darwin's theory of the origin of species by natural selection would be immensely upsetting to spokesmen of the former sort of design argument, yet could be welcome to those committed only to the latter.

The second important distinction is between those who appeal to some supposed synthetic a priori principle of causation, guaranteeing that things of such and such a sort either must be or cannot be caused in this or that way and those who, following Hume, insist that for all that can be known a priori "Anything may be the cause of anything."

Without that kind of guarantee, which the Humean will maintain that we neither can nor do have, we must be reduced to arguing from our accumulated experience of Gods and of Universes. But such experience is, of necessity, entirely lacking, for both the God whose existence it is desired to prove and the

Universe from which the whole argument must start are, by definition, unique. There can be no question of arguing that (experience of other cases teaches!) it is either immensely probable or immensely improbable that the Universe could have whatever regularity and integration it is found to have if that regularity and integration were not imposed upon it and sustained by God. Nor are we entitled to infer, without benefit of revelation, what sort of Universe, if any, a Being utterly beyond human comprehension could reasonably be expected to create. Indeed the Humean would go further, suggesting that the burden of proof must always lie upon anyone wanting to say that any characteristics that the Universe appears to have cannot be intrinsic to it. This is precisely the Stratonician atheism (see Strato of Lampsacus) that Hume found so sympathetically presented in the *Dictionary* of Pierre *Bayle, and that many believe to have been Hume's own final stance.

It should be noted that the idea of design or contrivance, though compatible, sits uneasily with that of an almighty Being.

argumentum ad baculum. (Latin for: argument appealing to the cudgel.) An argument employing an implicit or explicit threat. When in *The Godfather* the mafioso obeys the instruction to "make him an offer he can't refuse" the mafioso presents an *argumentum ad baculum.* See Pascal's wager.

argumentum ad hominem. (Latin for: argument appealing to the man.) See ad hominem argument.

argumentum ad ignorantiam. (Latin for: argument appealing to ignorance.) The label, introduced by *Locke (*Essay* IV (xvii) 20), for the move of those who "require the adversary to admit what they allege as a proof, or to assign a better."

argumentum ad judicium. (Latin for: argument appealing to judgment.) The label, introduced by *Locke (*Essay* IV

(xvii) 22), for the approved employment
of "proofs drawn from any of the foundations of knowledge or probability".
This is contrasted with *argumentum ad
hominem*, *argumentum ad ignorantiam*,
and *argumentum ad verecundiam*, all of
which he rejected.

argumentum ad verecundiam. (Latin
for: argument appealing to respect.) The
label, introduced by *Locke (*Essay IV*
(xvii) 19), for an appeal to respect for
and for submission to someone's
authority, where the authority is understood as not being authority relevant to
the particular area in question.

argumentum a fortiori. See a fortiori.

Aristotelianism. Aristotelianism and
*Neoplatonism stand like twin colossi
astride the medieval world arena of
philosophical thought. At various times
they clashed, mingled, and separated but
the product was always fruitful and
provided further scope for philosophical
development. Aristotelianism itself is an
umbrella term that covers both the
spread and study of Aristotle's doctrine
as well as the deliberate adoption and
practice, or, indeed, perversion, of that
doctrine by various groups. Its history
may conveniently be divided into a
Greek European branch and an Arabic
Middle Eastern branch.

The initial impetus for the development of the former was provided by
Aristotle's disciple, Theophrastus (d.
c.288 BC), who took over the headship of
the school, the Peripatos or *Lyceum,
on his master's death in 322 BC. Theophrastus elaborated some of Aristotle's
teaching, including his metaphysics, and
it was not long before the use of
Aristotelian logic by other groups like
the Stoics and the Sceptics led to a
deeper study, and absorption, of Aristotle's doctrines by intellectual circles.
The whole process was magnificently
crowned in the 1st century BC when
Andronicus of Rhodes (fl. 50-40 BC) and
a number of other scholars critically
edited most of the Aristotelian corpus.

Thereafter the Stagirite's teaching was
assured of a wide audience.

In the first centuries AD Neoplatonism appeared. Plotinus (204-70 AD), the
father of the new philosophy, took what
he needed from Aristotelianism and
rejected the rest. He accepted, for example, Aristotle's theory of the separate
Intellect and used, albeit in a modified
form, such Aristotelian contrasts as
matter and form, and potentiality and
actuality; but he attacked the ten
*categories and his vision of a threefold
emanationist hierarchy consisting of the
One, the Intellect, and the Soul clashed
strangely with Aristotle's theology.
Plotinus' disciple Porphyry of Tyre (234-
c.305) wrote an introduction (*Isagoge*)
to five concepts (species, genus, differentia, property, and accident) which had
featured many times in the work of
Aristotle. This *Isagoge* was adopted as
part of the *Organon*, was canonized for
future generations as Aristotelian in
inspiration, and was the origin of the
medieval doctrine of the five voices (*see
also* al-Kindī). Its popularity was assured
by *Boethius (c.480-c.524) whose intention was to reconcile Aristotelianism
with the teaching of Plato, and whose
thought was a mixture of Neoplatonism
and Aristotelianism. He produced a
famous commentary on Porphyry's
Isagoge which gave rise to the great
controversy on universals (*see* universals
and particulars) in the Middle Ages.

Of all Aristotle's works it was the
logical treatises that most fascinated the
scholars and that received most study in
the early Middle Ages; the Christian
Church began to develop such Aristotelian contrasts as substance and
accident, matter and form, and to use
these terms more and more in technical
theological senses. But in the 13th
century AD the hitherto comparatively
limited impact of Aristotelianism was
transformed out of all recognition. The
rendering into Latin of the Arabic
translations of Aristotle and, much more
importantly, of the Arabic commentaries
on his work by the major Islamic
philosophers (*see* Islamic philosophy),

provided the catalyst for an explosion of Aristotelianism in Western Europe. Indeed, Averroes (1126-98) became more honoured in the Latin West than in his own land, and provided much material to exercise two of the giant intellects of medieval *scholasticism. *Albertus Magnus (also called Albert the Great, c.1200-80) was exposed to Averroes' commentaries on Aristotle at the University of Paris, and his work reveals the influence of both Averroes and Avicenna. Albert's pupil Thomas *Aquinas (1225-74) tried to produce an acceptable synthesis of Christian thought and Aristotelianism, having become acquainted with the thought of Aristotle and Averroes while a student in Naples. But Averroes gave Aristotelianism a bad name and the 13th-century Church authorities looked with grave disquiet on the link which had developed between the Arab philosopher and the Greek. Was Christian orthodoxy to be tainted by such Averroist (and indeed, Aristotelian) doctrines as the eternity of the world? The result was that Aristotelianism and its Averroist interpretations were proscribed several times in the 13th century, beginning in 1210. This development culminated in the great condemnation by the Bishop of Paris, Stephen Tempier, on 7 March 1277.

However, the setback for Latin Aristotelianism was only temporary. A careful, though by no means uncontroversial, study of Aquinas, coupled with that scholar's canonization in 1323, helped in the rehabilitation of Aristotelianism, which had continued to influence such scholastic theologians as *Duns Scotus (c.1266-1308) and *William of Ockham (c.1285-1347). In the succeeding centuries Renaissance humanism produced a fresh crop of scholars interested in the classical languages who were forced, as a result of a revived study of Plato, to choose between him and Aristotle.

The 16th, 17th, and 18th centuries witnessed another reaction against Aristotelianism: this was partly the fruit of the astronomical work of thinkers such as *Copernicus (1473-1543), who challenged many of Aristotle's theories, as well as the later scientific ideas of physicists of the Enlightenment. Despite this, Aristotle's doctrines have continued to be studied up to the present day. The seal was set on a revived Catholic scholasticism with Pope Leo XIII's commendation of Aquinas in the encyclical *Aeterni Patris* in 1879. Furthermore, 20th-century students of Aristotle everywhere have benefited immensely from the careful translation into English of the Corpus Aristotelicum under the aegis of the Oxford scholar Sir W.D. Ross (1877-1971), and medieval Latin translations are being made available in the Aristoteles Latinus series.

The history of the Arabic Middle Eastern branch of Aristotelianism contrasts vividly with the Greek European. Whereas Aristotle's doctrines in Europe generally emerged from the filter of medieval scholastic thought as recognizably Aristotelian, the Middle Eastern alembic produced a form of Aristotelianism that would very often have been completely disowned by Aristotle himself. The latter has had, of course, numerous interpreters and has seemed many different things to many different people who have all invoked his authority to support their own varied dogmas. The Muslim philosophers were no exception and indeed, the 10th-century *Rasā'il Ikhwān al-Ṣafā'* (Epistles of the Brethren of Purity) quote a tradition about the prophet Muḥammad in which he observes that Aristotle would have become a Muslim had he lived in the age of Muḥammad (570-632). In the medieval Middle East, Aristotle's doctrines were viewed through Neoplatonic spectacles and these *Epistles*, which constitute, in effect, a Neoplatonic Muslim encyclopedia, provide excellent examples of the cavalier fashion in which many of Aristotle's doctrines were treated: in one place, for example, substance is described, Neoplatonically, as an aspect of form. Elsewhere, the Brethren of Purity observe, in a discussion of the four causes of plants, that the material cause is the four elements of fire, air, water, and earth; the efficient cause is the power of the Universal Spirit; the final cause is the provision of food and profit for animals; and the formal cause is bound up with "astral reasons which would take too long to explain". Furthermore, since the Brethren believed that all motion was due to the Universal Spirit and not to God, the problem of motion did not have the same status in the physics of the Brethren of Purity as it did with Aristotle. They also emphatically denied his doctrine of an uncreated world.

As a result of Islam's contacts with Hellenism, a wide variety of Aristotelian texts appeared in Arabic (see Islamic philosophy). These included not only the major authentic works but also such spurious texts as De Mundo, the Neoplatonic Theologia Aristotelis, and De Pomo. The latter became known in Arabic as Kitāb al-Tuffāḥah (The Book of the Apple) and portrayed the dying Aristotle discussing immortality with his students while inhaling the smell of an apple.

All the early Muslim philosophers were influenced by Aristotle, and especially by his terminology, as well as by Neoplatonism. Thus al-Kindī (d. after 866 AD), the father of Islamic philosophy, operated from a basically Aristotelian framework. Even philosophers such as *al-Fārābī (870-950) and *Avicenna (980-1037), who espoused Neoplatonism wholeheartedly, recognized the immense importance of studying Aristotle. Avicenna, who was Islam's greatest Neoplatonist, made repeated attempts at understanding his Metaphysics. After being invited to write a commentary on Aristotle, he produced the magisterial Kitāb al-Shifā' (The Book of Healing (of the Soul))—the Liber Sufficientiae of medieval Europe—which dealt with logic, the natural sciences, mathematics, and theology. Though the treatment of the latter two subjects was strongly influenced by Euclid, Ptolemy, and Neoplatonic thought, that of the former two may be said to fall within an Aristotelian mould.

The zenith of Arabic Aristotelianism was reached with the Spanish Muslim *Averroes (1126-98) whose great commentaries on Aristotle won him international fame (see Islamic philosophy). But his thought was too radical for some of his orthodox countrymen; in 1195 he was banished and an order was promulgated decreeing the burning of his philosophical works. Though Averroes regained the royal favour briefly before his death in 1198, his passing marked the end of Islamic Aristotelianism. Yet the translation of his Arabic commentaries in Europe ensured that Averroes' thought would live on and that his brand of Aristotelianism would rise, phoenix-like, in the West within a few years to disturb, perplex, and challenge another orthodoxy.

Aristotle (384-322 BC). Greek philosopher, born in Stagira, the son of the court physician to the king of Macedon. At the age of 17 he entered Plato's Academy in Athens where he remained, first as student, then as teacher, for the next 20 years, until Plato's death. The following 12 years were spent away from Athens; during three of these he acted as tutor to the young Alexander the Great. In 335 he returned to Athens and founded his own school, the Lyceum, where he taught for the next 12 years. Upon the death of Alexander, anti-Macedonian feeling in Athens forced Aristotle to take refuge in Euboea where soon afterwards he died.

The bulk of Aristotle's writings, which have survived more or less intact, consists of unpublished treatises that were either Aristotle's lecture notes or used as texts by his students. Of the dialogues and other works that Aristotle published during his life only fragments quoted by later writers have survived. The treatises that survive have traditionally been regarded as expounding a finished system of doctrine. It is only in this century that scholars have tried to discern development within Aristotle's writings. First attempts at tracing this development were guided by the assumption that Aristotle must have begun as a loyal Platonist and become more critical of Plato as he developed. More recent assessments find a hostility to Plato's philosophy in what are reckoned to be Aristotle's earliest treatises and detect the evolution of a more sophisticated position which, while by no means Plato's, is nevertheless closer to Plato's in spirit.

In *Metaphysics* (A9 and M4-5) Aristotle explicitly criticizes Plato's theory of Forms, alluding to the third man argument (*see* Plato) and complaining that the Forms are useless as explanatory devices and that the various arguments for accepting the Forms either prove nothing or establish the existence of unwelcome Forms such as negations and relations. Even where Plato's Forms are not the target of criticism, Aristotle advances theories that run contrary to the drift of Plato's thought. This is true particularly of the logical treatises which very probably date from Aristotle's days in the Academy.

In the *Categories*, for example, individual things such as particular men and animals are called primary substances; *species and genera (see* genus) of primary substances are called secondary substances. The species and genera are what an individual thing is; Socrates is a man (species) and an animal (genus). The word which 'substance' translates, '*ousia*', is more literally 'reality'. In claiming that individual things are primary realities Aristotle has stood on its head Plato's view that sensible particulars are only partly real, pale reflections of the full reality which is described by giving an account of what such particulars inadequately imitate.

Aristotle adds that it is characteristic of both primary and secondary realities (substances) not to have contraries. Many of Plato's Forms come in contrary pairs, for example, the large and the small. Aristotle would not classify the large and the small as secondary substances. These belong to one of nine other categories (in this case the category of relation) since they do not contribute

to an account of precisely what a primary substance is. 'Man' says what Socrates is because a definition of 'man' may be predicated of Socrates (he is a two-legged mammal); 'five feet tall', 'pale', 'married', do not say what Socrates *is* because he cannot be said *to be* a size, colour, or relation of any kind. The other nine categories depend on substance because qualities, quantities, etc., exist only as qualities, quantities, etc., of individual substances.

In the *Posterior Analytics*, a treatise on the logical structure of a science, Aristotle argues for the autonomy of various disciplines (geometry, astronomy, harmony) and against there being principles common to all sciences, from which the correct explanations given in those sciences could be deduced. Acceptance of this would undermine the hopes that Plato, at one stage at least, held of *dialectic. Plato's *Republic* speaks of dialectic as pursuing the most general principles from which even the principles of mathematics can be derived.

Aristotle never accords to dialectic the dignity of "the coping stone of the sciences", but like Plato his thought was profoundly shaped by his involvement in the peculiar debating activity which for Plato was the beginning of dialectic. The *Topics*, Aristotle's handbook of dialectical techniques, was very likely used in the Academy. Dialectic led Aristotle to a formal theory of valid inference built around the *syllogism. It also led him, through the need to spot equivocation, to a preoccupation with the different ways words are used (*see* equivocate).

One device for detecting equivocation was also put to work reinforcing the frontiers between autonomous disciplines. A word is not used univocally if it is applied to different kinds of things, for example, 'mule' said of an animal and a machine. For there to be a *single* science whose job it is to study all that is said to be a mule, 'mule' would have to be applied to one kind of thing only. The facts and explanations pertaining to different kinds of things belong to different sciences.

Combined with the categories, this principle provided further ammunition for attacking Plato's project of a master science. The categories are the most general kinds there are. But they are not species of a further more general kind of thing because the species of a kind can exist without one another, and nine of the categories could not exist without the category of substance. Thus there is no single kind which is everything there is, and there is therefore no science which encompasses everything there is. Plato says dialectic studies either Being or the Good, but 'to be' and 'good' are used in several categories and are therefore not univocal.

This argument appears in *Eudemian Ethics* I.8. But the line is softened considerably in *Metaphysics* Γ where Aristotle allows that a single science may encompass things that are systematically related in ways other than as species of a single genus. The categories show how various things that are said to *be* (quantities, qualities, relations, etc.) are related to substance and so there is, after all, the possibility of a discipline that studies everything that *is*. Aristotle calls this discipline 'First Philosophy', although the treatise devoted to it came later to be known as the *Metaphysics*. Undertaking an enquiry into First Philosophy represents something of a concession to Plato.

The central question of the *Metaphysics* (Books Z,H) is "What is substance?" The *Categories* gave the short answer, "Individual things like Socrates and this ox here". But it now appears that this answer is no longer adequate, probably because Aristotle's thought has developed as a result of applying the categories in an analysis of change. A typical change (analysed in *Physics* I.7) takes place when a substance, such as Socrates, which has some quality, such as a pallor, ceases to have that quality and comes to have a different quality, such as a tan. There is change that fits this analysis in the categories of quantity and place as well as quality (*Physics* V.1), but there is one

kind of change not covered by this analysis.

In a short treatise, *On Coming to Be and Passing Away*, Aristotle analyses the coming into existence (as opposed to coming to have some quality, etc.) and ceasing to exist (as opposed to ceasing to have some quality, etc.). He distinguishes within an individual substance, such as a statue, matter (bronze) and form (shape of a god). ('Form' here should not be confused with a Platonic Form or Idea; the Aristotelian form of the statue has no existence apart from matter of some kind.) A statue comes into existence when bronze is cast in a certain shape and ceases to exist when the bronze is melted down into something else. Why we should not regard the bronze as substance and the shape as belonging to some other category is explained in *Metaphysics* Z and Θ. The matter, bronze, by itself, does not have sufficient unity to be regarded as a substance.

But the *Metaphysics* does not follow the expected path of declaring that substance (what is primarily real) is a composite of form and matter. Aristotle wishes to have what is primarily real knowable and he follows Plato in holding that what is knowable must be eternal and definable. Composites of form and matter are perishable and not definable. Only the form (also said to be the essence) of a composite of form and matter can be defined. Aristotle also feels able to claim that forms do not come into or go out of existence when a composite is created or destroyed because the form will exist embodied in some other matter elsewhere. This implies that form is something common to many individuals and brings Aristotle's candidate for what is primarily real closer to Plato's separate ideal Forms.

But in the very same book of the *Metaphysics* (Z13-14) Aristotle argues that Plato's forms cannot be substances because they are universal or common to many things. This seems to cut with equal force against Aristotle's explicit identification of form with substance. There is no agreement among scholars as to how Aristotle avoids this contradiction, or even that he does avoid it. One suggestion is that Aristotle distinguishes, without clearly informing us, between what is primarily real (the composite of form and matter) and definable reality (the form). Another suggestion is that, in spite of appearances, forms are not common but peculiar to each individual. Yet another solution proposes that when Aristotle denied substance could be common, he meant common to many definitions. For example, animal would appear in the definitions of man and ox; man and ox could be substances, but animal could not. This view entails that it is species which are primary realities in the *Metaphysics*.

The second of the above views, that each individual thing has its own peculiar form, seems to be in harmony with Aristotle's favourite example: a man is a composite of form, *psyche* (translated 'soul') and matter (flesh and blood); and is not each man's soul peculiar to him? This is certainly true of Plato's *psyche*, an immaterial reality unhappily imprisoned in a body; but Aristotle's *psyche* is a different thing altogether. According to the treatise on the soul (*De Anima*), every living thing has *psyche*; it is that which makes a thing alive and consists in capacities for various activities characteristic of life. The lowest living things, plants, have a capacity only for nourishment and reproduction; animals have in addition capacities for sensation and movement; higher animals have in addition a limited memory; humans have in addition a capacity to reason. Matter that has lost these capacities is dead, and as these are capacities *of a body* it is, with one exception, absurd to speak of them as existing without a body and absurd to speak of them as existing in a body that lacks the organs needed to exercise them. Vision cannot exist in a body that lacks anything that could do what an eye does.

This close dependence of *psyche* on body makes it possible for Aristotle to say (*Metaphysics* Z8) that it is different matter that makes different men different. If there is a difference between the *psyche* of one man and that of another, this difference must derive from their different bodies and perish when they die. Any hope for personal survival after death must thus rest with the one exception to this close dependence of *psyche* on body. One rather obscure capacity involved in abstract thought is said not to involve any organ of the body and thus possibly to survive death. This is pure form and it is not clear how pure forms are to be individuated. Aristotle says so little about this that the view of the great 12th-century Arab commentator, *Averroes, that there is just one of these pure forms for the whole human race, cannot be ruled out.

The account of the human *psyche* plays an important role in Aristotle's ethical theory. The *Ethics* is a treatise on those characteristics that men acquire by habituation (*ethos* means roughly 'habit'). To determine which habits should be fostered Aristotle starts with what all men agree is the aim of life, *eudaimonia* (roughly 'happiness', but *eudaimonia* in ordinary Greek could not consist in a low grade contentment). There is, of course, little agreement on what happiness consists in. To settle the question Aristotle reasons that what is aimed at by something is the good for that thing and then, taking a step at which many balk, he identifies this with the actualization of the best potentiality of that thing. In other words, in seeking happiness all men are seeking to actualize the best that men are capable of. This conflates 'the good sought by men' with 'what it is to be a good man'. The next step is to determine the best that men are capable of by determining what is the distinctive activity (*ergon*) of man. This step is reasonable since one cannot say what is the best an *X* is capable of unless one knows what *X*s distinctively do. It follows from the account of the human *psyche* that it is distinctive of men to reason.

Aristotle does conclude that the best (and happiest) man spends as much time as possible in the purest activity of reason, theorizing (*Ethics* X). However, since he is a man, the rational part of his soul (*psyche*) is more than just an intellect, and intellectual excellence by itself does not make a good and happy man. Reason governs action as well as theorizing. Action is the response made to desire, and here, Aristotle insists, one can respond too much or too little. The correct response lies somewhere between the two extremes. This is the doctrine of the mean (*see* golden mean). It does not pretend to provide a moral decision procedure. It is a (meta-ethical) statement about the form of certain moral concepts: to every virtue there are two distinct vices.

So what is needed in addition to intellectual excellence is moral excellence. The man who has the latter has habits that lead him always to find the virtuous mean between two vicious extremes. These habits are not unthinking responses or natural instincts for doing the right thing. They involve a rational assessment of each new situation and a choice made in the light of a conception of what it is men should aim at, what they should regard as constituting happiness.

Arnauld, Antoine (1612-94). French theologian, priest, logician, and mathematician, born into a family of prominent Jansenist supporters, closely connected with the *Port Royal group. His book *De la fréquente communion* (1643) setting out Jansen's doctrines, as well as numerous pamphlets attacking the Jesuits, raised violent protest. Arnauld was deprived of his Sorbonne doctorate, and persecution for his continued support of Jansenism eventually forced him to seek refuge in Belgium in 1679.

During his time at Port Royal he collaborated with Nicole and *Pascal on *La logique, ou l'art de penser* (known as the *Port Royal Logic*) (1662). Though they were originally friends, Arnauld came to disagree with *Malebranche, whom he attacked in *Traité des vraies et des fausses idées* (1683).

arrow paradox. *See* Zeno's paradoxes.

artificial language. *See* natural language.

art, philosophy of. *See* aesthetics.

assertion sign. The symbol '⊢' placed by *Frege in front of a sentence to indicate that the sentence was being asserted (said to be true). Frege's use of '⊢' made it part of the *object language of his system. In modern use '⊢' is a sign in the *metalanguage used to indicate that the sentence which follows may be (a) derived from the axioms of the theory, or (b) derived without assumptions, that is, is a logical theorem. Written between sentences, or sets of sentences, '⊢' is a metalinguistic symbol used to indicate that what occurs on the right may be derived from, or may be asserted on the basis of, what occurs on the left; thus, for example, '$A_1 \ldots A_n \vdash B$' is read 'B may be derived from $A_1 \ldots A_n$', or 'given $A_1 \ldots A_n$, B may be asserted'.

assertoric. Describing a proposition that simply asserts that something is or is not the case. The term is used to contrast such propositions with modal (that is *problematic or *apodeictic) propositions.

associationism. A psychological rather than a philosophical theory, taking association to be the fundamental principle of mental life. Its first systematic presentation was by *Hume in the *Treatise*, where the author hoped that various sorts of association between atoms of consciousness would do for the mental world what classical mechanics had done for that of "hard, massy and impenetrable" bits of stuff. This associationist tradition continued through *Hartley, James Mill, J. S. Mill, and Herbert Spencer. Associationism has usually been combined with *sensationalism.

association of ideas. 1. A psychologistic explanation advanced by *Hume to refute certain philosophical "fictions", particularly in connection with the notion of *causation. The mind has a tendency to associate the ideas corresponding to types of events that have always been observed in close succession; consequently, whenever the idea of the first type of event is present to the mind, it evokes the idea and expectation of an event of the second type. The two types of events, termed 'cause' and 'effect', give rise to the assumption that there is a necessary connection between them; in fact there is no observable phenomenon and hence no "genuine idea" of a necessary connection.

2. In the *phenomenalism of J. S. *Mill, a law of inference that explains one's belief in the existence of material objects. By experience one learns that certain sensations occur together in the perception of any object; one forms a concept of an object in terms of the possible group of sensations associated with its perception.

asymmetric. See relation.

asymptotic. Denoting a line or series that approaches nearer and nearer to a curve or limit but will never reach that curve or limit within a finite distance. The moves of Achilles and the tortoise in Zeno's paradox are of this kind (see Zeno's paradoxes).

ataraxia. (Greek for: tranquillity of mind, unpeturbedness.) The goal and inspiration of the Greek Sceptics. It was to be achieved by the calm and reasoned suspension of judgment (epoche) about contentious issues.

atheism. The rejection of belief in God, whether on the grounds that it is meaningful but false to say that God exists, or, as the logical positivists held, that it is meaningless and hence neither true nor false (see logical positivism). It can be said with some point that atheism exists only in relation to some conception of deity, that the professed atheist can always reasonably be asked what God he denies, and that 'God' covers so many different conceptions, from crude anthropomorphism to sophisticated ideas of an Infinite Substance or Ground of all Being, that everyone is perforce an atheist in relation to some of them. However, the label 'atheist' is ordinarily, though probably not invariably, applied without qualification only to someone who denies God in any of the senses that current uses of the term allow.

Some atheists have maintained that the onus of proof is on the theist since atheism is *prima facie* the more reasonable position. There are also various standard arguments in defence of atheism: for example, that God as such must exist necessarily and the notion of necessary existence is logically incoherent; that the existence of God is incompatible with the presence of evil in the world; or that appeals to a *First Cause or Cosmic Designer (see argument from design) create only illusions of explanation. Many modern thinkers, however, while acknowledging the force of such arguments, see them as grounds for radical reappraisal of the function of the concept of God in the economy of human thought, rather than for outright atheism.

atomic sentence. A sentence containing no logical *operator, and which is thus logically simple.

atomic uniformity, principle of. The name given by J. M. *Keynes to the further assumption, additional to that embodied in the principle of *limited independent variety, supposedly required to justify *induction: "the material universe must consist ... of bodies ... such that each ... exercises its own separate, independent and invariable effect, a change of total state being compounded of a number of separate changes each of which is solely due to a separate portion of the preceding state" (A Treatise on Probability, p. 249).

atomic wff. A *wff containing no logical *operator.

atomism. The belief that matter consists of atoms. It is usually traced to the Greek philosophers *Leucippus and *Democritus (5th century BC). The belief derives its power partly from empirical and partly from metaphysical considerations: scientifically it is attractive to believe that the large-scale properties of objects are the result of, and can be explained as, the arrangements of a set of fundamental constituents; metaphysically it may be appealing to regard all change as the result of the rearrangement of enduring parts, rather than as involving the creation and destruction of matter itself. The classical atomists maintained that atoms possess only spatial extension, shape, solidity, and perhaps weight, but not properties such as colour, warmth, and smell. They thus anticipated the corpuscularian philosophy of *Gassendi, *Boyle, and *Locke in the 17th century, with its emphasis on the difference between the *primary and secondary qualities of material things.

Modern physics maintains the principle of explaining observations by seeking the structure of progressively smaller particles, but these particles can no longer be conceived as having solidity and shape, like miniature billiard balls: electromagnetic and other less familiar properties have superseded these in explanatory importance. The pull of atomism is still evident in the unease people feel when descriptions of the subatomic world do not allow them to picture what is going on in terms of the motions of small shaped solid objects. See also effluxes, theory of; logical atomism; quantum mechanics.

attributive. 1. Denoting a particular placing of an adjective. The adjective 'white' is in the attributive position in 'Silver is a white horse' and in the predicative position in 'Silver, the horse, is white'. **2.** An adjective. If an adjective in either position requires a substantive to supply part of its sense, it is said to be *syncategorematic or a logical attributive. For example, to say that a mouse is large involves the understanding that it is large-for-a-mouse, since a mouse is small-for-an-animal; Mary may be good at cooking, but indifferent at singing. So 'large' and 'good' are logical attributives. If the substantive cannot or need not apply on its own (an expectant mother is not necessarily a mother, a forged passport cannot be a passport) then the adjective ('expectant', 'forged') is said to be *alienans.

Aufklärung. German for: *Enlightenment.

Augustine of Hippo, St. (354-430). The greatest of the Latin Church fathers, born in North Africa. He studied and taught in Carthage, Rome, and Milan. After spells of Manichaeism and scepticism, he re-converted to the Christianity of his childhood in 386. He returned to North Africa to found a monastic community and was subsequently made Bishop of Hippo (395-430). Of his many theological treatises, mainly on the controversies of the time, the best known philosophically are the Confessions (400) and The City of God (composed over the period 412-27).

Although many passages in Augustine's work, like the famous analysis of time in the Confessions, suggest outstanding technical ability, his philosophy was almost always auxiliary to religious preoccupations. He saw both philosophy and religion as essentially quests for wisdom and, through wisdom, beatitude; the crucial difference was that Christian faith succeeded in the quest, while the unaided human reason of the philosophical schools could not. He did not, however, deny that some truths, including theological truths, were attainable by reason alone. *Neoplatonism certainly helped him to break free from Manichaean dualism (see Manichaeism), and Platonic concepts played an important role in his interpretations of Christian teaching. But the task of reason was essentially that of elucidating things already accepted by faith as divine revelation—an attitude later summed up in the formula "Credo ut intelligam" (I believe so that I may understand).

In opposition to *Pelagianism, which he helped to have declared heretical, Augustine insisted on man's need for grace, for a divine initiative to effect the reconciliation between God and man which fallen man is powerless to achieve for himself. This raises difficult problems, much discussed in subsequent Christian theology, about predestination and freewill, but Augustine appears to have allowed that man has a measure of freedom to respond to, or reject, the offer of grace.

In the *City of God*, he presents human history as in essence the conflict between the city of God, the community of those whose actions are, through divine grace, inspired by love of God, and the earthly city, founded on the love of temporal things—a conflict which will, eventually, end in the triumph of the city of God. Such a city, as he envisaged it, was a spiritual entity, not to be identified with any specific place or organization, though doubtless he regarded the Church as its primary manifestation on earth.

Augustine's writings, especially on divine grace and the role and authority of the Church, profoundly influenced both medieval and Reformation religious thought.

Austin, John (1790-1859). Perhaps the most influential philosopher of law of the 19th century. Austin was greatly influenced by the work of Jeremy *Bentham, especially in his 'positivist' approach to the nature of law (*see* law, philosophy of). In *The Province of Jurisprudence Determined* (1832), Austin argued for a strict separation between what the law is and what it ought to be. (On the latter question Austin took a utilitarian position.) Austin defined law as a command of the sovereign, expressing his wish, and backed by sanctions for non-compliance. The sovereign is in turn defined as that individual or body to whom the people have a habit of obedience. This picture of the law has the advantage of imparting clarity and factual verifiability to many legal questions. However, there are many kinds of law (for example, the law of contract, and other laws that enable people to undertake obligations) to which the model of command backed by sanctions cannot be applied without distortion.

Austin, John Langshaw (1911-60). British philosopher who spent his whole working life, except for wartime intelligence service, in Oxford. His main mission was to apply the methods and standards of a scholar of classical texts to some usually non-technical areas of contemporary English discourse. How else are concepts to be elucidated if not through meticulous attention to the usage of the words through which they are expressed?

The nature of this Austinian mission, and the philosophical profit to be won from it, is perhaps best seen in the articles 'Other Minds' (1946) and 'A Plea for Excuses' (1956), reprinted in his posthumous *Philosophical Papers* (1961). The former contains Austin's first account of performatory utterances, speech acts which are in themselves the performance of an action. Thus to say 'I promise' in the appropriate conditions is in itself the making of a promise, not a mere statement about a promise. (This insight finds unacknowledged anticipations in the account of promising in Hume's *Treatise*.) The latter article brings out the great richness and some of the detailed characteristics of our everyday vocabulary of extenuation and excuse. In this area of logical mapwork, as elsewhere, Austin was always very conscious of how much the Aristotle of the *Nicomachean Ethics* has to teach. The same page contains Austin's clearest repudiations of two silly views often but falsely attributed to him by hostile polemicists: first, that such mapwork is the be-all and end-all, as opposed to the begin-all, of philosophy; second, that our untechnical vocabulary never needs to be revised or supplemented. His other work in this period was the posthumously published lecture series *Sense and Sensibilia* (1962).

In his last years—represented by the 1955 William James Lectures, published as *How to do things with words* (1962)—Austin refined upon the notion of performative utterance. He distinguished, for instance, the illocutionary force of a speech act (what is done *in* saying something) from its locutionary force (what is the act *of* saying) and its perlocutionary force (what is effected in others *by* saying). Because Austin always somehow "failed to leave enough time in which to say why what I have said is interesting" his later work has often been thought to be philosophically irrelevant linguistics. *See also* speech acts.

autological. A synonym for *homological.

Avenarius, Richard (1843-96). German philosopher. In his major work, *Kritik der reinen Erfahrung* (Critique of Pure Experience) (1888-1900), he presented a theory of knowledge known as empirio-criticism. This is developed as an extreme form of *positivism, insisting on the elimination of all metaphysics and admitting as knowledge only that given in pure *experience. As such, it is extremely close to the philosophical views of Ernst *Mach, as well as to neutral monism (*see* monism). Avenarius rejected the differentiation between the psychological and the physical, or between private sensations and an independently existing external world, in favour of a single system of pure experience, of which the ego and its environment are constituents. This is the philosophy famously attacked by *Lenin as idealist (*see* idealism) in *Materialism and Empirio-Criticism*.

Avencebrol. *See* Ibn Gabirol.

average. 1. In one common sense, a word virtually synonymous with 'typical', 'ordinary', or 'in no way distinguished'. **2.** More technically, the average is the arithmetic mean: to find, for instance, the average height of the people in a room you must add up the heights of every individual and divide that total by the total number of people. It is false to say, as is quite often said, that half the members of any group must be below and half above average in whatever respect anyone chooses to specify. For instance, if the average height of these six individuals is six foot

this might result from the fact that one was six foot two-and-a-half and the other five all five foot eleven-and-a-half. **3.** The median is the middle number of a series of numbers arranged in order of magnitude. (Where the series has an even number of members the median is the figure halfway between the two middle terms.) The most common mistake here is to confuse the median with the mean; that is, the assumption that the total of the deviations above the median always must (as of course they always *may*) equal the total of the deviations below. **4.** The third technical sort of average is the mode. This is the most likely case. To calculate the modal mark in a set of examination results you must first establish the frequency distribution. In this instance the obvious move is to divide the whole range of possibilities into ten class-intervals: those from 0-9%; those from 10%-19%; and so on. You then count how many marks have been awarded within each of these ten class-intervals, and the modal mark is that at the halfway point between the limits of the most frequented.

Averroes (Arabic name: Ibn Rushd, Abū al-Walīd Muḥammad b. Aḥmad) (1126-98). Islamic philosopher and judge, who spent most of his life as a qāḍī (judge) in Seville and Cordova and wrote on jurisprudence and medicine, in addition to his voluminous philosophical output. Main works: *Tahāfut al-Tahāfut* (The Incoherence of the Incoherence) (written c.1180) and numerous commentaries on Aristotle.

Averroes was Islam's greatest medieval Aristotelian. A famous meeting (c.1169) with the Almohad prince Abū Ya'qūb Yūsuf, during which the subject of the eternity of the world was discussed, led to Averroes' agreeing to write commentaries upon Aristotle. He produced a series of magisterial works that ranged over the whole Corpus Aristotelicum (as well as Plato's *Republic* and Porphyry's *Isagoge*), and included three distinct lengths of commentary on each of the *Metaphysics*,

Physics, Posterior Analytics, De Caelo, and De Anima. It was this aspect of his work, revealing as it did the full profundity of his knowledge of Aristotle, that made him justly famous in Western Europe. He tried to remove some of the Neoplatonic elements that had crept into Aristotelian exegesis and in his most original work, The Incoherence of the Incoherence, he ably defended philosophy against *al-Ghazālī's attack. See also Islamic philosophy.

Avicebron. See Ibn Gabirol.

Avicenna (Arabic name: Ibn Sīnā, Abū'Alī al-Husayn) (980–1037). Islamic philosopher. Main works: Kitāb al-Shifā' (The Book of Healing (of the Soul)), abridged by Avicenna in Kitāb al-Najāt (The Book of Salvation), and Qānūn fī 'l-Tibb (The Canon of Medicine). (The latter two works were printed in Rome in 1593.)

Prodigiously erudite in many subjects before the age of 18, Avicenna claims to have found difficulty only with metaphysics. He read Aristotle's Metaphysics forty times without comprehension but eventually chanced upon a commentary by *al-Fārābī which illuminated the work for him. Indeed, Avicenna owed much to al-Fārābī and developed the latter's *Neoplatonism. Avicenna's Supreme Being was characterized by both necessity and complete unity; from It emanated all other being. While his work may not have been highly original, he wrote with a clarity which al-Fārābī lacked and this helped greatly in popularizing his ideas. More is known about Avicenna than any other Muslim philosopher since he took the unusual step of dictating his autobiography to one of his students. Although regarded primarily as a philosopher, his substantial contribution to medicine should not be overlooked. See also Islamic philosophy.

avowals. A term used by *Ryle to describe certain first-person utterances (such as 'I am in pain') and to distinguish them from their third-person counterparts ('He is in pain'). Ryle noted that the latter are (usually) normal, information-giving statements, and, as such, open to doubt. Avowals, on the other hand, seem (when sincere) to be infallible. Ryle argues that this may be because they are not ordinary assertions but are part of the behaviour that characterizes being in the state to which they refer.

axiology. The philosophical study of values, undertaken especially in the fields of ethics, religion, and aesthetics.

axiom. A statement for which no proof is required and which, thus, occurs as a premise of many arguments but as the conclusion of none. It may be accorded this status either because it is held to be a self-evident truth, as the axioms of Euclidean geometry were for a long time, or because it is thought to constitute an implicit *definition of the terms it contains or to contribute, with other axioms, to such a definition. An axiomatic theory is one in which all the claims of the theory are presented as theorems derivable from a specified collection, the set (or system) of axioms, which are the axioms of the theory (see theorem). Geometry, as presented in Euclid's Elements, provides a paradigm for such a presentation. The point of presenting a theory in this way is that it is then possible to see exactly what its assumptions are, or what must be postulated to be the case if the theory is to be accepted as correct. For this reason the terms 'axiom' and 'postulate' are sometimes used interchangeably. It is often possible to axiomatize the same theory in different ways, that is, to present two different sets A and A' of axioms such that whenever C can be deduced from A it either belongs to A' or can be deduced from A', and vice versa. A and A' would then be said to be alternative axiomatizations of the theory. In general, one aims at reducing the number of axioms to a minimum in order to show just how many basic assumptions must be made in accepting the theory.

In the presentation of a theory the axioms are sometimes divided into *logical* and *non-logical* axioms. In cases where this is not done the logic is assumed to be agreed and all the axioms are non-logical. The exception is when the theory being presented is itself a system of logic, in which case all the axioms are logical axioms. Non-logical axioms are those concerned with the content of the theory and involve terms specific to the theory, as, for example, 'Between any two points a straight line may be drawn'. The logical axioms, however, involve only *logical constants together with symbols abbreviating sentences or predicates, as for example $(x)(Fx \lor -Fx)$, and determine, together with the rules of *inference adopted, what are the means to be employed in drawing consequences from the non-logical axioms. An axiom such as $(x)(Fx \lor -Fx)$, which contains a letter abbreviating or marking the place of an unspecified expression, is more strictly speaking an *axiom schema* (*see also* variable). An axiom is obtained from an axiom schema by substitution—in this case a particular predicate, say 'is a closed curve' would be substituted for '*F*'. The corresponding axiom would then be 'For all *x*, either *x* is a closed curve, or *x* is not a closed curve', which is an example of a logical axiom, since the axiom schema from which it is obtained is a logical axiom schema. It is, however, also possible to have non-logical axiom schemata.

axiomatic method. A method of formalizing and studying a subject by using only the methods of formal logic in order to derive the truths of the subject from a list of undefined terms and a list of axioms. *See* axiom.

axiom of infinity. An axiom of *set theory that asserts, in one form or another, that there exists a set with infinitely many members: for example, there is a set, *A*, such that the empty set is a member of *A* and for any object, *b*, if *b* is a member of *A*, so is the set whose sole member is *b*. The reduction of mathematics to set theory requires the axiom of infinity, which *Russell originally and erroneously believed was provable from other accepted assumptions. The axiom is now known to be independent of the other axioms of set theory.

Ayer, Sir Alfred Jules (1910-). English philosopher who studied under *Ryle at Oxford and then in Vienna before returning to Oxford (1933) to lecture in philosophy. He became Grote Professor of the Philosophy of Mind and Logic at London University (1946) and Wykeham Professor of Logic at Oxford (1959). He was knighted in 1970.

Language, Truth and Logic (1936) presented the principal theses of *logical positivism, providing a link between the ideas of the *Vienna Circle and British linguistic analysis; it dealt with problems of reality, perception, induction, knowledge, meaning, and other minds. Ayer's original views were modified in the revised edition of this work (1946), *The Foundations of Empirical Knowledge* (1940), and *The Problem of Knowledge* (1956). He continued to adhere to the *verification principle as stated by *Carnap, but distinguished between 'strong' and 'weak' verification, between verifiability in practice and in theory, allowing that general statements of science and those about the past can be meaningful if experience can show them probable though not conclusively provable and if there is a conceivable (if not actual) method by which they can be verified.

B

Bacon, Francis (1561-1626). London-born philosopher who was the forerunner of the British empiricist tradition. His family belonged to the higher rank of the civil service and Bacon himself enjoyed an outstanding legal and political career, James I making him Lord Chancellor and later Viscount St.

Albans. However, in 1621 Bacon was charged with corruption, fined an enormous sum, and banished from court. Alexander Pope had in mind both Bacon's incomparable reputation for learning and his ultimate disgrace when he called him "the brightest, wisest, meanest of mankind" (*Essay on Man*, Part VI).

Bacon was the first in the great line of British empiricist philosophers, stretching through Locke, Hume, and J. S. Mill to Bertrand Russell, who found time to produce a wide range of theoretical and literary works. In Bacon's case these include, most notably, his *Essays* (first published in 1597; reissued and augmented until the final version of 1625); *The Advancement of Learning* (1605), a systematic survey of the various branches of existing knowledge leading to a new classification of the sciences, both present and future; the *Novum Organum* (1620), the title of which recalls the Aristotelian *Organon*; *De Augmentis Scientiarum* (1623), which was an expanded Latin version of *The Advancement of Learning*; and the *New Atlantis* (published posthumously in 1660). Bacon also produced numerous legal, historical, scientific, and aphoristic works.

In general Bacon's outlook was concrete, practical, and utilitarian. His thinking was, moreover, markedly forward-looking, sometimes even apocalyptic in its view of the possibilities for human progress once the allegedly cramping illusions of traditional theories and methods were shaken off. Hence the regular occurrence of the word 'new' in the titles and sub-headings of so many of his writings. He appears to have accepted the doctrines of Christianity as true, though his choice of words when discussing theology sometimes strongly suggests the later ironic postures of *Hobbes or *Hume. As part of an elaborate polemic against scholasticism he called for a separation of reason and revelation. He believed that this would have the advantage of facilitating the pursuit of genuine scientific knowledge

which, properly and systematically applied, would quite quickly transform human life for the better. In this sense he equated knowledge with power. His vision of the imminent likelihood of a large-scale technological mastery of nature was certainly utopian; thus the *New Atlantis*, where some of the means for this mastery are vividly set forth, might be described as the first notable work of science fiction.

Philosophically, Bacon is particularly interesting for two reasons.

(1) In Part II of the *Novum Organum* he tried to improve on existing conceptions of scientific method by expounding a method of *induction which was not simply induction by *simple enumeration. He insisted, quite rightly, that traditional syllogistic logic was not a means of empirical discovery but only an aid for exhibiting the deductive consequences of what is already known. He also stressed the need for checking generalizations by a search for "negative instances". Here he initiated that concern with the nature of inductive or probable reasoning characteristic of British philosophers, a concern culminating in J. S. Mill's *System of Logic* (1843). During the Enlightenment Bacon was held in the highest esteem, especially by the French *philosophes*. His classification of the sciences was largely adopted in the *Encyclopédie* (1751-65), and he was widely considered, as D'Alembert put it, to have first "made known the necessity for experimental physics". However, while Bacon was indeed perhaps the most eloquent advocate of the empirical scientific *spirit*, his understanding of scientific *method*, as actually practised by his scientific contemporaries, such as Galileo, was in fact very imperfect. Bacon notoriously failed to appreciate the sense in which mathematics was already the language of the new physics; he also gravely underestimated the use scientists need to make of imaginative hypotheses. On this last point his position was criticized memorably by *Kant (see *Critique of Pure Reason*, B xii ff).

(2) In Book I of the *Novum Organum*

and elsewhere Bacon made what was probably the first systematic attempt to expose the psychological motives and human interests that often lie behind various forms of philosophical outlook. He discusses what he calls the *idola mentis* (*idols of the mind) which had, he believed, up to his own time persistently stood in the way of objective knowledge. This particular critique of philosophical doctrines was taken up and much further extended in the 18th century, most notably by Hume and by *Condillac.

Bacon, Roger (*c.*1214-1292). English Franciscan, who worked in Oxford and Paris and earned the sobriquet *Doctor Mirabilis.* Main works: *Opus Maius* (Greater Work), *Opus Minus* (Lesser Work), *Opus Tertium* (Third Work), *Compendium of Philosophy, Compendium of Theology.*

Although an admirer of Aristotle, Bacon was by no means part of the mainstream developments in Parisian theology and philosophy that were taking place in his time. The Neoplatonic *Book of Causes,* the fantastic fabrications of the *Secret of Secrets* (both masquerading as Aristotelian), and the philosophy of science of *Grosseteste were among the influences that combined to make Bacon speculate on scientific matters. This he did with the prophetic insight of erratic genius. His words recommending mathematics as the sure foundation for other sciences come very close to those of *Descartes. Bacon placed a high value on experiment, with numerous but odd concrete illustrations. For him experience comprised not only the findings of the senses, but also the divine illuminations attributed to patriarchs and prophets. He accordingly believed that moral virtue clarifies the mind so that it can more easily understand the truth. He has also been credited with leaning towards that priority of the individual over the universal (*see* universals and particulars) later exemplified in *Duns Scotus and *William of Ockham.

bad faith. In the *existentialism of *Sartre, a form of deception of self and others; the attempt to rationalize human existence through religion, science, or any belief in operative forces that impose meaning and coherence. Man shapes his own destiny through a succession of free choices for which he is totally responsible. In 'bad faith' he denies the necessity of relying on his own moral insight and fallible will, trying to escape the burden of responsibility by regarding himself as the passive subject of outside influences, and his actions as being predetermined by these rather than freely chosen by himself. *See also* Angst.

Bain, Alexander (1818-1903). Scottish empiricist philosopher and psychologist. He became Professor of Logic and eventually Rector at Aberdeen and founded the philosophical periodical *Mind.* He was a close friend of John Stuart *Mill and a supporter of *utilitarianism. Bain's interest lay chiefly in the philosophy of mind, presented in *Senses and the Intellect* (1855) and *Mental and Moral Science* (1868), where he advocated the investigation of physical conditions influencing mental states.

barber paradox. A paradox illustrating a problem in *set theory. Suppose that the barber of Seville shaves all the men of Seville, except those who shave themselves. Does the barber shave himself? If he does shave himself, he is not to be shaved by the barber, that is, himself; if he doesn't, he should be shaved by the barber. Hence he both does and does not shave himself. So the original supposition is false. *Compare* Russell's paradox.

basic action. A thing that we simply *do*, without having to do anything else to make it happen. The contrast is with those of our actions that involve causing things to happen (for example, exploding a demolition charge by pressing the detonator). Raising one's arm is the stock example of a basic action. However, the causal powers involved in even such a simple case have seemed mysterious to some philosophers. *See also* action.

basic statements. A phrase coined by *Ayer in the context of arranging the beliefs of an individual. If epistemology is conceived as the project of arranging the statements we believe according to the reasons we have for believing them, then we are likely, sooner or later, to come to beliefs for which no reasons can be given. An empiricist asserts that this will indeed be the case, and that all such statements will report what we experience through our senses. These statements Ayer called 'basic statements'. *Neurath, in the context of arranging the (intersubjective) beliefs of a community, called them *protocol statements* (*Protokollsätze*).

battle of gods and giants. An image in Plato's *Sophist* describing the perennial conflict between two types of thinker: "One side drags down everything from heaven and the unseen to earth, rudely grasping rocks and trees in their hands. For they get their grip on all such things, and they maintain that that alone exists which can be handled and touched ... Terrible men ... Those who battle against them defend themselves very carefully from somewhere above in the unseen, contending that true existence consists in certain incorporeal Forms which are objects of the mind" (§§ 245-6). Plato himself is the first forefather of the gods; *Leucippus and *Democritus, *Hobbes and *Marx, fight in the front line for the giants.

Baumgarten, Alexander Gottlieb (1714-62). German philosopher of the Wolffian school (*see* Wolff). Major early works include the *Metaphysica* (1740), which was much admired by Kant, and the *Ethica Philosophia* (1740). Baumgarten remains best known for his long, unfinished treatise, *Aesthetica* (1750-8), in which he was the first to introduce the term 'aesthetics' in something resembling its contemporary use (*see* aesthetics). The principal claims of the *Aesthetica* are that art is founded upon mental representations that are both sensuous and bound up with feelings, and that in this respect *beauty is not a simple and distinct intellectual idea but an elaborate and confused complex.

Bayes's theorem. The theorem published posthumously in 1763 by Thomas Bayes (1702-61), giving an expression for the probability of a hypothesis, *h*, if some evidence, *e*, is added to antecedent knowledge, *a*. The theorem states that the probability of *h* relative to *e* & *a* is equal to the probability of *h* relative to *a* multiplied by the probability of *e* relative to *h* & *a*, and divided by the probability of *e* relative to *a*. This means that evidence improbable antecedently, but likely to obtain if the hypothesis is true, raises the probability of a hypothesis most. The application of the theorem can be controversial, since it is often unclear how assignments of antecedent probabilities are justified.

Bayle, Pierre (1647-1706). French philosopher, who studied philosophy under the Jesuits at Toulouse and became a Catholic for a while. Having reconverted to Calvinism he fled persecution to Geneva where he studied the works of *Descartes, then returned to France to become professor of philosophy at the Calvinist college at Sedan. After a fresh outbreak of persecution Bayle took refuge in Rotterdam where he continued to lecture until his dismissal from the university in 1693, following an accusation that he was a French agent and enemy of Protestantism.

His chief work, the *Dictionnaire historique et critique* (1696), is a compendium of sceptical arguments against theological and philosophical theories, drawing the conclusion that rational endeavour is useless and man must turn to faith to justify his belief that things exist and that God is not a deceiver. The work was widely attacked on grounds of alleged profanity and for its claim that morality is independent of religion; nonetheless it became influential in the sceptical philosophy of the *Enlightenment and its arguments were used by *Hume and *Voltaire in their attacks on traditional theology.

beauty. The sensible condition of aesthetic excellence considered to arouse the keenest pleasure. Until the 18th century, discussions that would now be thought to fall within the domain of *aesthetics were invariably expressed in terms of beauty and the *sublime, either in nature or art. Beauty was held to be either (as for *Plato) an intrinsic property of objects, measurable in reference to, for example, purity, integrity, harmony, or perfection, or (as for the British philosopher Francis *Hutcheson) an idea prompted in us by particular objects.

Since the 18th century, the term has virtually been displaced in favour of the concepts of art and creativity. For contemporary purposes, there are two principal difficulties with the concept of beauty: first, it is ambiguous between the idea of a universal standard of aesthetic merit and the idea of a particular quality standing in specifiable relation to, for example, elegance; second, while classical works of art may strike us as beautiful, the term seems wholly inapplicable to modern works such as Picasso's *Guernica.*

Bedeutung. (German for: meaning.) In the philosophical logic of *Frege, the term standardly translated as 'reference' (*compare* Sinn). *See* sense and reference.

begging the question. The procedure of taking for granted, in a statement or argument, precisely what is in dispute.

behaviourism. The theory, first propounded by the psychologist J.B.Watson in *Behaviorism* (1925), that psychological functioning is definable in terms of observed behavioural data. Initially introduced in order to establish a firm scientific basis for psychology, the theory has since had extensive elaboration, notably in the writings of B.F.Skinner.

Philosophical behaviourism has found favour in relation to problems raised by a dualistic model of the mental and physical, and by traditional introspec-tionist accounts of the mind. In his classic, *The Concept of Mind* (1949), Gilbert *Ryle argues that the Cartesian myth of the *ghost in the machine results from a *category mistake about the exclusivity of the mental and physical, and that in fact mental concepts may be analysed in terms of overt acts and utterances. In a modified, epistemological version of the thesis, *Wittgenstein provides a focus for current debate in arguing that the criteria for the occurrence of mental processes cannot be private, introspective acts, but must rather be publicly accessible forms of behaviour (*see* criterion).

Two philosophical difficulties with a behaviourist approach are considered to be, first, what precisely the concept of behaviour identifies (whether, for example, physiological movements or voluntarily performed acts); and second, after Wittgenstein, whether the criteria of first person *avowals of inner sensations (for example, pain) can be behavioural. *See also* dualism; introspection; operationalism.

being. Usually equivalent in the verbal sense to 'existence' (*see* is). As the most general property of all reality this is often considered to be the defining subject of metaphysical enquiry. Thus *Aristotle, in the work later called *Metaphysics,* reviewed the fundamental sorts of things there are (*see* categories). But he also insisted that being cannot be a *genus. Others taking this hint argued that 'there is' and 'there are' must be construed differently when applied to objects recognized as belonging to different categories. For instance, *Meinong dichotomized those that red-bloodedly exist from those constitutionally incapable of more than pale *subsistence; thus making 'being' equivalent to 'existence or subsistence'. Again, asked to justify time spent studying Aristotle's own doctrine of ten categories, J.L.*Austin replied, "Dreadfully important, ten senses of the word 'is'."

One question is whether being is a

property. Aristotle answered firmly that to say that anything exists is not to add to its description. By pointing out that being, unity, truth, and thinghood transcend his categories he occasioned the medieval doctrine of *transcendentals. Others, such as *Descartes, arguing that existence must be a perfection—perhaps a supreme perfection—deployed the *ontological argument for the existence of the Perfect Being, God. The criticism, above all in Hume and Kant, of its assumptions about existence persuaded modern logicians to introduce into their symbolisms a fundamental distinction betwen existential assertion and run of the mill predication (see existential import).

Another question is: "How do we tell to what ontology—what list of (sorts of) things there are—a philosopher commits himself?" *Quine answered, "To be is to be the value of a variable." We are, that is, committed to the reality of a kind of things iff we cannot state our views in a logical symbolism without using affirmative statements with variables ranging over things of this kind bound by the existential quantifier. Again, what ontology, if any, is presupposed by the employment of a logical symbolism? In particular, does this commit us to the existence of at least one object? If 'Everything is F or not F' implies 'a is F or not F', then this seems in turn to imply that 'At least one thing is F or not F'.

More generally interesting are two current debates: the existentialist contrast of being with existence, and the rash theological claim that God simply is being as such. The former distinguishes the mere being of animals and inanimate things from the more splendid existence of people. Yet this seems to be no more than a contorted reiteration of the inexpugnable, important truth that we can, and cannot but, make choices (see existentialism). The latter is rash because it appears to involve that God is only a concept, an abstraction, not the actual, dynamic, agent Creator "God of Abraham, Isaac, and Israel".

belief. The epistemic attitude of holding a proposition p to be true where there is some degree of evidence, though not conclusive evidence, for the truth of p. Clearly related to *knowledge, belief may be characterized as stronger than mere ungrounded opinion but weaker than full knowledge. Importantly, while knowing p would generally be considered to entail, among other things, that p is true, believing p is consistent with the actual falsity of p.

Traditionally, belief has been identified as a particular state of mind: either, as for Descartes, an active state in which assent to some proposition is granted or withheld; or, as for Hume, a passive state that occurs or fails to occur in respect of some proposition. In contemporary philosophy, however, the tendency has been, as, for example, for Ryle, to deny that belief is an introspectible mental state and to favour behavioural identification (see behaviourism). Thus, a belief that p is regarded as a disposition to act in ways that are not manifestly inconsistent with the truth of p: for example, it would be manifestly inconsistent to worship God while claiming to believe that there is no God. See also epistemology.

Bentham, Jeremy (1748-1832). London-born philosopher who studied law, and developed a lifelong critical interest in its foundations. He was an influential advocate of reform—legal, political, social, and educational, but best known to philosophers for his *Introduction to the Principles of Morals and Legislation* (1789).

Bentham is remembered primarily as a leading utilitarian (see utilitarianism). Starting from the principle (of which the precise sense and status are debatable) that "Nature has placed mankind under the governance of two sovereign masters, pain and pleasure", he developed the thesis that actions should be judged morally right or wrong simply according to whether or not they tend to maximize pleasure (and minimize pain) among those affected by them. (He elaborated a "hedonic calculus" to meet obvious difficulties about estimating effects of actions.) He explored at length the implications of this utilitarian principle for legal and other social institutions.

Bergson, Henri (1859-1941). French philosopher. He was appointed professor at the Collège de France in 1900, elected Academician in 1914, and awarded the 1927 Nobel prize for literature.

Dynamism characterizes Bergson's philosophy; the dualist view (see dualism) he adopts posits a vital principle (see élan vital) in contrast to inert matter; he rejects mechanistic or materialistic approaches to understanding reality and any deterministic view of the world, and claims, in L'Évolution créatrice (1907), that the creative urge, not natural selection, is at the heart of evolution.

Essai sur les données immédiates de la conscience (1889) points out the inadequacy of the intellect for grasping experience, which is an indivisible continuum and cannot be considered as a succession of demarcated conscious states. Bergson draws a distinction between the concept and the experience of time; the former might be subjected to the kind of analysis applied to the concept of space, but "real time" is experienced as duration and apprehended by intuition, not through separate operations of instinct and the intellect.

Berkeley, George (1685-1753). Irish philosopher of English descent, best known for the doctrine that there is no material substance and that things, such as stones and tables, are collections of "ideas" or sensations, which can exist only in minds and for so long as they are perceived.

Berkeley was born in Kilkenny, Ireland, and was educated at Kilkenny College and at Trinity College, Dublin. He became Dean of Derry in 1724. In 1728 he sailed with his wife for America to further his project for the establishment of St. Paul's College, Bermuda, for which the House of Commons had voted a grant. In the event the money was not

forthcoming, and the Berkeleys returned to England in 1731. Back in Ireland, Berkeley became Bishop of Cloyne in 1734.

Berkeley's most important works were published when he was still very young, the first of these—An Essay towards a New Theory of Vision—appearing in 1709. Here Berkeley argues that sight does not acquaint us directly with the objects we touch and feel, but rather with visual appearances that are distinct from them, at no distance from us, and indeed in our minds. Strictly, visual appearances are but "signs" giving us clues as to what objects we may perceive by touch, though we learn to interpret the clues so naturally and effortlessly that we end up by confounding the object seen with the tangible thing itself. Even the notion that what we see may in certain respects be like what we feel is an illusion. A man born blind and made to see would not at first be able to tell just by looking which of two objects was a sphere and which a cube; and he would have to learn through trials to correlate the visual appearances with those tangible shapes he could already identify by touch. In general, Berkeley holds that "the proper objects of vision constitute an universal language of the Author of nature, whereby we are instructed how to regulate our actions in order to attain those things that are necessary to the preservation and wellbeing of our bodies, as also to avoid whatever may be hurtful and destructive of them" (New Theory of Vision §147).

Throughout this work the reader is allowed to suppose that tangible objects really are outside the mind and at a distance from us, but in the Principles of Human Knowledge (1710) this is described as a "vulgar error" which "it was beside my purpose to examine and refute…in a discourse concerning vision" (Principles §44). In the Principles, however, there is no such limitation. Whatever we perceive by any sense, be it colour, hardness, odour, or whatever, is said to be an "idea" or sensation that cannot exist unperceived.

Things like trees and books are merely collections of such "ideas", and as such they can no more exist without a mind than their constituent "ideas" can. The bold claim comes out very clearly in §6 where we are told that "all those bodies which compose the mighty frame of the world, have not any subsistence without a mind, that their being is to be perceived or known; that consequently so long as they are not actually perceived by me, or do not exist in my mind or that of any other created spirit, they must either have no existence at all, or else subsist in the mind of some eternal spirit." Not suprisingly Berkeley's contemporaries found this doctrine strange and unpalatable, and in 1713 he published his *Three Dialogues between Hylas and Philonous* to elaborate on his notions and "to place them in a new light".

Berkeley's readers have often thought his basic doctrine to be quite patently false, so it may seem surprising that he thought its truth so obvious that "a man need only open his eyes" to see it (*Principles* §6). The explanation of his attitude lies in doctrines he was opposing. Berkeley found it widely accepted by philosophers that we come to know "outward" objects through "ideas" or sensations being produced in our minds. In *Locke, for example, he could find the claim that the mind "perceives nothing but its own ideas", together with the view that it is by virtue of their corpuscular or atomic structure that objects can act on each other and on *us* to produce "ideas" that represent them (*see* effluxes, theory of). But it seemed to Berkeley that this account gave rise to insoluble problems. In particular, if we allow, as Berkeley does, that we perceive only "ideas", it seems impossible that we should know anything about "outward" objects, even that they exist; and there is the additional problem of understanding how something material can act on an immaterial thing (or mind) to produce a sensation in it. Indeed, the more the account of a material thing is elaborated, the more problematic it seems to Berkeley to

become, and he claims that the notion is meaningless or contradictory. His own view he sees as the only viable alternative. Tables and the like are not "outward" objects hidden away behind a veil of "ideas"; rather they *are* "ideas", the very things we perceive.

Berkeley is traditionally seen as reacting against Locke, and so indeed he was. He could find in Locke a prominent supporter of the corpuscularian view of nature, and of the related view that objects really *have* "primary" qualities, such as shape and solidity, but that other qualities, such as colours and tastes, are mind-dependent. In Locke, too, he could find the view that the qualities of objects require the support of a "substratum" of which we can have no clear concept. He could also find in Locke the doctrine of *abstract ideas, which he attacks at length in the Introduction to the *Principles* and which he had said in the *New Theory of Vision* (§125) to be the source of "innumerable errors and difficulties in all parts of philosophy and in all the sciences". Once the impossibility of "abstraction" was appreciated we could, Berkeley held, see the foolishness of supposing that an object could have *just* those qualities Locke calls "primary", or of positing a material substratum underlying qualities. Even the notion that "houses, mountains, rivers, and in a word all sensible objects have an existence natural or real, distinct from their being perceived" will, Berkeley suggests, "be found at bottom to depend on the doctrine of *abstract ideas*" (*Principles* §§4-5).

It must however be stressed that Berkeley was not just attacking Locke, and that Locke was not the only important influence on him. For example, in the tradition associated with *Descartes he could find an acute awareness of the difficulty of explaining the interaction of matter and mind, and in *Malebranche in particular he could find the view that there is no interaction and that God produces the appropriate sensations in us on the occasion of the presence of material objects (*see* occasionalism). The notion was attractive to Berkeley in that it brought God to the centre of things while a more orthodox materialist system tended to push him to the background. However, to the problem of justifying belief in external objects it added the further problem of explaining why God should have needed to create objects which played no causal role. In Berkeley's system a new meaning is given to Malebranche's rather obscure doctrine that we see all things in God, God emerging both as the sole possible cause of our sense experiences and as the omnipresent perceiver in whose mind sensible objects can be said to exist even when no finite spirit perceives them.

Of the various points made in the *Principles* and *Dialogues*, mention should be made of the repeated claim that to equate sensible objects with mind-dependent "ideas" is in no way to make them less "real"; of the view that the person is an uncompounded and active spirit that, as emerges briefly in *Principles* §98, "always thinks"; and of the view that the natural sciences are concerned not with the discovery of strictly causal relationships but with phenomena standing in the relationship of "sign" to "thing signified". At a simple level, "the fire which I see is not the cause of the pain I suffer...but the mark that forewarns me of it" (*Principles* §65); the regularities we observe manifest "the goodness and wisdom of that governing spirit whose will constitutes the Laws of Nature" (*Principles* §32). It should be noted that the *Principles* as published was intended as the first part of a four-part work. The second part, which would have developed Berkeley's view of spirit as well as dealing with ethics, was never completed. *De Motu* (1721) covered some of the ground that would have been dealt with in a third part, and the *Analyst* (1734)—"A Discourse Addressed to an Infidel Mathematician"—takes Berkeley onto the area that would have been covered in a fourth.

Of Berkeley's later works mention should be made of *Alciphron* (1732), a

lively defence of the Christian faith against freethinkers and deists; the *Theory of Vision Vindicated* (1733); and *Siris* (1744). Both popular and controversial at the time, this last major work is now regarded as little more than a curiosity. In it Berkeley supports the cause of tar-water as an infusion useful against all diseases, and a train of reflections leads him to thoughts on God and the Trinity by way of an examination of the role given to aether by ancient and modern thinkers. Here again, however, familiar themes recur. Berkeley notes, for example, that "it passeth with many, I know not how, that mechanical principles give a clear solution of the phenomena [in nature]." He counters that "all phenomena are, to speak truly, appearances in the soul or mind" and that "it hath never been explained, nor can it be explained, how external bodies, figures, and motions, should produce an appearance in the mind" (*Siris* §251). Once again Berkeley's claim is that "the natural connexion of signs with the things signified...forms a sort of rational discourse, and is therefore the immediate effect of an intelligent cause" (*Siris* §254).

It will be apparent that throughout his life Berkeley's major concern was to focus his readers' attention on "the intimate presence of an *all-wise Spirit*, who fashions, regulates, and sustains the whole system of being" (*Principles* §151). In pursuing this end he opposes himself to "inert senseless matter", to the notion of a world distinct from appearances, and to the prevalent notion that the explanation of phenomena must lie in the corpuscular structure of objects and in principles such as that of gravitation. However, his writings have engrossed many who have not been attracted by his concern for theism. Whether he is writing on geometrical optics, the natural sciences, arithmetic, or perception, his grasp of his subject matter is always impressive and his criticism of his contemporaries often acute. His *New Theory of Vision* is generally regarded as a pioneer work in the psychology of vision even by those who would reject his claims about the status of what is perceived by sight; while aspects of his philosophy of science, including his criticisms of the ideas of absolute time, space, and motion and his opposition to what have been called "essentialist" explanations, are regarded as surprisingly modern. Certainly the full-blown immaterialism of the *Principles* and *Dialogues* has been found challenging and sometimes inspiring by philosophers, even though very few have accepted his main positive doctrines. In this connection, however, it is worth noting that we can find in Berkeley a foreshadowing of the respectable, though controversial, theory known as *phenomenalism. Indeed phenomenalism has been described as "Berkeley without God".

Berlin, Sir Isaiah (1909-). British moral and political philosopher and historian. Main works: *Karl Marx* (1939), *Historical Inevitability* (1954), *Two Concepts of Liberty* (1959). Berlin has argued against determinist philosophies of history (*see* history, philosophy of), rejecting, especially, the Marxist idea of an objective march of history and the view that all values are conditioned—and devalued—by the place and social situation that the valuers happen to occupy in time. He stresses the importance of moral values, and the necessity of rejecting determinism if we wish to keep hold of the notions of human responsibility and freedom. The historian's approach to his subject cannot be entirely objective or value-free (*compare* value-freedom), since, if we view humans as purposing, motivated creatures and not merely causal factors in a series of events, some degree of moral or psychological evaluation is inevitable.

Bernard, St. (1090-1153). Abbot of Clairvaux, monastic reformer, and theologian. Main works: *De Diligendo Deo* (On Loving God) and *De Gratia et Libero Arbitrio* (On Grace and Freewill). In religious controversy his method

was mystical rather than inferential and evidential. In this respect, however, his opponent *Abelard was a more thoroughgoing Neoplatonist than he was and St. Bernard found more favour than the former with the ecclesiastical authorities. In 1953 Pius XII eulogized St. Bernard as *Doctor Mellifluus*.

Bernoulli's theorem. A concept in *probability theory, also known as the law of large numbers. Suppose that there is a sequence of n trials, on every one of which an outcome A is possible and on every one of which the probability of A is the same, say p. The theorem states that the probability that the proportion of As in the sequence lies within the range $p \pm h$ (where h is any small fraction) approaches 1 as n approaches infinity. The law (sometimes misleadingly thought of as 'the law of averages') can be misinterpreted, for instance, if it is forgotten that it applies only to repetitions of independent trials, on each of which the outcome has the same probability. *See also* gambler's fallacy; randomness; statistics.

Berry's paradox. An informal version of *Richard's paradox. Consider the expression A, 'the least integer not nameable in fewer than nineteen syllables'. List all expressions of English (including A), starting, for example, alphabetically with expressions of one letter, then those of two letters, and so on. Now delete all expressions not naming integers. Should one delete A? If A, names m, then m is both nameable and not nameable in fewer than nineteen syllables, since A has eighteen syllables. *See* semantic paradoxes.

Bertrand's box paradox. A paradox suggesting that different ways of describing alternatives lead to different probability assignments (*see also* probability theory). Three boxes each hold two coins. In one box both are gold, in another both are silver, in the third there is one coin of each type. Given that a randomly chosen coin is gold, what is the probability that the remaining coin in the box is gold? On the one hand the box originally contained either two gold or one gold and one silver coin, so the probability is one half. On the other hand, if one imagines the coins in each box to be ordered in some way then the chosen coin is either the first or second in the box containing the two gold coins or the gold coin from the mixed box. Thus the probability that the remaining coin is gold is two thirds.

Bertrand's paradox. A paradox illustrating difficulties in assigning probabilities where there are infinite alternatives (*see also* probability theory). An equilateral triangle is inscribed in a circle. What is the probability that a random chord is longer than one of its sides? On the one hand, it is longer if the midpoint of the chord lies on the inner half of the radius which bisects the chord. Thus the probability is one half. On the other hand, it is longer if the midpoint of the chord lies within the concentric circle with half the original radius. Thus the probability is one quarter (since the area of this circle is one quarter that of the original).

best, principle of the. The Leibnizian principle of *perfection, satirized by *Voltaire in *Candide* through the hero's naive belief that "everything is for the best in the best of all possible worlds".

bhakti. (Sanskrit for: devotion.) In the *Vedânta and other Indian systems, love of God, expressed in prayer and meditation and ultimately in total self-surrender to the divine nature. *Bhakti* came to prominence during the medieval theistic period of Indian thought; its philosophical basis was chiefly provided by Rāmānuja (*c.*1100 AD).

biconditional. A statement in which it is asserted that possession of one property is a *necessary and sufficient condition for possession of another, as in 'A number is prime iff it has no divisors other than one and itself', or that the existence of one state of affairs is a necessary and sufficient condition for the existence of another, as in 'He will

be president iff he wins the election'. The expression 'if and only if (abbreviated to iff)' rarely occurs in ordinary discourse, but is employed widely in those disciplines where precise definitions are necessary. Such a statement is called a biconditional because to say '*p* iff *q*' is itself an abbreviated expression of the joint assertion of the two *conditional statements 'if *q* then *p*' and 'if *p* then *q*' (since '*p* only if *q*' implies that *p* cannot be true without *q* being true). The truth of both the conditional statements 'if *p* then *q*' and 'if *q* then *p*' requires that *p* and *q* have the same truth-value, for if *p* and 'if *p* then *q*' are both true, *q* must also be true (by modus ponens) and if *p* is false and 'if *q* then *q*' is true, *q* must be false (by modus tollens), and similarly for *q* (*see* affirming the antecedent). Thus in formal systems of propositional logic the symbol '$\equiv$' or '$\leftrightarrow$' used to stand for 'iff' is defined by the *truth-table

p	$\equiv$	q
T	T	T
T	F	F
F	F	T
F	T	F

See also equivalent.

binary operation. A two-place *operation.

bivalence, principle (*or* law) of. The principle that states that every statement is either true or false; that is, that every statement has a *truth-value and that there are just two truth-values. In the presence of a *negation operator, as standardly conceived, this principle entails that of the *excluded middle, but since it makes no mention of negation is not equivalent to it. The law of excluded middle is a logical law operating at the level of the *object language, whereas the principle of bivalence is a semantic principle, one governing the interpretation of the language to which it is applied. Belief in this principle is linked with realism—the idea that statements are determined as true or false by reference to an independent reality and thus may be thought to have determinate truth-values even though we may not be in a position to know what these are.

Black, Max (1909-). American philosopher of mathematics, logic, and language. His Cambridge education as a mathematician led to an early work on *The Nature of Mathematics* (1933). Black was to come under the influence of *Wittgenstein. His major works include *The Importance of Language* (1962) and the extensive and highly regarded study, *A Companion to Wittgenstein's Tractatus* (1964). He became editor of *The Philosophical Review* in 1946. Black's other writings include many articles in analytical philosophy, and translations of the work of Rudolf Carnap and (with P. T. Geach) of Gottlob Frege.

Boehme (*or* **Behmen**), Jacob (1575-1624). Silesian theosophist, known as 'the German philosopher' (*philosophus Teutonicus*). Main works: *Aurora, oder die Morgenröte im Aufgang* (1612), *Mysterium Magnum* (1623). His writings were widely admired in the 17th century. His supposed insights into the divine nature, the origin and structure of the Universe, and the hidden mysteries of the Bible and the sacraments were all, he claimed, directly vouchsafed by divine illumination. His terminology is notoriously difficult, drawing on occult, alchemical, and astrological sources. His belief that the entire creation is a manifestation of God led him to postulate two wills in God, one loving, one wrathful, to account for the problem of evil.

Boethius, Anicius Manlius Severinus (*c.*480-524). Roman philosopher and translator of Aristotle. He was a high official under the Gothic king Theodoric, but fell from favour, was imprisoned, and executed. He translated Aristotle's works on logic, including the *Prior Analytics*, *Posterior Analytics*, *Topics*, and the *Sophistical Refutations*, and translated and wrote a commentary on Porphyry's *Introduction to the Categories of Aristotle* (the *Isagoge*), which became the standard medieval textbook on logic. Among his original treatises were works on mathematics, logic, music, and theology, the last being notable for his application of classical logic to Christian revelation. His most famous work was the *Consolation of Philosophy*, written during his imprisonment at Pavia.

The *Consolation*, surprisingly, exhibits no explicitly Christian doctrine, depending purely on reason for solace in the face of disaster. Boethius probably considered faith and reason to be two distinct means by which a valid account could be given of the Universe, and, having chosen reason as his guide, did not introduce arguments properly pertaining to faith. In Book I Philosophy appears to the distraught writer and recalls to him his fundamental belief in a purposive Universe and the rationality of man. Books II and III discuss the unreliability of fortune, and other false means to happiness, concluding that God is the sole immutable good. This leads in Book IV to the problem of evil, and Book V tackles the puzzle of freewill and determinism; the conclusion is that divine foreknowledge is compatible with human freedom in moral choices.

Boethius' work provided medieval philosophy with both a methodology and a vocabulary. After the Bible, the *Consolation* was perhaps the most widely read, translated, and commented on book of the following millennium. Its author's role in transmitting the philosophy of antiquity to the Christian Middle Ages amply justifies the traditional assessment of Boethius as "the last of Romans; the first of the scholastics". *See also* Aristotelianism.

boo-hooray theory. The apt and widely employed nickname of the view of moral, and indeed of all evaluative, utterance expressed in *Ayer's *Language, Truth and Logic* (1936). Such utterances, or the evaluative elements in them, do not state anything, but, like ejaculations, simply express the reactions of the speaker.

Boolean algebra. The algebra developed by George Boole (1815-64) as a way of manipulating symbols by purely algebraic methods (for example, multiplication), without regard for any particular interpretation but merely reflecting basic laws of thought. The term now refers to abstract systems, similar in many respects to the original Boolean algebra, which may be applied to such diverse areas as probability and computer design.

Bosanquet, Bernard (1848-1923). British philosopher who taught at Oxford (1871-81) and St. Andrews (1903-08). His career was otherwise devoted to social work and writing. Main philosophical works: *Knowledge and Reality* (1885), *Logic* (1888), *History of Aesthetics* (1892), *The Principle of Individuality and Value* (1912).

Strongly influenced by Hegelian idealism, Bosanquet developed a system of thought in which a central role is played by the idea of the individual, characterized as the *concrete universal or harmony of opposites, which alone is capable of independence, of "standing by itself". Such individuality finds expression, not primarily in persons, but rather in their self-transcendence in art, religion, and society, and above all in the *absolute, the unity of all these lesser manifestations.

bound variable. *See* variable.

Bourbaki, Nicolas. The collective pseudonym of a group of French mathematicians who, since 1939 when the first volume of *Éléments de Mathématique* appeared, have been working on a definitive survey of mathematics. Their emphasis is on developing mathematics from a few basic axioms within a strict logical arrangement, and they do not make the traditional mathematical distinctions (into algebra, geometry, etc.) but divide mathematics into parts characterized by structure (for example, algebraic structures).

Boyle, Robert (1627-92). English chemist and physicist of Irish descent, who was influential in promoting the *corpuscular or atomistic view of matter, as a result of his experiments with gases. His book *The Sceptical Chemist* (1661) divorced chemistry from alchemy by insisting that the nature of material substances had to be based on experimental evidence rather than the Greek view, still then prevalent, that they were composed of the mystical elements (*see* four elements). This view is encapsulated in the motto of the Royal Society, of which he was a founder member, *Nullius in Verba* (nothing by mere authority).

Bradley, Francis Herbert (1846-1924). English idealist philosopher. He was appointed research fellow of Merton College, Oxford, in 1870 and awarded the Order of Merit in 1924. Main works: *Ethical Studies* (1876), *Principles of Logic* (1883), *Appearance and Reality* (1893). *Ethical Studies* is an attack on contemporary doctrines of moral philosophy, utilitarianism in particular. In *Principles of Logic*, he denounced uncritical *psychologism and denied that the nature of fact could ever be adequately expressed by any form of statement.

Though strongly influenced by *Hegel and *Kant, Bradley advanced his own notions of reality and the *absolute in *Appearance and Reality*, according to which no unitary thing can be viewed as the collection of properties attributable to it; the unity and character of any thing is imparted by the relatedness of its properties. The absolute is not merely a system of appearances, it is also the container of that system. Every appearance, even if misleading as to the true nature of a thing, is a constituent of reality. The idea of reality is given in sentient experience inseparably combining sensor and sensed; one's notion of the "self" is definable only in terms of what is "other".

brahman. In the traditions of *Indian philosophy influenced by the *Upaniṣads*, the name given to the ultimate being or world soul, which is both immanent and transcendent, existing both in the Universe and in itself.

Brentano, Franz (1838-1917). German psychologist and philosopher, ordained Catholic priest in 1864. He taught philosophy at Würzburg until 1873 when he left the clergy and continued teaching in Vienna until retirement in 1895.

In *Psychologie vom empirischen Standpunkt* (1874) Brentano introduced the doctrine of intentionality, distinguishing and characterizing mental events as "the direction of the mind to an object" in (1) perception, (2) judgment or belief, and (3) approval or disapproval.

Broad, Charlie Dunbar (1887-1971). English philosopher, Professor of Moral Philosophy at Cambridge (1933-53). His main concern was the appraisal and analysis of ideas and doctrines in several areas, including the philosophy of mind, metaphysics, and epistemology; most of his own views are presented in the commentaries in his major two-volume work *Examination of McTaggart's Philosophy* (1933, 1938). He also had a lifelong interest in parapsychology.

Broad distinguished critical from speculative philosophy; the former analyses the basic concepts and propositions of science and everyday life, but can give rise to a view of the world which is too narrow and rigid. Speculative philosophy, though it can make no claim to demonstrable truths, can take a synoptic view correlating the findings of the natural sciences with religion, art, and social theory, as well as common sense.

Brownson, Orestes Augustus (1803-76). American transcendentalist philosopher and religious thinker. A disciple of the French philosopher Victor Cousin (1792-1867), Brownson also closely related his transcendentalism to the theories of the Italian idealist, Vincenzo Gioberti (1801-52). Although a confirmed deist (*see* deism), Brownson regarded his philosophy as rational rather than as founded on mere faith. Most of his writings appeared in *Brownson's Quarterly Review* which he founded in 1844 and edited until 1875.

Bruno, Giordano (1548-1600). Italian philosopher and sometime Dominican friar, who was burnt at the stake for his unorthodox views. An enthusiastic champion of Copernicanism (*see* Copernicus), he wrote several treatises promoting an extreme form of *pantheism: God is the unifying substance from which all things in the Universe are derived. But like *Nicholas of Cusa, by whom he was influenced, he considered that the Universe could afford no genuine knowledge of the divine. His work was influential in certain scientific and occult circles in the 17th century, but then suffered neglect. In the 19th century his name became the rallying cry for an anticlerical movement in Italy.

brutes. All animals other than man. A famous passage in Descartes' *Discourse* deals with "the difference between men and brutes". The crucial point about animals, for Descartes, is their lack of language: animal "utterances" are always elicited by a specific stimulus and never amount to genuine speech. It follows that animals have no thoughts and that all their behaviour can be explained on purely mechanical principles. Hence the notorious Cartesian doctrine of the *bête-machine*, the claim that animals are simply "natural automata". This doctrine aroused considerable opposition (see the article on animals in Voltaire's *Dictionnaire Philosophique*). Hume (in the *Treatise*) argued that belief and some degree of inferential reasoning can be attributed to animals. In recent times a revival of the Cartesian thesis of a radical difference in kind between men and brutes (hinging on the claim that animals are incapable of genuine "stimulus-free" speech) has been associated with the work of *Chomsky. Current empirical research, however, seems to indicate that chimpanzees at least have the ability to acquire a substantial degree of linguistic competence.

Buber, Martin (1878-1965). Jewish philosopher and theologian, born in Vienna. From 1925 Buber lectured on Jewish religion and ethics at the University of Frankfurt-am-Main until the rise of Nazi power forced him to leave in 1933. Settled in Palestine (1938), he became professor of social philosophy at the Hebrew University. After his retirement in 1951, he lectured extensively outside Israel and also became the first president of the Israel Academy of Science and Humanities.

The basic formulation of Buber's philosophy (the philosophy of dialogue) is contained in *Ich und Du* (1923) where he makes a radical distinction between two basic attitudes of which men are capable, described as I-Thou and I-It. I-Thou designates a relation between subject and subject, a relation of reciprocity and mutuality; I-It is the relation between subject and object, involving some form of utilization or control, the object being wholly passive. The I in the two situations also differs: in the I-Thou it appears only within the context of the relationship and cannot be viewed independently, whereas in the I-It situation the I is an observer and only partly involved. The I-Thou situation cannot be sustained indefinitely and every Thou will at times become an It; through this situation objective knowledge is acquired and finds expression. In a healthy man there is a dialectical interaction between the two situations; every I-It contains the potential of becoming I-Thou—the situation in which man's true personality emerges within the context of his world.

Buber's notion of God is that of the eternal Thou, the only I-Thou situation that man can sustain indefinitely; in it God is recognized in all things as the wholly other, not observed but revealing himself.

Buddhist philosophy. Buddhism is an originally Indian religion, founded in the 5th century BC by Siddhârtha Gautama, the 'Buddha' (enlightened one). In the beginning its teachings were restricted to ethics and meditational exercises, and it separated from Hinduism on purely religious grounds (rejection of Hindu scriptures, ritual, and social system). However, by consistently maintaining

the belief in the ineffability of the ultimate (*nirvāṇa*), which only meditational trance could realize, and in the transience and lack of essence of all empirical phenomena, a typically Buddhist form of thought developed at the time when full systems of philosophy were being created.

Already in the last centuries BC attempts were made (in the *Abhidharma* literature) to classify the various factors of existence (*dharmas*) in a systematic manner, and in one branch of Buddhism (known as the Thēravāda) this developed into an increasingly rationalistic and formalized pursuit, culminating in the *Sarvâstivāda. Other tendencies in Buddhism (the Mahāyāna) reacted against this scholasticism by emphasizing the mystical side. A philosophical interpretation of Mahāyāna was then provided by the *Madhyamaka and *Vijñānavāda (or Yogâcāra). From the 8th century AD Buddhist philosophy declined in India, and by 1200 Buddhism had practically disappeared in its country of origin. But many other countries in Asia had accepted Buddhism, without however developing its strictly philosophical side beyond the Indian models. *See also* Hindu philosophy; Indian philosophy.

Burali-Forti's paradox. The paradox of the greatest ordinal (*see* number), and one of the *logical paradoxes. Consider the set of all ordinals; call it *O*. *O* can be *well ordered, by the 'less-than' relation, and there is a proof that all well ordered sets have an ordinal. So the ordinal of a set of consecutive ordinals (starting with the lowest) will be greater than every ordinal in the set. Thus *O* has an ordinal, *w*, greater than all the ordinals in *O*. But *w* is itself an ordinal, and therefore is a member of *O*. So *w* both is, and is not, a member of *O*. In most versions of set theory, paradox is avoided by insisting that there is no set of all ordinals.

Buridan, Jean (*c*.1295-1356). French nominalist philosopher, who studied and taught at Paris (*see* nominalism). Buridan also contributed to the study of mechanics and optics. He wrote a number of commentaries on Aristotle and some original works on logic, notably *Consequentiae* and *Sophismata*. In philosophy he rejected both extreme Ockhamism (*see* William of Ockham) and some of the more radical Arabic additions to the Aristotelian tradition. *See also* Buridan's ass.

Buridan's ass. The traditional illustrative example, first found in Aristotle but now associated with *Buridan, of the problem of decision making when there is no reason for preferring one of the possible alternatives. The ass, faced with two equally desirable hay-bales, starves to death through indecision since, ex hypothesi, there are no grounds for preferring one bale to the other.

Burke, Edmund (1729-97). British statesman, essayist, and philosopher. Burke's major contribution to philosophy was his *Philosophical Inquiry into the Origin of Our Ideas of the Sublime and the Beautiful* (1756) in which his central argument is that our enjoyment of beauty consists in the way in which the imagination is engaged by obscurity and suggestiveness rather than by intellectual clarity, and, in respect of the *sublime, by a pleasurable form of terror and ignorance. In his later political career, Burke lent his support to both the Irish cause and American independence. However, his *Reflections on the Revolution in France* (1790) strongly opposed what he saw as the altogether unWhiggish and anti-historical tendencies of the French radicals.

Butler, Joseph (1692-1752). Anglican priest, Bishop of Bristol (1738-51) and Durham (1751-52). His main contributions to moral and religious philosophy are contained in his *Fifteen Sermons* (1726) and *The Analogy of Religion*, with its supplementary dissertation *Of the Nature of Virtue* (1736).

In his *Sermons*, Butler approaches the examination of morality through empirical considerations regarding human nature. He insists on its complexity, and

hence on the one-sidedness of accounts, like those of *Hobbes and *Shaftesbury, that presented it as dominated by a single governing principle, whether self-love or benevolence. For Butler, these principles are not, as they are often assumed to be, necessarily opposed to each other, and both are manifested in an indefinite variety of forms in human conduct. More importantly, man is distinguished from the rest of creation by the superior faculty of reflection or conscience, which "... without being consulted... magisterially exerts itself...", and pronounces on the rightness or wrongness of the various human "affections" and actions stemming therefrom. Since conscience is our God-given guide to right conduct, its demands are absolute. But they are not arbitrary, and Butler believed that in the long term they would be found to coincide with the requirements of self-love and benevolence alike. In his *Analogy of Religion* he attempts to show that the evidence for the design and creation of Nature by an intelligent Being, which contemporary deists admitted —and the difficulties to which their position is exposed —are closely analogous to those encountered by theists who regard this Being as also the moral guide and judge of mankind (*see* deism; theism). Hence belief in revealed religion is in principle no less rational than deism.

C

Cabbala. *See* Kabbalah.

Cajetan, Thomas de Vio, Cardinal Cajetan (1469-1534). Italian theologian and exegete, who wrote an influential commentary on Aquinas' *Summà Theologiae* (1507-22). As papal legate in Germany, he examined Luther's doctrines (1518), and later helped to draft the condemnatory bull, *Exsurge Domine*. *See also* analogy.

calculus. Essentially a system of rule-governed symbols (which may be marks on paper but which might equally well be beads on an abacus), designed to facilitate reasoning of various kinds. The rules for using the symbols are such that they can be learnt by rote and applied without any grasp of the rational or computational processes that they represent. The paradigm example of a calculus would be the system of arabic numerals together with the rules for addition, subtraction, multiplication, and division. One can get the 'right answer' to an arithmetical problem by a mechanical application of these rules to the symbolic representation of the problem without knowing why they should give the right answer, that is, without grasping the nature of the arithmetical operations they represent. (This indeed is the criticism levelled at the 'old-fashioned' way of teaching mathematics by drilling children in multiplication tables, etc.)

If the validity (see validity and truth) of an argument is due to its form or structure, then, once one has a means of representing types of argument structure, the study of validity can become a purely formal matter. One has only to study argument forms, not arguments; and one need only look at the structure of an argument, ignoring its content, in order to assess whether it is valid. This suggests that it would be possible to reduce the process of constructing valid arguments to a matter of following rules that do not require one to pay attention to the content of the argument or even to understand its premises and conclusion. This was, in effect, what occurred in the scholastic development of Aristotelian logic during the Middle Ages, when all sorts of mnemonic devices were used to assist recall of the valid patterns of inference, patterns that could be mindlessly applied. But this development was unsystematic and would scarcely count as a 'calculus'.

In the 16th and 17th centuries, with the development of algebraic techniques, the ideal of a systematic formulation of the means of representing argument forms and of the rules for constructing valid arguments took shape as the ideal of presenting a *calculus ratiocinatur* — a calculus of reasoning. The conception of this ideal has undergone a considerable evolution and has become more precisely articulated. To reduce reasoning to a calculus is not just to make reasoning like arithmetical computation or the solving of algebraic equations, but to make it mechanical in the strong sense of being something that a machine (computer) could do. (This sense can be made fully precise through the theory of computing machines.) The rules must be such that they could be programmed into a computer. This requires that it be possible to treat all proof as a matter of symbol manipulation, each *proof being only of finite length. The rules for its construction are rules for processing symbols. These rules must be such that there are effective (mechanical) procedures (see effective procedure) for checking whether any given sequence of symbols is, or is not, a proof.

The two logical calculuses most commonly encountered are (classical) *propositional calculus* and (classical) first order *predicate calculus*. Any *formal system of logic can be called a (system of) *propositional calculus* if it consists of the following: (1) a specification of a *formal language the symbols of which are either propositional variables or propositional connectives, where the latter are intended to represent some or all of the connectives 'and', 'or', 'not', 'if...then', or are such that symbols representing some of these connectives could be defined from them; (2) a set of axioms and/or rules of inference (see axiom; inference, rule of) governing the connectives of the language. Different axioms or rules may determine distinct propositional calculuses, although there are, in general, many equivalent ways of formulating the same system. (Two formulations are equivalent when exactly the same inferences are valid in each of them.) However, the phrase 'propositional calculus' is usually used to refer to any system in which the formally valid arguments are exactly those that can be shown to be valid by application of the standard two-valued truth-table definitions of the logical connectives (see truth-table).

Similarly, any formal logical system can be called a (system of) *predicate calculus* if it consists of at least the following: (1) a specification of a formal language containing the following categories of symbols (a) a *denumerable set of individual variables (say, x_i); (b) a finite or denumerably infinite, but not empty, set of *predicate letters (say, P_i^n, where n indicates the number of argument places); (c) a finite, denumerable, or empty, set of individual constants (say, a_i); (d) propositional connectives; (e) either the existential or the universal *quantifier, or both. (i ranges over the integers throughout); (2) a set of axioms and/or rules of inference governing the propositional connectives and quantifiers of the language.

When used without qualification, the phrase 'predicate calculus' usually means 'classical first order predicate calculus'. This is the system obtained by extending the axioms and/or rules of propositional calculus by adding axioms and/or rules for the quantifiers which are designed to treat universally quantified sentences as infinite conjunctions and existentially quantified sentences as infinite disjunctions. The adjective 'classical' is used to mark the contrast between those systems of propositional and predicate calculus that reflect the notion of validity derived from the truth-table definitions of the logical operators and the systems developed by the intuitionist mathematicians (see intuitionistic logic). Higher order predicate calculuses can be defined by stipulating axioms and/or rules of inference governing the logical operators of higher order languages (see higher order logic).

Cambridge Platonists. A group of philosophers and theologians active in Cambridge in the middle and later years of the 17th century. Its main members were Ralph *Cudworth, Nathanael *Culverwel, Richard *Cumberland, Joseph *Glanvill, Henry *More, John *Norris, and Benjamin *Whichcote. At a time when religion was under attack, the Cambridge Platonists endeavoured to establish a reasonable philosophical basis for Christian theology. Aristotelianism, particularly Aristotelian mechanics, had been discredited by recent scientific advances (see Galileo; Newton) and the old hierarchical order of society was no longer a satisfactory model to counter the onslaught of Hobbist rationalism (see Hobbes). The Cambridge Platonists therefore looked to the Platonic and Neoplatonic traditions (between which they made no critical distinction) as their authorities (see Neoplatonism; Platonism). They opposed what they saw as three sinister tendencies in English intellectual life at the time: Hobbism, 'enthusiasm' (that is, the eccentric doctrines of the obscure religious sects active after the 1640s), and hollow ritualism (as practised by the followers of Archbishop Laud (1573-1645)). Their thought, as a group, is characterized by religious tolerance, a tendency towards mysticism, and an emphasis on an absolute standard of right and wrong, viewed as rooted in reason and independent of appeals to divine authority. The first and last of these traits were influential in English thought during the succeeding two centuries.

Cantor, Georg (1845-1918). Professor of Mathematics at Halle University, Germany (1872-1913). His main works are collected in *Gesammelte Abhandlungen*, edited by E. Zermelo (1932).

Cantor, regarded as the father of *set theory, provided the first formal theory of the infinite. By means of a *diagonal procedure he demonstrated that the set of all natural numbers, N, is not equivalent to (does not have the same number of members as) the set of all real numbers (the set of those numbers representable as points on a straight line segment—the continuum), thus showing that there exists more than one infinite number (see number). He tried unsuccessfully to show that the *power set of

N (the set of all subsets of N) is equivalent to the continuum, a problem only solved in 1963 by Paul Cohen.

Cantor's paradox. A paradox in *set theory discovered by Georg *Cantor. The paradox is generated by the question of whether the set of all sets is (a) equal to or (b) greater than its own *power set. If (a), a contradiction arises in that it can be proved that the power set of any given set is greater than the set itself. If (b), a contradiction arises since the power set of any set is itself a set of sets and therefore a subset of the set of all sets, and it can be proved that the subset of any given set is not greater than the given set. *Compare* Russell's paradox.

cardinality. The cardinality of a *set, X, is any property possessed by all and only those sets equivalent to X. (Two sets are equivalent iff members of one set can be paired off with members of the other set in such a way that each member of either set is paired with exactly one member of the other, that is, there is a one-to-one correspondence between members of the two sets.) The set of all those sets equivalent to X is sometimes taken as a cardinal number. Intuitively, two sets share the same cardinality iff they have the same number of members.

cardinal number. *See* number.

Carlyle, Thomas (1795-1881). Scottish historian and social critic. After attending Edinburgh University he taught in schools for a while and then turned to freelance journalism. Some years of poverty and obscurity were followed by moderate success when Carlyle became the chief interpreter of German literature to the early Victorian public, notably through his translation of Goethe's *Wilhelm Meister* (1824) and his *Life of Schiller* (published in book form in 1825). He also published two pieces of influential social criticism 'Signs of the Times' (1829) and 'Characteristics' (1831), (1831), and the semi-autobiographical *Sartor Resartus* (1833-4). Carlyle moved to London, formed a

somewhat uneasy friendship with J. S. Mill, and quickly became famous after the publication of his *French Revolution* (1837). Among Carlyle's most important later works of history and social criticism are: *Chartism* (1839), *On Heroes, Hero Worship, and the Heroic in History* (first delivered as lectures in London in 1840), *Past and Present* (1843), and *The History of Friedrich II of Prussia* (1858-65).

Early in his life Carlyle became disenchanted with the theology (though not with the moral fervour) of the Scottish Puritanism in which he was brought up. He then sought and found, especially in the writings of *Goethe, a sense of the wholeness that he considered to be disastrously lacking both in the actual social life of Victorian England and in the prevailing utilitarian social philosophy. Perhaps the most interesting thing about Carlyle philosophically is that he, along with S. T. *Coleridge, first imported into British social thinking a number of powerful and, to some minds, peculiarly seductive concepts and paradigms, which then became useful in criticizing industrial society; for example, he naturalized that cluster of images centring round a contrast between 'organic and dynamical' outlooks, forms of life, etc. (which are allegedly good), and 'mechanical and static' ones (which are allegedly bad). Originating in late 18th-century Germany, these metaphors have been persistent in Hegelian and Marxist thinking right up to the present time.

Carnap, Rudolf (1891-1970). German positivist, Professor of Philosophy at Chicago from 1935 to 1952, and at the University of California at Los Angeles until 1961. His works include *Der Logische Aufbau der Welt* (1928), *Logische Syntax der Sprache* (1934), *Introduction to Semantics* (1942), *Meaning and Necessity* (1947), and *Logical Foundations of Probability* (1950).

For many years Carnap was one of the most influential logical positivists, and the one who did the most to offer a thoroughgoing philosophy of knowledge on positivist principles (see logical positivism). This demanded a 'construction theory' that showed how highly theoretical statements, that do not apparently describe immediate experience, are reduced by definitions to ones that do. The *Aufbau* provided such a system, based firmly on descriptions of immediately given experience, and Carnap was zealous in promoting the view that sentences that did not have this rigid relation to experience, particularly those of metaphysics, were meaningless answers to pseudo-problems. He later came to relax the standards for meaningfulness, through realizing that the relation between good scientific theory and experience is not definitional, but rather that the former should be confirmable by the latter (see *also* confirmation theory). Carnap's investigations of this notion culminated in his great classic *The Logical Foundations of Probability*.

Carnap firmly believed that progress in philosophy needs scientific analysis of the concepts involved, and he regarded the development of a formal language as the first essential step in such an analysis (*compare* Frege; Russell). His own contributions to semantics, although controversial, have been important, especially to the development of modal systems. His view of the connections between parts of a theory has been criticized as excessively tied to the particular linguistic formulation in which the theory is couched.

Carneades (*c*.214–129 BC). Sceptical philosopher, leader of the 'New Academy'. A brilliant dialectician with an acknowledged debt to *Chrysippus, Carneades continued and extended the Academic attack on Stoic and other dogma. As head of the Academy, he went in 155 BC to Rome, where he caused a sensation by arguing first in favour of and then against righteousness. Notoriously capable of arguing from any point of view, while committing himself to none, Carneades was known for his systematic classification (the *Carneadea divisio*) of all possible ends for human action (which he could then play off against each other) and for a doctrine, serious or otherwise, of sense impressions that are 'persuasive' and credible, though not indubitably certain. See Academy of Athens; Scepticism.

Carroll, Lewis. The pseudonym employed in the non-professional writing of Charles Lutwidge Dodgson (1832–98). As an undergraduate Dodgson achieved first class honours in mathematics, and thereafter remained as a Student (Fellow) of the same Oxford college (Christ Church) for the rest of his life. His apparently Platonic enthusiasm for the company of well brought up children of the opposite sex continues to provide field days for the psychoanalytically minded or the merely prurient. As a conventional don Dodgson produced a pathbreaking essay on the mathematical theory of voting and a useful edition of *Euclid* I and II (1882). But his place among the immortals was earned as the author of *Alice in Wonderland* (1865), *Through the Looking Glass* (1871), *The Hunting of the Snark* (1876), and even *Sylvie and Bruno* (1889, 1893). The first of these hardy perennial children's tales, in particular, is at the same time a logical-philosophical causerie, garnished with innumerable examples of elegant and unforgettable absurdity. M. Gardner's *The Annotated Alice* (1960) and *The Annotated Snark* (1962) are witty guides to their respective works.

Cartesian. Of or relating to René *Descartes.

Cārvāka. See Indian materialism.

casuistry. In ethics, the systematic discussion of the applicability of general moral laws to particular cases of conduct, accommodating new ideas that enter and challenge social order. It is often used pejoratively to refer to over-subtle reasoning that has a tendency towards greater moral laxity than the dictates of the unsophisticated individual conscience would allow.

categorematic. In traditional logic, denoting a word that can stand on its own as a term (either a subject or a predicate) in a categorical proposition. In modern logic, its meaning is extended to include any symbol that has independent meaning, for example 'red', 'animal', 'Aristotle'. *Compare* syncategorematic.

categorical imperative. A term introduced into ethics by *Kant to distinguish the guidance to action given by morality from that of other forms of prescription. Whereas most advice is of the form 'If you want *X*, do *Y*' (Kant calls this a *hypothetical imperative*) moral injunctions take the categorical form: 'Thou shalt not kill'. Thus morality is seen as being an objective requirement, independent of what anyone may want.

categorical proposition. *See* syllogism.

categories. 1. (in Aristotelian philosophy) A technical term used to refer to ten classes that together 'covered' all modes of being. A predicate in one category might, in certain conditions, and on account of its category membership, be thought inappropriate to apply to a subject in another. The medieval tradition seems to have regarded Aristotle's list as a total inventory of the highest genera of being. 2. (in Kant's philosophy) A theory that did not have as its focus the elements of subject and predicate, but rather whole statements, or 'judgments'. He made a twelve-part *logical* classification of statements, each part of which he believed corresponded to a function of the human understanding. Within that classification his main divisions were quantity, quality, relation, and modality; these applied to phenomena or appearances rather than to 'things-in-themselves' (*see* Ding-an-Sich). Kant's categories were therefore categories of the understanding, and he was concerned more with how the presupposed forms of the understanding might be arrived at than with what the complete list of the genera of being was. *Hegel, *Husserl, and *Peirce sub-

sequently provided developments of Kantian theory. 3. (in modern philosophy) Any basic concepts, like classes, sections, or isolable systems. Categories have been conceived as types or genera limiting operations with the notions belonging to them in such a way as to set the limits of cognitive meaning and avoid the unintelligibility found, for example, in 'This teapot is emotional' or 'That bed is arrogant'. *Russell invented his theory of types in order to resolve a paradox he found in Frege's logic of classes. Sentences which were meaningless, which were 'sound without sense', he thought to be the result of combining member elements that belonged to differing and distinct logical types. It was found that a Russellian hierarchy of logical types was better interpreted as the aggregate of *expressions* within a given language, rather than an aggregate of entities. This programme appeared to apply most convincingly not to natural languages, such as English or German, but to logical 'ideal' languages. *Ryle, however, sought to establish that types are found among the expressions of a natural language rather than imposed by the inflexible rules of a calculus in an artificial language. To determine category differences Ryle relied on the notion of absurdity. Where an expression cannot be substituted for another within a hitherto meaningful sentence without making that sentence absurd, the former expression was said to belong to a different category from the latter. *See also* category mistake.

category mistake. A notion, prominent in Ryle's philosophy, depending upon one or another theory of *categories. In *Aristotle it is a sort of equivocation. For Ryle, "Philosophy is the replacement of category-habits by category-disciplines..." (*The Concept of Mind*, p.8). This approach appears to suggest that progress in philosophy consists in acquiring a correct theory of categories and then avoiding, for philosophical purposes, "the presentation of facts belonging to one category in the idioms appropriate to another" (*ibid.*, p.8). Ryle had earlier employed the notion of "systematically misleading expressions" in an effort to show how we can be misled by purely grammatical structure into unwarranted belief in the existence of unnecessary entities, of which he cited Satan as one example. He criticized Descartes' dualism of body and mind as "one big mistake and a mistake of a special kind. It is, namely, a category mistake. It represents the facts of mental life as if they belonged to one logical type of category (or range of types or categories) when they actually belong to another" (*ibid.*, p.16).

causal theory of perception. The view that, although we can never be directly acquainted with more than the *veil of appearance, material things can nevertheless be known as the hypothesized causes of our *sense data. Those who reject the negative assumption of this philosophical theory, maintaining instead that in having sense data we are often also directly acquainted with physical things and events, usually insist nevertheless that the sense data occurring in genuine perception must be caused by what is perceived. See perception; representative theory of perception.

causa sui. (Latin for: cause of itself *or* himself.) An expression applied mainly to God, by those who, while insisting that God cannot have been produced by or be dependent on anything else, are nevertheless reluctant to say that God is uncaused. See also First Cause.

causation. The relationship between two events or states of affairs such that the first brings about the second. When the switch is turned on, the light shines. An apparently simple causal relationship clearly exists between the two events. But do all events have to have an antecedent cause and how, if at all, can one event necessitate the occurrence of another? According to quantum theory, it is not always the case that events at the atomic level do have causes; some

occur at random (*see* quantum mechanics; uncertainty principle). *Hume argued, as some scholastic precursors had done, that there neither are nor have to be any truly physical necessities. The idea, or the pseudo-idea, of causal necessity is just an empty shadow of our own mind's throwing and all there really is out there are regularities of nonnecessary constant conjunction.

The causal relation is a main locus of dispute between rationalist and empiricist philosophers (*see* empiricism; rationalism). The former are prone to search for a priori principles governing what kind of thing may or cannot cause some other kind of thing. All such principles, could they be established, would enable us to say is what kind of thing must have been responsible for the existence of the Universe or of human beings, or what kind of thing minds and bodies must be if they are to interact. The definitive critic of this type of search was Hume, who argued that knowledge of causes must come from experience. We know nothing of what kind of thing must or cannot cause another, or of whether every event must have a cause, except in so far as we can justify our claims by reference to actual experience of constant regularities.

Hume and later J. S. *Mill were unable to supply a satisfactory positive account of just what causal connection is. Russell was subsequently to claim that an advanced scientific understanding of the world needs no such notion. Modern analyses regard it as explicable through the subjunctive conditional 'If e_1 had not occurred, e_2 would not have occurred', but little is clear about what makes such a remark true. See also Mill's methods; science, philosophy of; space and time, philosophy of.

causes: material, formal, efficient, and final. These distinctions are known collectively as Aristotle's doctrine of the four causes. The description is unfortunate, because in English the word 'cause' would by anyone quite untouched by Aristotelian influences be applied only to the third. Although it remains necessary to know the traditional labels, it is perhaps best to think of Aristotle as here distinguishing four fundamentally different sorts of questions and their corresponding answers.

In the *Metaphysics* he picks out the material cause as "that from which, as its constitutive material, something comes, for example the bronze of the statue...". The formal cause in that case must be the account of what the statue is—a statue, perhaps, of the goddess Athena. The efficient cause is "the source of the first beginning of change,... for example ... the father is the cause of the child". The final cause is the purpose, "that for the sake of which [something is done], as health is of walking around ..." (1034A–B). More than one, and sometimes all, of these four sorts of questions can be asked and answered of the same thing: "since the term is multiply *ambiguous there are regularly several causes of the same thing."

It is important to appreciate that all these four notions of cause are closely tied in with other distinctive features of Aristotle's thought. Thus the distinction between material and formal relates to his fundamental contrast between form and matter. The efficient cause is always thought of as a substantial agent rather than as, possibly, an occurrence. The final cause for Aristotle is by no means always or typically, as here, a matter of conscious purpose or intention. It can simply be the end towards which something tends naturally to develop, but blindly and without conscious direction; his physics is in this sense teleological (*see* teleology) without being animistic (*see* animism).

cave, image of the. Plato's illustration in the *Republic* (Book VII) of the difference between knowledge and illusion, reality and appearance. Men chained in a cave, facing a blank wall, with a fire burning behind them, can see only shadows, which they take for real objects. When one who has been made to leave the cave and see the real world

by the light of the sun returns, it is hard for him to adapt to the dim light; he is ridiculed by his former companions and in unable to convince them that what they see are but vague reflections of reality. *See* Plato.

certainty *and* doubt.   Concepts that play an important part in Cartesian theory of knowledge. In the first of his *Meditations*, Descartes argued that if one is to know that a proposition p is true, then (a) one must be certain that p, and (b) one must be unable to doubt that p. The first of these conditions is necessary but not sufficient for knowledge; that is, one must be certain in order to know, but one can be certain and be wrong, that is, not know. Descartes says, then, that certainty must be supplemented by indubitability. He seems to have argued as follows. If someone doubts that p, he is in effect saying that the reasons produced for believing in the truth of p are not good enough. The doubter does not go so far as to deny the truth of p, but he does say that the reasons brought in support of p leave open the possibility that p is false; one *may be wrong* in asserting p. The move from this to the conclusion that knowledge implied indubitability seems to be made as follows. One cannot logically say, "I knew that p, but I turned out to be wrong." So if one is to say, with justification, "I know that p", one must not be in a position in which one may at some time have to take back one's assertion that p; the assertion that p must be such that one cannot doubt the truth of what one says.

Descartes' celebrated 'methodical doubt' used indubitability as a criterion of knowledge. It incidentally shows that to doubt the truth of a proposition p is to assert that the reasons advanced for believing that p are inadequate. Descartes asks, "Which, of the propositions I have previously accepted as true, do I not really *know*; that is, which of them are such that the reasons advanced for believing in them leave room for doubt? For example, can I doubt that the external world exists, as long as I base my belief solely on my sense-perceptions?" He answers that he can doubt this; in other words, he asserts that the reasons sometimes brought to justify a particular belief are inadequate.

chain of being. A metaphor for the order, unity, and completeness of the created world, thought of as a chain extending to include all possibilities of existence, from God to the tiniest particle of inanimate matter. The idea has a long history, originating in Plato's *Timaeus* and forming the basic medieval and Renaissance image for a hierarchical arrangement of the Universe. *See also* Lovejoy.

chaos. The term first used in the *Theogony* of Hesiod (8th century BC) to describe the gap resulting from the separation of heaven and earth during the emergence of the world from an undifferentiated state; it was interpreted by *Aristotle as the pre-philosophic concept of space. The Stoics, (allegedly because of an etymological error) understood the term as referring to the "watery state" which, they believed, follows the periodic destruction of the universe by fire and precedes its reconstruction (*see* Stoicism). A characteristic feature of all Greek philosophy is its conception of the world coming into being through the imposition of order on pre-existing chaos and the concept passed into Christian tradition through interpretations of the account of the creation in Genesis chapter 1. *Compare* cosmos.

ch'i. (Chinese for: material force *or* matter-energy.) In early Chinese philosophy the term associated with the psychophysiological state of possessing the attributes of life. Subsequently it was contrasted with the Neo-Confucian concept of *li*. *See* Neo-Confucianism; yin yang.

Chinese philosophy. The first flowering of philosophy in China occurred between the 6th and 3rd centuries BC; this period, which saw the appearance of the two great traditions of *Confucianism and *Taoism as well as the rich variety of thinkers known as the Hundred Schools, has ever since been regarded as its golden age. It was a time during which the Chinese states asserted their independence from the feudal league over which the old Chou dynastic power had presided, and vied with one another in a struggle for supremacy that ended only with the unification of China under the ruler of Ch'in in 221 BC. Contemporaneously, important economic and social changes were taking place within the states; artisan and merchant classes began to develop and an emerging bureaucratic class increasingly usurped the functions of the old aristocracy. As previously accepted values—the Chou king and the feudal lords had originally ruled through clan ties and religious authority as well as force—lost their hold and ceased to apply, Chinese thinkers sought to come to terms with the changing situation. The philosophy of the period consists to a large extent of a series of alternative diagnoses of the existing situation and rival proposals for dealing with it, which these thinkers tried to persuade various rulers to adopt. From the first, moral philosophy and political theory were thus interrelated.

The focal point of philosophical concern was the Way (*tao*) of man in the natural world and in society. Answers were sought to such immediately relevant questions as: what is the nature of man, and what kind of society corresponds to it? Chinese philosophers believed that the ancients, blessed with sage rulers, had lived according to the true Way, whereas their own generation had to rediscover it. Most would have maintained, as did Confucius (551-479 BC), who rationalized the ancient ritual code and hierarchical social structure in new moral terms, that they were "transmitting not inventing" (*see* Confucianism). Indeed the appeal to ancient precedent has remained an important feature of Chinese argumentation throughout history. Even the opponents of Confucius, the amoral and irrational Taoists (*see* Taoism), held that man had lost the primitive Way, known to his ancestors, of existing in harmony with nature. (Clearly the religious cult of the ancestors was an influential if unconscious factor in such attitudes.) Ancient precedent also figured among the famous three tests of a proposition advanced by Mo-tzu (fl. c.400 BC), the other two being present evidence and actual utility. It was the utilitarian emphasis of Mo-tzu and his followers, along with their doctrine of loving all one's fellow men alike, that antagonized Confucians. They, like *Mencius (372-289 BC), who insisted on the primacy of the family, considered all wider manifestations of love as springing from affection for one's parents and tended to regard indiscriminate utilitarianism as inimical to true morality. This Confucian attitude was certainly in part a reaction against both Mo-tzu and another school, that of *legalism. The legalists made state-oriented utilitarianism the basis of an amoral political system that for a short time during the Ch'in dynasty (221-207 BC) triumphed over all its rivals.

One concern which the legalists shared with other schools, however, was that which centred on the relationship between language and reality. In the context of legalist theory this concern referred to the correspondence of the actual performance of officials with their designated function. For Confucius and Mencius the "rectification of terms" (cheng ming) meant making the actual correspond to the ideal: unless one behaved like a true ruler, for example, one could not be termed a ruler. (Compare Thrasymachus in Book I of Plato's Republic.) During the Warring States period (403-221 BC), a naive excitement at the logical possibilities of language is a characteristic of several schools, including the Taoists. (But whereas the interest of his Confucian predecessors was only ethical, that of Hsün-tzu (313-238 BC) was logical. He examined the logical fallacies contained in the statements of rival schools, explored the origins and nature of linguistic communication, and on the basis of his conclusions evolved a simple epistemology in which the empirical and rational are nicely balanced.

The triumph of philosophical legalism in 221 BC came to an end with the establishment of the Han dynasty (206 BC-220 AD), although much that was legalistic in the administrative apparatus survived. Confucianism became the recognized state orthodoxy, but it was the Confucianism of Tung Chung-shu (179-104 BC). This was an amalgamation of Confucian morality with elements culled from the *yin yang school and other early superstitious beliefs in the framework of a cosmology that correlated the human, natural, and supernatural spheres and emphasized portents and numerology.

The Taoist revival at the end of the Han and during the Six Dynasties (221-589 AD) was characterized by a similar eclecticism (see Neo-Taoism). Moreover its emphasis on metaphysical problems prepared the ground for the gnostic Mahāyāna Buddhism (see Buddhist philosophy) that ousted Confucianism, and even to a lesser extent Taoism, in the minds of the ruling elite from the 5th century onwards. More popular forms of Buddhism (introduced into China in the 1st century AD) had already begun to exert a strong influence over the masses, and continued to do so up to the Neo-Confucian revival in the Sung Dynasty (960-1279).

*Neo-Confucianism aimed at nothing short of the social and political reform and moral regeneration of the whole country. Neo-Confucians like earlier Confucians opposed Buddhism, not only because they regarded its theory as erroneous, but also because of its serious social and political consequences. These anthropocentric, life-affirming moralists attacked—because they undermined the Confucian Way—such doctrines as those that rejected existence as an illusion, denied the reality of personality, and advocated celibacy and mortification of the body (both unfilial acts). As in earlier times it was still a question of convincing the ruler of the validity of their case, but now there was also a large bureaucratic class to be won over. This task, begun through the instruction of those who would be candidates for the civil service recruitment examinations, was consolidated when the interpretations of the Confucian classics set out by Chu Hsi's school were adopted as orthodox for the examination system in 1313—a position they retained until 1905.

The Neo-Confucians based their metaphysical system on the interpretations which Ch'eng Yi and Chu Hsi gave to classical works such as the *Ta hsüeh* (Great Learning), *Chung-yung* (The Mean), and *Meng-tzu* (Mencius—particularly his theory of human nature), and the more recent works of Chou Tun-yi (1017-73) and Shao Yung (1011-77). For their central concept of the Way as the universal principle, immanent in all phenomena and immanent in man as his moral nature, however, they drew on Buddhism itself. But it was Chang Tsai (1020-77) who provided the framework that set this concept firmly in the world of reality, in his description of all existence as a material flux informed by this principle. The Rationalist school of Ch'eng and Chu sought it in external phenomena, while Lu Hsiang-shan (1139-92), Wang Yang-ming (1472-1529), and others of the School of Mind looked for it in themselves. Until the introduction of European philosophy all subsequent Chinese thinkers tended to adopt positions between these extremes.

choice, axiom of. An *axiom of *set theory. Given any set *X*, the members of which are non-empty disjoint sets (that is, no two member sets of *X* have any members in common and each member set has at least one member), the axiom of choice states that there exists a (choice) set that consists of exactly one member of each of the members of *X*. The axiom has been shown to be independent of the other axioms of set theory. *See also* Gödel.

Chomsky, Avram Noam (1928-). American linguistic scientist and philosopher,

Ferrari P. Ward Professor of Modern Language and Linguistics, Massachusetts Institute of Technology. Some main works on linguistics: *Syntactic Structures* (1957), *Aspects of the Theory of Syntax* (1965), *Cartesian Linguistics* (1966), *Language and Mind* (1968), and *The Logical Structure of Linguistic Theory* (1975).

In learning a language we learn rules that tell us how to produce grammatical strings of words, and one task of linguistics is to set out these rules (the grammar) of a language. Chomsky's studies of grammar have revolutionized the scientific study of language. In discussing grammar Chomsky stressed that language users have the creative ability to produce and understand indefinite numbers of new sentences. Hence the grammar of a natural language must be generative, that is, must allow those who know its rules to generate and understand sentences never before encountered. In *Syntactic Structures* Chomsky discusses three possible grammars. Only one, transformational grammar, provides an adequate generative grammar for a natural language such as English. (The grammar is called 'transformational' since it contains *transformation rules, rules that tell us, for example, how to transform sentences from active to passive and how to derive idiomatic sentences from formal grammar.)

Chomsky makes important applications of his work to psychology. He criticizes behaviourist psychology, in particular its account of language learning. (By that account we learn language by associating words with stimuli.) Chomsky allows that this may explain how we form expectations and associations; what it does not explain is how, after hearing relatively few utterances, children gain the creative ability to understand and produce indefinitely many different grammatical sentences.

His work in linguistics also has a bearing on philosophy, notably on disputes between empiricists and rationalists. He argues that languages have underlying structural similarities and claims that we must be born with knowledge of this 'universal grammar'. As children we use it in analysing the utterances we hear. Only so can we explain why, on the basis of an acquaintance with a few utterances, we are quickly able to produce and understand new ones. This need to posit innate capacities counts *against* *empiricism (the view that our minds, wholly empty at birth, obtain all knowledge from postnatal experience) and *for* *rationalism, with which the belief in innate ideas is typically associated.

Chrysippus (*c.*280-207 BC). Third and greatest head of the Stoa (*see* Stoicism) and author of over 700 writings, all now lost. A convert to Stoicism from the sceptical Academy of *Arcesilaus (*see* Academy of Athens; Scepticism), Chrysippus elaborated and defended the Stoic system with unsurpassed energy and success. "Without Chrysippus, there would have been no Stoa", went the saying; and Chrysippus' teaching, different in certain minor respects from that of his predecessors, became identified with Stoic orthodoxy.

Church's theorem. The theorem stated in 1936 by Alonzo Church to the effect that there is no *algorithm for the first order functional calculus or any stronger theory, such as arithmetic. A formal theory may consist of a number of assumptions (axioms) and rules for obtaining (proving) new sentences (known as theorems) from such assumptions. The question is whether there is an algorithm or mechanical procedure that, after a finite number of steps, tells us whether an arbitrary sentence of the language is a theorem or not. Although there is such an algorithm for the propositional calculus, Church's theorem denies that there is such a solution for more complex systems.

Cicero, Marcus Tullius (106-43 BC). Roman politician, orator, and writer on rhetorical and philosophical questions. As a young man, Cicero had studied philosophy in Greece, but his philosophical writings, apart from the political *Republic* and *Laws* (*c.*55-52 BC), were all produced in one short period of retirement from public life (Feb.45-Nov.44 BC). They included the incompletely preserved *Academica* (on the impossibility of sure knowledge), the *De Finibus* (on the ends of human action), the *Tusculan Disputations* (on practical questions of death, pain, the emotions, and happiness), *Laelius on Friendship, Cato Major on Old Age*, the theological *On the Nature of the Gods* and *On Divination*, and the *De Officiis* on the rules for right conduct. Written at speed, these works are diffuse and often muddled adaptations of various Greek originals. Philosophically, Cicero was eclectic, professing an Academic scepticism. His aim was to create a literature in Latin on the principal questions of philosophy. This he largely achieved, thereby greatly fostering the development of Latin as a philosophical language. Since, moreover, their originals are lost, his works are a major source for Hellenistic epistemology, theology, ethics, and political thought.

clairvoyance. *See* extrasensory perception.

Clarke, Samuel (1675-1729). English philosopher, theologian, and philologist, who studied at Cambridge where he became a friend and disciple of *Newton.

In two sets of Boyle lectures, 'A Demonstration of the Being and Attributes of God' (delivered 1704) and 'A Discourse Concerning the Unchangeable Obligations of Natural Religion' (delivered 1705), Clarke expressed his disagreement with the 'freethinking' of *Hobbes and *Spinoza and set out to prove God's existence by a method "as near mathematical as the nature of such discourse would allow". He also claimed that moral principles could be known by reason alone, being as certain as the propositions of mathematics. In extensive correspondence with *Leibniz (published in 1717) he defended the Newtonian view of the universe and of space and time as absolute entities rather than mere relations between objects and events (see absolute space).

class. Intuitively, a collection of entities of any kind that is typically specified by giving a condition for belonging to the class. Thus the people who live in York form a class, the class of inhabitants of York, to which a person belongs by satisfying the condition for being an inhabitant of York, namely, living in York. This class would be denoted by {x: x lives in York}. Classes determined by different conditions are the same iff they have the same members, so that {x: x has a heart} = {x: x has kidneys}. In general, it seems, any *predicate 'F' will determine a class—the class of things to which it may be correctly applied, symbolically {x: Fx}—and that an object a belongs to this class, written a ε {x: Fx}, iff 'Fa' is true.

The terms 'class', 'set', 'collection of objects', and 'extension' (of a concept or of a general term) were used almost interchangeably and without any clear distinctions being drawn between them until the discovery of *Russell's paradox. Even prior to this discovery there was debate about whether all classes must be determined in this way, that is, whether it is a necessary condition (see necessary and sufficient conditions) for a group of entities to form a class that they have some property in common. This, then, is a debate over whether all classes are extensions of concepts, or whether 'class' is a more inclusive notion, covering also arbitrary collections of objects such as that consisting of Tom, his house, the Houses of Parliament, and the Union Jack. What Russell's paradox demonstrated was that a contradiction arises from the assumptions that every predicate determines a class and that classes are themselves entities that may be formed into classes. There have been a variety of 'solutions' to this paradox, all of which involve placing restrictions on one or both of these assumptions and drawing a distinction between classes and sets. The term 'class' is more often used for 'extension of a concept' whereas 'set' covers arbitrary listable collections of objects, together with the extensions of certain kinds of predicates. Exactly which predicates determine sets is stipulated by the axioms of *set theory. See also extension; set.

classical theory of probability. See probability.

class paradox. See Russell's paradox.

clinamen. (Latin for: a turning aside, swerve.) See Epicureanism.

clock paradox. A paradox that arises from the special theory of *relativity, which predicts that clocks run more slowly in a frame of reference moving at speeds approaching the velocity of light when observed from a stationary frame of reference. Thus, if one of a pair of twins embarks on a high-speed space journey, he will, when he returns be younger than his brother who has remained on earth. The resolution to this form of the paradox is that the departure, turn-around, and return of the space-travelling twin involve accelerations and decelerations, which are not covered by the special theory.

clocks, image of the two. An illustration provided by *Geulincx, and later used by *Leibniz in presenting his own response to the Cartesian *mind-body problem. If two clocks are seen to keep perfect time with each other, there are three ways that this could arise: (1) through mutual influence; (2) through constant adjustments by the mechanic who cares for them; (3) through their own inbuilt individual exactitude. If one substitutes mind for one clock and body for the other, the three ways of agreement become three possible responses to the Cartesian problem: (1) two-way *interactionism; (2) *occasionalism; and (3) Leibniz's own preferred solution, harmonious parallel functioning (see psychophysical parallelism).

closed wff. See wff.

cogito ergo sum. (Latin for: I think, therefore I am.) The most common formulation of the Cartesian argument for the basic certainty of one's own existence. *See* Descartes.

cognitive. 1. Denoting mental processes connected with understanding, formulation of beliefs, and acquisition of knowledge, and thus distinct from volitional processes, such as wanting or intending. 2. Denoting utterances that are both significant and either true or false, in contrast to other utterances, such as commands and exclamations, that are significant and intelligible but cannot be classed as either true or false (sometimes called 'non-cognitive'). In particular, some analyses of ethical utterances (for instance, the *boo-hooray theory) are called non-cognitive. This, again, contrasts with, for instance, G. E. *Moore's account of goodness as a nonnatural quality that something might in truth either possess or not possess.

cognitive achievement word. A word that, when used correctly in a claim about a proposition (or an object) entails the truth of that proposition (or the existence of the object). For example, 'John knows that it is raining' (if it is true that he knows) entails that it is raining; or 'I see (or feel) the table' entails that there is a table there to see (or feel). Such words are to be contrasted with ordinary propositional words, such as 'believe', 'think', 'think of', and so on. 'I believe that *p*' entails nothing about the truth or falsity of *p*.

Cohen, Hermann (1842–1918). Professor of philosophy at Marburg (1876–1912). Cohen's early works were critical studies of Kant, and he developed the *Marburg school of *Neo-Kantianism. At Marburg he wrote *Die Logik der reinen Erkenntnis* (1902), *Die Ethik des reinen Willens* (1904), and *Die Ästhetik des reinen Gefühls* (1912). After his retirement he taught at a rabbinic seminary in Berlin, and in the last years of his life he changed his attitude to religion, no longer subordinating it to reason but according it an independent role. The works of this period, *Der Begriff der Religion im System der Philosophie* (1915) and *Die Religion der Vernunft aus den Quellen des Judentums* (1919), established him as the dominant influence in subsequent German Jewish philosophy (*see* Jewish philosophy).

coherence theory of truth. A theory of the nature of truth, associated with objective *idealism. It states that truth is essentially system, by which is meant that the progress of knowledge is a progress towards a single complete system of thought, and that truth is predicable of this system alone. This leads logically to the view that what are normally called 'true' or 'false' propositions should really be called *partly* true or *partly* false. Supporters of this theory insist that the coherence of which they speak attaches only to a concrete system, of which human experiences form a part; it does not attach to the abstract systems of mathematics or logic, where several mutually incompatible systems are possible. The coherence theory must also be distinguished from the view that coherence is a criterion of truth. According to this, a proposition may be accepted as true if it coheres with other propositions which are known to be true; but it is not suggested that the truth of these propositions lies in their coherence.

Coleridge, Samuel Taylor (1772–1834). Romantic poet, philosopher, theologian, and social theorist. Coleridge was one of the earliest British thinkers to be profoundly affected by the philosophy of Kant, and later by Schelling's *System of Transcendental Idealism* (1800). Coleridge's account of his own mental development is given in his *Biographia Literaria* (1817), a key document in the intellectual history of early 19th-century England.

Coleridge was a prolific but very disorganized writer, and this makes it difficult to discover exactly what he thought about particular philosophical issues. Some of his best insights were hastily penned in the margins of his copies of the philosophical works of others, and his views on a given topic are usually widely dispersed among his highly miscellaneous prose works. These works are themselves characterized by strange digressions, autobiographical revelations, and undigested learning reminiscent of writers of the 16th and 17th centuries, from whom, indeed, much of this learning derives. Coleridge frequently addresses his readers in patronizing, homiletic tones. He has an occasionally unfortunate penchant for word-coinage; for instance he called creative imagination 'esemplastic' because he mistakenly thought the ordinary German word for imagination, *Einbildungskraft*, had colloquial connotations suggesting 'organic unity'. Yet, for all this, Coleridge certainly possessed considerable philosophical talent. Moreover, as his remarkable *Notebooks* show, he was a great introspective psychologist.

Among the many places where Coleridge discusses topics of specifically philosophical interest are: *On Logic and Learning* (ed. A. Snyder, 1929); *Treatise on Method* (1818; ed. A. Snyder, 1934), *The Friend* (1818; second section, Essay 11) and *Table Talk* (12 September 1830, 17 March, 14 April, and 29 June 1833) where Coleridge consideres the merits of different philosophical and scientific methods and defends his own; *Confessions of an Enquiring Spirit* (1840) on the nature of religious belief; *Biographia Literaria* (chapter 13) on imagination; *The Friend*, I, 15, for criticisms of utilitarianism; *Aids to Reflection* (1825), pp. 224 ff., gives Coleridge's version of the Neo-Kantian distinction between 'reason' and 'understanding' and one formulation of his dialectical conception of 'truth' as subsisting only in 'ideas' (compare *Statesman's Manual* (1816), Appendix). *The Philosophical Lectures* (ed. K. Coburn, 1949) contains Coleridge's lectures on the history of philosophy. These are heavily dependent for information on W. G. Tennemann's *Geschichte der Philosophie* (1798-1819) but contain many original observations;

they should be compared with chapters 7 to 9 of *Biographia Literaria*.

Coleridge's interest in the Germans sprang from dissatisfaction with the prevailing British and empiricist theory of knowledge, according to which the human mind was relatively passive and its operations entirely explicable in terms of the *association of ideas. Coleridge had a special interest in the psychology of artistic creation which, he felt, the empiricist theory did little to explain. He came to regard the most important associationist treatise of the day, David Hartley's *Observations on Man* (1791), as too "mechanistic" and "necessitarian". The German philosophers, on the other hand, conceived the mind as fundamentally active and they used organic (as opposed to mechanical, atomistic) metaphors to describe its formative operations. This strongly appealed to Coleridge since, as he put it in one of his famous conversations later in life, "The pith of my system is to make the senses out of the mind—not the mind out of the senses, as Locke did" (*Table Talk* (1835), 25 July 1832). The general epistemological outlook of the Germans appealed to Coleridge for another reason as well: it appeared to give rational support to the main doctrines of Christianity, in which he fervently believed. Although Coleridge also found Kant's account of the foundation of moral judgments by no means wholly acceptable, it was, at any rate, in important respects more consonant with his own religious feelings than the utilitarianism of Bentham or Paley.

None of this meant, however, that Coleridge was incapable of being sometimes acutely critical of German philosophy. For example, in his copy of Kant's *Dreams of a Ghost-Seer* (1766) he registered the following disagreement with Kant's idea that duty should be done simply for the sake of duty: "Away with Stoic hypocrisy!... Let thy maxim be capable of becoming the Law of all intelligent Beings—well! but this supposes an *end* possessible by intelligent Beings. For if the Law be barren of all consequences, what is it but words? To obey the Law for its own sake is really a mere sophism in any other sense". Again, Coleridge's irritation with Hegel's use of 'Nothing' as a name in the *Science of Logic* (1812-16) was equally to the point: "'To be' (*Sein, Tò ειναι*) is opposed to the 'Nothing' (*Nichts*)", noted Coleridge in the margin of his copy of Hegel's *Logic*, "Whereas", he continued, "the true opposite of 'To be' is 'Not to be'."

Apart from the pervasive effect of his writings on Victorian theologians, Coleridge is best known as the most important English literary critic and aesthetician in the early 19th century, though here too he borrowed much from German sources, especially from *Schlegel. Coleridge's one book on social philosophy, *On the Constitution of the Church and State* (1830), with its central dialectical (but non-revolutionary) ideal of social harmony achieved through a reconciliation of forces working for permanence with forces working for progression, was influential not only on conservative thinkers. In a now famous article on Coleridge, published in the *Westminster Review* (March 1840), J. S. *Mill also acknowledged his own debt to Coleridge and to the 'Germano-Coleridgeans' who had helped him to gain a more comprehensive conception of the "philosophy of human culture" than that afforded by classical utilitarianism.

collective. In von Mises' treatment of *probability, an infinite sequence of elements some of which correspond to a certain attribute or result, and which satisfies the conditions of convergence and *randomness.

collective unconscious. In the psychology of C. G. *Jung, the inherited *unconscious that contains the "archetypes", the symbolic epitomes of the experience of the whole human species.

collectivism. Another name for political *holism.

Collingwood, Robin George (1889-1943). British philosopher, Waynflete Professor of Metaphysical Philosophy at Oxford (1935-41). Main philosophical works: *Speculum Mentis* (1924), *An Essay on Philosophical Method* (1933), *The Principles of Art* (1938), *Essay on Metaphysics* (1940), *The New Leviathan* (1942), *The Idea of Nature* (1945), *The Idea of History* (1946).

Apart from philosophy, Collingwood's chief interests were ancient history and archaeology; the nature of history and its relation to philosophy were longstanding preoccupations. At some points (for example, in the *Essay on Philosophical Method*) he seemed to allow that philosophy is a discipline distinct from history, tackling, by its own distinctive methods, its perennial problems about the nature of reality. Later, he moved towards a thoroughgoing historical relativism, in which any statement, of a philosophical thesis or anything else, can be understood or evaluated only when seen as the answer to a question raised in and by a particular historical situation, and against the background of the presuppositions, interests, concepts, etc., of a particular culture at a particular stage of development.

common consent arguments. Arguments from the (almost) universal acceptance of a belief, especially belief in God, to the truth of that belief. Apart from difficulties of determining how nearly universal belief in God has been throughout human history, or what should count as such belief, any argument of the form "(Almost) everyone believes *p*, therefore *p* is true" is clearly invalid. Nonetheless, if essentially similar beliefs are widespread among mutually independent cultures, it can reasonably be argued that they probably embody in some fashion important truths (perhaps about human nature or needs) and should not lightly be dismissed as mere errors.

common sense. 1. In general, the kind of opinions about life at large (for example, that the world has existed for a long time or that our minds are incorporeal) that philosophers believe unphilosophical people take for granted. The attempt solemnly to justify these notions appears comical, pedantic, or esoteric, except in circumstances in which they are being doubted or denied. When they are defended, the defence characteristically relies on an appeal to the general or universal consent that exists about them. Thomas *Reid, among others, emphasized this particular line of justification. He and such successors as Sir William *Hamilton are often described as the Scottish Philosophers of Common Sense.

In this century the leading defender of common sense against philosophical scepticism was G. E. *Moore. Some of his admirers argued—though he himself was never fully persuaded—that his defence should be interpreted as a defence of ordinary language. The ultimate rationale of this has to be the contention that the key terms, the application of which the sceptic challenges, can only be understood at all on assumptions that rule out such philosophical scepticism (see also linguistic philosophy; private language). Those out of sympathy with this style and tone associate common sense with an uncritical refusal to recognize complexity for what it is.

2. (in Aristotle) The faculty that integrates the data of the five senses into unified apprehensions of objects.

compatibilist. See freewill and determinism.

complete. Denoting, very roughly, a *formal system in which the rules and axioms of the system allow one to construct enough proofs (see axiom; proof). But what counts as 'enough' may be judged relative to different purposes, and there are a variety of non-equivalent requirements giving rise to non-equivalent notions of completeness. A system that is not complete is said to be *incomplete*.

1. (as applied to *formal systems, or formalized theories) (a) A formal system S is *simply complete* (or *decidable*) iff,

for every sentence A of the language of S, either A or its negation is provable in S. (b) S is *complete with respect to an *interpretation I* iff all sentences of the language of S which are true in I are provable in S. (c) S is *absolutely complete* iff for every sentence A of the language of S, either A is provable in S or the addition of A to the axioms of S has the effect of making all sentences of the language of S provable.

(a) is a notion that is syntactically defined and thus the methods of *proof theory can be employed to determine whether any given system is complete in this sense. Using such methods, Gödel showed that no formal system of arithmetic, if it is consistent, could be complete in this sense (see Godel's theorem). No system that is incomplete in sense (a) can be complete in sense (b), since for any sentence A of the language of S, either A or its negation must be true in I, and hence if S were complete in sense (b), either A or its negation would be provable in S. This means that by showing that a system S is incomplete in sense (a) one in effect shows that S cannot be regarded as a complete formalization of an informally developed theory concerning some domain D of entities, in the sense that it will not capture all the features of that domain—there will be things true of entities in D which are not provable in S. A system which is complete in sense (c) (another syntactically defined notion) is, in a sense, maximal. It allows one to prove as many things as is possible within the constraints of consistency.

2. (as applied for formal systems of logic) A formal system L of logic is complete (with respect to interpretations in the class Υ) iff, for every sentence (closed *wff) A of the language of L, if A is true in all interpretations in Υ, then A is a theorem of L, that is, there is a proof of A in L. L is *complete with respect to entailment* (in interpretations in Υ) iff, for any set Γ of sentences and any sentence A of the language of L, if A is true in every interpretation in Υ in which every member of Γ is true, then there are sentences $P_1 \ldots P_n$ in Γ such that there is a proof in L of A from $P_1 \ldots P_n$ as assumptions. Since Γ may be empty, if L is complete with respect to entailment, then L is also complete, but the converse does not automatically hold unless a deduction theorem (*see* inference, rule of) can be proved for L.

Here the intuitive idea is that a logical system is complete if it allows one to produce proofs corresponding to all the valid inference forms that can be represented in the language. This assumes that there is an independently defined notion of validity based either on an intuitive interpretation of the logical operators of the language, or on a class Υ of interpretations (in the sense of valuations) of the language of the system. If an intuitive interpretation of the logical operators is assumed, this will determine the relevant class Υ of (admissible) interpretations, and the relativization of completeness to a class of interpretations is omitted, as is the case when it is shown that both propositional and predicate *calculus are complete.

complex number. *See* number.

composition *and* division. There are two different ways in which the terms 'composition' and 'division' are used, and different fallacies are associated with each. The first is concerned with the reference of terms used in an argument; the second with changes of meaning obtained by different combinations of terms.

1. Composition applies to a whole or class considered collectively, and division applies to it considered as its individual parts. Thus the *fallacy of division* is arguing from the fact that something is true of a thing considered as a whole, to the conclusion that the same is true of parts of that whole. An example would be an argument that proceeds invalidly from 'All the men can build the house in a month', that is, collectively they can, to the erroneous conclusion that every single man, individually, can build the house in a month. *The fallacy of composition* is an

equally invalid argument in the reverse direction.

2. These two terms are also used in an Aristotelian sense to describe the ways in which the same words or phrases can be interpreted to give different meanings. Thus the sentence 'When John is talking, he could be silent' can be given a composite sense, to mean that he can talk and be silent at the same time, which is obviously false, or a divided sense, to mean at some particular time John talks, and could instead at that time be silent.

composition, fallacy of. *See* composition and division.

Comte, Auguste (1798–1857). French positivist philosopher. He studied contemporary science at the École Polytechnique and became secretary to *Saint-Simon. Denied university appointments, he lectured to private audiences. Main philosophical work: *Cours de philosophie positive* (6 vols., 1830–42).

Comte traced the development of human thought (and human society) from its theological and metaphysical stages to its positive stage; this last stage was characterized by systematic collection and correlation of observed facts and abandonment of unverifiable speculation about first causes or final ends. He claimed to have pioneered sociology as the positive study of social structures and development. *See also* positivism.

concept. 1. (in general philosophical use) That which a person has when he understands or is able to use some portion of his language. Criteria for possessing a concept may be weak, requiring only an ability to pick out or distinguish that to which an expression applies. For example, to possess the concept sheep could require no more than the ability to say 'sheep' in the presence of sheep. Stronger criteria might involve the grasp of the logical or grammatical behaviour of the expression ('sheep' is a common noun, not a proper name), factual knowledge (sheep are a source of meat), or the ability to define or give the *essence of a sheep.

2. (in Frege) A concept (*Begriff*) expression is what is now known as a predicate *term. Because concept expressions contain a place either to be filled by a singular term or bound by a *quantifier, Frege regarded them as essentially incomplete expressions, requiring for their reference (*see* sense and reference) entities that are similarly incomplete, that is, concepts. For this reason concepts are to be sharply distinguished from objects of all kinds including classes (*see* class). *See also* function.

concept *and* **object.** *See* formal mode of speech.

conceptualism. The theory of universals (*see* universals and particulars), according to which general or abstract terms (such as 'substance' or 'humanity') have meaning because they name or otherwise refer to corresponding non-physical entities, called concepts. In the most substantial, but perhaps least plausible view, these concepts are taken to be mental images. *See also* nominalism; realism.

concomitant variations, method of. *See* Mill's methods.

concrete universal. A term used in Hegelian philosophy to encapsulate Hegel's view that thinking must be universal (that is, in terms of universal law), but not *abstractly* universal. Hegel illustrates his meaning (*Encyclopaedia*, par. 163, Addition) by Rousseau's concept of the general will. The laws of the state, which spring from the general will, are universal in form, so the general will may be called 'universal'; but this will is also the will of a particular historical community, and in this respect it is concrete.

Condillac, Étienne Bonnot de (1715–80). French philosopher who, in spite of being an ordained priest, associated himself with the secularizing and rationalizing tendencies of the *Encyclopedists. He greatly admired *Locke and, in his *Essai sur l'origine des connaissances humaines* (1746; re-edited by the author, 1771) and *Traité des sensations* (1754; re-edited 1778), he followed Locke in tracing all human faculties back to their origins in sensation. Man's will and understanding are modifications of the accumulation of impressions, associations, etc., arising from the stimulation of the sense organs.

conditional. 1. (adj) Describing a statement in which it is claimed that something is, or will be, the case, provided that, or on the condition that, some other situation obtains. 2. (n) A conditional or *hypothetical* statement. Such statements are charcteristically expressed using the word 'if'. Thus both (1) 'If James was born in Wisconsin, then he is American' and (2) 'He will come only if he is invited' are conditional statements. In (1) it is claimed that the truth of 'James is American' follows from, or is guaranteed by, the truth of 'James was born in Wisconsin', whereas in (2) it is claimed that the truth of 'He will not come' will result from its being true that he is not invited so that (2) might also have been expressed by 'If he is not invited, he will not come'. When a conditional statement is expressed in the form 'If *p*, then *q*', *p* is called the *antecedent* or *protasis* and *q* the *consequent* or *apodosis* of the conditional.

The logical nature of conditional statements, that is, the conditions under which they can be held to be true or false (if they can indeed be thought to be, strictly speaking, true or false at all) and the nature of the rules of *inference that should be thought to govern their use in arguments has been, and remains, one of the most controversial points in the logical formalization of everyday discourse. It has been held that a conditional statement cannot be true unless there is some connection between its antecedent and consequent: this connection can be derived from the meanings of the words involved, as in 'If he is unmarried, he is a bachelor', from the presence of a causal connection between the states said to obtain, as in 'If it is raining, the ground will be wet', from a connection established by some legal code, as in 'If you discriminate on the basis of race or sex, you are liable to be prosecuted', or from some other source. Others have denied this, some saying that it is acceptance of the conditional statement itself that establishes a connection between its antecedent and consequent and that a conditional statement thus has the status of a rule entitling one to infer the truth of the consequent from that of the antecedent, but which, in so far as it is a rule, is not itself open to assessment in respect of truth or falsity. Others deny that there is any connection either established or implied by a conditional statement.

The most commonly adopted course in formal propositional logic is either to deny that the truth of a conditional statement requires that there be any connection between its antecedent and consequent, or at least to concentrate on those uses of conditional statements that do not seem to require such a connection. This is done by giving the minimum possible force to a conditional statement, seeing 'If p, then q' as asserting only that it is not in fact the case that p is true and q is false. In other words, 'If p, then q' is treated as being equivalent to 'Not (p and not-q)' (symbolically -(p & -q)). Conditional statements interpreted in this way are being treated as *material conditionals*. If 'not' and 'and' are both treated as *truth-functional operators, then material conditionals will also be regarded as truth-functional compounds of their component statements. In this case the symbolic representation of 'If p, then q' is $p \supset q$' where '$\supset$' is defined by the *truth-table

$$
\begin{array}{ccc}
p & \supset & q \\
T & T & T \\
T & F & F \\
F & T & T \\
F & T & F \\
\end{array}
$$

which is also the truth-table for -(p & -q). The symbol '$\rightarrow$' is sometimes used

in place of '$\supset$', but is also used for other interpretations of conditional statements.

A material conditional may be true even when there is obviously no connection whatsoever between its antecedent and its consequent, as for example 'If England is part of Europe, then grass is green'. It is for this reason that it is not always regarded as being an adequate representation of the normal use of conditional statements. Cases in which the inadequacy of this representation become particularly acute are those in which the antecedent and consequent of the conditional are given in the subjunctive mood, as in 'If the polar ice caps were to melt, 90% of Europe would be under water'. Such conditionals are known as *subjunctive conditionals*.

The problems are most dramatic when the antecedent is a past tense subjunctive statement, as in 'If this match had been struck, it would have lit', which carries the implication that the corresponding past tense indicative statement, 'This match was struck', is false. Such statements are commonly called *counterfactual conditionals*. If the counterfactual conditional 'If this match had been struck, it would have lit' is represented as having the force of the material conditional 'This match was struck $\supset$ this match lit' it would automatically be judged to be true, because it is a notable feature of material conditionals, as defined by the above truth-table, that they must be judged to be true whenever their antecedent is false (one of the paradoxes of material implication—*see* implication and entailment). But this would hold equally for the most implausible statement, such as 'If this leaf had been struck, it would have lit', so that the material interpretation of conditional statements gives no obvious basis for discriminating between true, or reasonable, counterfactual conditionals and those which are false, or highly implausible.

conditional proof, rule of. *See* inference, rule of.

configurationism. The English term occasionally used for *Gestalt theory.

confirmation. The relation between propositions when one supports or adds credence to another. Confirmation theory hopes to delimit what kind of proposition or theory is confirmable (that is, capable of gaining support from experience), this being a necessary task of any kind of *positivism. It is plagued by paradox (*see* Goodman's paradox; Hempel) and its lack of success has led some philosophers to regard the relation as non-logical and entirely subservient to what scientists at any particular time regard as a good theory. Some, such as *Popper, even deny that experience ever confirms the hypotheses of a scientific theory, and others such as Feyerabend, advocate epistemological anarchy, under which there are no established criteria to separate rubbish from sensible theory. *See also* Carnap; probability.

Confucianism. Philosophy of the school founded by Confucius (551-479 BC), whose name in its familiar Western form is a Latinization of Chinese K'ung fu-tzu 'Venerable Master K'ung'. For this doctrine the only reliable source is the *Lun-yü* (Analects), a collection of brief dialogues and sayings recorded— often without indication of context—by his disciples, mostly young gentlemen whom he was preparing for government office. The philosopher who emerges from the *Lun-yü* is a teacher primarily concerned with moral values as the basis of social and political order. Defending the Way (*tao*) of the ancients at a time when the old religious imperatives and rituals which regulated all social and political intercourse had lost their force, he invested them with a new moral justification. His Way presupposed that the hierarchical structure of the old society corresponded to a natural moral order: the onus was thus on each individual to assume the moral obligations inherent in his position as son, father, subject, ruler, etc. The cardinal virtue *jen*, usually translated 'benevolence' or 'humanity', is a homophone of the

Chinese for 'man', and in fact embraces all the moral qualities of the true man: loyalty, reciprocity, dutifulness, filial and fraternal affection, courtesy, good faith, and friendship. For a time Confucius travelled from state to state in an unsuccessful attempt to win the support of their rulers for his Way, but although some of his followers eventually gained high office he regarded himself as having failed in his mission. *See also* Mencius; Neo-Confucianism.

conjunction. *See* and.

connected. *See* relation.

connective. A word or group of words that can be regarded as joining two or more sentences to form a single complex sentence. Examples are 'either...or...', 'and', 'because', 'since'. Most common are connectives joining two sentences; these are termed *binary connectives*. Although there are many expressions that function grammatically as connectives, the term is often, in the context of logic, restricted to the *logical connectives*: 'and', 'or', 'if... then...', and 'if and only if (iff)'. A connective may be used to join sentences that are already complex in the sense of themselves containing a connective, as when 'If... then...' is used to connect 'It stays fine and there are no high winds' with 'There will be a good harvest' to form the sentence 'If it stays fine and there are no high winds, then there will be a good harvest.' In such a case the last connective used, in this example 'If... then...', is called the *main*, (or *principal*) *connective* of the sentence.

connotation. *See* denotation.

conscience. The holding of a conviction that some action is morally obligatory (or wrong) and to be firmly committed to doing (or refraining from doing) it. Those who consider that all moral beliefs provide overriding reasons for acting thereby make them all matters of conscience.

Conscience has often been regarded by theists as the voice of God (*see*

Butler). However, conscience could not deliver new moral information from God, since it can err, and, therefore, in order to know if a particular deliverance came from God we should have to know already what his commands were.

Many philosophers believe that a man should be excused from blame for following his erring conscience since he is, by definition, doing his best. The possible social consequences of this belief might be somewhat limited by the (equally controversial) claim that there are beliefs too extreme to be conscientiously held.

consciousness. A term with two related philosophical uses: first, as for example, for Locke, in the sense of self-knowledge acquired by virtue of the mind's capacity to reflect upon itself in introspective acts analogous with perception; and second, in a broader modern sense, opposed to anaesthesia, designating what is held to be the general property of mental states.

The principal philosophical issues that surround these conceptions are (a) in what ways it is possible for a subject to be made the object of its own awareness (how can introspection occur?), and (b) whether consciousness necessarily accompanies every mental state. Introspectionist theories have been widely discredited in contemporary philosophy (*see* mind, philosophy of), but there is considerable interest in the question of the relation of consciousness to mental states. For example, it would commonly be agreed that one could not fail to be conscious of the fact that, for example, one was in pain; on the other hand, there are cases in which one may deceive oneself about, and in that way fail to be conscious of, the mental state one is in; and again, as Freud held, there are certain mental states that appear to be inaccessible to consciousness.

consequence. If S is a set of statements, the statement A is said to be a consequence of S if the truth of A follows from the joint truth of members of S. The force of 'follows from' may be interpreted in various ways, each inter-

pretation giving rise to a different *consequence relation*. When taken to mean that A is true whenever all members of S are true, the relation is that of *logical consequence*, which is a semantically defined notion (*see* semantics). When taken to mean that A can be deductively derived from members of S according to the rules of some formal logical system, then the relation is that of *formal consequence*, which is a syntactically defined notion (*see* syntax). There are other, not strictly logical, relations, such as that of causal consequence. *See* conditional; implication and entailment.

consequent. *See* affirming the antecedent; conditional.

consequential characteristics. An alternative name for *supervenient characteristics.

consequentialism. An umbrella term for any moral theories that state that the rightness or wrongness, goodness or badness of an action is solely dependent on the results the action produces. In its pure form this doctrine refers to the actual results of individual actions, but variations on the theme include reference to the foreseeable or possibly the intended results alone or to the results of *classes* of actions. The most popular and influential version of this approach to morality is *utilitarianism.

consistent *and* **inconsistent.** A set of statements is inconsistent if it entails a *contradiction or has contradictory consequences, and is consistent otherwise. The bifurcation of the notion of consequence into semantic and syntactic notions creates a corresponding division between notions of consistency (*see* semantics; syntax). A set S of sentences written in a formal language L is (semantically) *consistent* iff it has a *model, that is, there is an *interpretation of L under which all sentences belonging to S are true. It is (syntactically) consistent, or *consistent with respect to provability*, iff there is no *wff A of L such that both A and its negation can be proved from the members of *S*. An axiomatic theory is consistent if its axioms form a consistent set of sentences (*see* axiom).

A person holding a consistent(inconsistent) set of beliefs may be said to be consistent(inconsistent) and may also be said to be being consistent(inconsistent) when the statements he makes are consistent(inconsistent) or the actions he performs can be seen as according(or failing to accord) with a consistent set of principles. To assert or believe a contradiction is to hold that something both is and is not the case at the same time. Since something cannot both be and not be the case at the same time, one is therefore being irrational in attempting to hold as true what cannot be true (*see also* non-contradiction, law of). Consistency is thus a requirement of rationality. In so far as a person is not consistent, he is held to be being irrational.

Systems of logic, as paradigms of reasoning, are obviously required to be consistent, as are deductive theories, the representations of rationally acquired knowledge. A system of logic *L* is said to be *consistent with respect to negation* iff there is no wff *A* of the language of *L* such that both *A* and its negation are theorems of *L* (*see* theorem). Many systems of logic (particularly those which use the material *conditional) have the property that, for any wffs *A* and *B*, *B* will be derivable from 'A and not-A'. Thus a set *S* of sentences will be consistent with respect to provability in such a logic iff there is some wff that is not provable from *S*. Since negation is not mentioned in this condition, it gives rise to a further syntactic notion of consistency that is applicable to languages that do not include negation. A set *T* of sentences in a language *L* (logical system *S*) is said to be *absolutely consistent* iff there is some wff of *L* which is not provable from *T* (not provable in *S*).

constant. *See* logical constants.

constants. Logical symbols, usually divided into logical and descriptive (or non-logical) constants. For the former, *see* *logical constants. The latter can be seen as functioning like names; that is, they stand, in a particular interpretation of a logical language, for something absolutely definite, and as such should be contrasted with *variables. There are *individual constants*, which stand for particular individuals (as 'Socrates' does), and *predicate constants*, which can stand for properties (as 'red' or 'flies' do) or relations (as 'taller than' does).

constative. A term coined by J. L. *Austin to refer to an utterance *with* which one makes a true or false statement. It was initially contrasted with *performative.

construct. *See* logical construction.

constructivism. The view that mathematical entities exist only if they can be constructed (or, intuitively, shown to exist), and that mathematical statements are true only if a constructive proof can be given. It is thus opposed to any view of mathematics—for example, platonism (*see* mathematics, philosophy of)—that sees mathematical objects and truths existing or being true independently of (our) apprehension. Constructivism encompasses *intuitionism, *finitism, and *formalism.

contextualism. A theory of aesthetic interpretation that holds that a work of art should be understood in its total cultural context, and that every work is historically conditioned. *Compare* isolationism.

contingency. 1. (of entities) The property of not *having* to exist. 2. (of events) The property of not *having* to occur. 3. (of propositions) The property of not *having* to be true, or of risking the possibility of being false.

Contingency is usually contrasted with *necessity, and the kind or kinds of necessity represented by the italicized words above are distinguished as, variously, logical or causal. Medieval thinkers sometimes took the view that God exists necessarily and hence that his existence is not a (logically) contingent matter, to be doubted, debated, and investigated (see Anselm, St.).

Logical empiricists, however, have doubted whether 'necessary truths' can yield fresh information about the world, on the ground that they are logically analytic, or tautological. Thus it has been thought that most or even all of our experience and knowledge is of a contingent kind. This has not greatly disturbed recent philosophers in the Anglo-American tradition, but in the philosophical novel, La Nausée, and elsewhere, *Sartre appeared to lament the contingency of all existence.

contingent falsehood. See necessary and contingent truth.

contingent truth. See necessary and contingent truth.

continuum problem. The problem of how many subsets of natural *numbers there are; equivalently, of how many real numbers, that is, points on the continuum, there are. *Cantor showed that infinite sets could be discriminated according to size by attempts to pair off their members. Assuming the *axiom of choice, sizes (usually called cardinalities) of sets can be ranked in order linearly, such that each cardinal has an immediate successor. Cantor demonstrated that the cardinality of the power set (set of subsets) of X is greater than that of X. Now the set of real numbers has the same cardinality as the power set of the natural numbers. Hence the continuum or set of real numbers has greater cardinality than the set of natural numbers (the smallest infinite set). *Gödel, and later Cohen, showed that the hypothesis that the cardinal of the continuum is the immediate successor, in the linear order, of the cardinal of the natural numbers is completely independent of the rest of set theory. In other words, we do not know how many real numbers there are.

contradiction. A simultaneous assertion and denial of one and the same *proposition occurring within or between contentions, assumptions, suppositions, and other forms of assertive discourse. Much less usually, contradictions are said to obtain between conflicting imperative sentences (see phrastic and neustic). The word is also sometimes confusingly applied to tensions or conflicts within or between physical things or social groups. *Mao Tse-tung's pamphlet On Contradiction is thus concerned almost exclusively with such tensions and conflicts, rather than with logical questions. See also self-contradiction.

contradiction, principle (or law) of. A logical principle, which in Aristotle's formulation, states that "The same attribute cannot at the same time belong and not belong to the same subject and in the same respect" (Metaphysics, 1005 b19-20). It is also stated more concisely as "It is impossible for the same thing to be and not to be" (compare Aristotle, Metaphysics, 1006 a1). Modern logicians often give the name to a theorem of the propositional calculus, namely: 'It is not the case both that p and not p' (where p is any proposition).

contradictory. 1. (adj) Describing a discourse containing *contradictions. 2. (n) Either of two propositions so related that both cannot be true or both cannot be false. Thus the proposition 'It is not the case that p' (symbolized as $-p$, and read 'not p') is the contradictory of the proposition p, and the other way about. Compare contrary.

contraposition. A valid form of immediate inference (see syllogism) in which a conditional or universal statement appears as premise and its *contrapositive as conclusion.

contrapositive. The contrapositive of the *conditional statement 'If p, then q' is 'If not-q, then not-p' and of a universal statement 'All As are B' is 'All non-Bs are non-A'.

contrary. Either of two propositions so related that both may be false but only one can be true. To contradict such a proposition as 'All human differences are determined by the environment' it is both sufficient and necessary to say only that 'Not all human differences are determined by the environment': each of these two propositions is the *contradictory of the other. The contraries are 'All human differences are determined by the environment' and 'No human differences are determined by the environment'. Each of the second two propositions is contradictory to, but not the contradictory of, the other. Champions of all such extreme views are apt to make controversy easier for themselves by wrongly assuming that everyone who contradicts what they say must therefore be committed to the contrary position.

contrary-to-fact conditional. A counterfactual *conditional.

conventionalism. The view, first expressed by *Poincaré and developed by *Mach and *Duhem, that scientific laws are disguised conventions reflecting the decision to adopt one of various possible descriptions. Conventions govern not only the use of words in a given language, but also the formulation of any coherent system in logic, mathematics, and mechanics. Scientific objectivity derives from general agreement over the conventions adopted.

convention T. See truth definition.

converse. 1. (in Aristotelian logic). The proposition derived by *conversion of the original. The converse of 'No S are P' is 'No P are S' and of 'Some S are P' is 'Some P are S'. Conversion in both these cases is called *simple conversion*. The converse of 'All S are P' is 'Some P are S' and the inference in this case is called *conversion per accidens*. 'Some S are not P' has no converse. 2. (in propositional logic) The converse of a conditional statement 'If p then q' is 'If q then p'. In this case the converse is *not* a logical consequence of the original.

converse fallacy of the accident. The mistake of arguing from a qualified principle, or a particular case (such as, it is never wrong to kill in order to save your own life), to an unqualified or general principle (such as, it is never wrong to kill). The (rarer) error of arguing from a general rule to a particular case without taking account of factors (accidents) that vitiate the rule is known as the *fallacy of the accident*. Both fallacies are sometimes known by their Latin scholastic tag *secundum quid*.

conversion. A form of immediate inference (*see* syllogism) in which the order of the terms is reversed. *See also* converse.

Copernicus, Nicolaus (1473–1543). Founder of modern astronomy. Born at Torun, Poland, he attended Cracow University, studied Greek philosophers at Bologna, and completed his studies of mathematics, astronomy, medicine, and theology at Padua. He settled in Frauenburg (Prussia) where he was canon of the cathedral.

Dissatisfied with the *Ptolemaic system, Copernicus revived the *heliocentric theory advanced by Aristarchus of Samos, a contemporary of Euclid. In *De revolutionibus orbium caelestium* (On the Revolution of the Celestial Orbs) (1543) he used the system of *Pythagoras to prove mathematically that the earth is spherical and in uniform motion around the sun. His work was a milestone in the emergence of undogmatic scientific thought in the 16th century; it faced violent opposition from the Church, on account of the supposed implications of a discovery that the earth, and hence mankind, is not at the physical centre of the Universe. *See also* Kepler.

copulatio. See suppositio.

corpuscularian. An obsolete synonym for 'atomic', used particularly in the 17th century in connection with the philosophy of *Gassendi, *Boyle, and *Locke. *See* atomism.

correspondence theory of truth. Considered in its widest sense, the claim that truth is agreement with reality—that it consists in a correspondence between (for example) a statement and 'the way things are'. More narrowly the claim that truth is a relational property, that whatever is true—sentence, proposition, statement, belief—is so by its relation to something else, usually a fact. The correspondence may be elaborated as naming, or picturing, or into heterogeneous relations (say, naming and expressing). One difficulty is clearly to distinguish between what is stated or believed and the fact, to discriminate the two *relata*. For if facts have constituents, and are like propositions in structure, so that there are, for example, negative and general facts, then perhaps facts are just (true) propositions. But it is not at all clear how—or if—the structure discernible in a proposition or statement mirrors or corresponds to the structure of a fact or state of affairs. We might try, as *Tarski did, to give the truth-conditions for complex propositions in terms of those for the simplest propositions, which in turn are true if they are constructed from elements which can be shown to combine in a systematic way to say what is the case, or how things are. Another view, raised by F. P. Ramsey and by A. N. Prior claimed that talk of correspondence could be removed, but the spirit of the theory be retained, by analysing 'X believes truly that p' as simply 'X believes that p, and p'.

corroboration. A notion introduced by Karl *Popper in *The Logic of Scientific Discovery* to replace that of confirmation (see confirmation) in the process of testing scientific hypotheses. However much corroboration is found for a hypothesis it is still not conclusively proved true. *See also* acceptance; falsifiability.

cosmogony. A scientific or mythic account of the origin of the Universe. Among primitive races, a cosmogony is portrayed as a single act of creation in time, with the world emerging or being shaped from one, or a few very simple, principles or elements. In Western culture the first chapter of Genesis provides the best known of such creation myths. The first attempt at a philosophical cosmogony was by *Thales of Miletus. *Plato and subsequent philosophers based their cosmogonies on what they understood to be the qualities and propensities of the *four elements, and no really scientific account was offered until *Newton and *Kant. *See also* cosmology.

cosmological argument. Usage of this expression to denote one of the major arguments for the existence of God is confused and inconsistent. Since it is primarily to *Kant that it owes its present wide popularity it is surely best at least to start from his account of the only three possible ways of trying to prove the existence of God "on the grounds of speculative reason"(see natural theology). All such attempts, in Kant's own words,"either begin with determinate experience and the special constitution of the world of sense experience...or they begin with a purely indeterminate experience, that is some empirical existent; or abstraction is made from all experience and the existence of a Supreme Cause is inferred from a priori concepts alone." In the first of these categories, called by him the *physico-theological argument, Kant would have had to include all the *Five Ways of St. Thomas *Aquinas, for these all start from what Aquinas takes to be obvious general facts about the Universe around us. The third category is that of the *ontological argument. It is the second category that is relevant here.

The defining characteristic of any form of cosmological argument is, therefore, that it must start, not from any actual or supposed general characteristics of the Universe, but from the mere fact that there is a Universe. What is thus taken to require explanation, and not to be a possible ultimate in terms of which other things might perhaps be explained, is the mere fact that there is anything at all. The most radical objection to all such cosmological arguments rises here. The point is that any system that seeks to explain why things are as they are must always ultimately be made in terms of general facts that themselves are not, and cannot be, further explained. So why should the existence of the Universe, and perhaps the fact that it has whatever fundamental regularities it does have, not themselves be accepted as the fundamentals, requiring no further explanation?

The version of the cosmological argument that was familiar to and criticized by Kant he found in *Leibniz. This is sometimes called the argument from the contingency of the Universe (a contingentia mundi). Leibniz applies to the cosmological question, "Why is there something rather than nothing?", his own basic principle of *sufficient reason. Those who press the radical objection indicated in the previous paragraph would here insist that this principle must, for the reason given, be false. The cosmological question, in the view of Leibniz, requires an answer because the existence of the Universe is a contingent fact, as opposed to a logically necessary truth (see necessary and contingent truth). In The Principles of Nature and of Grace founded upon Reason he writes, "Now this sufficient reason for the existence of the Universe cannot be found in the procession of contingent things...So the sufficient reason, which needs no further reason, must be found outside the procession of contingent things, and is found in a substance which is the cause of that procession and which is a necessary being containing the reason for His existence in Himself...And this final reason for things is called God" (§7-8).

The outcome of this Leibnizian argument, which is paralleled in Samuel *Clarke and many other rationalists, is that God is a logically necessary Being, so that the existence of God must be a logically necessary truth (see rationalism). It is therefore, as Kant urged,

exposed to all the objections deployed against the ontological argument and against the peculiarly philosophical concept of God from which that takes its start.

The second kind of cosmological argument is defined as eschewing this particular conception, and the attendant contrast between a logically necessary Being and logically contingent beings. The key positive idea is that the mere existence of the Universe somehow demands explanation, though not in the way indicated by Leibniz; whereas the existence of its creator God, a Being perhaps still necessary, albeit in some other sense, would not. The great difficulty here precisely is to spell out and to justify this desired contrast. For to reject the Leibnizian alternative is to accept the objection that all explanation of logically contingent facts has to end in some other such contingent fact, or facts, which is itself, or which are themselves, not further explained.

It should be noted that the third of the Five Ways, which is often misconstrued as a cosmological argument, and which is even sometimes misrepresented as the prime target of the Kantian criticism, in fact employs the expressions 'necessary being' and 'contingent being' in quite different senses, deriving from *Aristotle. Necessary beings here are all those that are not by their natures liable to cease to exist; for Aquinas this class included heavenly bodies, human souls, and the angels.

See also creation; explanation; First Cause; First Mover; universe and Universe.

cosmology. 1. The branch of philosophy, often considered a subdivision of *metaphysics, that deals with the Universe as a totality of phenomena, attempting to combine metaphysical speculation and scientific evidence within a coherent framework. The problems generally falling within its province include those of space, time, eternity, necessity, change, and contingency. Its method of rational enquiry distinguishes it from purely mythic accounts of the origin and structure of the Universe (*see* cosmogony).

The *Presocratics discussed cosmological issues, which were modified and systematized in the works of *Plato and *Aristotle. In medieval philosophy, Christian theology significantly coloured the whole approach to cosmology, until Renaissance science caused a radical revision of the world-picture. *Kant maintained that the problems of cosmology were of a kind that could never be solved. While some elements in cosmology have tended to be subsumed in metaphysics, others have become increasingly the concern of the physical sciences.

2. The modern scientific study of the origin and structure of the universe based on such things as the spectral investigation of the distribution of elements throughout the universe and the study of the red shift associated with the recession of the galaxies.

cosmos. The Pythagorean notion of the world as a rational ordered whole. The Greek word implies fitness and beauty as well as orderedness within finite limits. Various accounts of cosmos as the totality of natural phenomena were given by Parmenides, Democritus, and Empedocles; *Plato used the term in his theory that the goodness of anything is dependent on the proper ordering of·its parts.

counter-example. An instance of the kind of thing over which a generalization or universal statement has been made, which lacks the property said to be possessed by all things of that kind. One might say 'All swans are white' but the exhibition of one black swan would scotch the idea that all swans are white and would be an instance of the form of argument known as *refutation by counter-example*. Counter-examples are·used widely in logic to demonstrate that a given form of argument is not *valid. To say that a form of argument is valid is to make the general claim that all instances of that form which have true premises

also have a true conclusion. An example of an argument having the form in question but with true premises and a false conclusion thus provides a counter-example to the claim that it is a valid form of argument. Thus the obviously invalid 'If 5 is divisible by 2, 5 is not a prime number. 5 is not divisible by 2. Therefore 5 is not a prime number.' provides a counter-example to the claim that 'If p, then $-q$. $-p$ Therefore $-q$.' is a valid form of argument.

counterfactual. *See* conditional.

count noun. A term standing for an item in a countable class. Thus, girls being countable, 'girl' is a count noun. *Compare* mass noun.

Couturat, Louis (1868–1914). French philosopher and logician. In *L'Infini Mathématique* (1896) he argued— against the prevailing finitistic view of mathematics (*see* finitism)—for the concept of the actual infinite. His views led him to become interested in *Leibniz, another great proponent of infinity, whose logical papers were almost unknown until Couturat published *La Logique de Leibniz* in 1901. Couturat also did much in articles and in *L'Algebra de la logique* (1905) to introduce into France and defend the new mathematical logic of *Russell and Peano.

covering law model. The model that represents explanation as a matter of finding a law that covers, in the sense of entailing, the phenomenon to be explained. It is unclear that finding such a law is a necessary condition for explaining a phenomenon, for many explanations in everyday life proceed without apparently demanding such laws. And it is also unclear that such a law is sufficient for explanation: for instance, it is unsatisfactory to explain why the train is late today by saying that it is always late. The model represents a formal approach, rather than one which demands explanation in terms of antecedently understood mechanisms.

See also Hempel; science, philosophy of; social science, philosophy of.

Craig's theorem. The proof, provided by William Craig in 1953, that if we axiomatize a scientific theory formally and partition the vocabulary into two parts (one supposedly 'theoretical' and the other 'observational'), then there will be an axiomatization from which all the sentences involving only observational terms are deducible, and which itself contains none of the theoretical terms. This might seem to have reductionist implications, by suggesting that theoretical terms are expendable. But the methods used in the proof do not support this suggestion.

creation. The action required both to produce the Universe out of nothing and to be its indispensable sustaining cause (*see* universe and Universe). Thus, on the first count, the Demiurge of Plato's *Timaeus*, presented as shaping already existing raw materials, is precisely not a Creator, whereas, inasmuch as he produces the Universe *ex nihilo* (from nothing), the God of Mosaic theism is. On the second count, the crux is that to say the Universe has a Creator is essentially to say that, were the Creator's support at any time to be withdrawn, then the whole Universe, in which everything both animate and inanimate is his creature, must—in a striking phrase of the British Archbishop William Temple—"collapse into non-existence".

These crucial points come out very well when we consider a famous contention of St. Thomas *Aquinas. He maintained that it is possible to prove by arguments of *natural theology that there is a Creator, "which all men call God". But that the Universe in fact had a beginning—as in accordance with the teachings of his Church he, of course, most firmly believed—could be known to us only thanks to God's special revelation. This position Aquinas defended against murmuring charges of heresy—most memorably in the polemical pamphlet *de Aeternitate Mundi contra Murmurantes* (Concerning the Eternity of the Universe, against Murmurers). That he was thus concerned to prove the existence of the Creator as the continually sustaining cause, rather than the more popular conclusion of initiation "in the beginning", must never be forgotten in examining his *Five Ways. This warning is the more necessary since he himself, most unfortunately, there neglected to remind his readers of this fact. *See also* First Cause; First Mover.

credo quia impossibile. (Latin for: I believe because it is impossible.) A tag deriving from a statement made by the eventually heretical Latin Father Tertullian in his *De Carne Christi* (II v): "It is certain because it is impossible."

credo ut intelligam. (Latin for: I believe in order that I may understand.) A key idea of St. *Augustine of Hippo, often put by him in the imperative.

Crescas, Hasdai ben Abraham (d. 1412?). An Aragonese courtier, Jewish communal leader, and Hebrew poet, born in Barcelona. His *Or Adonai* (Light of the Lord) (1410) is a rational refutation of the Aristotelian position formulated by *Maimonides. He stresses the limitations of human reason, God's love, and the need for love and joy in man, leading to a mystical communion with God. Crescas betrays the influence of the *Kabbalah (despite his fundamental rationalism), and perhaps also of Christian scholastics, and in turn he exerted an important influence on Pico della Mirandola, Bruno, Spinoza, and other later thinkers.

criterion. A word that has various uses in philosophical discourse, that of the later *Wittgenstein being currently the most important. His main (though arguably not his only) use is such that, if X is a criterion of Y, then it is a necessary or non-inductive truth (that is, a truth grounded in meanings rather than empirical data) that X is evidence for Y. For example, 'pain' is so used that certain overt physical conditions or behaviour-patterns are criteria of pain, that is, so that pain as such is necessarily identifiable through (though not identical with) such conditions, etc. Hence, it is equally mistaken both to deny possible knowledge of someone else's pain and to equate pain with pain-behaviour.

critical idealism. Another name for Kant's transcendental *idealism.

critical realism. The doctrine accepted by some philosophers sympathetic to the view of R.W.Sellars, as published in *Critical Realism* (1916). Critical realism retains the belief of common-sense realism in independent physical things, but admits that these are not directly and homogeneously presented to us in perceptual situations. These latter are thought to be very various, and our understanding of them must depend in part on the state and findings of the natural sciences. Thus the *after-image and the double image, the foot that is felt after the leg has been amputated, and other cases call for different explanatory accounts. In general, critical realists hold that knowledge of the world can be gained because there is some sort of reliable correspondence between sensa, or some sort of intuitive data, on the one hand, and external objects on the other. Critical realism is historically the successor to *idealism. It conceded to idealism that whenever something is perceived it is an object for a mind, but insisted that it does not follow from this that that something has no existence except in its being perceived.

Croce, Benedetto (1866-1952). Italian philosopher, known for his work on aesthetics and cultural history. In 1903 he founded the periodical *La Critica* in which most of his writings were published, including reviews of contemporary European philosphical and literary works.

The fundamentals of Croce's system, "the philosophy of spirit", are contained in *Estetica come scienza dell'espressione e linguistica generale* (1902), *Logica* (1905), *Filosofia della practica* (1909), and *Teoria e storia della storiografia*

(1917). He distinguishes between two distinct moments within spirit: thought and action; the first is further divided into poetry (art) and logic, the second into economics and ethics. The relation between these moments is one of reciprocity, giving rise to unified, circular, self-generating spirit.

Cudworth, Ralph (1617-88). English scholar and a leading member of the *Cambridge Platonists. His main works, *The True Intellectual System of the Universe* (1678) and the posthumously published *Treatise concerning Eternal and Immutable Morality* (1731), exemplify the group's concerns respectively in metaphysics and ethics.

Culverwel, Nathanael (c.1618-c.1651). One of the *Cambridge Platonists, whose premature death forestalled his ambitious project of demonstrating the compatibility of the gospel revelation with reason. His *Discourse of the Light of Nature* (1652) confidently announces his stance as a Christian rationalist.

Cumberland, Richard (1631-1718). English philosopher and Bishop of Peterborough (from 1691). The sub-title of his main work, *De Legibus Naturae* (On the Laws of Nature)(1672), indicates his intention of refuting Hobbism in both its moral and its social aspects. In contrast to the overriding egoism of *Hobbes, Cumberland's vision was of universal benevolence as the pre-eminent moral good. His belief that no action could be morally excellent unless it contributed to the happiness of mankind anticipates *utilitarianism. *See also* Cambridge Platonists.

Cusa, Nicholas of. *See* Nicholas of Cusa.

Cynics. "Dog-like" (Greek: *kynikoi*) disciples of *Diogenes of Sinope (c.400-325 BC), known as 'kyon' (dog) on account of his shamelessness. Diogenes was a primitivist: happiness, he taught, means "living according to Nature"— that is, satisfying one's simplest "natural" wants in the simplest manner. Desire for anything beyond the minimal bodily satisfactions should be condemned as "unnatural"; so, too, should any convention that inhibits the satisfaction of the basic requirements. The reduction of one's wants to a "natural" minimum demands self-discipline, but leads to self-sufficiency and to freedom. Diogenes conveyed his principles by bon-mots and drastic action (for example, by masturbating in public to show how simply one's sexual desires can be satisfied). His followers (Crates of Thebes, Onesicritus, Cercidas, Bion the Borysthenite, Teles, and others) developed these principles in various directions; there was never an organized Cynic school. Equally, Cynic ideas and attitudes—cosmopolitanism and an emphasis on universal human nature, flamboyant individualism, a contempt for convention and culture—are commonplaces of early Stoic and Epicurean moralizing. The Cynic sect flourished in the 3rd century BC and had a notable revival in the 1st century AD.

Cyrenaics. Adherents of a school of philosophy flourishing in the 4th century BC, purportedly founded by Aristippus of Cyrene, *bon viveur*, and disciple of Socrates. The Cyrenaics maintained that pleasure is the supreme good, identifying "pleasure" with immediate bodily gratification and denying any positive value to "mental pleasures" of anticipation and memory or to the cessation of pain. Their grounds were that only our present "feelings" of pleasure and pain, themselves simply physical motions internal to us, can be truly known to us. Cyrenaic teaching was often compared, contrasted, and confused with Epicurean hedonism (*see* Epicurus).

D

Darwin, Charles Robert (1809-82). English biologist. In 1831 he joined an exploratory expedition to study flora and fauna, and published his observations in *The Voyage of the Beagle* (1839). His theory of evolution, set out in *The Origin of Species* (1859) and *The Descent of Man* (1871), stated that all kinds of living things developed from very few simple forms through natural selection. In particular, Darwin denied that the evolution of man as a biological species was governed by forces fundamentally different from those influencing other forms of life, although he did not infer that human beings must or should model their own conduct on "nature red in tooth and claw".

Darwinism. *Darwin's view of organic evolution through natural selection, which favours individuals and species best suited to a given environment. This theory undermined beliefs about man's being the supreme product of God's design and was certainly incompatible with any literal reading of Genesis. By showing that living things are not patterned after prototypes, each sharply differentiated from all others, it made it necessary to revise the view that all natural things have real, though often unknown, essences that can serve as a basis for their differentiation into species. The idea that life is subject to natural laws guaranteeing the survival of the fittest influenced, by action or reaction, many later ethical and sociological theories.

Dasein. (German for: being there.) A term employed by *Heidegger in the investigation of human existence. Man's particular mode of being-in-the-world is characterized by relatedness to surrounding objects and members of his community, in terms of being concerned with and caring about them. Heidegger distinguishes three constitutive features of Dasein: (1) factuality, (2) existentiality, or the apprehension of his purposive being and potential, and (3) fallenness, man's tendency to become lost in present preoccupations, forfeiting his unique possibilities and "authentic" existence. "Unauthenticity" consists in a depersonalized and objectivized mode of being, with no temporal significance other than that of sheer presence. Anxiety (indeterminate fear) is occasioned by the confrontation with possibility and the apprehension of death as the "limit of possibility"; in the effort to overcome it, man retreats into unauthentic anonymous existence, envisaging himself as merely one unit in the totality of things. *See also* Angst.

death. *See* survival and immortality.

death of God. A reference to a passage called 'The Madman' in *Nietzsche's The Gay Science*: the madman reports the greatest deed of mankind, the killing and hence the death—even the decomposition—of God. Those Protestant thinkers who accept this 'death of God' cannot but prejudice their own claims still to be theologians.

decidable. Denoting a system or theory expressed in a logical language where there is an *algorithm for determining, for any correctly formed sentence of the language, whether that sentence is or is not a theorem of that theory. A theorem is a sentence that is derivable from a theory using rules of logical inference.

decision problem. The problem of finding a *decision procedure for a theory. A positive solution consists in a proof that a decision procedure exists. A negative solution is a proof that no such procedure exists.

decision procedure. The *algorithm for determining that a theory is *decidable.

decision theory. A theory whose subject matter is the situations in which a *decision problem arises. In a decision problem one may be typically faced with a set of alternative actions and uncertainty as to the consequences of all or some of these actions. The problem is in deciding which action to undertake, that is, which action is most rational relative to the information available.

One common approach is to assign probabilities to the occurrence of the consequences of each action, estimate utilities (welfare, happiness, etc.) associated with each consequence, and to

select as most rational the action with the maximum expected utility. However, in many situations inadequate information may make it impossible to assign probabilities or estimate utilities with certainty or near certainty. The approach also takes no account of risk aversion.

In response weaker principles have been adopted, such as the minimax (maximin) principle which recommends choice of the action which has, as its worst outcome, a consequence which is better than the worst consequence of any alternative action. The principle is often criticized as being too conservative except in a small class of situations (zero sum games in which one's opponents are rational).

One of the main problems facing decision theory is that there is no adequately accepted notion of what is involved in rational decision. Attempts have been made to develop axioms (assumptions) which any intuitive concept of rationality must satisfy. It seems that suggested decision criteria do not satisfy all such axioms. *See also* game theory.

de dicto. *See* modality.

deduction. A valid argument in which it is impossible to assert the premises and to deny the conclusion without thereby contradicting oneself. The word is not confined within the restrictions of the traditional syllogistic (*see* syllogism) form.

deduction theorem. *See* inference, rule of.

deductive logic. *See* logic.

deep structure. *See* structure, deep and surface.

defeasible. Open to objection. The term is used particularly in connection with concepts, such as legal responsibility, which are presumed to apply unless one or other of a perhaps indeterminate list of defeating conditions obtains. Every person is thus presumed to be legally responsible for what he did: unless the balance of his mind was disturbed; or he could not have known what he was doing; or he acted under intolerable duress; or..., etc. In so far as responsibility is thus a defeasible concept, the question should be not 'When is a person responsible?', but 'When is a person not responsible?'

definiendum. *See* definition.

definiens. *See* definition.

definist fallacy. One aspect of the *naturalistic fallacy: that of confusing two notions by defining one in terms of the other. *Moore thought that if 'good' is defined in terms of some natural property, say 'that which produces pleasure', then the *open question argument would show that the two were, nevertheless, distinct. That is, one can still ask whether that which produces pleasure *is* good. Whether this is indeed a fallacy is unclear, since surely it makes sense at least to ask of things that may (in fact, or by definition) be identical, whether they are identical.

definite description. An important kind of singular *term. Understanding a description, for example, 'bald man', requires understanding what criteria an object must satisfy if the description is to apply to it. For a proper name to be applied, on the other hand, its bearer does not need to satisfy any such criteria. A large man may be correctly named Tiny, but not correctly described as tiny. A definite description (often marked by the definite article 'the') is used in such a way that it is clearly intended to apply to one and only one object, for example, 'the smallest prime number' or 'the 14th President of the U.S.'.

Definite descriptions are important in connection with singular terms, as a singular term without a bearer (or reference) presents problems for the theory of meaning and for logical formalization. For this reason *Russell proposed to replace sentences containing definite descriptions by sentences that did not contain them and which, he claimed, were equivalent to the original sentences. In effect, 'The present King of France is bald' was to be replaced by 'There is something which at present is a King of France, and at most one thing at present is a King of France, and that thing is bald' (*see* descriptions, theory of). *See also* logical fiction; logically proper names.

definition. A process or expression that provides the precise meaning of a word or phrase. A definition (*definiens*), correctly made, will be logically equivalent to the word or phrase being defined (*definiendum*). The one may therefore be substituted for the other, perhaps at the cost of some stylistic sacrifice, but without loss or change of meaning. Definition may be either of a present established meaning or of a meaning proposed for the future. In the former case the definition is said to be *descriptive*, in the latter *prescriptive* or *stipulative*.

Again, definition may be either *ostensive* or *verbal*. In the former a meaning is explained by some sort of pointing or showing. In the latter it is spelt out by saying it in alternative words.

Another contrast is between *explicit* and *implicit definitions* within a *calculus. In the former the symbol so defined has to be synonymous with some other symbol, or combination of symbols, that has already been given an interpretation. In the latter the meaning of the terms so defined is limited by their occurrence in initial formulae. From these, further formulae are derived, which are interpreted as empirical generalizations.

The term *contextual definition* (rather than *implicit definition*) is used when meaning is defined implicitly by the context rather than spelt out explicitly; the expression *definition in use* is also employed here. A *recursive definition* begins by giving examples of the class of object represented by the word to be defined; it then specifies a procedure for generating further examples.

Earlier generations used to characterize definitions as *nominal* or *real*. A nominal definition simply explicated a meaning that a term happened to have according to existing verbal usage. A real definition would characterize a structure common to all the objects to which that term should be applied. The *nominal definitions* of the words 'gold' or 'God', the *nominal *essence* of gold or God, can be known by anyone familiar with the meanings of those two English terms. But the *real definitions*, the *real essence* of gold or God, might be at the same time unknown to anyone, the latter being perhaps forever beyond human understanding.

A special case is *persuasive definition*. This expression was introduced by the American philosopher C. L. Stevenson first in an article and then in his book *Ethics and Language* (1944). The notion is best explained in Stevenson's own words: "Our language abounds with words which like 'culture' have both a vague descriptive meaning and a rich emotive meaning. The descriptive meaning of them all is subject to constant redefinition. The words are prizes which each man seeks to bestow on qualities of his own choice. Persuasive definitions are often recognizable from the words 'real' or 'true'...Since people usually accept what they consider true, 'true' comes to have the persuasive force of 'to be accepted'. This force is utilized in the metaphorical expression 'true meaning'. The hearer is induced to accept the new meaning which the speaker introduces."

When Adolf Hitler claims that "National Socialism is true democracy", and when the Communist governments of North Korea or East Germany maintain that they preside over real democracies, attempts are thereby being made, usually with some appearance of reason given, to annex a prestigious word. A similar exercise in persuasive definition can also be seen in Book IX of the *Republic*, where *Plato argues that only approved pleasures count and that those of disfavoured activities are not real and true pleasures.

degrees of perfection argument. The fourth of the *Five Ways, which

contends that, since whatever is the most φ must be the cause of whatever else is φ, all being and goodness in the *Universe must be the work of One who is in these respects The Mostest; "and this we call God." Any force that this argument possesses derives from Plato's theory of Forms or Ideas (*see* Plato).

deism. The doctrine that belief in God can commend itself to the human mind by its own inherent reasonableness, without either being supported by appeals to alleged divine revelations or imposed by religious institutions. It has appeared in various forms in various periods of history, but its best known manifestations are found in the thought of the 18th-century *Enlightenment and, especially, of *Voltaire. It is usually taken to involve God's leaving the Universe to its own lawful devices, without any particular interventions, once the process of creation had been completed.

Deism is sometimes seen as exemplifying the vast confidence in reason of the post-Newtonian era; the human intellect, now at last come of age, and aware of its own powers, no longer needs any assistance in demonstrating the existence of an originator of the whole scheme of things, or of a source of natural or moral law. But there is also a deism that is part of the "religion of the heart"; this says, with *Rousseau, that "The more I strive to prove the infinite Being of God the less do I understand it. But I feel that He is. That is enough for me." Either way, there is obvious attraction in the idea of a simple creed that can convince any human mind, or heart, by its own merits, and owes nothing to the traditions or institutions of a particular culture. But beliefs based on rational arguments are always a target for counter-arguments, and the arguments on which deists relied have fared badly at the hands of modern critics of metaphysics and natural theology. And an appeal to feeling is obviously highly subjective, capable of yielding many strange and mutually incompatible beliefs. Hence orthodoxy, despite its difficulties, is in some important respects in a stronger position—and has shown much greater survival-value—than deism.

delusion. *See* illusion, arguments from.

Demiurge. A term derived from the Greek for craftsman. **1.** In Plato's *Timaeus*, the maker of the physical world. **2.** The maker acknowledged by most gnostic systems, whose cosmogonic myths depict a demonic being either collaborating with God in creation or seeking to destroy the world by introducing evil.

Democritus of Abdera (*c.*460–*c.*370 BC). A younger contemporary of *Leucippus and a prolific expositor of *atomism. He was nicknamed 'the laughing philosopher'. The only fragments of his work that survive are from his ethical writings. These expounded the first rigorously naturalistic (as opposed to supernaturalistic) Greek ethics, and were clearly free of any sophistical amoralism. Democritus was also the subject of the Ph.D. thesis of *Marx.

demonstration. *See* proof.

De Morgan's Laws. Laws named after Augustus De Morgan (1806–71), one of the pioneers of the algebraic approach to logic. (1) is formally stated as $-(p \& q) \equiv -p \lor -q$, that is to deny a conjunction is to assert the *negation of at least one of the conjoined statements (and vice versa); (2) is formally stated as $-(p \lor q) \equiv -p \& -q$, that is to deny the disjunction of p and q is to assert both the negation of p and the negation of q (and vice versa).

denotation. In logic (as opposed to ordinary use), the denotation of a word refers to the particulars to which the word can correctly be applied, while the connotation is the abstract or dictionary definition of the word. Thus the denotation of the word 'mother' is all the particular existing mothers that there are, while the connotation is the abstract definition or meaning 'female animal parent'. In certain cases, for example 'unicorn', there is no denotation (one cannot refer or point to a particular existing unicorn), although there is a connotation (a deer-like animal with a single horn in the centre of its head). It should be noted that this philosophical use is different from the ordinary, literary use of denotation and connotation, where the denotation of 'mother' is 'female animal parent' and the connotation refers to the overtones or associations of the word (home, maternal love, etc.).

denote. A word put to quite different uses by different writers. It is sometimes used as equivalent to 'designate', sometimes used to translate Frege's *bedeuten* (*see* sense and reference), and sometimes used to express the relation between a predicate *term and everything to which it applies, that is, its extension. Russell used 'denoting phrase' as a term to contrast with 'logically proper name'. He included among denoting phrases, *definite descriptions, indefinite descriptions (such as 'a man'), and phrases such as 'all men', 'every man', 'any man', and 'no men'. *See also* denotation; logically proper name.

denoting phrase. *See* denote.

denumerable *and* **non-denumerable.** The set of natural numbers has, as members, the numbers 0, 1, 2, 3,.... A *denumerable* set is one whose members can be matched one for one (put in a one-to-one correspondence) with the members of the set of natural numbers. A *non-denumerable* set is an infinite set that is not thus denumerable.

deny. *See* negation; refute.

denying the antecedent. *See* affirming the antecedent.

denying the consequent. *See* affirming the antecedent.

deontic logic. The formulation of logical principles specific to the concept of obligation, such as the impossibility of something being at once both morally obligatory and forbidden (*compare* modal logic). *See* logic.

deontology. The ethical theory taking duty as the basis of morality; the view that some acts are morally obligatory regardless of their consequences. Although the term was used as the title of a work by *Bentham, deontological ethics can be contrasted with any sort of *utilitarianism, which must always be teleological (*see* teleology). *See also* Kant.

de re. *See* modality.

Descartes, René (1591-1650). French philosopher and mathematician, born in La Haye. After attending the Jesuit college of La Flèche he went on to study law at Poitiers, graduating in 1616. In 1618 he travelled, first to Holland, and then to Germany with the army of the Duke of Bavaria. It was in Bavaria, in the winter of 1619, closeted in his famous "stove-heated room" that Descartes conceived the mission that had such profound effects on the philosophical world. "Ancient cities that have become large towns in process of time are as a rule badly laid out", he later wrote, "as compared with those…that are laid out by a designer." Descartes' unique ambition was not to add a contribution, however great, to the existing body of knowledge, but to reconstruct the whole of philosophy from new. For the next few years Descartes continued travelling in Germany, Holland, Italy, and France. In 1628 he left Paris to return to Holland, where he lived quietly in the countryside for most of the remainder of his life.

Descartes' earliest work was *Regulae ad directionem ingenii* (Rules for the Direction of the Understanding) composed in the late 1620s, but not completed, and only published posthumously in 1701. Here Descartes makes it clear that mathematical reasoning was to be the paradigm for his new system of knowledge: "those who are seeking the strict way of truth should not trouble themselves about any object concerning which they cannot have a certainty equal

to arithmetical or geometrical demonstration." Such mathematical reasoning, moreover, is applicable to the whole of science; knowledge, for Descartes, is a unified system: "all the sciences are interconnected and dependent on one another." (It should be noted in passing that Descartes was not simply interested in mathematics as a model; he made major contributions to the subject, particularly in the reform of algebraic notation and in the development of coordinate geometry.)

By 1632 Descartes had ready a substantial treatise, *Le Monde*, which contained a complete theory of the origins and working of the solar system. The crucial feature of the kinds of explanation Descartes offered was that they abandoned the old Aristotelian apparatus of substantial forms and natural kinds; qualitative explanations (for example, that a body falls because it possesses the quality of heaviness or '*gravitas*') were to be replaced by mathematical laws dealing with the quantifiable—the sizes, shapes, and motions of matter. *Le Monde* also followed the Copernican hypothesis that the earth moves annually round the sun. After the notorious condemnation of Galileo by the Inquisition in 1634, when the Copernican hypothesis was forbidden to be taught, Descartes cautiously withheld his book from publication.

In 1637, however, Descartes was ready to publish a selection of his scientific views, the *Dioptric, Meteors, and Geometry*. He wrote in French rather than Latin as the book was planned for a popular rather than a scholarly audience. He added a philosophical introduction, which has since become his best known work—the *Discours de la Méthode*.

In 1641 Descartes published his philosophical masterpiece, the *Meditationes de Prima Philosophia* (Meditations). Three years later the mammoth *Principia Philosophiae* (Principles) appeared, providing a full account of Descartes' metaphysical and scientific theories. These included the Copernican hypothesis, carefully presented as an expository device rather than the literal truth.

Among Descartes' many correspondents was Princess Elizabeth of Bohemia (niece of Charles I of England); an exchange of letters with her over the relation between mind and body (a crucial theme of the *Meditations*) stimulated the writing of his last book, the *Passions of the Soul*, published in French in 1649. The same year Descartes left Holland for Stockholm at the invitation of Queen Christina of Sweden. The move proved fatal. Descartes' habit was to stay in bed meditating until midday; in Sweden he had to rise at five in the morning to tutor the queen in philosophy. He contracted pneumonia and died on 11 February 1650.

Two features mark out as unique Descartes' definitive statement of his philosophy in the *Meditations*. The first is its intensely individualistic standpoint. The *Meditations*, like the *Discourse* before it, was written in the first person. Descartes offers not a formal exposition of his theories but a dramatic voyage of discovery from doubt to certainty. Indeed the very title 'Meditations' conveys the character of the work—a private mental exercise, which the reader must 'make his own'.

The second distinctive feature, already referred to, is Descartes' insistence on beginning philosophy afresh; of starting from scratch by ridding the mind of all accumulated preconceptions, however indispensable they may seem. Descartes' device to this end is his famous 'method of doubt'. He begins with a systematic examination of hitherto accepted beliefs. The testimony of the senses is first scrutinized: it is sometimes found that the senses deceive, and "it is prudent not to trust entirely anything that has once deceived us." Yet some sensory evidence, Descartes admits, is so clear that only a madman would doubt it, "for example that I am here seated by the fire wearing a dressing gown." But then a new doubt arises: one might be dreaming, in which case one's belief (about the fire and the dressing gown) might well be false. The upshot of the long and involved "dreaming argument" (the interpretation and validity of which is still hotly debated) is that any judgment made about the external world, any existential claim, may be suspect.

To reinforce the dreaming argument, Descartes introduces the famous device of a malignant demon, "who has employed all his energies in deceiving me. I shall consider the sky, earth, colours, shapes, sounds, and all external things are not more than the delusions of dreams... I shall consider myself as having no hands, no eyes...." The *First Meditation* ends on a note of apparently universal doubt.

But the *Second Meditation* unearths at least one proposition that is immune from the diabolic doubt. For however great the demon's deceptions, "he can never cause me to be nothing so long as I think I am something." Descartes concludes, "I am, I exist, is, necessarily, true as often as I put it forward or conceive of it in my mind." This argument is expressed in the *Discourse* in the form "I think therefore I am" (*je pense, donc je suis*; in its Latin form perhaps the best known quotation in all philosophy—*cogito ergo sum*).

Descartes thus arrives at at least one existential truth—that something, which he calls "I", exists. But how much farther can he get without abandoning his rigorous method of doubt? As he puts it elsewhere, in the mouth of an imaginary objector: "If you proceed by this path you will go neither far not quickly. For how shall you always find truths of which you are as certain as of your own existence?"

The way Descartes then proceeds is by offering two notoriously debatable 'proofs' for God's existence. The first starts from the premise that men know they are imperfect, yet find in their minds an idea of supreme perfection; it then continues, using the curious principle that "a cause must contain at least as much reality as its effect", to the conclusion that the cause of the idea of perfection must itself be a perfect being—

God. The second argument is Descartes' version of an ancient (and still much discussed) 'proof', known as the *onto-logical argument. Existence, being a perfection, can no more be separated from the concept of a supremely perfect being than the fact that its angles equal two right angles can be separated from the concept of a triangle. So just as a triangle must, by definition, have angles which total 180 degrees, so the supremely perfect being (God) must by definition exist.

Whatever the merits of these arguments, they serve a vital function for Descartes—that of making scientific knowledge possible. For once God's existence is established, one is no longer limited to the private momentary certainty of one's own existence; one can now, since God is benevolent and non-deceiving, have a reasonable degree of confidence in the existence of an external world, in one's powers of memory, in the normal reliability (suject to careful scrutiny) of the senses. The construction of a systematic body of truths becomes possible.

The other interesting feature about the 'proofs' of God's existence is that they show that 'Cartesian doubt' is very much less radical than is often supposed. In order to arrive at knowledge of God's existence, Descartes has to rely on many premises (for example, "the cause is as real as the effect") whose truth is supposed to be self-evident. For of course God cannot be invoked to guarantee the truth of the very premises needed to prove his own existence, or else Descartes' whole procedure would be circular—a charge many contemporary critics did in fact raise. To avoid the 'Cartesian circle', Descartes had to maintain that there are some basic logical truths that, so long as they are entertained, cannot be doubted. Such truths Descartes regards as present in us from birth: an example he gives is the law of *non-contradiction—that something cannot both be and not be at the same time. These truths are evident to the 'natural light' of reason and are never really

questioned by the doubts of the *First Meditation*. In fairness one should add that Descartes seems to have toyed with a more radical scepticism: at one point in the *First Meditation* he throws out the suggestion that he may be mistaken even about such simple truths as "2 + 3 = 5". If this is taken seriously then the morass of doubt is indeed inescapable, and there would be no hope of proving God's existence, or indeed of doing any coherent reasoning at all.

Perhaps the most influential and provoking aspect of Cartesian metaphysics is Descartes' theory about the human mind and its distinction from the body. From the proposition "I think therefore I am", Descartes proceeds by a series of dubious moves to "*sum res cogitans*"—or, as the *Discourse* puts it, "I am a being whose whole essence or nature is to think, and whose being requires no place and depends on no material thing."

This is not quite the austerely intellectualist doctrine that it appears at first sight to be. For by thinking (*la pensée, cogitatio*) Descartes means to include not only intellectual but also volitional activities, such as willing and affirming, and even the mental awareness involved in the operations of imagining and perceiving: "Thought is a word that covers everything that exists in us in such a way that we are immediately conscious of it." Nonetheless, Descartes' theory has some startling consequences. For Descartes the world is made up of two incompatible kinds of substance—mind or consciousness (*res cogitans*), which is unextended and indivisible, and matter (*res extensa*), which is extended and divisible. It follows that our physical bodies, including our brains, being part of the extended divisible world of matter, can have no part in our essence as thinking beings.

Man is thus not the rational animal of Aristotelian tradition, but an incorporeal mind lodged mysteriously in a mechanical extended body. The 'mysteriously' is in place here, for it is hard to understand how two such radically distinct and incompatible substances can interact. Yet interact they indubitably do; when I tread on a drawing pin (physical event), the consequence is that I feel a pain (mental). As Descartes himself had to admit, "Nature teaches us by the sensations of hunger, thirst, etc., that I am not merely lodged in my body as a pilot in a ship, but that I am very closely united and as it were intermingled with it" (*Sixth Meditation*).

The mystery of this 'intermingling' was never unravelled by Descartes, and leaves a lacuna in his system that later Cartesians made some elaborate and bizarre attempts to fill. Descartes' own researches on the brain led him to locate the seat of the mind or soul (the two terms are interchangeable for Descartes) in the pineal gland, but finding a location for the strange psychophysical transactions that his system requires does not explain how they are possible in the first place.

'Cartesian dualism', as Descartes' conception has come to be known, has exerted so profound an influence on the philosophy of mind as has his method of doubt on the theory of knowledge. A great deal of work in our own century has been devoted to trying to avoid Descartes' absolute division between the mental and the physical. But unless and until the phenomenon of consciousness and its relation to physics is better understood, the Cartesian picture is unlikely entirely to lose its hold on the imagination.

If the pervasive influence of Descartes on epistemology and philosophical psychology is unquestionable, his contribution to the philosophy of science is harder to assess. On the one hand, the details of his physical system, which postulated a system of 'vortices' or whirlpools to explain the movements of the celestial bodies, were largely swept away by Newtonian physics. On the other, the central conception that physical phenomena must ultimately be reducible to quantifiable treatment by means of mathematical laws has re-

mained a paradigm for scientific explanation.

Textbooks often describe Descartes as a rationalist, by which is meant that he attempted to construct a world system purely a priori, in contrast to the observational methods of the empiricists (*see* empiricism; rationalism). It is by now clear that this distinction is too facile to cope with the complexities of actual scientific reasoning. While some of Descartes' procedures, such as the attempt to deduce the laws of inertial motion from premises about the nature of God, support the caricature of the armchair scientist deducing the structure of the world by the unaided light of reason, many passages show that he accorded a crucial role to experiment. Descartes' actual conception of scientific method often resembles the more respectable *hypothetico-deductive model, where a hypothesis is advanced, and the results logically deduced from it are then compared with actual observation.

"The whole of philosophy", Descartes once wrote, "is a tree whose roots are metaphysics, whose trunk is physics, and whose branches are the other sciences." The organic figure of a plant with its slow growth is a surprising choice; Descartes' more usual metaphor was of laying the foundations for a new and unified structure. Judged by the overwhelming standards of his own ambition, Descartes' achievement must be classed as wanting. By any other standards, his contribution to human thought is prodigious.

descending induction. An alternative name for the method of infinite descent. *See* infinite descent, method of.

description, knowledge by. *See* acquaintance and description, knowledge by.

descriptions, theory of. The theory proposed by *Russell in order to reveal the underlying logical form of denoting phrases containing descriptions (*see* denote). For example 'the first man in space' is a description that picks out one unique individual. But some denoting phrases may seem to refer to non-existent people or things and yet be part of a meaningful sentence. A non-Russellian analysis of the sentence 'The present King of France is bald' would attempt to isolate a non-existent individual and predicate baldness of him. This would render the sentence meaningless because, having failed to perform an act of reference, the sentence could not be said to be either true or false. Russell's theory of descriptions would analyse the sentence into two parts, connected by a conjunction: 'There is a unique individual ruling France, and if someone rules France then he is bald'. The sentence is now meaningful because: (1) the analysis eliminated the putative act of reference by dividing the original sentence into two new sentences, one a claim about existence and the other a conditional sentence; (2) the existence sentence is clearly false; (3) a sentence containing a conjunction is false if either of the parts is false; (4) the whole sentence as now analysed is therefore false, and being false can be said to be meaningful.

descriptive definition. *See* definition.

descriptivism. The view that moral judgments have only descriptive, and not prescriptive, meaning and can thus be proved by being deduced from statements all straightforwardly factual. Descriptivism is thus a form of ethical naturalism. R. M. *Hare, who coined the term, claims the weakness of this account to be that to accept a moral judgment does not, in itself, provide a reason for acting on it. *Compare* prescriptivism.

design, argument to (*or* **from**). *See* argument to (or from) design.

designate. *See* rigid designator.

designated value. *See* many-valued logic.

designation. *See* denotation.

determinism. *See* freewill and determinism.

Deus sive Natura. (Latin for: God or Nature.) The phrase used by *Spinoza to denote the one infinite "substance" to which all "attributes" must be ascribed. *See also* pantheism.

Dewey, John (1859-1952). American philosopher, psychologist, and educationist. He became Professor of Philosophy at Columbia University and one of the leading exponents of *pragmatism.

Dewey synthesized the views of *Peirce and *James, developing pragmatism as a theory of both logical and ethical analysis (*see also* instrumentalism). In *Reconstruction in Philosophy* (1920) he presented his view of philosophy as the clarification of ideas of the natural sciences, art, and social and cultural institutions, and criticism of the beliefs that influence the life of the human community. In *Experience and Nature* (1925) and *The Quest for Certainty* (1929) he rejects the "spectator" theory of knowledge; experience sets problems to be solved, and modern man has learnt to modify nature and need not be its passive subject.

dharma. *See* Buddhist philosophy.

diagonal procedure. The method by which *Cantor proved that there are infinite sets that cannot be counted. The real numbers, unlike the rational numbers, are such a non-denumerable set (*see* number)—that is, they cannot be put in a one-to-one correspondence with the natural numbers. Any real number can be expressed as an infinite decimal. Suppose that the set of real numbers is countable. Then we can make a list of all the real numbers, using a function f that matches the first real number, r_0 with 0, the second, r_1 with 1, and so on. (Symbolically, $f(0) = r_0$, $f(1) = r_1$, ..., $f(n) = r_n$). Cantor showed that we can never make such a list, for we can always construct a real number c that is not in the list, by the diagonal procedure. That is, if r_0 has 1 in its first decimal place, we write 2 in the first decimal place of c;

otherwise we write 1. If r_1, has 1 in its second place, we write 2 in the second place of c; otherwise we write 1. So, if (for example)

$$r_0 = 6.8181....$$
$$r_1 = 0.1454....$$
$$r_2 = 5.1367....$$
$$r_3 = 1.0213....$$

then

$$c = 1.212....$$

and by continuing in this way we can be sure to construct a number different from every number in the list—it will be different from the first number in the first decimal place, from the second in the second place... and so on. (That is, there is no r_n such that $c = r_n$, for the nth decimal of r_n will be different from the nth decimal of c.) So, there is no natural number n such that $f(n) = c$. In other words, there is no one-to-one correspondence between the natural numbers and the set of real numbers; the real numbers constitute an uncountable set.

dialectic. 1. (Socratic) The term 'dialectic' is derived from a Greek word that means 'to converse' or 'to discourse', and the dialectic that is ascribed to Socrates is close to this sense. It refers to his conversational method of argument, involving question and answer. *Compare* eristic. 2. (Platonic) In Plato's *Republic*, 'dialectic' is the supreme kind of knowledge, which "gives an account" (*logos*) of everything—that is, explains everything—by reference to the "Idea of the Good". In Plato's later dialogues (see especially *The Sophist*), 'dialectic' is the name given to the study of the interconnection of the Platonic Forms or Ideas, and appears to refer to a method of definition by *genus and species. 3. (Aristotelian) In Aristotle's logical works, 'dialectic' refers to reasoning from premises that are probable, in the sense of generally accepted. 4. (Kantian) Kant asserted (falsely) that, in the ancient world, 'dialectic' was a type of specious argument, dressing up fallacious reasoning in pseudological garb. He proposed to give the name 'dialectic' to a branch of philosophy that exposes

such sophistries; so, for example, the part of the *Critique of Pure Reason* called 'Transcendental Dialectic' includes a criticism of arguments put forward to prove the existence of God. 5. (Hegelian) 'Dialectic' is Hegel's name for the logical pattern that thought must follow. Broadly, Hegel argued that thought proceeds by contradiction and the reconciliation of contradiction, the overall pattern being one of thesis, antithesis, and synthesis (*see* Hegel). Since, for Hegel, thought *is* reality, the laws that thought must follow are also the laws that govern reality. 6. (Marxist) Marxists borrow Hegel's views about the pattern that thought and reality must follow; but since, unlike Hegel, they deny that thought is the fundamental reality, they distinguish between 'subjective' and 'objective' dialectics. Objective dialectics hold in nature; subjective dialectics is the reflection in thought of objective dialectics.

dialectical materialism. A metaphysical doctrine held by many Marxists. It asserts that matter is primary or fundamental, and states general laws governing the motion and development of all matter. As such, it is distinguished from *historical materialism*, which is the Marxist theory of history, dealing with the more particular laws governing the development of human society and thought. In asserting the primacy of matter, dialectical materialists do not advance a reductive theory; they do not assert that everything that exists is *nothing but* matter. Rather, they are concerned to oppose *idealism; in their view, matter is not a product of mind, but mind is the highest product of matter. This explains how Marxist historians of philosophy can say that Locke and Spinoza, for example, were materialists. Both these philosophers believed that mind is as real as matter, but they were 'materialists' in the sense that they were not idealists. Dialectical materialists argue that the laws that govern matter are not mechanistic, but are dialectical. Borrowing from Hegel, they assert that these laws are: (a) the transformation of quantity into quality; and conversely, (b) the law of the interpenetration of opposites (that is, the denial of the principle of *contradiction); (c) the law of the negation of the negation (that is, the view that reality develops by way of contradiction and the reconciliation of contradiction, the reconciliations producing fresh contradictions). *See also* Engels; Hegel; Marxism.

dichotomy paradox. The alternative name for the stadium (or racecourse) paradox of Zeno of Elea. *See* Zeno's paradoxes.

dictum de omni et nullo. (Latin for: the statement about all and none.) The principle, first formulated by *Aristotle in the *Prior Analytics*, "That one term should be included in another as in a whole is the same as for the other to be predicated of all the first" (26 B 26-7); that is, that whatever can be asserted of every member of a class can also be asserted of every member of any class contained in the first class.

Diderot, Denis (1713-84). French essayist, philosopher, and playwright, one of the leading figures of the *Enlightenment. He studied in Paris where he became acquainted with *Rousseau and translated the works of Locke and Shaftesbury. In 1750 he became editor of the *Encyclopédie* (*see* Encyclopedists), to which he contributed several articles on aesthetics, ethics, social theory, and the philosophy of history.

The essay *Lettre sur les aveugles* (1749) advocated a materialist interpretation of nature and examined the influence of the senses on the acquisition of ideas; its atheistic overtones led to Diderot's imprisonment for five months. His main philosophical works include *Le Rêve d'Alembert* (1730) and *Pensées sur l'interpretation de la nature* (1754), in which he emphasizes the complementary roles of observation and reflection in empirical enquiry. Experimental science is possible because a single causal principle is operative in nature. Sub-

stance is neither unitary nor uniform, but composed of essentially different "elements" divisible into molecules. Diderot's views foreshadowed later theories in suggesting that all species of living beings pass through stages of development (*see* Darwinism) and that the formation of moral values is traceable to childhood influences (*see* Freud).

difference, method of. *See* Mill's methods.

difference of degree. A concept contrasted, always unfavourably, with difference of kind, the former being taken to be by comparison essentially trivial and unimportant. A difference of degree between *A* and *B* can be defined in terms of a spectrum of actual or possible gradations, with no apparently natural delineations between them (*see* vagueness). The differences between age and youth, poverty and riches, insanity and sanity—all in human terms of the utmost importance—are of this wrongly despised sort. *See also* heap, the.

differentia. That part of the essence of a thing that distinguishes its *species from all other species in the same *genus.

Dilthey, Wilhelm (1833-1911). German philosopher and historian of ideas. His main works, including previous publications, were collected posthumously and published as *Gesammelte Schriften* (1913-36). Dilthey was influenced by *Kant and by British *empiricism, and placed central importance on a theory of knowledge that involves consideration of human volition as well as of sensations and thought. He criticized metaphysical speculation on empiricist grounds, while viewing metaphysics as still important in expressing a world-outlook (*Weltanschauung*). His central theme was the creation of a true philosophy of life, based on examining human and social studies (*Geisteswissenschaften*). He was especially interested in the relations between lived experience, expression, and understanding (*Verstehen*): that is, understanding of the mind and how it directs and manifests itself in literature, languages, and history.

Ding-an-sich. (German for: thing-in-itself.) The meaning of this phrase is explained by *Kant in his *Prolegomena to any Future Metaphysics*: "As the senses...never and in no single instance enable us to know things in themselves, but only their appearances, and as these are mere representations...all bodies, together with the space in which they are, must be held to be nothing but mere representations in us, and exist nowhere else than merely in our thought. Now is this not manifest idealism?" (§13 Note II).

Kant himself answered this question in the negative. His grounds were that he did not deny that there are things-in-themselves but only that we can know anything of them as they are. *See also* idealism; representationalism.

Diogenes of Apollonia. A *Presocratic philosopher who lived late enough to be guyed in a comedy of 423 BC. He apparently argued that everything must be constituted of fundamentally the same sort of matter, on the ground that radically different kinds could not interact. This basic substance is air, which is always endowed with intelligence but with more or less according to its different forms and conditions. His physiological interests gave, he thought, clues to cosmology.

Diogenes of Sinope (*c*.400–325 BC). Greek philosopher, founder of the Cynic sect. Author of epistles, dialogues, and tragedies, now lost, Diogenes spent most of his adult life in Athens. Perhaps inspired by *Antisthenes, he preached and practised an ideal of "self-sufficiency", attained through "simplicity" and rigorous self-discipline allied with a "shameless" disregard for conventional decencies. Moralist, iconoclast, and showman, Diogenes rapidly became a legend and a symbol, and remained one for centuries. *See* Cynics.

Dionysius the pseudo-Areopagite (*c*.500 AD). Mystical theologian, who was probably Syrian, wrongly identified with the Athenian converted by St. Paul (*Acts* 17.34). His extant works, notably *Mystical Theology, Celestial Hierarchy, Ecclesiastical Hierarchy,* and *Divine Names,* are a synthesis of Christian dogma and Procline Neoplatonism (*see* Proclus; Neoplatonism). Translated into Latin by John Scotus *Erigena, they became the basis for much medieval theological and mystical writing.

disconfirmation. The opposite of *confirmation. It is sometimes called infirmation.

disjoint. A set-theoretic term describing sets that have no members in common.

disjunction. *See* or.

distributed. Denoting an assertion that is made of all the members of a class. An *undistributed* assertion is made of less than all the members of a class. 'All Xs are ϕ' is distributed; 'Some Xs are ϕ' and 'This particular X is ϕ' are not. *See also* undistributed middle.

distribution. In statistics, the property of a random variable that is identified when a probability is attached to each value of the random variable. *See* randomness.

division, fallacy of. *See* composition and division.

Doctor Angelicus. (Latin for: Angelic Doctor.) The traditional scholastic nickname for St. Thomas *Aquinas.

Doctor Mirabilis. (Latin for: Miraculous Doctor.) The traditional scholastic nickname for Roger *Bacon.

Doctor Subtilis. (Latin for: Subtle Doctor.) The traditional scholastic nickname for *Duns Scotus.

Doctor Universalis. (Latin for: Universal Doctor.) The traditional scholastic nickname for *Albertus Magnus.

Dodgson, Charles Lutwidge (1832-98). *See* Carroll.

domain. 1. (of quantification) *See* quantifier. **2.** (of a function) *See* function.

double aspect theory In Abbagnano's doctrine of positive *existentialism, the theory that every concrete possibility open to man has a positive and a negative aspect. For example, knowing entails having the right answer, but has the negative aspect of not being mistaken, or the 'non-possibility' of error. Errors do, in fact, occur and therefore cannot be regarded as 'impossibilities' — their falsehood is demonstrable. See also Abbagnano, mind-body problem.

double effect, principle of. A principle characteristic of, but not confined to, Roman Catholic moral theology. Where some course of action is likely to have two quite different effects, one licit or mandatory and the other illicit, it may be permissible to take that course intending the one but not the other; for example, to give a terminally ill patient a dose of morphine to relieve pain knowing that it might perhaps also prove fatal (see euthanasia). Contraceptive slot machines labelled 'For the prevention of disease only' appealed to the same principle.

double negation. The principle that any proposition implies and is implied by the negation of its negation. Sometimes considered a law of logic, it is the combination of (1) the law of *non-contradiction (not both p and not-p) and (2) the law of *excluded middle (either p or not-p). These can both be put into the form of an implication, (1) if p, then not not-p, and (2) if not not-p then p, to yield the principle of double negation: p, iff not not-p. Intuitionist logic rejects the law of excluded middle, and hence double negation is not admitted as valid in the system (see intuitionism).

double truth. The notion that something might be false in philosophy yet true in religion. Though it certainly had earlier Arab sources, it is first spoken of in Western Europe in 1277, when it was formally condemned by the Bishop of Paris, along with many other heretical and scandalous doctrines allegedly taught in the Sorbonne. If and in so far as any

such notion really was maintained, it must have been a self-contradictory cover for conclusions inconsistent with the imperatives of orthodoxy.

doubt. See certainty and doubt.

dualism. A theory concerning the fundamental types into which individual substances are to be divided. It asserts that substances are either material or mental, neither type being reducible to the other. Dualism is to be distinguished, first from *monism, and then from *pluralism. The latter is a theory about the number of substances rather than about their type, and states that there exists more than one substance. Some pluralistic philosophies, such as Cartesianism, are dualistic, but others are not. For example, Berkeley asserts the existence of a plurality of substances, but he is a monist in saying that these are all of the same kind, in that all are mental substances.

Ducasse, Curt John (1881–1969). French-born American philosopher with wide interests. The most important book is perhaps his Carus Lectures, *Nature, Mind and Death* (1951). He had a lifelong interest, both theoretical and practical, in *parapsychology.

Duhem, Pierre Maurice Marie (1861–1916). French physicist and philosopher of science. His main philosophical work is *La Théorie physique: son objet, sa structure* (1906).

Duhem espoused a formalistic view of scientific theory, according to which a theory is a useful calculus enabling us to predict the course of our experience, but its elements do not themselves refer to anything. He believed that models in terms of which scientists picture their theoretical entities are just psychological aids. He developed the view that for any accumulation of evidence there would always be many different theories, equally good at producing predictions, and he is remembered too for the view that a failure in prediction strikes only at a whole theory and its auxiliary hypotheses, never at one particular part of it. *See also* Quine; science, philosophy of.

Duns Scotus, John (*c.*1266-1308). Scholastic philosopher, born in Scotland. Documentation on his short life is scanty and sometimes controversial. He entered the Franciscan order and was ordained at Northampton in 1291. He studied at Oxford and Paris and may well have taught at Cambridge. He became master at Paris in 1305, but also apparently taught briefly at Cologne, where he died and was buried.

His premature death left his works in an incomplete state and his associates and pupils used a variety of sources— notes taken at his lectures, earlier drafts, and marginal notes—to fill them out, sometimes with chaotic results. Only recently have the researches of scholars and the volumes of a critical edition enabled the genuine to be distinguished from the spurious. The state of the canon is roughly as follows. The notes of his Parisian lectures (*Opus Parisiense*), as recorded by someone present, contain the usual commentary on the *Sentences* of Peter Lombard (*see* scholasticism). The *Opus Oxoniense*, or Oxford Work, is also known as the *Ordinatio*, a title that implies that it is a version based on notes taken at lectures and revised by the author. We also have the *Tractatus de Primo Principio* (Treatise on the First Principle); discussions of points from Aristotle's *Metaphysics, Categories, De Interpretatione*, and *Sophistical Refutations*; and the *Quodlibetal Disputations*; as well as the more dubious *Theoremata*.

Given that Scotus rightly bears the title of 'Subtle Doctor', and has been capable of arousing the interest and admiration of moderns as diverse as Heidegger, C. S. Peirce, and G. M. Hopkins, any attempt at summarizing the thought of the original 'dunce' can yield only inadequate approximations. He may be seen, for instance, as restoring the primacy of the individual, and in particular the freedom of the individual will, in opposition to the necessitarian

tendency of previous Aristotelian intellectualism. In the *Aristotelianism (and *Platonism) of this period, the universal form is the prime object of the intellect: what is involved in being a man, a horse, or a tree, can be intelligibly specified in a general abstract definition. The problem is then to account for the comparative unintelligibility of the specific individual (*see* universals and particulars). According to an answer deriving from *Aristotle it is the *matter (in the special Aristotelian sense of the word) that is responsible for individuation. But if the connection of form with definition makes form a principle of intelligibility, then the contrasting individuating matter may be seen as a source of unintelligibility; this results in the individual becoming fundamentally unintelligible —perhaps even to the divine intellect. Scotus, however, restores intelligibility to the individual by making *haecceitas* (Latin for: haecceity or 'thisness') a principle of individuation which is formal, that is, of the same logical type as the universal. (This is betokened by the abstract terminations '-ness' and '-*eitas*'.) It contracts the universal or common nature (for example, of man) to a "this", so that Scotus is able to conclude (in the *Opus Oxoniense*) that "a singular is intrinsically intelligible", although perhaps not to our intellect.

The resulting situation may be used as an approach to another well-known Scotist device, namely the "thing-centred formal distinction" (*distinctio formalis a parte rei*). Thus there exists such a distinction between Socrates' general nature (humanity) and his "Socraticity" (defined as the thisness appropriate to Socrates); its statement is not merely a "distinction of reason", but is about how things *are*, while still not amounting to a statement of real non-identity (like that which holds between Plato and Socrates). It is also used to characterize the distinction between essence and existence, between one divine attribute and another, between the faculties of the soul, and so forth.

Another phase of Scotus' thought is

his doctrine of the will (see scholasticism), which is a reaction against Aristotelian intellectualism, especially as influenced by Arabic Neoplatonic thought (see Neoplatonism). This tradition had presented a vision of a Universe so shot through with necessary connections that little or no place remained for contingency or freedom. According to this interpretation, an eternal world eternally proceeds by way of necessary emanation from an immutable First Cause. Free creation is eliminated as the origin of the Universe, as this would entail mutability, and hence contingency, on the part both of the First Cause and its effects. Such doctrines, which are described in several of the articles of the 1277 Paris condemnation of Averroists, motivated reaction in favour of an accent on the power and will of free omnipotence and on the autonomy of human willing. Hence the prominence of 14th-century speculations centred around the distinction between the absolute power of God (potentia absoluta dei) and the ordered, or ordained, power of God (potentia ordinata dei). For Scotus, the will is never necessarily subordinated to the intellect's appreciation of values; it is thus released from cool self-interested seeking of perfection in the Aristotelian style, to fly freely and spontaneously to the disinterested love of the supreme object of love. The Universe, in its turn, is the product of the free loving activity of God—as opposed to the purely intelligible quasi-geometrical necessity of eternal emanation. In contrast to *Aquinas, Scotus allows that certain commandments do not pertain to the natural law in the strict sense (and are hence dispensable according to the will of God). He cannot, however, concede that those that concern the honouring and loving of God could ever be other than indispensable.

This loosening of the web of the intellectualists' necessary connections naturally affected Scotus' view as to the possibility of proofs of the existence of God in the style of Aquinas. The argument from moved finites to a First Mover now appeared to lack the background that it must presuppose. Indeed, there is clearly a gap between a God who is merely the final phase of an Aristotelian physical theory (and thus, in a sense, part of the physical order) and the unique, infinite, and transcendent God of religion. It is therefore on God as the metaphysical ground of possibility, rather than on God as inferred from the physical, that Scotus' proofs of the existence of God tend to turn. A further consequence is the movement away from abstract a priori dogmatism as to how things are, towards a greater appreciation of the need for reliance on observation and experiment as a guide to how God happens to have willed things to be in the world. Consequently the problems of induction, grounds of certitude, and the difficulties raised by the illusions of dreams and madmen (since made familiar by *Descartes and the British empiricists) are all present in the lengthy discussions of human knowledge contained, for instance, in the Opus Oxoniense.

duration. See space and time, philosophy of.

dyadic. In logic, denoting a *predicate or relation, that requires the addition of two singular terms in order to make a well-formed sentence. '... is larger than...' is dyadic (or two-place).

E

Ebreo, Leone (c.1460–1535). Portuguese Jewish doctor, philosopher, mathematician, and astronomer, also known as Judah Abrabanel. He fled persecution to Spain, then to Italy where he lectured at Naples and Rome. Influenced by Plato, Aristotle, and Plotinus as well as religious doctrines, his chief work Dialoghi di Amore (1535) treats aesthetics, metaphysics, and ethics, and identifies God with love, the essential principle of all life and activity.

eclecticism. The principle or practice of taking one's views from a variety of philosophical and other sources. The tendency is manifested in many individuals and systems that make no strenuous effort to create intellectual harmony between discrete elements (for example, *theosophy), but it can also form the basis of creative *syncretism.

economy, principle of. A modern name for *Ockham's razor.

education, philosophy of. Until the early 1960s philosophy of education in Britain secured a sporadic place in educational studies under the titles 'history of educational ideas' and 'principles of education'. The historical approach surveyed the educational works of thinkers who varied greatly in philosophical quality and who usually ranged in time from *Plato to *Dewey. The study of principles was less personalized and more contemporary, offering generalized discussion of curricular aims, teaching methods, and organization. Chiefly under the impact of R.S. Peters and his associates such philosophy as there was in these two conceptions gave place to a more disciplined and analytic approach rooted in general philosophy.

However, even as a newly emerging and self-conscious discipline, philosophy of education could take more than one form. A common American practice was to identify distinctive philosophical schools, such as realism, idealism, pragmatism, and existentialism, and then to explore the possible educational implications of each in a holistic way. Apart from causing unease by its generalized grouping into schools, such an approach has been thought unbalanced in its educational relevance, and has been strongly challenged in America by Israel Scheffler.

Analytic philosophy of education has drawn freely from general philosophy for models of argument, methods of analysis, and substantive positions. In this way educational principles and practices have been revealed as genuinely problematic where problems might not have been thought to exist. On the other hand, openness to already existing educational controversies has in turn generated some new interests in philosophical enquiry.

Four main branches of philosophy have been found of most help. Questions raised in *ethics concerning value relate to the aims and justification of overall conceptions of education and to the more particular area of moral education. *Social philosophy is most relevant to principles of organization both within schools and in the pattern of institutional provision, raising issues to do with freedom and authority, rights, equality, and political accountability. *Epistemology is a third important area, especially for such questions of curriculum construction as whether certain sorts of knowledge are fundamental, how far integration is possible, and whether all knowledge is ideological. And, since the learner is at the centre of the educational process, the philosophy of mind (see mind, philosophy of) is a fourth area of major relevance that can contribute to a better understanding of learning and teaching, emotions, and behaviour.

More specific areas of philosophy may have insights to offer for particular curriculum subjects, as is the case with aesthetics and the philosophies of history, science, religion, and mathematics. Philosophy of education itself is not a "philosophy of" in quite the same way as these latter specialisms. Its topic is so wide in scope that no branch of philosophy can be excluded as being without some relevant commentary to offer. Almost echoing Dewey, it might be said that philosophy of education is simply general philosophy when it more specifically addresses itself to educational concerns as these arise both inside and outside formal institutions.

Edwards, Jonathan (1703–58). The first major philosophical talent to be born and raised within what became the US. A hardline Calvinist divine with a bent for philosophy, Edwards was educated at Yale, and later became President of Princeton. He was active in the Great Awakening of 1740, his report on this being a major contribution to the psychology of religious conversion. His philosophy was entirely in the British tradition of Locke and Berkeley, Hutcheson and Shaftesbury. The philosophical and biblical case for Calvinism has surely never been presented more formidably than in his *Enquiry into Freedom of the Will* (1754).

effective procedure. A procedure (for solving a problem, answering a question, etc.) that consists of a finite number of mechanical steps before reaching the answer (to the problem, question, etc.). For instance, we may consider the question 'Is p a prime number?' An effective procedure is to divide p by each integer greater than one and less than p + 1. If any such division yields no remainder the number is not prime; otherwise it is prime. *See* algorithm.

efficient cause. *See* causes: material, formal, efficient, and final.

effluxes, theory of. The view held by the Greek atomists that the surfaces of objects are constantly emitting thin films of atoms (known variously as *idola*, *effluvia*, or *simulacra*) that impinge upon the eye and thus produce the sensation of sight. This account of vision as essentially a tactile process is discussed at length by *Lucretius (*De Rerum Natura*, Book IV). *Locke in the *Essay on Human Understanding* gives a broadly similar explanation of the way in which the primary qualities of objects (*see* primary and secondary qualities) are perceived: "And since the extension, figure, number, and motion of bodies of an observable bigness may be perceived at a distance by sight, it is evident some singly imperceptible bodies must come from them to the eyes, and thereby convey to the brain some motion which produces these ideas which we have of them in us" (Book II, chapter 8).

ego. 1. The experienced 'I' not coextensive with either mind or body, but the centre of organization of attitudes towards the body, the physical and social world, and all experience that determines identity and individuality. It is the personal point of reference, providing continuity and consistency in thinking, perceiving, planning actions, and relating past, present, and future experiences through memory, imagination, and anticipation. **2.** (in Freudianism) The part of the psychic structure concerned with orientation in the world, balancing the dictates of impulse and instinct with the demands of conscience, or 'superego'. *See also* Freud.

egocentric particular. Russell's term for a *token-reflexive.

egoism. *See* altruism and egoism.

eidetic images. Mental imagery defined as having the vividness of *sense data, but distinguished from hallucinatory sense data as precluding the inclination to believe that there is a genuine *perception of a public reality. Eidetic imagery is experienced as projected onto 'the external world'. Those capable of it, usually children, are called eidetikers.

eidos. (Greek for: form.) The term used by *Plato to denote his abstract Forms or Ideas. From it were developed in medieval philosophy the notions of substantial and accidental forms. Objects were to be classified according to their substantial forms, while their accidental forms consisted in any adventitious properties they happened to have had. *See also* Aquinas.

eightfold path. *See* nirvāna.

Einstein, Albert (1879-1955). German physicist whose formulation of the special and general theories of relativity laid the foundations of modern physics. Einstein's departures from classical physics include the philosophically central step of making the observer a physically important part of the world he is describing, so that, for example, the temporal relation between two events is only determinate with respect to an observer in a defined state of motion relative to them. Einstein's work on space and time has often been regarded as a triumph for the stringent empiricism of *Hume and *Mach, to each of whom he paid tribute. *See also* operationalism; relativity; space and time, philosophy of.

Eleatic. Denoting the philosophy of *Parmenides and his followers *Zeno of Elea and *Melissus of Samos. *See also* Presocratics.

elenchus. In Socratic *dialectic, a form of cross-examination that refutes an opponent's thesis by drawing out contradictory or otherwise intolerable consequences from him. Aristotle uses the word to mean 'refutation', as in the title of his work *Sophistici Elenchi* (Sophistical Refutations).

emanationism. A theory particularly associated with *Neoplatonism, which accounts for the source and structure of reality in terms of a perpetual, spontaneous flowing out (emanation) from a transcendent principle, usually called God or the One. Traces of emanationism occur in earlier Greek philosophers, but it was formulated in its clearest and most influential guise by *Plotinus, and from him passed into medieval Christian, Jewish, and Islamic thought. Man's task in an emanationist Universe is to 'turn back' and contemplate his divine origin. Except in certain mystical contexts, evolutionist theories have completely discredited emanationism. *See also* gnosticism; Kabbalah.

Emerson, Ralph Waldo (1803-82). American transcendentalist writer and romantic. More a literary figure than a mainline philosopher, Emerson was nevertheless deeply influenced by the German 19th-century philosophers, particularly F. W. J. von *Schelling, and by the studies in romanticism of *Coleridge and *Carlyle. The latter became a close friend. In his major work, *Nature* (1836), Emerson sought to present a manifesto of transcendentalism focused on the romantic ideals of self-knowledge and self-reverence, and his views were much admired by *Nietzsche and *Bergson.

More recently, there has been a revival of interest in Emerson's social criticism and his opposition to mass civilization.

eminently. *See* formally and eminently.

emotivism (*or* **emotive theory**). A meta-ethical theory (see ethics) concerned with the meaning of ethical terms. It came to prominence in the late 1930s, first through the account of moral judgments given by *Ayer in *Language, Truth and Logic* (1936) (see boo-hooray theory), and reaching its fruition with the publication of C. L. Stevenson's *Ethics and Language* (1944). This doctrine has since been the target of much criticism. But even though it is now unlikely that anyone could hold it in its purest form, it has had a profound effect on the course taken by moral philosophy.

To outline the theory one may best start by a comparison with orthodox subjectivism (see subjectivism and objectivism). The simple subjectivist claims that a moral utterance of the form, 'X is good' is equivalent to 'I like X' or 'I approve of X'. In other words it is a statement by the speaker about his own feelings, a report of his attitude to X. For an emotivist, however, an expression such as 'X is good' is not a statement at all, whether about the speaker or anything else. It is neither true nor false, but an expression of emotion, best compared perhaps to laughing at a joke or crying over bad news. Such reactions may be appropriate or inappropriate, they may be genuine or fraudulent, but they cannot be literally true or false.

Stevenson, the most sophisticated exponent of emotivism, adds more to the analysis. For him all moral utterances are essentially an attempt to persuade others to share one's own attitude: in saying, 'Abortion is always immoral' we not only express our hostility to abortion but also try to make others share that hostility. Stevenson's emphasis on the persuasive element in moral arguments arises from his starting point—the nature of ethical disagreement. Whereas previous moral philosophers often write as though we are all agreed on ethical matters, Stevenson is interested in the extent to which we disagree. He draws the conclusion that the purpose of moral discussion is to reach agreement through persuasion.

Three criticisms of the theory are common: (1) it cannot distinguish moral arguments from propaganda; (2) there are clear cases where moral utterances are not attempts to persuade anyone (for instance, talking to someone whose views you know to be similar to your own or trying to reach a moral decision in private); (3) it excludes rationality from moral arguments. On this last point the charges against it are similar to those against subjectivism.

Empedocles of Acragas (d. *c*.433 BC). An ardent democrat practising as a doctor. Empedocles thought in a world shaped by *Parmenides, and the problem posed by his work is how to relate, and if possible to reconcile, the this-worldly speculations of his work *On Nature* with the other-worldly doctrines of a fall, *transmigration, and possible escape from the wheel of birth found in his *Purifications. See* Presocratics.

empiricism. Usually defined as the thesis that all knowledge—or at least all knowledge of matters of fact as distinct from that of purely logical relations between concepts—is based on *experience. The phrase 'is based on' is sometimes replaced by 'comes from', 'derives from', or 'has its source in'—but it has to be admitted that all of these are more or less overtly metaphorical and can do little to specify just what relationship between knowledge and experience is intended.

Empiricism can perhaps be better characterized in terms of what it denies. To begin with, it is a rejection of the doctrine, found in various forms in *Platonism and *idealism, that when the human mind first encounters the world it is already furnished with a range of ideas or concepts, that accordingly owe nothing to experience. By contrast empiricists maintain that at birth the

mind is, as *Locke put it, "white paper, void of all characters", and that only experience can provide it with ideas. (Hence the time-honoured problem for empiricism about how we acquire ideas not instantiated in experience, for example, ideas of mathematical points or lines.) Granted that ideas, the raw material of knowledge, originate thus, some empiricists, though not all, have claimed that the truth of factual statements can only be established inductively from paticular experiences, and have denied any intuition or Cartesian "natural light" (*see* Descartes) which enables us to grasp general truths about reality independently of experience. The inductive method can, in its turn, be variously interpreted either, more liberally, as justifying claims to truth and knowledge for statements about a mind-independent reality, or, more strictly, as justifying only statements about the immediate data of experience. Understood in this latter fashion, empiricism leads to a radical scepticism about many of our ordinary claims to knowledge, as is manifested in *Hume and the logical positivist school (*see* logical positivism).

Empiricism, then, has taken several forms; but one common feature has been the tendency to start from experimental science, as a kind of prototype or paradigm case of human knowledge—in contrast with *rationalism which assigned a similar role to pure mathematics. (Empiricism has gravitated towards a view of pure mathematics as achieving independence of sense experience at the expense of dealing only in tautology.)

The development in the 17th and early 18th centuries of what became known as the British empiricist school of philosophy—with Locke, Berkeley, and Hume as its major figures, and Francis Bacon and Hobbes as important forerunners—was closely linked with the steadily increasing success and importance of experimental science, and its gradual discovery of its own identity as something distinct from pure mathematics and other disciplines. As a result, empiricism has characteristically seen the acquisition of knowledge as a slow, piecemeal process, endlessly self-correcting and limited by the possibilities of experiment and observations, and has been characteristically sceptical about the claims of all-embracing metaphysical systems.

empiriocriticism. An empirical, positivist approach to epistemology, developed by Richard *Avenarius and criticized by *Lenin in *Materialism and Empirio-Criticism* (1909). *See also* experience.

empty set. The *null set.

enantiomorphs. A pair of objects related to each other as a right hand is to a left, or as opposite spirals are, or mirror images. *Kant, in the *Prolegomena* used them in an argument in favour of the concept of absolute (as opposed to relative) space. A purely relational description of a universe containing only one hand could not discriminate between its being a right or a left hand, since the spatial relations between the parts of a right hand are exactly the same as those between corresponding parts of a left hand. Thus, if the concept of space were purely relative, there could be no distinction between a universe containing only a left hand and a universe containing only a right hand. But there must be a distinction, because an enantiomorph cannot be superimposed on its counterpart.

Encyclopedists. A group of 18th-century French writers who, under the editorship of *Diderot and D'Alembert, collaborated in the compilation of the *Encyclopédie* (1751-65), described as "an analytical dictionary of the sciences, arts, and trades". Including articles by *Voltaire and *Helvetius, the work was characterized by its sceptical attitude to religion and the advancement of liberal and tolerant social and political views. *See also* Enlightenment.

Engels, Friedrich (1820-95). The life-long collaborator of Karl Marx, Engels wrote many works on politics and history. Unlike Marx, he also wrote at length on philosophical topics. His major works in this field are: *Herr Eugen Dühring's Revolution in Science* (1877-8: abbreviated, *Anti-Dühring*), *The Dialectics of Nature* (written 1873-86; first published in 1925), and *Ludwig Feuerbach and the end of classical German philosophy* (1886). The writings of Engels contain the classical exposition of what is now called *dialectical materialism. Some writers (both Marxist and non-Marxist) have tried to draw a sharp line between Marx and Engels on this issue, saying that Marx was not a dialectical materialist, but this seems unjustifiable. There was certainly a division of labour between the two men, but there is no evidence of a fundamental divergence of views.

The *Dialectics of Nature* consists only of fragments, and is chiefly about the dialectical character of science; Engels' main views about philosophy are to be found in the other two works mentioned. In *Ludwig Feuerbach*, Engels divides philosophers into two classes, idealists and materialists; the former assert the primacy of mind over matter, the latter assert the primacy of matter. Engels argues that scientific thinking is dialectical (a thesis illustrated in *The Dialectics of Nature*) and adds that science has taken over much of what was formerly the province of philosophy. In this connection, he remarks that philosophy (in the sense of speculation about the nature of reality) came to an end with Hegel. But there is still a place for philosophy in the sense of the theory of thought and its laws. *Anti-Dühring* contains most of what Engels has to say about such laws (*see* dialectical materialism).

Enlightenment (*or* Age of Reason). The era characterized by the emergence, in 18th-century France, of progressive and liberal ideas that led to the Revolution and remained influential in western philosophy. Increasing scientific knowledge gave rise to the development of empiricist, naturalist, and materialist doctrines and strong opposition to clericalism. It was the era that saw the publication of the *Encyclopédie* (*see* Encyclopedists).

The prevailing ideas were systematized and published by d'Holbach (1723-89) in his *Système de la nature* (1770). His introductory remark, "Man is unhappy because he is ignorant of Nature", represents a summary of the work's aims. Nature, he maintains, is knowable through human experience and thought, and explanations should not be sought in traditional beliefs or the alleged "revelations" of the Church. There is a fundamental continuity between man and the rest of nature, between animal and human behaviour; all natural phenomena, including mental ones, are explicable in terms of the organization and activity of matter. Religion and extranatural beliefs inculcate habits inhibiting enquiry and the acquisition of the knowledge that is necessary to achieve the fundamental aims of man: happiness and self-preservation.

Nature makes men neither good nor evil but malleable by education and experience. Reason shows man's need of others and is the foundation of moral systems determined by what is useful to a society. Politics must conform to the essence and aims of society, not to the passions of rulers. The power of man over man is justifiable only by utility; education and legislation can be effective only when men are convinced that their interests will be served thereby.

en soi. *See* Sartre.

ens realissimum. (Latin for: the most real being.) God, the absolute possessor of all realities and all the attributes of perfection. The term is used in *Kant's discussion of proofs of God's existence.

entailment. *See* implication and entailment.

entelechy. 1. Realization or actuality as opposed to potentiality. In the works of *Aristotle (*De Anima, De Genera-*

tione) treating of the relationship between the soul and the material body, the soul (psyche) is defined as the form or actuality (entelechy) of an organic body that is potentially endowed with life. **2.** (in *vitalism) The vital principle, characteristically present in living bodies only.

enthymeme. 1. A *syllogism with a suppressed premise. **2.** A *conditional holding on formally-reducible material grounds.

entropy. Originally a thermodynamic concept measuring the extent to which the energy of a closed system is available to do work, entropy now has wider implications.

According to the first law of thermodynamics, no energy can be lost or gained by a closed system. The second law says that although its total energy may not change, not all the energy will be available to do work. In the form given to it by Lord Kelvin (1824-1907), the second law says that heat cannot flow spontaneously from a cold to a hot body. In other words, the heat of a body can only do useful work if the body is at a higher temperature than its surroundings. The heat of the ocean, for example, cannot be used to drive a ship, because they are both at the same temperature.

In 1854 Rudolf Clausius restated the second law in terms of entropy, which he defined as the property of body that increases when an infinitesimal amount of heat is added to it at a constant temperature: the increase in entropy being equal to the amount of heat added divided by absolute temperature.

Because heat can only flow spontaneously in one direction, every spontaneous energy change in a closed system must be irreversible. Moreover, every irreversible change must be accompanied by a loss in the amount of energy available to do work. Entropy measures this loss: the greater the loss in available energy, the greater the entropy.

As all real energy changes are, at least to some extent, irreversible, it follows that the entropy of the universe must be continuously increasing. When it reaches its maximum, the universe will reach its heat death—no more energy will be available to do work.

This gloomy though remote prediction is open to a number of objections, most of which are based on Boltzmann's hypothesis that the entropy of a system is related to the probability of finding it in a particular state. While a state of thermal equilibrium may be the most probable state of the universe, the statistical nature of entropy must not be ignored. There may be regions of the universe in which there is a substantial deviation from the statistical mean of equilibrium. In this statistical interpretation, entropy becomes a measure of the disorder of a system, and in this form it is used in several non-thermodynamic fields. In information theory, for example, an increase in the information about a system can be regarded as an decrease in its entropy. In linguistics, the concept has been applied to a statistical study of the structure of language.

epagoge. Greek for: argument from *induction.

Epictetus (*c.*55-135 AD). Stoic philosopher and moralist. A freed slave, Epictetus taught philosophy first at Rome and then at Nicopolis in Epirus. His discourses there were written down by a pupil, Flavius Arrianus. Four books of these survive, along with a compendium of Epictetus' teaching, the famous *Enchiridion* or *Manual*. Recalling in style the Cynic *diatribe* or sermon, they reveal Epictetus as a moralist preaching, with an often religious fervour, a gospel of inner freedom to be attained through submission to providence and a rigorous detachment from everything not in our power.

Epicureanism. The philosophy of *Epicurus and his followers, combining an ethical *hedonism with a theory that all things are really atoms and void. Reformulating these doctrines in such a way as to counter various points in Plato and

Aristotle, Epicurus built them into a recognizably Hellenistic system, with ethics supported by physics and epistemology.

Knowledge, according to Epicurus, derives from sensations. These are impressions made on the soul by images, or films of fine atoms from the surface of physical objects. Repeated sensations give rise to general concepts that make judgments possible. Always corresponding to something real, sensations are never false; but they can be "unclear" and hence misjudged. The test of any theory about things that cannot be seen is that it should accord with our "clear view" of things that can.

Atomism is such a theory. Our clear perceptions confirm that there must be indestructible and therefore indivisible elements, and that there must be a void in which they can move. Perceptible qualities result from the geometrical properties and arrangement of atoms, change from their rearrangement. Infinite in number, the atoms rain downwards. But some of them "swerve" at random (a fact that, incidentally, guarantees a certain indeterminacy and freedom to human action), causing collisions and rebounds (*see* clinamen). Our world, one of several in an infinite universe, is the fortuitous and perishable result of one such collision. Its development, including the evolution of animal species and human culture, can be explained by mechanisms such as the "survival of the fittest", without our having to posit any "natural purpose" or divine providence. The gods exist—men have "clear knowledge" of them—but only in the intercosmic spaces. They do not intervene in this world, or punish the wicked in the hereafter. Indeed, there is no hereafter; the human soul is a combination of atoms that perishes with the body.

Here atomistic theory serves a moral purposes. Epicurus taught that pleasure is our "primal and congenital good", maintaining the superiority of "mental" over "physical", and of "static" over "kinetic" pleasure. The latter distinction is between the pleasant *process* of satisfying a desire (for example, by eating) and the normal agreeable *state* of well-being restored thereby. Pain, as the interruption of this state, is its contradictory, and there is no intermediate or mixed condition. The completest possible pleasure is reached with the total elimination of pain—anything further is just variation. Desires should therefore be limited to those which are "necessary" or are "natural" and easily gratified; some obvious "pleasures", notably those of the intemperate, should be avoided, if we calculate that they will bring us more pain than pleasure. We can speak not only of "physical" but also, since we are capable of memory and anticipation, of "mental" pleasures or pains; and these are far more serious. The worst mental anguish comes from fear of divine intervention and of punishment after death. To be free of such disturbance, and thus happy, we need Epicurus' teaching on Nature.

The school that Epicurus founded was as much a commune as a college. He denied that man is naturally a social animal; so Epicurean communities provided an escape from ordinary society and also a substitute for it (hence the importance of friendship in Epicurean thinking). The enduring attraction of Epicureanism was due largely to the success of these communities, employing pastoral techniques that anticipated those of the Catholic Church, in guiding their adherents to a serene and happy life.

Epicurus (341-270 BC). Founder of Epicurean philosophy Epicurus' voluminous writings are all lost, apart from fragments, two collections of moral sentences, and three letters. The first of these 'To Herodotus' outlines his theory of Nature, the third 'To Menoeceus' is a manifesto of his moral position. Originally active on the east Aegean coasts, Epicurus founded his school in Athens around 307 BC. Philosophically, his principal debt was to *Democritus. But he himself stressed his own originality; and his disciples stood somewhat apart from

the other philosophical schools. *See also* Hellenistic philosophy.

epiphenomenalism. A doctrine concerned with the relationship between mind and body, advanced in the late 19th century as an alternative to the theories of *interaction and *parallelism. One of its proponents, T. H. Huxley, in his paper 'On the Hypothesis that Animals are Automata' (1874), considered consciousness to be an *epiphenomenon of molecular changes in the brain and hence all mental events to be the effects of physical events but never the causes of either physical or other mental events. *See also* mind-body problem; vitalism.

epiphenomenon. A secondary or added accompaniment to a process, considered as merely incidental and having no part in the further development of the process.

epistemics. A term coined in Edinburgh University in 1969 to label a new school dedicated to the scientific, as opposed to the philosophical, study of knowledge. *Compare* epistemology; sociology of knowledge.

epistemology. The branch of philosophy concerned with the theory of *knowledge. Traditionally, central issues in epistemology are the nature and derivation of knowledge, the scope of knowledge, and the reliability of claims to knowledge.

Philosophers have frequently been divided over the question of how knowledge is derived. Rationalists (for example, Plato and Descartes) have argued that ideas of reason intrinsic to the mind are the only source of knowledge. In opposition to this view, empiricists (for example, Locke and Hume) have argued that sense experience is the primary source of our ideas, and hence of knowledge (see empiricism; rationalism).

A significant turning-point in the debate between rationalists and empiricists occurred with Kant's discussion of whether there could be *synthetic a priori knowledge—knowledge which is not derived from experience but which is a condition of the comprehensibility of experience. For example, Hume had maintained that our knowledge of causation consists in our experience of the constant conjunction of events. But Kant took the view that the concept of cause is not empirical but rather a pure category of the understanding, required to make sense of the relation of events within experience.

Although Kant's epistemology is anti-empiricist in denying that all knowledge is *derived* from experience, it nevertheless stands in opposition to, for example, Platonic epistemology over the question of the *scope* of knowledge; for, while Plato considered true knowledge to be confined to the suprasensible world of the Forms or Ideas, Kant insisted, with the empiricists, that knowledge is limited to the world of experience.

With respect to the question of the reliability of knowledge, a potent influence in the history of epistemology has been the role of the sceptic in demanding whether any claim to knowledge can be upheld against the possibility of doubt. *Descartes' epistemology, indeed, was to pivot precisely upon the sceptic's method of doubt in his setting aside any claim that was open to doubt until he discovered some indubitable truths, for example, *cogito ergo sum.*

In contemporary epistemology the sceptic's role has diminished. G. E. *Moore and *Wittgenstein, in particular, have been influential in redirecting philosophical attention from the defence of claims to knowledge against doubt to the analysis of their meaning. For instance, it would now commonly be held, in A. J. Ayer's standard formulation, that what is meant by the claim to know proposition *p* is that at least (a) *p* is believed, (b) *p* is true, and (c) there are good reasons for believing that *p* is true (*see* belief).

equivalence relation. Any transitive, symmetric, and reflexive relation (*see* relation). Whenever two things *a* and *b* are equivalent, or identical in some respect *P*, the relation expressed by '*x* is

the same as *y* in respect of *P*' will be an equivalence relation. For example, two rods, of whatever material, may or may not have the same length. For some purposes all rods of the same length are equivalent and the relation given by '*x* is the same as *y* is respect of length' is an equivalence relation over the class of rods.

One important characteristic of equivalence relations is that they divide up, or partition, the class over which they are defined into non-overlapping sub-classes. Thus 'has the same length as' divides the class of material rods into sub-classes according to length, so that two rods will belong to the same sub-class only if they have the same length, and all rods with that length will be in that same sub-class. No rod can belong to more than one of these sub-classes, for no rod can have more than one length, or, more precisely, be the same length as two rods *a* and *b* where *a* and *b* are of unequal length. To put this more formally, if *R* is an equivalence relation over *C*, let $[a]_R$ stand for the class of all members *b* of *C* such that $R(a,b)$. $[a]_R$ is termed an *equivalence class*. *R* then partitions *C* into disjoint equivalence classes. In other words, every member *x* of *C* belongs to some equivalence class (to $[x]_R$ at least, because *R* is reflexive) and no member of *C* belongs to more than one such class.

equivalent. 1. (material) Two statements are said to be *materially equivalent* when they have the same *truth-value. Symbolically the material equivalence of *p* and *q* is expressed by '$p \equiv q$' which is true only when *p* and *q* have the same truth-value. '$p \equiv q$' is also the symbolic representation of the *biconditional '*p* iff *q*' when 'iff' is treated as a *truth-functional connective and hence as an expression of material equivalence. If *p* is materially equivalent to *q*, then if *q* is replaced by *p* in any truth-functional compound, the truth-value of that compound will not be altered. Hence it is said the *p* may be substituted for *q* *salva veritate.*

2. (formal) Two statements *A* and *B* are said to be *formally equivalent* when *A* may be deduced from *B* alone by valid argument, and vice versa.

3. (logical) Two statements *A* and *B* are said to be *logically equivalent* when it is impossible that they should have different truth-values. If *A* and *B* are truth-functional compounds, this amounts to saying that *A* and *B* are logically equivalent iff 'A $\equiv$ B' is a *tautology.

equivocal. Having two meanings. *Compare* ambiguity; univocal.

equivocate. To employ *equivocal words or expressions, confounding their meanings.

Er. *See* myth of Er.

Erasmus, Desiderius (1466–1536). Dutch humanist, philologist, and theologian, ordained into the Augustinian order. He studied and taught in Paris and later in most cultural centres of Europe, including England, where he published his most famous work *Encomium moriae* (The Praise of Folly) (1509).

Strongly opposed to dogmatic scholasticism, Erasmus was dedicated to ecclesiastical reform, regarding Christianity not as a mere doctrine of salvation but as a religion of the spirit based on confidence in human reason. Although he added his support to procuring a hearing for Luther at the Diet of Worms, he was opposed to the violent and dogmatic theology of the Reformers. Yet his *Colloquia* (1519), attacking the pedantry and frivolity of the Roman Catholic Church, is generally regarded as a work that prepared men's minds for the ideas of the Reformation. *See also* humanism.

Erastianism. The belief that secular authority should have supremacy over the Church in all matters.

Erigena, John Scot (*c*.810–*c*.877). Irish theologian and philosopher, the translator of works by pseudo-Dionysius and Gregory of Nyssa, and author of various commentaries. Main works: *De Praedestinatione* (On Predestination) and *De Divisione Naturae* (On the Division of Nature).

Erigena is an enigmatic figure in that his origins, the sources of his Greek learning, and the closing years of his life, have long been the subject of myths and controversies. He worked on the continent, had connections with the court of Charles the Bald, and was engaged in the 9th century's most animated controversy concerning predestination. His appeal to purely rational methods and the unorthodoxy of some of his conclusions shocked his contemporaries. In the dialogue on the so-called divisions of nature he discusses and invents ways of talking about God that are sometimes alleged to tend towards agnosticism and pantheism. The divisions are: (1) that which creates and is not created (that is, God as the first origin of things); (2) that which is created and creates (the divine ideas or exemplars); (3) that which is created but does not create (creatures outside God); and (4) that which neither creates nor is created (the divine final accomplishment of the process of return to and absorption (*adunatio*) into God). The reign of the notion of the procession of creatures from God and their return to God was prolonged by those medieval thinkers (including *Aquinas) who continued to use Erigena's translation of the pseudo-Dionysius.

eristic. 1. (as a noun) The art of disputation, especially as practised among the *sophists, but also used in the Platonic Academy. The word often has pejorative overtones, suggesting argument by dubious means for the purpose of victory, rather than the disinterested pursuit of truth (*compare* dialectic). *See* Plato. **2.** (as an adjective) Controversial, particularly with the implication of arguing for a victory regardless of the actual truth of what is contended.

erotetic. Concerning questions, interrogatory. The term is used especially in connection with the logical analysis of questions (also called *erotetic logic*). The term *erotetic quantifier* is used for any of various devices functioning similarly to ordinary quantifiers (*see* quantifier). For instance, the question "When did you get home?" might be reformulated as a propositional function bound by a quantifier: (?*t*) (you got home at *t*), in other words, "what time *t* was it such that you got home at *t*?"

ESP. *See* extrasensory perception.

esse. (Latin for: to be.) A term used in scholastic philosophy for existence. *See* Aquinas.

esse est percipi. (Latin for: to be is to be perceived.) Often mistaken to be an epitome of the metaphysics of Berkeley, the tag was in fact by him applied only to sensible things—in effect, *sense data. The true epitome is the disjunction *esse est aut percipere aut percipi* (to be is either to perceive or to be perceived), which makes room both for experiences and for experiencers.

essence. The notion of a fixed and timeless possibility of existence, derived from *Aristotle by his medieval interpreters. Aristotle had taught that the definition of a thing expressed the thing's essence, the characteristics it had to have to be the thing it was. Empiricist thought in and after the 17th century leaned towards the view that a full definition was not a correct analysis of a thing's nature, but a complete account of how the expression employed to denote that particular thing was to be used. This seemed to make essences matters of linguistic practice, notoriously a field of growth and alteration. *Locke made a celebrated distinction between real and nominal essences, the former being the "unknown constitution" of a thing which produces its properties the latter being the thing's possession of those (known) properties in virtue of which it is correctly called by its name. *See also* Aquinas; essentialism.

essentialism. A term designating three separate philosophical positions. **1.** The doctrine, in *Plato, of the existence of Forms, that is, of really existing abstract entities of which physical objects are imperfect copies. **2.** A position holding that something can have an essential property in virtue of a definition, or as described in a certain way. For instance, a man can be essentially two-legged but only if described, say, as a bicyclist. **3.** Perhaps the most important, a metaphysical view dating back to Aristotle, certain aspects of which are currently much discussed. It maintains that some objects—no matter how described—have essences; that is, they have, essentially or necessarily, certain properties, without which they could not exist or be the things they are. This is often seen as equivalent to the claim that there are *de re* modalities (*see* modality). There is also a related essentialist view, presented originally by *Locke, that objects must have a 'real'—though as yet unknown—'essence', which (causally) explains their more readily observable properties (or 'nominal essence'). Recently the issues raised by this third view have been reconsidered and revived, by such philosophers as Saul *Kripke and Hilary Putnam. They have applied essentialist considerations to problems raised by quantified *modal logic and the analysis of the meaning of modal assertions, and, more generally, to issues in the philosophies of science and of language.

eternal. 1. Everlasting. **2.** Non-temporal. Plato's Forms or Ideas should surely be thought of as the latter rather than the former; and, if so, his attempt in *Phaedo* to base a doctrine of the temporal immortality of the soul upon that theory must have been misconceived. *See* Plato.

ethical jurisprudence. *See* law, philosophy of.

ethics. To the layman the word 'ethics' suggests a set of standards by which a particular group or community decides to regulate its behaviour—to distinguish what is legitimate or acceptable in pursuit of their aims from what is not.

Hence we talk of 'business ethics' or 'medical ethics'. But not all uses of the term need be associated with a specific activity. If it makes sense to talk of following principles within a restricted area like medicine or commerce, then equally there can be standards of morality that apply to men not simply in virtue of their particular roles but in respect generally of their being men who live among other men. In Western countries the clearest example of such a system would be Christian moral teaching.

As a philosophical term 'ethics' has clear connections, though it is not identical, with this everyday usage. Like all philosophical endeavour it is an investigation into the fundamental principles and basic concepts that are or ought to be found in a given field of human thought and activity. Being a branch of philosophy it is a theoretical study. As such it differs from 'ethics' in the lay sense outlined above, in that any actual body of ethical belief, for example, Christian ethics, will be intended to be a practical guide to living and not merely an exposition and analysis of certain theoretical doctrines. Where philosophical 'ethics' does correspond to lay 'ethics' is in its subject-matter; it is just those systems that are intended to guide the lives of men qua men that are scrutinized by moral philosophers. It is, however, important not to overemphasize the distinction between the layman and philosopher in this context; in so far as the man in the street thinks critically about his own moral views or those of others, or ponders on their justification, or compares them with rival attitudes, to that extent he is a moral philosopher.

Classically, ethics has been concerned with activity of this kind. But speculation has led away from direct concern with matters that a non-philosopher would regard as bearing on ethics. Here we should notice three roads along which philosophers may travel, all of which may properly be seen as highways in the state of ethics, but which in one way or another tend away from the day-to-day business of moral life.

(1) A moral philosopher may take a set of principles, virtues, and attitudes recognized by an existing group or institution, a set which is not primarily philosophical (in that its purposes are practical rather than theoretical), and try to explain and analyse this set's basic moral tenets. Any critique of Christian ethics would be in this category. More usually the moral philosopher will investigate a moral theory itself invented and modified by other philosophers. They have either believed it to be a better account than any existing pre-philosophical doctrine of "what we all really believe" or have advocated it as an improved guide to practical action. The best example of this, at least in the Anglo-Saxon philosophical tradition, is the theory of *utilitarianism. Of all views of how a man should live, this is now the most widely discussed, analysed, criticized, attacked, and defended. Yet it was created entirely by philosophers and has no group or institution of its own.

(2) In returning to the comparison with specific ethics, like those of commerce or medicine, we come to the question of justification. Presumably the rules that demarcate on these shop-floors are not arbitrary, established and maintained at the whim of capricious authority. To refute such a charge a defender of the system of medical ethics for instance, would try to show that the rule under investigation was necessary for, or anyway an aid to, the purposes of medicine. Thus he might support the principle that whatever a patient tells his doctor in the consulting room is confidential by showing that this creates trust in the patient, which in turn inclines him to greater honesty, which means that the doctor receives more evidence on which to base his diagnosis. This form of argument works because there is an agreed end for medicine, the prevention and cure of disease. However, if we are to give a similar form of support to the rules that are supposed to apply to people, not in any special capacity, but

just as people, then we need some parallel agreed aim. This has led moral philosophers into some very rarefied speculation indeed. The human condition may be characterized in terms of generalizations on human nature, on God and his relation to Man, or on the necessary conditions of social life. But, whatever the base, there will be some attempt to show that these essential factors determine, in a way not always obvious, a purpose or meaning of life. Once this purpose has been clearly established, any moral principle or virtue can be assessed in terms of the contribution it makes, or possibly fails to make, towards this end. Thus the move from investigation into morality itself to what makes it either possible or necessary becomes almost inevitable.

So far what has been described is what would today be called *normative ethics*. That is the investigation into the content of moral principles and virtues, and their justification in terms of the human condition. Although some of the classical writers on moral philosophy—among them Aristotle, Aquinas, Spinoza, Hobbes, Hume, Kant, and J. S. Mill—would not have recognized themselves and their work from this account (and indeed some of their ethical concerns *are* outside this framework) in general terms philosophical ethics consisted in this type of enquiry until the present century.

(3) However there are questions about morality that are not concerned with its content, being neither questions on what principles there should be nor how we must live. These spring instead from puzzles about the logical form of morality. For example, the question of the objectivity or subjectivity of moral judgments and the problem of the logical relation between moral beliefs and factual beliefs (*see* naturalistic fallacy) are not directly concerned with the content of any particular form of moral life, whether real or imaginary, but with what the general logical rules of *any* morality or any moral argument, whatever it advocates or condemns, must be. This type of question is distinguished

from those of normative ethics and is characterized as *meta-ethical*. Now plainly such meta-ethical considerations are in a logical sense prior to those of normative ethics. For example, until you have decided whether moral beliefs reflect some objective truth or are dependent on the personal desires of their holders you cannot know what form of argument is appropriate for the support or refutation of any given belief. Indeed you may not know if rational argument about morality is possible at all. So it has been the claim, sometimes implicit, sometimes explicit, of many 20th-century moral philosophers, for example, Moore, Stevenson, and Hare, that the primary task of ethics is to deal with meta-ethical problems, leaving it an open question whether the more substantive questions of morality (those of normative ethics) can be tackled at a later date.

Euclid (fl. *c*.300 BC). Mathematician, who founded a school and taught at Alexandria. His treatise on *geometry in 13 books, the *Elements*, was the preeminent textbook on the subject for over 2000 years, and it was not until the middle of the 19th century that the possibility of a *non-Euclidean geometry was seriously considered. Until not long before World War I, geometry in British schools was often called simply 'Euclid'.

Eurytus of Croton. A follower of *Pythagoras, known only for his procedure of associating particular creatures with, and representing them by, particular numbers of pebbles. The most plausible interpretation of this practice is that he considered that the essence of a sort of objects consists in the points required to bound the surfaces of those objects. *See* Presocratics.

euthanasia. In its etymological origins 'good dying', but currently confined to an easy death as an escape from some condition, usually terminal, and felt by the patient to be intolerable. Everyone working for legalization insists that euthanasia must be only voluntary, seeing the desired legal change as an important extension of the rights of the individual. Passive euthanasia is when death results from the simple cessation of unwanted life-sustaining measures. Active euthanasia requires that someone, preferably the patient himself, takes positive steps to kill. This killing is morally equivalent, in another person, to assisting suicide and, in the patient, to suicide.

Euthyphro dilemma. The question put by Socrates in Plato's dialogue *Euthyphro*: "Is the holy loved by the gods because it is holy, or is it holy because it is loved by the gods?" (§ 9E). Such questions can be put about any moral term, and with reference to any proposed authority, human or divine. If you choose the first option you have a standard of holiness, or whatever else, which is logically independent of your authority; and one which that authority may sensibly be praised for meeting, but may also in fact fail to meet. If you choose the second, then for you the rulings of your authority are simply as such to be accepted; and, since there is now no question of that authority either measuring up or failing to measure up to some logically independent standard, you cannot sensibly praise your God, or state, or party, for being itself superlatively whatever it may be.

evaluative. Tending to concern or suggest rules or standards, as opposed to purely descriptive. An evaluative statement implies a value judgment on the part of the person making it. *See also* normative.

event. An occurrence (as opposed to a material object), usually thought of as happening at a determinable time and place. It need not involve the participation of human agents. It is often conceived as subsisting with other events in causal relationships; one event may be said to cause another to occur, as its effect. *See* causation.

evidence, paradox of ideal. *See* ideal evidence, paradox of.

examination paradox. *See* prediction paradox.

excluded middle, principle (*or* **law**) **of.** The principle or law the acceptance of which commits one to holding that for any statement *p*, the statement '*p* or not-*p*' is true as a matter of logical necessity. This is not to be confused with the related principle of *bivalence.

existence. *See* being.

existential import. The existential import of a proposition is, strictly, whatever existence is entailed by that proposition. The sentence 'There is a bull in that field' commits a speaker to the existence of the bull and the field. A problem arises in the translation of natural language sentences into quantificational logic. The existential *quantifier, as in 'Some men are mortal' is usually interpreted as 'There is at least one thing (which is both male and mortal)'. Its import is thus existentially affirmative; it implies the existence of something, in this case, one thing both male and mortal. But the universal quantifier, as in 'All men are mortal', is taken as 'If anything is a man then it is mortal' and this last sentence is still true even if there are no men. Thus its import is existentially negative, which in many cases seems counter-intuitive. A solution proposed by *Strawson is that the sentence presupposes the existence of men (*see* presupposition), but does not entail it.

existentialism. A philosophical trend or attitude, as distinct from a particular dogma or system. Its origins are attributed to *Kierkegaard. It became influential in continental Europe in the second quarter of the 20th century, the writings of *Heidegger, *Jaspers, *Marcel, and *Sartre. Existentialism is generally opposed to rationalist and empiricist doctrines that assume that the universe is a determined, ordered system intelligible to the contemplative observer who can discover the natural laws that govern all beings and the role of reason as the power guiding human activity.

In the existentialist view the problem of being must take precedence over that of knowledge in philosophical investigations. Being cannot be made a subject of objective enquiry; it is revealed to the individual by reflection on his own unique concrete existence in time and space. Existence is basic: it is the fact of the individual's presence and participation in a changing and potentially dangerous world. Each self-aware individual understands his own existence in terms of his experience of himself and of his situation. The self of which he is aware is a thinking being which has beliefs, hopes, fears, desires, the need to find a purpose, and a will that can determine his actions. The problem of existence can have no significance if viewed impartially or in abstraction; it can only be seen in terms of the impact that experiences make on a particular existent. No individual has a predetermined place or function within a rational system and no one can discover his supposed duty through reasoning; everyone is compelled to assume the responsibility of making choices. Man is in a condition of anxiety arising from the realization of his necessary freedom of choice, of his ignorance of the future, of his awareness of manifold possibilities, and of the finiteness of an existence that was preceded by and must terminate in nothingness.

Existentialist thinkers distinguish between "authentic" and "inauthentic" forms of existence. Some make the distinction on the basis of the individual's endeavour to transcend a particular situation, the alternative being a denial of liberty and abandonment to a form of anonymity as a creature of circumstances. Others deny the possibility of transcending one's own point of view and claim that moral life is an illusion: authenticity is the preservation of an individual personal identity which is in danger of being eroded by deceptions, under the influence and demands of society. Yet others regard the recognition of other free individuals and communication with them as a criterion of authentic existence.

existential quantifier (*or* **operator**). A logical *operator, usually written as ∃. *See* quantifier.

experience. Philosophical *empiricism, as against philosophical *rationalism, holds that all our knowledge, or at any rate all our knowledge of what *Hume would call "matters of fact and real existence", must be based upon, and vindicated by reference to, experience.

A crucial distinction has to be made between two enormously different interpretations of the word 'experience', the ambiguity of which is paralleled in many other associated terms. In ordinary nontechnical usage, to say that someone has had experience of computers, or to speak of the sights they have seen, or the perceptions which they have enjoyed, is to imply something both about the existence of actual computers and about that person's cognitive dealings with real material objects. Philosophers, however, impressed by all the demoralizing arguments of the sceptics, often employ the word 'experience' to refer only to how it appears to the subject, specifically disowning all implications for what may or may not be the case in any objective and *external world. The guiding or misguiding idea is that for each of us certainty is possible only with regard to our own experience, in this cribbed and 'private' interpretation, and that any claims to experience in the everyday and 'public' sense must be incorrigibly reckless.

Such philosophers make it much harder to appreciate what is going on, and perhaps also what is going wrong, by thus insisting on employing in their own special and 'private' senses common words that are commonly used in precisely that 'public' way which they themselves are here concerned to reject. Ordinarily to say that someone saw or otherwise perceived something entails that that something was there to be perceived, existing independently of the perceiver: hallucinatory rats on a drunkard's lost weekend are not seen but 'seen' (in snigger quotes). Hume was, therefore, wrong to speak of "perceptions of the mind" when he proposed to maintain that we have no philosophically adequate reason for believing in the existence of any material things ontologically independent of such (private) "perceptions". It is similarly misleading today to talk of *sense* data when you are labouring not to commit yourself about either the existence or our knowledge of (public) material things.

One popular fallacy of equivocation is to argue that because you have had, in the 'private' sense, experience of God, therefore you have also had, in the 'public' sense, experience of God: the first claim (this is how it seemed to you) must not be confounded with the second (that you have in fact knowingly confronted an actual Creator). *See also* a priori and a posteriori; analytic and synthetic; empiricism; necessary and contingent truth.

explanation. *See* historical explanation; mechanical explanation.

explication. 1. In general, explanation. 2. (in logic) A form of analysis by which an imprecise concept is given a precise formal definition in order to make it suitable for formal logical use.

extension. 1. That which has spatial dimensions. The concept was used by *Descartes to distinguish matter, which is extended or has extension, from mind, which he regarded as a thinking substance having no spatial dimensions. 2. *See* extension and intension.

extension *and* **intension.** A distinction introduced in the *Port Royal Logic* (1662) (*see* Port Royal) as that between extension and comprehension. Since the 19th century, English writers have followed either Sir William Hamilton in replacing 'comprehension' by 'intension'—which has no other use in ordinary language—or J.S. Mill in replacing the distinction by that between connotation and *denotation. The *exten-*

sion of a general *term, *predicate, or *concept is made up of all those entities to which the term or predicate correctly applies, or which fall under the concept (*see also* class). Intension is a more difficult notion to define and one whose definition is not universally agreed. Following the *Port Royal Logic*, one would say that the *intension* of a general term or concept *A* was made up of all those general terms or concepts *B* for which 'All *A*s are *B*' is a necessary truth, either because *B* forms part of the explicit definition of *A* or because it can be proved that anything which is an *A* must also have the property of being *B*. Thus 'having interior angles equal to the sum of two right angles' forms part of the intension of 'triangle' although it is not part of the definition of that term. Others have included only those terms forming part of the explicit definition of a complex term in its intension, and some have used 'intension' simply as a means of marking the contrast between the extension of a general term and its meaning or significance.

In contemporary logic, with its emphasis on propositions rather than on general terms, the contrast which more frequently occurs is that between extensional and intensional occurrences of expressions. An expression is said to occur extensionally in a sentence iff the expression is either (1) a singular *term, *a*, (2) a *predicate, *F*, or (3) a sentence, *p*, and the following substitutions do not affect the *truth-value of the sentence: (1) '*b*' for '*a*' where '*a*' and '*b*' have the same denotation, (2) '*G*' for '*F*' where '*G*' and '*F*' have the same extension, (3) '*q*' for '*p*' where '*p*' and '*q*' have the same truth-value. Thus 'The author of *Mysticism and Logic* was a member of the House of Lords and a Cambridge don' is extensional throughout in that the following substitutions can be made without altering its truth-value: 'Bertrand Russell' for 'The author of *Mysticism and Logic*', 'A British peer' for 'A member of the House of Lords', and 'Grass is green' for 'The author of *Mysticism and Logic* was a Cambridge don'. On the other hand, in 'Tycho Brahe believed that the earth was the centre of the universe', although Tycho Brahe occurs extensionally, substitution of '1 + 1 = 3' for 'the earth was the centre of the universe' reveals that the latter expression does not occur extensionally, for this substitution turns the original sentence, which is true, into one which is false. When an expression occurring extensionally in a sentence is removed from it, the remainder is said to form an *extensional context*. Contexts which are not extensional are *non-extensional* or *intensional*. An operator is said to be extensional if its application to purely extensional contexts results in a purely extensional context, and intensional or non-extensional otherwise.

extensive magnitude. *See* magnitudes.

external world. The philosophical problem set by *Descartes when, in his "room with a stove", he argued that his only rock bottom certainty was his immediate present consciousness: "I think, therefore I am." The problem was to show whether, starting from there, anyone could know, and how he could know, that there was a universe around him, containing things and other people. It should be remembered that the Cartesian starting point is a subject of consciousness both solitary and incorporeal. *See* ghost in the machine; veil of appearance.

extrasensory perception (*or* ESP). The various putative phenomena of acquiring information without any employment of the senses (*see* parapsychology). ESP is telepathic if the information is acquired from other people, or brutes, and clairvoyant if it is not. If this information is acquired before it becomes available to the other person, or in the events and objects themselves, then the ESP is called precognitive (*see* precognition). Given these definitions it is wrong, though tempting and common, to accept the suggestion, which is implicit in such positive-sounding labels as 'ESP', 'telepathy', and 'clairvoyance', that investi-

gators must be investigating a previously unknown means of acquiring or transferring information. All the key concepts are in experimental practice defined in terms not of some (however vaguely) hypothesized new means, but rather of the complete absence of any sensory or other known means at all.

One corollary of this would seem to be that ESP phenomena are essentially statistical, although not, of course, for that reason either insignificant or unreal. The evidence for their genuineness is all either singular and anecdotal or quantitative and experimental. But, since 'ESP' is not a name for some means or mechanism, it can make no sense to ask, of any series of correspondences between the guesses or other materials produced by the subject and their supposed targets, which particular correspondences are due to ESP and which are those just bound to happen 'by the law of averages'. We can only notice, in conditions in which we hope preclude sensory means and ordinary inference, that the amount of correspondence between guess and target series is statistically significant.

Until recently most parapsychologists, assuming a Cartesian view of man, have seen telepathy as direct communication between essentially incorporeal minds or souls, and clairvoyance as such a soul's substitute for perception.

F

fact/value distinction. The argument against rationalistic ethics, first advanced by *Hume, claiming that reason alone cannot grasp or be the grounds for moral approval or disapproval. Distinction is made between two classes of assertions: the factual and the moral (evaluative). Premises and conclusions of one class can neither entail nor be derived from those of the other. *See also* naturalistic fallacy.

fallacy. An argument involving an invalid, rather than a valid, form of reasoning. For example, it would be fallacious to argue: given that 'All Communists claim to repudiate racial discrimination', and given that 'Dr. Angela Davis claims to repudiate racial discrimination', then it must follow that 'Dr. Angela Davis is a Communist'. For, although the conclusion was at the time of writing true, it cannot validly be deduced from those premises. The argument is thus one *token of the type traditionally labelled the fallacy of the *undistributed middle. The word 'fallacy' is often used loosely in general language to characterize any supposed error, and a clear distinction must be made between this general usage and the strictly logical usage in which its function is to distinguish one particular kind of error.

fallibilism. A theory presented by *Peirce describing enquiry as an activity generated by a state of unease and aiming to attain a state of rest through finding the right answer to a question. But rest is never assured, since no one can know what fresh evidence might present itself to necessitate a change in position.

false. See truth and falsity.

falsidical. Saying what is false; a word created by philosophers as an opposite for *veridical.

falsifiability. See verifiability.

fatalism. The doctrine that what will happen will happen, and nothing we do or do not do will make any difference. It can of course be held either about everything and everyone or in more restricted forms. It is distinguishable from a causal determinism that holds that everything, including everything which we do, is completely caused, but that still leaves room for the possibility that human action may be causally effective in ensuring that this happens rather than that. Leibniz sometimes speaks of fatalism as Mahommedan Fate. See freewill and determinism.

feeling. Broadly, a state of non-perceptual awareness or bodily sensation, which is sometimes a component of an emotion.

It often involves some bodily sensation, not necessarily of the localized kind found in apprehensions by any of the five 'external' senses, but possibly, for example, of general comfort or discomfort. Again, it may be associated with the occurrence of fear, relief, anger, joy, etc., or with concurrent respiratory, digestive, cardiac, or other sensations. It can be a fear, or it can be an accelerated heartbeat, or the word can be used to refer conjointly to both of these when they occur together. There is little convergence of view about whether one's present state of feeling is entirely open to one's own *introspection. It has sometimes been argued that a feeling is not merely accompanied by appropriate overt behaviour, but that it simply *is* this behaviour (see behaviourism). In criticism of this it is pointed out that one can, for example, be frightened without showing one's fear externally. Feelings have similarly been identified with people's measurable physiological states, although, again, negative or neutral instances occur. Before the 18th century feeling was not distinguished from what had been called 'the passions' or 'affections', a general concept used in the then psychology of motivation. In the Hobbist version of this, elements of feeling would probably have fallen within the category of passions. By Kant, however, feeling was taken to be one of the basic elementary faculties of mind.

Feuerbach, Ludwig Andreas (1804–72). Bavarian philosopher and theologian, who was influenced by *Hegel and himself influenced *Marx and *Engels (see Hegelianism). His writings are critical of Hegel's idealism and of current Christian theology, the most famous being *Das Wesen des Christentums* (1841), which was translated into English by Mary Ann Evans (George Eliot) as *The Essence of Christianity.* Feuerbach defined religion as "the dream of the human mind", and he viewed all spiritual development as properly relating to man, rather than God. This should be made a conscious activity tending towards the good of the human species.

Fichte, Johann Gottlieb (1762-1814). German philosopher, who studied and taught at Jena and Berlin. Strongly influenced by *Kant, he published *Versuch einer Kritik aller Offenbarung* (1792) investigating the conditions under which religious belief is possible. Religion is the belief in the divinity of moral law; practical (moral) reason is the foundation of all knowledge and satisfies the needs of its subjects, rational beings.

His *Wissenschaftslehre*, written and revised over many years, shows a departure from the Kantian system, presaging the absolute idealism of *Hegel and of some later *existentialism. Fichte's doctrine of the *ego describes the autonomous experiencing active being in a system determined by Nature. The ego affirms itself as a primitive act of consciousness, constructing the objective world, or non-ego, from appearances.

Ficino, Marsilio (1433-99). The head of the Platonic *Academy of Florence and a major influence in the Renaissance revival of *Platonism. In 1484, Ficino produced the first standard translation of Plato's dialogues, and his commentaries on Plato and *Plotinus commanded wide respect. Although his reputation later diminished, he has recently come to be regarded as one of the philosophically more original Platonists. In particular, there is renewed interest in his chief work, *Theologia Platonica de Immortalitate Animarum* (Platonic Theology of the Immortality of Souls) (1482)—a sustained defence of the doctrine of the immortality of the soul—and in his philosophical letters.

fideism. The view, recurrent throughout religious history, that essential religious doctrines cannot be established by rational means, but only accepted, if at all, by acts of faith. Its extreme form (for example, in *Kierkegaard) holds that religion requires the acceptance of doctrines actually absurd or contrary to

reason (*compare* credo quia impossibile). In its more moderate forms (for example, in St. *Augustine or *Pascal) reason is not antithetically opposed to faith, but plays an auxiliary role in formulating or elucidating what must first be accepted by faith.

fides quaerens intellectum. (Latin for: faith seeking understanding.) A slogan coined by St. *Augustine to characterize the Christian intellectual quest.

figure. In logic, one of the four possible arrangements of the terms in a categorical syllogism. Aristotle distinguished only three figures; the isolation of the fourth is traditionally attributed to Galen. *See* syllogism.

final cause. *See* causes: material, formal, efficient, and final.

finite set. A set that is either empty, or is such that there exists a one-to-one correspondence between its members and a subset of the set of natural numbers less than a specified natural number. Alternatively, a set *A* is finite if it has no proper subset *B* such that the members of *A* can be put in one-to-one correspondence with the members of *B*. *Compare* infinite set.

finitism. An approach to mathematics that admits to the domain of mathematics only a finite number of objects (numbers) each of which must be capable of construction in a finite number of steps. Any general theorem that asserts something of all members of the domain is acceptable only if it can be proved, in a finite number of steps, to hold of each particular member of the domain. David Hilbert was the major proponent of finitistic methods in mathematics. *See also* mathematics, philosophy of.

First Cause. The second of the *Five Ways of St. Thomas *Aquinas, an argument to a "a First Efficient Cause, to which everyone gives the name 'God'." The adjective 'efficient' is there to show that Aquinas is concerned with the third of the four kinds distinguished in Aristotle's doctrine of four causes (see causes: material, formal, efficient, and final). Such efficient causes are always expected to be substantial agents rather than mere events.

The premise of this second way is that "In the observable world we discover an order of efficient causes, but no case is found or ever could be found, of something efficiently causing itself." It is however, Aquinas urges, "impossible to go on forever in a series of efficient causes…if the series goes on forever, then there will be no first efficient cause; and so there will be no final effect and no intermediate efficient cause, which is obviously false."

To understand this argument we have to realize two things. First, here, as elsewhere in the Five Ways, the aim is to prove, not a first initiation "in the beginning", but the continuing existence of the Creator as the sustaining cause of the *Universe (*see also* creation). It would therefore miss the point to object that nothing has been said to show that these series of efficient causes could not go back indefinitely in time. Aquinas himself elsewhere argued that it is perfectly conceivable that the Universe might have had no beginning. So he is not arguing, as often is thought, that everything must have a cause, that this series could not go back indefinitely in time, and hence that there must have been an uncaused First Cause; an argument in which the proposed conclusion actually contradicts the first premise. Yet it remains hard to see that Aquinas is not arguing, in a different but equally self-contradictory way, that all efficient causes require other efficient sustaining causes, and that if there are to be—as there are—efficient causes, then there must be at least one efficient sustaining cause that does not require an efficient sustaining cause or, which amounts to the same thing, that is itself its own such cause (*causa sui*).

The second thing to recognize is the background of a rather astrological element in Aristotle's physics. Aquinas followed Aristotle in believing that heavenly bodies, and in particular the sun, are very much more than necessary conditions for, for instance, the production of children by parents here on earth. It is these heavenly bodies that by their presence or absence cause "the phases of generation and corruption of bodies here on earth". The consequence is that "whatever begets here below, reproduces its kind as an instrument of a heavenly body." It is this sort of continuing supportive activity that everything in the Universe all the time requires, and that, Aquinas is arguing, is all the time provided by his First Cause "to which everyone gives the name 'God'". *See also* First Mover; natural theology; physico-theological argument; quantifier-shift fallacy; secondary causes.

First Mover. The origin of all motion in the *Universe, an origin that is itself unmoved. The idea was introduced by Aristotle and developed by philosopher-theologians in all the three great traditions of Mosaic theism—Judaism, Christianity, and Islam. It provides the first, and he himself thought the most obvious, of the *Five Ways of St. Thomas Aquinas. The premise is that there is, in a broader than our now more usual sense, motion in the Universe. So, Aquinas urges, "everything which is in motion is moved by something else. But this cannot go on forever: because if it did there would be no First Mover, and consequently no other mover at all, since second movers do not move except when moved by a First Mover, just as a stick does not move anything except when moved by a hand. And so we must reach a First Mover which is not moved by anything: and this all men think of as God."

To understand this argument, though not necessarily to accept it, two points must be appreciated. First, here, as elsewhere in the Five Ways, the aim is to prove not initiation by a Creator, "in the beginning", but the continuing existence of that Creator as the sustaining cause of the Universe (*see* creation). Second, Aquinas is there taking for granted one of the fundamentals of

Aristotelian physics. Aristotle and his followers required explanations, not only for every initiation of change, but also for all continuations of it; whereas Newton's First Law of Motion states that a body will, unless it is subject to some impressed force, either remain at rest or continue in uniform motion in a straight line. Aquinas thus saw motion not as intrinsic to but as impressed upon the Universe, and sustained by an outside Force. His choice of example is significant: if a man is waving a stick the stick stops moving when he stops waving it, whereas an arrow shot from a bow continues towards its target after the archer's work is done. (Aristotelians laboured to explain this second sort of phenomenon by appealing to putative continuing pressures in and from the surrounding air.)

From the time in the 1400s when these Aristotelian ideas first began seriously to be challenged, farseeing people on both sides of the dispute appreciated that their abandonment would encourage the rejection of the theist notion of a Creator as a sustaining cause, in favour of the deist idea that the Universe was wound up "in the beginning", and then left to run on its own "like clockwork". See also deism; First Cause; quantifier-shift fallacy.

first order language. See calculus; higher order logic.

first order logic. See calculus; higher order logic.

Five Ways, the. The five attempts made in the Summa Theologiae by St. Thomas *Aquinas to deduce the existence of God from very general natural facts about the universe: "We must say that it is possible to prove the existence of God in five ways" (IQ2A3). See also argument from (or to) design; cosmological argument; degrees of perfection argument; First Cause; First Mover; natural theology.

flux, doctrine of. See Heraclitus.

flying arrow paradox. The arrow paradox of Zeno of Elea. See Zeno's paradoxes.

foreknowledge. See precognition.

form The term 'Form' is used to translate the Greek term 'eidos'. In the philosophy of *Plato, 'Form' and 'Idea' are interchangeable terms. Although Aristotle's account of the nature of forms differs from Plato's, he is concerned with broadly the same problems. In Plato, to know the Form of X is to understand the nature of X; so the philosopher who, for example, grasps the Form of justice knows not merely what acts are just, but also why they are just. Similarly, Aristotle regards a form as that which makes something intelligible, and which (like Plato's Forms) is grasped by the intellect.

However, Aristotle rejects Plato's view that all forms are 'separable', that is have an independent existence. For Aristotle, what exist independently are substances (see substance), and substances (with a few important exceptions, such as God) consist of both matter and form. Matter is that which has form; for example, the human soul is the form of the human body, which is its matter. The human body is again a form, whose matter is constituted by the bodily organs, and so on. In the case of the products of skill, form is imposed on matter; for example, when a carpenter makes a table out of wood he imposes on matter (the wood) a form, which is what is grasped when it is understood what makes a table a table. But many forms (such as the form of the human body) are not imposed on matter in this way, but are in a sense immanent. A form of this kind explains a thing's development; it is the intelligible structure that a thing has when fully developed, and the growth of the thing is regarded as a striving to make actual its form. Forms in this sense figure not only in Aristotle's biology but also in his physics. For example, he explains the fall of an unsupported body in terms of its endeavour to realize its form—namely, its proper place in the universe.

When the scholastic philosophers spoke of 'substantial forms', they had in mind forms of this immanent kind. The theory of substantial forms was sharply criticized by many philosophers and scientists of the 17th century, who saw such forms as inconsistent with the mechanistic concepts of the new physics.

formal cause. *See* causes: material, formal, efficient, and final.

formal implication. *See* implication and entailment.

formalism. 1. (mathematics) A view pioneered by D. Hilbert (1862–1943) and his followers, in which it was claimed that the only foundation necessary for mathematics is its formalization and the proof that the system produced is consistent. Numbers (and formulae and proofs) were regarded merely as sequences of strokes, not as objects denoted by such strokes. Hilbert's programme was to put mathematics on a sound footing by reducing it (via arithmetic) to consistent axioms and derivation rules, the former being certain series of strokes, the latter ways of manipulating them. Later *Gödel showed that the consistency of arithmetic cannot be proved within the system itself, thus demonstrating the impossibility of achieving part of the Hilbert programme.. **2.** (in ethics and aesthetics) Emphasis on formal issues at the expense of content. The term is generally employed by opponents of such attitudes.

formal language. An uninterpreted system of signs. The signs are typically of three sorts: (1) variables, for example, sentence letters p, q, r, s; (2) connectives, for example, $\lor$, $\&$, $\to$, by which signs are joined together; and (3) punctuation devices, such as brackets, to remove ambiguity. There are also *formation rules telling how to string signs together to form well-formed formulae, and *transformation rules telling how to transform one string of signs into another.

Formal languages in this sense are just sets of marks permutable by rules, much as chess notation is. They may, however, be interpreted. Thus, if (1) the variable letters are made to stand for propositions, (2) $\lor$, $\&$, $\to$ to stand for 'or' 'and' 'if—then' and (3) the transformation rules are made deduction rules, then the formal language has been interpreted as a system of logic.

Distinction must be made between formal languages (uninterpreted systems of marks) and artificial languages (interpreted formal languages which are, however, not natural languages as vernacular English is).

formally *and* **eminently.** Scholastic technical terms still used without explanation by *Descartes. Thus *Meditation VI* argues that the power producing what would now be called *sense data "resides in some substance different from me, in which all the reality subjectively in the ideas produced is formally or eminently contained." The second term means in a pre-eminent manner or degree, the first specifies a straightforward correspondence with what is found in the effect. Descartes here appeals to that supposed a priori knowledge of causality which *Hume was later to deny.

formal mode of speech. The employment of all the various devices for making it unequivocally clear that the true subject of discourse is, where it is, concepts and the logical relations between concepts, rather than objects or events and the supposed contingent facts about those objects or events. The contrast is with *material mode of speech*. Both expressions were introduced by Rudolf *Carnap.

The concept of God, or of tomato, or of anything else, is the use to which we put the word 'God', or 'tomato', or whatever else; and this, of course, must be exactly the same as the use of any precisely equivalent term in any other language. Those who talk about concepts are not by so doing referring to the objects to which the concepts under discussion would apply. It is possible to say things about the concept of centaur altogether without prejudice to the question whether there in fact are, or could be, centaurs.

It is wrong, but common, to confuse such conceptual discourse with either philological discussion of the words of one particular language or psychological commentary upon the mental imagery that may be coming before the minds of those who employ this or that particular word for some concept. To compare the English English terms 'lift' and 'car' with their American equivalents 'elevator' and 'automobile' is not to converse about either concepts or means of transport (or transportation). Nor, as Gottlob *Frege insisted so vehemently, do any facts about the mental pictures with which individuals may happen to associate the symbol '100' have anything to do with questions about what is or is not a correct arithmetical calculation.

The person who says that threehood necessarily involves oddness, that the idea of a triangle contains the idea of the equality of its three angles to two right angles, or that existence is part of—or is—the essence of God, is employing the material mode of speech. The alternative formal mode is more long-winded, but does make clear that the subject is concepts and their logical relations, and it avoids the two sorts of confusion just mentioned. Thus say 'There are three of them' and to deny 'There are an odd number of them' would be a contradiction; to say 'This is a triangle' and to deny 'This has three angles equal in sum to two right angles' would be a contradiction; and to suggest that there may be no God would be to contradict yourself (see ontological argument).

formal system (or **theory**). Any set of axioms and/or rules of inference written in some specified *formal language L. The axioms will be closed wffs (see wff) of L, and rules of inference (or *transformation rules*) are rules according to which *proofs can be constructed out of

wffs of L. See also axiom; calculus; inference, rule of.

formation rules. Rules defining, often inductively, the notion of a *wff (well-formed formula) of a language.

Forms (or **Ideas**). See Plato.

forms of argument. See logic.

four causes, doctrine of the. See causes: material, formal, efficient, and final.

four elements. The four entitiès considered by the Greek philosophers to be the basic constituents of the physical universe: earth, air, fire, and water. Each possessed two qualities: earth (cold and dry), air (hot and wet), fire (hot and dry), water (cold and wet). Elements with common qualities were able to change into one another, for example, water could change into earth as both included the quality of coldness. The doctrine of the four elements remained pivotal to the explanation of the physical world until the 17th century. Compare quintessence.

four humours. The four body fluids that *Galen believed must be held in equilibrium to maintain mental and physical well-being. They were blood, choler (yellow bile), phlegm, and melancholy (black bile). The doctrine, like that of the *four elements, survived until the 17th century, forming the basis of medieval physiology and clinical medicine.

four-term fallacy. A form of defective *syllogism that is deficient because the *middle term occurs in two distinct senses. Thus 'All kids cry. That goat is a kid. Therefore that goat cries'.

Frankfurt School. A movement associated with the Institute for Social Research founded within the University of Frankfurt in 1923. It has included Max Horkheimer, Theodor Adorno, and Herbert Marcuse. The uniting idea is the need for a critical Marxism, construed as involving rejection of *positivism, *value-freedom, and (crude) *materialism, while stressing the actual Hegelian and alleged idealist side of *Marx himself. *See also* idealism.

freedom. *See* liberty.

free variable. *See* variable.

freewill *and* **determinism.** Two apparently opposed philosophical concepts: the former postulating that man is able to choose and act according to the dictates of his own will, the latter that all events including human actions, are predetermined. Perplexities arise for both the secularist and still more the theist. We cannot but assume in most everyday life that on many occasions we are free agents, able to do or to abstain from doing this or that at will. Yet it may also seem to be both a presupposition and an implication of the achievements of the sciences, and most importantly of the aspiring sciences of man, that there are in truth no such alternatives; and that everything, human conduct not excluded, really happens with absolute *inevitability. The philosophical problem is to discover what the presuppositions and implications of the two areas actually are, and whether they can or cannot be reconciled. Adherents of the one view are compatibilists, of the other incompatibilists. The special theist problem substitutes the existence of God for the achievements of the sciences; if the doctrine of *creation is true, then can this leave any room for human responsibility and choice? In the theistic context it is usual to speak of predestination, implying that everything, including particularly every choice, has been fixed in advance by divine decree.

The philosophical issues are indeed philosophical, and hence concerned with logical presuppositions and logical implications, logical compatibilities and logical incompatibilities (*see* Preface). Too often they are prejudicially misrepresented to take incompatibilist answers for granted, leaving open only the factual and not philosophical questions of which of the two incompatibles is true. In particular the terms 'freewill' and 'determinism' are frequently so defined that

one explicitly excludes the other. No philosophical dispute is settled, of course, by appeal to authority. Yet it is worthwhile, precisely and only in order to dissolve such prejudice, to notice that many—perhaps most—of those classical philosophers who published in this area were compatibilists: *Hobbes, *Leibniz, *Locke, and *Hume.

Ordinarily we contrast acting of our own freewill with acting under compulsion. But even the person who acts under compulsion is an agent, whereas the person who is simply picked up by main force and thrown as a missile victim is not. The crux here is what is essentially involved in *action, not freewill in the everyday sense. Determinism too may be considered only in terms of physical causes necessitating their effects. But it is also possible to speak of conduct determined by the agent's motives; and to say this is not so is clearly to imply that there was no alternative.

Modern problems in this area have centred round the claim that human actions are, or are capable of being (had we the knowledge), causally explained (*see* causation); that is they either (a) fall under (causal) physical laws, or (b) are physically determined (in the sense that the movements of inanimate physical objects are held to be physically determined). This might mean, of a given event c (falling under a law), that its effect e (a) could have been predicted, or (b) could not but have happened. When e is a human action, the tension is between describing it as free or voluntary—if this means 'within our power to do or not to do, as we choose'—and claiming that it could have been predicted, or (given circumstance c) e could not but have happened. But to deny that human actions do not fall into the realm of causality as ordinarily understood creates problems. In what sense then can we be said to *cause* our own actions (and hence be responsible for them, as the concept of freewill is said to imply—*see* responsibility) rather than have them accidentally happen to us? Compatibilists believe that the concept of freewill must involve causality.

Frege, Gottlob (1848-1925). Professor of mathematics at the University of Jena. Main philosophical works: *Begriffsschrift, einer der arithmetischen nachgebildete Formelsprache des reinen Denkens* (1879), *Die Grundlagen der Arithmetik* (1884), translated by J. L. *Austin as *The Foundations of Arithmetic*, and *Grundgesetze der Arithmetik*, in two volumes. (1893-1903), the first part of which was translated by M. Furth as *The Basic Laws of Arithmetic* (1965). Frege also wrote numerous articles, and some of the most important of these, together with parts of the *Begriffsschrift* and the *Grundgesetze* are translated in *Translations from the Philosophical Writings of Gottlob Frege* (1952), edited by P. Geach and M. Black.

Frege was the founding father of modern mathematical logic, philosophy of mathematics, and philosophy of language. He believed that proof in mathematics should be exhibited in a way that lays bare the deductive validity of each step, leaving nothing to unbridled intuition. The axioms from which proof starts must be as firm as possible—preferably truths of logic (*see also* logicism). To satisfy this programme proofs must be translated into a *formal language with a settled vocabulary and set modes of construction. In such a notation the construction of each sentence, hence its meaning, and hence the question of whether it follows from previous steps, are all explicit. Frege's greatest achievement in developing this idea was the invention of the *quantifier and variable construction to formalize expressions of generality in natural languages. This success of his step-by-step approach to meaning not only created the most important tool of modern logic, but remains the inspiration of most recent philosophy of language. *See also* semantics; variable.

Freud, Sigmund (1856-1939). Austrian physician, founder of psychoanalysis. He was appointed to an extraordinary professorship at Vienna University in 1902. His extension of the ideas of unconscious desires, beliefs, etc., required and involved the introduction of a new criterion of the mental, challenging the established Cartesian identification of the mind with consciousness. His work is often seen as in a special way emancipatory, since his psychoanalytic therapy was supposed to put more of the total psychic energy at the disposal of the deciding agent: "Where Id was Ego shall be." *See also* unconscious.

function. One of the most central concepts in mathematics. It comes to have application in logic as a result of Frege's insistence (in 'Function and Concept') on the analogy between concepts and functions (*see also* concept). However, with the increasing use of formal logic in the study of the foundations of mathematics, functions themselves have become objects of study in logic itself.

Intuitively speaking, a function is an operation which, when applied to one or more objects (*arguments* for the function), yields another object (the *value* of the function for that argument). The value of the function f for the argument t is denoted by '$f(t)$' or sometimes just 'ft'. To specify a function, as opposed to some value of it, and at the same time indicate what operation is to be performed in obtaining the value of the function from the given argument(s), variables (x, y, z) are used. The square function might be specified by writing 'x^2' and addition by '$x + y$'. Sometimes, to make it absolutely clear that it is the function that is being referred to, rather than any of its values, the notation '$\hat{x}^2$' (due to Russell) or '$\lambda x.x^2$' is used. In these notations, 'x' appears as a bound variable (*see* variable), whereas in 'x^2' it is free. Thus, for example, '3^2' denotes the number 9, which is the value of the function $\lambda x.x^2$ for 3 as argument; '$4+5$' also denotes 9 as the value of the function $\lambda x.\lambda y.(x+y)$, when $x=4$ and $y=5$.

One can also think of expressions

such as 'the capital of' as analogous to 'the square of' and 'the sine of', and so as standing for a function which, for a country as argument, gives a city as its value. Thus 'the capital of France' denotes Paris. Frege urged that the analogy be further extended to expressions such as 'is a mountain', seeing them as functions which, for an object as argument, yield a truth-value as their value. Thus, 'Everest is a mountain', being a true sentence, is said to denote the truth-value True, whereas 'London is a mountain', being a false sentence, denotes the truth-value False. Put in the language of functions, this would be expressed by saying that 'is a mountain' takes the value True for Everest as argument and the value False for London as argument.

Any function will be applicable only to, or is only defined over, a certain class of objects. For example, x^2 is defined only for numbers and not for objects such as the moon, whereas 'the capital of' is not defined for numbers, since 'the capital of 2' does not stand for anything. The class of objects for which a given function f is defined, is called the *domain* of f and the class of objects which are values of f is the *range* of f. In other words, D is the domain of f iff, for each object a belonging to D, $f(a)$ is defined (denotes an object), and R is the range of f iff, for each object b belonging to R there is some object a such that $b = f(a)$ (b is the value of f for some object a). If D is the domain of f, R the range of f, and S some class in which R is included, then f is said to be a *function from D to S*. So 'sine(x)' is a function from angles to real numbers, whereas 'is the capital of x' is a function from countries to cities. If $S = R$ then f is said to be a function from D *onto* S; otherwise f is a function *into* S. A function which, for each pair of distinct objects in its domain, takes distinct values, is said to be *one-one*. More formally, a function f is one-one iff, for all a, b in D, if $a \neq b$, then $f(a) \neq f(b)$. So, for example, '$x + 1$' is a one-one function from the real numbers onto the real numbers, whereas 'x^2' is

not a one-one function over the real numbers ($3^2 = -3^2$) and is not onto the real numbers, since negative numbers are not the squares of any real numbers.

Two functions are identical iff, they have the same domain and for each argument from that domain they take the same value. The actual way in which the value is determined is thus not regarded as being crucial to the identity of the function. This leads naturally to the suggestion that, from a logical point of view, functions should be identified with *relations of a special kind. One can define a relation $F(a,b)$ from a function f by saying that $F(a,b)$ holds iff $b = f(a)$. F is then the relation between an argument of f and the value of f for that argument. It is evident that if $\lambda x.f(x) = \lambda x.g(x)$, then the corresponding relations $F(x,y)$ and $G(x,y)$ will have identical extensions, so that a function f can, for most purposes, be identified with the extension of the corresponding relation F (*see* extension). (Within co-ordinate geometry this would amount to identifying a function with its graph.) As relations, functions are distinguished by having the property that if $b \neq c$ and $F(a,b)$ ($b = f(a)$), then $F(a,c)$ is not true ($c \neq f(a)$), because the value of f for a given argument must be uniquely determined. This is not generally true of relations; for example, 5 is greater than 2 and 5 is greater than 3, so that 'x is greater than y' does not denote a function. As the extensions of two-place relations are represented by classes of ordered pairs, the identification of functions with relations leads to the representation of functions of one argument by classes of ordered pairs (and more generally, of functions of n arguments, treated as $n+1$ term relations, by classes of ordered $(n+1)$-tuples). *See* relation.

fundamentum divisionis. (Latin for: basis of division.) *See* per genus et differentiam.

future contingents. *See* seafight.

G

Galen (129–199). Greek physician whose immensely influential writings dominated western medical theory until the Renaissance. *See* four humours.

Galileo Galilei (1564–1642). Italian mathematician, astronomer, and physicist who founded modern mechanics and cogently argued for the Copernican *heliocentric theory of the universe. His views brought him into constant conflict with the religious authorities. In 1633 he was forced to recant and was placed under house arrest for the remainder of his life. His works had an important effect on 17th-century thought: the most influential were *Letter to the Grand Duchess Christina* (written in 1615, but not published until 1636), *The Assayer* (1623), *Dialogue on the Two Chief World Systems* (1632), and *Discourse on Two New Sciences* (1638).

Galileo first came to prominence in 1610 with the publication of his telescopic observations of the heavens. These threw great doubt on the geocentric theory of the universe, which was then generally accepted; with the current scholastic physics (*see* Aristotelianism), it constituted the orthodox natural philosophy. Considerable criticism was provoked, some of which was supported by appeal to religious authority. Galileo's reply was his *Letter to the Grand Duchess Christina*, in which he argued for the strict separation of theological and scientific issues, on the grounds that different expertise was required for each discipline and that the truths of one could never conflict with the truths of the other. In essence, it was a plea for the autonomy of science.

Galileo's method in science owed much to his mathematical background, his admiration for Archimedes, and his great ability to devise experiments, many of which (like Einstein's) were "thought experiments". His philosophy of science found clear expression in *The Assayer*. Here he stated that the book of nature is written in the language of mathematics (thus setting himself strongly against the qualitative approach of scholastic thinkers) and held that the properties of bodies could be distinguished into primary and secondary (*see* Locke; primary and secondary qualities).

In 1632 Galileo published the *Dialogue on the Two Chief World Systems*, which, despite a ban imposed by the Church, argued the superiority of the heliocentric hypothesis. Although under arrest, he published his most important scientific work, the *Discourse on Two New Sciences*, in 1638. Here he revealed his discovery of the law of falling bodies and provided the foundation for the central concept of classical mechanics, that of inertial motion.

gambler's fallacy. The belief into which a gambler may be tempted, to the effect that a system such as a roulette wheel or a tossed coin has a "memory", so that after a run of one kind of result another outcome becomes more probable. The fallacy lies in supposing that the so-called law of averages (*see* Bernoulli's theorem) implies this. In fact the theorem applies only where probabilities are constant from repetition to repetition and so can offer no support to the gambler's belief.

game theory. A mathematical theory dealing with game-like situation in which participants wish to maximize some property (such as utility) in positions of uncertainty, not only with respect to the state of nature but also the actions of other players whose interests may be opposed or parallel to those of the participant. Typically, when deciding what to do, one must predict the actions of others with the knowledge that they themselves when deciding which action to perform will predict the actions of others including oneself. Complexity may be increased by allowing coalitions between players. Game theory has been used to analyse and calculate best possible strategies in game-like situations such as business, war, politics, and social activities. It has been extensively developed in the 20th century by John Von Neumann (1903-57) and Oskar Morgenstern (1902-). *See also* decision theory.

Gassendi, Pierre (1592-1655). The distinguished contemporary of *Descartes, born in Provence. He became professor of philosophy at Aix (1617) and in 1645 was appointed professor of mathematics at the Collège Royal, Paris. Gassendi is best known as the author of the Fifth Set of *Objections* (1642) to the *Meditations* of Descartes. Among many telling criticisms which Gassendi raises is the question of how we are supposed to tell whether our knowledge is "clear and distinct". In his earlier *Exercitationes Paradoxicae adversus Aristotelicos* (1624) Gassendi had argued the impossibililty of deriving scientific knowledge from a basis of sensory experience, but a detailed study of the doctrines of Epicurus (Gassendi published three books on the subject in the 1640s) led him to modify his scepticism. In the *Syntagma Philosophicum* (published posthumously in 1658) Gassendi put forward an atomistic theory of the universe based on the Epicurean model. However, he was careful to insist that the soul and its activities were outside the domain of atomistic explanations.

general will. *See* Rousseau.

generative grammar. The rules that allow speakers to construct (generate) infinite numbers of new sentences in a language. Language speakers, though exposed during language learning to only a finite number of sentences, acquire the ability to understand and produce an infinite number of new ones; this has led linguistic scientists to assert that speakers possess rules that allow the construction of an infinite number of new sentences using a finite vocabulary. These rules are called a 'grammar'. They also enable interpretation of new combinations of words on a first hearing. Chomsky's transformational grammar is one kind of generative grammar (*see* Chomsky).

genetic fallacy. The mistake of arguing that because something is now such and

such, therefore it must already have been such and such at an earlier stage; or, because it was such and such then, therefore it must be the same now. Because, for instance, mankind evolved from some species of higher ape, therefore people now must be, really, higher apes; and because, it is alleged, the state originated as an instrument of class coercion, therefore now too states must be that and, perhaps, only that.

Gentile, Giovanni (1875-1944). Italian idealist philosopher, professor at Palermo, Pisa, and Rome, editor of *Enciclopedia italiana*, and minister of education under Mussolini. He collaborated with *Croce in editing the periodical *La Critica* until 1922; their association was severed due to their disagreement over fascism.

Gentile rejected Croce's differentiation between the theoretical and practical categories of mind. In *Teoria generale dello spirito come atto puro* (1916) the only reality is taken to be the act of thought, which is also the act of creation. Nature is simply dead thought: so conceived, it can be intelligible —as a 'thing-in-itself' it must remain unknowable.

Gentzen, Gerhard (1909-45). German logician and mathematician. In 1934 he presented a system of natural deduction for elementary logic, that is, a formalization of logical principles that proceeds by giving simple rules governing the use of logical connectives. This was in contrast to previous formulations of the propositional and predicate calculuses, which had used the *axiomatic method. In 1936 he gave a proof of the consistency of classical pure number theory, using transfinite *induction.

genus. In Aristotelian logic, a very wide and comprehensive class or kind, sub-classes of which may be called species. Generally in philosophy neither term carries its peculiar biological implications.

geometry. A science that has its origins practically located in the need of the ancient Egyptians to redraw field boundaries each year as a result of the Nile floods; the laws concerning lines, angles, etc., being arrived at by empirical generalization. The Greeks, in particular *Euclid (c.300 BC), turned geometry into a deductive theoretical science based on certain postulates, which in recent times has been rigorously axiomatized using only the primitive terms 'point', 'between', and 'congruent'.

One of the main philosophical problems of geometry is whether Euclid's postulates are to be taken as describing physical reality or not. If they are thus taken, then according to Einsteinian physics they falsely describe the world—space, for instance, being non-Euclidean; if they do not describe physical reality, then the subject matter of geometry is non-physical. See also non-Euclidean geometry.

Gerson, Jean de (1363-1429). French academic theologian and religious reformer. Although versed in *nominalism, Gerson was attracted to the doctrines of *Aquinas. He was critical of the technicalities of the received speculative theology of the followers of *Duns Scotus, holding that their liking for technical jargon had made current theology unnecessarily recondite. He himself sought a pious mysticism that stressed love of God rather than union with God. He tried to repair the split, known as the Great Schism, between Eastern and Western branches of the Church.

Gersonides (or **Levi ben Gershom,** also known by his initials as Ralbag) (1288-1344). Provençal philosopher, physician, natural scientist, and biblical commentator. His philosophy is contained in his commentaries on the Bible and on *Averroes, and in his theological treatise *Milhamoth Adonai* (Wars of the Lord) (1329). A supreme rationalist, Gersonides followed in the footsteps of *Maimonides, but differed from him on some important points: he favoured a teleological, rather than a cosmological, proof of God's existence; he denied creation from nothing, asserting instead

the eternity of matter; he maintained that God could be known through positive, not negative, attributes only; and he allowed full range to man's freewill by limiting God's foreknowledge of human actions (compare Ibn Daud). See also seafight.

Gestalt. An organized, coherent whole whose parts are determined by laws intrinsic to the whole rather than being randomly juxtaposed or associated. The concept gives its name to the 20th-century school of psychology founded by Max Wertheimer, Wolfgang Köhler, and Kurt Koffka.

Gestalt theory was originally set up on general principles in opposition to the prevailing psychological atomism of the empiricist tradition (see psychology, philosophy of). But its most significant contributions have occurred in the field of psychology of perception, in virtue of a number of classic experiments designed to show how the eye naturally tends to organize, for example, a series of lines or dots into coherent patterns. For Gestalt theory, seeing is essentially a phenomenological process in so far as what is 'seen' is what appears to the seer rather than what may actually be there (see phenomenology).

Geulincx, Arnold (1624-69). Belgian philosopher, who studied and lectured at the Catholic University of Louvain until his conversion to Calvinism. Seeking refuge in Holland, he became philosophy professor at Leyden University and published several treatises on logic and method.

A disciple of *Descartes, Geulincx advanced the theory of *occasionalism to meet objections to the Cartesian mind-body antithesis (see also clocks, image of the two). His views are expounded in two posthumously published works: *Ethica* (1675) and *Metaphysica* (1691).

ghost in the machine. A label introduced by Gilbert *Ryle in *The Concept of Mind* (1949) to describe a thesis of *Descartes to the effect that, while the human body may be regarded as an enormously subtle and complicated machine, it only becomes a person when it is joined by an incorporeal soul. Although for Descartes the official defining characteristic of soul is consciousness, when he comes in Part V of the *Discourse on Method* to offer "two most certain tests" of the presence of a soul within the bodily machine these seem to be tests only of rationality (*see* other minds). Although the *brutes (animals other than man) are supposed not to possess souls, Descartes seems never actually to have drawn the conclusion, so often held against him, that the brutes must be altogether insensible.

given, the. An obsolete term for the putative raw data of *experience—uncontaminated by theoretical, ordering, or inferential impositions or additions.

Glanvill, Joseph (1636-80). English philosopher and divine. *The Vanity of Dogmatizing* (1661) is a rejection of the arid Aristotelianism of Oxford, where he was educated, in favour of the views of the *Cambridge Platonists. In *Lux Orientalis* (1662) he supported Henry More's belief in the pre-existence of the soul, and after Glanvill's death More edited his most notorious work, *Sadducismus Triumphatus* (1681). This is an attack on the rationalizing sceptics who, supposedly as the first step towards atheism, denied the existence of ghosts, witches, and other manifestations of the spirit world (*see* Sadducism).

gnoseology. An obsolete synonym for *epistemology.

gnosticism. A religious movement blending Christian doctrine with esoteric pagan philosophy, that flourished in the first two centuries AD. It manifested itself in many forms, ranging from serious philosophical enquiry to debased magic ritual. Its defining characteristic, however, was its adherents' belief in *gnosis* (knowledge)—the knowledge of God supposedly revealed to initiates to enable them to attain salvation. Like *Manichaeism, with which it shares many features, gnosticism is fundamentally dualistic, drawing a sharp distinction between the "good" spiritual world and the "evil" material world. To evade the problem of how a supremely good God could have created a material world in which evil exists, the gnostics insisted that the world was the work of a *Demiurge. In this world particles of spirit were trapped and Christ was seen as an ambassador from God to the unliberated spiritual fragments. The esoteric and elitist aspects of gnostic teaching earned it the wrath of orthodox Christians, but the metaphysical attractions of dualism ensured gnosticism's survival in one form or another throughout the Middle Ages, for instance in the Albigensian heretics of 13th-century France.

God, arguments for the existence of. *See* argument from (or to) design; common consent arguments; cosmological argument; degrees of perfection argument; First Mover; First Cause; Five Ways; moral argument for the existence of God; natural theology; ontological argument.

Gödel, Kurt (1906-78). Mathematical logician, born in Czechoslovakia, who worked at Princeton, U.S. from 1938. His three major achievements, produced in the 1930s but stimulating much new mathematical work in subsequent decades, were: the completeness proof for the first-order functional calculus; *Gödel's theorem, which had major repercussions on the philosophy of mathematics; and a demonstration that if standard axiomatic *set theory is consistent, it remains consistent upon the addition of the *axiom of choice and the generalized continuum hypothesis.

Gödel's theorem. The proof, published by Kurt Gödel in 1931, of the existence of formally undecidable propositions in any *formal system of arithmetic. More precisely, his *first incompleteness theo-*

rem (which is what is usually meant when people talk of Gödel's theorem) states that in any formal system S of arithmetic, there will be a sentence P of the language of S such that if S is consistent, neither P nor its negation can be proved in S. The technique used in proving this result is to translate the *syntax of the language of S into arithmetic, thus making S capable of representing its own syntax. This makes it possible to show that there must be a sentence P of S which can be interpreted (very roughly) as saying 'I am not provable'. It is shown that if S is consistent, this sentence is not provable, and hence, it is sometimes argued, P must be true. It is this last step which had led people to claim that Gödel's theorem demonstrates the superiority of men over machines—men can prove propositions which no machine (programmed with the axioms and rules of a formal system) can prove. But this is to overlook the point that the proof of the theorem only allows one to conclude that *if S is consistent*, neither P nor its negation is provable in S. One cannot go on to conclude that P is not provable in S, and hence must be true, without having proved the consistency of S. Indeed, because Gödel's proof is formalizable in S, it could be said that one machine T *could* prove of another machine T' that if T' is consistent, there is a proposition that T' cannot prove. But T' could prove exactly the same thing about T. The theorem does not therefore *prove* that men are superior to machines (*see also* complete).

The fact that the first incompleteness proof can be formalized in S allows one to derive Gödel's *second incompleteness theorem* as a corollary. This theorem states that the consistency of a formal system of arithmetic cannot be proved by means formalizable within that system. This result was damaging to the prospects of completing Hilbert's programme for the foundations of mathematics (*see* formalism), for Hilbert had hoped to justify the use, in calculus for example, of the notion of infinity by showing that a formal system governing its use could be shown to be consistent using only finitistic methods (*see* finitism). This would have demonstrated that the notion could be regarded merely as a calculating device whose use was legitimate, in that it would never lead one astray, and justified in terms of economy of labour. But the finitistic methods envisaged are formalizable within a formal system of arithmetic and were thus shown to be inadequate to Hilbert's task.

God of the gaps. The hostile phrase applied to theories appealing to the concept of God to explain anything science currently finds inexplicable, for instance, the origins of life or of consciousness. Theologians now generally regard such appeals as creating only the illusion of explanation, and providing no valid basis or support for *theism.

Godwin, William (1756-1836). British political theorist, essayist, and novelist. In both early and late life, Godwin was regarded as a hack of no great distinction, but in the 1790s he had achieved wide prominence, even notoriety, with his major work, *Enquiry concerning Political Justice* (1793), in which he expressed the view that all types of government and society are necessarily corrupt on account of vested interests in prejudices of nationality and class. His anarchism, which was founded on strict determinist and utilitarian principles (*see* utilitarianism), exercised considerable influence over the radical intellectuals of his time, and particularly attracted the romantics, including *Wordsworth and *Shelley (later Godwin's son-in-law). Godwin's *Enquiry* was one of the main targets of the *First Essay* of *Malthus. *See also* romanticism.

Goethe, Johann Wolfgang von (1749-1832). German poet, writer, and scientist. Goethe's literary reputation was established throughout Europe with his early romantic novel, *The Sorrows of Young Werther* (1774). It was subsequently confirmed by his major work,

Faust (1808 and 1831), and several important novels. While at court in Weimar, he was able to pursue his interest in science, publishing a work on the metamorphosis of plants—highly regarded by *Darwin—and a classic study in the theory of colour.

Although not regarded as himself a philosopher, Goethe maintained a deep interest in philosophical ideas, particularly Spinoza's *pantheism, Leibniz's *panpsychism, and Kant's aesthetics. His influence on German philosophers, especially his friends *Schiller and *Schopenhauer, was considerable. His importance in the development of *romanticism is reflected in the work of the principal philosopher of romanticism, F. W. J. von *Schelling.

golden age. In Greek mythology, a time of paradisal innocence under the rule of Cronus, son of Uranus (Heaven) and Gaea (Earth). The idea of the golden age became a potent literary and artistic emblem for a perfect and harmonious relationship between man and Nature and between man and man.

golden mean. Moderation in a person's course of life. Aristotle saw the mean as the rational and virtuous course between extremes of excess—for example, temperance shunning both asceticism and profligacy. Extolled by Horace (65- 8 BC) as *"aurea mediocritas"* (*Odes* 2.10.5), the golden mean has had widespread appeal as a practical ethical guide. The *Doctrine of the Mean* is, for instance, one of the Four Books of the wholly independent Confucian canon (*see* Confucianism).

golden rule. The maxim 'Do unto others as you would have them do unto you'. Various expressions of this fundamental moral rule are to be found in the tenets of most religions and creeds through the ages, testifying to its universal applicability. Confucius, for instance, was asked whether the true way could be summed up in a single word, and answered, "'Reciprocity' is such a word" (*Analects* XV 23).

Goodman, Nelson (1906-). American philosopher. His main works are *The Structure of Appearance* (1951), *Fact, Fiction and Forecast* (1954); and *Languages of Art* (1969).

Goodman is associated with an extreme nominalism, which he develops through a prolonged attack on the notion of a similarity. It is because people objectify similarities that they think that properties and qualities exist, as well as individual things in space and time. This critique gained much impetus from the discovery of *Goodman's paradox, which Goodman uses to argue for the sway that accidental linguistic history holds over our thinking about the world. He has treated this topic from his first book, a critical study of Carnap's *Aufbau*, right to his last, which applies his view to pictorial as well as linguistic representation.

Goodman's paradox. A linguistic paradox of *confirmation or prediction. We predict by projecting regularities beyond our experience (*see* induction). Goodman showed how to define a vocabulary so that hypotheses that look to us as though they predict change have the linguistic form of projecting a regularity. Goodman introduces a new predicate 'grue', which applies to an object if it has been examined before a certain time *t* and is green, or has not been examined before *t* and is blue. Suppose all emeralds examined up to time *t* have been green. Then these two inductive hypotheses (1) All emeralds are green, and (2) All emeralds are grue, are both equally well supported by the evidence. But we would not choose (2) and predict that emeralds examined after *t* will be grue (and hence blue). The paradox is that there is no evident asymmetry between the vocabularies, so that prediction of change looks as reasonable as prediction of similarity. Goodman's view is that only historical accident makes one system natural to us, since there are no language-independent similarities in things.

grammar, deep and surface. *See* structure, deep and surface.

grammar, generative. *See* generative grammar.

grammatical form. The apparent surface form of an expression, in comparison with the underlying logical structure. In any language some expressions may resemble others in appearance, yet differ fundamentally in their kind of meaning. Such expressions may then be said to be similar in grammatical but different in logical form. In *Through the Looking Glass* Alice said she saw nobody on the road, and the King envied her her eyes: "It's as much as I can do to see real people, by this light!" Lewis Carroll was thus representing him as being misled by the similarity in grammatical form between 'nobody' and 'somebody' into construing both words as having the same logical form, that is, as both referring to a person. *Compare* logical form.

greatest happiness principle (*or* **principle of utility**). The basic tenet of *utilitarianism, which holds that the supreme good is the greatest happiness of the greatest number of people. Happiness is construed as the maximization of pleasure and minimization of pain; it is contended that only in terms of this programme do concepts like 'good', 'duty', and 'right' have meaning and application.

Green, Thomas Hill (1836–82). English philosopher, influential in the 19th-century tradition of philosophical *idealism and political liberalism. His most important writings were the introduction to his edition of Hume's works (1874) and *Prolegomena to Ethics* (1883). In the former he attacked *empiricism, particularly Hume's principle that nothing is real but sensation (*see* sensationalism). Green claimed that to be real is to be related to other things, and that relations are the work of the mind, which is thus not confined to the production of mere feelings. In the latter he again attacked the empiricist doctrine that made feelings the only cause of

human action, rather than the motives of a rational consciousness.

Grelling's paradox (*or* **paradox of heterologicality**). A semantic paradox presented by K. Grelling (1886–) in 1908. Some words have the same property as that which they name: for example, 'short' is a short word and 'polysyllabic' has many syllables. These words are called 'autological'. In contrast, heterological words such as 'useless' or 'monosyllabic' are not instances of the properties they name. The paradox arises when considering the word 'heterological' itself: if it is heterological, then it does not instantiate its meaning—but this *is* what 'heterological' means, therefore the word is autological. Conversely, if 'heterological' is autological, then it must have the characteristic of applying to itself and therefore 'heterological' is heterological.

Grosseteste, Robert (*c.*1170–1253). English philosopher of science, Chancellor of Oxford University, and, from 1235, Bishop of Lincoln. Main works: *De Luce* (On Light), *De Motu Corporali et Luce* (On Corporal Motion and Light), and influential commentaries on Aristotle's *Physics* and *Posterior Analytics*. An important mediator of Arabic and Jewish *Aristotelianism, Grosseteste is chiefly remembered for his metaphysics of light, in which he held that light was God's dynamic agent in the creation, by which unextended matter was expanded to make the finite Universe. Light is also the means by which the soul causes motion in the body.

H

haecceity. (Latin: *haecceitas*) A term originally employed by *Duns Scotus to denote the formal property of an object or person in virtue of which it is uniquely individuated (*see* individuation, principle of) as just *this* object or person. C. S. *Peirce later revived the notion as a means of non-descriptive reference to an individual.

Hallevi, Yehudah (Judah) (before 1075-1141). Born in Spain, Hallevi is primarily remembered as a Hebrew poet. His philosophy is set out in his Arabic prose work *Kitāb al-Hujja waal Dalīl fī Nasr al-Dīn al-Dhalīl* (Book of Argument and Proof in Defence of the Despised Faith), commonly known as the *Kuzari* (The Khazar). Within the literary framework of the conversion of the Khazar king, Bulan, to Judaism (*c.*740), the work expounds the superiority of Judaism to (Aristotelian) philosophy, Christianity, and Islam. Hallevi's attitude to philosophy is complex and romantic. He accepts the need for logical argument, but rejects the primacy of philosophical systems. His attitude is similar to, and perhaps reflects the influence of, that of *al-Ghazālī. History is a more trustworthy guide than unaided reason; this leads Hallevi to a view of the role of the Jewish people and the Land of Israel which has endeared him greatly to modern Zionists.

Hamilton, Sir William (1788-1856). Scottish philosopher, whose main work was published as *Lectures on Metaphysics and Logic* (1859-60). He argued that perception gives us immediate direct (as opposed to representative) knowledge of objects. However, for three reasons, this knowledge is not absolute, but relative. First, the knowledge is purely phenomenal; that is, we perceive only appearances, but these are appearances of an object, which though inconceivable apart from its phenomena, must exist absolutely. Second, knowledge is contributed by the object itself, and then modified by the senses and the media through which we perceive it. (Though as J. S. *Mill pointed out, in *An Examination of Sir William Hamilton's Philosophy* (1865), this only shows that the knowledge not contributed by the object itself is relative.) Third, to think of something is necessarily to think of it under conditions; that is, as a thing of a certain sort, classified under a concept.

Thus the objects of our knowledge are always conditioned in some way.

Hampshire, Stuart Newton (1914-), British philosopher, who has been Grote Professor of the Philosophy of Mind and Logic at University College London (1960-63), Professor of Philosophy at Princeton, U.S. (1963-70), and Warden of Wadham College, Oxford (1970-).

Hampshire's theory of knowledge, metaphysics, ethics, and philosophy of mind are set out in *Thought and Action* (1959). In his view, thought and the use of language presuppose that objects and persons are identifiable persistent beings; the world cannot be analysed in terms of sense impressions. Self-consciousness is awareness of one's situation in the world; personality is not contemplative intellect alone but is also expressed through will and action. Freedom is achieved through knowledge of the factors that make intentions ineffective and of means of modifying these factors. The idea of goodness, though permanently open to reconsideration, is indispensable in providing reasons for action.

Hare, Richard Mervyn (1919-). British moral philosopher, and White's Professor of Moral Philosophy at Oxford (1966-). In *The Language of Morals* (1952) and *Freedom and Reason* (1963) he presents the argument against ethical *naturalism, claiming that moral judgments are not descriptive but imperative, since they have action guiding functions.

harmony of the spheres. *See* music of the spheres.

Hartley, David (1705-57). English philosopher, physician, and psychologist. His major work was *Observations on Man, His Frame, His Duty and His Expectations* (1749), in which he offered an account of human nature based on the doctrine of the association of sensations with sets of ideas. Complex thought processes were to be analysable into clusters and sequences of elementary sense impressions, and all psychological acts should then be explainable by a single law of association. His view that body and mind are a unitary physical and causal system was more influential than the suspect physiology on which he based it. *See also* associationism.

Hasidism. A pietistic mass movement that began among Jews in early 18th-century Russia. Its philosophical roots were in the *Kabbalah.

hatha-yoga. The Indian system of mental and physical training, which is based on certain speculative physiological theories and is intended to give an individual control over his own physical and spiritual well-being. It is commonly known in the West as yoga, but is not to be confused with the *Yoga school of philosophy, with which it shares certain techniques of meditation.

heap, the. *See* millet seed paradox.

hedonism. 1. (in ethics) The principle that happiness (defined in terms of pleasure) is the sole and proper aim of human action. 2. (in psychology) The doctrine that no one in fact ever does or ever can act save to further his own pleasure.

The earliest and most extreme version of the former was advocated by the *Cyrenaics (4th century BC), who claimed that the art of living consists in maximizing the enjoyment of each moment through pleasures of the senses and of the intellect. In contrast, the Epicureans laid emphasis on the attainment of enduring pleasures and the avoidance of pain, stressing the role of prudence and discipline in securing the supreme good: peace of mind (*see* Epicureanism).

In the late 18th century hedonism was revived by *Bentham, both as a theory of normative ethics (*utilitarianism), and as a psychological theory of motivation. Bentham started from the dictum: "Nature has placed mankind under the governance of two sovereign masters, pain and pleasure." He claimed that the only rational and consistent criterion by which the rightness of human action could be judged is that of the beneficial consequences.

The equation of happiness with pleasure had been rejected by philosophers and theologians from the time of Socrates. Psychological hedonism was effectively assailed by *Butler. In the 20th century *Moore pointed out the illegitimacy of deriving the conclusion that pleasure ought to be desired from the fact that men do desire it. Advocates of various forms of utilitarianism have attempted to distinguish between acts that one believes to be conducive to happiness and those that in fact achieve it.

Bentham differentiated betwen various sources of pleasure on the basis of the intensity, duration, immediacy, and certainty of gratification, suggesting that the quantity rather than the quality of pleasure attainable should guide one's choice. In contrast, J.S. *Mill introduced a qualitative distinction between 'higher' and 'lower' pleasures. The charge that egoism characterizes hedonist ethics could be met by the principle of utility (*see* greatest happiness principle) differentiating between acts performed for one's own benefit and those morally commendable actions that afford the greatest possible sum of pleasure for everyone.

Hegel, George Wilhelm Friedrich (1770-1831). German idealist philosopher, born in Stuttgart. His career as a university teacher, which began in 1801, was interrupted by Napoleon's victory at Jena in 1806, and was not resumed until 1816, when Hegel became a professor at Heidelberg. He was professor of philosophy at Berlin from 1818 until his death in 1831. His written works are notoriously obscure; of these his relatively early book *Phänomenologie des Geistes* (1807) referred to hereafter as *The Phenomenology of Mind*, which is often stressed in Marxist writings on Hegel, is the most difficult. Other major works include the *Encyklopädie der philosophischen Wissenschaften im Grundrisse* (1817) and *Naturrecht und Staatswissenschaft im Grundrisse* (1821), referred to hereafter as *The*

Philosophy of Right. His philosophy is perhaps best approached by way of the notes that his pupils took of his lectures, the introductions to the lectures on the philosophy of history and the history of philosophy being particularly helpful.

If there is a key to Hegel's philosophy, it lies in the important position occupied in it by history, and by the history of thought in particular. Hegel's works often refer to earlier philosophers, whom he sees, not as mere providers of an interesting store of fallacies, but as necessary stages in a developing thought process, which cannot be comprehended fully without a knowledge of these stages. A short article cannot put Hegel within the context of the whole history of philosophy, but a little must be said about his relations to his great German predecessor Kant. In the *Critique of Pure Reason*, Kant had been concerned with what he called 'synthetic a priori' truths—truths that are necessary, but not logically necessary. To explain how such truths can be known, Kant argued that the mind is not in a purely passive relation to its objects, but contributes much to them. Much, but not all; there are also 'things-in-themselves', that are wholly independent of any mind, and contribute something to the objects that we know. Things-in-themselves can be thought, but not known, in that they are beyond the reach of experience, whereas the knowledge of objects involves the possibility of experience. Like Kant, Hegel was concerned with truths that are necessary, but not necessary in the way that the truths of formal logic are necessary. But whereas Kant's main concern was with the necessary truths presupposed by the natural sciences, Hegel was more concerned with the necessary truths provided by history, which he regarded as a process that follows necessary laws. (Curiously, he did not extend the idea to cover the evolution of Nature.) Hegel agreed with Kant that necessary truths must be mind-imposed, but, like other critics of Kant, he rejected the idea of the thing-in-itself

as unintelligible. This led him to the view that all that exists must be mental.

Hegel's philosophy is not only a form of *idealism, it is also a form of *monism. For Hegel, there must exist just *one* thinking substance, one subject—where 'subject' means, not so much the logical subject of a proposition, as an agent who thinks of certain things, the objects of the agent's thought. Hegel seems to have been led to monism by considerations about the nature of truth. Like every idealist philosopher, he was faced with a problem that may be put crudely as follows: if everything is in the mind, how is one to distinguish the subjective from the objective, the true from the false? Hegel's reply took the form of a version of the *coherence theory of truth. For him, truth means system; it means, moreover, a unique and complete system. As Hegel put it in the Preface to the *Phenomenology of Mind*, "The true is the whole." His argument is that any single proposition or set of propositions that is less than the complete system of propositions will turn out to be self-contradictory; only in the complete system are contradictions reconciled and falsity removed. This complete system does not *correspond* to reality, it *is* reality—the one reality, the one subject.

Hegel's views about truth have been seen to involve the notion of contradiction, and indeed this notion is a fundamental one in his philosophy. The whole of which he speaks is a developing whole, and it develops through the medium of contradiction. This is the view presented by Hegel's theory of dialectic. The word 'dialectic' is connected with the Greek word 'dialegein', meaning to discourse or argue. Though Hegel did not actually use the terms in this way, his dialectic is generally regarded as a process of argument that proceeds by triads, each triad consisting of thesis, antithesis, and synthesis. One starts with an initial proposition, the thesis; this proves to be inadequate, and generates its opposite, the antithesis. This in turn proves inadequate, and the opposites are taken up into a synthesis.

The synthesis is what Hegel terms the "Aufhebung" (usually rendered as 'sublation') of the thesis and antithesis; that is, it preserves what is rational in them, but cancels what is irrational. This whole triadic process may be repeated, the synthesis leading to a new thesis, and so on.

An example of a triad will help to clarify what is meant. The triad comes from Hegel's major work on moral and political philosophy, *The Philosophy of Right*, and consists of three views about right. Hegel calls these abstract right (the thesis), morality (the antithesis), and ethics (the synthesis). In the first of these, which Hegel ascribes to the Stoics, certain lines of conduct are laid down as universally binding. To that extent, this concept of right is a rational one; however, there is no reference to the individual's conscience, and so the concept is also abstract and legalistic. The opposite view, morality, is ascribed by Hegel to Rousseau; it says that something is right in so far as the individual's conscience approves of it. This, however, is mere subjectivism, as it fails to do justice to the fact that the right thing to do is also the rational thing, and rationality implies universal laws. So we have two contradictory views, neither of which is adequate; they are sublated in the ethical life, the concept of right entertained by a society. Such a concept is not abstract (as abstract right is), yet it is binding on all (which morality is not). This example also illustrates another feature of the dialectic. According to Hegel, a false philosophical doctrine is not refuted by counter-arguments; it collapses of itself, of its own internal weakness. Something of this idea survives in the Marxist view of the collapse of social systems.

So far, Hegel's dialectic has been discussed in terms of the part played in it by contradiction. But the reality that develops by way of contradiction is also a subject, and it is important to grasp Hegel's view about the relation between subject and object. He has said that all that exists is really mind. We may seem to find ourselves confronted by objects, in the sense of entities that are independent of thought, but these objects have no genuinely independent existence, and it is a sign of philosophical progress when this fact is recognized. Hegel describes this situation—the initial illusion and the overcoming of illusion— as the estrangement ("Entfremdung") of mind from itself, and its eventual return to itself. All this is closely linked to what has just been said about sublation; the mind's self-estrangement and return *is* the triadic process, described in another way. Both have to do with the mind's gradual achievement of full awareness of the nature of reality, which is also an awareness of its own nature. There is an important point about terminology to be made here. In place of the word 'Entfremdung' (estrangement) Hegel sometimes uses the term 'Entäusserung', often translated as 'alienation'. These terms reappear in the context of the complicated theories of *alienation to be found in the early writings of Marx and in much modern Marxism. It should be stressed, however, that 'alienation' is not a good term for what Hegel has in mind when he speaks of 'Entfremdung' or 'Entäusserung'. His concern is with a philosophical analysis of the concept of an object; he thinks of an object as that which is extraneous (fremd) to the human mind, external (ausser) to it.

So far, very little has been said about what sublates what; by what stages the mind "returns to itself". Hegel gives a systematic account of these stages in his *Encyklopädie*. This work has three parts. The first is called 'Logic' (also termed 'The Lesser Logic', to distinguish it from the two-volume *Wissenschaft der Logik* (1812-13, 1816)); the second is called 'The Philosophy of Nature' and the third 'The Philosophy of Mind'. Hegel's 'Logic' is not a treatise on formal logic. Hegel calls logic "the science of thought"; and since, for him, thought is reality, the science of thought turns out to be a metaphysics. It differs from the other parts of Hegel's philosophy by virtue of its relative abstractness; it presents abstract patterns which the philosophies of nature and mind—called by Hegel "applied logic"—present in a more concrete form. Hegel divides logic into three main parts, the theories of being, essence, and the notion, the third of which is the sublation of the others. The theory of being is subdivided into accounts of quality, quantity, and measure; in the course of the last of these, Hegel discusses the transformation of quantity into quality, which reappears in Marxist dialectics. His main concern here seems to be to attack the traditional doctrine that "nature makes no leaps." This doctrine, says Hegel, is simply false; there are many cases (for example, the transformation of water into steam or ice) in which a new state does not appear gradually, but appears as a leap. In general, Hegel's theory of being is devoted to the analysis of that kind of thinking in which we regard things as simply given to us and leave the matter there, without asking the question, "Why?". When we do ask this question we are employing a different kind of thinking, described by Hegel under the title of "essence". In effect, when Hegel speaks of essence he is referring to the way in which the natural scientist, and in particular the physicist, reasons. The physicist tries to establish necessary relations, and as such, his thinking is superior to thought at the level of being, where things are taken for granted and no attempt is made to explain them. However, essence is in turn inferior to the notion; that is, physics is not the paradigm of rational thinking. It is deficient, Hegel argues, in that it is unable to explain processes of a teleological kind (see teleology). Here, Hegel is not referring simply to the growth of living things of all kinds. If he were, the whole of his section on the notion would be open to serious scientific criticism, in that Hegel could be accused of clinging to a now outmoded *vitalism. Really, however, Hegel's chief concern here is with conscious agents. In the technical terms of his philosophy, what is involved in the section on the notion is not so

much the category of *substance* (that belongs to the realm of essence) as that of *subject*. At the level of the notion we understand *that substance *is* subject, *is* mind, is a self-developing conscious whole.

'The Philosophy of Nature' is Hegel's attempt to fit natural science into his dialectical scheme. Hegelian scholars have noted the great efforts that Hegel made to keep abreast of the science of his day, but it cannot be said that he grasped the direction in which science was moving. In chemistry he rejected the atomic theory and tried to defend Aristotle's theory of the *four elements; in optics he rejected *Newton in favour of the German poet *Goethe. Of much greater value is the third part of his system, 'The Philosophy of Mind'. This consists of three parts: 'Subjective Mind', 'Objective Mind', and 'Absolute Mind'. The first of these studies the mind of the individual in abstraction from his social relations; the second studies mind in its social context; the third and highest stage is concerned with art, religion, and philosophy. Hegel's strength as a philosopher is perhaps best displayed in his account of objective mind, particularly as developed, not in the restricted space available in the *Encyklopädie*, but in *The Philosophy of Right*. The relations between the three main parts of this work—'Abstract Right', 'Morality', and 'Ethics'—have already been described. The main point made by Hegel is that an adequate account of moral virtue cannot be given if the individual is divorced from society. Hegel answers the question, "What kind of society?" in the third part of *The Philosophy of Right*, in which he distinguishes between the family, civil society, and their sublation, the state. Civil society is called by Hegel "the external state", and "the state based on need". This does not just mean a society viewed in purely economic terms, though this is an element in Hegel's meaning. In calling civil society the external state, Hegel is also saying that in such a state there is a distinction between us and them. This is eliminated in what Hegel calls the state, in which controllers and controlled are the same; a society in which there is not determination from outside, but self-determination—in other words, freedom.

Hegel is often accused of state-worship; still worse, of worshipping Prussian autocracy. This is unjust. As a young man he had, like many of his contemporaries, greeted the French Revolution with enthusiasm. But he was disgusted by the excesses of the Terror, to which he devoted some of his most powerful pages (see the section entitled 'Absolute Freedom and Terror' in *The Phenomenology of Mind*). This does not mean that the mature Hegel turned into a reactionary defender of Prussianism. Rather, Hegel's politics were those of a cautious liberal; the constitutional monarchy which he describes approvingly in *The Philosophy of Right* is not an absolute monarchy of the Prussian type. Nor, indeed, can Hegel be accused of state-worship of any kind. As has been seen, the highest level of mind for Hegel is not the state, which is only the highest level of objective mind; the highest level is absolute mind.

To grasp the relations between objective and absolute mind it is necessary to consider the state not as an entity that is relatively fixed and independent, but as something that has a history and relations to other states. The Hegelian state is a nation-state, and each nation or people (*Volk*) has its own mind or spirit (*Volksgeist*). Each "mind of a people" has a history of its own, a history of development, maturity, and decline. But history as a whole forms an intelligible pattern; each mind of a people is a link in a chain of progress, the culmination of which is the "world-mind" (*Weltgeist*). This world-mind differs only in subtle respects from what Hegel calls "absolute mind". For Hegel, then, thought culminates in art, religion, and philosophy. He insists that art is not just a means of expressing or evoking feelings, but is a kind of thought; it is a way of apprehending reality, which it presents in the form of what can be

sensed. Religion, too, is a way of apprehending reality, but it works through the medium of "Vorstellung", which may be freely rendered as 'pictorial thinking'. But because religion works through the medium of images, it is not the highest form of thought. Hegel reserves this place for thinking of a pure, imageless kind, namely, philosophy.

Hegelianism. The views of those who claim to uphold the doctrines of Hegel have shown considerable differences, not only because of the obscurity of Hegel's writings, but also because there was a fundamental ambivalence in his views. Hegel had argued that history is a process which has a rational end, and soon after his death there was disagreement among his followers about the rationality of the state that history had reached. The so-called Old Hegelians argued that contemporary political conditions were rational; the Young Hegelians disagreed, and said that the business of philosophy was to promote a revolution—more specifically, a revolution of ideas. There was also disagreement about the religious implications of Hegel's thought, the Old Hegelians saying that Hegel had reconciled religion and philosophy, the Young Hegelians arguing that a Hegelian approach to religion must be a critical one. As philosophers, most of the Young and Old Hegelians are of little intrinsic interest; the chief exception is Ludwig *Feuerbach (1804-72), who began as a disciple of Hegel but who later rejected Hegelianism, and whose views, along with those of some other Young Hegelians, influenced the young Marx.

Adverse political conditions led to the extinction of Hegelianism in Germany soon after 1840, and interest in Hegel was not revived there until the first decade of this century. Meanwhile, there were Hegelian movements elsewhere. The British idealists (*see also* idealism), who may be said to date from the 1870s, resembled the Old Hegelians in that they saw Hegel as reconciling science with religion; politically, they viewed Hegelianism as an answer to Victorian *laissez faire.* In Italy, Benedetto *Croce and Giovanni *Gentile have in this century presented versions of Hegelianism. Gentile compromised with Italian fascism, but Croce remained faithful to liberal ideals. In France, interest in Hegel was stimulated in the 1930s and afterwards by Alexandre Kojève, who interpreted Hegel from a Marxist-existentialist point of view. The influence of Hegelianism in Britain declined as a result of the attacks on idealism made by Russell and Moore in the early years of this century. However, there has recently been a revival of interest in Hegel among English-speaking philosophers, though it cannot be said that this amounts to a new Hegelian movement.

Heidegger, Martin (1889-1976). German philosopher. He studied under *Husserl and became Rector of Freiburg University in 1933. After World War II, Heidegger resumed lecturing to a restricted circle of students. Main philosophical treatise: *Sein und Zeit* (1927).

Although Heidegger did not regard himself as an existentialist, he was influenced by *Kierkegaard. Heidegger's *ontology is echoed in existentialist writing, including the works of *Sartre. Heidegger adopted Husserl's phenomenological method (*see* phenomenology) in order to examine the data of immediate experience, discarding preconceived epistemological and logical constructions that make a distinction between consciousness and the external world; any theory formulated in terms of a perceiving subject as a spectator demanding proof of an objective world is absurd in failing to give an account of that which can demand such proof.

Existence can be apprehended only through the analysis and description of human 'being' (*see* Dasein), the basic mode of being in the world through participation and involvement. The world is conceived and conceptualized as structurally differentiated into regions (existential modalities and their modifications). The environment (*Umwelt*) is constituted of objects that are accessible

and utilizable for purposive action. Action and knowledge are inseparably related: the concept of a utensil (*Zuhandsein*, or 'being-at-hand') is epistemologically prior to the objectivized conception of a thing (*Vorhandsein*, or 'being-onhand') that can be scientifically investigated. *Dasein* is also communality; the modifications of the communal region (*Mitwelt*) are the 'authentic' recognized unique being among other human agents 'at-hand' and the 'unauthentic' retreat into anonymity, reducing the self and others to 'on-hand' existents. The notion of time is also subjected to this distinction: objective time is a succession of discrete moments (on-hand entities); as an area of subjective human concern time is revealed as inseparable phases of existence, past and future being as 'real' as the present.

The 'authentic' self is potentiality for action, characterized by its orientation towards the future, entailing possibilities and the constant necessity of choice. Every choice is understood as the exclusion of the alternative, through which the 'nothingness' aspect of existence is expressed. The past is significant in terms of unrealized possibilities that relate to the present and future; from these unrealized possibilities stem guilt and anxiety (*see* Angst), recognizing the 'nothingness' in present and future choices and the finiteness of the time allotted.

heliocentric theory. The theory, first advanced by Aristarchus of Samos (310-230 BC) that the earth and planets revolve round the sun, which remains fixed, and that the earth rotates on its own axis throughout its orbit. Revived by *Copernicus in refuting the *Ptolemaic system, and upheld by *Galileo, the idea of the earth not being at the centre of the universe was opposed as much in the times of Aristarchus as in 16th and 17th-century Europe, on the grounds that it depreciated man's place in the Universe.

Hellenistic philosophy. The Hellenistic period in Greek history runs from 323 BC, the year of Alexander the Great's death, to 30 BC when the last major Hellenistic empire was annexed by Rome. Philosophy in this period centred on Athens. Of the four major schools there (Academic, Peripatetic, Epicurean, and Stoic), the Epicureans, with their hedonistic ethics and denial of providence, were the outsiders. The contrary belief (derived ultimately from Socrates) in a purposive universe and in the right exercise of reason as the supreme human good found its most forceful advocates in the Stoics. Their principal opponents came from the *Academy of Athens with its "sceptical" rejection of all positive "dogmatic" belief. Controversy between Stoics and Academics dominated the philosophical scene in the 3rd and 2nd centuries BC. Later there arose a tendency, variously represented by Panaetius, Posidonius, and Antiochus, to combine Stoicism with the Platonic and Aristotelian doctrines, that ultimately submerged it.

Hellenistic philosophy was characterized by the systematic organization of its subject matter into logic, physics, and ethics. Ethics was the supreme study, since the accepted purpose of philosophy was to secure the happy life. Its two leading systems, *Stoicism and *Epicureanism, concentrated here on personal morality, paying little, if any, attention to problems of political or social organization. The ethics of both groups were naturalistic and "this-worldly", a characteristic reflecting the thoroughgoing materialism of their physics. By 30 BC, however, a portentous revival of "other-worldly" Platonic and Pythagorean speculations had begun. Stoic, Epicurean, and sceptical philosophies continued for another three centuries, and most of our sources for them date from this 'Roman' period. But the preoccupations of philosophers in later antiquity became ever more religious, a development that led to the *Neoplatonism of Plotinus and his successors.

Helvétius, Claude-Adrien (1715-71).

French philosopher and philanthropist, one of the *Encyclopedists.

In *De l'esprit* (1758) he advanced the view that the source of all intellectual activity is physical sensation; self-interest—the love of pleasure and fear of pain—is the foundation of action and affection. All intellects are equal, differing only in the degree of their desire for instruction. The book was translated into the principal European languages and strongly influenced *Bentham and advocates of *utilitarianism. But it was denounced by the Sorbonne, and publicly burnt in Paris.

Hempel, Carl Gustav (1905-). German empiricist, who worked in America after 1937. In addition to the important articles collected in *Aspects of Scientific Explanation* (1965), his work includes 'A Definition of "Degree of Confirmation"' (*Philosophy of Science*, 1945), written with Paul Oppenheim, and *Fundamentals of Concept Formation in Empirical Science* (1952).

Hempel belongs, with *Carnap, to the sober aftermath of *logical positivism, when it was realized that the distinction between "respectable" science and "disreputable" metaphysics badly needs an account of the way scientific theory relates to experience. His work on the way in which an observation report confirms a generalization led to the paradox that bears his name. Observing a black raven ought to confirm the hypothesis that all ravens are black; equally, observing a non-black non-raven ought to confirm the hypothesis that all non-black things are non-ravens; yet the second hypothesis is logically equivalent to the first, so observation of a white shoe ought to confirm that all ravens are black. But intuitively, it does not. This is one example of the difficulties that formal confirmation theory meets. Hempel also originated the influential model of scientific theory in terms of covering laws deduced from other laws further up a hierarchy of increasing generality. *See* covering law model.

henological argument. An alternative name for the *degrees of perfection argument for the existence of God.

Heraclitus of Ephesus (died after 480 BC). Greek philosopher known as "the obscure", "the riddler", and "the weeping philosopher". The most famous doctrine attributed to him was that all things are in a state of flux: even the unchanging hills change, but more slowly than most other things. This doctrine was, however, certainly balanced by a notion of *logos, the word or reason, which keeps everything in order, and there was also some doctrine, hailed by *Hegel, of the unity of *opposites. Heraclitus postulated fire as the basic matter of the universe; for him the fire of the human soul was related to the cosmic fire, which virtuous souls eventually join. *See* Presocratics.

Herbert of Cherbury, Edward, Lord (1583–1648). British philosopher of religion. Main works: *De Veritate* (1624), *De Causis Errorum* (1645), *De Religione Gentilium* (1663). Herbert is regarded as the first English author of a purely metaphysical thesis. He was unconcerned by the appearance of new scientific ideas, and appears to have believed that the wider the acceptance of a proposition, the more likely it was to be true. Divine Providence had given all mankind the "Common Notions" (including religion and law), about which, he believed, all those of sound mind, including pagans, were in general agreement. For Herbert ecclesiastical institutions and ecclesiastics obscured natural religion ('natural' in contrast to varied and uncertain 'revelation') so that it was necessary to investigate historically the origins of all religions. (*De Religione Gentilium* is one of the first treatises on comparative religion.) Where religion is concerned, the Common Notions (whose presence in a religion certifies its universality and truth) were that: (1) there is one supreme God; (2) he ought to be worshipped; (3) moral rectitude and piety are the main part of worship; (4) humans must repent their sins; (5) divine goodness will requite merits and demerits during and after mortal life. Herbert's theory of (God-given) innate ideas was attacked by *Locke, who not only did not believe in innate ideas but thought that, if there were any, their innateness would not guarantee their truth.

Herder, Johann Gottfried von (1744–1803). German philosopher and critic. Main works: *Abhandlung über den Ursprung der Sprache* (1772), translated as *Treatise upon the Origin of Language* (1827) and *Ideen zur Philosophie der Geschichte der Menschheit* (1784–91), translated as *Outline of a Philosophy of the History of Man* (1800). Herder's philosophy of psychology, language, art, and history, and criticism of the *Enlightenment, were formative in the development of the romantic movement (*see* romanticism). He attacked the prevailing compartmentalized view of the mind, insisting that perceiving, reasoning, feeling, etc., were not separate faculties and, especially, that reasoning and the use of language could not be separated.

In aesthetics Herder argued against the ideas of a constant innate faculty of taste and an unchanging uniform standard of beauty, holding that historical, environmental, and psychological factors mould artistic concepts at different times. His most influential and wide-ranging work was in the philosophy of history, where he again argued against imposing an overall immutable standard by which to judge historical periods, behaviour, and ideals. These could not be understood unless treated sympathetically and seen as growing organically in response to a particular temporal and spatial environment.

hereditary property. A term used in formal logic. An R-hereditary property (where R is a relation) is any property P such that for any objects b and c, if c has the property p and b stands in the relation R to c, then b also has the property, p. For instance, if R is the relation 'is greater by three than' the property of being exactly divisible by three is *R*-hereditary among numbers, since, for any numbers *b* and *c*, if *c* is exactly divisible by three, and *b* is greater by three than *c*, then *b* is exactly divisible by three.

hermeneutics. **1.** (in theology) The interpretation of the spiritual truth of the Bible. **2.** (in social philosophy) The term imported from theology by *Dilthey, used to denote the discipline concerned with the investigation and interpretation of human behaviour, speech, institutions, etc., as essentially intentional. **3.** (in existentialism) Enquiry into the purpose of human existence.

hermeticism. The occult tradition based on the late antique treatises known by the collective title of the *Corpus Hermeticum*. In the Renaissance, its imaginary author, the Egyptian priest, Hermes Trismegistus, was often credited with an antiquity equal to that of Moses and held to be the spokesman par excellence for gentile philosophy as Moses was for the Hebrew tradition. *Ficino, for instance, who translated part of the *Corpus* into Latin, believed that he was dealing with the ancient Egyptian sources of Platonic philosophy. The treatises contain a blend of philosophical, religious, magical, and mystical material that was absorbed into Renaissance *Neoplatonism, *alchemy, and other similar esoteric traditions. In 1614 Isaac Casaubon demonstrated the post-Christian origins of the *Corpus Hermeticum*; its history is still obscure, but recent scholarship has suggested both a composition date between 100 and 300 AD and that the *Corpus* may constitute the literature of a gnostic sect. *See also* gnosticism.

Herodotage. A colloquial name for anthropological literature in which human habits, customs, and beliefs are compared (*see* relativism). The reference is to a confrontation, recorded in the Greek historian Herodotus, between rival commitments to burying, burning, or eating dead relations (*History* III 37-8).

Heschel, Abraham Joshua (1907-72). American philosopher of religion and historian of Jewish philosophy. Main philosophical works: *Man is Not Alone* (1951), *Man's Quest for God* (1954), *God in Search of Man* (1956). Heschel's standpoint is one of religious existentialism rooted in a profound knowledge of classical Jewish philosophical and mystical sources. He also published critical studies of earlier Jewish thinkers, among them, Sa'adya (1944) and Maimonides (1935), in which he stressed the limitations of the rationalistic approach to religious thought and the correspondingly greater significance of personal faith.

heterological. Inapplicable to itself. For example, 'French' is heterological because it is not a French word (*compare* homological). *See* Grelling's paradox.

heuristic. Serving to indicate or stimulate investigation. In many cases it involves proceeding to a solution by trial and error in the absence of an *algorithm. In modern logic, the word describes a process that may solve a particular kind of problem but offers no guarantee of success.

higher order logic. The study of validity in languages of second, or higher, order. The order of an expression can be defined as follows. Expressions standing for individual objects have order *O*. A predicate (open *wff) is of order $n+1$ if it contains free variables for which expressions of order *n* may be substituted and no variables (free or bound) for expressions of order greater than *n* (*see* variable). Any expression formed from a predicate of order $n+1$ by substitution of constants for variables, or by quantification, is also of order $n+1$. Thus if $x_1,\ldots,x_n$ are individual variables, '$Px_1,\ldots,x_n$' is a first order predicate, as are 'Fx_1', 'Gx_2', Fx_1 & Gx_2' and '$(x_1)Px_1,\ldots,x_n$', where '*P*', '*F*', and '*G*' contain no variables other than those indicated. '$(x_1)Fx_1$' would then be a first order sentence. A first order language is one all of whose sentences are first order expressions. A second order language is one containing first order predicate variables, and hence open wffs of second order, but no expressions of any higher order.

An example of a second order predicate would be 'ϕ is a transitive relation', where ϕ is a variable that can be replaced by some expression standing for a first order predicate. For example, '"weighs more than" is a transitive relation; "is the father of" is not a transitive relation'. An English sentence that invites representation by a formal sentence involving quantification over first order predicates is 'The Smiths have everything that the Joneses have'. This sentence does not mean that the Smiths jointly own the Joneses' colour T.V., washing machine, etc., but rather that for *every kind of appliance* (each kind of appliance being distinguished by means of a predicate such as 'is a colour T.V.', 'is a washing machine', etc.) if the Joneses own an appliance of that kind, the Smiths do as well.

To provide singular terms to replace first order variables, a second order language may contain an *operator which, when applied to a first order predicate expression yields a singular term. For example, Russell used the notation '$P\hat{x}$', which since it contains a bound individual variable, is a first order expression. A second order language need not contain such an operator; it may contain only first order predicate variables and no singular terms for first order predicates.

It is often, but not always, possible to treat predicate variables as set variables, and since set theory can be expressed in a first order language, this avoids the use of higher order languages. Another way of avoiding the use of higher order languages is to distinguish between object language and metalanguage, where the individual variables of the metalanguage range over all expressions of the object language, but if the languages are distinct, each can be treated as a first order language. Such moves are felt to be desirable because of the complications involved in the definitions of 'interpretation' and 'validity' (*see* interpretation; validity and truth) for higher order languages.

Hindu philosophy. Just as it is impossible satisfactorily to define Hinduism as a religion, no definition of what is typically Hindu philosophy is possible. It can only be described as those forms of philosophical thought that, regardless of their origins and original motivation, allied themselves with, and were accepted by, the very complex religious superstructure called 'Hinduism', which set itself in opposition to materialism, Jainism, and Buddhism. For most practical purposes, the *Vedānta and *Mīmāmsā alone are strictly 'Hindu', by virtue either of their adherence to the fundamental scriptures and rites of Hinduism, or simply because they were accepted as such by the Hindus (thus the *advaita* Vedânta of Śankara, strictly speaking, transcends Hindu religion). The four other systems (*Sāmkhya, *Yoga, *Nyāya, and *Vaiśeṣika), which Hinduism includes in its traditional list of six 'orthodox' systems (*darśanas*), are only nominally Hindu (or religious in the general sense of the word). In particular, the Vaiśeṣika and the Nyāya differ far more from the Vedânta than do the Buddhist *Madhyamaka or *Vijñānavāda. *See* Indian philosophy.

historical explanation. A topic that has been the focus of considerable discussion and argument in the philosophy of history. Recent controversy, which echoes earlier disputes concerning the relations between the human studies and the natural sciences, has largely revolved round two opposed claims: the contention that such explanation conforms in its essential structure to explanations of the kind typified in scientific contexts, and the contrary contention that it is *sui generis*, being susceptible to a quite different pattern of analysis. Proponents of the first position, originally favoured by logical empiricists eager to uphold the unity of scientific method, have invoked the deductive-nomological (or *covering law) model of explanation; an event is explained, in history as elsewhere, in so far as the assertion of its occurrence is derivable from premises comprising descriptions of initial conditions together with 'universal hypotheses' or laws. Proponents of the second, on the other hand, have stressed the crucial role played by notions like meaning and intention in the understanding of human behaviour; it is argued that these set historical accounts within a teleological or rational framework of interpretation that has no counterpart at the level of scientific thought and enquiry.

historical materialism. *See* dialectical materialism.

historicism. A term somewhat confusingly used to designate a variety of distinguishable methodological views relating to history and society. The following may be singled out as central. **1.** Doctrines, often held to have relativist implications, to the effect that all systems of thought and knowledge must be judged within a perspective of historical change or development. **2.** Claims about the specific nature of historical enquiry that typically stress empathetic understanding and the interpretation of past events in their unique particularity. **3.** Conceptions of social science as being concerned with the discovery of 'laws of development' that govern the historical process and permit long-term social forecasts and predictions. *See also* Collingwood; Popper; Spengler; Vico.

history, philosophy of. Two separate branches of enquiry, commonly distinguished as *speculative* and *critical*.

1. *Speculative philosophy of history.* Enquiry characteristically undertaken with the aim of providing an interpretation of the human past considered as a whole. Those who have embarked upon such an enterprise have regarded the course taken by history as conforming to some general order or design, the task of the philosopher (unlike that of the ordinary practising historian)

being one of eliciting a comprehensive pattern in terms of which the historical process in its totality can be seen to have a 'meaning' or to exhibit an overall direction. In its earlier manifestations this mode of approaching the past often mirrored theological concerns and was primarily inspired by the thought that whatever happened in history unfolded in accordance with a divinely ordained plan.

Later developments, however, were influenced by quite different considerations. The 17th century witnessed rapid advances in the physical sciences and in the succeeding two centuries it was widely assumed that social and historical phenomena must be subject to universal laws comparable to those successfully established within the sphere of Nature. From such a standpoint the claim that history followed a predictable course or direction was held to be justifiable on purely empirical grounds rather than by an appeal to religious or metaphysical dogma; at the same time, it was treated by many Enlightenment and post-Enlightenment thinkers (for example, Condorcet, Comte, and Marx) as lending support to programmes of political or economical reform. Even so, not all historical theorists of the period conceived their function to be one of constructing interpretations along lines suggested by the natural sciences; systems of the kind propounded by *Vico and *Hegel, for instance, were imbued with a belief in the unique status and character of historical knowledge and were structured according to teleological, as opposed to causal or 'mechanistic', principles. During the 20th century the assumptions underlying all forms of historical speculation have been subjected to severe re-appraisal and criticism, with the result that the most recent large-scale contributions to the genre (those by Spengler and Toynbee) have tended to meet with a predominantly sceptical response.

2. *Critical philosophy of history.* Enquiry primarily concerned, not with the human past itself, but with modes of

thought and enquiry about that past. Thus it takes as its subject matter the categories in terms of which the historian seeks to comprehend and interpret his material and the presuppositions that underlie his procedures. As such, it is a second-order discipline, which in the first instance evolved in response to methodological issues arising from the proliferation of historical studies during the 19th century. The contention that history had finally taken shape as an autonomous form of thinking, distinguishable from other types of investigation but not for that reason inferior, was central to the work of continental philosophers such as *Dilthey and *Croce at the turn of the present century, and it was later to be given eloquent expression by the British writer, R. G. *Collingwood. Although originally strongly influenced by idealist preconceptions, critical philosophy of history in its subsequent development has tended to reflect aims and methods associated with contemporary analytical trends. Controversy has chiefly focused upon the historian's use of explanatory concepts and upon the question of whether historical understanding is essentially different from understanding in other fields. Problems relating to the possibility of achieving objectivity in historical description and to the role and responsibility of historical agents have also attracted considerable attention. *See also* historical explanation; historicism.

Hobbes, Thomas (1588-1679). British philosopher and political scientist. Born the second son of a wayward country vicar, Hobbes was sustained throughout a long life and many works by the patronage of the great, mainly and most happily that of William Cavendish, first Earl of Devonshire. The only nearly complete edition of the English and Latin *Works* of Hobbes (published 1839-40) is by the *Philosophical Radical Sir William Molesworth. The series begins with a translation of Thucydides' *History of the Peloponnesian War* and ends, when the author was in his late eighties,

with two swan songs in the shape of translations into English verse of both the *Iliad* and *Odyssey* of Homer.

Like Locke and Kant, but unlike Berkeley and Hume, Hobbes matured late. His friend John Aubrey in *Brief Lives* tells how the intellectual great awakening of Hobbes occurred "in a gentleman's library" when he chanced upon the theorem of Pythagoras in Euclid. This at once "made him in love with geometry", sweeping him away by its irresistible deductive power and compulsive certainty. Rationalist inspiration mated with the theoretical concern with politics that had led Hobbes to translate Thucydides, whom he was to describe, with reason, as "the most politic historiographer that ever writ". The first births of this union were hastened by the foresight of impending civil war; just—as Hobbes always used to say in order to explain and excuse his supposed constitutional timorousness— "His mother fell in labour with him upon the fright of the Invasion of the Spaniards."

One offspring was "a little treatise in English" of which "though not printed, many gentlemen had copies". Since its immediate implications were royalist, on the assembly of the Long Parliament in 1640 "Mr. Hobbes, doubting how they would use him, went over into France, the first of all that fled". There *Mersenne immediately persuaded him to write the Third Set of Objections to be published with the forthcoming *Meditations* of *Descartes. The other and more substantial first birth was the Latin *De Cive* (Concerning the Citizen), a treatise expounding what Hobbes saw as his new science of the state. This was specifically not the mere political geography which, since Aristotle founded the subject, had passed as political science. Hobbes, as he thought, was on to the real thing, a new science strictly on a par with the work of his friends Harvey and Galileo. (It was Galileo who "was the first that opened to us the gate of natural philosophy universal", while "the science of man's body ... was first discovered ... by our countryman Dr. Harvey". However, "civil philosophy", the political equivalent of the natural philosophy which we call physics, "is no older ... than my own book *De Cive*".)

That putative new political science was represented, along with the best of what Hobbes had to say about everything else, in *Leviathan*, which is, by common consent, his masterpiece. It was in the year of this publication, 1651, that Hobbes returned home and, in full accordance with his own undemanding political principles, made his peace with the now firmly established parliamentary regime. Like Descartes, Hobbes believed that the secret of success was to find and use the right method. But for him this was the method that Galileo and Harvey learnt in the University of Padua. In the Preface to *De Cive* Hobbes writes: "... everything is best understood by its constitutive causes. For as in a watch ... the matter, figure, and motion of the wheels cannot be well known, except it be taken insunder and viewed in parts; to make a more curious search into the rights of states and duties of subjects, it is necessary (I say, not to take them insunder, but yet that) they be so considered as if they were dissolved".

Hobbes therefore proceeds to consider what men are like, and, more particularly, what they would be like if all the restraints of law and society were removed. From Galileo Hobbes had caught a vision of a Universe in motion. Just as the restless atoms are the sole components of a through and through mechanical Universe, so we ourselves are the turbulent creatures that alone compose every social machine. To understand the nature and the function of the state, we have to consider what our condition would be if there were no state; what sometimes indeed, when that machinery has collapsed, it actually is. This is the Hobbist state of nature and, Hobbes insists, it would be "a war of every man, against every man". This often quoted purple passage ends: "And the life of man, solitary, poor, nasty,

brutish, and short" (*Leviathan*, chapter 13).

Whereas for *Locke the state of nature was going to be a condition in which some of everyone's ancestors did once live, and from which they in fact escaped by making a social contract, for Hobbes the crux is not historical but hypothetical. This is what would happen if..., and what will happen unless.... Our only security lies in concentrating all the powers of the sovereign state into the hands of "one man or assembly of men"; though Hobbes expresses a personal preference for monarchy as opposed to any form of collective leadership. How such sovereign powers first originated Hobbes does not speculate, although he recognizes that they can be and are extended when peoples defeated in war pledge obedience in return for their lives. Once Hobbist man is clearly seized of this lesson about the nature and function of the sovereign state, then he is bound to submit to and sustain all such established powers, including the new regime that succeeded and executed Charles I: "For every man is desirous of what is good for him, and shuns what is evil, but chiefly the chiefest of natural evils, which is death; and this he doth by a certain impulsion of nature, no less than that whereby a stone moves downward."

In detail Hobbes is concerned to show what various capacities the state must have if it is to perform its function, and by this he makes a major contribution to the definition of 'sovereignty'. He also works with a distinctive notion of a law of nature as "a precept or general rule, found out by reason, by which a man is forbidden, to do that which is destructive of his life or taketh away the means of preserving the same, and to omit that by which he thinketh it may best be preserved" (chapter 14). This is very different from the prescriptive moral law of nature found later in Locke as well as in earlier tradition. It is like nothing so much as the popular so-called law of self-preservation, which possesses an effective prescriptive force based on the pretence that it expresses an inescapable descriptive law of human conduct.

What has been and is most studied and valued in Hobbes is his contribution to political thought. But he was also the founding father of modern metaphysical *materialism: "the Universe, that is the whole mass of things that are, is corporeal, that is to say body" (chapter 46). This commitment Hobbes followed right through to the end. Where every contemporary was careful to provide for incorporeal spiritual substances, exemplified in God and the human soul, Hobbes argued with a perhaps reckless and certainly characteristic audacity that all such talk is quite simply incoherent and absurd. God? God is a great corporeal Spirit; yes, altogether corporeal, albeit of an exceptionally refined constitution. And people? Here Hobbes takes the Aristotelian and Rylean line that talk about our minds or souls is just a special sort of talk about the corporeal creatures that we are. It is no better than absurd, "when a man is dead and buried", for anyone to say that "his soul (that is his life) can walk separated from his body, and is seen by night amongst the graves" (chapter 46).

Descartes—that "French cavalier who set forth with so bold a stride"—saw reason to maintain only that all inanimate nature, the brutes, and the human body, are or may be regarded as machines. Hobbes has no orthodox or Cartesian inhibitions. The whole Universe is mechanical; not excluding, indeed particularly including, the state and man.

Two sets of suggestions in Hobbes are of special interest. First, he maintained, both in a long controversy with Bishop Bramhall and elsewhere, a compatibilist position about freewill (see freewill and determinism): "Liberty and necessity are consistent: as in the water, that hath not only liberty but also a necessity of descending by the channel." Second, Hobbes had a general interest in the use and abuse of language. He believed that a deal of pretentious technical sounding talk could be utterly deflated by trying

and failing to discover its cash value in the down to earth vernacular. Particularly in the philosophy of religion—especially in the final anti-Catholic chapters of *Leviathan*—Hobbes attacks doctrines not as unscriptural or as merely false but as incoherent and absurd. To Hobbes as an erastian, anti-clerical materialist the doctrine of transubstantiation was peculiarly offensive: "they say that the figure, and colour, and taste of a piece of bread, has a being, there, where they say there is no bread … . The Egyptian conjurors, that are said to have turned their rods to serpents, and the water into blood, are thought but to have deluded the senses of the spectators by a false show of things, yet are esteemed enchanters. But what should we have thought of them, if there had appeared in their rods nothing like a serpent, and in the water enchanted, nothing like blood, nor like anything else but water, but that they had faced down the King that they were serpents that looked like rods, and that it was blood that seemed water?" (chapters 46, 44).

holism. 1. The contention that wholes, or some wholes, are more than the sum of their parts. One special version is organicism, urging that some systems that are not literally organisms are nevertheless crucially like organisms, whose parts can only be understood in relation to their functions in the complete and ongoing whole. **2.** (in the social sciences and history). A theory that claims that society may, or should, be studied in terms of social wholes: that is, that the fundamental data of social analyses are not individuals or individual manifestations but rather societal laws, dispositions, and movements (see methodological holism and methodological individualism). **3.** (in politics) Views that, like the Platonic or the Marxist, grant little political authority or significance to the role of the individual. Holism, which in this sense is sometimes called collectivism, is central to idealist theories of the state, particularly those inspired by *Hegel. 4. The philosophical system of Jan Smuts (1870-1950), South African statesman, who published his views of the operation of the "holistic factor" in history in *Holism and Evolution* (1926).

homological. Describing an association or similarity based on a correspondence in structure, origin, and development, though not necessarily in function. It is also used to express a particular relation that a word may have to itself, that is, when it applies to itself. For example, 'English' is an English word.

homonym. A word with the same form or sound as another but different in meaning, as pole (flag) and pole (magnetic) or bear (grizzly) and bear (children). *Compare* antonym; synonym.

Hook, Sidney (1902-). New York philosopher profoundly influenced by John *Dewey. Hook was for some years a spokesman for Marxism as conceived in his own *Towards an Understanding of Karl Marx* (1933). But he later became very active in the defence of democracy, in the western sense, as, for instance, in *Heresy, yes. Conspiracy, no* (1953).

humanism. A term that has been given a wide variety of often very vague meanings, two being more important than the rest. 1. The intellectual movement that characterized the culture of Renaissance Europe. Renaissance students of the literature of classical Greece and Rome—especially Greece—were called humanists. Such students were optimistic about human possibilities, attended enthusiastically to human achievements, and eschewed refined enquiries into theological niceties. However, in this sense, humanism was perfectly consistent with belief in God and a particular Christian and even Roman Catholic devotion, as, for instance, in *Erasmus. 2. In this century the label has been appropriated by those who reject all religious beliefs, insisting that we should be exclusively concerned with human welfare in this, allegedly, the only world.

Hume, David (1711-76). Scottish philosopher, historian, and man of letters. Born in Edinburgh the second son of a minor laird, Hume accumulated a modest fortune from copy-money on his various publications, supplemented by the proceeds of some spells of well-rewarded public employment. He spent his last years too in Edinburgh, where he died the much loved and universally respected leading figure of the Scottish *Enlightenment. He survived just long enough to hear the long foreseen and welcome news of the American Revolution.

The British Library catalogues Hume as 'the historian'. Certainly his *History of England* constituted both in bulk and circulation the greater part of his writings. A landmark in the development of historiography, accepted until Macaulay as the standard work, it was a best-seller for nearly a hundred years. Hume saw his *History*, like everything else, as a contribution to the human sciences: all these, called in his day 'moral subjects', were his chosen field. His economic writings, recently collected into a single separate volume, were again a landmark, recognized as such by Hume's much younger friend Adam Smith; Hume read *The Wealth of Nations* on his deathbed, hailing it at once as the achievement it is. Hume's political essays were, along with those of his pen-friend *Montesquieu, and Locke, among the main intellectual influences on the founding fathers of the U.S. constitution.

Hume published four major philosophical works. First and by far the longest is *A Treatise of Human Nature*, significantly subtitled 'An attempt to introduce the experimental method of reasoning into moral subjects'. (Since the Introduction denies the possibility of truly scientific experiments in (introspective) psychology, it should have been not 'experimental' but 'experiential'.) Between the appearance of Books I and II of the *Treatise* in 1739 and that of Book III in 1740 Hume published, again anonymously, *An Abstract of a Treatise of Human Nature*, a commendatory pamphlet decisively identified as his only in the present century. Disappointed by the reception of the *Treatise*—"It fell dead-born from the press"—and persuaded that it was his fault for premature publication, Hume later "cast ... anew" whatever of Book I he saw as fit for salvage into *An Inquiry concerning Human Understanding* (1748); adding two things apparently excised—"out of my abundant prudence"—from the manuscript of the *Treatise*. In 1752 *An Inquiry concerning the Principles of Morals* (the second *Inquiry*) re-covered some of the ground of Book III. At about the same time Hume started work on *Dialogues concerning Natural Religion*. These he was indeed too cautious to issue in his lifetime. But most careful arrangements for posthumous publication, incorporating deathbed revisions, were faithfully executed in 1777 by Hume's nephew.

One main aim of the many-sided *Treatise* was to discover, in *Locke's words; "what objects our understandings were, or were not, fitted to deal with." In this aspect it is one great work in a succession beginning with Locke's *Essay* and continuing in *Kant's *Critique of Pure Reason*. Like Kant, Hume sees himself as conducting an anti-Copernican counter-revolution. Through his investigations of the heavens *Copernicus knocked the Earth, and by implication man, from the centre of the Universe. Hume's study of our human nature was to put that at the centre of every map of knowledge.

In the *Treatise*, for instance, he argues that we cannot found any knowledge of the external world upon our sensory experience, we can only examine the psychology of our beliefs about that world; notwithstanding that it is an irresistible and also fortunate part of our nature to have such beliefs. In the first *Inquiry* he develops an equally aggressive *agnosticism about religion. The established rational apologetic proceeded in two stages: first, a minimum knowledge of God is provided by *natural

theology; second, this is supplemented by a more abundant revelation, identified as genuine by the historically well-evidenced occurrence of constitutive and endorsing miracles. To the first Hume responds with an unprecedentedly powerful general offensive against all the supposed proofs of natural theology, but particularly the most popularly persuasive, the *argument to design. Against the second Hume sketches a contention belonging both to the philosophy of history and the philosophy of religion. In interpreting and assessing detritus from the past as historical evidence the historian must appeal to all that he knows, or thinks he knows, of what is probable or improbable, possible or impossible. But a miracle would be an overriding of a descriptive law of nature, while what is incompatible with such a genuine law of nature is, by definition, physically impossible (*see* laws of nature). It would therefore seem that—quite apart from special considerations of the particular unreliability of testimony in such religious cases—the historian is professionally committed to dismissing any case for the miraculous as at best warranting the appropriately Scottish verdict 'Not proven'.

Another ambition of the *Treatise*, later largely abandoned, was to produce a sort of mental mechanics. Hume accepted from Cartesian tradition the doctrines both of the *veil of appearance and of a great divide between consciousness and stuff. Where Locke had overworked the word 'idea' to cover everything of which he allowed us to be immediately aware, Hume preferred to speak of "perceptions of the mind", proudly subdividing these into "impressions" (primary) and "ideas" (derivative). But, for him, it was still appearances in our own minds rather than objects in the external world of which alone we can be immediately aware.

The incomparable Newton had worked out the fundamentals of the science of stuff. It remained to develop a parallel mechanics of consciousness. The mental atoms were "perceptions of the mind". The forces operating on and between them were associations: in the *Abstract* the author of the *Treatise* presents his main claim to originality as "the use he makes of the principle of the association of ideas".

A more successful, and more philosophical, consequence of imitating a Newtonian model is Hume's account of value, and particularly moral value. The inspiration here was the distinction, prominent in the *Opticks*, between *primary and secondary qualities. Newton had maintained that physical objects and light rays are not really coloured: "In them there is nothing else than a certain power and disposition to stir up a sensation of this or that colour." These sensations occur only in our minds, "our little sensoria" (*see* sensorium). But we project them out onto the external realities which the vulgar uninstructedly and erroneously describe as coloured. Hume argued that the same applies to virtue and vice, beauty and ugliness. Thus the *Treatise* says: "The vice entirely escapes you, as long as you consider the object. You can never find it, till you turn your reflexion into your own breast, and find a sentiment of disapprobation, which arises in you, towards this action....". Again, the second *Inquiry* declares: "Euclid has explained fully the qualities of the circle; but has not in any proposition said a word of its beauty. The reason is evident. The beauty is not a quality of the circle."

Hume therefore proceeds to ask what are the actual characteristics that provoke in us the reactions that are thus projected. In doing this he produces the first systematic treatment of value in the modern period to be through and through secular, this-worldly, and man-centred. Even in the more cautious *Treatise*, religious beliefs are noticed only as distorting fundamentally sound principles of human nature. So there is one very good sense in which Hume's handling of the problems of value, as of everything else, is radically naturalistic. But it is not by the same token naturalistic in another sense, the sense in which a

naturalist in ethics is one who takes the *naturalistic fallacy to be no fallacy. For it was Hume who in the *Treatise* penned what is today its most quoted description (III (i) 1). It was he too, labouring to avoid *descriptivism, who wrote such careful statements as: "Nothing remains but to feel...some sentiment of blame or approbation, whence we pronounce the action criminal or virtuous."

Reading such anticipations of the contemporary *boo-hooray theory, however, we must never forget that Hume's own prime concern here, as so often elsewhere, is psychological description rather than analytical philosophy. When, for instance, in the same context, Hume explains that his hypothesis "defines virtue to be whatever mental action or quality gives to a spectator the pleasing sentiment of approbation", it is tempting to construe him as contributing to the *definition of the word 'virtue'. This would be anachronistic and wrong. Hume is not explicating the concept. He is reviewing what goes on when people employ the word.

For causation Hume clearly employs the same Newtonian model. He has two aims here. The first is to establish a negative thesis. Descartes and other rationalist predecessors believed that it is a logically necessary truth, knowable a priori, both that everything must have a sufficient cause, and that certain things or sorts of things either must be or cannot be the causes of other things or sorts of things. About the first part of this negative thesis, so persuasively put in the *Treatise*, Hume seems to have become embarrassed. But the second is crisply restated in the first *Inquiry*: "If we reason a priori anything may appear able to produce anything. The falling of a pebble may, for ought we know, extinguish the Sun, or the wish of man control the planets in their orbits." With this conclusion Hume makes joyous general havoc of natural theology; only the argument to design, appealing to experience, survives for separate special treatment.

Hume's second aim is to show that

the idea of necessity essential to the concepts both of *causation and of natural law cannot be drawn from our observation of the external world, but must instead be derived from the felt force of our habitual associations of "perceptions of the mind". The resulting notion, or pseudo-notion, is then projected out onto a world which in itself knows nothing of the kind: out there events are "entirely loose and separate" and, although some sorts are in fact constantly conjoined, there are no real connections. Hume makes no distinction between logical and natural or physical necessity. So he systematically dismisses every warrant suggested for believing that there are natural necessities and natural impossibilities, for the insufficient reason that these constitute no grounds for rejecting his cherished negative contention.

Given this, Hume developed his account of argument from experience, which successors have labelled the problem of *induction. Its nerve is represented as an irreparably broken-backed syllogism, leaping invalidly from 'All known Xs are π' to 'All Xs are π'. Hume deduces that since such procedures are manifestly not founded on reason they must be referred to another principle of our nature—habit.

Hume himself wanted to say this, and to rejoice in the scandal so caused, while never relaxing his commitment to 'the experimental method of reasoning' both in 'moral subjects' and elsewhere. This is one of many cases where the sceptical outcome of the general philosophy of Book I of the *Treatise* apparently or actually clashes with Hume's deep concern for scholarship and for general enlightenment, to say nothing of *common sense. How, to take another instance, are we to reconcile his commending in the *Treatise* of the supposedly unevidenced 'natural belief' in the external world with his insistence in the first *Inquiry* that, confronted by the "impertinent solicitations [of] arrogant bigotry and superstition,...A wise man...proportions his belief to the

evidence?" Certainly Hume was aware of these tensions, and toiled to overcome them, first in the *Treatise* and then, rather differently, in the first *Inquiry*. There is no consensus that he succeeded.

The *Dialogues* appear to have begun to be generally accepted as the mature masterpiece they are only with Kemp Smith's critical edition of 1935. He contended that the character Philo comes nearest to Hume's own ultimate position. If this is right—and every possible alternative view has since been propounded by someone—then Hume died, in unruffled and unterrified high good humour, a 'Stratonician atheist' (*see* Strato of Lampsacus).

Hume's fork. The increasingly popular nickname for an aggressive employment of *Hume's fundamental distinction between propositions stating or purporting to state only "the relations of ideas" and propositions stating or purporting to state "matters of fact and real existence" (*Inquiry concerning Human Understanding* (IV(i)). This distinction is substantially the same as that between truths of reason and truths of fact in *Leibniz earlier (*see* necessary and contingent truth). But it is its aggressive employment in Hume that makes his version the classical anticipation of logical positivism's challenge to choose between, on the one hand, analytic, a priori, and logically necessary and, on the other hand, synthetic, a posteriori, and contingent. Logical positivists insisted that these three distinctions, though different, separated propositions into the same two groups in all three cases. Against Hume *Kant argued that we must allow for a vitally important third group: propositions that are both necessary and a priori yet nonetheless synthetic. It was in terms of this third, intermediate category that Kant toiled both to answer his own question "How is metaphysics possible?" and to meet the challenge put in Hume's concluding words: "When we run over libraries, persuaded of these principles, what havoc must we make? If we take in our hand any volume—of divinity or school metaphysics, for instance—let us ask, *Does it contain any abstract reasoning concerning quantity or number?* No. *Does it contain any experimental reasoning concerning matter of fact and existence?* No. Commit it then to the flames, for it can contain nothing but sophistry and illusion" (XII (iii)).

Hume's law. The increasingly popular label for Hume's insistence that the *naturalistic fallacy is indeed a fallacy; and hence that conclusions about what ought to be cannot be deduced from premises stating only what was, what is, or what will be—and the other way about.

humours, doctrine of the four. *See* four humours.

Husserl, Edmund Gustav Albert (1859-1938). German philosopher, who studied mathematics at Leipzig, Berlin, and Vienna where he attended lectures by *Brentano. He taught philosophy at Halle, Göttingen, and Freiburg.

Husserl set out to develop the doctrine of *phenomenology into a pure, non-empirical science. In *Logische Untersuchungen* (1900, 1901) he criticized *psychologism and *naturalism, claiming that a study of the meaningful use of words must rest on insight, not generalizations from experience. *Ideen zu einer reinen Phänomenologie und phänomenologischen Philosophie* (1913) presents a programme for the systematic investigation of consciousness (the fundamental undeniable existent) and its objects. It is of the essence of objects to be correlative to states of mind; no distinction can be made between what is perceived and the perception of it. Experience is not limited to apprehension through the senses but includes whatever can be an object of thought (mathematical entities, moods, desires).

Hutcheson, Francis (1694-1746). British moral philosopher and aesthetician of the empiricist tradition. Hutcheson's primary philosophical contribution was his development of the theory of moral

sense, first articulated by *Shaftesbury. In his major work, *Inquiry into the Original of Our Ideas of Beauty and Virtue* (1725), Hutcheson sought to establish an empiricist basis for moral judgment through the idea of an inner sense by which virtue is apprehended and found pleasurable in itself. His aesthetic theory constitutes an extension of this view of the operation of inner sense with respect to beauty. In later work, Hutcheson devoted himself to further analysis and explication of the theory of moral sense. *See also* aesthetics; empiricism.

hylomorphism. The metaphysical doctrine that every natural object is somehow composed of matter and form. The character, relationship, and function of matter and form are central problems in the *Physics* and *Metaphysics* of *Aristotle, and his solution, the doctrine of hylomorphism, was taken up by the scholastic philosophers, notably *Aquinas. It was prominent in discussions of the relation of body and soul and of such theological enigmas as the nature of the Eucharist.

hylozoism. The doctrine that all objects in the universe are invested with life and are responsive to each other. The doctrine has had several adherents from the Greeks onwards, the most notable modern being F. C. S. *Schiller. It contrasts with anthropocentric metaphysical theories such as *idealism. *Compare* panpsychism.

hypostasis. (*pl.* hypostases) **1.** (in the metaphysics of *Plotinus) One of the three orders or realms of incorporeal reality. Literally, the Greek word indicates something that underlies other things and serves as a support. **2.** A *substance (Latin: *substantia* or *suppositum*).

hypothesis. 1. *See* hypothetico-deductive method. **2.** From *Newton onwards, a theory or suggestion that still has overtones of the arbitrary or the speculative. Sometimes, even after all reasonable doubt has been dispelled, a theory retains the title of a hypothesis (for example, Avogadro's hypothesis).

hypothetical. 1. (statement) See conditional. 2. Describing a valid *syllogism consisting of two premises, both conditional in form, and a conditional conclusion. The three statements forming the argument contain between them just three distinct component propositions each of which appears twice, as for example in 'If the crops fail, the villagers will starve. If there is a drought, the crops will fail. Therefore, if there is a drought, the villagers will starve.'

hypothetical imperative. See categorical imperative.

hypothetico-deductive method. The method of creating scientific theory by making an hypothesis (or set of hypotheses) from which results already obtained could have been deduced, and which also entails new experimental predictions that can be verified or refuted. There is controversy over the credit that accrues to such hypotheses when a prediction is verified (see confirmation; Popper; verification). It is historically uncertain to what extent the method describes actual scientific procedure, where the fit between theory and observation often does not seem as tight as that of strict deducibility. See also covering law model; science, philosophy of.

I

Ibn Daud, Abraham ben David Hallevi (c.1110–80). The first Jewish Aristotelian philosopher. In his Al-'Aqīda al-Rafī'a (The Exalted Faith) (1160) Ibn Daud asserts (following *Sa'adya) the essential harmony of philosophy and Torah (revealed religion). He expounds his theme in the tradition of Ibn Sīnā (see Avicenna) and the other Muslim Aristotelians, and with an extreme rationalism that leads him to limit God's omniscience in the interest of man's freewill.

In general, God can be known only through negative attributes. A concluding section concerning ethics combines Platonic and Aristotelian ideas. As a Jewish Aristotelian Ibn Daud was soon eclipsed by the more brilliant figure of *Maimonides. His Sefer hak-Kabbalah (Book of Tradition) (1161), an apologetic work of history directed against Karaism (rejection of rabbinic tradition in favour of literal interpretation of the Bible) and Christianity, remains an important historical document of the time.

Ibn Gabirol, Solomon (c.1020–c.1057). The first philosopher of Spain and one of the foremost Hebrew poets of the Middle Ages. Most of his prose writings are lost: we have only an Arabic ethical treatise, Improvement of the Qualities of the Soul (1045), and the Fountain of Life, surviving in Latin translation (Fons Vitae). Cast in the form of a dialogue between master and pupil, the latter is a discussion of the principles of matter and soul, and reveals the author as primarily a Neoplatonist. It was most influential among Christian scholastics (who knew Ibn Gabirol under the Latinized name of Avicebron or Avencebrol), the theory of a universal matter being a bone of contention between *Duns Scotus and the Franciscans, who accepted it, and the Dominicans, led by *Aquinas, who did not. Ibn Gabirol's philosophical ideas also appear, mingled with mystical motifs, in his poems, especially Kether Malkhuth (The Kingly Crown); in this way they entered the Hebrew liturgy, and they also figure in the literature of the *Kabbalah.

Ibn Khaldūn, 'Abd al-Raḥmān (1332–1406). Islamic historian. Main work: al-Muqaddimah (The Introduction) (first version completed 1377).

Ibn Khaldūn is Islam's philosopher of history par excellence, though the originality of his thought should not be exaggerated. His formative years in North Africa were passed amid great political and social upheavals and this must inevitably have influenced his views in maturity. His basic cyclical theory of history was brilliantly simple. He examined his environment and, seeing a mixture of desert and city oasis, he divided mankind into two parts: primitive and nomadic, and civilized and settled. The first preceded and produced the second: the nomads became civilized and attained a peak of culture. But their nomadic virtues were corrupted by the power and luxury which civilization brought, and they were finally destroyed by a less civilized people. The whole cycle took about 120 years.

Ibn Rushd. See Averroes.

Ibn Sīnā. See Avicenna.

icon. A *sign that has some of the characteristics of that which it signifies, for example, a cloth sample or a portrait.

idea. 1. (in Plato) The term 'Idea' is equivalent to the term 'eidos' (form). Both are connected with the Greek word 'idein' (to see); an idea (or Idea) is something that is seen—but seen by a kind of intellectual vision. The question is precisely *what* is seen in this way. The Idea of, say, justice is not the same as a correct definition of justice; Aristotle says that Socrates gave definitions, but had nothing that corresponded to a Platonic theory of Ideas (*Metaphysics* 1078 b28-32). Yet it seems clear that a Platonic philosopher who has seen the Idea of justice will be able to define justice correctly. Plato also asserts that only Ideas are real. Much of the detail of his argument is obscure, but in saying that Ideas are real he seems to be making the point that there exist objective standards, that are not dependent on anyone's decision. So the definition of a circle, for example, is not an arbitrary matter. In saying that *only* Ideas are real, Plato may be saying that, for example, no real or genuine circle is presented to our senses; the real circle is the Idea of the circle, that is grasped by the mind.

2. (in Cartesian philosophy) In the 17th century, Descartes gave the word 'idea' a new sense. He agreed with Plato that an idea is an idea *of* something, but whereas Plato insisted that an idea is something objective, quite independent of minds, Descartes said that an idea is "whatever the mind directly perceives" (Reply to Third Set of Objections to the *Meditations*, No. 5). This was connected with Descartes' search for what cannot be doubted (*compare* certainty and doubt). One may doubt, for example, whether one really is looking at a tree; what one takes to be a tree may be some other physical thing, or one may be dreaming the whole affair. But, said Descartes, in such a situation one cannot doubt that there is present to one the *idea* of a tree. Other philosophers followed Descartes in this usage; for example, Locke (*Essay concerning Human Understanding*, Epistle to the Reader) says that by 'idea' he understands "Some immediate object of the mind, which it perceives and has before it".

ideal. Of or connected with a Platonic Idea. Plato is often said to write about, for example, the 'ideal' state, and to the extent that the Idea of the state (*see* idea) is a *paradigm*, this is legitimate. In modern usage, however, one tends to contrast ideal with real, and it is important to remember that for Plato, the so-called 'ideal' state is the *real* state, in the sense that it, and only it, is worthy of the name of 'state'. Plato would have said that the Athens in which he lived was not a real state—meaning by this, not that it was an illusion, but that it lacked some of the features of a genuine state.

ideal evidence, paradox of. A paradox affecting assignment of probability. If a very small probability is assigned to an event, but on slender evidence, then ideal evidence could emerge that further justifies that low valuation. The paradox is that this evidence does not alter the probability assignment, yet it might make the observer more confident than before that the event will not happen. But the supposition is that the probability assignment reflects confidence that the event will not happen, so that the valuation *must* alter if the expectation changes strength.

idealism. A name given to a group of philosophical theories, that have in common the view that what would normally be called 'the external world' is somehow created by the mind. Idealism does not quarrel with the plain man's view that material things exist; rather, it disagrees with the analysis of a material thing that many philosophers have offered, according to which the material world is wholly independent of minds. There are three principal types of idealism. **1.** *Berkeleian idealism.* According to Berkeley, a correct analysis shows that a material object consists of nothing but ideas, whether in the mind of God or of the conscious agents that he has created. This is close to *phenomenalism, but not every phenomenalism is a type of idealism, in that some phenomenalists argue that material objects are reducible to *sense data, which differ from ideas. **2.** *Transcendental idealism.* A term applied by Kant to his theory of the external world. It is also called critical idealism. It refers to his view that the objects of our experience, in the sense of things existing in space and enduring through time, are nothing but appearances, and have no independent existence outside our thoughts. The adjective 'transcendental' indicates Kant's reason for this view: namely, that only by accepting it can we account for our a priori knowledge of objects. **3.** *Objective idealism* (also called *absolute idealism*). A type of idealism first developed fully by Hegel. Whereas Berkeleian idealism and transcendental idealism are pluralistic, objective idealism is monistic, maintaining that all that exists is a form of one mind ('Absolute Mind'). The so-called British idealists (for example, T.H.*Green, F.H.*Bradley, and B.*Bosanquet) belong to this school of thought.

The term *subjective idealism* is used by Hegel and by Marxists to refer to the views of philosophers such as Kant, who argue that what is known of objects is contributed by the human beings who perceive them. It is therefore that form of idealism that is the opposite of objective or absolute idealism.

Ideas (*or* **Forms**). *See* Plato.

identity. The relation expressed in mathematics and logic by the 'equals' sign, ' = '. The force of saying that $2 + 3 = 5$ is that the number obtained by adding 2 and 3 is (identical with) 5. In ordinary English the relation of identity is expressed using the word 'is', but this word has so many other uses that one has to try to isolate the cases in which it is used to express identity (*see also* is). Consider the following four sentences: (1) London is a city. (2) London is the capital of England. (3) Rhodesia is in Africa. (4) Rhodesia is Zimbabwe. In (1) and (3) a particular entity is described in some way. When 'is' is used in this way, in the giving of descriptions, it is called the '*is*' *of predication.* By contrast, in (2) and (4), where 'is' has the sense of 'is the same as' it is called the '*is*' *of identity.*

Two features that help to distinguish the 'is' of identity from other uses of 'is' are (a) it can be replaced by 'is the same as' without significantly altering the sense of the sentence in which it occurs, and (b) the phrases standing on either side of it can be interchanged without significantly altering the sense of the sentence. For example, taking (3), 'Rhodesia is the same as in Africa' does not make much sense, nor does 'In Africa is Rhodesia', whereas both 'Rhodesia is the same as Zimbabwe' and 'Zimbabwe is Rhodesia' preserve the force of (4). The expressions occurring on either side of an 'is' of identity must be singular terms; that is, either proper names, such as 'John', *definite descriptions, such as 'the North Pole', pronouns, such as 'I' or 'he', or demonstrative words or phrases such as 'this', 'this cat', and 'that mouse'. The formal logical representation of (4), for example, would be '*r* = *z*' where '*r*' abbreviates 'Rhodesia' and '*z*' abbreviates 'Zimbabwe', whereas that for (3) would be $A(r)$, where '*A*' abbreviates 'is in Africa'.

Identity is distinguished among relations by being the only *logical relation*. This means that in an axiomatic theory (*see* axiom) axioms for '=' are counted among the logical axioms, and in a *natural deduction system, rules governing the use of '=' are counted among the rules of *inference. The relation of identity is an *equivalence relation, but is distinguished from other equivalence relations by having the further property of licensing substitutions. This characteristic is embodied in a principle sometimes known as *Leibniz's law, which states that if *a* is identical with *b*, then any property of *a* is a property of *b*, or whatever is true of *a* is true of *b*. Formally this would be $a = b \rightarrow (\phi)(\phi a \leftrightarrow \phi b)$. The converse principle, that if *a* and *b* are identical in all respects, then they are identical objects, is called the principle of the *identity of indiscernibles (formally, $(\phi)(\phi a \leftrightarrow \phi b) \rightarrow a = b$).

Intuitively the first of these principles seems obvious, but its formalized counterpart presents problems that arise from the difficulty of getting an adequate specification of the predicates over which the variable 'ϕ' should be allowed to range. The second principle is less obvious in that it would seem that one could have qualitatively identical objects, differing only in their spatial location (two indistinguishable billiard balls, for example). Here again, much depends on what counts as a *property (that is, whether spatial location is a property) and whether indistinguishability has to be at a given time or throughout the whole history of *a* and *b*. *See also* sense and reference.

identity of indiscernibles. The principle that if *x* has every property that *y* has, and *y* has every property that *x* has, then *x* and *y* are identical. The term was first used by Leibniz in 1716 (Fourth Paper to Clarke, sec.5).

identity theory of mind. A materialist theory of consciousness (*see* materialism), which identifies being in such and such a state of consciousness with being

in some corresponding neurophysiological state. It maintains that the modes of consciousness involved in the occurrence of thoughts, feelings, or wishes cannot be considered as constituting a separate class of entities or happenings, nor are mental and physical events merely correlated in any particular way (*compare* epiphenomenalism; psychophysical parallelism). Mentalistic or physicalistic terms in fact describe one and the same event. The identity claimed is empirical or contingent, not logical: statements about mental events are not synonymous with nor analysable into statements about neurophysiological states (*compare* behaviourism).

identity theory of predication (*or* truth). If predicates, like subjects, are ultimately noun phrases (the two-term theory) and name objects (the two-name theory), then sentences containing those predicates are true just if subject and predicate are names of the same thing. That is, whatever are named by subject and predicate are identical.

ideology. 1. Generally, any system of ideas and norms directing political and social action. **2.** As used by *Marx and *Engels in *The German Ideology* (written in 1845-6 but published first in 1932), the word refers to such general systems only in so far as they are recognized to contain falsehood and distortion generated by more or less unconscious motivations. In this sense the writers did not, of course, consider their own work ideological. **3.** In other Marxist contexts, and where the emphasis is on *metaphysics, the word embraces all ideas of every sort, and the contrast is between ideological superstructure and material foundations: in this sense the most disinterested and objective science is also ideology. *See* materialism; sociology of knowledge.

idols of the mind. The false assumptions and illusions, identified by Francis Bacon in *Novum Organum* Book I; 39-44, as the four main sources of error besetting the human mind in its pursuit of truth.

These are: (1) the idols of the tribe "inherent in human nature and the very tribe or race of men, for man's sense is falsely asserted to be the standard of things"; (2) the idols of the den (or cave), which are peculiar to each individual; (3) the idols of the market-place, "formed by the reciprocal inter-course and society of man with man", particularly as a result of "bad and unapt formation of words"; and (4) the idols of the theatre, attributable to false philosophies.

if. A term usually introducing a condi-tional; for example, 'If Tom is invited (then) he will come'. In ordinary language use, an 'if p then q' statement presupposes a link between p and q — for example, p would be a ground or reason for, or a cause of, q. Also, the truth or reasonableness of the statement does not depend on the truth-value of p or q (it may be perfectly true, or justi-fiable, to assert that if Tom is invited he will come, whether or not he *is* invited, or comes). For purposes of formal logic, however, any connection between p and q is denied, and the truth of if-then statements is completely dependent on the truth-value of p and the truth-value of q. *See* conditional.

iff. The standard abbreviation for 'if and only if'. *See* biconditional.

ignoratio elenchi. (Latin for: ignorance of the refutation.) In English the phrase is used more widely to cover the ignoring, rather than ignorance, of any contention, not just a refutation. A person is, in modern usage, guilty of an *ignoratio elenchi* if his contribution to the discus-sion fails to meet what his opponent actually said.

illicit major. A fallacy associated with the categorical *syllogism in traditional logic. It is committed when the major term is *distributed in the conclusion but not in the premise. For example: 'All men are mortal, and no women are men. Therefore no women are mortal'. 'Mortal' is the major term here (the predicate of the conclusion).

illicit minor. A fallacy associated with the categorical *syllogism in traditional logic. It is committed when the minor term is *distributed in the conclusion but not in the premise. For example: 'All Anglicans are Christians, and all Anglicans are Protestants. Therefore all Christians are Protestants'. 'Christians' is the minor term here (the subject of the conclusion).

illocution. An utterance in which an illocutionary act (act done *in* speaking) is performed. Thus *in* uttering, for ex-ample, the words, "Look out", I may *warn* someone. *See* J. L. Austin.

illusion, arguments from. The collective name given to all appeals, made for the purpose of casting doubt upon perceptual beliefs, to the possibility and actual occurrence of perceptual error. The term 'illusion' here covers much that would not in non-philosophical contexts be so called. First, there are the exemplary illusions of the psychology textbooks: equal lines appearing unequal against a particular background; and so on. Second, there are those vivid dreams, visions, and hallucinations by which the subject may be deluded into the belief that he has perceived something, though there is nothing public and perceivable there at all: one favourite example is the dagger not seen but 'seen' by Macbeth (*Macbeth* II, i). Third, there are the cases where some public object has in fact been perceived but not what the subject might be inclined to think: he believes, for instance, that he has seen an oasis, whereas what he actually has seen is a photographable mirage; or—a more sophisticated example—she thinks she can see a distant star, but that star has in fact perished since the light now striking her retinas left it (*see* time-lag argument). Fourth, it is suggested that many of the familiar phenomena of the most ordinary perception are similarly deceptive: a round coin observed askew supposedly appears to be not round but oval; the experienced table (as experienced from different distances) occupies different total proportions of the subject's visual field, while the real table stays obstinately the same size; and so on. Fifth, Descartes noticed that people may report sensations as felt where a limb would have been had it not been amputated, while Plato and Berkeley remarked that the same water may feel warm to a cold hand and cool to a warm hand. Considerations of these sorts, taken together, have often been thought to show that all that anyone can be immediately aware of, in what they might uninstructedly describe as *perception, is their own private sensory experiences; their *sense data, that is, constituting a forever impenetrable *veil of appearance between them and the external world. See also private language.

imagination. A form of mental activity held to be distinct from cognitive or rational processes; a free, creative ordering of the contents of mind. Imagination in this sense is often confused with the production of mental imagery, which would be better called 'imaging'.

Philosophers have frequently disdained the imagination on grounds of its lack of cognitive authority. Plato's condemnation of art, for instance, derives substantially from this view (see aesthetics). However, in *Kant's epistemology, the imagination is held to be a condition of all possible knowledge in virtue of its synthesizing power over the raw contents of mind, and in Kantian-influenced aesthetics the imagination at free play is held to be the condition of art. This view of the centrality of the imagination was further developed by such philosophers as Friedrich *Schiller, *Schopenhauer, and *Hegel, and, through *Schelling, was influential in *romanticism, where the imagination is often held actually to provide access to knowledge and truth, and where art is thought of supreme value.

In contemporary philosophy, the imagination has been a focus of interest for existentialist philosophers such as *Sartre. Against this trend, the British philosopher Gilbert *Ryle has argued that the imagination is not a single

mental faculty—that, indeed, it is not an inner mental activity at all—but rather that 'imaginativeness' can characterize many very different kinds of observable behaviour (see behaviourism).

immanent. In-dwelling. The word is often used by pantheists (see pantheism) to describe the way in which God dwells in, or is in some sense identified with, the created world. Compare transcendent.

immortalist. A person who believes that somehow people, or some crucial elements in people, survive death and last for ever.

immortality. See survival and immortality.

imperative. The characteristic mood of the main verb in sentences (imperative sentences) with which conduct-guiding *speech acts, such as requests and orders, are standardly performed. Imperatives, that is imperative sentences, are of interest to moral philosophers and logicians. One influential theory states that moral judgments imply imperatives, and hence that, for example, 'If you ought to do X, do it' is a valid inference when the 'ought' is a moral 'ought'. According to this view, if a moral judgment can occur as the conclusion of an argument then so also can an imperative. Yet arguments as conceived by traditional logic cannot contain imperatives whether as conclusions or as premises; for traditional logic deals only with arguments whose premises and conclusions can be true or false, whereas imperatives can be neither. There appear however to be valid arguments containing imperatives, for example, 'Shut all the As. This is an A. So shut this A'. The view that this is a valid argument can be maintained by supposing that just as propositions are true or false, so imperatives are satisfied (carried out) or unsatisfied. Thus it could be held that an argument containing imperatives is valid if the truth or satisfaction of the premises implies the truth or satisfaction of the conclusion. For example, if 'Shut all the As' is satisfied, and 'This is an *A*' is true, it follows that 'Shut this *A*' is satisfied. By thus demonstrating the possibility of a logic (see logic) of imperatives it is shown that the possibility of drawing moral conclusions is not precluded by the imperatival implications of moral judgments.

implication *and* **entailment.** A family of closely related notions, attempts to provide an adequate account of which have occupied many volumes. Problems arise when one seeks to determine relationships within the family, and, as a result, clear and agreed definitions are not available. To assert the conditional statement 'If *A*, then *B*' is thought to be equivalent to saying that *A* implies *B*, and this in turn is often taken to mean that *B* is deducible from *A*. But if *B* is deducible from *A*, then to reason *A*, therefore *B* is to argue validly, which means that *B* follows from *A* or that *A* entails *B*. This train of connections might lead one to suppose that all these claims about the relation between *A* and *B* are just different ways of saying the same thing. But there are other considerations that show that this certainly cannot be said without qualification. There are many conditional statements, such as 'If Albert has taken a large dose of arsenic, he will die', which might be accepted as true, but where the corresponding inference 'Albert has swallowed a large dose of arsenic, therefore he will die', while reasonable, could not be claimed to be formally *valid, because the truth of 'Albert will die' follows from that of 'Albert has swallowed a large dose of arsenic' only by virtue of the properties of arsenic in relation to the human metabolism and not because of the logical form of the two statements. A conditional statement of the same form, such as 'If Fred has swallowed a large dose of vitamin C, he will die, probably will not be regarded as true. Thus, if by 'validity' one means 'formal validity', there are cases where 'If *A*, then *B*' is true but 'A, therefore *B*' is not a valid inference.

This distinction between the truth of a conditional statement and the holding of an entailment relation becomes even more necessary when conditional statements are, as is most common in logical formalizations, treated as material conditionals (see conditional). The material conditional '*A* ⊃ *B*' is true if as a matter of fact it is not the case that *A* is true and *B* is false, whereas for 'A, therefore *B*' to be a valid inference it must be *impossible* for *B* to be false when *A* is true (see also validity and truth). Since it is generally accepted that 'A' entails '*B*' iff 'A, therefore *B*' is a valid inference, this means that to say that 'A' entails '*B*' is to say that '*A* ⊃ *B*' is not merely true, but is necessarily true. It is in this way that the study of the entailment relation has been thought to fall within the province of *modal logic, pioneered by C.I. Lewis in his systems of *strict implication.*

Implication is a notion that is left sitting between conditional statements on the one hand and entailment on the other, and as a result various 'kinds' of implication are distinguished in terms of their relation to these other notions. *Material implication* is the relation holding between *A* and *B* when the material conditional *A* ⊃ *B* is true. Dissatisfaction with the material conditional as an adequate representation of the logical force of conditional statements largely stems from the so-called *paradoxes of material implication.* These are that, for any statement *A*, (1) if *A* is false, '*A* ⊃ *B*' is true, and (2) if *A* is true, '*B* ⊃ *A*' is true, no matter what statement *B* is. Thus, on the material interpretation, all of the following would be true: 'If grass is blue, hedgehogs are cuddly', 'If grass is blue, hedgehogs are not cuddly', 'If grass is not blue, hedgehogs are not cuddly'. However, one normally presumes that part of the point of asserting 'If *A*, then *B*' is to deny that 'If *A*, then not *B*' by ruling out the possibility that *B* be false when *A* is true. If this is correct, then, it is argued, the logical representation of conditionals should ensure that 'If *A*, then *B*' and 'If *A*, then not *B*' are contradictories (*see* contradictory).

The relation of *formal implication*, introduced by Russell, suffers from similar paradoxical features. A generalized conditional statement, such as 'If any piece of iron is heated, it will expand', when symbolized as $(\forall x)$ $(Px \supset Fx)$ is said to express a formal implication, and if it is true, '*Px*' is said formally to imply '*Fx*'. The label 'formal' here is unfortunate, for it is by no means true that all such implications hold in virtue of the *logical form of the component statements; $(\forall x)$ $(x$ is a dinosaur $\supset x$ is dead) provides a *counter-example. The paradoxical properties of material implication extend to formal implication, making it possible to make any general claim about non-existent objects, such as that $(\forall x)$ $(x$ is a unicorn $\supset x$ has three horns).

Logical implication is a notion much closer to entailment. *A* logically implies *B* if *B* cannot be false when *A* is true. The difference between the two notions is that implication is always a relation between two statements, whereas entailment is a relation between one or more statements and a statement. This still would not make any essential difference if entailment were restricted to a relation between a finite number of statements and a statement, for then the *conjunction of that finite number of statements would logically imply the statement in question. But if it can be said that a statement is entailed by an infinite collection of statements this reduction is not possible.

Other notions of implication have been introduced and their formal characteristics described. In general there is always scope for introducing a new notion of implication. This is because each logical system *S*, in determining certain forms of argument as valid, partially determines the relation of entailment. One can then introduce conditional statements '$A \rightarrow_s B$' which are defined to be true just when '*A*, therefore *B*' is a valid inference in *S*. This will introduce a new sort of impli-

cation, implication$_s$, defined by '*A* implies$_s$ *B*' iff '$A \rightarrow_s B$', or iff *A* entails *B* relative to the criteria provided by *S*. Whether this is a genuinely new sort of implication is then a matter for further investigation. In so far as *S* is not a universal system, that is, does not exhaust the criteria for determining validity, implication$_s$ will not coincide with logical implication and may or may not coincide with any forms of implication already dealt with in *S* or in some other system.

incompatibilist. *See* freewill and determinism.

incomplete. *See* complete.

incomplete symbol. *See* logical fiction.

incongruent (*or* **incongruous**) **counterparts.** Another name for *enantiomorphs.

inconsistent. *See* consistent.

inconsistent triad. A set of three statements of which at least one must be false because from any two of them the *negation of the third may be deduced. Where the deduction is syllogistic, this form of inconsistency is sometimes called an *antilogism*. For example, 'Evils are not created by God', 'Evils are real', and 'Everything real is created by God' form an inconsistent triad and so cannot be simultaneously true.

incontinence. An alternative term for *weakness of will or for acrasia.

incorrigible. Directly and conclusively verified, not subject to any further tests. A class of so-called *basic statements or propositions that are descriptive of present contents of experience (for example, 'I have a headache') are generally regarded as incorrigible in so far as they express nothing about which one could be uncertain or mistaken. Such statements may, however, be false, even when the claim is sincere, not because experience itself can be in any way fallible but because it might be misidentified or incorrectly formulated in words. *See* protocol statements.

independent. 1. A proposition C is (*logically*) independent of propositions $B_1,\ldots,B_n$ iff neither C nor its negation is a (logical) *consequence of $B_1,\ldots,B_n$. **2.** A sentence Q is (*formally*) independent of sentences $P_1,\ldots,P_n$ in a *formal system S iff neither Q nor its negation can be derived from $P_1,\ldots,P_n$ in S (in which case neither Q nor its negation is a formal *consequence of $P_1,\ldots,P_n$ in S).

indeterminism. *See* freewill and determinism.

indexical. An alternative name for *token-reflexive.

Indian materialism. A somewhat marginal but long-lived aspect of *Indian philosophy, that appears under various labels, such as Cārvāka, Lokāyata, and Ājīvika. None of the original writings of these schools, which flourished as early as *c*.600 BC, are extant, and information about their teaching can be gained only from indirect accounts. These mention as typical examples of their doctrine the following attitudes: the refusal to accept the notion of transmigration and/or an ethical rationale behind it; the denial of any form of personal survival after death; the rejection of any means of knowledge (including the means of 'inference' and 'verbal testimony', which are important to other schools of Indian thought) other than that obtained by perception; and the opposition to belief in freewill (instead, an absolute determinism is postulated). In most materialist schools man is analysed purely in terms of material components and their interaction. This analysis is usually connected with a pessimistic attitude; hedonism appears only quite rarely. The influence of this type of thinking was less philosophical (though the *Vaiśeṣika may exhibit it) than sociological, for the teaching was used in attacking ritual and mystical religion.

Indian philosophy. Although Indian thought developed in an intellectual climate which in many ways was different from, and almost certainly not influenced by, the ancient Greek world, abundant and often striking similarities with Western philosophical thought justify the application of the term 'philosophy' to it. The nature of the world-view taken for granted by the majority of schools and, in the course of time, an increasingly religious preoccupation nevertheless led Indian philosophy in a somewhat different direction from occidental. But the great variety of approaches even during the medieval period disproves the myth that all Indian philosophy is 'mystical' or 'theological' or that (*advaita*: non-dual) *Vedânta is its sole, or most typical, representative.

A typology of Indian philosophy is complicated by the fact that the Indian tradition itself classifies schools according to *religious* criteria, a practice that tends to obscure the philosophical character of the individual systems. Thus six systems are classified as *Hindu philosophy, while three others are separated as heterodox: *Indian materialism, *Buddhist philosophy, and *Jain philosophy. A periodization is equally difficult, since many traditions continued over long periods parallel to each other. We may, however, distinguish four periods: (1) formative; (2) realistic or nature-philosophical; (3) monistic—mystical and illusionistic; and (4) theistic.

Philosophical ideas are first expressed in various hymns composed between *c.* 1000 and 800 BC, in primarily ritual contexts. Interested in controlling the powers that govern the universe, archaic magical thought began to speculate on the *one* central power that underlies all others and from which the world of phenomena derives its being. Many different suggestions eventually crystallize in the notion '*brahman*', which figures as the one ultimate principle of unity in a basically realistic cosmological system.

The (older) *Upaniṣads* (from *c.* 800 BC onwards) appear to combine this conception with an altogether different and new complex—meditationally obtained altered states of consciousness. The interpretation given to these was eventually to become universal to the Indian *religious* world-view. A fundamental distinction is made between matter and spirit; since eternity man's spiritual essence (*ātman*) finds itself entangled in a material frame and passing through a potentially endless sequence of rebirths (*saṃsāra*). By meditation and other means it is however capable of discarding the material fetters and obtaining the state of liberation (*mokṣa*), free from space, time, matter, and rebirth. This state of liberation, in which the *ātman* realizes its true nature, is now identified with *brahman*, the source of the universe, and conceived of as a monistic merger of the *ātman* into *brahman*.

Both Jainism and Buddhism (founded in the 5th century BC) participate in the *religious* interpretation, but reject the *metaphysical* frame which the *Upaniṣads* derive from earlier thought. While Jain philosophy utilizes a nature-philosophical interpretation, Buddhism restricts itself to a rationalistic analysis of *saṃsāra*, in order to encourage meditational practices. This analysis emphasizes the transitory nature of the world of phenomena—suffering (*duḥkha*) being its basic characteristic—and explains human entanglement in it through desire (which comprises all forms of clinging to transitory phenomena, particularly the everyday notion of a 'person'). *Duḥkha* can however be overcome through meditation, in which the total antithesis to *duḥkha*—*nirvāṇa*—is realized. In order to stress that empirical reality does not contain anything essential or lasting, transmigration is explained in a purely functional manner, as a series of processes that condition each subsequent one, and without reference to any permanent entity ('soul') that transmigrates. Any statement about the nature of *nirvāṇa*, or about which aspect of the empirical person is capable of the liberating realization of *nirvāṇa*, is avoided. Various motives for this silence have been suggested: it could reflect a scepticism concerning the power of human thought to grasp what lies beyond the world of phenomena, which is also documented elsewhere in Indian writing, or a pragmatism which, in view of the urgency of meditation, discarded metaphysical speculation as useless waste of time.

Buddhist thought has remained the most elusive form of Indian philosophy, and only in the *Vijñānavāda will a somewhat less rigid attitude be noticed. Certain schools of Thēravāda Buddhism, collectively known as the Pudgalavāda, have in fact postulated the existence of a person (*pudgala*) to simplify the description of the process of transmigration and to allow for the existence of transcendental saviour figures, but all other schools of Buddhism have rejected the Pudgalavāda as heterodox.

An entirely different approach is shown by developments in the area of natural philosophy. The interest is restricted here to a critical analysis of the external world, including language and thinking itself. This tradition is represented by *early* strata in the teachings of the Vaiśeṣika, Nyāya, and Jain philosophy, and influences are seen in the Buddhist *Abhidharma* speculation, and in the Mīmāṃsā and Sāṃkhya. Its beginnings appear to go back to the first half of the first millennium BC. The vast variety of phenomena in the external world is reduced to a limited number of basic factors, and the structure of the world is explained in terms of these basic factors and the laws governing their interaction. The purely empirical interest accounts, among other things, for a strictly functional notion of a 'soul' and for the absence of any ultimate principle of unity. Important results of this approach are (besides a highly formalized description of language) atomistic theories, the distinction of basic categories, such as substance, attribute, etc. (see Vaiśeṣika), the formulation of a system of logic (see Nyāya) and exegetics or hermeneutics (see Mīmāṃsā), and a quasi-scientific world-view. Even many centuries after the flourishing of these schools, the principles of their approach remain influential.

The Buddhists participated in these developments only partially. While the general character of the world-view and the analytical approach expressed in the *Abhidharma*, and in a fully systematic manner in schools like the *Sarvâstivāda, are very similar to those described above, the Buddhist schools differ fundamentally in one respect. The notions of a substance, of eternal souls (however functionally they be defined) and of equally eternal atoms are rejected, and the concept of '*dharma*' is formulated instead. A *dharma* is a basic factor of existence, belonging to the categories of substance, attribute, and action indiscriminately, and covering the whole range of matter, emotions, thought, etc.; it is atomic when material and lasts only one single moment.

Originally, this whole line of thought appears to have been interested in a purely mechanistic description of the external world, generally in a neutral position relative to religious preoccupations. Only in the schools of *Indian materialism have mechanistic ideas been utilized for anti-religious purposes. But the intellectual climate moved more and more away from a quasi-scientific approach to religious problems. Later strata therefore attempted to accommodate these in some form by making reference to transmigration and liberation and by acknowledging some form of moral order besides the mechanistic laws. Sometimes also a god-figure was introduced into these basically atheistic systems (as a specially privileged monad in the Yoga, and as creator of the world in the Nyāya).

But the general trend of Indian thought moved away from fundamentally pluralist and realistic systems towards a monistic, and often illusionistic, approach. In Buddhism we have first the *Madhyamaka where all phenomena are described as 'empty' and as constituting the basically illusory level of relative reality, and where 'emptiness' figures as the one universal, absolute reality. The question of how this world of empty phenomena originates was dealt

with in the slightly later school of *Vijñānavāda. Here Consciousness was regarded as the absolute, and the world of phenomena as an illusory mental projection. During the same period also, the teachings of the *Upaniṣads* were formulated in a systematic manner, which marked the beginning of the Vedânta as a distinct philosophical system. Initially, the monistically conceived merger of the individual *ātman* with *brahman* in the state of *mokṣa* remained attached to the old idea of *brahman* as the source of a real world. But under the direct influence of the two Buddhist schools mentioned, this was reinterpreted during the 7th century AD according to illusionistic thought. The world of the phenomena was considered purely an unreal imposition upon the one real, the universal Consciousness, *brahman*. This form of Vedânta was embedded in typically Hindu material; it accepted the *Upaniṣads* as a scriptural basis, employed Upaniṣadic terminology like *brahman* and *ātman*, and was consciously anti-Buddhist. Along with the Mīmāṃsā which during this period produced a remarkable atheistic theory of revelation in defence of the Hindu scriptures, the Vedânta emerged as the representative of a Hindu renaissance which pushed Buddhist thought into the background. The influence of monistic *brahman* speculation can also be recognized in the area of philosophy of language where (for example, in Bhartṛhari's *Vākyapadīya*, composed in the 7th century AD) the plurality of words is derived from the one transcendental Word-*brahman*, or in aesthetics where aesthetic experience is related to the realization of *brahman*.

From the very end of the first millennium AD, an altogether different complex came to the fore—theistic thought. As a feature of Hindu religion, the belief in a personal absolute is documented from at least the 4th century BC, and in the *Bhagavadgītā* (3rd or 2nd century BC?) had already found a somewhat unsystematic and syncretistic expression. During the following centuries other popular religious works (*Purāṇas,* Āgamas, Saṃhitās, etc.) continued this approach, usually under the banner of (a theistic, non-classical form of) *Sāṃkhya*. But the very vague and imprecise statements which were made about the relationships between the absolute God and primal matter and the individual souls cannot claim to be philosophy. But after the establishment of monistic Vedânta, Hindu theism reacted by formulating, under the same title of Vedânta, a systematic and fully philosophical expression of theistic thought. The first person to do this was Rāmānuja (12th century AD), and he was followed by many others during the succeeding centuries. Theistic thought gained increasing popularity, and also influenced the later developments of certain schools of the illusionistic Vedânta; but the strictly philosophical material diminished. Only from the 19th century onwards, in a very small segment of Hindu society, has Western philosophy stimulated new developments, for instance in thinkers like Aurobindo (1872–1950) or Vivekānanda (1863–1902).

Indian philosophy has by and large been school-philosophy, the domain of professionals who hand down their teaching through consecutive generations of disciples. This can throw light on a number of peculiarities of Indian philosophizing. Philosophical writings, particularly the older works, have come down to us on the whole in the form of teaching manuals. The basic ideas of a school, developed and formulated over many generations, were contained in extremely concise *sūtras* (formulae) and *kārikās* (summary verses). Oral teaching would then take the form of commenting on these, and commentaries of outstanding teachers appeared also in written form. Independent works exist, but are much less common.

Furthermore, a certain correlation between the range of subjects discussed (and the historical shifts of emphasis) and the professional, institutionalized nature of philosophizing may be suggested. Thus logic grew out of the popular custom of holding public debates between representatives of different schools; analysis of language evolved from the study of the Sanskrit language which, although not used outside the schools since the beginning of the Christian era, remained the almost exclusive medium of teaching and debating; philosophy of mind was the outcome of meditational practices that naturally began to dominate the scene once monastic institutions (in Buddhism and Jainism from the 4th century BC, in Hinduism from the 7th century AD onward) participated in the philosophical discussion. More generally, once the belief in transmigration and the ideal of liberation gained universal acceptance (probably in the last centuries BC), the kind of pursuit typical of the nature-philosophical schools became decreasingly rewarding as a professional career. The rivalry between Buddhist and Hindu philosophers proved to be one of the most fertile stimuli for the development of increasingly critical and sophisticated systems of thought (till the end of the first millennium AD), but it also tended to restrict the discussion to topics disputed between them. Thus Buddhists, Jains, and Hindus share the same ethical presuppositions, which have never been reflected upon in a philosophical manner. Furthermore, any discussion of the social or political order, relevant to Hinduism alone, has never gone beyond a fundamentalist and pragmatic attitude derived from established customs and ancient religious works which provide details, but no theory. *See also* Buddhist philosophy; Hindu philosophy; Jain philosophy.

indicative. The characteristic mood of the main verb in ordinary statements and questions. For example, in the sentence 'Mary was skating', the verb 'was skating' is in the indicative mood. The assumption that logic and philosophy should be concerned only with statements was by *Ryle polemically nicknamed "the fetish of the indicative sentence". *Compare* imperative.

indicator word (*or* **term**). An alternative name for a *token-reflexive.

indifference, principle of. The principle made prominent by *Laplace, allowing us to regard events as equally probable if we can see no reason why one should occur rather than the other. It can be used to justify the regarding of various hypotheses as antecedently equiprobable, so giving an input into *Bayes's theorem. Unfortunately, unless formulated very carefully it leads to inconsistencies. Its critics deny that our ignorance should justify anything at all. *See also* probability theory.

indiscernibility of identicals. The principle that if *x* and *y* are identical, then *x* has every property that *y* has, and *y* has every property that *x* has. The converse of the *identity of indiscernibles, it is sometimes called *Leibniz's law.

individual. 1. Anything that can be separated and individuated or made the referent of the subject of a sentence or thought. Individuals, though they are sometimes taken narrowly to mean particulars, such as a man or a book, can be universals, such as whiteness or goodness (*see* universals and particulars). **2.** (in logic) The subject of a sentence of the first-order predicate *calculus.

individuation, principle of. A principle that uniquely identifies one individual. A scholastic dispute concerned whether individuation is effected materially or in virtue of a formal property of uniqueness or *haecceity; the term most commonly occurs now in discussions of *personal identity and of the way in which one individual is to be identified in relation to others.

indubitable. An epistemological term denoting the property of being certain, or beyond rational doubt. The indubitability of a proposition is not equivalent to its logical necessity, since some contingent propositions may also be said to be effectively beyond doubt. *See* certainty and doubt; epistemology.

induction. 1. A method of reasoning by which a general law or principle is inferred from observed particular instances. The word 'induction' is derived from the Latin translation of Aristotle's '*epagoge*', which seems in turn to have been taken from earlier Greek writers on military tactics. The term is employed to cover all arguments in which the truth of the premise, or premises, while not entailing the truth of the conclusion, or conclusions, nevertheless purports to constitute good reason for accepting it, or them. The expression 'ampliative argument', suggested by C. S. Peirce, is also used. There is no generally accepted subclassification of inductive or ampliative arguments, though induction by simple enumeration is often thought to be the fundamental form: from A1 is ϕ, A2 is ϕ, A3 is ϕ, and so on, this proceeds to the conclusion that all As are (probably) ϕ.

With the growth of natural science philosophers became increasingly aware that a deductive argument (*see* deduction) can only bring out what is already implicit in its premises, and hence inclined to insist that all new knowledge must come from some form of induction. It was in this understanding that Francis *Bacon was the prophet of inductive science, who "rang a bell to call the wits together."

What is now called the problem of induction was set by *Hume, who himself did not actually use the word in this context. Hume represented the nerve of all argument from experience as an attempted *syllogism, the problem being to show how we can be entitled to move from a first premise that all observed so-and-sos have been such and such to the conclusion that all so-and-sos without restriction have been, are, and will be such and such.

A second premise that would complete a valid syllogism is that all so-and-sos have in fact been observed. But this suggestion is disqualified, since where it applies we have an *analysis of* not an *argument from* experience. This latter essentially involves a going beyond what is given, a use of cases examined to guide expectations about those that have not been examined. The only alternative second premise considered by Hume would make reference to the *uniformity of nature. This he ruled out on the grounds that it could only be known to be true by a question-begging appeal to arguments of the very kind here in question (see begging the question). It could be objected, even more powerfully, that when formulated as a second premise in the desired syllogism such a reference would be directly known to be false simply by *appeal to* but *without argument from* experience. For it would have to claim that all the so-and-sos experienced by anyone you like, up till any point in time you care to stipulate, constitute in all respects a perfectly representative sample of so-and-sos. And everyone knows from his own experience of novelties that this is false.

The moral that Hume drew is that argument from experience must be without rational foundation. He seems nevertheless to have felt few scruples over the apparent inconsistency of going on to insist, first, that such argument is grounded in the deepest instincts of our nature, and, second, that the rational man everywhere proportions his belief to the evidence—evidence which in practice crucially includes the outcome of procedures alleged earlier to be without rational foundation.

Hume's successors have explored every avenue in their efforts to meet his challenge. Some have rested their case upon our success in employing inductive procedures and meet the objection that this is question-begging by countering that deduction itself is susceptible only of deductive justification. Others have contended that such procedures presuppose a metaphysical principle—known perhaps, if at all, by faith alone—expressing the fundamental uniformity of nature. Others again, following Sir Karl *Popper, maintain that Hume did indeed succeed in demonstrating the invalidity of induction, but then go on to say that respectable science advances by

*hypothetico-deductive rather than inductive methods. Still others assail Hume's form of representation, urging that argument from experience ought to be seen, not as an irreparably fallacious attempt to deduce conclusions necessarily wider than the available premises can possibly contain, but rather as a matter of following a tentative and self-correcting rule, a rule that is part of the very paradigm of inquiring rationality. This rule could be stated in these terms: when all known cases of so-and-so have been found to be such and such, expect and presume that other so-and-sos have been and will be until and unless you discover some particular reason to revise these expectations. **2.** (in mathematics) An inference from statements of the form 'the first term of a series has the property P' and 'if the nth term of the series has the property P so does the $n+1$th term' to a statement of the form 'all terms of the series have the property P'. Complete induction allows the move from 'the first term of a series has the property P' and 'if all terms of the series before the nth term have the property P so does the nth term' to 'all terms of the series have the property P'.

inductive logic. *See* logic.

inevitability. 1. Logical necessity; if q follows inevitably from p this simply means that it follows necessarily. **2.** Contingent inescapability; if some occurrence is inevitable, this means that it will happen regardless of all attempts to prevent it. *See* fatalism; freewill and determinism; necessary and contingent truth; seafight.

inference, mediate *and* **immediate.** *See* syllogism.

inference, rule of. A rule for the construction of arguments which says what may be inferred from one or more statements whose logical structure is specified. An almost universally accepted rule of inference is *modus ponens* (see affirming the antecedent) which, for any statements A and B, says that from A together with 'If A, then B' one may infer B. It has been held that there is no difference between accepting a rule of inference, that from A together with B one may infer C, and adopting as an *axiom or logical law the statement 'If A and B, then C'. For this reason attention in logical theory was, in the early part of this century, focused almost exclusively on axiomatic presentations of logic, on logical laws, and on logical truths rather than on rules of inference.

Three points should, however, be noted. (1) Without at least one rule of inference, no conclusions can be drawn from any axioms. (2) The attempt to embody *all* rules of inference in axioms leads to an infinite regress, as was observed by Lewis Carroll in his 'What the Tortoise said to Achilles' (*Mind*, 1895). This point can be illustrated by taking the axiom corresponding to *modus ponens*, which is $(A \& (A \rightarrow B)) \rightarrow B$. To know that from this axiom together with A and $A \rightarrow B$ one can infer B requires another rule of inference and hence another axiom, this time $(((A \& (A \rightarrow B)) \rightarrow B) \& A \& (A \rightarrow B)) \rightarrow B$, and so *ad infinitum*. (3) To accept that from the fact that from A together with B one may infer C, one may further infer 'If A and B, then C' is, in itself, to accept a rule of inference, albeit of a slightly different kind, since it permits the drawing of a conclusion not from statements as premises but from the fact that a certain inference can be correctly made.

Such rules, which are rules for forming arguments out of arguments, were called by the Stoics '*themata*', as distinct from '*schemata*', which are patterns for inferring statements from statements. Depending on the system of logic, and its treatment of *conditional and universally quantified statements in particular, this rule, which is required to convert rules of inference into statements of an equivalent deductive force, may not be available either as an explicitly stated rule (the rule of conditional proof) or as a rule which is introduced on the basis of a set-theoretic proof of the deduction theorem. This theorem states that the rules of the system would, in every case in which they permit C to be inferred from A and B, also permit 'If A and B, then C' to be proved as a theorem. In other words, the deduction theorem does not hold for all systems of logic, so that rules of inference cannot always be replaced by logical axioms.

infinite descent, method of. A type of argument in mathematics, also called descending induction. Consider any property or condition; if it can be shown that for any number, if it satisfies the condition or has the property, then there is a lesser number that does also; the method then allows the inference that no number satisfies the condition or has the property. Infinite descent has connections with the *least number principle.

infinite divisibility. A concept that many philosophers, from *Zeno of Elea onwards, have considered to be impossible, since it supposedly leads to paradox. If, they have argued, a (finite-sized) existent is infinitely divisible, then it must consist of infinitely many parts. These must either have some size, or lack size and be nothing. If each part has some size or other, however minute, then the aggregate of an infinite number of these parts will be infinitely large. But if each part has no size, then the aggregate would have no size, that is the original existent would be made up of nothing. Another view of the problem is to contend that to be infinitely divisible is to be divisible indefinitely, into as many parts as anyone chooses, and not to consist in an actual infinity of parts. *See also* Zeno's paradoxes.

infinite set (*or* **collection** *or* **number**). A set (collection or number) that is not finite. A set, X, is finite only if there is a non-negative integer n such that X has n members. Alternatively a set, X, is infinite if its members can be matched one for one (put in a one-to-one correspondence with) some proper subset of X. The set, N, of all natural numbers, $\{0, 1, 2, 3, \dots\}$ is the smallest infinite set, *Cantor showed that there were infinite sets larger than N.

infinity. A notion used since the time of the ancient Greeks who applied it to substance. It also occurred in the paradoxes of *Zeno of Elea. The concept of the infinite was vague, loosely being taken as 'that which has no beginning or end' or 'that which has no boundary, internal or external'. A distinction was drawn between the potential infinite and the actual infinite, some philosophers, notably Aristotle and Kant, allowing the former but not the latter. A potential infinity of Fs is an indefinitely large number of Fs in the sense that for any finite number one selects, the number of Fs is greater. An actual infinity of Fs is such that the number of Fs is (actually) greater than every finite number. It is unclear that the distinction can be maintained, but it was of some traditional importance; for example, *Descartes' argument for the existence of God requires the actual rather than the potential infinite.

In the 19th century, *Cantor and Dedekind dispelled much confusion surrounding the infinite by noting that talk of an infinite property, substance, etc., can be reduced to talk of an infinite number, numbers themselves being regarded as certain classes. Thus Cantor's theory of the actual infinite was a theory of infinite classes.

infirmation. Disconfirmation. See confirmation.

innate ideas. Ideas or knowledge in the mind prior to and independent of sense experience. For *Plato, knowledge of the *Forms derives from innate ideas which are accessible to memory (see reminiscence, argument from). For *Descartes, all principles of science and knowledge are founded on clear and distinct ideas, or *incorrigible truths, which are innate in the mind and which may be captured by the method of reason.

Innate ideas came to be the focus of attack by empiricist philosophers who sought to argue that the mind is at first a *tabula rasa only subsequently informed by sense experience. The classic objection to innate ideas occurs in *Locke's Essay Concerning Human Understanding, where it is argued that if there were ideas innate in the mind then we should expect to find them expressed by infants and untutored savages; but experience conclusively shows that this is not the case.

inscription. A linguistic entity, such as a sentence. The term figures in some analyses of propositional attitudes, for example, belief.

instinct. In psychological theory, an habitual pattern of behaviour that is innate or inherited rather than learned or acquired. The concept of instinct is particularly significant in Freud's psychological theory, where the libido is considered the reservoir of instinctual energy which issues in sexual or aggressive behaviour. In behaviourist theory, J. B. Watson distinguished instinctual patterns of responses from those that are conditioned or conditionable.

instrumentalism. 1. A theory of the nature of thought, logic, and acquisition of knowledge, advanced by *Dewey, developing the *pragmatism of William *James. Ideas, concepts, and judgments are instruments functioning in experienced situations and determining future consequences. Propositions are to be regarded as means in the process of enquiry; as such, they cannot be true or false but are characterizable only as effective or ineffective. Judgments may have truth-values relative to whether or not their assertion is warranted. Ideas and practice work together as instruments: ideas relate experiences, making prediction possible, and are in turn tested by experience. **2.** A term applied to a view about the status of scientific theories held by some anti-realist philosophers of science, including *Berkeley and *Mach. Theories are merely instruments, tools, or calculating devices for deriving some observation statements (predictions) from other observation statements (data). Consequently, there is no question as to the truth or falsity of these theories—they *can* be neither true nor false. Instrumentalism is thus opposed to most realist theories of science. *Compare* realism.

insufficient reason, principle of. An alternative name for the principle of indifference. *See* indifference, principle of.

intension. *See* extension and intension.

intensive magnitude. *See* magnitudes.

interactionism. A dualistic theory of the relation between mind and body, according to which physical events can cause mental events, and vice versa. Examples are feeling an emotion making the heart beat faster, or a piece of music causing a poignant memory. *See* mind-body problem.

inter finitum et infinitum non est proportio. (Latin for: there is no proportion between infinity and finitude.) A maxim with an important bearing on *Pascal's wager.

interpretation. The assigning of meanings to the expressions of a *formal language. Any language can be treated as a system of symbols in which sentences, and other kinds of expression, are constructed according to syntactical rules (rules of grammar). To do this is to ignore any meaning that the expressions of the language might have; it is to treat the symbols as constituting an uninterpreted structure or formal language.

1. In its most general sense, to give an interpretation of a formal language is to give *any* means of assigning truth-values to sentences of the language (*see* truth-value). In an interpretation each sentence receives no more than one value from a set of truth-values, that may contain as few as two members (usually called 'true' and 'false') or any finite or infinite number of members. (This article will be confined to discussing two-valued interpretations; *see also* many-valued logic.) If the language under consideration, say

L, is governed not only by grammatical rules, but also by rules of inference, giving it a formally defined logical structure, then an interpretation in this most general sense may not render the rules of inference of L valid. That is, if a sentence B can be derived from sentences $A_1,...,A_n$ by application of the rules of inference of L, there may be an interpretation of L in which all of $A_1,...,A_n$ are assigned the value 'true' and B is assigned the value 'false'. Such an interpretation is not an *admissible* interpretation of L. Where a language has a formally defined logical structure it is common to restrict 'interpretation' to 'admissible interpretation'.

In this general sense any *one* assignment of truth-values to the propositional (sentential) variables of the propositional (sentential) *calculus together with the *truth-table definitions of the *truth-functional connectives will provide an admissible interpretation of the propositional calculus. Interpretations in this most general sense are often called *valuations* to distinguish them from interpretations as discussed under 2.

2. In a narrower and more common sense an interpretation is an assignment of truth-values to the sentences of a formal language which makes use of the predicate structure of the sentences. Consider first a simple elaboration of the propositional (sentential) calculus discussed under 1: imagine that each proposition (sentence) variable has the form Fa where a is a name and F a *predicate. Then instead of interpreting the calculus by assigning values directly to each proposition (sentence) variable, one could assign to each name one member from a set of objects, called the *universe* (*of discourse*) and to each predicate expression a criterion for when that expression is true of an object of the universe (in other words, when an object of the universe satisfies the expression). Such criteria are called *truth* or *satisfaction conditions*. For example, the universe might be numbers and one might assign to the predicate F, a

procedure for testing whether a number is prime. This would have the effect of assigning to Fa the sense or meaning of 'a is a prime number' and the sentence Fa would be true iff the name a has been assigned a prime number.

Another way of supplying truth conditions for predicate expressions is to assign to each a subset of the universe of discourse. Fa is then true iff the object assigned to a belongs to the subset assigned to F. This would amount to a *set-theoretic interpretation* of the simple language introduced in the previous paragraph.

The previous two paragraphs set out the fundamental ideas of interpretation. The next step to be taken here is to remove the simplifying assumptions. To begin with, the propositional (sentential) variables might have the form Gab or $Habc$, or in general involve n-place predicates. Interpretation in that case requires a universe of discourse, assignment of objects to names, and criteria for when an *n-tuple satisfies an n-place *predicate. For example, the universe might be people, and the two-place predicate, G, assigned the procedure for comparing weight, so that Gab would be true iff the person assigned to a was heavier than the person assigned to b. A set-theoretic interpretation would require assigning to each n-place predicate a set of n-tuples of objects in the universe of discourse. For example, Gab would be true iff the pair $<a,b>$ belonged to the set of ordered pairs assigned to G. Formal and mathematical logicians work with set-theoretic interpretations to such an extent that it is common to define 'interpretation' in such a way that it covers only set-theoretic interpretations.

Another simplification made above involved ignoring the possibility that sentences might contain quantifiers. Thus far the discussion has proceeded on the assumption that all sentences are either simple or are complexes constructed out of simple sentences by one or more connectives, and that the truth-values of complex sentences are to be determined from the values already assigned to components of the complex by means of the truth-tables. For example, the sentence $Gab \lor Fb$ is true iff one of Gab or Fb is true (*see* or). Thus, given the interpretation of the names and predicates, one can determine, step by step, the truth-value for every sentence. The truth-tables are thus said to provide a *recursive determination of truth-values*.

The principal achievement of Tarski's truth theory was to extend this recursive determination to cover quantified sentences. To do this Tarski first used the truth-tables to define what it would be for an object to satisfy a complex predicate (or *open sentence*), such as Gxb & Fx. (For a to satisfy this open sentence it must satisfy both Gxb and Fx, that is both Gab and Fa must be true.) A universally quantified sentence, then, is true iff the open sentence which results from removing the quantifier is satisfied by all objects in the universe. An existentially quantified sentence is true iff the open sentence which results when the quantifier is removed is satisfied by at least one object in the universe.

Given Tarski's theory, an interpretation for any language that has the logical structure of the predicate calculus can be specified by choosing a universe, assigning objects to names, and satisfaction conditions to the predicate and relational expressions of that language. Often the formal languages that interest logicians contain only quantified sentences and no assignment of objects to names is required. With Tarski's theory and a preference for set-theoretic interpretations, an interpretation may be defined simply as the objects and sets needed for the interpretation of the names and predicates, together with a function assigning objects to names and sets to predicates. *See also* model.

intersubjectivity. The property of holding in reference to more than one subject, rather than purely subjectively. For example, the proposition 'hydrogen sulphide smells like rotten eggs', may be said to hold intersubjectively because there is common agreement upon its truth.

introspection. Awareness *by* an individual of his *own* states and condition, with particular reference to his mental and emotional activity. The notion that introspection is an adequate guide to complete self-knowledge is problematic. If every mental act or process is introspectable, one must, for example, be able simultaneously to do an addition sum and to observe oneself doing it. But then the act of introspection is a part of one's total mental activity, so it, also, must be introspectable. However if, in principle, one needs to be able to observe oneself observing, in order to allow the ubiquitous access to the psyche of introspection, one surely needs to observe oneself observing oneself observing one's calculation of the addition sum. It is not hard to see that one would have to be able to accomplish, in principle, an infinite number of synchronous mental acts, if it is to be believed that one can 'know oneself' entirely by introspection. *Ryle pointed out this and associated difficulties in *The Concept of Mind*. Both in psychology and philosophy it has been thought more plausible to assign the role of introspection to immediate retrospection.

intuition. A form of uninferred or immediate knowledge. Two principal philosophical uses of the term may be distinguished: first, uninferred knowledge of the truth of a *proposition; second, immediate knowledge of a nonpropositional object. In the latter sense, four kinds of nonpropositional object have been claimed as intuitable: (a) universals; (b) concepts, as in the case of correctly applying a concept without being able to state its rules of application; (c) sensible objects, as in Kant's account of our immediate, nonconceptual relation to sensible objects; and (d) ineffable objects, as in Bergson's account of the inexpressible awareness of duration, or in certain religious accounts of our awareness of God.

intuitionism. 1. (in ethics) The view that (at least some) moral judgments are known to be true by *intuition. **2.** The view that there are several distinct moral duties, that cannot be reduced to one basic duty, in contrast, for example, to *utilitarianism. While both views can be, and are, held separately, they often go together. *See* Moore. **3.** (in mathematics) A system propounded by L.E.J. Brouwer, identifying truth with being known to be true, that is, proven. The main theses of intuitionism are: that a mathematical entity exists only if a constructive existence proof can be given; and that a (mathematical) statement is true only if there is a proof of it, and false only if a proof of its denial can be given. Brouwer's idealist inclinations led him to describe mathematics as investigation of the (ideal) mathematician's "mental constructions". The view is notable for its rejection of classical (or realist) logic, in particular the law of *double negation, the law of *excluded middle, and classical *reductio*.

intuitionistic logic. The logic employed and developed by intuitionistic mathematicians (*see* intuitionism). It arises out of a view concerning the way in which meaning can be conferred on mathematical statements. Mathematical objects, such as numbers, are held to be mental constructs—products of our own mental operations. This means that they can have only those properties which we, as a result of our mental operations, recognize them as having. They are not independently existing objects capable of having properties that we may never be able to discover. On this view, to grasp the meaning of a mathematical statement is to know what mental construction would constitute a proof of it. The statement is true iff there is such a proof.

This account of the meaning of mathematical statements requires the intuitionist to re-examine the logic employed in mathematical reasoning. For classical logic, that employing *truth-functional operators, is based on the supposition that each statement is determinately true or false, whether we can ever come to know this or not. This is the principle of *bivalence, which is presupposed in the construction of *truth-tables. The truth-table definition of a propositional connective, 'or', for example, shows how the *truth-value of 'A or B' is determined from the truth-values of 'A' and 'B' (see or). Since, for the intuitionist, the truth of a statement consists in there being a (constructive) proof of it, his account of the meaning of 'or' proceeds by saying what counts as a proof of 'A or B', given that we know what counts as a proof of 'A' and what counts as a proof of 'B'. A proof of 'A or B' is anything that is either a proof of A or a proof of B. Similar accounts are given for all the other logical operators. In particular, to have a proof of 'not-A' is to have a demonstration that any proof of A can be converted into a proof of something absurd (such as $0 = 1$). Given any statement A, it is not necessarily the case that we either have a proof of A or a demonstration that any proof of A can be converted into a proof of '0 = 1'. That is, we may lack a proof of 'A or not-A' and lacking this we cannot say that it is true. (An undecided statement such as Goldbach's conjecture that every even integer greater than two is expressible as the sum of two primes, would be an example of an A for which this is the case.) Thus the law of *excluded middle cannot be asserted as a law of intuitionistic logic. There are many other respects in which intuitionistic logic diverges from classical logic, but rejection of the law of excluded middle is perhaps the best known and most fundamental of the differences.

What is crucial in the reassessment of the validity of logical principles is the rejection of *realism for a certain class of statements (for what is rejected is the idea that there is an independently existing domain of mathematical objects described by mathematical statements). Similar considerations might also be thought to apply to reasoning in other areas where a non-realist approach is thought to be appropriate (talk about

virtues and vices, for example). Thus the relevance of intuitionistic logic is not restricted to discussions in the foundations of mathematics.

invalid. See valid and invalid.

inventio medii. (Latin for: discovery of the middle.) The formal name for the logical *pons asinorum.

inversion. See obversion.

Ionian school. See Milesian school.

irrational number. See number.

irreflexive. See relation.

is. A word with three fundamentally different uses. In 'The Morning Star is the Evening Star' it indicates identity; in 'This oaf is drunk' predication; and in 'There is a green hill far away' existence. The second reading is in a way redundant, for predication or attribution could be indicated, and in some languages and logical systems is, not by a separate symbol, but through the relative positions of subject and predicate. The problematic relationship between 'ought' and 'is' underlies *Hume's fork and the *naturalistic fallacy. See also being; identity.

Islamic philosophy. Early Islamic philosophy is characterized by a profound tendency towards *syncretism. The theological simplicity of the nascent Islamic religion, which prevailed during the lifetime of its founder, the prophet Muḥammad (570-632), later suffered an assault from such diverse elements as 'Irāqī gnosticism, Christian Hellenism, Persian dualism, and Greek thought. The easily understood profession of the Islamic faith, "There is no god but God and Muḥammad is His prophet", was confronted with the concepts and dialectic of Greek philosophy. These last manifested themselves as possible means to the solution of problems that swiftly arose in early Islamic thought. So the study of Islamic philosophy in its early stages is inevitably the study of the influence of Greek philosophy on Islam.

Furthermore, philosophy and theology are inextricably mingled.

The problems with which the Muslim thinkers wrestled were not new. They included such questions as freewill and predestination, anthropomorphism and allegory, and divine justice. There is a marked similarity between the subjects that preoccupied some of the early Fathers of the Christian Church, such as *Origen and John of Damascus (c.675-749), and those that preoccupied Islam. Indeed, during the centuries following the death of Muḥammad, Christian theology strongly influenced Islamic thought.

M. S. Seale (*Muslim Theology*, London, 1964) has shown that the Christian influence was very obvious in some of the unorthodox Islamic movements. The Damascene Ghaylān (d. 743), one of the first Muslims known to have expressed a belief in freewill, was a contemporary of John of Damascus. He was executed by the caliph because of his views. The thought of the theologian and political activist Jahm b. Ṣafwān (d. 745), who instigated a revolt against the Umayyad dynasty, is a microcosm of Greek Christianity. His allegorization is like that of *Philo, while his ideas about a transcendent God parallel those of Clement of Alexandria (c.150-c.215). Furthermore, Jahm, like Origen, denied the eternity of heaven and hell.

It will be readily appreciated that discussion of such theological subjects called for a high degree of sophistication and ability in dialectic. Both were lacking in Muslim thought until the introduction of Greek philosophy and the logical tools that came with it, such as the syllogism. An infant theology may thus be said to have provided the impetus for Muslims to study the Greeks.

It is easy to trace the general outlines of the transmission of Greek philosophy: many of the peoples whom Islam had conquered were culturally rooted in Hellenism. There was a large Hellenistic element present among the secretaries of the ʿAbbāsid court. At first, it was not the technical concepts of Greek philoso-

phy that gained currency but notions derived from popular philosophy. Later, after the establishment of the ʿAbbāsid caliphate in Baghdād (762 AD), an industry of translating Greek texts into Arabic and Aramaic grew up. This was spurred initially by the caliphs' concern with their health, and belief that Greek medical science could help them. Soon there were translations available, not only of nearly all the medical corpus of Galen and Hippocrates, but also of many important Aristotelian works (the *Categories*, *Metaphysics*, both *Analytics*, and the *Nicomachaean Ethics*), as well as Euclid's *Elements* and Porphyry's *Isagoge*.

However, the Greek work that had the greatest impact on early Islamic thought was the so-called *Theologia Aristotelis*. Despite its name, it was very far from the thought of Aristotle. It was a Neoplatonic compilation that embodied *Plotinus' doctrine of emanation from the One and of the way in which the whole order of being and the material world beneath It took shape. Scholars have shown that this work was in fact a paraphrase of Books 4, 5, and 6 of Plotinus' *Enneads*. The *Liber de Causis* ranks with the *Theologia* as another major source of *Neoplatonism in Islam, partially modified by the 5th-century Neoplatonist Proclus. These two works together contain nearly all the important features of Islamic Neoplatonism, such as an utterly transcendent deity or First Principle, the doctrine of emanation, and the primacy of the Second Principle, Intellect, whose main activity was the generation of the Third Principle, Soul.

While Aristotelian terminology and methods of reasoning quickly spread into Islam, the original thought of Plato, by contrast, had a more muted impact, except perhaps with *al-Fārābī (870-950). While there are obvious *Phaedo*-inspired Platonic references to the world being a prison for the soul, Plato's doctrine of Ideas or Forms, for example, does not seem really to have caught the imagination of the early Muslim thinkers. The ideas of Plotinus had a far greater influence and thus Aristotle often emerges in Neoplatonic guise.

Furthermore, there is frequently an unresolved conflict within the same Arabic work between two views of Allāh. An example is to be found in the 10th century *Rasā'il Ikhwān al-Safā'* (Epistles of the Brethren of Purity). On the one hand, the deity is endowed with some characteristically Islamic features such as unity, the guiding of souls, and the direct granting of gifts such as the ability to read and write. It is He, not the emanations, who sends the prophets. On the other hand, to remain at the pinnacle of a Neoplatonic hierarchy, He is treated Neoplatonically, in that He creates with the aid of the first two emanations (Intellect and Soul) and is unknowable, almost in the Plotinian sense, for no attributes may be ascribed to Him.

The introduction of Greek thought produced a split between progressives and traditionalists, but such was its impact that all sides were ultimately obliged to have recourse to the weaponry of Greek dialectic. The spirit of free enquiry that accompanied the philosophical awakening obviously constituted a grave fundamental threat to many basic Islamic beliefs. Some groups, like the Mu'tazilah school, which began the process of examining Islamic doctrine in Greek terms, were able to remain, for the most part, within the broad pale of Islam, despite occasional persecution. The Mu'tazilah were not freethinkers, as was claimed in the last century, nor rationalists, as has been claimed in this, but speculative philosophers with fundamentally authoritarian instincts. Other thinkers, however, such as al-Rāzī (well known in Europe as Rhazes) (d. 923 or 932), were led further astray by their speculation. His nonconformist thought, which embodied both Platonic and Neoplatonic elements, and his rejection of prophecy, led to his being anathematized by most orthodox Muslims.

*al-Kindī (d. after 866) represents the first major attempt to harmonize philosophy with traditional dogma. For him, God remained the only real cause in the world, but did not believe that there was a conflict between philosophy and revelation. His eclectic work contained both Aristotelian and Neoplatonic elements, which were developed by Abū Nasr *al-Fārābī (known in the medieval West as Abunaser or Alfarabius) (870-950). al-Fārābī was the first true Islamic Neoplatonist. He identified The One of Plotinus with the Islamic Allāh and described a hierarchy in which all other things emanated by a 'necessity' of nature from this First Being, beginning with the First Intellect and proceeding through a series of nine other Intellects.

The work of al-Ash'arī (873/4-935/6) marks a halt in the onslaught of Hellenistic thought. He has been likened, with good reason, to *Aquinas. Groups like the Mu'tazilah had attempted to draw together the strands of the Greek and Islamic intellectual traditions, but they had generated many intellectual problems in the process. al-Ash'arī's significance lay not in solving such problems but in exploiting Greek dialectic for his own orthodox ends. He was principally concerned with defending the omnipotence of God, which he did by using reason to support the truths of Islamic revelation. He did not accept that any of the Aristotelian *categories, except substance and quality, had an objective reality; his views led to the Islamic school of atomists or occasionalists epitomized in the name al-Bāqillānī (d. 1013).

Neoplatonism in Islamic philosophy perhaps reached its climax in the thought of one of the greatest thinkers ever to write in Arabic, Ibn Sīnā (known in the West as *Avicenna) (980-1037). Yet his thought was tinged with a mystical element that made it quite distinct from what had gone before and, at the same time, foreshadowed the later mystical philosophers. Together with al-Fārābī, Avicenna was devastatingly attacked by *al-Ghazālī (1058-1111) in the work *Tahāfut al-Falāsifah* (The Incoherence of the Philosophers). al-Ghazālī elaborated 20 propositions against which the careless believer was to be on his guard.

For him, the world was deliberately created by God and did not just emanate, in Neoplatonic fashion, from a First Being.

After al-Ghazālī there are a number of interesting philosophical developments. The increasing aridity of medieval Muslim thought produced a reaction among many Muslims who began to yearn for a more personal communion with God than was possible in orthodox Islam with its prevailing philosophical systems. The result was Ṣūfism or Islamic mysticism; this word was probably coined from the Arabic word 'ṣūf' meaning 'wool', in reference to the woollen garments worn by the early mystics. It has been well pointed out that soon after the death of al-Ghazālī, who had tried to reconcile the Islamic sciences and Ṣūfism, the first great organized Ṣūfī orders began to appear at the popular level.

A mystical element invaded philosophy as well, and produced what might be termed the Ishrāqī (Illuminationist) school of Islamic philosophers. Its best known exponent was al-Suhrawardī (1155–91) of Aleppo, whose thought was bound up with the science and nature of light. Light permeated everything and he envisaged a hierarchy of pure lights at the top of which stood the Light of Lights or Necessary Light whose principal attribute was unity. al-Suhrawardī's greatest work, Ḥikmat al-Ishrāq (The Wisdom of the Illumination), was a mixture of Neoplatonism and mysticism derived from various oriental sources.

Ṣūfism could also be said to be a popular reaction against the Peripatetics: Aristotle's greatest Muslim disciple Ibn Rushd (called in the West *Averroes) (1126–98) was born in Muslim Spain. His defence of Aristotle, expressed in wide-ranging commentaries on the Stagirite's philosophy and original works that show how his philosophical predecessors, al-Fārābī and Avicenna, departed from Aristotle's thought, has given Averroes a unique place in the history of Islamic philosophy. Furthermore, just as al-Ghazālī attacked al-Fārābī and Avi-

cenna in Tahāfut al-Falāsifah, so Averroes in turn attacked al-Ghazālī in his most famous work Tahāfut al-Tahāfut (The Incoherence of the Incoherence), accusing al-Ghazālī, among many other things, of misunderstanding the whole question of the attributes of God and how such concepts as speech and sight might be predicated of the Supreme Being. Averroes' impact on Islamic thought, however, was slight when compared to the enormous influence which he had in medieval Europe, which was rocked by a wave of "Averroism" when 15 of his 38 commentaries were translated from Arabic into Latin in the 13th century.

But by the end of the 13th century the great vigour of Islamic philosophy and thought was more or less spent. Commentaries gave birth to supercommentaries and glosses and, as in the field of Arabic literature, little great and original work was produced between 1300 AD and 1800 AD. A variety of reasons has been adduced for this: politics, in the form of the devastating invasions of the Mongols, must have played a part. The ever increasing rigidity of Islamic theology and law, epitomized early in the 10th century in the legal phrase, 'the closing of the door of ijtihād (independent reasoning)', must also have been a major factor.

The invasion of Egypt by Napoleon in 1798 AD, and the ideals of the French Revolution which were thereby introduced, produced an enormous culture shock in a Muslim world which was in decline culturally, politically, and philosophically. The ensuing problem of how—or even, whether—to try to reconcile Western thought and culture with Islamic thought and traditional sciences is one that has still not been solved satisfactorily. Muslim thinkers such as al-Afghānī (1838–97) and Muḥammad 'Abduh (1849–1905) wrestled with this problem but, though imbued with Western ideas, they were at heart distrustful of the West and its culture. Western philosophies have, of course, gained adherents, such as the Egyptian

A. R. Badawī who espoused existentialism and wrote such works as *Existential Time* (1943), and others who have written on logical positivism. But these Western orientated thinkers can hardly be characterized as Islamic; modern Arab philosophers have yet to produce a system of philosophy that may be described as both truly Islamic and truly modern.

isolationism. A theory of aesthetic interpretation that holds that a work of art may, or should, be understood without reference to its cultural and historical context. *Compare* contextualism.

isomorphic. Having the same structure, due to resemblance between corresponding parts (*see also* structuralism). The term is applicable in relating material objects, social organizations, works of art, and abstract concepts. Often the resemblance referred to is determined on the basis of the functions of the parts. In logic and mathematics, the term is applied to models (interpretations of wffs) and sets, if there is a one-to-one correspondence of parts and structure (between two or more models or sets). *Carnap, in *Meaning and Necessity*, applied the term *intensionally isomorphic* to sentences that are logically equivalent and share the same structure.

J

Jain philosophy. Jainism is an Indian religion founded in the 5th century BC by the 'Jina' (conqueror) Mahāvīra. Its philosophy combines archaic Indian nature-philosophical speculations (*compare* Vaiśeṣika) with the quest for liberation from the cycle of rebirth. It soon ossified in doctrinalism, but it is possible to point to some creative thinkers, like Kundakunda (4th century AD).

The Jain system is presented under seven headings. (1) Lifeless substances (*ajīva*), comprising space, the media of movement (*dharma*) and rest, time, and matter (*pudgala*), which consists of homogeneous atoms. (2) An infinite number of souls (*jīva*). Essentially possessed of unlimited knowledge, power, and bliss, the souls become deprived of these qualities through (3) the influx (*āsrava*) of subtle matter on account of words, thoughts, and deeds. Weighed down by it, the souls suffer (4) bondage (*bandha*) in the world of phenomena, in the form of transmigration. By (5) refusing to allow further matter to enter (*saṃvara*), and by (6) exterminating (*nirjarā*) the already present matter by means of a strict ethical discipline and severe penance, the soul obtains (7) liberation (*mokṣa*), and moves upwards to the top of the universe.

James, William (1842–1910). American psychologist and philosopher. He graduated in medicine at Harvard where he taught comparative anatomy, eventually becoming Professor of Philosophy and later of Psychology.

James' philosophy of radical empiricism developed the ideas of *Peirce and was expounded in his collection of essays *The Will to Believe* (1897), the treatise *Pragmatism* (1907), and *The Varieties of Religious Experience* (1902), an important account of the nature and cognitive status of religion. James claimed that all metaphysical disputes could be either resolved or trivialized by examining the practical consequences of alternative answers; scientific theories are instruments to guide future action, not final answers to questions about nature. In religion and ethics man is free to decide which of various conflicting hypotheses to accept; if the choice is of vital concern to him and if he cannot rationally settle a question then it is right and necessary to follow his inclination. Ideas must have "cash-value": an idea is right and true if it has fruitful consequences. *See also* James-Lange theory; pragmatism.

James-Lange theory. A theory of emotions formulated (independently) by William *James and Carl Lange, stating that subjective feelings are generated by bodily changes that follow perception of some "exciting fact". The theory as presented by James in *Principles of Psychology* (1890) is that "...we feel sorry because we cry, angry because we strike...".

Jaspers, Karl (1883-1969). German philosopher and one of the founders of *existentialism, the themes of which he introduced in his *Psychologie der Weltanschauungen* (1919), and elaborated more profoundly in his three-volume *Philosophie* (1932). He presents existentialism as an attempt to deal with the problem of '*Existenz*' (a special sense of 'existence') through reason. But this cannot be through objective thought since existence is not an external object, but is transcendent. By existence Jaspers means three things. (1) The human condition, limited and revealed by ultimate situations of suffering, guilt, and death, which man experiences and is part of and thus cannot make objective. (2) Existence implies freedom, and the free existent is responsible for (and thus guilty of) his actions. (3) Existence means communication between existents, and man's search for truth becomes his striving to transcend his own existence and thus communicate.

jen. (Chinese for: humanity *and* benevolence.) The basic principle of Confucius' moral and social philosophy. *See* Confucianism.

Jewish philosophy. A concern with the ultimate questions of the nature of the Universe and the human condition has been characteristic of Judaism from its beginnings. There has, however, always been a plurality of approaches determined to a large extent by the historical conditions governing Jewish life and the external influences that have operated on Jewish thought. Like Christianity and Islam, Judaism represents a constructive synthesis of biblical monotheism and Greek philosophy. There has been considerable reciprocal influence between thinkers of the three religious traditions.

The earliest written source for Jewish ideas is the Hebrew Bible. Considered as a divinely revealed or inspired text, this became the foundation for all subsequent Jewish thought. The Bible does not present a systematic philosophy. The product of different authors and times, its ideas are expressed by means of myths, proclamations, parables, and poems more often than in continuous reasoned argument. Despite the diversity, certain common strands stand out, notably the belief in a single, personal God, creator of the Universe and of man, caring for his creation, intervening in history, and sanctioning an elaborate code of social regulations. There is also a strong belief in the destiny of the people of Israel, sometimes interpreted in universal terms. Later books, such as Proverbs and Ecclesiastes, present folk wisdom interspersed with general philosophical reflections, and Job contains a profound treatment of the problem of human suffering.

The centrality of the Bible was already established when Greek and Hebrew thought first came into direct contact, after the conquests of Alexander. The earliest Greek references to the Jews describe them as a race of philosophers. The object of the Hellenistic Jewish thinkers was to reach an accommodation between Greek and Hebrew ideas, and between the rival claims of revealed religion and rational philosophy. They identified many common elements, and even asserted the essential harmony of the two traditions, but they insisted on the primacy of Jewish teachings, and maintained that the ideas of the Greek philosophers derived from Jewish origins. The surviving writings of the period, notably the voluminous works of *Philo and Josephus and shorter treatises such as the *Wisdom of Solomon* and *4 Maccabees*, reveal the influence of the Greek philosophical schools of the time, particularly *Platonism, *Stoicism, and *Pythagoreanism. These writings exercised a profound influence on early Christian thought.

From the 3rd century AD the main centres of Jewish thought were for several centuries in the Aramaic-speaking East. The literature of this period, notably the *Talmud*, presents little systematic philosophy. It consists largely of collections of fragments, presented in dialectical form, expressing widely differing opinions and betraying the influence of Greek and Persian ideas. With the rise of Islamic *Kalām there is a significant resurgence of philosophical activity, beginning among the Karaites, who rejected the oral tradition of the rabbis, but soon spreading to their Rabbanite opponents, beginning with *Sa'adya. From the 10th century on there is a rich Jewish philosophical literature in Arabic, paralleling the work of Muslim philosophers, following the same trends (Kalām, *Neoplatonism, *Aristotelianism), and grappling with similar problems: the conflicting claims of reason and revelation, the existence and attributes of God, divine providence versus human freewill, and questions of law and ethics (*see* Islamic philosophy). The best known of the medieval Jewish rationalists is Moses *Maimonides, but there is a vast literature, much of which remains to be edited and studied.

At the same time there was a parallel stream of mystical speculation, partly deriving from ancient gnostic sources but incorporating many different elements, and issuing in the theosophical system of the *Kabbalah. Although the medieval Kabbalah is essentially a reaction against the extreme rationalism of the philosophers, it must also be considered as a philosophic attempt to reconcile Jewish monotheism with Greek naturalism, and some thinkers combined rationalism and mysticism to a high degree, for example, the Kabbalistic philosopher Moses Naḥmanides (1194–1270) and the philosopher-poets Solomon *Ibn Gabirol and Yehudah *Hallevi. In due course, mysticism came to replace rationalism as the dominant factor in Jewish intellectual life; it has

exercised a profound influence even on rationalist thinkers down to the present day. Meanwhile, the rationalist philosophy was also attacked from within, notably by Ḥasdai *Crescas and Isaac Abrabanel (1437–1508), who felt that Maimonides and others had gone too far in identifying Judaism with Aristotelianism.

Most of the authors mentioned so far lived in Muslim lands, or in the Spain of the Christian Reconquest. In most Christian countries the oppressed conditions of Jewish existence did not permit free participation in the general intellectual life, even though Jews played an important part as mediators of culture by translating Arabic works into Latin, and Christian thinkers were greatly influenced by translations of the works of Jewish philosophers such as Maimonides and Ibn Gabirol. However, with a gradual improvement in the treatment of the Jewish communities, Jewish thinkers did emerge in Christian lands, noteworthy examples being Judah (son of Isaac) Abrabanel (*see* Ebreo) in Renaissance Italy or Baruch *Spinoza in 17th-century Holland. In Germany the first Jewish philosopher of importance was Moses *Mendelssohn (1729–86), and from the later 18th century on Jews participated increasingly in the intellectual life of Western Europe, although in Eastern Europe the process of integration was much slower.

Jewish reaction to the *Enlightenment and to political and social emancipation took many forms. At one extreme there were those who turned their backs on the new developments and sought to maintain the traditional structures of Jewish life and thought; at the other there were many who abandoned Judaism entirely. Between these two extremes there was a wide spectrum of responses, expressing not a superficial diversity but a radical fragmentation in conceptions of the essence and meaning of Judaism. Under the influence of prevailing modes of thought in the wider society there was a polarization between religion and secularism that represents a genuinely new departure. On the one hand there was a tendency to define Judaism purely as a religion, which gave rise to rival religious movements such as Reform, Conservatism, and Neo-Orthodoxy, each with its own theological rationale: on the other hand there was a secularist tendency, minimizing the theological content of Judaism and focusing rather on ethical or national concepts. All these new movements are more or less products of the prevailing rationalism, although to a greater or lesser extent they might all also accommodate supernaturalistic, mystical, or romantic elements.

Given this extreme diversity of attitudes, it is hard to judge what may legitimately be called 'Jewish philosophy' in the modern period. Many modern philosophers have been Jews, without their thought presenting any distinctively Jewish features. Again, some exponents of Judaism must be categorized as theologians rather than philosophers. It is possible, however, to define certain philosophical tendencies in the understanding of the nature and destiny of Judaism, and to identify certain external philosophical influences on Jewish thought.

Foremost in the latter category were the theories of *Kant, *Schelling, and *Hegel. Several 19th-century thinkers sought to produce a philosophy of Judaism under one or more of these influences, for example, Nachman Krochmal (1785-1840), Solomon Formstecher (1808-89), Samuel Hirsch (1815-89), and Moritz Lazarus (1824-1903). Krochmal also pioneered the critical study of historical sources with a view to defining the essence of Judaism, thus preparing the ground for the *Wissenschaft des Judentums* (Science of Judaism) movement, chiefly represented by Leopold Zunz (1794-1886) and Abraham Geiger (1810-74). Meanwhile, other thinkers, such as S. L. Steinheim (1789-1866) and S. D. Luzzatto (1800-65), rejected the primacy of philosophic rationalism and insisted on revelation as the foundation of Judaism.

Another response to the new situation was Zionism, a political philosophy many of whose advocates—for example, A. H. Ginsberg ('Aḥad Ha'am') (1856-1927) and A. D. Gordon (1856-1922)—saw the life of the nation rather than religion as the cardinal feature of Judaism. Others, however, such as A. I. Kook (1865-1935) and Martin *Buber, developed a religious philosophy of Zionism, often blended with mystical ideas.

Hermann *Cohen (1842-1918), with his original synthesis of *idealism and Judaism, exercised a seminal influence on Jewish thinkers in the early 20th century, foremost of whom were Leo Baeck (1873-1956), Buber, and Franz *Rosenzweig (1886-1929). Each of these developed his own understanding of the essence of Judaism and the role of Judaism in the world. While sympathetic to the claims of rationalism (and of Zionism), they all developed distinctively religious, theocentric philosophies of Judaism, and all devoted close attention to the differences between Judaism and Christianity. The standpoint of Buber and Rosenzweig is close to that of the existentialists, and forms the basis of most subsequent philosophy of Judaism.

The Nazi holocaust, which destroyed the life of European Jewry, marks the end of an era. It brought to a close the German phase of Jewish thought, with its effort to harmonize Judaism with German idealism. Henceforth the language of Jewish philosophy is English, and its home, with a few isolated exceptions (for example, Ignaz Maybaum (1897-1976), a pupil of Rosenzweig, who worked in Britain), is North America. The crisis of the holocaust, with the challenge it presents to faith in a benign God, in human progress, and in the destiny of Israel, still dominates most Jewish thinking, and has produced a variety of responses. The debate between Reform and Orthodoxy, centring on the nature of *halakhah* (religious law), continues to highlight the old problem of the conflict of revelation and reason. An original American development is the Reconstructionist movement (founded by M. M. Kaplan (1881-), which combines an extreme form of naturalism with the maintenance of traditional forms of religious observance. In general, however, rationalism has yielded to a more existential philosophy of dialogue, of which the outstanding modern exponent is A. J. *Heschel (1907-72).

Johnson, Alexander Bryan (1786-1867). American philosopher who settled in Utica, N.Y., in 1801, where he had a long and successful career in business and finance. His claim to philosophical fame rests on three publications: *The Philosophy of Human Knowledge* (1828), *A Treatise on Language* (1836), and *The Meaning of Words* (1854). These anticipate many moves familiar now from the writings of the logical positivists and *Ryle; for instance, "The word 'gravity' names many interesting and important phenomena; but if, in addition to these, we look for gravity itself, we act as ignorantly as the child at the opera, who, after listening with impatience to the music, singing and dancing, said: 'I am tired of these; I want the opera'."

judgment. *See* proposition.

Jung, Carl Gustav (1875-1961). Swiss psychiatrist and psychologist; from 1907 collaborator and disciple of *Freud. They split when, following independent clinical investigations, Jung published *Die Psychologie der unbewussten Prozesse* (1913), rejecting Freud's theory of the sexual etiology of psychoneurosis and advocating instead 'analytical psychology' to tackle the patient's current conflicts and tensions.

Jung distinguished four primary functions of the mind: thinking, feeling, sensation, and intuition. He classified personalities into introvert and extravert types, according to the individual's attitude to the external world. Man's aim in life, he stated, is the achievement of psychic harmony between cultivation of the self and devotion to the outer world.

justice. A concept traditionally defined by the Latin tag *suum cuique tribuere* (to allocate to each their own). This essentially backward-looking and individualistic ideal of securing for all their presumably diverse and several antecedent deserts and entitlements is properly to be contrasted, not identified, with the forward-looking Procrustean and collectivist ideal of imposing an equality of outcome. The distinction can be collapsed only if it is assumed that all concerned are, in whatever respects it is thought determine desert and entitlement, indistinguishable. This can arise, for instance, if it is argued that neither the environmentally nor the hereditarily conditioned characteristics of the individual can be essential. Certainly justice requires the equal treatment of equals, and campaigns for justice are often compaigns for equality (in certain respects) for previously disadvantaged groups. But it does not follow that all individuals are relevantly equal, nor that refusing to discriminate by, say, race or sex requires that no distinctions be made within such irrelevant groupings themselves.

Distributive justice has been since Aristotle distinguished from corrective; the former being concerned with who ought to get what goods, the latter with punishment for offences committed. *See also* law, philosophy of.

K

Kabbalah. (Hebrew for: tradition.) The mystical Jewish tradition in general, and in particular the theosophical system whose classical text is the *Zohar*. Jewish mysticism has its roots in antiquity, and shows strong signs of gnostic influence. Its two main preoccupations were cosmogony (*Ma'aseh Bereshith*) and the nature of God (*Ma'aseh Merkabah*); it also had a practical side, aiming at wonderworking and especially the artificial creation of a man.

In the Middle Ages, despite an inherent conflict with rationalism, there were close links between speculative Kabbalah and philosophy, which are particularly evident in the thought of such men as *Ibn Gabirol and *Hallevi. For the kabbalists, as for *Maimonides, God is in his essence unknowable: he is called simply 'Infinity' (*Ein Sof*). The chasm between the Infinite and the finite world is bridged by means of a series of emanations (*sefiroth*), which are progressively more accessible and knowable (*see* emanationism). God can thus be known through his action in the world, and also through a parallelism that exists between the lower and upper worlds.

Kabbalistic thought reached its first peak in 13th-century Spain, with Moses ben Naḥman (Naḥmanides) (1194-1270) and the *Zohar* (written in Aramaic by Moses of Leon, c.1283), and a second in Safed (in Galilee) in the 16th century, with Joseph Karo (1488-1575), Moses Cordovero (1522-70), Isaac Luria (1535-72), and Ḥayyim Vital (d. 1620). Kabbalah has exercised a profound influence on Jewish thought up to modern times, and furnished the intellectual basis of *Ḥasidism. It enjoyed a considerable vogue among Christians in the 15th and 16th centuries, for example, J. Reuchlin (1455-1522) and Paracelsus (1493-1541), and was also influential in the modern theosophical movement (*see* theosophy).

Kalām. (Arabic for: speech.) In *Islamic philosophy the adducing of philosophical proofs to justify religious doctrine. The word is often translated as 'Muslim scholastic theology'; those who practised it were called 'mutakallimūn'.

Kant, Immanuel (1724-1804). German philosopher who labelled his own position "transcendental" or "critical" idealism. No name can do justice to his profound and complex philosophy, which arose out of the two most important philosophical theories of his time: the *rationalism of Descartes and

Leibniz and the *empiricism of Locke, Berkeley, and Hume. Kant was Hume's junior by thirteen years and was well acquainted with at least some of his work. In Kant's own words, it was Hume's account of causality "that first interrupted my dogmatic slumber and gave a completely different direction to my enquiries in the field of speculative philosophy" (*Prolegomena*).

Kant was born in Königsberg, Prussia, which today is in the U.S.S.R. and called Kaliningrad. Kant never left the town, and for most of his life taught at the University, at which he became professor of logic and metaphysics in 1770. He was deeply interested in the natural sciences, and his early publications were concerned with problems in astronomy and geophysics. One of his pupils wrote that "nothing worth knowing was indifferent to him".

Kant produced his most influential work late in life. Although his output was large, his most important works are the three Critiques: *Kritik der reinen Vernunft* (Critique of Pure Reason) (1781), *Kritik der praktischen Vernunft* (Critique of Practical Reason) (1788), and *Kritik der Urteilskraft* (Critique of Judgment) (1790). These works will be referred to as the first, second, and third *Critiques*.

The first *Critique* is one of the masterpieces of philosophy, although also one of the most unreadable. Kant himself described it as "dry, obscure, contrary to all ordinary ideas, and on top of that prolix". The second *Critique* is disappointing in comparison, although the views Kant expressed in it on moral philosophy have been widely influential. The third *Critique* is concerned with the nature of aesthetic and teleological judgments.

Kant aimed, in the first *Critique*, to examine whether metaphysics, once queen of all the sciences, could be restored to her rightful place. The most important questions in philosophy had become the subject of endless and apparently irresolvable controversy. Kant hoped to make progress comparable to the recent advances in science (such as those of Newton, whom Kant greatly admired) by undertaking a critical examination of the nature of reason itself. The 'pure reason' of the title means 'a priori reason'—what can be known by reason apart from anything derived from experience. Kant agreed with the empiricists that there cannot be *innate ideas in the sense of anything known prior to any sense experience, but he was not prepared to say that therefore all knowledge must be derived from experience. Hitherto philosophers had assumed that "our knowledge must conform to objects. But all attempts to extend our knowledge of objects have, on this assumption, ended in failure." So he tried a different method of approach. "We must therefore make trial whether we may not have more success in the tasks of metaphysics, if we suppose that objects must conform to knowledge." Kant suggested that the apparatus of human sensibility and understanding, that is, the way in which we perceive, identify, and reflect upon objects might itself have a form or structure which in some way moulds or contributes to our experience.

Kant compared his new approach to that of Copernicus. Rejecting the idea that the sun and stars revolve round the spectator, "he tried whether he might not have better success if he made the spectator to revolve and the stars to remain at rest." Thus the apparent movement of the stars was in fact in part the movement of the spectator. In the same way, some of the properties that we observe in objects may be due to the nature of the observer rather than the objects themselves. This is indeed Kant's conclusion. There are two sources of human knowledge: sensibility and understanding—"through the former objects are given to us; through the latter they are thought." It is only through the workings of the understanding that sense experience comes to be ordered and classified into experience of an objective world, the world of nature. "The order and regularity in objects, which we

entitle *nature*, we ourselves introduce. The understanding is itself the lawgiver of nature."

Kant claimed that there were some concepts (twelve in all) that were not learnt from experience but were thought by the understanding independently of experience and then applied to it. These twelve concepts, the "categories", enable us to make sense of our experience, but have no significance apart from their application to our sense experience. He thought the categories indispensable for experience. They are concepts that are essential if any creature is going to be able to make judgments about his experience. The twelve categories form a sort of minimum conceptual apparatus for making sense of the world.

Kant's procedure differed significantly from the generally psychological empiricist method, for rather than seeking for the impressions upon which certain ideas are based, he investigated the relationships that exist between the fundamental concepts related to a subject's having experience of objects. He was concerned with theoretical questions of a sort he calls "transcendental", such as "under what conditions is experience of an objective world possible?"

One of the conclusions of the main, positive part of the first *Critique*, the "Analytic", is that the conditions of knowledge are such that it is not possible to apply the concepts which we employ in our knowledge of the objects of sense experience to anything that lies beyond or transcends such experience. Any attempt to apply our concepts in such a way leads to inconsistency and error. Consequently Kant believed that the claims of speculative metaphysics are worthless (a conclusion very close to Hume's in his *Inquiry concerning Human Understanding*). However, he believed that the human mind is naturally disposed to fall into such error by attempting to employ concepts beyond the sphere in which alone they can be legitimately used, and the second part of the first *Critique*, the "Dialectic", demonstrates the confusions and illusions that can arise through such misemployment.

The core of the "Analytic" is the portion known as the "Transcendental Deduction". Kant's arguments are dense and complex, but one of the conclusions for which he is arguing could be expressed as follows. Instead of trying to explain how the idea of an enduring physical object could ever be arrived at by building up from small pieces of experience, such as *sense data, Kant takes an entirely different line. It is fundamentally mistaken to take knowledge of tiny pieces of sense experience as the primary data, for even to have such knowledge already assumes knowledge of an objective world—"our inner experience is possible only on the assumption of outer experience." Kant argues that even the simple fact of being self-conscious, being aware of oneself, assumes an objective world: "the mere consciousness of my own existence proves the existence of objects in space outside me." So what for Descartes was the starting point is for Kant somewhere near the finishing post.

The first *Critique*, the critique of pure theoretical reason, is concerned with a priori grounds for judgment about experience. Pure practical reason is concerned with the a priori grounds for action, and, especially, moral action. For Kant, in the second *Critique* and his other writings on moral philosophy, such as the well known *Grundlegung zur Metaphysik der Sitten* (Groundwork of the Metaphysic of Morals) (1785), this involves awareness of the moral law, and a motive for acting in accordance with that law. He claims that this motive, if we are concerned with *pure* reason, must be different in kind from any natural, empirically conditioned interest.

Kant makes it plain that he is not attempting to dismiss our ordinary moral judgments or to produce a new morality: "no new principle is set forth in it [the second *Critique*], but only a *new formula*." Kant's most famous contribution to moral philosophy does in fact appear to be a formula. This is the categorical imperative, the best known version of which is "Act only on that maxim which you can at the same time will to become a universal law." This appears to provide us with a necessary, but not sufficient condition for a moral principle, namely, that one should only adopt and act on principles which everyone could adopt, but it doesn't tell us which of such principles—for there are many—we ought to adopt. So the categorical imperative is best seen not as a *source* of moral principles, but as a test of those principles we already have.

In calling his imperative 'categorical', Kant contrasts it with hypothetical imperatives, which are imperatives we can choose to take note of, *if* we have a particular aim. A hypothetical imperative might be offered as prudential advice: for example, "Go to bed early." This advice might be offered because it is believed that going to bed early maintains good health. So it is only if we wish to maintain our health that we need take note of the advice; for it is really in the hypothetical form, "If you wish to maintain your health, go to bed early." Similarly, a hypothetical imperative may concern the performance of a skill: "If you wish to hit the ball, keep your head still." But morality, Kant claims, depends on no such "if's", nor does it depend on the particular wishes, inclinations, or idiosyncratic nature of the agent.

If the motive action is not any particular wish, what is it? For Kant, to act morally is to act for the sake of duty. Feelings and inclinations cannot be the motive for moral action, for however desirable and admirable they may seem to be, they are not, he claims, subject to the will. We cannot order ourselves to love someone, or summon up sympathy at will, and it cannot be our duty to do what we are unable to do—'ought' implies 'can'. Nor should we assess the worth of actions by their results or consequences, for these may turn out quite differently from the way the agent anticipated, for reasons outside his control. The only test of a moral action is whether it is done in accordance with and for the sake of duty.

These principles led Kant to maintain that it was never right to tell a lie: the obligation to be truthful cannot be limited by any expediency. "To tell a falsehood to a murderer who asked us whether our friend, of whom he was in pursuit, had not taken refuge in our house, would be a crime."

Kant does allow one type of feeling as morally important, the feeling that arises from awareness of the moral law, which he calls 'respect': a respect which is a sort of awe, expressed by Kant at the conclusion of the second *Critique*. "Two things fill the mind with ever new and increasing admiration and awe, the oftener and more steadily we reflect on them: *the starry heavens above and the moral law within*."

Kant's attempts in the third *Critique* to provide an objective basis (that is, a basis in external objects) for aesthetic judgment mirror his ethical theory. True aesthetic judgment, or judgments of taste, as Kant calls them, must be distinguished from judgments as to what is merely agreeable, which are idiosyncratic to particular individuals. Aesthetic judgments must be based not on the contingent likes and dislikes of individuals but on what is common to everybody: "the judgment of taste exacts agreement from every one; and a person who describes something as beautiful insists that everyone *ought* to give the object in question his approval and follow suit in describing it as beautiful. We are suitors for agreement from every one else, because we are fortified with a ground common to all." This ground is what Kant calls "common sense", which is the ability to recognize what is beautiful by taking delight in it. This ability is related to, but different from, our cognitive abilities.

The third *Critique* is in fact concerned with very much more than just aesthetics, for the second part of it is concerned with an ability Kant connects with "common sense", that is, the ability to identify purposiveness in nature, or

teleological judgment, as he calls it. He regards the unity of Nature or science as an unprovable but useful postulate, the assumption of which leads to the constant endeavour of scientists to subsume particular scientific laws under more general ones. The principle of the purposiveness of Nature is related to this idea, and it is a principle which Kant claims to be "a special a priori concept." It is a postulate whose assumption makes scientific laws possible, rather than an empirical principle. Purposiveness, or a hierarchical system of empirical laws, is not something necessarily inherent in objects, but rather something we are bound to regard Nature as possessing.

Kant connects the idea of purposiveness with aesthetic judgment by claiming that our recognition of the purposiveness of an object leads to a certain sort of pleasure which it is open to everybody to have, if they similarly recognize this quality. "*Beauty* is the form of *finality* [purposiveness] in an object, so far as perceived in it *apart from the representation of an end*."

Kant has had a very great influence over subsequent philosophy. Immediately, in Germany, he influenced the school of speculative idealism, whose adherents included *Fichte and *Hegel. Although Kant in his more positivist moods might well have rejected their speculations, nevertheless it must be said that there is much in his writings that lays the foundations for speculative metaphysics and which in this summary has been ignored, such as his discussions of "things in themselves" (*see* Ding-an-Sich) and "noumena" (*see* noumenon).

karma. (Sanskrit for: action.) In both Hinduism and Buddhism, action very generally conceived as a way of life and a moral force. In the *Bhagavadgītā* the way of action (*karma-yoga*) is presented as one of the three ways in which man can attain union with God, the other two being the way of wisdom (*jñāna-yoga*) and the way of devotion (*bhakti-yoga*). *Karma* determines whether a person is born again in a fortunate or an unfortunate condition (see saṃsāra).

Kepler (or **Keppler**), Johannes (1571-1630). German astronomer, who studied at Tübingen, taught mathematics at Graz and Linz, and worked under Tycho Brahe. Following *Copernicus, Kepler upheld the application of mathematical principles in astronomy, but corrected the Pythagorean description of the uniform motion of planets in spherical orbits. Kepler's three laws, explicated by *Newton, showed planets moving in ellipses of which the sun is one focus; their motion is not uniform, and their period of revolution around the sun is proportional to their distance from it.

Keynes, John Maynard, 1st Baron Keynes (1883-1946). British economist, son of J. N. *Keynes. His *General Theory of Employment, Interest and Money* (1936) was revolutionary, and policies supposedly derived from it guided or misguided many countries until a counter-revolution got under way in the 1970s.

Keynes wrote an important philosophical work *A Treatise on Probability* (1921) on *probability and *induction, in which he argued that probability attaches only to propositions (rather than events), and is *objective* in that a proposition always has a certain probability, independently of our recognition of it. However, probabilities are assigned to propositions only in relation to some other proposition or propositions taken as premises (or evidence). That is, we can only talk of the (objective) probability of p, given premise q; or the probability of p, given evidence r and s. Induction and probability are linked by equating 'p is highly probable' with 'p has been arrived at by a justifiable induction'. Keynes' account of justifiable induction shows a similarity with Mill's (see Mill's methods), whereby the variety, rather than the number, of confirming instances (see confirmation) is of central importance (see limited independent variety, principle of).

Keynes, John Neville (1852-1949). British logician and economist, who lectured in moral science at Cambridge. His chief work was *Formal Logic* (1884).

Kierkegaard, Søren (1813-55). Danish philosopher and religious writer. In 1830 Kierkegaard enrolled at the University of Copenhagen, ostensibly to study theology; in fact, he spent most of his time reading literature and philosophy, which were then in Denmark under the spell of contemporary German culture, especially the philosophy of *Hegel. In 1840 he became engaged to Regina Olsen, but soon broke this off, having decided that his personal mission from God to be a writer was incompatible with the married state.

Kierkegaard's first significant book was his M.A. dissertation, *Om Begrebet Ironi* (The Concept of Irony) (1841), a brilliantly original work that criticized prevailing Hegelian assumptions and is even now an important contribution to its subject. Kierkegaard's polemic against Hegel was continued in his early philosophico-aesthetic ('pseudonymous') works, sometimes even in their very titles: for example, *Enten-Eller* (Either-Or) (1843), *Philosophiske Smuler* (Philosophical Fragments) (1844), and the *Afsluttende Uvidenskabelig Efterskrift* (Concluding Unscientific Postscript) (1846), the latter actually being a massive tome containing Kierkegaard's doctrine of 'subjective truth'. Among his later, more directly Christian books, are: *Kjerlighedens Gjerninger* (Works of Love) (1847), *Christelige Taler* (Christian Discourses) (1848), and *Sygdomen Til Døden* (The Sickness unto Death) (1849).

Kierkegaard's stress on the primary importance of the "existing individual", together with his analysis of such features of religious consciousness as faith, choice, despair, and dread, became widely influential after 1918, above all in Germany. In particular, Kierkegaard has deeply affected many protestant theologians and existential philosophers, including Barth, Heidegger, Jaspers, Marcel, and Buber. *See* existentialism.

knowledge. Philosophical questions about the nature of knowledge belong either to *epistemology or to the philosophy of mind (*see* mind, philosophy of). The two groups of questions may be roughly separated by saying that the first group concentrates on the nature of knowledge, whereas the second concentrates on the nature of the knower. **1.** (in epistemology) Philosophers recognize three main kinds of knowledge. (a) Knowledge that, or 'factual knowledge'. There is fairly general agreement that the following are necessary and sufficient conditions of *X*'s knowledge that *p*. (i) *p* must be true. (ii) *X* must believe that *p*, in the sense that he sincerely asserts, or is ready so to assert, that *p*. (iii) *X* must be in a position to know that *p*. The sufficiency of these conditions has been challenged (*see* E. L. Gettier, in A. Phillips Griffiths (ed.), *Knowledge and Belief*, Oxford, 1967, pp. 144-6). But even if the conditions are sufficient, there is much room for debate as to what (iii) properly involves. For Descartes, the grounds are adequate only if one's assertion is indubitable (*compare* certainty and doubt), but this view is now generally rejected. (b) Knowledge how, or 'practical knowledge'. The importance of this kind of knowledge has been emphasized by Ryle, who argued in *The Concept of Mind* (1949) that to suppose such knowledge to be reducible to a knowledge of truths is a mere legend—the 'intellectualist legend'. (c) Knowledge of people, places, and things, or 'knowledge by acquaintance'. Such knowledge often involves knowledge of types (a) or (b), but does not seem necessarily to do so. For example, one may have a vague knowledge of a person, even though one cannot state any facts about him, and does not know how, say, to interest or amuse him. In his earlier writings, for example *The Problems of Philosophy* (1912), Bertrand Russell took 'knowledge by acquaintance' to be knowledge only of that of

which we are directly aware, that is sense data. He distinguished such knowledge from 'knowledge by description', and argued that many cases of what would normally be regarded as knowledge by acquaintance, for example the knowledge of persons, are really cases of knowledge by description.
2. (in the philosophy of mind) If *X* has knowledge of any of the three kinds mentioned above, one is apt to say that *X* must have a mind; so to ask philosophical questions about knowledge can be a way of asking questions about the nature of mind. Modern philosophers emphasize that to say that *X* knows this or that is not to say that something is happening in an immaterial substance directly accessible to *X* alone; it might be no more than to say that *X* has a disposition to behave in certain ways, for example, in the case of practical knowledge, to perform certain tasks successfully.

Kripke, Saul (1941-). American logician and philosopher who has made important technical advances in *modal logic and *truth theory, and had influential insights in philosophy of language and metaphysics. In papers such as 'Naming and Necessity' (1972), he argues that *proper names have meaning in virtue of their reference, those things for which they stand, and not because of descriptions associated with them, and that true identity statements using proper names or equivalent expressions are necessarily true. He has given new meaning to the notion of a thing or natural kind possessing essential properties, and argued against the materialist thesis that mental states are identical with brain states (*see* identity theory of mind).

L

Langer, Susanne K. (1895-). American philosopher, influential in the fields of linguistic analysis and aesthetics, and author of *An Introduction to Symbolic Logic* (1937). Her main work, *Philosophy in a New Key* (1942), puts forward a theory of art as an articulation of human emotions.

language game. A key concept in the later work of *Wittgenstein. According to his famous analogy between using language and playing games, we have in both various sets of rules or conventions, and these determine what moves are permissible or impermissible, successes or failures, each set of rules identifying a distinct game. A given move can be judged only according to the rules of the game to which it belongs. Many time-honoured philosophical problems result from judging moves in one game by the rules of another, and can be dissolved only by systematic clarification of the relevant differences; hence such clarification should be philosophy's main concern.

language, philosophy of. The phrase covers a variety of activities.

1. Philosophers interested in problems, for example, about mind and knowledge, may frame their questions in various ways. They may ask directly about mind or knowledge; they may talk about the concept of mind or knowledge; or they may begin by asking how the *words* 'mind' and 'knowledge' are used. The belief that philosophical questions may be approached by asking questions about the use of words underlies what is sometimes called *linguistic philosophy. Those who practise linguistic philosophy are sometimes said to be practising the philosophy of language. (In view of common misapprehensions it is as well to stress that this way of doing philosophy is not new. When in Book I of *The Republic* Plato asks, "Would it be just to return weapons to a mad man?", he is inviting his hearers to consider whether *they* would *call* that action just. He hopes that reflection on this matter will throw light on the notion of justice.)

2. The procedure of investigating philosophical questions by reflecting on the uses of words generates another meaning of 'philosophy of language'. Here there are two questions. First, there is a general question about the justifiability of approaching philosophical questions via a study of how words are used (*see* J.L. Austin; Wittgenstein). Second, philosophers who study the use of words *use* such key terms as 'meaning', 'reference', 'truth', and 'use'. It is possible to make these terms, used by philosophers and others in talking about language, objects of study. Philosophy of language, on this interpretation, then becomes a higher level study of 'linguistic philosophy' and of its terms of art.

3. Although an interest in such terms as 'meaning', 'truth', 'reference', and the like can arise as philosophers deliberate on their methods, it can also arise because philosophers become interested in a study of the nature and workings of language as a subject in its own right, rather than as a means to the solution of further philosophical problems. 'Philosophy of language' then becomes the search for an understanding of the nature and functioning of language. This may lead, as in the later Wittgenstein, to the consideration of the sorts of conditions that have to be met for language to be possible at all; or it may lead to the detailed discussion of such topics as meaning and reference (*see* denotation; sense and reference). In this kind of philosophy of language we can detect a difference: between those, such as Austin and Wittgenstein, who are happy to study the actual workings of natural languages; and those who believe natural languages to be overly vague, confused, or imprecise and in need of tidying up. Some of the latter believe the workings of language are best explored through the construction of more precise artificial languages. *See also* meaning.

4. 'Philosophy of language' is also used to describe the discussion of theoretical problems that arise when linguistic scientists attempt to describe the syntax (grammar) and semantics (meaning) of a language. This discussion, sometimes called 'philosophical linguistics' is not

uncommonly classed as a branch of philosophy of language.

Lao-tzu. *See* Taoism.

Laplace, Pierre Simon de (1749-1827). French mathematician and philosopher. His main philosophical publications are *Exposition du système du monde* (1798) and *Essai philosophique sur les probabilités* (1814).

Laplace is best known for his belief in mechanical determinism, and for his foundation of probability theory upon consideration of combinations of equipossible cases. Alternatives are shown to be equipossible by an application of the principle of *indifference, and Laplace embraced the subjective air of this principle. He made many contributions to the mathematical theory of probability. Laplace's determinism was based on the enormous success of Newtonian mechanics, and in particular he himself proved the mechanical stability of the solar system. He thus removed the need for the adjusting hand of God; hence the famous remark about God to Napoleon, "Je n'ai pas besoin de cet hypothèse".

large numbers, law of. *See* Bernoulli's theorem.

law, philosophy of. 1. The analysis of the nature of law and legal systems; analytic jurisprudence. 2. The critical evaluation of the basis of legal authority and of the moral rationale behind legal decision making; ethical jurisprudence.

1. Historically there have been two distinct and incompatible views concerning the nature of law. According to the "natural law" tradition (developed in the Middle Ages, but with roots going back to the Stoics and Aristotle), the law must necessarily conform to the universal "law of nature". In its Christian form, this doctrine asserts that human law must ultimately be subject to the divine law. In a secularized version, the claim is that the law must reflect certain goals or ends that are "natural" for mankind. Both versions insist on an essential moral content to the law, so that, in the words of the ancient maxim

"*lex injusta non est lex*" (an unjust law is no true law).

By contrast, the *positivist* view, first fully articulated in the 19th century by *Bentham and the jurist John *Austin, claims that law can be defined without any reference to its content. "The existence of law is one thing, its merit or demerit another", wrote Austin. According to Austin, law is simply the command of the sovereign, backed by appropriate sanctions. The distinguished present-day philosopher H. L. A. Hart, in his seminal work *The Concept of Law* (1961), has produced a highly sophisticated version of positivism. Law is not merely a list of arbitrary commands. It is a complex union of "primary and secondary rules" whose legitimacy depends on their being ultimately derived from a basic "rule of recognition" (for example, the rule that what the Queen in Parliament enacts is law). This remains a positivist view, since law is still defined by reference to its pedigree, not its content. More recently, Hart's critics have questioned whether the deductive model of a hierarchical system of rules can cope with the complexity (and sometimes innovative character) of the actual judicial process.

2. The chief problem in ethical jurisprudence concerns the difficult notion of responsibility. Under what circumstances are the courts justified in holding a man responsible for his acts (or omissions)? In this connection, the time-honoured maxim "*actus non facit reum nisi mens sit rea*" (an act does not make a man guilty unless the mind is guilty) has received much philosophical scrutiny. What exactly is the "mental" element (*mens rea*) that is supposed to be necessary for guilt? Following the Aristotelian tradition that makes voluntariness the basic requirement for responsibility, many jurists have defined *mens rea* in terms of a prior act of will or *volition. But this seems inadequate to cope with the cases where people are held responsible for inadvertence or negligence (for example, failing to notice a stop-light).

Intention provides another stumbling block for the theory of responsibility. "I did not mean to do it" is in ordinary life, often taken as some kind of excuse; but the courts have sometimes held it to be murder when a death is the unintended (though foreseeable) consequence of some other intentional act (for example, when a policeman thrown off the bonnet of a moving car subsequently died, and the accused claimed he intended merely to shake him off). Philosophical problems abound, when, as in this case, the meanings given by lawyers to the term 'intention' differ from its ordinary sense.

Even when an act is fully intended, the law sometimes excuses from responsibility, most notably in in the case of insane offenders. The definition of legal insanity provides some of the richest terrain for philosophical analysis (particularly in the light of the awkward concept of "diminished responsibility" which is now a part of English law).

Interwoven with problems about responsibility is the philosophical puzzle about the justification for punishment. The longstanding dispute about whether retribution or deterrence should be seen as the justifying aim of the penal system has now been complicated by a more radical view that the whole notion of punishment should be abandoned in favour of a reformatory or even "curative" approach. In this area philosophy of law can be seen to overlap with general ethics (especially with the question of whether human beings possess genuine freedom of action) and also with political theory (since a "curative" approach to crime would raise serious worries about individual liberty).

Of the many other areas where philosophy of law overlaps with other disciplines, three are worth special notice. The first is the question of whether the law should be used to enforce the prevailing morality in a society (for example, laws against pornography and indecency). The second problem, a focus of much recent interest, concerns the nature and moral status of legal rights. Finally, there is the question of legal obligation—that is, whether the mere fact that a certain statute has been duly enacted places an obligation on the citizen to obey it. The answer here seems to hinge on whether the acceptance of the benefits of a legal system, such as the security it provides, carries with it any reciprocal obligations, and if so, what is their scope.

laws of nature. Principles that may be either prescriptive or descriptive, but must always be in some sense necessary. 1. The prescriptive law of nature is conceived as a basic system of moral norms, the necessity of obedience being moral. This conception is often linked with *natural theology, and then the contrast is with revelation. Mandates issued by divine authority are supposed to be accessible to natural reason, although they can be and in fact often are violated. 2. Descriptive laws of nature are supposed to hold with a (non-logical) necessity, and cannot be broken: a genuine exception (*see* miracle) would show only that what had been thought to hold as such a law does not. The nature and indeed the reality of this necessity has been much disputed, many philosophers taking it that *Hume showed that the non-linguistic world contains no necessity, neither logical nor any other. Propositions stating such laws of nature, called nomological propositions, are of the form; not 'Not as a matter of fact *X* and not *Y*'; but 'Any *X* must be *Y*'. The crucial difference is that the former cannot, while the latter must, imply subjunctive and counterfactual conditionals (*see* conditional). *See* inevitability.

lazy sophism. The nickname used by *Leibniz and others for the argument that, since from '*X* will be' it follows necessarily that '*X* will be', therefore it must also follow that '*X* necessarily and inevitably will be'. *See* fatalism; freewill and determinism; inevitability; seafight.

learning paradox. An old problem raised in Plato's Socratic dialogues and later found in some writings on education and certain medieval approaches to the knowledge of the nature of God. A person can learn only that which he doesn't know, but if he doesn't know it, how does he know what he is seeking to learn?

least number principle. The principle that if a property or condition holds for some number then there is a least number that satisfies the condition. This principle is equivalent to the principle of complete induction. See induction.

legalism. (Chinese *fa chia*: the school of law) A school of thought that flourished in the state of Ch'in. The policies of this school were instrumental in the unification by that state of the central Chinese kingdoms in 221 BC. The leading theorists, Shang Yang (d. 330 BC) and Han Fei (d. 233 BC) rejected all traditional moral values, making utility to the state the supreme criterion. Through a system of rewards and punishments, set out in a rigid code of law, all human activity was directed towards increasing the power of the state and its ruler, both internally and externally. To this end, the people were set to pursuing only agriculture and warfare, and all alternative forms of social activity were prohibited.

legal positivism. See law, philosophy of.

Leibniz, Gottfried Wilhelm (1646-1716). German philosopher, born in Leipzig. He spent most of his life in the service of various members of the German nobility, but this did not prevent him from following an intellectual career of great variety. Not only was he a philosopher and a mathematician, he was also a historian and a jurist. Perhaps because of these manifold activities he left behind no philosophical *magnum opus*. Neither of his two philosophical books, the *New Essays on the Human Understanding* (c.1705) and the *Theodicy* (1710), gives a complete account of his philosophy; it is necessary to supplement them by reference to his many short papers.

The general outlines of the philosophy of Leibniz are clear enough. In contrast to Spinoza's view that there is only one substance, Leibniz declares that there is an infinity of substances, created and maintained in existence by God. The world that these substances compose is the best possible, created by God precisely because it is the best possible world. Each substance is simple, that is without parts, and for this reason Leibniz calls it a 'monad', a term that means 'unit' or 'unity'. A substance is also immaterial, and therefore may be called a soul. But Leibniz does not take a phenomenalist view, reducing material substances to classes of the ideas that conscious agents have. In his view, material substances have an independent existence, being composed of classes of substances that, although immaterial, are not conscious. Strictly speaking, no created substance acts on any other; the monads, says Leibniz, "have no windows, by which anything could come in or go out" (*Monadology*, par. 7). But this does not imply that to talk of causes and effects is to talk nonsense. Although no created substance really acts on any other, God has pre-established a harmony between the states of all created substances, such that it is in principle possible to infer from any state of any one substance to a corresponding state of any other substance (see clocks, image of the two). In the language of Leibniz, God has created substances such that each one "expresses" all others. When it is easier to infer from the states of substance A to the states of substance B than conversely, then we say that A is the "cause" of B.

Each substance expresses the whole universe by virtue of perceiving it. A substance also has what Leibniz calls "appetition"; for although it does not act on any other, it *acts*, and its action takes the form of appetition, a striving towards an end. Using Aristotelian terminology, Leibniz often calls this end the "form" of the substance. A substance's acts are not random, but are part of a law-governed series, such that "the present is big with the future and laden with the past" (*New Essays*, Preface). An omniscient being, such as God, can tell in advance all that a substance will do; indeed, it is just because, for example, Adam will choose to eat the apple that God decides to create the Adam that he does create. Despite this, Leibniz insists that the human will is free.

Although one may have doubts about its consistency, the system itself seems fairly clear. But it is by no means so clear why Leibniz put forward such strange sounding views. In 1900 Bertrand Russell published an important study, *A Critical Exposition of the Philosophy of Leibniz*, in which he drew attention to the part played in that philosophy by logic. Russell took logic in a broad sense, so as to include theories about the structure of the proposition and the nature of truth. This approach to Leibniz is still a helpful one. Leibniz held that, in the last analysis, every proposition is of the subject-predicate form; and, furthermore, whatever assertion we make, we are in effect saying that the concept of the predicate is contained in the concept of the subject. So, for example, to say that Julius Caesar is renowned is to say that the concept of being renowned is contained in the concept of Julius Caesar. If the proposition is true, the concept of the predicate is contained in the concept of the subject; if false, then the concept of the predicate is not contained in that of the subject. The idea of the inclusion of predicate in subject is familiar from the use that Kant made of it later; but whereas Kant was speaking only of those propositions that are logically true, Leibniz, however, applied his thesis to all true propositions. From his view of truth, Leibniz derived the consequence that every substance must have a "complete concept", that is, a concept that contains everything that can truly be said of the substance. Human beings do not possess such concepts—the concept that even the most learned historian has of Julius Caesar is far from being the complete concept of Caesar—but there are such concepts,

and an omniscient being such as God has complete concepts of all individual substances.

The notion of a complete concept has important metaphysical consequences for Leibniz. First, since a knowledge of all that happens to an individual substance can in principle be derived from its complete concept alone, Leibniz argues that each substance is independent of all others in the universe. In this way, Leibniz establishes the "windowless" character of substance. Second, since the complete concept of a substance contains all its states at all times, Leibniz argues that a substance must be a law-governed whole, such that from any one of its states it is in principle possible to infer any other. Leibniz seems also to think that this is possible only if a substance strives towards an end, in the way that Aristotle viewed the soul as striving towards an end, so the soul-like character of substance is also demonstrated. Another consequence is the so-called *identity of indiscernibles. The complete concept of a substance must be sufficient to identify that substance, from which it follows that a complete concept can have only one instance. In other words: if we are given complete descriptions of what are ostensibly two substances, A and B, and the two descriptions are exactly alike, then 'A' and 'B' must be different names for the same substance.

The logical views of Leibniz involve him in great difficulties. The thesis that all propositions are basically of the subject-predicate form was attacked by Russell on the grounds that those logical arguments that depend on the properties of *relations cannot be recast in subject-predicate form. Some modern scholars have argued that Leibniz never intended to reduce relational propositions to subject-predicate propositions; certainly, if he did, he was mistaken. Leibniz is faced with another serious difficulty. It was pointed out above that what Leibniz asserts of all truths, Kant asserts only of those propositions that are logically true. The question is, how Leibniz is to distinguish those propositions that are logically necessary from those are not. Leibniz gives two different but related answers to this. First, he says that, although the predicate of a truth that is not logically necessary is indeed included in the subject, to show it is would require an infinite analysis. A truth is logically necessary, not simply because the predicate is in the subject (as it is for Kant), but because the inclusion of predicate in subject can be demonstrated in a finite number of steps. Second, a truth that is not logically necessary depends for its truth on the will of God; logically necessary truths, on the other hand, are eternal truths that do not depend on God's will. The two answers are related, in that what God wills to create is an infinite universe, and since each substance must express all others it must, although indivisible, be of infinite complexity.

It is evident from this that the concept of the will of God has an important part to play in the philosophy of Leibniz. In fact, it plays a dual role. First, it enables him to mark an important respect in which he differs from Spinoza; second, it serves as an instrument of a priori construction. To begin with the first of these: Leibniz agreed with Spinoza that everything is explicable. "There cannot", he wrote, "be any true or existent fact, or any true proposition, without there being a sufficient reason why it should be so and not otherwise" (*Monadology*, par. 32), and he called this the principle of *sufficient reason. He differed from Spinoza, however, in that he denied that all explanation is deduction from logically necessary truths. For example, there could be *laws of nature different from those that actually hold; the ones that do hold are due to the will of God. The laws of nature are indeed necessary; it does not, for example, just happen that light travels in straight lines. But they are not *logically* necessary, they are *hypothetically* necessary. That is to say, they are necessary *given that* such and such is the case—namely, that there is a

creative deity who makes such and such decisions.

The concept of hypothetical necessity also provides Leibniz with answers to problems about human freedom. He wanted to maintain that the will is free; yet his philosophy seems to menace freedom in two ways. First, if each substance has a complete concept that covers all that it does—a concept, incidentally, that God has before he created the substance—then how can a human being be free? Second, the principle of sufficient reason means that every human action is explicable. But if to explain something is to show it as following from necessary laws, then how can a human being do other than what he does? Leibniz replies that the existence of, say, an Adam who will eat the apple is not logically necessary; it is only hypothetically necessary, given that God wills to create the best possible world, and an Adam of such a kind is an indispensable part of such a world. As to the necessary laws that determine the acts of a human being, Leibniz would say that it is indeed true that we must follow the strongest motive. But motives "incline without necessitating", by which Leibniz means that what we do is only hypothetically necessary, and that it is always logically possible for us to choose something other than what we in fact choose.

The other role played by the concept of God's will in the philosophy of Leibniz is that of an instrument in the a priori construction of the Universe; something that enables Leibniz to say, independently of experience, what the Universe *must be* like. God wills to create the best possible world, and Leibniz holds that we can state certain features that such a world must possess. Since Leibniz was a great mathematician, it is not wholly surprising that these features of the best possible world correspond to features that a mathematician looks for in his deductive systems. His axioms (*see* axiom) should be fertile—should generate the required theorems—and should also be economical; similarly, Leibniz says that God creates, by the most economical means, a world that is the richest possible. The principle that God follows in doing this is sometimes called by Leibniz the "principle of the best"; sometimes, confusingly, he calls it the "principle of sufficient reason", here restricting the principle to those truths that are not logically necessary. In this sense, the principle of sufficient reason plays an important part in a controversy that Leibniz carried on with *Newton during the last years of his life. Leibniz argued that the Newtonian idea of *absolute space, that is, of space as independent of spatial objects, contradicted the principle of sufficient reason, and he put forward another view, according to which space is an order of co-existences, and as such is really inseparable from objects in spatial relations. Leibniz, however, failed to upset holders of the Newtonian theory of absolute space, which remained dominant throughout the 18th century.

Leibniz's law. The principle that if one thing is identical with another then anything that is true of the one must also be true of the other. This sounds obviously true. Yet if it is indeed to be true, then it has to be construed as in one particular way limited in scope. For, although it holds of the actual properties of identicals, it does not hold of those peculiar and factitious properties constituted by people's beliefs about those identicals and about all the reactions that may be guided or misguided by those beliefs. People may not know, for instance, that the Morning Star is the Evening Star and so their beliefs about and their reactions to what is in fact one and the same planet can be quite different according to the description under which it is considered. See masked man fallacy.

Lenin, Vladimir Ilyich (1870-1924). Russian Marxist revolutionary whose major contribution to philosophy was his book *Materialism and Empirio-Criticism* (1908), in which he attacked certain professing Marxists for defending a

Berkeleian 'subjective idealism' (see idealism). In this book, Lenin expounded a theory of knowledge that is still part of orthodox Soviet Marxism; according to this, ideas are "copies" or "reflections" of reality. When in exile, Lenin also made a close study (1914-16) of Hegel, and his notes were published after his death as *Philosophical Notebooks*. In them, Lenin stressed the importance of a study of Hegel for a correct understanding of Marxism.

Lessing, Gotthold Ephraim (1729-81). German dramatist, aesthetician, historian, and theologian. In his best-known work, *Laocöon* (1766), Lessing sought to oppose the influence of French classical aesthetics in arguing for the idea of an art unrestricted by formal considerations and founded on the free expression of feeling. The view was later to attract several of the romantics, though Lessing himself is not considered a romantic theorist.

In later life, Lessing turned increasingly to the theory of history and to theology. His theological studies were influential in 19th-century religious thought and were greatly respected by Kierkegaard.

Leucippus of Miletus (fl. 450-420 BC). Greek philosopher who seems to have taken hints from Melissus, Empedocles, and Anaxagoras to produce the first unequivocally atomistic cosmology. This was developed, and very much more fully expounded, by his younger contemporary *Democritus. Their work, mediated through *Epicurus, is for us best displayed in *De Rerum Natura* (On the Nature of Things) by *Lucretius. See Presocratics.

Lévi-Strauss, Claude (1908-). French anthropologist and proponent of *structuralism. From 1934 he was professor of sociology at the University of São Paulo until, in 1938, he led an extensive expedition for anthropological investigations in central Brazil. He subsequently worked in New York and after 1950 held various academic posts in France.

Lévi-Strauss' writings investigate the relationship between culture (an exclusive attribute of humanity) and nature, based on the distinguishing characteristic of man: the ability to communicate in a language. In the four volumes of *Mythologiques* (1964, 1966, 1968, 1972) he analyses myths not as explanations of natural phenomena but as attempts at resolving problems of human existence and social organization.

li. (Chinese for: order, principle.) *See* Neo-Confucianism.

liar paradox. A *paradox traditionally attributed to Epimenides the Cretan and supposedly strengthened by Eubulides. The statement, 'I am lying', is true only if it is false, and false if it is true. This was an example used by *Russell in developing the theory of types, showing that certain formulations of words, though grammatically correct, are logically nonsensical.

libertarianism. 1. The view, opposed to *determinism, that certain human actions are not (or not entirely) governed by causal laws. *See* freewill and determinism. **2.** Wholehearted political and economic liberalism, opposed to any social and legal constraints on individual freedom. The term was introduced in this sense by people who believe that, especially but not only in the U.S., those who pass as liberals are often much more sympathetic to socialism than to classical liberalism.

liberty. 1. The freedom of the will (*see* freewill and determinism). **2.** Political freedom, which consists in the absence of external constraint. "The free man", wrote *Helvétius, "is the man who is not in irons, nor imprisoned in a gaol, nor terrorized like a slave by the fear of punishment." No one is free in all respects. Someone may be in some respect free through unable or unwilling to exercise that freedom, and unfree despite content with unfreedom. Because the word 'freedom' sounds to many good

(whereas the reality is abhorrent to authoritarians) and because political freedom is indeed, like peace, essentially negative, some commend as positive, true freedom the actual pursuing of some favoured course rather than the liberty so to do or not.

likelihood. In connection with a statistical hypothesis on a body of data, the chance of those data occurring if the hypothesis is true. This likelihood does not give directly the probability of the hypothesis, because the sum of the likelihoods of rival hypotheses may be much greater than 1. But often the best estimate of a *distribution may be that which has the maximum likelihood on the given data, and the method of maximum likelihood counselled by R. A. Fisher recommends this estimation. *See also* probability.

limited independent variety, principle of. The name given by J. M. *Keynes to the contention that to justify inductive generalizations it has to be assumed "that the objects in the field, over which our generalizations extend, do not have an infinite number of independent qualities" (*A Treatise on Probability*, p. 256). *See also* atomic uniformity, principle of; induction.

limit number. Any number, α, other than 0, such that for any number, β, if β is less than α then the successor of β is less than α.

line, image of the. Plato's illustration in the *Republic* (Book IV) of the putative four different kinds of reality and of our possible knowledge of these. The basic division of the line is into "two unequal parts, corresponding to the visible and the intelligible worlds". These parts are then both subdivided in the same proportions. *Compare* cave, image of the.

linguistic philosophy. An approach to philosophy that holds that a careful study of how language is actually used, taught, and developed in everyday discourse can illuminate, and even transform or dissolve, time-honoured philosophical problems. These problems are seen as arising, often if not invariably, because thinkers, misled by superficial grammatical similarities or their own fondness for uniformity, have ignored relevant differences in the functions of terms and hence misused them (see grammatical form; logical form). Which features of language linguistic philosophers explicate are largely determined by the specifically philosophical problems they wish to clarify, but the boundary between such philosophy and linguistics proper is ill-defined. Philosophy thus understood is an activity of analysis, usually relying less on a set of doctrines or a vigorously prescribed method than on sensitivity to niceties of language. This approach has been since World War II especially characteristic of English-language philosophy but traces its origins much further back. Its most influential exponents have been *Wittgenstein, J. L. *Austin, and *Ryle.

Locke, John (1632–1704). Probably the greatest, and certainly the most influential, English philosopher, whose thought became the foundation both for classical British *empiricism and for liberal democracy. His two most important philosophical works, both first published in 1690, were the *Essay Concerning Human Understanding* (the *Essay*) and the *Two Treatises of Government* (the *Treatises*). His other major philosophical works were *A Letter Concerning Toleration* (1689), *Some Thoughts concerning Education* (1693), and *The Reasonableness of Christianity, as Delivered in the Scriptures* (1695). His extensive surviving correspondence is now mainly published. In general, the usual characterization of his writings as exhibiting moderation, common sense, and an earnest concern to discover the truth, is justified.

Locke came from a Somerset family of minor gentry. His father supported the Parliamentary cause in the Civil War and some aspects of his Puritan background are discernible in Locke's mature thought. In 1647 he went to Westminster School, which was Royalist in sympathy, and from there, in 1652, he proceeded to Christ Church, Oxford.

Oxford was then under Puritan control. It was also the centre for much scientific activity associated with John Wilkins and Robert *Boyle. It was not long before Locke, too, was involved with practical studies of medicine and chemistry. Locke found the largely scholastic undergraduate course dull, but nevertheless he became a don at Christ Church after graduating in 1656.

By this time Locke was well acquainted with Robert Boyle, who was to have a substantial influence on his thought. Boyle, the leading scientist in England, was committed to an empirical and experimental method. He was also the spokesman for the corpuscular philosophy, which held that most changes in the properties of physical objects could be explained as resulting from the rearrangement of the basic particles of matter. Locke came to share Boyle's account, though he always recognized its hypothetical status. At about this time Locke's interest in philosophy was also awakened, largely as a result of reading *Descartes. Certainly the *Essay* is closely related to Descartes' work, though often in conscious opposition.

Locke's knowledge of medicine brought him into contact with the leading Whig politician, Lord Ashley, later first Earl of Shaftesbury. In 1667 Locke left Oxford to join Ashley's household as his personal physician. Ashley was soon calling for Locke's advice on matters unrelated to medicine, and through Ashley Locke obtained a succession of official appointments, coming into contact with the political and scientific circles of London. In 1668 he was elected Fellow of the Royal Society, and collaborated with the great physician Thomas Sydenham on the latter's research. Between 1675 and 1679 Locke was in France, mostly for reasons of health, though possibly also because of political danger. He travelled extensively and met many foreign scientists.

In 1683, following the fall and death

of Shaftesbury, Locke, not without reason, felt himself threatened and retired to Holland, where he remained until after the Glorious Revolution of 1688. While there Locke continued work on his *Essay* (which he had begun in 1671) and the *Treatises*, and came into close contact with the Remonstrants' movement, whose theological views were very similar to his own.

Soon after his return to England, when Locke was 58, the *Essay* was published, and it quickly established a considerable reputation for its author, especially in those circles most closely associated with the Royal Society. The *Treatises* were published anonymously. His other major works soon followed. Although Locke was far from well in his later years, he nevertheless took on demanding and important work as a Commissioner for Trade (1696), which he carried out with the same success that had characterized his earlier appointments. However, he was not well enough to take on an even more important position which the King personally asked him to fill in 1698, and the remainder of his life was spent at Oates, Essex, reading, revising his texts, and conversing with such friends as Isaac *Newton and Anthony Collins.

The *Essay Concerning Human Understanding* is a critical assessment of the origins, nature, and limits of human reason. Locke's concern with this issue arose from the implications of new scientific ideas and methods for current beliefs about morality and religion. The old scholastic philosophy was found wanting, and Locke, in common with his empirically minded scientific colleagues, could not accept the rationalist response of Descartes. Locke's answers to the problem were sustained and deeply thought. They were the first attempt in modern times to offer a detailed account of human understanding in the empiricist idiom that also took account of the current achievements in science. The same answers supplied the base for the empirical philosophy of *Berkeley, *Hume, and the French *Encyclopedists.

The *Essay* begins with an identification of the role of the philosopher as an underlabourer whose task is to clear the ground and remove "some of the rubbish that lies in the way of knowledge" (Epistle to the Reader). The actual acquisition of knowledge Locke leaves to scientists like Boyle and Newton.

Book I is an attack on the then widely held doctrine that men have innate knowledge of some truths, either moral or speculative, which supply us with the foundations of knowledge. None of the proffered arguments, Locke maintains, begin to make it plausible that there are any such innate notions. Rather, Locke argues in detail in Book II, we can account for all of the ideas in our minds by *experience*. Experience is of two sorts. There are ideas of sensation, derived from the outer senses, and ideas of reflection, which are those ideas of which we become aware by introspection, for example, thinking, believing, and willing.

Book II gives an account of the origins of a large cross-section of our ideas, which Locke distinguishes into simple and complex. Simple ideas, such as yellow, hot, and sweet, have no other ideas contained within them, and, like atoms, can neither be created nor destroyed by us. Complex ideas are compounded out of simple ideas, and the mind is quite capable of imagining complex arrangements of simple ideas that do not in fact correspond to anything in the world, for example, a unicorn.

In his discussion of our ideas of material substances (physical things), Locke distinguishes between the primary and secondary qualities of objects (a distinction drawn before him by *Galileo, Descartes, and Boyle). Primary qualities, Locke says, are those qualities to be found in all bodies whatsoever; he includes solidity, extension, figure, and mobility among them. Locke held that in perception these qualities produce ideas in us which resemble their cause. The secondary qualities, on the other hand, are nothing but powers in the object to produce in us ideas which do not resemble their cause. The ideas so produced include those of colour, taste, and smell. Locke's account of our knowledge of the physical world via the mediation of ideas was to be a source of much criticism by later philosophers, but critics often misunderstood Locke's position.

Locke attempts to give plausible explanations for the origins of all of our ideas by giving an analysis of complex ideas into their basic simple ideas. There are, however, some difficult cases. One is our idea of power, understood in a causal sense. Another, which Locke himself saw as generating a major difficulty, is the idea of substance. This Locke believed we can acquire neither by sensation nor by reflection, since it is the thing in which qualities are held to subsist, rather than itself being a quality, to which there corresponds an idea. Book II remains nonetheless a formidable achievement, not only in its breadth but also because of its insights into many key concepts, for example those of identity, power, and—despite the difficulties —that of substance.

Book III of the *Essay* offers an account of language. Although it has major faults (for example, the central claim that words name ideas) it also makes undoubted contributions, not least in Locke's recognition of the importance of a satisfactory account of language to any account of the intellect. Locke recognizes major imperfections in language. His contention that the language of our classification of things in the world must be based upon *our* view of the essential qualities of objects (the nominal essences) rather than on a certain knowledge of the real essences of objects themselves, was a telling criticism of the rationalist programme for science advocated by Descartes and *Spinoza.

In the fourth and last book of the *Essay* Locke gives his positive account of knowledge. Although in important respects Locke follows Descartes, the differences underline the gulf between their two approaches. Like Descartes,

Locke sees the fundamental unit of knowledge to be that of intuition. We have immediate intuitive knowledge of our own existence. We can also know things by deduction or demonstration, for example, in mathematical calculation, where each step in the argument is intuitively certain. Locke held that we can demonstrate the existence of God similarly. He also held that we have certain knowledge through our senses of the existence of particular physical objects that we can see, touch, etc. Where Locke differed from Descartes was in his view that we could have no certain knowledge of general truths about the world. The natural sciences could never aspire to be other than highly probable. This was, Locke was quick to point out, in no way to condemn them but it was to deny false aspirations after a totally demonstrative science of nature.

The *Essay* was soon the object of much criticism, the most able being supplied by Berkeley and Leibniz. Despite this the *Essay* remained the single most influential work in European philosophy for at least a hundred years.

The *Two Treatises of Government* have often been seen as written by Locke to vindicate the Revolution of 1688, but they were in fact largely completed several years before. They are, however, very much a product of their time and reflect Locke's great concern to supply a justification for constitutional rule and the liberty of the individual at a time when both were threatened.

The first *Treatise*, an attack on Filmer's *Patriarcha* (1680), argues that there is no foundation for the view that God has placed some men above others, and that men are therefore not naturally free. There is no divine right of kings to rule, and God did not appoint Adam and his descendants to rule over the world.

The second *Treatise* offers a substantial positive political philosophy. In the state of nature, man is free, and in this condition all men are equal. Man's freedom is not, however, a state of licence, for there is a law of nature, ordained by God, by which men should regulate their behaviour. The law of nature grants to each man natural rights. We each have a right to life, and a right to liberty so long as our actions do not infringe the natural rights of others, and we have both property in our own body and in the product of our own labour. Before the creation of civil society man has a right to amass private property only so far as he has use for it. For example, a man has a right to as much corn as he and his family need, but he has no right to a surplus which will only spoil.

Unfortunately the state of nature is in practice unstable, because men, unless coerced, often infringe the natural rights of others. It is soon apparent that in order that men may enjoy their natural rights they must join together by means of a social contract. The function of the contract is to form a civil society in which men may enjoy their natural rights under a government established to enforce laws protecting those rights and to adjudicate disputes. The ruler, say the king, has the primary function of providing the conditions under which the citizens may enjoy their rights. If he either violates the rights of individual citizens or fails to provide the conditions under which citizens may enjoy their rights, then the people are entitled to remove him. On issues that do not threaten any natural rights Locke held that majority opinion should prevail. The commitment to natural rights, the rule of law, the function of the state as the guarantor of these conditions, and the rule of the majority were powerful ideas that helped to shape both the American and French Revolutions and provided the key concepts for the development of liberal democracy.

A similar concern to achieve a balance between individual liberty and consti-tutional rule is exhibited in the *Letter Concerning Toleration*, whose subject was religious toleration in a political society. Toleration was a primary virtue of the true Church and persecution was quite contrary to charity. Individual liberty to worship should only be limited by restricting religious practice to activities that do not infringe the rights of others.

locution. A grammatically well formed and meaningful utterance. A locutionary act is the use of a locution to say something. *See* J. L. Austin.

logic. In its broadest sense logic is the study of the structure and principles of reasoning or of sound argument. Hence it is also a study of those relations in virtue of which one thing may be said to follow from or be a consequence of another. Within this very loosely defined area one can distinguish various kinds of logic according to the kind of reasoning considered and the kind of sentences in which it is conducted. Within the study of reasoning which aims to establish the truth of propositions, the major dis-tinction is between *deductive* and *induc-tive logic* (*see* deduction; induction). Another important use of reason occurs in practical reasoning, where one seeks to establish what ought to be done. Such reasoning may be expressed using both indicatives and imperatives, although the conclusions of trains of practical reason-ing are characteristically expressed in the imperative. The study of this form of reasoning is termed *deontic logic*, the *logic of norms*, or the *logic of imperatives* (*see* imperative).

However, in its narrower sense, logic is the study of the principles of deduc-tive inference, or of methods of proof or demonstration. This study is not conduc-ted by collecting data about the ways in which people do in fact argue, for logic is a theoretical rather than an empirical science. It is the study of winning strategies in the game of argument and of legitimate inferences; it is concerned with the possible means of establishing propositions. The relation between logic and actual inferences is thus similar to that between the theory of a game and the actual playing of it. This analogy is worth pursuing in that it reveals where empirical considerations are, or should be, the concern of the logician. The theoretical discussion of a game cannot proceed without knowledge of (a) the object of the game (what it is to win) and (b) the rules according to which the game is actually played. The object in presenting an argument is to get the audience addressed to believe its conclusion, and there are, of course, all sorts of ways of doing this, ranging from appeal to abstract principles, through bribery, to threats either of immediate physical violence or of fire and brimstone to come. But the object of the particular game in which the deductive logician is interested is more narrowly defined than this. Deductive arguments aim to induce belief in their conclusions by *force of reason* (arguments which succeed in this being called logically *valid). Then the question to ask is whether the analogy with a game is a good one—whether there are accepted rules for conducting arguments that have this objective, and if so, what these accepted rules are.

If an argument is to induce belief by force of reason, it must be such that it shows that it would be irrational not to accept its conclusion, after having agreed to its premises. 'Irrational' is here taken in the sense of 'inconsistent', so that denying the conclusion of a valid argument after having accepted its premises must amount to holding contradictory beliefs. But how does one recognize such an argument and how construct one in support of a given proposition? These are the questions to which the study of logic should provide some answers, but which it cannot answer without also taking a look at what are the accepted standards of rationality—at what inferential moves are regarded as being rationally compelling. The aim is to make explicit the rules which are implicitly recognized as rules according to which arguments ought to be constructed, at the same time pointing out any anomalies that may appear in the process. In this way the situation is not unlike that of trying to pick up and formulate the rules of, say, American football by watching a game and the referee, noting what play is regarded as legitimate and what foul (bearing in mind that the referee may not be perfect).

But here one has also to be careful to distinguish between those inferences which it is regarded as reasonable to accept and those whose acceptance is compelled by force of reason. It might be unreasonable to reject the former, but it would not by the same token be irrational in the sense of committing one to belief in a contradiction. For example, if one has found that the 8:30 train is persistently late, it would be unreasonable to expect that it will be on time tomorrow, and one could be justly criticized for arriving late for an appointment as a result of having assumed that the train will run to schedule. But one could not be criticized for holding contradictory beliefs, for one can accept both that the train has been late on the last six occasions on which one has caught it and that it will run to time tomorrow. Indeed, it might be that work on the track, which was causing the delays, is due to be completed today, in which case it would be entirely reasonable to believe that the train will run on time tomorrow. On the other hand, if one is presented with a proof that the interior angles of a triangle add up to 180°, understanding the proof involves seeing that if one accepts the axioms of Euclidean geometry one cannot but accept the conclusion. This does not, of course, mean that one must accept these axioms; if one does not, but takes instead the axioms for a non-Euclidean geometry, one will be able to prove that the sum of the interior angles of a triangle is not 180°. The difference between the two kinds of case is that in the former one can, even in the light of the premises, refuse to accept the conclusion and even sustain this refusal by the introduction of further premises, whereas in the latter one can only refuse to accept the conclusion of the proof by rejecting one of the axioms used as premises.

Thus, the fact that a given inference is regarded as legitimate (reasonable) is not sufficient for it to be logically valid; the inference must also be such that conformity to it is a requirement of reason. The irrationality of accepting its premises and rejecting its conclusion must be demonstrated before it can be accorded the status of logical validity. This requires a theoretical argument to show *why* it would be inconsistent to reject the conclusion while accepting the premises. Thus, writing down rules of inference and claiming that they are logical principles requires justification, unlike writing down the rules of a game. This justification must come from a theory concerning the basis of the law of *non-contradiction, for it is by reference to this same basis that other logical laws will have to be justified.

The science of (deductive) logic, then, has its roots in the conception of establishing propositions by means of arguments that are such that it would be irrational to reject their conclusions, having accepted their premises. Here it should be noted that there is no requirement that a logically valid argument be an argument from *true* premises (*compare* fallacy). If the premises are not true, the argument may still be valid, but its validity will not compel acceptance of its conclusion. A valid argument establishes its conclusion only conditionally—on the condition that its premises are correct.

One's view of the nature of this science will depend on one's views on the nature of truth, knowledge, and our cognitive capacities. If knowledge is knowledge of an independent reality, and if the truth of a proposition consists in its presenting a picture that is an accurate representation of this reality, then laws of logic, as regulative principles governing the pursuit of knowledge and the construction of scientific theories, will appear as laws founded in the nature of the reality we seek to know. Seen in this way, logic is the most general of all sciences; its study is a "limning of the most general traits of reality" (W. V. Quine, *Word and Object*, (1960)). To assert a contradiction would be to depict things

as being one way and yet at the same time not that way. But nothing can be *p* and not-*p* at the same time. To believe a contradiction is thus to hold as true something that is necessarily false.

On the other hand, because a logically valid argument is one whose acceptance is a dictate of reason, the laws of logic have also been regarded as laws of thought—laws governing the operation of the intellect or the faculty of reason—and thus as having their foundation in the nature of the human intellect, rather than in any external reality. Thus George Boole, one of the pioneers of the mathematical approach to logic, said (in *The Mathematical Analysis of Logic* (1847)): "The laws we have to examine are the laws of one of the most important of our mental faculties. The mathematics we have to construct are the mathematics of the human intellect" (Introduction). The human intellect might have operated differently, in which case logical principles would be different.

Since talk of faculties and their operation is out of fashion in 20th-century philosophy, so too is the term 'law of thought'. Boole's attitude toward logic, translated into the idiom of contemporary linguistic philosophy, would be that the laws of logic are laws governing the functioning of our language and that they thus have their foundation in socially instituted conventions for the use of words; conventions that determine the nature of a language in that they provide the framework within which particular expressions of the language acquire meaning. Thus the law of non-contradiction is founded on the meaning of the sign for negation: to assert a contradiction is to violate the conventions for the use of this sign. But the conventions for the use of negation are not isolated and arbitrary in that they also, in helping to determine what can and cannot be asserted, contribute to a determination of the possible content of a statement.

However, whether laws of logic are regarded as logically necessary truths or as laws of thought or of language, in being the rules according to which arguments are to be judged, they must be independent of particular subject matter, for they must be applicable in general, no matter what the argument is about. They are concerned with the forms of arguments and not with their content. Thus a prerequisite of any theoretical approach to the principles of argument is the development of means of representing the logical form or structure of an argument. But what is logical form? Is it just grammatical structure? A consideration of the following pairs of grammatically similar, but logically dissimilar inferences should be sufficient to demonstrate that whatever logical form is, it is not *just* grammatical structure (*see also* logical form).

Fido is a father.
Fido is yours.
Therefore, Fido is your father.

Brian is a snail.
Brian is mine.
Therefore, Brian is my snail.

All dogs have canine teeth.
No canine teeth are molars.
Hence, no dogs have molars.

All dogs are mammals.
No mammals are cold-blooded.
Hence, no dogs are cold-blooded.

In a theoretical study of logic one thus has first to explain what is meant by logical form and say how it is manifested in ordinary linguistic expression, and then to give an explicit formulation of rules for the construction of valid arguments by saying what their logical structure should be. A theory of logic thus involves (a) a discussion of the principles for formalizing ordinary language in order to reveal its logical structure, and (b) the development of a formal system of rules for the construction of valid forms of argument. The formal system should be such that given any formalized argument—an argument whose logical structure has been exhibited—one can tell, by reference to the explicitly formulated rules of the system, whether the argument has been constructed in conformity with the rules

and hence whether it is (formally) valid. The successful formal system would thus reduce reasoning to a mechanical procedure, analogous to those involved in making arithmetical computations, by making it a matter of following explicitly formulated rules, the application of which merely requires the recognition of structural patterns and requires no grasp of the subject matter under discussion. Thus Leibniz claimed that by the provision of a *lingua characteristica* (a logical notation together with rules for its use), "the mind will be freed from having to think directly of things themselves, and yet everything will turn out correctly." Leibniz is here giving expression to the ideal of a logically perfect language; one in which logical and grammatical structure coincide. Where logical and grammatical structure fail to coincide, complete mechanization of the processes of inference is out of the question because the principles of formalization will not be completely mechanical rules, but only rules of thumb.

The pursuit of knowledge through rational debate is an ideal presented in the dialogues of Plato, but it was Aristotle who first engaged in a systematic and theoretical study of the principles according to which such debates should be conducted. The kind of question debated in Plato's dialogues was whether, for example, "being loved by the gods" is part of what is meant by 'piety', or whether it is only a matter of contingent fact that the gods do love what is pious (*see* Euthyphro dilemma). To establish that the first alternative holds, one would have to establish that whatever is pious is necessarily loved by the gods. To give the principles according to which such debates should be conducted is thus to give a list of general rules for the construction of arguments that can establish that all As are B and of rules for refuting claims of this form. To this end one must consider (a) how any two terms can be related and the nature of the propositions in which these relations are expressed and (b) how the information conveyed in such propositions can be combined to give further relations between the terms mentioned. Aristotle's answer to (a) is that given any two terms *A* and *B*, there are four possible relations that could hold between them. These find expression in the four kinds of categorical proposition (*see* syllogism). His answer to (b) is contained in the theory of the syllogism, presented in his *Prior Analytics*.

It is this concentration on the relations between terms that characterizes both Aristotelian and scholastic logic. It was only with the work of *Frege (late in the 19th century), whose approach was adopted by *Russell and *Whitehead in the writing of *Principia Mathematica*, that the focus of attention was shifted firmly away from terms to propositions and their relations. The advance made in Frege's system (set out in his *Begriffsschrift* (1879)) is the introduction of quantifiers (*see* quantifier) and of the treatment of concepts by analogy with mathematical *functions. This enabled him to unify the logic of propositions (propositional *calculus) with the study of those logical relationships which had previously been treated in the theory of the syllogism. Thus he made it possible to exhibit the relation between singular and universal propositions within a single system, that of predicate calculus. Frege's system also allows for the representation of relations and so makes possible a treatment of the logic of relations, something which is highly problematic in a term-orientated logic (*see* relation).

Even prior to the Fregean innovations, the study of logic had become increasingly mathematical, since it is possible to treat a formal logical system as just another system of algebra giving rise to an algebraic structure that can be studied using mathematical techniques. Such study is differentiated from that more closely geared to the application of actual arguments by being accorded the title 'mathematical logic'.

logical atomism. The philosophy expressed in Wittgenstein's *Tractatus Logico-Philosophicus*, written during World War I, and in a number of contemporary papers by *Russell. The belief was that analysis of the conditions necessary to give a sentence a definite meaning reveals that ordinary (molecular) sentences must be compounded from fundamental (atomic) units of meaning. The elements of such 'atomic' sentences must refer directly to the basic entities whose relations make up states of affairs in the non-linguistic world. In Russell, although not in Wittgenstein, anyone understanding the sentence must be directly acquainted with these entities. Russell's version thus gives rise to a reductionist programme, and may be said to be the precursor of *logical positivism. For Wittgenstein the nature of these atoms was of no interest: they had simply to exist in order to make possible our actual understanding of everyday language. This atomistic philosophy was subsequently abandoned by both writers.

logical constants. Symbols that represent certain of the devices, independent words, prefixes, suffixes, and inflections in any language that enable one to discern the grammatical structure of a sentence. Expressions such as possessives, tense markers, pronouns, and connectives perform this structuring function independently of content or subject matter. Amongst these expressions some, in some of their uses, are singled out as indicating not just the grammatical but also the logical structure or *logical form of sentences in which they appear. In order to represent the logical structure of a sentence, symbols are introduced to stand for these expressions of ordinary language. The logical symbols thus have a single, precise function whereas their linguistic counterparts may have several, related grammatical and/or logical roles. The logical symbols introduced to represent the logical structure of sentences are what are known as the logical constants.

Those most commonly employed are '-', '&', '$\vee$', '$\rightarrow$' or '$\supset$', '$\forall$', and '$\exists$'. Sometimes the *modal operators '$\square$' and '$\lozenge$' or the symbols $\perp$ (the False) and $\top$ (the True) are also included amongst the logical constants of a formal language. Additional logical constants may be used in logics seeking to represent more logical structure than is customary or in systems that differ in their overall conception of the nature of logical relations and of what is indicative of logical structure.

logical construction. A term used by philosophers, such as *Russell and *Wisdom, to characterize those things whose status and/or existence we are in doubt about or find problematic. Examples might be: the average family, the English, material object. (The words referring to them are often called *incomplete symbols*—see logical fiction.) We might find them problematic because (like the average family) they don't exist but we find it useful to talk as if they do; or (like the English) we might feel that statements about them are reducible to statements about more basic particulars (for example, that the history of the English is nothing over and above the history of individual English persons); or (like material objects) they may exist, but in any case we cannot ever be directly aware of them (but only experience, for example, sensations or sense data). For all these entities, there seem to be unproblematic or ultimate entities out of which the problematic kind can be *constructed*. Logical constructions are not necessarily reducible to those things out of which they are constructed; it is just that statements about them (say, material objects) are translatable into statements about more basic, unproblematic entities (say, sense data).

logical fiction. An object that is only apparently invoked by a sentence. When a logical analysis represents a portion of discourse that appears to refer to (or involve quantification over) objects of some kind by a form of words free from such reference (or quantification), these

objects may be called logical fictions. For example, if a sentence such as 'There is a possibility it will rain' is represented by 'It is possible it will rain', the possibility is said to have been shown to be a logical fiction. Russell called expressions that disappear upon analysis *incomplete symbols*. His theory of *definite descriptions, he believed, showed such descriptions to be incomplete symbols and enabled him to speak of the supposed reference of a non-referring description as a logical fiction. Russell also aimed to show that symbols for classes were incomplete and that classes were logical fictions (*see* class).

logical form. The form of an argument expressed in a symbolic representation from the structure of which the reasoning procedure adopted is apparent. It is by reference to this structure that the argument is judged to be formally *valid or invalid according as the reasoning procedure adopted is or is not such that, in general (that is, no matter what the subject under discussion) and given true premises, it will lead to a true conclusion. In order to give the form of an argument it is necessary to give a representation of the logical structure of its component sentences—to assign them a logical form. This representation is obviously required to be such that it makes the interdependencies of the sentences more evident, since one is interested in knowing how the truth or falsity of one bears on the truth or falsity of another.

Opinions as to what constitutes logical form and of how it is to be represented may thus differ according to one's philosophic position, and in particular one's views on the nature of truth, meaning, and the assessment of truth-values. For instance, there is the classic debate between Russell and Strawson over the logical form of 'The King of France is bald'. Strawson assigned it the form of a straightforward subject–predicate statement, namely 'Bk'; Russell, on the other hand, while admitting that it is grammatically of this form (*see* grammatical form), denied that this could be its logical form. The form he gave was '$(\exists x) (Kx \& Bx \& (\forall y) (Ky \supset x = y))$'. The difference that this makes vis-à-vis inferences is that Russell would recognize the inference 'There is no King of France. Therefore it is not the case that the King of France is bald.' as formally valid, seeing it as an instance of the valid form '$-(\exists x) Kx$. Therefore $-(\exists x) (Kx \& Bx \& (\forall y) (Ky \supset x = y))$'. Strawson, however, would assign it the form '$-(\exists x) (x = k)$, Therefore, $-Bk$' which, on his view, cannot be valid because the truth of the premise would ensure, not the truth of the conclusion, but that the conclusion lacks a *truth-value. *See also* definite description.

logical implication. *See* implication and entailment.

logically-black-is-white slide. The abusive nickname for the *fallacy of arguing that, because the difference between two extremes is a *difference of degree, therefore those extremes are really the same.

logically perfect language, A language in which logical and grammatical structure entirely coincide. *see* grammatical form; Leibniz; logic; logical form.

logically private language. A language in which all words must be defined in terms of the logically private experience of the individual language user. The later *Wittgenstein suggested that most philosophers since *Descartes have talked as if all language must be of this sort. He argued that the whole notion is, nevertheless, incoherent. *See also* privacy; private language.

logically proper name. A proper name of the kind required by Russell's logical atomism. Such names had meanings that were strictly identifiable with their bearers and were meaningless if their bearers did not exist. Russell thought demonstratives (for example, 'that' and 'this') were logically proper names. Ordinary proper names cannot have their meanings strictly identified with their bearers since we associate a variety of

descriptions with the proper names we use (for example, 'Moses' names the man who led the Children of Israel out of Egypt). If an ordinary name turned out not to have a bearer such descriptions would ensure the name was not meaningless. *See also* definite description.

logical operator. *See* operator.

logical paradoxes. Usually distinguished from the *semantic paradoxes in that they can be expressed using only logical or set-theoretic terms. The most well-known examples are *Cantor's paradox, *Burali-Forti's paradox, and *Russell's paradox. *See* paradox; set theory.

logical positivism. The range of ideas characteristic of the *Vienna Circle in the 1920s and 1930s. Logical positivism was strongly influenced by the empirical tradition, and especially the work of *Hume; its distinctive feature was its attempt to develop and systematize empiricism with the aid of the conceptual equipment furnished by modern research on logical and mathematical theory, in particular the early works of *Russell and *Wittgenstein.

According to its famous *verifiability principle, the meaning of a proposition consists in the method of its verification, that is in whatever observations or experiences show, whether or not it is true. Mathematics and logic, which are consistent with all observations, are admitted as meaningful at the price of being tautological. They simply explicate the meanings of terms, telling us nothing about how things are in the world (*see* tautology). But any nontautological proposition, that is in principle unverifiable by any observation, is *ipso facto* devoid of meaning. This verifiability principle is the basis of logical positivism's attack on theology and metaphysics; its characteristic propositions (about the creation of the world, the nature of reality as a whole, etc.) being thus unverifiable, are neither true nor false, but simply meaningless. Therefore, all arguments either for or against them are equally pointless. At best, the (pseudo-)propositions of metaphysics, like those of ethics or aesthetics, can be allowed to function as expressions of emotional attitudes, as slogans or exclamations rather than statements of fact. The task of philosophers now becomes essentially one, not of establishing philosophical doctrines, but of elucidating meanings or calling attention to the lack of them—this latter especially in the work of their predecessors.

The status of the verifiability principle itself, however, was suspect. (Is *it* either tautological or empirically verifiable?) And there were serious problems about how to formulate it in order to exclude metaphysics without also excluding such things as historical propositions or scientific generalizations. (Neither of these can be conclusively verified by observation). Such difficulties have turned philosophers of broadly empirical outlook away from logical positivism towards more flexible and less dogmatic forms of linguistic and conceptual analysis. But it had at least the merit of focusing attention sharply on the questions of meaning which must be settled before questions of truth and falsity can usefully be raised. See *also* Comte; verification.

logical product.   See and.

logical subject.   The subject of a sentence expressed in a *logically perfect language, or the object that that subject denotes. The logical subject of a sentence is often revealed to be different from its apparent subject when a sentence in a natural language is analysed into its *logical form. For example, the logical form of 'All men are mortal' is 'If anything is a man, then it is mortal', which reveals 'anything' to be the logical subject.

logical sum.   See or.

logicism.   The view, pioneered by *Frege and *Russell, that received mathematics, in particular arithmetic, is part of *logic. The aim was to provide a

system of primitives and axioms (which on *interpretation yielded logical truths) such that all arithmetical notions were definable in the system and all theorems of arithmetic were theorems of the system. If successful the programme would ensure that our knowledge of mathematical truths was of the same status as our knowledge of logical truths. Arithmetic was eventually reduced to *set theory, but this cannot be genuinely regarded as part of logic.

logistic method.   The method of studying a subject by formalizing it. For example, philosophers of science often analyse scientific theories into statements exhibiting their *logical form in order to clarify their interrelations and entailments.

logos.   (Greek for: word.) An ancient term with many uses, generally fulfilled by other words in modern languages. 1. *Heraclitus held an obscure *logos* doctrine, in which *logos* appears as a kind of non-human intelligence that organizes the discrete elements in the world into a coherent whole. 2. The use of the word by the *sophists approaches the modern uses of its derivatives 'logic' and 'logical'; for them *logos* could mean an argument, or the content of an argument. 3. The Stoics (see Stoicism) equated it with that sort of God who is the supposed source of all the rationality in the universe. 4. The *logos* with which most modern people are familiar appears in the opening words of St. John's gospel where it is equated with Jesus Christ in his creative and redemptive aspect. Its meaning here is, of course, derived from Greek influences, especially that of the Stoics.

Lokāyata.   The Indian philosophical doctrine that holds that this world is the only one that exists and that there is no after-life. See Indian materialism.

lottery paradox.   A paradox arising from the principle that a rational man who believes each of two propositions ought to believe their conjunction. But suppose there is a lottery with one hundred tickets 1,2,3,...100. A rational man may, it is said, believe that 1 will not win, 2 will not win, and so on for each ticket. So he ought, by the principle, to believe the conjunction of all these, which is equivalent to believing that no ticket will win. But one will! So the natural principle of combining rational beliefs has a false consequence.

Lovejoy, Arthur Oncken (1873-1962). American philosopher and historian of ideas. In Lovejoy's first major work, *The Revolt Against Dualism* (1930), he defended epistemic dualism (the view that the objects of our knowledge in the world are not identical with our ideas or images of them). Lovejoy accepted the idea that they are both spatially distinct—our image of a table is within us while the actual table is located at a distance from us—and temporally distinct—at the time we receive the image of a star it may already be extinct (*see* time-lag argument). He was also influential in the history of ideas. *The Great Chain of Being* (1936) traces, from Plato onwards, the significance of what Lovejoy called the 'principle of plenitude', that is the notion that all real possibilities are realized in this world.

Löwenheim-Skolem theorem. The proof, provided by Löwenheim in 1915, that any finite set Γ of sentences which has a *model, has a *denumerable model, which result Skolem generalized in 1920 to the case where Γ is a denumerably infinite set of sentences.

This gives rise to the so-called *Skolem paradox*, because it is possible to formalize the theory of real numbers in a system with denumerably many axioms. Within this system it is possible to prove that the set of real numbers is nondenumerably infinite. Yet application of Skolem's result to the system means that if the system is consistent (has a model), it has a denumerable model (one in which there are only denumerably many 'real numbers').

Lucretius, Titus Lucretius Carus (99/94-55/51 BC). Latin philosophical poet. He wrote a didactic poem *De Rerum Natura* (On the Nature of Things), an exposition of Epicurean natural philosophy in six books (*see* Epicureanism). These deal with atomic theory (I and II), with the mortality of the soul (III), with sensation and thought (IV), with the origins and development of the world (V), and with various natural phenomena (VI).

Lyceum. The public garden in Athens that gave its name to the school of philosophy founded by *Aristotle in 335 BC. *See also* Peripatetic.

M

Mach, Ernst (1838-1916). Austrian philosopher and physicist. Mach's scientific writings contain much of his philosophy, and include *Die Geschichte und die Wurzel des Satzes von der Erhaltung der Arbeit* (1872), *Die Mechanik in ihrer Entwicklung historisch-kritisch dargestellt* (1883) translated as *The Science of Mechanics* (1893), and *Beiträge zur Analyse der Empfindungen* (1906), translated as *The Analysis of Sensations* (1914).

Mach is widely regarded as the father of logical positivism. His philosophy is radically empiricist. The mind is allowed no power to know or understand things beyond its own sensations, and scientific theory is not the discovery of real things apart from our sensations, but a device for predicting their course. The logical positivists took from this not only the foundational approach to knowledge based on sense experience, but also the consequence of the fundamental unity of science—all sciences have the same subject matter: sensation. Mach's criticism of concepts that try to go beyond their empirical role influenced *Einstein. His philosophy was criticized by Lenin as surreptitiously idealist and solipsistic. *See also* logical positivism; science, philosophy of.

Madhyamaka. A school of Mahāyāna
*Buddhist philosophy. Nāgārjuna (*c.*
200 AD), in his *Madhyamakakārikās*, and
his disciple Āryadeva, author of the
Catuhṡatakam, developed the school on
the basis of certain ideas expressed in
earlier religious (particularly the *Prajñā-
pāramitā-*) literature. The external world,
whose nature is 'plurality' (*prapañca*),
was conceived of as ultimately unreal,
without essence, 'empty'. All phenomena
are embedded in the one absolute
'emptiness' (*ṡūnyatā*), which in itself is
without essence, 'empty'. Thus the
remarkable conclusion was drawn that
the absolute emptiness and the world of
phenomena are identical. Since all
concepts are 'conditioned', that is, denote
only by virtue of their opposites, nothing
can be said about this emptiness which
lies in between the notions of being and
non-being; realization of this fact constitutes liberation.

Subsequent achievements in the area
of logic were applied by Buddhapālita
(*c.* 5th century AD) and Candrakīrti (7th
century AD) to Nāgārjuna's often erratic
and paradoxical statements, though
solely for the purpose of a *reductio ad
absurdum* of the propositions of other
schools.

magnitudes. A magnitude is intensive
if it is possible to order things of a
certain type according to it; it is extensive if it is both intensive and different
numerical values can be assigned to
differing positions in the ordering, such
that the ordering by magnitude is preserved when ordered by the relation less
than. Thus *mass* is an extensive magnitude since physical objects can be
ordered in accordance with it and it
makes sense to assign numerical values
to the masses. *Beauty* is intensive but
not extensive since it makes little or no
strict sense to say that a painting has
such-and-such units of beauty or that it
is twice as beautiful as another.

Mahommedan fate. *See* fatalism.

Maimonides (*or* **Moses ben Maimon,**
also known by his initials as **Rambam**)
(1135–1204). Physician, and head of the
Jewish community of Fostat (Old Cairo).
Maimonides' major philosophical work
is the *Dalālat al-Ḥa'rīn* (Guide for the
Perplexed; in Hebrew: Moreh Nevu-
khim) (*c.*1190), but aspects of his thought
are also presented in his *Sharh al-
Mishnah* (Commentary on the Mishnah,
also known as *Sirāj*, (Luminary)) (1168),
Mishneh Torah (Code of Jewish law),
(1178), *Treatise on Resurrection* (1191),
and other works, including a vast corpus
of legal responsa.

The *Guide*, in which Maimonides
attempts to harmonize the teachings of
Judaism with Aristotle, is generally
recognized as one of the great works of
medieval philosophy. It is directed at the
initiate, not at a general public, and the
style and arrangement of material are
often deliberately obscure. For Maimonides, metaphysics is the highest form of
human activity, but it is not open to all
men. He examines and rejects the
method of *Kalām, and insists that only
philosophy can lead to a true understanding of the nature of God and the
world, despite the objection that Aristotle maintained the eternity of the world
and thus ruled out *creation or a creator.
Whereas the exponents of Kalām proved
the existence of God from the religious
dogma of the creation, Maimonides
proves it purely on the basis of Aristotelian principles. However, he also
demonstrates that the eternity of the
world cannot be established by rational
arguments, and hence there is no objection to the scriptural account of the
creation, which he defines as creation *ex
nihilo* (from nothing).

Maimonides is commonly described
as an Aristotelian, but his departure
from Aristotle on this point has such far-
reaching ramifications that the epithet is
not entirely appropriate. Although the
basis of his thought, in contrast to that
of most of his Jewish predecessors
(except *Ibn Daud), is Aristotelian, his
conception of God is not. The idea of
God's absolute unity and perfection
makes it impossible to describe him by
means of positive attributes; he can only

be known in negative terms, that is, by a denial of imperfection. Thus, for all his faith in human reason, Maimonides is conscious of its limitations. Again, while he accepts that everything in the world has a purpose, which may be discovered by science, he refuses to allow that the purpose of the world itself can be determined.

Maimonides acknowledges a debt to earlier Islamic philosophers and he had a high regard for his contemporary *Averroes. His own influence on contemporary and subsequent philosophers, Jewish, Muslim, and Christian, was enormous. The Guide, in Latin translation, was eagerly studied by Christian scholastics such as Albertus Magnus and Aquinas, and in more recent times was admired by Spinoza, Leibniz, Mendelssohn, and others.

major premise. In a categorical *syllogism, the premise containing the *major term.

major term. The *predicate term of the conclusion of a categorical *syllogism.

Malebranche, Nicolas   (1638–1715). Philosopher, theologian, and principal developer of Cartesianism. In his De la Recherche de la Vérité (1674/5), Malebranche advanced a theory of the relation between mind and body known as *occasionalism. As to the causal interaction between physical objects, Malebranche asserts that when two bodies collide, the motion of one has no power to affect the motion of the other, since there is no necessary connection between the two (compare Hume). A corollary of Malebranche's view of causation is his famous thesis that "we see all things in God": since an idea cannot be produced by external objects "all our ideas are in the efficacious substance of the divinity". This curious doctrine was taken by Malebranche to explain our alleged knowledge of eternal and necessary truths. Compare Berkeley.

Malthus, Thomas Robert (1766–1834). English clergyman and classical economist, author of the influential but bitterly controversial Essay on Population (First Essay 1798; Second Essay 1803). He argues that mankind is endangered by the geometrically expanding growth rate of world population compared with the arithmetical growth rate of increasing food production. The checks on this "law of population" are twofold: causes of death and causes preventing birth. Disease, war, and famine will keep the population steady at near starvation level unless positive steps are taken to contain the birth rate. These steps include moral restraint (sexual abstinence) and "vice" (including birth-control methods).

Manichaeism. A religious movement named after its Persian founder Mani, "the apostle of God" (c.216–76 AD). Manichaeism is best seen not as a heretical movement within Christianity but as a separate religion. It was for some time a quite serious rival, embodying Buddhist and Zoroastrian as well as Christian elements. St. *Augustine was briefly an adherent.

Manichaeism was radically dualistic, seeing the world, and especially human life, as a struggle between totally independent principles of good and evil (light and darkness, God and matter). Manichaeans saw themselves as taking the side of light, and through a rigorous asceticism, striving towards ultimate freedom from the darker, material elements in human nature.

manifold. (German: mannigfaltigkeit.) A term used by *Kant, in the Critique, to mean the various and discrete elements of sensory experience—that which is presented to the senses and which the mind then organizes through concepts, in order to perceive the world (as made up of material objects and so on).

Mannheim, Karl (1893–1947). German sociologist, influenced by *Marx but advocating the improvement of society through piecemeal reformist effort rather than revolution. In Ideologie und Utopie (1929) Mannheim contrasted the attitude of commitment to preservation, producing ideologies (*see* ideology) and overemphasis on stability, with the commitment to change, envisaging possible future utopias. *Mensch und Gesellschaft im Zeitalter des Umbaus* (1935) maintains that individual freedom is threatened equally by extreme liberalism and by totalitarian dictatorship. Economic stability and education leading to radical democratization are the fundamentals of a viable social system.

many questions, fallacy of. A mistake consisting of putting or accepting a question that tacitly takes for granted a false or at least disputatious answer to some prior question or questions. It is a common form of intellectual error, though not perhaps in the strictest sense a *fallacy.* Compare Chapter Six of *Alice's Adventures in Wonderland:* "How am I to get in?" asked Alice again, in a louder tone. "Are you to get in at all?" said the Footman. "That's the first question, you know."

The traditional example is the question: "When did you stop beating your wife?", put to a man who is either not married at all, or else has not started, or perhaps has started but not stopped, beating his wife.

many-sorted logic. The study of validity in many-sorted languages. A formal language with *predicate structure is many-sorted if typographically distinct kinds of names and variables are used with the intention that interpretation of the language will involve assigning, to each kind, different categories of objects for their universes of discourse (*see* interpretation). For example, in sentences like $(\exists x)(\exists \phi)(K\phi \,\&\, F\phi x \,\&\, B\phi b)$ the Roman names and variables might be assigned a universe of physical objects and the Greek variables a universe of events. Many logicians prefer other ways of achieving this effect of restricting the domains of the quantifiers, ways that enable them to continue to work in one-sorted languages.

many-valued logic. The study of validity and consequence under an inter-

pretation that assigns three or more possible values to the sentences of a *formal language. It is, however, more usual for an interpretation of language to assign one of two *truth-values to the sentences of that language.

Providing a many-valued interpretation requires not only choosing a set of values, but also specifying the functions that will enable one to determine the value of a complex sentence from the values assigned to its components. For example, if the language contains the connective '$\vee$' (*see* or), then for any sentences, 'A' and 'B', the value to be assigned to '$A \vee B$' should be determined once values have been assigned to 'A' and 'B'. If the values are $1,\ldots,n$, this requires that '$\vee$' be interpreted by a *function f such that for any pair j, k of values, $f(j,k)$ is defined and is one of the values $1,\ldots,n$. This is, in fact, what a *truth-table does for the usual *two* values, true and false.

Furthermore, some of the values used must be singled out as *designated values.* Intuitively, designated values can be thought of as ways of being true or as degrees of truth, whereas undesignated values are ways of failing to be true, or degrees of falsity. If an admissible valuation is defined as one which is obtained from an assignment of values to atomic wffs of the language by application of the functions interpreting the logical operators, then each set of values, together with functions interpreting logical operators and a specification of which values are designated, determines a (different) many-valued logic, L. For the notions of validity (*see* validity and truth) and *consequence are defined in terms of the designated values and admissible valuations. B is said to be a *consequence of $A_1,\ldots,A_k$ in L* (or the inference, $A_1,\ldots,A_k$ therefore B, is *valid in L*) iff for all admissible valuations, B is assigned a designated value whenever each of $A_1,\ldots,A_n$ is assigned a designated value. A is *valid in L* iff A has a designated value in all admissible valuations.

An important application of many-valued logics lies in the provision of proofs that one logical axiom or rule of inference is *independent of others. Given a formal system, L, of logic, it is sometimes possible to devise a many-valued logic L' such that all rules of inference of L are valid in L' (can never lead from designated to undesignated values) and such that all axioms $A_1,...,A_k$ are valid in L'. To show that sentence C cannot be proved from $A_1,...,A_k$ in L it is then sufficient to show that C is not valid in L'.

Attempts have also been made to use many-valued logics as models of the use and/or understanding of natural languages.

Mao Tse-Tung (1893-1976). Chinese revolutionary leader and Chairman of the Chinese People's Republic. His contribution to the development, indeed transmogrification, of the Marxism of *Marx was enormous, since he led, and wrote to justify as Marxist, a revolution based not on the proletariat but on the peasantry. In philosophy his pamphlet *On Contradiction* is orthodox and traditionally Marxist. It therefore collapses the crucial distinction between *contradictions (between utterances) and conflicts and tensions (in the non-linguistic world). The famous little red book interestingly resembles both in form and content the classics of *Chinese philosophy, for Chairman Mao's thoughts are presented in aphoristic paragraphs rather than continuous prose and contain next to nothing of philosophical argument.

Marburg school. One of the most important divisions of *Neo-Kantianism. Founded by Hermann *Cohen (1842-1918) and Paul Natorp (1854-1924), the Marburg school was mainly concerned with philosophy of science. Using the methods of Kant's 'transcendental logic', it enquired especially into scientific presuppositions. Prominent members were Ernst Cassirer (1874-1945) and Rudolf Stammler (1856-1938).

Marcel, Gabriel(1889-1973). French Catholic existentialist philosopher. Critical both of *Sartre's undisciplined view of morality and of his insistence on the essential loneliness of the human soul, Marcel considered *existentialism to be compatible with Christian doctrines. The aim of life is "communication" between men as well as between man and God, but relationships must be based on and retain the freedom and uniqueness of individuals, not be dependent on the joint acceptance of rules and goals. *Les Hommes Contre l'humain* (1951) warned against the ethical consequences of generalization and the substitution of abstractions ('fascist' or 'communist') for the real and particular human existent.

Marcus Aurelius (121-80 AD). Roman Emperor and Stoic, the author of *Meditations* or *Writings to Himself* in twelve books. Converted to Stoicism as a young man, Marcus was never a professional philosopher. His *Meditations* are personal reflections and aphorisms, written for his own edification during a long career of public service and arranged, after the acknowledgments filling Book I, in next to no order. Conservative in content, they show no signs of the other-worldly speculations that were coming to dominate philosophy in his time. They are valuable primarily as a personal document, as evidence of what it could mean to be a Stoic.

Maritain, Jacques (1882-1973). French philosopher, converted to Catholicism under the influence of *Bergson. Maritain studied biology at Heidelberg under *Driesch. He later rejected the Bergsonian doctrine to become a leading exponent of *Neo-Thomism.

Known outside France chiefly for his writings on art and politics, Maritain also gained recognition for his philosophical treatise, *Les degrés du savoir* (1932), in which he argued that sensation, reason, revelation, and mystical union are grounds of different but equally significant kinds of knowledge. Science and faith can cooperate without friction if the right distinction is made between their respective claims.

Marx, Karl (1818-83). German social theorist, interested mainly in economics and history. He had little to do with the philosophical doctrines that now form part of *Marxism. In the first volume of *Das Kapital* (1867) Marx made use of, and to some extent discussed, a theory of method that owed something to *Hegel. Marx called this a dialectical method, but said that it turned Hegel's dialectic the right way up, in that it was materialistic and not idealistic. But though Marx's dialectic may in a broad sense be called a philosophy of history, it is really an account of socio-historical development rather than a philosophical theory, and so is the concern of the historian rather than of the philosopher. *See also* dialectical materialism.

Marxism (*or* **Classical Marxism**). The body of doctrines originally propounded by Marx and Engels, which involves certain philosophical views. These views (propounded mainly by Engels) rely heavily on the philosophy of Hegel, and in particular on his thesis that change has to be explained in terms of contradiction. But whereas Hegel's philosophy is a form of *idealism, Marxism declares itself to be a form of *materialism. Not, however, 'mechanistic' materialism, but 'dialectical' materialism, where due weight is given to 'the transformation of quantity into quality' (*compare* Hegel). This means that mind is not reduced to matter, but is seen as coming from matter, though qualitatively different from it. Early in the 20th century, in the course of a polemic against idealism, Lenin laid stress on the view that knowledge is a 'copy' of reality, and this now forms part of official Soviet Marxism. Since World War I, many different versions of Marxism have been propounded. A large number of these are not philosophies, but rather types of social theory; those that are genuinely philosophical, for example, the theories of Georg Lukács (1885-1971) or Ernst Bloch (1885-1977),

often develop certain Hegelian aspects of Marxism. *See also* dialectical materialism.

masked man fallacy. The mistake of arguing that because someone knows (or does not know) something under one description, they must therefore know it (or they therefore cannot know it) as the same thing when it appears under another description. For instance, from the facts that my father knew Lloyd George, and that my father did not know who the masked man was, it does not follow that the masked man was not Lloyd George. *See also* Leibniz's law.

mass noun. A term referring to an uncountable thing. Glasses of water can be counted, water cannot. Hence 'water' is a mass noun. *Compare* count noun.

material adequacy condition. *See* truth definition.

material cause. *See* causes: material, formal, efficient, and final.

material implication. *See* implication and entailment.

material implication, paradoxes of. *See* implication and entailment.

materialism. As most commonly understood in philosophy, the term denotes the doctrine that whatever exists is either *matter, or entirely dependent on matter for its existence. The precise meaning and status of this doctrine are, however, far from clear. What are the properties that matter in the relevant sense must, could, or could not possess? Is matter to be regarded simply as that which is extended in both space and time (so that rainbows and shadows are examples of matter as well as trees and stones)? Or if not, what further properties are essential to it? Is there a relevant distinction to be drawn here between existence or occurrence and being, or reality? And how exactly are the space and time in which matter extends, the forces moving it, and the consciousness perceiving it, dependent on it? The range of possible answers, or attempted answers, to such questions makes materialism in effect a somewhat ill-defined group of doctrines rather than one specific thesis. It is easier to see what materialists deny—that is, the existence of such things as the Cartesian non-extended "thinking substance" or mind (see Descartes), and the reality of spirits, angels, or deities in most traditional senses—than what they positively assert.

Further, even supposing the content of the doctrine is sufficiently clarified, why should it be accepted? There are certainly no observational or analytical methods of establishing it as true. Often it appears to function as a *policy* of research rather than a statement of a *result* of research; the materialist in his explanations of the phenomena of nature and consciousness proposes to do without the postulate of immaterial entities (whatever this expression is taken to mean) and to rely exclusively on material things and their inter-relations. But while we may, of course, adopt such a policy if we wish, is there any compelling reason why we should? It could doubtless be recommended to researchers by an appeal to *Ockham's razor, or to the notorious difficulties created, for example, by the Cartesian mind/body dualism. It is, however, questionable whether the difficulties of giving a materialistic account of consciousness are any less intractable, and recent thought, especially that of the later *Wittgenstein and his followers, has challenged the necessity of restricting our options to either Cartesian dualism or materialism (*compare* identity theory).

Forms of materialism appear in the history of thought as far back at least as *Democritus and *Epicurus, who attempted to describe natural processes and human experience in terms of arrangements and rearrangements of changeless atoms, or indivisible material particles, in empty space. Despite inevitable religious opposition there have been various revivals of such ideas, beginning in the 17th century in conjunction with the new physics of Galileo and, later,

Newton. *Hobbes produced a drastic and brilliant account of such materialism and the promise of an all-explaining scientific world-view was subsequently pursued by, for example, La Mettrie (1705-51) and Holbach (1723-89).

In more recent times, Marxist thinkers have attempted to replace such "mechanistic materialism"—and resolve some of its difficulties—by their own "dialectical materialism". This sees matter, not as something static on which change and development have to be imposed *ab extra*, but as containing within its own nature those tensions or "contradictions" which provide the motive force for change—a vision which, it is claimed, is lacking in earlier materialists (see dialectical materialism; Marxism). *Compare* Indian materialism.

material mode of speech. *See* formal mode of speech.

mathematical logic. *See* logic.

mathematics, philosophy of. The study of the concepts of and justification for the principles used in mathematics. Two central problems in the philosophy of mathematics concern what, if anything, mathematical statements, such as '2 + 2 = 4', are about, and how it is that we come to have knowledge of such statements.

Although mathematics is a useful tool in science, few believe that the subject matter of mathematics is physical objects or that empirical observation is the ultimate ground for deciding the truth or falsity of mathematical statements. Many mathematicians—sometimes only implicitly—take a realist view about mathematical truth and the existence of mathematical objects. They hold that the latter exist independently of our thought and hence that mathematical statements are true (or false) independently of our knowledge of them or our ability to prove them. This view is known as *platonism*, since it derives from and often includes, Plato's view that the subjects of mathematical statements — *numbers—are abstract entities and that, if true, these statements describe relations holding between the entities. Abstract entities are timeless, do not exist in physical space, and do not causally interact with the physical world. This leaves open the question as to how we attain knowledge of such entities, that is, mathematical knowledge. *Kant believed that (true) mathematical statements were self-evident and capable of being known a priori by intuition alone. In the proof of such statements we employ particular instances of the concepts used as we represent these instances to ourselves. The logicists, notably *Frege and *Russell (see logicism), unhappy with the subjectivist bent of Kant's approach, sought merely to show that our knowledge of mathematical truth was as certain as our knowledge of logical truth. By adopting a rigorously formal approach they attempted to demonstrate that received mathematics was reducible to *set theory and that this in turn was part of logic. Although this yielded important results in the foundations of mathematics, set theory was not shown to be part of logic (in the narrow sense) and the postulates of classical logic seemed to be indubitable in a way that the postulates of set theory did not.

There have been various reactions against the view, with its attendant epistemological difficulties, that 'mysterious' or platonic abstract entities are the subject matter of mathematics. Conventionalists hold that true mathematical statements are true merely by convention or fiat. This is compatible with the possibility of the rejection of present conventions and the adoption of new conventions more useful in the light of empirical experience—for instance, in particle physics. Intuitionists (see intuitionism) restrict the scope of mathematics to that which can be proved by constructive processes alone. Entities referred to in such proofs must themselves be capable of being so constructed. Hence intuitionists eschew the plethora of actual infinite numbers and sets that the Platonists consider admissible.

*Formalism is the view that mathematical sentences are not about anything but are rather to be regarded as meaningless marks. The formalists are interested in the formal properties of systems of these marks. In 1930 Gödel's incompleteness theorems (see Gödel) showed that in the theory of arithmetic (and in most of useful mathematics) there would be true statements that could not be proved in the theory. This suggests that the truth of a mathematical statement cannot merely consist in its proof from a set of axioms.

matrix. See normal form; truth-table.

matter. That which has traditionally been contrasted either with form or with mind. The two contrasts are not entirely unrelated. But it is important to remember, when, for example, we are concerned with Greek ideas of matter, what is the relevant contrast there (in this case not with mind but with form). This makes matter simply the basic stuff or raw material from which the diverse elements of the world are composed (that is, something analogous to the craftsman's wood or clay). This does little, of course, to determine what matter positively is, and we find a long history of varied speculations, from *Thales and *Anaximander through *Democritus, *Plato, and *Aristotle to the Epicurean and Stoic schools (see Epicureanism; Stoicism), about such questions as the different kinds of matter, whether it consists of discrete atoms or a single continuous medium, and whether its potentialities can be explained in terms of its arithmetical or geometrical properties. Such speculations, though guided merely by unsystematic observations or preconceptions of the world, can still be seen as remote ancestors of modern systematic science, in so far as they sought for unifying principles underlying the world's surface diversity.

Modern post-Cartesian thought has contrasted matter primarily with mind. But Descartes' radical dualism, apart from raising very serious problems about how mind can have knowledge of the material world, or indeed how the two can interact at all, also leaves uncertainty about the precise nature of matter (see Descartes; mind-body problem). Is it simply, in the Cartesian phrase, "extended substance", that is, extended in space as well as time? Are only geometrical properties, then, essential to it, or are some dynamical properties essential also—and, if so, which? How are we to characterize such things as space, time, energy, and light, which clearly do not belong to the mind side of the dichotomy, and yet do not seem examples of matter either? Do we need some further principle to explain the difference between organic and inorganic? And are motion and development imposed *ab extra* on matter, or should they, as, for example, *dialectical materialism has claimed, be seen as inherent elements of its nature?

Despite such theoretical difficulties, however, there were undoubtedly great benefits for modern science, during its earlier phases, in the idea of the world of matter as a more or less isolated and self-sufficient system, the elements of which interacted according to immutable and unbreakable laws—laws which science could set itself to explicate. And over a long period of its history, a basic distinction between matter—in the Newtonian sense, distinguished by mass as well as extension—and energy, each with its own principle of conservation, served the purposes of science admirably. In the present century, however, this distinction has been challenged by Einstein's famous demonstration that for some purposes the two conservation principles have to be combined, that in some circumstances matter and energy are mutually transformable. The development of atomic and subatomic physics has largely dissolved traditional ideas of the ultimate constituents of the material world as discrete parcels of inert and impenetrable stuff. No longer are they seen as wholly distinct from the forces acting on them, but instead as themselves consisting, at least in essential part, of patterns of interaction with their environment. Also, indeterminacy theory has called attention to fundamental difficulties in the way of establishing precisely defined laws governing events in the subatomic world, and hence raised arguments over our justification for assuming that such laws do in fact operate in this field (see uncertainty principle).

In brief, the history of thought yields no single concept of matter, but rather a large and still growing family of interrelated concepts. See also materialism.

maximin principle. See decision theory.

McTaggart, John McTaggart Ellis (1866-1925). British idealist philosopher, who studied and taught philosophy at Cambridge. Main philosophical works: *Studies in Hegelian Dialectic* (1896), *Studies in Hegelian Cosmology* (1901), *A Commentary on Hegel's Logic* (1910), and *The Nature of Existence* (2 volumes, 1921, 1927).

Starting from his Hegelian studies, McTaggart developed an original and ingeniously argued *idealism in which reality is envisaged as essentially spiritual, a closely interrelated society of minds and their contents. Matter, space, and time are relegated to the realm of appearance. He denied the existence of God, as traditionally understood, but, despite the alleged unreality of time, defended a theory of individual immortality.

mean. See average.

meaning. The philosophy of meaning explores the various aspects of our understanding of words and sentences, and our ability to endow them with a symbolic function. The important goal historically was to delimit the extent of human understanding, and to that end a succession of principles connecting meaning with experience has been offered, each refining the idea that you cannot know what something means unless you know what you would experience if it were true. This enterprise has been retarded by the difficulties encountered by *confirmation theory, which have even allowed empiricists such as *Quine to doubt whether the single sentence of a scientific theory has any meaning.

Another aspect of the notion of meaning is its connection with other psychological conditions, such as wanting or intending, and with human conventions and rules. Following H. P. Grice, many writers have hoped to analyse the fact of a sentence's meaning something in terms of its being normally used by those intending to bring about a certain result in an audience. It is through this work that light may be thrown on the relation between human and animal communication systems and on the role of convention in language using.

A third aspect of meaning concerns the connection between meaning and other semantic notions, such as reference and truth. Here philosophers have been impressed by the success of *model theory in interpreting *formal languages; by equating meaning with truth-conditions they hope to show how recognition of the meaning of grammatically complex sentences can be reduced to rule. See also empiricism; logical positivism; semantics; translation.

meaning postulates. Devices used by Rudolf *Carnap to introduce *analytic sentences into a formal language. Under all interpretations (see interpretation) for a formal language L, only logical truths (such as 'No married woman is not married') will remain true invariantly. Analytically true sentences (such as 'All spinsters are not married') will not, however, remain true under all interpretations, since their truth depends on the particular meanings of their non-logical words (such as 'married' and 'spinster'). Formal semantics (the analysis of formal languages and their interpretations) admits only two sorts of truths—logical and non-logical—thus disregarding the analytic/synthetic distinction which has seemed important to many philosophers of language. Carnap proposed meaning postulates as an addition to the *truth definition for L.

As well as giving truth conditions for predicates, a particular relation must be stipulated to hold between certain predicates. For example, to guarantee the analyticity (and thus invariant truth) of 'All spinsters are not married', (using Sx for 'x is a spinster' and Mx for 'x is married') we shall have: $(\forall x)(Sx \rightarrow -Mx)$ as a meaning postulate.

mechanical explanation. An expression employed with different and often rather vague connotations, to cover various substantially different areas of denotation. Vitalist and organismal biologists, for instance, are inclined to describe all their opponents as such as mechanists, notwithstanding that these opponents themselves always place enormous emphasis upon the chemistry of organisms and that chemical is often contrasted with mechanical explanation. Confusion about what should and should not count as mechanical explanation is encouraged by the linguistic fact that in ordinary non-philosophical usage the word 'mechanism' covers a great deal more than the word 'machine' (see also mechanism). Most typically a machine is some man-made device for performing a task that could be and previously was performed by people, for example, a sewing machine or a milking machine. But we are prepared to describe as a mechanism almost any system some of the elements of which act upon the others.

Talk about mechanical explanation and ambitions vastly to extend its scope first became prominent in the 1600s. Thus the Introduction to the *Leviathan* of *Hobbes starts from the suggestion that all living things are, as it were, natural machines; while automata must be, correspondingly, artificial organisms. From there Hobbes proceeds to promise his new science of the state, an artefact with its own artificial life. Again, *Descartes conceives the familiar fundamental principles of direct contact, push-and-pull, mechanical operation to be the universal and necessary laws of all possible matter. Part V of his

Discourse recommends not that we should *assert that* the brutes and even people actually are machines but that we should "*consider* ... *as* a machine ... the body of every animal" (italics supplied).

But the traditional paradigm of mechanical explanation has been provided, almost from its first publication, by "the incomparable Mr. Newton's" *Philosophiae Naturalis Principia Mathematica* (1687). *Newton himself inclined to the view that this work was defective in allowing for *action at a distance in gravitational attraction. He sometimes suggested that gravitational forces must somehow be transmitted through a continuous intervening corporeal medium, so far undetected. In subsequent centuries this assumption of the impossibility, even inconceivability, of action at a distance was abandoned, while the system of Newton's *Principia*, now construed as unequivocally providing for such action, remained the paradigm.

mechanism. 1. A scientific philosophy developed principally by Descartes. In place of the traditional scholastic kind of scientific explanation which invoked 'real qualities', Descartes claimed that his science was "like mechanics in that it considers merely shapes, sizes, and motions." An example is the phenomenon of gravity, which Descartes attempts to explain purely in terms of the interaction of particles of a certain shape, size, and velocity: no reference is made to matter possessing the 'quality' of *gravitas* or 'heaviness'. "I recognize", wrote Descartes, "no matter in corporeal objects other than that susceptible of what the geometers call quantitative analysis."

Apart from the elimination of qualities in favour of quantifiables, another crucial element in 'mechanism' (also to be found in Descartes) is the rejection of Aristotelian 'final causes'. The mechanist holds that purposes have no place in good scientific practice: teleological explanations (for example, that 'the plant turns its leaves in order to catch the sunlight') should always be replaced by a mechanistic account (for example, one specifying the molecular structure of the leaf that makes it move in the direction of sunlight).

2. The thesis that genuine scientific explanation involves a search for mechanical models. Such models, based on known processes, describe the true mechanisms underlying the phenomenon to be explained. (Elements of this conception are to be found, again, in Descartes, who explains, for example, the behaviour of celestial particles by using a model of wooden balls in a box.)

3. A 'clockwork' universe of the Laplacean type—that is, one governed by strictly deterministic laws. *See* Laplace.

median. *See* average.

medium. *See* syllogism.

Megarian school. A philosophical school active at Megara, near Athens, between the late 5th and early 3rd centuries BC. No writings of the Megarians have survived and our knowledge of their doctrines and interests is based on references in the works of their contemporaries. They were influenced by Socrates and the Eleatics and were critical of Plato and Aristotle. Some of their contributions to logic are of lasting interest. Eubulides, the refiner of the *liar paradox, was one of their number.

Meinong, Alexius von (1853–1928). Austrian philosopher, disciple of *Brentano. In *Über Gegenstandtheorie* (1904) he distinguished between three distinct elements in thinking: the mental act, its content, and its object. Object is defined as that towards which a mental act can be directed; it may or may not be an existing entity. Content is that attribute of the mental act that enables attention to be directed towards any particular thing.

Melissus of Samos. A statesman who also commanded a victorious Samian fleet against the Athenians in 441–440 BC. His philosophical contribution was to argue that the unitary reality (the One) of *Parmenides must be infinite in extent as well as without end and without beginning; moreover, since everything bodily must have parts, the One must be incorporeal. Yet it seems to have remained still spatial, not purely abstract. Melissus' contention that "if there were a plurality each one of the many would have to be just as I say the one is", was intended as a refutation of plurality. It later became the first principle of the atomism of *Leucippus and *Democritus. See Presocratics.

memory. The capacity to bring to mind (a) an event from one's past experience ("I remember my first day at school"), (b) a fact about the past beyond one's own experience ("I remember the date of the battle of Waterloo"), or (c) a proposition relating to the past ("I remember that the book was removed from the shelf"). The variety of these and other uses of the verb 'to remember' does not provide a generally accepted paradigm of memory, though there have been attempts to establish one standard use to which all others may be reduced. It is commonly agreed, however, that memory is closely related to *knowledge, either as a special case of knowledge, or in so far as it is only possible to remember what was once known.

A central problem about memory concerns how it is possible to acquire present knowledge of that which is no longer present. A standard resolution here, found in different forms in Aristotle, Locke, Hume, and Russell, has been to identify something now present in the mind (for example, an image, idea, or impression) as a representative of that which was in the past. More recently, however, the problem has been reconceived, not as how present knowledge of the past is *acquired*, but rather as how past knowledge is *retained* in the present.

Mencius (371–289 BC). Chinese philosopher who devoted his life to persuading the rulers of the warring central Chinese states to base their government on Confucian morality (see Confucianism). The Western form of his name is a Latinization of the Chinese Meng-tzu 'Master Meng'. Mencius argued that a truly moral ruler would receive the spontaneous support of the people in all the states, which would then unite under his rule. His appeal to morality was based on the argument that human nature was good: that men had an innate predisposition to goodness, revealed in the instinctive reaction of anyone who sees a child about to fall into a well. He insisted however that like any plant the moral nature required cultivation to grow and function properly. His conversations with rulers, disciples, and others are recorded in the *Meng-tzu*, a much fuller exposition of Confucian ideas than Confucius' *Lun-yü*.

Mendelssohn, Moses (1729–86). German philosopher, a leader of the Aufklärung (Enlightenment) movement. Mendelssohn's thought reflects his staunch adherence both to Judaism and to rationalism. His *Phaedon* (1767) (inspired by the Platonic *Phaedo*) is an attempt to justify the doctrine of the immortality of the soul, while in *Morgenstunden* (1785) he demonstrates the rationality of the belief in the existence of God. In *Jerusalem* (1783) he explains Judaism as a religion of reason, placing it far above Christianity in this respect. He was a strong supporter of the separation of Church and State. The great reputation Mendelssohn commanded made him a cardinal figure in the movement for Jewish emancipation.

mention *and* **use of words.** If I remark that the (German) word 'Gott' has four letters, then I am mentioning that word not using it. So what is being talked about is not God but, strictly, a four-letter word. Where a word is mentioned it is a word in a particular language; if the sentence in which such a mention occurs is translated, that word is left as it was. But the *use* of a word, the task to which it is put, must be the same for all its synonyms, both in the same and other languages. See formal mode of speech (especially for hints as to the importance of this distinction); metalanguage.

Merleau-Ponty, Maurice (1908-61). French philosopher who worked on problems of consciousness and ethics. He taught in various lycées, and after World War II, he held professorships at the University of Lyons and the Sorbonne. He was editor of the journal *Les Temps modernes* which he founded with *Sartre.

In his major works *Le structure du comportement* (1942) and *Phénoménologie de perception* (1945) he investigated the relationship between consciousness and the world, rejecting dualist theories of body and soul as well as extreme realist and subjectivist views of the world as something "given" to the perceiving subject or wholly constructed by him. Merleau-Ponty's "philosophy of ambiguity" stated that the objects of one's experience are by nature enigmatic.

Mersenne, Marin (1588-1648). Friend and principal correspondent of Descartes. Friar Mersenne was responsible for collecting for publication the first six sets of *Objections* to Descartes' *Meditations.* His own prolific writings include *La Vérité des Sciences contre les Sceptiques* (1625).

meta. Originally a Greek preposition, now employed by English-speaking philosophers as a prefix. The usual meaning is 'about' as in 'meta-ethics', 'metahistory', and 'metalanguage'. But the etymology of the word 'metaphysics' involves the other meaning 'after': Aristotle's *Metaphysics,* and hence later its subject, was so called because it followed the *Physics.*

meta-ethics. *See* ethics.

metahistory. In the broad sense, philosophy of history. The term is often restricted to the discipline's speculative aspect, which attempts to establish a framework of principles that can account for the course of historical developments. *See* history, philosophy of.

metalanguage. The language used to talk *about* an *object language and its component words. Thus if a treatise on the Russian language is written in English, Russian is the object language and English the metalanguage. If, however, we write about English using English, then English is both object language and metalanguage. The distinction between object language and metalanguage is entirely relative since what may be used as a metalanguage in one discussion may become the object language in another.

In many works on formal logic the object language may be a *formal language consisting of uninterpreted symbols. The writer may talk about that formal language using a natural language, such as English, perhaps supplemented by technical terms.

When both metalanguage and object language are the same natural language, as when we talk about English using English terms, it is essential to distinguish those terms that are being talked about (mentioned) from those metalanguage words that are used to talk about them (*see* mention and use of words). One way of doing this is to put quotation marks round the object language expressions. Thus "'True' has four letters" does not use 'true' but makes a metalinguistic remark about it. Many paradoxes, including some of the so-called semantic paradoxes, result from failure to distinguish object language and metalanguage expressions. *See also* formal mode of speech.

metamathematics. The study of formal systems, and, especially, of the concepts used in mathematics. It is also called *proof theory. The term is often restricted to analyses employing finitary methods (*see* finitism).

metaphysics. A central element in Western philosophy from the Greeks onwards, 'metaphysics' has meant many different things. It can be an attempt to characterize existence or reality as a whole, instead of, as in the various natural sciences, particular parts or aspects thereof. *Materialism and *idealism, Spinoza's *monism and Leibniz's *monadology, are examples of metaphysics in this sense. It can also be an attempt to explore the realm of the suprasensible, beyond the world of experience; to establish indubitable first principles as a foundation for all other knowledge; or to examine critically what more limited studies simply take for granted.

Not surprisingly, many critics have argued that the achievement of some at least of these aims is in principle impossible. Thus, it has been held that the human mind has no means of discovering facts outside the realm of sense experience; also that pure mathematics, the inspiration of many metaphysicians, achieves independence of experience only at the expense of dealing entirely in tautologies. Another criticism is that since no conceivable experience could enable us to decide between, for example, the statements that reality consists of only one substance (monism) or of infinitely many (monadology) neither serves any purpose in the economy of our thought about the world, and they are alike neither true nor false but meaningless. Furthermore, any attempt at characterization of reality as a whole must perforce use concepts originally developed to distinguish particular elements within reality and hence can only *misuse* them (*see* empiricism; logical positivism; positivism).

Nonetheless, in our natural sciences (and even in our most practical relationships with the world) we use an extensive apparatus of concepts, principles, etc., that it is no part of the function of science to examine or establish. And, from *Kant onwards, many philosophers have held that the proper outlet of the metaphysical impulse lies in the systematic study, not of reality, but of the fundamental structure of our thought about reality. Kant tried to show that there was a fixed conceptual framework that every rational mind as such must adopt. Later thinkers held that the framework might vary from one time or culture to another. Thus R.G. *Collingwood in his *Essay on Metaphysics* (1940) saw metaphysics as the explication of the "absolute pre-suppositions" underlying the characteristic thought of this or that period of history. And P.F. *Strawson, in his *Individuals* (subtitled *An Essay in Descriptive Metaphysics*) (1959) distinguishes between descriptive metaphysics, which "is content to describe the actual structure of our thought about the world", and revisionary metaphysics, which "is concerned to produce a better structure" (p. 9). An attempt, however, to show that a given structure is the right one, or better than its rivals, faces the difficulty that any assessment process itself presupposes some such structure; the metaphysician has to be content to describe, or propose, ways of thinking, rather than to establish the right one. Arguably also, any given language is biased towards a particular metaphysic and is therefore an intractable medium for the development of alternatives—one reason for the notorious obscurity of many essays in revisionary metaphysics.

metempsychosis. The idea, found in Buddhism and other religions originating in the Indian subcontinent, that our souls have lived before in the bodies of other men or of non-human animals, and that after death they will in due course be reincarnated into other human or non-human bodies. This doctrine, also known as that of the transmigration of souls, was apparently held by *Pythagoras of Samos and his followers, and is certainly entertained by *Plato in the *myth of Er. In *Meno* and *Phaedo* Plato presents what are supposed to be philosophical proofs of the pre-existence of the human soul, but their conclusions are not there linked with any claims about pre-existence in other bodies either human or non-human.

methodological holism *and* **methodological individualism.** Rival banners in an imbroglio in the philosophy of social science. One side presses for explanation in terms of social structures and social wholes, the other insists that everything must be reduced to statements about the component individuals. Both have more or less in the forefront of their minds metaphysical convictions, convictions about what ultimately there is or is not. *See* holism; Popper.

methodology. The study of method, usually covering the procedures and aims of a particular discipline, and enquiry into the way in which that discipline is organized.

Middle Platonism. The developments in *Platonism that took place between the establishing of the so-called Middle Academy (*see* Academy of Athens) by *Arcesilaus and the advent of *Plotinus. *See also* Neoplatonism.

middle term. *See* syllogism.

Milesian (*or* Ionian) school. The group of *Presocratics who came from the then Greek cities of the Aegean coast of what is now Turkey. The known figures are *Thales, *Anaximander, and *Anaximenes (all from Miletus), and *Anaxagoras of Clazomenae (who spent all his working life in Athens until he was expelled, nominally for godlessness). It was no accident that Western philosophy began in the independent capitalist trading city of Miletus, in close touch with the religion and science of both Babylon and Egypt. What the Milesians had in common was a fresh and radical this-worldly naturalism, and their various key ideas were all secularizations of elements in some previous supernaturalist religion. Thales' remark that 'The earth is full of gods' expresses this conviction that all forces are forces of the *Universe itself.

Mill, James (1773–1836). Scottish philosopher, historian, and economist, disciple of *Bentham, and one of the leaders of the *Philosophical Radicals. He published several articles on government and jurisprudence and was one of the founders of University College London. A profound believer in the efficacy of education, he maintained that in politi-

cal matters men could be persuaded by argument to make rational assessments before taking action. His *Elements of Political Economy* (1821), based on the works of Ricardo, can be seen to have influenced *Marx. His philosophical teachings are reflected in the works of his son and pupil, John Stuart *Mill.

Mill, John Stuart (1806–73). English empiricist philosopher and social reformer, educated by his father, James *Mill, through whom he became acquainted with *Bentham, Ricardo, and other *Philosophical Radicals. He sponsored and supported *Comte, only dissenting from his ideas on social planning on the grounds that they jeopardized individual liberty.

The major work that established Mill's reputation and has remained influential in the 20th century (as is evidenced in the writings of Frege and Russell among others) was his *System of Logic* (1843). Discussing the limits and characteristics of meaningful discourse, Mill made three fundamental distinctions: (1) between general terms (referring to an infinite number of similar things) and singular terms (proper names and complex names referring to specific objects); (2) between concrete terms ('man', 'white') and abstract terms ('humanity','whiteness'); and (3) between the connotation and the *denotation of expressions. One can speak significantly only of the sensible effects of properties characterizing different objects (*see* phenomenalism). Syllogisms do not represent a form of proof by inference from general to particular statements, but they relate inductive generalizations (*see* induction) and conclusions, inductive inference itself being based on the principle of the *uniformity of nature (*see* Mill's methods).

Utilitarianism (1863) modified the ethical theory of Bentham, considering self-interest to be an inadequate criterion of goodness and making a qualitative distinction between pleasures (*see also* hedonism). Mill attempted to show that men's notions of obligation can be made compatible with the *greatest happiness principle.

On Liberty (1859) related three fundamental freedoms of the individual (those of belief, of tastes and pursuits, and of uniting with others) to the powers of authority and social demands. Men must be encouraged to express their individuality. Actions, however, have consequences and it is the duty of rulers and society to restrain men from damaging others' interests and to require them to assume responsibility in furthering the interests of their community.

millet seed paradox. A puzzle, also known as the heap, that arises out of the attack on plurality and on the evidence of the senses by *Zeno of Elea. If one millet seed makes no sound in falling but 1000 millet seeds do make a sound, this would seem to suggest the nonsense that 1000 nothings become something. The puzzle's interest, such as it is, resides in the questions it suggests about the scope and validity of sense experience and the importance of differences of degree.

Mill's methods. The four "methods of experimental inquiry" distinguished by J. S. *Mill in his *Logic* (III (viii)). Mill held that all *induction involves a search for causes (*see* causation) and the methods are thus also contributions to the definition of 'cause'. He offers five canons: (1) "If two or more instances of the phenomenon under investigation have only one circumstance in common, the circumstance in which alone all the instances agree is the cause (or effect) of the given phenomenon" (method of agreement); (2) "If an instance in which the phenomenon…occurs, and an instance in which it does not occur, have every circumstance in common save one…[that] is the effect, or the cause, or an indispensable part of the cause…" (method of difference); (3) "If two or more instances in which the phenomenon occurs have only one circumstance in common, while two or more instances in which it does not occur have nothing in common save the absence of that circumstance, the circumstance in which alone

the two sets of instances differ, is the effect, or the cause, or an indispensable part of the cause…" (joint method of agreement and difference); (4) "Subduct from any phenomenon such part as is known by previous inductions to be the effect of certain antecedents, and the residue of the phenomenon is the effect of the remaining antecedents" (method of residues); and (5) "Whatever phenomenon varies in any manner whenever another phenomenon varies in some particular manner, is either a cause or an effect of that phenomenon, or is connected with it through some fact of causation" (method of concomitant variations).

Mīmāṃsā. One of the systems of *Indian philosophy. Originally it concerned itself solely with the *hermeneutics of the ancient ritualistic scriptures; this discipline was systematized by Jaimini in the *Karmamīmāṃsāsūtras* (before the 2nd century AD). It was drawn into the general philosophical discussion from the middle of the 1st millennium AD onwards: on the basis of Śabarasvāmī's commentary on the *sūtras* (5th century) Kumārila and Prabhākara (both 7th century) established fully fledged systems. In the context of a philosophy of nature similar to the *Vaiśeṣika, a detailed analysis of language produced the peculiar theory of the eternal prototype of language. Human speech only actualizes the eternal word whose sound-form and meaning are inseparably joined. This theory aims at demonstrating that the sacred scriptures, the Vedas (which contain the ritualistic works), do not require any God to be revealed to man and are in themselves the eternal highest form of knowledge.

mind-body problem. The philosophical problem of how the mind is related to the body, and of what properties, functions, and occurrences should be regarded as, respectively, mental or physical. This problem is central to both the philosophy of mind and the philosophy of psychology.

Both its prominence in modern philosophy and the established ways of representing it are primarily due to *Descartes. Systematic doubt led him to conclude that the sole irrefragable certainty must be his own immediate *consciousness as an incorporeal *substance. The essence of this substance is to think, which, in Descartes' made-to-measure sense, embraces all (but only) modes of self-consciousness. Besides such thinking he recognized also material substances. The problem thus comes to be conceived as that of the relations, or the lack of relations, between consciousness and stuff. Although Descartes was inclined to believe that his two sorts of substance must be too totally different to affect each other, he nevertheless settled for the idea that two-way causal interactions do occur—in the pineal gland in the brain (see ghost in the machine).

Dissatisfaction with this account soon led to alternative theories. For example, *Malebranche suggested *occasionalism (according to which God is the sole causal agent of the systematic correlations of mind with body, while each item in each pair is only the occasion not the cause of the other). Another theory was *epiphenomenalism (according to which mental occurrences are exclusively effects, never causes, of physical changes in the body). Occasionalism in its religious form may regard the non-causal correlations between the physical and the mental as involving a divinely "pre-established harmony" (see Leibniz). *Psychophysical parallelism also recognizes such non-causal correlations and denies interaction, but it avoids theological speculation. Epiphenomenalism is most happily illustrated by the analogies of phosphorescence on water or "the halo on the saint" (C. J. *Ducasse). *Spinoza argued that the mental and the physical are simply two aspects of the same underlying reality, God or Nature; while in our time P. F. *Strawson contends that it is the concept of the person that is fundamental, and to which both mental and physical predicates properly attach.

*Berkeley and other idealists conten-

ded that really there is no causation either way, because there is no such thing as matter (see idealism). Metaphysical behaviourists (see behaviourism) reached the same conclusion, from the opposite direction; for them consciousness is the misconception. In other monistic (but always in fact idealist) theories, mind and body have been presented as complex but differently constructed collections of entities of the same kind: these entities being ideas, or perceptions, or *sense data (see monism). Most recently there have been powerful supporters for an *identity theory, urging that being in a certain state of consciousness and being in a corresponding physical state just are the same: like—a favourite example—the Morning Star and the Evening Star.

Given the Cartesian criterion of the mental, it is self-contradictory to speak of unconscious mental processes. But in this century Freud and other psychologists have introduced an alternative or supplementary criterion, the purposive. A new philosophical classic such as Ryle's *The Concept of Mind* thus prefers to challenge the Cartesian framework rather than to attempt an answer to his questions (see Ryle). But Ryle's attempt at an analytical behaviourism does not succeed, or even claim to succeed, in reducing all consciousness to behaviour. So, although the mental is no longer to be identified with the conscious, the old problem of the relation between that and stuff remains.

mind, philosophy of. The philosophical study of the mind and mental functioning. While the principal task of the philosophy of mind may be regarded as the attempt to provide an account of what mind is, the complexity of the task is such that there is little in philosophical literaturé that will seem to constitute an integrated theory of the mind *per se.* Rather, issues that are central to the philosophy of mind occur throughout metaphysics, epistemology, logic, aesthetics, and, particularly, in the contexts of the philosophy of psychology and what is called the *mind-body problem. In contemporary philosophy, most discussions take the form of analyses of specific mental concepts: for example, *consciousness, emotion, *imagination, *introspection, intention, *thinking, and the will.

For the Greek philosophers, the primary concern was not so much mind as the more general concept of the *soul. Both Plato and Aristotle, for example, regarded mental and intellectual activity as merely one of the several functions of the soul. This preoccupation with the soul is also evident in medieval thinkers, such as St. Augustine and Aquinas. Here again, as for the Greeks, problems of the mind are more or less incidental to epistemological, ethical, and religious interest.

With the development of the natural sciences, however, philosophers became increasingly concerned with the application of scientific method to the study of mind. *Hobbes, for example, sought to provide a mechanistic theory of the mind founded on Galilean principles of motion; while *Hume was to adapt Newton's ideas in his view of the mind as operating upon principles of association. Hume, in fact, may be regarded as significant in the ultimate development of empirical psychology, for in holding mental operations to be definable in terms of customary associations of ideas, he was to open up the possibility of an empirical rather than philosophical approach to the nature of mind.

Partly in reaction to Hume, *Kant was to challenge the idea of empirical psychology as the proper concern of philosophy. For Kant, the mind actually structures our experience, and thus the principal task ought to be the investigation of what the workings of the mind contribute to our conception of the world. In this regard, Kant, rather more than Hume, may be said to stand behind contemporary practice in analysing specific mental functions in a manner that is held to be philosophically independent of empirical scientific research into the mind.

Since Descartes, it has been traditional to regard the workings of the mind as covert or private, and open only to introspective examination. But this view has been vigorously attacked in recent philosophy, particularly by *Ryle and *Wittgenstein and their followers. As a result, a great deal of current philosophy of mind is given over to questions about the accessibility of mental life: that is, not only with whether, and how, it is possible for me to know what occurs in the minds of others, but indeed how it is possible for me to have the kind of *privileged access which I appear to have to what occurs in my own mind. This problem about the accessibility of mind has in turn led to a concentration upon the idea of expression and on the way in which the mind manifests itself in language and action, and also in specific enterprises like art.

minimax principle. *See* decision theory.

minor premise. In a categorical *syllogism, the premise containing the *minor term.

minor term. The subject term of the conclusion of a categorical *syllogism..

miracle. A term that has been variously understood, but is most commonly taken to mean an act that manifests divine power through the suspension or alteration of the normal working of the *laws of nature. The idea of laws of nature is thus essential to the idea of the miraculous, but is also, clearly, a major barrier to belief that miracles actually occur.

Much philosophical discussion stems from the claim by *Hume (*Inquiry concerning Human Understanding*, especially section X) that belief in such occurrences is never rationally justified, since it must always be more probable that the favourable testimony is erroneous than that regularities confirmed by countless observations have been interrupted. If so, acceptance of miracles, while still logically possible, must be based on faith and so cannot provide independent support for it.

Some recent thought has explored the

idea that miracle stories have a primarily theological, rather than historical or confirmatory, role in religious discourse.

Miraculous Doctor. The traditional scholastic nickname for Roger *Bacon.

modality. The way in which a sentence may characterize another related sentence or proposition as true, that is, the mode in which it is true. For instance, a logical modality may be attributed to a proposition p, by saying that it is logically necessary, or contingent, or logically impossible that p. To say that it is now, or will be, or was, the case that p attributes a temporal modality; to say that it is obligatory, permissible, or forbidden that p is said to mark a moral or deontic mode; to say that it is known, unknown, or known that it is not true that p, the epistemic mode, and so on. Logicians have occasionally needed to curb their enthusiasm for proliferating modalities: it is written that p or it is *de fide* true that p do not characterize ways in which p is true.

*Modal logic has concentrated upon the logical modalities, whose formal properties are now well known, but whose interpretation frequently gives rise to logical and metaphysical difficulties. In particular, the distinction between a *de dicto* claim (where necessity is attributed to a whole assertion) and a *de re* claim (where necessity attaches to a thing's possession of some property) excites much discussion. *See also* essentialism; logic.

modal logic. The logic of necessity and possibility. A *modal statement* is one in which something is said to be necessarily, or possibly the case (*see also* apodeictic; problematic). In the *Prior Analytics*, Aristotle includes a discussion of modal statements and modal syllogisms. A *modal syllogism* is one in which at least one of the premises is a modal statement, as for example, 'Necessarily, no male is female. Only females are capable of bearing young. Therefore, no male is capable of bearing young'. Inferences involving modal statements also received

considerable attention from medieval logicians (especially in the context of attempting to reconcile the necessity of God's foreknowledge with the contingency of the future, and of one's own future actions in particular). Some of them, notably John of Sherwood, developed a highly sophisticated classification of kinds of modal statement and of their logical interrelations.

The modern, formal approach to modal logic is largely due to the work of C. I. Lewis (starting with a publication in 1912) and his development of axiomatic theories of strict implication (*see* axiom). These arose out of a dissatisfaction with the notion of material implication (standardly used in systems of propositional and predicate calculus), which is subject to the so-called paradoxes of material implication (*see* implication and entailment). The intuitive idea behind strict implication is that it should be such that A strictly implies B iff it is necessarily the case that A materially implies B. It is this connection between strict implication and necessity that means that systems of strict implication are systems of modal logic. Lewis proposed a number of axiomatizations of the theory of strict implication and the properties of these have since been extensively studied by modal logicians.

mode. A term derived from Latin *modus* (measure, manner), which has several different philosophical applications. **1.** (in medieval Aristotelianism) A combining of cognitive elements into a compound whose denotation is not antecedently decided; for example, 'union' of form and matter. A modern description might construe the term for such a mode as one having what Waismann called "open texture". **2.** (in *Locke) The notion was developed by Locke, who distinguished simple from mixed modes. A simple mode of an idea is the manner of thinking in which a simple idea is conceived either in simple multiples or in some other straightforward combination; thus, a score of whatever it may be. Locke instances as mixed modes concepts such as those required for moral discourse—murder, sacrilege, glory, gratitude. Mixed modes are "assemblages of ideas put together at the pleasure of the mind…whereby it designs not to copy anything really existing, but to denominate and rank things as they come to agree with those archetypes or forms it has made…. Names, therefore, that stand for collections of ideas which the mind makes at pleasure must needs be of doubtful signification, when such collections are nowhere to be found constantly united in nature…. What the word *murder*, or *sacrilege*…signifies can never be known from things themselves" (*Essay Concerning Human Understanding*, III (ix), 7–9). **3.** (in statistics) The item in a group that occurs most frequently. *See* average.

model. **1.** (of a set of sentences) An *interpretation (usually a set-theoretic interpretation) of the language in which the sentences are written, which assigns to each sentence of the set the value 'true'. **2.** (of a *formal system) An interpretation of the set of axioms of that system.

model theory. A branch of mathematical logic devoted to the study of logical relations and of the properties of formal systems via their models, that is, set-theoretic interpretations (*see* formal system; model). This is in contrast to the proof-theoretic study of such systems (*see* proof theory). The notions of validity, consequence, and independence receive model-theoretic definitions. Thus if *S* is a formal system, and *A* and *B* are sentences of the language of *S*, then *B* is a consequence of *A* in *S* iff *B* is true in all models of *S* in which *A* is true; *A* is valid in *S* iff *A* is true in all models of *S*; *B* is independent of the axioms of *S* iff there is a model of *S* in which *B* is true and a model in which *B* is false.

modus ponens. (Latin for: mood that affirms.) In its basic form, an argument that runs 'If *p*, then *q*. *p*. Therefore *q*.' *See* affirming the antecedent.

modus tollens. (Latin for: mood that denies.) In its basic form, an argument that runs 'If *p*, then *q*. But not-*q*. Therefore not-*p*.' *See* affirming the antecedent.

mokṣa (Sanskrit for: liberation.) In most systems of Indian thought, final release from the cycle of rebirth (*saṃsāra*) and the sorrows and perplexities of the material world. In this eternal repose the soul recovers its innate integrity; how this is thought to be achieved—whether by merging with *brahman or by eternal existence as a pure spirit—differs from system to system. Only the heretical materialists (*see* Indian materialism) denied the doctrine, together with the related doctrines of *saṃsāra and *karma. *Compare* nirvāṇa.

monadic. In logic denoting a *predicate that requires only the addition of one singular *term in order to make a well-formed sentence. '…flies' and '…is large' are monadic (or one-place) predicates.

monadology. The title given by one of Leibniz's editors to a metaphysical work written by Leibniz in 1714, and now applied to any metaphysical system such as Leibniz's. The term 'monad' originally meant 'unit' or 'unity', and Leibniz argued that only true unities can be substances (*see* substance); in his words, "What is not truly *one* being is not truly one *being*" (letter to Arnauld, 30 April 1687). A monadology is also usually regarded as asserting (as Leibniz's philosophy did) that the true unities are absolutely independent of one another.

monism. **1.** A philosophical theory that maintains that there is one, and only one, *substance. Examples of this type of theory are provided by the philosophies of Spinoza and Hegel. **2.** (in the context of discussions of mind-body relations) A theory of mind-body relations that is not dualistic. The theory of *neutral monism*, to be found in the philosophy of William *James and in Bertrand Russell's *logical atomism, is a monism of this type. According to this theory, minds and bodies do not differ in their intrinsic nature; the difference between them lies in the way that a common ('neutral') material is arranged. But this common material is not regarded as one entity (as it would in a monism of type 1), but rather as consisting of many entities (for example, experiences) of the same fundamental kind. *Compare* dualism.

Montaigne, Michel Eyquem de (1533-92). French humanist and essayist, influential in reviving and popularizing Greek sceptical theories during the Renaissance. His influence is reflected in the writings of Pascal, Descartes, Malebranche, and their several followers.

Montaigne's own sceptical philosophy was set out in his essay 'Apologie de Raimond Sebon' (1580), defending the views of a 15th-century Spanish rationalist theologian. Supported by examples from *Sextus Empiricus, Montaigne argued that rationality is no more than a form of animal behaviour. Despite their alleged superiority, men can often be shown to be, through vanity, stupidity, and immorality, inferior to animals; we do not succeed in living as happily as they do (*see also* noble savage). Failure of all attempts to achieve knowledge, shown by disagreements through the ages between the experts in every science, leads to the conclusion that the only true principles men can possess, and their only hope of achieving contact with reality, is through divine revelation.

Montesquieu, Charles-Louis de Secondat, Baron de (1689-1755). French philosopher and jurist, counsellor and president of the *parlement* of Bordeaux. He was elected to the French Academy in 1728 and contributed an essay on taste to the *Encyclopédie* (*see* Encyclopedists).

De l'esprit des lois (1748) was written after 14 years' study of political history and comparative legislation, including the political writings of *Locke. It classified forms of government not on the basis of the location of power but on that of the "animating principle": virtue being the principle of republics, honour of monarchies, and fear of despotism. The theory of the separation of powers, emphasizing the need for assigning legislative, executive, and judicial powers to independently acting bodies, had an enormous influence on the Founding Fathers of the American republic.

mood. One of the various ways in which (valid) syllogisms may be constructed within the four figures of the categorical syllogism (*see* syllogism). The valid syllogisms in each figure are called the moods of that figure. In the 13th century the 19 moods were given names that served as a mnemonic, the construction of each syllogism being deducible from its name. The most well known of these names is 'Barbara', which indicates any syllogism having the form 'All *M* are *P* and all *S* are *M*, therefore all *S* are *P*'.

Moore, George Edward (1873-1958). British philosopher, who came to philosophy from the study of the Classics. He was lecturer in philosophy (1911-25), and Professor of Mental Philosophy and Logic (1925-39) at Cambridge. He edited *Mind* from 1921 to 1947. Main philosophical works: *Principia Ethica* (1903), *Ethics* (1912), *Philosophical Studies* (1922), *Some Main Problems of Philosophy* (1953), *Philosophical Papers* (1959). These last three contain the most important of the lectures and papers in which many of his ideas were originally formulated.

Moore progressed through a variety of philosophical positions, and though the appearance in 1903 of *Principia Ethica* and the paper 'Refutation of Idealism' (*Mind,* N.S., vol. 12) can be seen as marking the beginning of his distinctive contribution to philosophy, he was rarely satisfied with his own treatment of any philosophical problem and kept tackling everything afresh. His greatest influence was perhaps in the example he set of honesty, the tireless pursuit of clarity, and his approach to philosophical problems through the meticulous analysis of the concepts involved.

In *Principia Ethica*, goodness is seen as a non-natural quality of certain things or situations, that is, one not given in sense experience, but nonetheless directly experienced, by a kind of moral intuition. Goodness is the fundamental ethical concept which cannot be defined or analysed in terms of anything simpler. Our other ethical concepts, right, duty, etc., can be defined in terms of producing and preserving so far as possible whatever possesses this quality of goodness, which Moore himself found most obviously exemplified in the experiences of friendship and aesthetic enjoyment.

In the field of theory of knowledge, while Moore's standpoint is essentially empiricist, he rejects the sceptical conclusions that have often been drawn from empiricism. Although the exact relationship between sense data and material things continued to puzzle him, in the main he was prepared to come to the "defence of common-sense", to quote the title of one of his papers. He endeavoured to show that the plain man is substantially right in thinking that our experience yields a great deal of knowledge properly so called, about the constituents of the mind-independent world, and yields it with, in some cases at least, a greater certainty than that possessed by the premises on which the sceptic's arguments are based.

moral. 1. Opposed to immoral. 2. Opposed to non-moral or amoral. Since the word is employed in the second sense in the expression 'moral philosophy' it would not be on this account paradoxical for a professor of that discipline to be immoral. *Compare* rational.

moral argument for the existence of God. An argument best known in the formulation by *Kant, which attempts to find sufficient grounds for *theism in the specifically moral experience of mankind. According to the Kantian form of the argument, the highest good is a state of affairs in which happiness is distributed in strict proportion to moral virtue. Our obligation to pursue this highest good becomes intelligible only if we see the world as so created and controlled that it (that is, the highest good) is in principle realizable, and hence only if we postulate God (in something like the theist's sense). This argument has not been accepted generally as any more successful than other defences of theism. *See* God, arguments for the existence of.

moral philosophy. *See* ethics.

moral sense. A supposed faculty for detecting moral properties. Moral sense theory, a form of *intuitionism popular in the 18th century, holds that the perception of certain actions (or events) arouses distinctive feelings of pleasure or pain in the spectator. These feelings serve both to enable him to distinguish right actions from wrong, and to provide motives to moral behaviour. *See* Hutcheson; Shaftesbury.

More, Henry (1614–87). English philosopher and theologian, one of the leaders of the *Cambridge Platonists. His numerous works reflect the group's main interests: among these writings are *Philosophical Poems* (1647), *An Antidote against Atheism* (1653), *Enthusiasmus Triumphatus* (1656), *The Immortality of the Soul* (1659), *Enchiridion Ethicum* (1667), and *Divine Dialogues* (1668). An early champion of *Descartes, More gradually turned against the French philosopher's mechanism: "Descartes, whose mechanical wit I can never highly enough admire, might be no master of metaphysics to me" (*Antidote*). Although he was never able to make good his claim that the "truth of the existence of God [is] as clearly demonstrable as any theorem in mathematics" (*Antidote*), More's chief concern in his works was to demonstrate the consonance of reason and faith. *See also* Glanvill.

mortalist. A person who believes that when people die that is that, and there is no survival.

Moses ben Maimon. *See* Maimonides.

moving rows (*or* blocks) paradox. *See* Zeno's paradoxes.

music of the spheres. The superb music believed by Pythagoreans to be produced by the regular movements of the heavenly bodies. No earthly ears—except perhaps those of *Pythagoras himself— have had the good fortune to hear it. This strange and haunting notion has captured the imagination of poets in successive generations. In *The Merchant of Venice* Lorenzo explains to Jessica:

There's not the smallest orb which thou behold'st
But in his motion like an angel sings,
Still quiring to the young-ey'd cherubins;
Such harmony is in immortal souls,
But whilst this muddy vesture of decay
Doth grossly close it in, we cannot hear it.

Muslim philosophy. *See* Islamic philosophy.

mysticism. What is claimed to be direct or unmediated experience of the divine, in which the human soul momentarily approaches union with God. Many of the great mystics have stressed that this is not primarily or essentially a matter of visions or ecstacies, as is sometimes supposed, but of total submission of the human will and intellect to God. Furthermore, they maintain that (despite the fears of some Christians that mysticism tries to achieve salvation by unaided human effort) their rigorous self-discipline is only preparation for mystical experience, which is itself the gift of grace, and that their detachment from this world is by no means lack of appreciation or care for it.

There are serious problems about what evidence (if any) mysticism can provide for the existence of God (in any traditional sense of 'God', at least). But, despite the difficulties of describing mystical experience, except negatively or metaphorically, there is an often noted unanimity between the various accounts, even by writers in quite different religious traditions. This unanimity, together with the intellectual and moral qualities shown by mystics like St. Teresa of Avila or St. John of the Cross, makes it difficult simply to reject mysticism out of hand as mere delusion or self-deception.

myth of Er. The concluding parable in Plato's *Republic* (Book X), concerning the fate of souls after death and the choices available to them before reincarnation. The warrior, Er, apparently slain in battle, returns to the world to narrate his vision of the afterlife, in which the pursuit of wisdom and justice is shown to be the soul's only safeguard against present folly and future degradation. It is noteworthy that Plato, having insisted in the *Republic*, as elsewhere, that the soul is essentially incorporeal, is quite unable, and makes no attempt, to describe the doings and sufferings of supposedly disembodied souls in any terms other than those appropriate to flesh and blood persons.

N

Nagel, Ernest (1901-). Czechoslovak-born American philosopher of science, professor at Columbia University, New York. He was the author of *The Structure of Science* (1961) and (with M. R. Cohen) of *An Introduction to Logic and Scientific Method* (1934).

naive realism. The simplest form of the view that sense perception is direct awareness of external things: that we do actually perceive objects in the 'external world', and are not forever cut off from them all by a *veil of appearance. Naive realism is generally challenged and supposedly refuted by arguments from illusion, pointing out, for instance, that a round thing may appear as elliptical from a certain angle, and that its colour seems to change under different illumination. *See also* perception; realism.

name, logically proper. *See* logically proper name.

natural deduction system. A set of rules for the construction of deductive arguments (*see* inference, rules of) without any axioms or postulates. The idea of constructing logical systems in this way, rather than axiomatically, is due to Gerhard *Gentzen.

naturalism. 1. In general, the philosophical belief that what is studied by the non-human and human sciences is all there is, and the denial of the need for any explanation going beyond or outside the *Universe (*see* Stratonician presumption). All such naturalists since Darwin insist especially upon the evolution, without supernatural intervention, of higher forms of life from lower, and of these in turn ultimately from non-living matter. **2.** (in philosophical *ethics) Particularly since G. E. *Moore, the view held by those who, taking the *naturalistic fallacy to be not really a fallacy, insist that value words are definable in terms of neutral statements of fact—not excluding even statements of putative theological fact. Earlier, and surely better, usage allowed any secular and this-worldly accounts of value to score as naturalistic; including those—for instance in *Hume—which expose and eschew that fallacy.

naturalistic fallacy. The mistake (which it is not universally agreed always is a mistake) of deducing conclusions about what ought to be from premises that state only what is the case; or the other way about. This was first labelled by G.E. Moore in *Principia Ethica* (1903). But everyone now refers, as Moore did not, to a much better and characteristically ironic statement in *Hume's *Treatise*: "In every system of morality, which I have hitherto met with, I have always remark'd, that the author proceeds for some time in the ordinary way of reasoning…when of a sudden I am surpris'd to find, that instead of the usual copulations of propositions, *is*, and *is not*, I meet with no proposition

that is not connected with an *ought*, or an *ought not*. This change is imperceptible, but is, however, of the last consequence. For as this *ought*, or *ought not*, expresses some new relation or affirmation, 'tis necessary that it shou'd be observ'd and explain'd; and at the same time that a reason should be given, for what seems altogether inconceivable, how this new relation can be a deduction from others, which are entirely different from it" (III(i)1).

Those who deny that the fallacy is a fallacy are also inclined to construe Hume as not really describing it as such in this passage. Others have taken him, as the French would say if only they spoke English, at the foot of the letter; supposing him to be claiming that all actual utterances already are unambiguously and unconfusably divided into either the *is* or the *ought* category. Yet, surely, a large part of Hume's point here, as in the parallel case of *Hume's fork, is to insist not that this fundamental distinction always is and has been made (although people needed to be told to notice this fact and to appreciate its significance) but that it always can and should be made, and that the making of it is the first step to further understanding. The insistence that the naturalistic fallacy is indeed a fallacy is now commonly called *Hume's law.

The label 'naturalistic fallacy' is apt, since many specimens centre upon some idea of what is natural. For instance, because a certain kind of conduct is natural to most of us, because that is something to which most of us are naturally inclined, therefore it must be at least licit if not positively obligatory.

natural language. An ordinary language, such as English, Russian, or Chinese, contrasted *either* with an artificial language such as Esperanto or Ido, *or* with a *formal language which may be no more than an uninterpreted logical calculus. *See* logic; metalanguage.

natural laws. *See* laws of nature.

natural number. *See* number.

natural theology. The attempt to prove the existence of God, and sometimes human immortality too, from premises provided by observation of the ordinary course of nature. The *Five Ways of St. Thomas Aquinas constitute one most famous specimen; William Paley's *Natural Theology* (1802) contains another. It is, however, sometimes thought that the putative object of these studies has taken special steps to reveal itself in another way, and much more fully; *revealed theology* is defined as the examination of the contents and implications of such a revelation. Paley's *Evidences of Christianity* (1794) is concerned with how the one genuine article can be identified as such. Some at least of these evidences are believed to be miraculous, and hence supernatural rather than natural. Of these some may be constitutive elements in the message itself, while others offer external endorsements of its authenticity (*see* miracle).

Nature, concepts of. The term 'Nature', as most commonly used in philosophy, is applied to the content, structure, and development of the spatio-temporal world as it is in itself. Sometimes man is allowed to be part of Nature and sometimes not, whereas for the theist Nature is always the work but never a part of God. It is the subject matter, roughly speaking, of 'natural science' as ordinarily understood.

Attempts at a general characterization of Nature thus understood have occupied many thinkers and can be traced back at least as far as Presocratic speculations about the basic substance or stuff of which the world is formed (*see* Presocratics). Ideas recurrent in such attempts include *atomism (all natural processes consist essentially in successive rearrangements of indivisible and unchangeable material particles) and determinism (all such processes are subject to unbreakable laws). Since, however, there seems to be nothing in the nature of material particles as such to explain why their arrangements change at all, or change in accordance with laws, such accounts of Nature had to treat its order like *dialectical materialism or Whitehead's philosophy of organism, (*see* Whitehead), have tried to present the ultimate constituents of Nature as containing the source of such order and development within themselves.

Problems have arisen over the status and possible justification of any such theory. For example, is determinism a result or presupposition of research? Also, since research itself is a form of human intervention in Nature, there is a question as whether, or in what sense, it can yield knowledge of Nature as it really is.

necessary *and* **contingent truth.** A *proposition is said to be necessarily true, or to express a logically *necessary truth*, iff the denial of that proposition would involve a *self-contradiction; a proposition which happens to be contingently true, or to express a logically *contingent truth*, is one which could nevertheless be denied, or asserted, without self-contradiction. With appropriate alterations the same holds of *necessary falsehood* and the necessarily false and of *contingent falsehood* and the contingently false.

Questioned about what the ghost of his father said, Shakespeare's Hamlet replies (I (vi)):

"There's ne'er a villain dwelling in all Denmark

But he's an arrant knave."

His friend Horatio responds:

"There needs no ghost, my lord, come from the grave

To tell us this."

There needs no ghost because Hamlet's proposition is logically necessary. What, very understandably, Horatio wanted was some contingent proposition, one the truth or falsity of which could not be known merely by fully understanding its meaning, and one the contradictory of which would be neither thus necessarily true nor necessarily false.

Had Hamlet claimed—however ana-chronistically, unpoetically, and irrele-vantly to Shakespeare's purposes—that all Danish villains were the product of maternal deprivation, then his proposi-tion would have been not necessary but contingent, and it could be known to be true—if it were true—only and ultimately by reference to some actual study of the deprived home backgrounds of Danish villains. What Hamlet said was not only logically necessary but also analytic, tautological, and a priori. What the sociologist Hamlet might have said would have been, besides contingent, synthetic and a posteriori. *See also* analytic/synthetic; a priori and a posteriori; Hume's fork.

necessary *and* **sufficient conditions.** This is a *necessary condition* for that iff that cannot be without this. This is a *sufficient condition* for that iff this is by itself enough to guarantee that. Neces-sary and sufficient conditions may both be either logically necessary or logically contingent (*see* necessary and contingent truth).

To say that this is a logically necessary condition of that entails that to affirm that and to deny this must be to contradict yourself: being a man is thus a logically necessary condition of being a husband. To say that this is a logically sufficient condition of that entails that to affirm this and to deny that must be to contradict yourself: being a husband is thus a logically sufficient condition of being a man. From which it becomes clear that if this is a logically necessary condition for that, then that must be a logically sufficient condition for this.

To say that this is a contingently necessary condition for that implies at least that in fact you will not, and at the most that in fact you cannot, have that without having (or having had) this. To say that that is a contingently sufficient condition for this implies at least that in fact you will not, and at the most that in fact you cannot, have that without having (or having had) this. In the weaker of these two interpretations both relations are indifferent to time, and the latter simply is material implication (*see* impli-cation and entailment). In the stronger interpretation both relations are con-strued as referring to causal connections, which certainly are not indifferent to time: if the sufficient condition is the causally sufficient condition, then it can only be simultaneous with or precedent to its effect, that of which it is the causally sufficient condition.

In the heat of controversy the tempta-tion is to make things easier for ourselves by attributing to an opponent, who has said that something is a necessary condition, the corresponding stronger thesis about a sufficient condition. He says, for instance, that state ownership of the economy is a necessary condition for establishing the New Jerusalem; and we reply, irrelevantly, that it will not do everything. She says that a pluralist economy is a necessary condition of liberal politics; and we reply, again irrelevantly, that some pluralist econo-mies suffer very authoritarian political regimes.

necessary falsehood. *See* necessary and contingent truth.

necessary truth. *See* necessary and contingent truth.

necessity. *See* categorical imperative; causation; freewill and determinism; impossibility; inevitability; law of nature; modal logic; modalities; neces-sary and contingent truth; necessary and sufficient conditions; seafight, problem of the.

negation. The denial of a proposition. In logic it is assumed that every *proposi-tion has a unique negation and that to assert the negation of the proposition *p* is in effect to deny *p*. Thus a statement and its negation are contradictories (*see* contradictory). However, in ordinary language there are often several, non-equivalent ways in which a negative particle can be inserted into a sentence. For example, the affirmative statement 'All philosophers are male' may be converted into various negative statements: (1) All philosophers are not male. (2) Not all philosophers are male. (3) No philosophers are male. (4) All philosophers are non-male. It is therefore not possible to introduce a symbol for negation simply as an abbreviation of the words 'not' or 'no'. The expression of ordinary language that captures the logical sense of negation is the somewhat clumsy 'It is not the case that...'. Thus the negation of 'Green is a soothing colour' would be 'It is not the case that green is a soothing colour' or 'Not (green is a soothing colour)', the latter indicating that it is the whole proposition which is negated, or denied to be true, and that no other positive but contrary assertion, such as that green is a garish colour, is implied. When used in this way, 'not' is variously symbolized by '-', '¬', or '∼', so that the negation of the proposition p is written '-p', '¬p', or '∼p'. In this use 'not' is often claimed to be a *truth-functional operator and to be defined by the *truth-table

$$
\begin{array}{cc}
- & p \\
F & T \\
T & F
\end{array}
$$

Neo-Confucianism. (Chinese *tao hsüeh*: the learning of the Way) A vague term often applied to all developments in *Confucianism from the Sung revival in the 11th century onward. This began as a deliberate effort to restore Confucian authority over a society in which, since the 5th century, Buddhism had become entrenched at every level. It was characterized by the reaffirmation and revitalization of classical Confucian ethics, the advocacy of political and social reforms, a new historical consciousness, and a heightened awareness of the moral and political role of the bureaucracy. Philosophically, however, its most important feature was a new metaphysics, evolved in response to the Buddhist challenge, and in certain respects indebted to it. At the core of the new metaphysics was the concept, borrowed from Mahāyāna, that behind all universal phenomena there lies a unifying principle or noumenon which is

present in man as his true nature (*see* Buddhist philosophy).

In the Rationalist school of Neo-Confucianism, Ch'eng Yi (1033-1107) and Chu Hsi (1130-1200) use the Chinese terms *li* (principle, structure) and *ch'i* (matter-energy) (*see* yin yang), the former being immanent in the latter in the multiplicity of phenomena which embraces moral as well as natural principles. Thus for Chu Hsi moral action required the investigation of the principles (each an aspect of the one great principle, the Way) inherent in the world around him, and exemplified in the Confucian classics and histories. For the Neo-Confucians of the School of Mind, however, from Ch'eng Hao (1032-85) and Lu Hsiang-shan (1139-92) to Wang Yang-ming (1472-1529), the moral criteria for action lay in the principles in one's own nature (as *Mencius had taught), and they advocated a form of moral *intuitionism.

Neo-Kantianism. An umbrella term for several philosophical movements in Germany between about 1870 and 1920, often very disparate but all tracing their inspiration back to the spirit, critical method, and works of *Kant. They diverged over the emphasis that they placed on different parts of Kant's work, but shared a reaction against speculative metaphysics and a return to the Kantian intention of a synthesis of empiricism and rationalism. Six different (and often opposing) schools are usually distinguished, perhaps the most influential being the *Marburg school. There were also: the Physiological school, represented by Hermann von Helmholtz (1821-94) and Friedrich Lange (1828-75); the Realist school, represented by Alois Riehl (1844-1924); the Heidelberg or Baden school, represented by Heinrich Rickert (1863-1936) and Wilhelm Windelband (1848-1915); the Göttingen school of Leonard Nelson (1882-1927), following the ideas of Jacob Fries (1773-1843); and the Sociological or Relativist school, represented by Georg Simmel (1853-1918).

Neoplatonism. A modern term for the recasting of Plato's philosophy, as first completed by *Plotinus (c.205-270 AD). Preceded by three centuries of revived Platonist speculation (sometimes called 'Middle Platonism'), Plotinus effectively combined Platonic with Pythagorean, Aristotelian, and Stoic doctrines to form a philosophical system in line with the religious preoccupations of his time. His central doctrine of three hypostases (The One, Nous, and Soul) with its metaphysical, exegetical, and experiential aspects, remained basic; but his philosophy was found, at least in the Greek-speaking world, to be insufficiently precise on some metaphysical points, inadmissibly casual in its exposition of Plato, and too austerely intellectual to function in the way that 4th-century Neoplatonists wanted, that is as a rival religion to Christianity.

The hallmark of later Neoplatonism, inaugurated by Iamblichus (c.250-c.325 AD), was its metaphysical elaboration (for example, its proliferation of hypostases and its replacement of Plotinus' "procession and reversion" with a triadic process of "abiding—procession—reversion"), its systematic exegesis of Platonic and other texts, and its stress on theurgy or ritual magic in place of intellectual contemplation. By the mid 5th century, there were two main schools of Neoplatonism, one at Alexandria which became Christian (*see* Alexandrian school), and one at Athens which was finally closed down in 529 AD as a centre of paganism. (Its best-known member was *Proclus.) For a millennium (c.250-1250 AD), Neoplatonism was the dominant philosophy in Europe. A link between ancient and medieval thought, it was revived during the Renaissance by Ficino, Pico, and others. Its influence continued into the 19th century. *See* Platonism.

Neopythagoreanism. A movement, originating in the 1st century BC, the main tenets of which were a blend of the teachings of *Pythagoras with Platonic, Stoic, and Peripatetic material. Mysti-

cism, number symbolism, and astrology were characteristic of Neopythagorean thought, and it was an important precursor of *Neoplatonism. *See also* Aristotelianism; Platonism; Pythagoreanism; Stoicism.

Neo-Taoism. (Chinese *hsüeh*: mysterious learning) An eclectic form of *Taoism that flourished in China c. 225-375 AD. Its exponents used the *Lao-tzu*, *Chuang-tzu*, and *I-ching* (Book of Changes) as a basis for discussing problems such as the relation between being and non-being, and the nature of absolute knowledge and communication. They expressed their ideas both in commentaries and in conversations, blending metaphysics and sophistry, which are recorded in the 5th century *Shih-shuo hsin-yü*. A crucial debate centred on conformity and naturalness. Some regarded Confucius as the supreme sage, maintained that spiritual detachment was compatible with a career in public office, and that human society was an extension of the natural sphere. Others argued that true Taoist naturalism implied aloofness from social or political involvement, and these withdrew into individualistic—often hedonistic—seclusion, associating only with people of like mind.

Neo-Thomism. The movement reviving the actual or supposed ideas of St. Thomas *Aquinas. It was stimulated by the encyclical letter *Aeterni Patris* issued in 1879 by Pope Leo XIII. Prominent names in Neo-Thomist circles are those of Cardinal Mercier, the University of Louvain, Etienne Gilson, and Jacques *Maritain.

Neurath, Otto (1882-1945). Influential Austrian philosopher and member of the *Vienna Circle, also actively interested in sociology, politics, and education. He is best known philosophically through papers in *Erkenntnis* (the Circle's journal).

Neurath developed *physicalism, the view that all empirical (including psychological and sociological) statements—that is all utterances neither tautological nor nonsensical—can in principle be formulated as statements about spatio-temporal objects. This explains the possibility of intersubjective understanding and of a unified scientific language. Neurath held also that *verification consists essentially in comparing statements with other statements, rather than directly with experience.

neustic. See phrastic and neustic.

neutral monism. See monism.

Newton, Isaac (1642-1727). British mathematician and physicist who formalized Galilean mechanics, discovered the inverse square law of universal gravitation, and made notable contributions to the theory of light. In 1666 Newton was appointed Lucasian Professor of Mathematics at Cambridge, but it was not until 1672, when he submitted a paper on optics to the Royal Society, that he became widely known in the scientific community. He also worked on alchemy, theology, and world chronology, but the publication that had the widest philosophical repercussions was his *Philosophiae Naturalis Principia Mathematica* (1687) usually known as the *Principia*.

The *Principia* is a closely argued work that cannot be followed in detail without a sound knowledge of mathematics. It provides a comprehensive system of mechanics (see mechanical explanation), which accounts not only for the motion of bodies on or near the surface of the earth but also for all motion throughout the universe, including that of the moon around the earth, and the earth and other planets around the sun.

Newton claimed that his method was empirical and inductive, in contrast with the method of *Descartes, who was both a source for much of Newton's thought and a target for attack. He also claimed that his discovery of universal gravitation was supporting evidence for belief in a deity. However, his scientific method was not as close to *positivism as has sometimes been held. His belief in

*absolute space and time, amongst other things, led him—through his defender, Samuel *Clarke—into conflict with *Leibniz for the second time. (The first was the controversy over which of them has invented the calculus.)

Newton's major work in physical optics (the *Opticks*) appeared in 1704. It was much more accessible to non-mathematicians than the *Principia*, and was widely read. In later editions Newton included 31 queries; these are a rich source for his more speculative thoughts on matters relating to optics, mechanics, religion, and morals.

Many 17th- and 18th-century philosophers, especially the British empiricists and *Kant, were profoundly influenced by Newton. For example, the motivation for much of *Locke's philosophy can be seen as working out the philosophical implications of Newtonian mechanics, for instance, Locke's discussion of *primary qualities and his *causal theory of perception.

Nicholas of Cusa (or **Nicholas Cusanus**) (c. 1400-64). German cardinal, whose "*theologia negativa*" was influential in the Renaissance. Main philosophical work: *De Docta Ignorantia* (Of Learned Ignorance) (1440). Using the methods of medieval logic, Cusanus examined the nature of God (Book I) and the Universe (Book II). His view of their relationship was fundamentally Neoplatonic; the Universe (*maximum contractum*), seen as the totality of finite things, flows out from and returns to God (*maximum absolutum*), whose nature is unknowable (see Neoplatonic). Hence all human knowledge is simply learned ignorance. In Book III he discussed the human nature of Christ as the existential identity of the *maximum absolutum* and *maximum contractum*. His work contained concepts important to later writers, notably his cosmology, which was non-geocentric, and his denial of the Aristotelian principle of non-contradiction.

Nietzsche, Friedrich (1844-1900). German writer and philosopher born at

Röchen, the son of a Lutheran pastor. Educated at the famous *Schulpforta* and at the Universities of Bonn and Leipzig, he was an outstandingly brilliant student, who at the age of 24 was appointed professor of classics at the University of Basel. Here Nietzsche had the historian Jacob Burckhardt as a colleague and Richard and Cosima Wagner, who lived nearby, were among his friends. Recurrent psychosomatic illness forced him to give up his chair in 1879. He spent most of the next ten years at resorts in Italy, France, and Switzerland, writing and trying to recover his health. He became insane in January 1889, after which his sister, Elizabeth, looked after him until his death in 1900. The following are the most significant of his numerous writings: *Die Geburt der Tragödie* (1872), the four *Unzeitgemässe Betrachtungen* (1873-6), *Die Fröhliche Wissenschaft* (1882), *Also Sprach Zarathustra* (1883-92), *Jenseits von Gut und Böse* (1886), *Zur Genealogie der Moral* (1887), and *Der Antichrist* (1895).

In the English-speaking world Nietzsche has only rarely been considered an important philosopher. Instead, he is still popularly seen as, at best, an impressive aphorist whose psychological *aperçus* partly anticipated the theories of Freud, and, at worst, as one of the latest and perhaps the most inflammatory of a long line of German opponents of the ideals of liberal enlightenment. Nietzsche's ambiguous reputation is not undeserved. In particular, his contemptuous dismissal of democracy in favour of the aristocratic ideal of the *Übermensch* or Overman; his atheism, expressed with unprecedented vehemence in *Der Antichrist*; his attacks on Christian and utilitarian ethics, notably in *Jenseits von Gut und Böse* and *Zur Genealogie der Moral*; his stress, from the time of his first book—*Die Geburt der Tragödie*—on the unconscious, voluntaristic, orgiastic, and self-destructive ('Dionysian') sides of human nature, seemingly at the expense of the calm, conscious, individuated, and rational ('Apollonian') sides; to which might be

added his unsqueamishly chauvinistic attitude towards women—all these elements in Nietzsche's thought have acted as barriers to his obtaining anything like general acclaim in the English-speaking world.

Nietzsche was a very radical thinker and, in some respects, one of the greatest prose stylists of modern times. He was also a considerable poet, a fact that needs to be firmly borne in mind when reading *Also Sprach Zarathustra*. For whatever else it may be, *Zarathustra* is poetry and consequently not the best place to look for Nietzsche's 'ideas', let alone his arguments. Quite apart from what Nietzsche actually said, then, his extraordinary use of language goes far to explain the great impact he has had, and continues to have, on poets, novelists, critics, even musicians, of many persuasions and nationalities.

For various reasons, Nietzsche is not easy to interpret objectively. In reading him due account has to be taken of the deceptively informal structure of his books, and of his manifold use of irony. His bold display of personal obsessions can easily lead one to forget that he can also think objectively and reason cogently. Nietzsche's delightful intimacy of tone, which unhappily degenerates into megalomania in later works, and his frequent shifts in mood and emphasis, are further characteristics that give his books a very special place in the modern literature of ideas. It is certainly a mistake simply to bracket Nietzsche with professional German philosophers. Because of their peculiarities of form and intention, Nietzsche's writings are best seen as belonging to the great tradition of European moral essayists and aphorists, beginning with Montaigne, continuing in the 17th and 18th centuries with writers like La Rochefoucauld and Vauvenargues, and later, during Nietzsche's formative years, with the essays of *Schopenhauer and R.W. *Emerson. Nietzsche studied all these writers carefully and learned more from them than he ever did from, say, Kant or Hegel.

Unfortunately, the peculiarities of Nietzsche's output have had a consequence he would himself have found deeply annoying: he has become nearly all things to all men. Instead of approaching him in a scholarly manner, European philosophers have acquired the habit of blatantly assimilating Nietzsche—or, rather, some myth about him—to their own concerns, often with bizarre results. And this is, in effect, the chief way Nietzsche has become of 'philosophical' importance on the European continent today. Such symbiotic relations to Nietzsche are to be found, most notably, in the 'existentialist' *Nietzsche* (1936) of Karl *Jaspers, in Jaspers' further influential linking of Nietzsche with *Kierkegaard, and in Martin *Heidegger's 'ontological' *Nietzsche* (1961). More recently, Michel Foucault has placed Nietzsche in the uncongenial company of Marx and Freud who, as a trinity, are said to have provided 'the postulates of modern hermeneutics'.

Although Nietzsche's books defy easy summary there are at least three central and closely connected areas of his thought that are of genuine philosophical interest.

(1) In his posthumously published Notebooks (called by his editors *Der Wille zur Macht* (1901)), Nietzsche develops an instrumentalist theory of knowledge and a 'perspectivist' analysis of truth (*see* perspectivism). "Against positivism, which halts at phenomena— 'There are only facts'—I would say: No, facts are precisely what there are not, only interpretations." Such views about knowledge and truth had preoccupied Nietzsche since at least 1873 when he began writing an important essay 'Über Wahrheit und Lüge in Aussermoralischen Sinn'. Both in that essay and throughout his major works Nietzsche touches on epistemological questions that are very much alive at present. Among these are questions raised by the *sociology of knowledge, about the relation between the truth of a doctrine or belief and its historical or social genesis. In fact, Karl *Mannheim, like many theorists associated with the so-called *Frankfurt school, was himself directly influenced by Nietzsche's 'perspectivism'. As we shall see, Nietzsche's ideas are also relevant to related debates about objective standards of rationality and truth in which contemporary philosophers of science like T. Kuhn and P.K. Feyerabend have sometimes adopted positions strikingly close to Nietzsche's own.

(2) Nietzsche is probably the greatest psychological critic of what Schopenhauer called 'Man's need for Metaphysics'. Especially in *Die Fröhliche Wissenschaft* and in *Die Götzendämmerung* Nietzsche brings to bear on this 'need' his conjectures about the 'will to power' as the basic drive behind all human endeavour, including all philosophizing. With considerable panache, he launches an attack on traditional beliefs in a 'true' or 'more real' world to which not only theologians but also philosophers like Plato and Kant have unfavourably contrasted the empirical world of everyday life. Essentially, Nietzsche sees such dualistic outlooks as springing from the aspirations of 'life-denying' and hence 'decadent' or physiologically weak individuals or groups of persons (for example, priests) who seek by these ideological means (though usually unconsciously) to dominate the 'strong and healthy'. Here again, the realms of rationality and truthfulness are not, Nietzsche suggests, above the battle of 'life'. ('Life', *Das Leben*, is an important, if somewhat elusive, concept in Nietzsche. His treatment of it is particularly interesting in the third of his *Unzeitgemässe Betrachtungen*, 'Von Nutzen und Nachteil der Historie für das Leben' — 'On the Use and Disadvantage of History for Life'.) Appeals to reason and truthfulness are merely one means among others (such as physical force) by which one 'will' can, in appropriate circumstances, assert its power over another. All reasoning, Nietzsche often suggests, is rationalization; all 'truth' a perspective issuing from the

centre of some ascendant 'will'. Moreover, since really "the concepts 'true and untrue' have...no meaning in optics", it follows, Nietzsche thinks, that "the falseness of a judgment is no objection to it". What actually matters about a belief is not so much whether or not it is 'true' but whether or not it is 'life-affirming', that is, capable of giving to those who entertain it feelings of strength, power, and freedom. Here Nietzsche is not talking about value-judgments alone; certainly, he says, "there are no moral facts", but "physics, too, is only an interpretation and exegesis of the world (to suit us...)." What is more, "Behind all logic and its seeming sovereignty of movement, there also stand valuations or, more clearly, physiological demands for the preservation of a certain type of life."

These are interesting ideas; it is a pity Nietzsche did not handle them more carefully. For, to take him up on just one point, if *admittedly false* propositions need not be rejected, then clearly nothing need be. Conceptual permissiveness on this scale is bound to attract a large following. Still, it must be said that Nietzsche is often exceedingly perceptive when criticizing particular outlooks and particular arguments. Consider, for example, his comments on Descartes' *cogito* argument (*Der Wille zur Macht*, section 484), his characterization of the Platonic Socrates (especially in *Die Götzendämmerung*), and some, but not all, of his remarks on Kant. Moreover, many of those passages where he seeks to lay the ghost of metaphysical otherworldliness are, even intellectually, second to none.

(3) Nietzsche is one of a number of German-speaking philosophers, from the late 18th century onwards, who have held that a critique of language should be at the very centre of philosophical thinking. It is indeed possible to select passages from Nietzsche that read very much like the later Wittgenstein. But the similarity is only superficial. For Nietzsche had at once a much more startling and a much less carefully thought out view about the relation between language and the world than Wittgenstein had. Thinking is inseparable from language and, Nietzsche believes, language necessarily 'falsifies' reality. This is because through language we artificially order and simplify our raw experience. We do this in order to survive biologically. Yet Nietzsche insists that neither individual concepts nor the structural features of language can really afford us any genuine knowledge about the world apart from language. Not unlike his contemporary *Bergson, Nietzsche conceives reality as a kind of ineffable flux that can be trapped within the categorical net of language only at the expense of fatal distortion. This alleged incommensurability between language and the world is what Nietzsche actually has in mind when he writes, "A philosophical mythology lies hidden in language which breaks through at *every* moment, *no matter how careful we may be*" (italics added). There is, then, strictly speaking, no place in Nietzsche's philosophy for Wittgensteinian, or any other, notions of conceptual enlightenment. Of course, Nietzsche goes on to use his views about the essentially 'falsifying' nature of language, and therefore of rational thought, to give theoretical backing to his favourite belief in the superior veracity of action and 'will'. But here the central paradox in Nietzsche's theory of knowledge emerges: he cannot himself, in all consistency, take that theory too seriously. *See also* death of God.

nihil in intellectu nisi prius in sensu. (Latin for: nothing in the intellect which was not first in the senses.) A scholastic formulation of a much older empiricist principle. *See also* empiricism; scholasticism.

nihilism. A term popularized through its employment to characterize his own position by Bazarov, a character in Turgenev's *Fathers and Sons* (1862). Turgenev himself detested Bazarov, who was modelled on his own pet aversion

N. A. Dobrolyubov. Yet this character became a model for a whole generation of radicals—believing in nothing save science, *materialism, revolution, and (in the abstract) the People. The word has since been employed, usually by opponents, of various other destructive tendencies. It was, for instance, applied to the National Socialist ideology described in Hermann Rauschnigg's *Hitler Speaks* (1939) and *Germany's Revolution of Destruction* (1940).

nirvāṇa. Roughly, the Buddhist equivalent of *moksa* (liberation from the cycle of death and rebirth). Precise definitions of the concept vary between the different Buddhist schools. It is generally conceived negatively as freedom from ignorance, suffering, and self-interest, and more positively as the achieving of disinterested wisdom and compassion. It is attained by the famous eightfold path of morality outlined in the *Samyutta-nikāya*: right views, right intention, right speech, right conduct, right livelihood, right effort, right mindfulness, right concentration. *See also* Buddhist philosophy; Indian philosophy.

noble savage. The romantic conception of man as enjoying a natural and noble existence until civilization makes him a slave to unnatural wants and seduces him from his original freedom. The theme was elaborated by *Rousseau in *Discours sur l'origine de l'inégalité parmi les hommes* (1755), where he maintained that only the uncorrupted savage is in possession of real virtue. *See also* romanticism.

noetic. 1. In general, cognitive. 2. In contrast to empirical and sensuous, pertaining to that which can be apprehended by reason alone. *Compare* nous.

nomic. Pertaining to a law (of nature). *See* laws of nature.

nominal definition. *See* definition.

nominalism. 1. (in scholastic philosophy) The view that universals (*see* universals and particulars) have no existence independently of being thought

and are mere names, representing nothing that really exists. The nominalist thus denies anything like Plato's theory of Forms or Ideas. But he is not by his profession therefore committed to denying that the things rightly characterized as φ do in reality resemble one another in relevant respects. *William of Ockham was a leading nominalist, declining to interpret universals as names of entities distinct from the individual things denoted by the general terms. *Abelard made a strenuous attempt to reconcile the realist and nominalist positions.

2. (in modern philosophy) The explanation of the use of general terms that accounts for their meaning, and denotation, in the mutual resemblance of the particular things to which they can be applied, or the recurrence in them of the general property indicated. In the former case, the general concept of, say, 'redness' is meaningful because all red things resemble each other in colour. The application of the word 'red' is not therefore arbitrary, since although it does not denote a special existing entity, 'redness', red things are called red because they share a common property. This tradition has continued from *Hobbes to some modern analytic philosophers, particularly the logical positivists.

nomological. *See* laws of nature.

nomothetic. Proposing or prescribing a law (of nature). *See* laws of nature.

non-cognitive. *See* cognitive.

non-contradiction, principle (*or* law) of. The principle or law the acceptance of which commits one to holding that for any statement p, the statement 'p and not-p' is false as a matter of logical necessity. *See also* consistent and inconsistent.

non-Euclidean geometry. A geometry that denies the parallel postulate of *Euclid. Euclid's *Elements* provides the postulates from which all the theorems of classical (or Euclidean) geometry may be deduced. A version of Euclid's fifth postulate (the parallel postulate) is that, given a straight line and a point not on this line, there exists exactly one straight line through the point parallel to the first line. One may insist, as Lobachevsky did, that there are many parallel lines, or, with Riemann, that there are no parallel lines. The simplest statement of Einstein's theory of *relativity uses Riemannian geometry.

non sequitur. (Latin for: it does not follow.) The expression is usually applied only to the drawing of conclusions without even an appearance of valid argument, rather than to those drawn invalidly by argument that happens to be fallacious.

no-ownership theory. A metaphysical doctrine of the *self, labelled by *Strawson. It arises from Cartesian mind-body dualism (*see* mind-body problem) and maintains that conscious experiences associated with a subject cannot be said to 'belong' to that consciousness: "Only those things whose ownership is logically transferable can be owned at all."

normal form. A notion that plays an important role in *proof theory. In trying to prove a result about a language L in which proofs can be constructed according to stipulated rules of *inference, it is useful to know that, or whether, all propositions expressible in the language can be expressed in some standard (or normal) form. That is, whether, for any given sentence S of L there is some sentence N_s of L conforming to this standard pattern and such that one can, using the rules of inference available in L, derive S from N_s, and N_s from S (in which cases S and N_s will be formally *equivalent). If this can be shown to be the case, then in considering what can be proved in L, it is sufficient to consider only proofs of sentences expressed in the standard form.

All propositions expressible in the language of propositional calculus can be expressed in either conjunctive or disjunctive normal form. A sentence is in *conjunctive (disjunctive) normal form*

iff it has the form $A_1 \& \ldots \& A_n$ ($A_1 \lor \ldots \lor A_n$) where each of $A_1, \ldots, A_n$ is either a propositional variable (*see* calculus), a negated propositional variable, or has the form $B_1 \lor \ldots \lor B_k$ ($B_1 \& \ldots \& B_k$) where each of $B_1, \ldots, B_k$ is either a propositional variable or a negated propositional variable. For example, $p \&$ ($p \lor -q \lor r$) & ($-r \lor s$) is in conjunctive normal form, whereas $p \lor$ ($p \& -q \& r$) $\lor$ ($-r \& s$) is in disjunctive normal form.

All propositions expressible in the language of first order predicate calculus can be expressed in *prenex normal* form. A sentence A is in *prenex normal form* iff it has the form $Q_1 \ldots Q_n M$, where M is a *predicate containing no quantifiers (*see* quantifier), each Q_i is either (x_i) or ($\exists x_i$) ($i = 1, \ldots, n$), and where $x_1, \ldots, x_n$ are variables which are all different and each of which has at least one (free) occurrence in M. M is then called the *matrix* of A.

normative. Tending to establish a standard of correctness by prescription of rules; evaluative rather than descriptive. Normative ethics—any system dictating morally correct conduct—is distinguished from meta-ethics—the discussion of the meanings of moral terms without issuing directives (*see* ethics).

Norris, John (1657-1711). English philosopher and divine, notable for his *Essay towards the Theory of an Ideal and Intelligible World* (1701-04). In this he expounded to an English readership the system of *Malebranche, in opposition to Lockean and sensualist views. Influenced by the *Cambridge Platonists Cudworth and More, he wrote a number of works asserting the harmony of human reason and divine truth, between which he saw only a difference of degree, not of kind.

no-true-Scotsman move. A nickname for a manoeuvre that meets the falsification of some cherished generalization by maintaining that the predicate in question, while not perhaps applicable to all run of the mill so-and-sos, is nevertheless essential to *true* so-and-sos.

"No Scotsman would do such a thing, But one did. Well, no *true* Scotsman would." The danger, and the appeal, of this manoeuvre is that the manoeuverer may persuade himself, and others, that this piece of arbitrary *redefinition has shown the original contingent contention after all not to be false. One classical example is the claim by Thrasymachus in Book I of the *Republic* of Plato that the *genuine* ruler can make no mistakes in determining his own interests.

noumenon. (*pl.* noumena) 'Thing-in-itself', contrasted with appearance or *phenomenon in the philosophy of *Kant. Noumena are the external source of experience but are not themselves knowable and can only be inferred from experience of phenomena. Although inaccessible to speculative reason, the noumenal world of God, freedom, and immortality is apprehended through man's capacity for acting as a moral agent. *See also* Ding-an-sich.

nous. (Greek for: mind.) A term used by the *Presocratics to indicate knowledge and reason. For *Plato it meant the rational part of the soul. For *Aristotle it was the intellect, in which he distinguished between active and passive reason, the former alone being immortal and eternal.

n-place operation. *See* operation.

n-place predicate. *See* polyadic.

null (*or* **empty**) **set.** The set with no members. It is usually symbolized as $\emptyset$.

number. The idea of number is closely and generally associated with counting. The most primitive way to establish the number of *F*s is to count the *F*s. Traditionally there have been three main approaches to number. According to platonism (*see* mathematics, philosophy of), numbers are abstract entities that exist independently of human thought; they are timeless and non-spatial, and therefore do not interact causally with the physical world. Various forms of *nominalism account for numbers as

non-abstract entities, such as ideas in the mind (*psychologism) or marks on pieces of paper (*formalism). *Intuitionism regards numbers as being the product of a process (for example, counting). In the 19th and 20th centuries, it was shown that numbers may be viewed as sets, in the sense that the axioms of arithmetic, say, are true of certain kinds of sets. The properties of, operations on, and relations between numbers are represented as properties of, operations on, and relations between these sets.

There are various sorts of numbers. A *natural number* is any one of the non-negative integers 0, 1, 2, 3,.... A *rational number* is any number of the form b/c where b is a positive or a negative integer or 0 and c is a positive integer, for example, 3/4 (also written $\frac{3}{4}$). A *real number* is any number representable as a non-terminating decimal, while an *irrational number* is any real number that is not rational. A *complex number* is any number of the form $b + c\sqrt{-1}$, where b and c are real numbers. An *algebraic number* occurs as any solution to any polynomial equation with integral coefficients. A *transcendental number* is any number real or complex that is not algebraic.

The mathematical definitions of cardinal and ordinal differ from their more ordinary usage. A *cardinal number* is commonly taken as that which distinguishes how many elements there are in a group. In mathematical sets it is any object b that is associated with a set X of equivalent sets (that is, X is a set all of whose members can be put in one-to-one correspondence with each other); one such candidate is the set X (*see also* cardinality). An *ordinal number* is commonly taken as that which indicates position in an ordered series (for example, 10th). In mathematics an ordinal number is the *order type* of a *well-ordered set. An order type is the set of all sets ordinally similar to a given set; and sets are ordinally similar iff they can be put into a one-to-one correspondence that preserves their ordering.

numbers, law of large. *See* Bernoulli's theorem.

Nyāya. One of the systems of *Indian philosophy. The earliest extant work are the *Nyāyasūtras* of Akṣapāda Gautama (1st century AD); these emphasize the rules for correct (and successful) debating and also deal with logic. Important later works are the commentaries on the *sūtras* by Pakṣilasvāmī (*Nyāya-bhāṣyam*, possibly 5th century) and Uddyotakara (*Nyāyavārttikam*, 7th century), and Jayanta Bhaṭṭa's independent exposition *Nyāyamañjarī* (9th century). The last two works are moving already into the direction of the *navya*-Nyāya, which Gangêśa's *Tattvacintāmaṇi* established *c*.1200 in Bengal. This work and its vast, often scholastic, commentarial literature restrict their attention to the discussion of formal logic. The older system concerned itself also with a philosophy of nature which is closely related to that of the *Vaiśeṣika, and thus we also find the title 'Nyāya-Vaiśeṣika' ('Nyāya' being restricted here to denoting the epistemology and logic of the combined system). It is assumed that all correct knowledge points to an objective reality beyond and independent of it. The Nyāya school formulated the Indian form of the syllogism, which rather laboriously proceeds in five steps.

O

objectivism. *See* subjectivism and objectivism.

object language. 1. (relative to a *metalanguage) A language discussed in a metalanguage. Such a language may itself be a metalanguage relative to some third language. **2.** (absolute) A language used to talk only about non-linguistic subjects, such as physical objects or numbers.

obligation. A duty that a person is under a moral compulsion to perform if he has a role in society and there are moral rules in that society dictating that anyone playing this role must thereby perform that act. Thus a father has obligations, qua father, to his children, a promiser, qua promiser, to the promisee, etc. Not all duties or obligations are voluntarily self-imposed. A citizen may have obligations to the state even though that role was not one which he chose to adopt.

There are clearly things that a person morally ought to do that are not obligations in this sense. Thus one ought, perhaps, to save someone in danger of drowning, yet it would be odd to say that one was under an obligation to do so. To say the latter would imply that the person in distress (or society in general) had a right to demand one's assistance, which would only be the case if one were, say, a lifeguard.

Many philosophers extend the word 'obligation' to cover all cases in which a person morally ought to do something. Some do so because they maintain that all those things one ought to do are really duties that may be exacted from one. This revisionary implication is avoided by those who distinguish our sense from a weaker use of the word 'obligation'. For many, the extension is merely a convenience, partly sanctioned by ordinary usage, since there is no other suitable noun covering the range of all the things one morally ought to do. But careless usage produces confusion.

obverse. The statement derived by obversion of the original and logically equivalent to it. Obversion of a categorical statement (*see* syllogism) is performed by negating the predicate term and changing the statement from negative to affirmative, or vice versa. The obverse of 'All *S* are *P*' is 'No *S* are non-*P*', of 'No *S* are *P*' is 'All *S* are non-*P*', of 'Some *S* are *P*' is 'Some *S* are not non-*P*', and of 'Some *S* are not *P*' is 'Some *S* are non-*P*'.

obversion. In scholastic logic, a form of immediate inference (*see* syllogism). Aristotle did not regard it as a valid form of inference. *See* obverse.

Occam's razor. See Ockham's razor.

occasionalism. A doctrine, put forward by *Malebranche, which attempts to plug a notorious gap in Cartesian thinking on the *mind-body problem. How can mind and body, supposed to be two radically distinct substances, causally interact? The occasionalists baldly deny any such interaction to be possible: the will of man is incapable of moving the smallest body. How then does my arm go up when I will it? The true cause, claim the occasionalists, is divine intervention, my willing being merely the occasion for that intervention: "We are the natural causes of the movement of our arm; but natural causes are not at all true causes, they are only *occasional* causes which act only via the power and efficacy of God's will" (Malebranche). *Compare* psychophysical parallelism.

Ockham's razor. The principle of ontological economy, usually formulated as 'Entities are not to be multiplied beyond necessity' (*Entia non sunt multiplicanda praeter necessitatem*). These actual words are not in fact to be found in the extant works of *William of Ockham.

Ockham, William of. See William of Ockham.

Oedipus effect. The impact of the making of a statement, in particular a predictive statement, upon the human situation to which that statement refers. The label was introduced by Sir Karl *Popper in *The Poverty of Historicism* (1957), with special reference to the fact that the publication of predictions about human affairs may have a tendency to bring about either their verification or their falsification. This important effect had been noticed but not named by earlier thinkers. Hume, for instance, in his first *Inquiry* (VIII (i)) argued that anyone may, if we tell them what they are going to do, do something else, just to prove us wrong; this, however, is not a good reason for believing that human conduct is in principle unpredictable.

omnipotence, paradox of. The difficulty arising when, for example, it is claimed that God, having given man freedom, *cannot* prevent, and is therefore not responsible for, its misuse. Can God then create what he cannot thereafter control? Either answer seems inconsistent with God's omnipotence, and hence an apparent need for some modification of our simple concept of omnipotence as capacity to do anything logically possible.

omniscience, paradoxes of. Problems arising over how God's omniscience can be consistent with his timelessness or his granting freewill to mankind, given that omniscience includes *fore*knowledge of future events (including human actions). It has been variously argued that foreknowledge cannot meaningfully be ascribed to the timeless, hence our concept of omniscience must be modified; that foreknowledge of actions *is* consistent with their freedom; or that even God cannot foreknow genuinely free actions, but has thus limited his own omniscience as a condition of granting human freedom. See also scientia media.

one-many problem. The problem of how we should account for the fact that we can correctly apply one and the same word to many distinct things. See Plato; universals and particulars.

one-one. See function.

one over many principle. See Plato.

one-place operation. See operation.

one-place predicate. See monadic.

ontological argument. The attempt to prove, simply from an examination of the concept of God, that the being to which that concept would apply must in fact exist. This argument was developed first by St. *Anselm. It was criticized and somewhat ambivalently rejected by St. Thomas *Aquinas. Revived by *Descartes, it was accepted by *Spinoza and *Leibniz, the latter with some qualifications. It was criticized and rejected by both *Hume and *Kant.

St. Anselm formulated the idea of God as that of "something than which nothing greater can be conceived" (*aliquid quo nihil maius cogitari potest* (*Proslogion* II)). He then argued that something that exists in reality must be greater than something that exists in the mind only; so God must exist outside as well as in the mind, for if he existed in the mind only and not in reality he would not be "something than which nothing greater can be conceived".

The Thomist objection seems to allow the basic principle that the proposition 'God does not exist' is self-contradictory, while distinguishing what is self-evident in itself from what may or may not be self-evident to this person or that: "So I maintain that this proposition 'God exists' is self-evident in itself, since its subject and predicate are identical; for, as we shall see later, God is his own existence...." Aquinas nevertheless proceeds almost at once to insist on a distinction between what exists in reality and what exists only in thought.

It was in terms of this distinction that Kant was later unequivocally to reject the argument as it appeared in Descartes and Leibniz: "A hundred real thalers [dollars] do not contain the least coin more than a hundred possible thalers ... My financial position is, however, affected very differently by a hundred real thalers than it is by the mere concept of them (that is of their possibility)" (*Critique of Pure Reason* A599/B627).

Contemporary followers of Kant urge that existence is not a(n ordinary) predicate in that it is presupposed by the categorical attribution of any others; while to say that something exists is to take it for granted that it has many (other) attributes. Thus, to borrow an example from G. E. *Moore, while we can say 'Some tame tigers growl, and some do not', it would be a significant semantic solecism to claim that 'Some tame tigers exist, and some do not'. Before Kant, Hume had dismissed the whole business in the shortest of short order: "But that Caesar, or the angel Gabriel, or any being never existed may

be a false proposition, but still is perfectly conceivable and implies no contradiction" (*Inquiry concerning Human Understanding* XII (iii)).

Most mainstream philosophers since Hume and Kant have followed them in rejecting the ontological argument. However, it is occasionally revived—as it was, for instance, by *Hegel and R. G. *Collingwood. The debates about it have left their mark on modern symbolic logic; thus the *Principia Mathematica* of *Russell and *Whitehead provides for a fundamental notational distinction between those propositions which assert existence and those which do not (*see* existential import; quantifier). Those too who advocate regular recourse to the *formal mode of speech make a main point of the failure of champions of the ontological argument to distinguish between concept and object, and to appreciate the categorial difference between manoeuvering with the definition of a word and discovering whether that word—however defined—does or does not have actual application.

The caveat upon which Leibniz insisted and which had been entered much earlier by *Duns Scotus, was that a complete and valid ontological proof of the existence of God must be prefaced by a demonstration that the relevant concept of God is itself legitimate and proper, and not through some concealed contradiction or in any other way vicious: 'If God is possible, God exists.' An ontological argument has played a key role in most rationalist systems (*see* rationalism), since it promises to provide an enormously rich and necessarily true existential premise from which the rationalist philosopher can hope to deduce many and various detailed consequences. It was this function which *Plato in the *Republic* would have liked his Form of the Good to fulfil, serving as the "unhypothetical first principle" of his deductive dialectics.

It should be noted that in Descartes the ontological argument needs to be distinguished from what is sometimes called, following a Cartesian hint, the *trademark argument.* That proceeds not from a concept of God itself, but from the psychological fact that we are now equipped with that concept. The argument is that this is too splendid a notion for mere humans to have constructed, that it must instead have been produced by God, and that it is in fact implanted in all our souls "as the mark of the workman imprinted on his work". *See also* cosmological argument; creation; physico-theological argument.

ontology. 1. The branch of metaphysical enquiry (*see* metaphysics) concerned with the study of existence itself (considered apart from the nature of any existent object). It differentiates between 'real existence' and 'appearance' (*see* noumenon; phenomenon) and investigates the different ways in which entities belonging to various logical categories (physical objects, numbers, universals, abstractions, etc.) may be said to exist. **2.** The assumptions about existence underlying any conceptual scheme or any theory or system of ideas. Widely differing assumptions about 'what there is not' and 'what there is', are found in *Parmenides and *Plato, in *Leibniz and *Kant, and in modern phenomenological and analytical schools.

opacity *and* **transparency.** Terms used in theories of reference (*see* sense and reference) and *modal logic, which are used to explain cases where the principle of the substitutivity of identicals apparently breaks down (*see* Leibniz's law).

When a definite singular term is used simply as a means of specifying its object, the sentence in which it occurs will remain true if another term, specifying the same object, is substituted. For example, 'Cicero was a Roman senator' remains true if 'Tully', or 'The man who denounced Catiline', is substituted for 'Cicero'. Contexts that permit such substitution are said to be 'referentially *transparent*'. They can be distinguished from contexts which are '*opaque*', that is containing definite singular terms which are not regarded as having a purely

referential function. The sentence 'The police are looking for Jones's murderer' will not necessarily remain true if 'Jones's murderer' is substituted by 'The man in a black hat', even if both terms are, in fact, applicable to the same individual. Modal contexts also create opacity. If the term 'nine' in the true statement 'Nine is necessarily greater than seven' is replaced by the term 'The number of planets' (which happens to specify nine) it yields a false statement 'the number of planets is necessarily greater than seven'. (It is surely contingent that there are nine planets. There could have been, as was once thought, only seven.) *See also* extension and intension.

open question argument. A test, introduced by G. E. *Moore, for demonstrating the failure of any proposed definition of 'good'. If '*X* is *Y*' is a definition, then the question 'Is *YX*?' cannot be substantial or, as some say, 'open'. But all questions of the form 'Is *Y* good?' are, Moore claims, 'open' in this sense; therefore 'good' is indefinable.

open texture. The expression introduced in an influential 1945 article by Friedrich *Waismann as a translation of his original German coinage *Porosität der Begriffe*. It is not, he explained, to be confused with *vagueness, being rather the possibility of vagueness. It characterizes most though not all empirical concepts: "Take any material object statement. The terms which occur in it are non-exhaustive; that means that we cannot foresee completely all possible conditions in which they are used … and that means that we cannot foresee completely all the possible circumstances in which the statement is true or in which it is false."

open wff. *See* wff.

operation. A *one-place operation* is a *function of one argument whose range is included in its domain. For example, adding one to an integer n to get $n+1$ is an operation on integers. The distinctive feature of one-place operations is that they can be repeatedly applied to generate a sequence of objects. Starting from n, one gets the sequence n, $n+1$, $(n+1)+1$, $((n+1)+1)+1,\ldots$ by repeatedly adding one. This characteristic of one-place operations is a consequence of the inclusion of their range within their domain. If the operation f is not a one-one function the terms of the sequence a, $f(a)$, $f(f(a)),\ldots$ may not all be distinct. An *n-place operation* is a function $f(x_1,\ldots,x_n)$ of n arguments such that (1) the domain of f is the set of all ordered n-tuples (*see* ordered n-tuple) of members of some set X, and (2) the range of f is included in X. For example, addition is a *two-place* (or *binary*) operation on integers, and can be repeatedly applied, as in $(2+3)+(4+5)$.

operationalism (*or* **operationism**). The theory in the philosophy of science that holds that all physical entities, processes, and properties are definable in terms of the set of operations and experiments by which they are apprehended. The principal aim of the theory, first propounded by P.W. Bridgman in *The Logic of Modern Physics* (1927), is to establish the meaning of scientific concepts in strict accordance with the practice of scientific research and experimentation. In psychology, an operationalist approach is exemplified in *behaviourism.

operator. That which effects an *operation. In logic it is usually expressed as a symbol. Corresponding to each *function on objects there is a symbolic operation effected by the symbol for that function. Thus if $f(x)$ is a function and a an object, $f(a)$ is an object —the object generated from a by application of $f(x)$. But '$f(a)$' is a name formed by conjoining the symbol 'f' for the function with the name 'a', 'f' is then an operator on names of objects, and is a name-forming operator; that is, when applied to the name of an object, the result is another name. The *truth-functional operators and quantifiers are termed *logical operators*. The truth-functional operators are also called *sentential operators* because,

when applied to sentences, they yield another sentence.

optimism *and* **pessimism.** Contrasting attitudes concerning the predominance of good or evil in the world. The former represents general hopefulness regarding the balance of pleasure and pain; the latter the view that hope is unreasonable and that happiness, if attainable, lies beyond the sphere of ordinary experience. The prevailing tone of a particular philosophical system depends mainly upon that system's *cosmology and its account of man's role in the Universe.

A pessimistic attitude is evident in the Orphic-Pythagorean tradition, reflected in some of the writings of *Plato. This regards earthly existence as a period of penance, with philosophical contemplation helping to achieve a purification of the soul and passage from the world of illusions to the domain of realities. Similar views are present in the teachings of the main eastern as well as western religions, emphasizing the corruptness of this world and the possibility of redemption and joy only in a hereafter.

One of the earliest examples of systematic philosophical optimism is *Leibniz' doctrine that God could not but have created the "best of all possible worlds". A generally optimistic philosophical mood characterized the 18th-century *Enlightenment. In *Kant's later writings, his original support of Leibnizian optimism is modified by the recognition of "radical evil" in the world, which prevents men from exercising good will.

Philosophical pessimism was prevalent in 19th-century Europe. Represented in the writings of *Schopenhauer and *Nietzsche, it was carried into the 20th century through the existential doctrines of *Heidegger and *Sartre, which concentrate on death, nothingness, and *Angst.

or. A *connective that has two principal, logically distinct uses: *exclusive*, as in (1), 'All flowering plants are either monocotyledonous or dicotyledonous', and *inclusive*, as in (2) 'He is either stupid or lazy'. In (1) the possibility of a flowering plant being both mono-cotyledonous and dicotyledonous is excluded, whereas in (2) the implication is that he may well be both stupid and lazy. It is the inclusive use that logicians take as primary, treating it as a connective between statements; thus (2) is taken to be short for 'He is stupid or he is lazy'. If p and q stand for statements, the inclusive use of 'or' is symbolized as '$p \lor q$'. '$\lor$' is here used to form the *disjunction* or *logical sum* of p and q. The exclusive use of 'or' is treated as secondary since it is definable from the inclusive use by 'p or q but not both' (symbolically: $(p \lor q)$ & -$(p$ & $q))$. In its inclusive use to form the disjunction of two statements, 'or' is often claimed to be a *truth-functional connective or a truth-functional operator whose definition is given by the *truth-table

p	$\lor$	q
T	T	T
T	T	F
F	T	T
F	F	F

and '$p \lor q$' is said to be a truth-functional compound of p and q.

ordered n-tuple. The ordered n-tuple of $b_1,\ldots,b_n$ is denoted by $<b_1,\ldots,b_n>$, and is the *sequence* of objects $b_1,\ldots,b_n$. $b_1,\ldots,b_n$ need not necessarily be distinct objects; in other words it is possible that for some $1 \leq i,j \leq n, b_i = b_j$. The ordered n-tuple $<b_1,\ldots,b_n>$ is to be distinguished from the (unordered) set B containing $b_1,\ldots,b_n$ as its only members; for example, if $b_1 \neq b_2$, $<b_1,b_2,\ldots,b_n> \neq <b_2,b_1,\ldots,b_n>$, as these are different sequences formed out of the members of the set B. (To specify B it does not matter in what order its members are listed.) This essential property of ordered n-tuples is encapsulated in the following condition for the identity of ordered n-tuples. $<b_1,\ldots,b_n> = <c_1,\ldots,c_n>$ iff $b_1 = c_1$, $b_2 = c_2,\ldots, b_n = c_n$, that is, they must contain the same objects in the same order. Thus $<2, 4, 2> \neq <2, 4>$ and $<4, 3, 2> \neq <2, 4, 3>$. An ordered 2-tuple is called an *ordered

pair; an ordered 3-tuple is called an *ordered triple*.

ordered pair. A pair the basic property of which is that two pairs are identical iff the first members of each are identical and the second members of each are identical. The ordered pair of b and c is written $<b, c>$. Thus $<b, c> = <d, e>$ iff $b = d$ and $c = e$. The ordered pair $<b, c>$ may be taken as the set $\{\{b\}, \{b, c\}\}$, its basic property following by elementary set theory. This notion of order is generalizable to an n-tuple (*see* ordered n-tuple).

ordering relation. In set theory, the relation R on a set X that imposes some order on the members of X.

Partial ordering: X is partially ordered by R iff for all members b, c, d, of X (1) if bRc and cRd then bRd, and (2) it is not the case that bRb. For example, let X be the set of positive integers and R the relation 'is an even number greater than'. R partially orders X since (1) if b is an even number greater than c and c is an even number greater than d then b is an even number greater than d, and (2) it is not the case that b is an even number greater than b. The relation 'is greater than' also orders X.

Simple ordering: X is simply ordered by R iff (1) X is partially ordered by R, and (2) for all non-identical members b, c of X either bRc or cRb. For example, 'is greater than' orders the set of positive integers but 'is an even number greater than' does not.

Well ordering: X is well ordered by R iff (1) X is simply ordered by R, and (2) R picks out a first member for every non-empty subset of X.

order type. The set of all sets ordinally similar to a given set. *See* number.

ordinal number. *See* number.

ordinary language. Ordinary (for example, non-technical and plain) language contrasts with esoteric (for example, technical or jargon). Note however, the difference between 'the use of ordinary language' and 'the ordinary use of "..."'.

'Ordinary use' means 'standard use' and even specialist words may have standard uses.

organicism. *See* holism.

organism, philosophy of. *See* Whitehead.

Organon. (Greek for: instrument, tool (Latin *Organum*).) The name traditionally given to *Aristotle's six treatises on *logic: *Categories*; *De Interpretatione*; *Prior Analytics*; *Posterior Analytics*; *Topics*; and *Sophistical Refutations*. It is the subject of the third and fourth of these to which the eponymous hero of Marlowe's *Dr. Faustus* refers: "Sweet analytics, 'tis thou hast ravished me."

Origen (*c.*185–254 AD). Christian theologian. Origen's works included a major critical edition of the Old Testament (the *Hexapla*), commentaries on most books of the Bible, sermons and devotional writings, the *De Principiis* (a pioneering attempt at a *summa theologiae*) and a defence of Christianity *Against Celsus*. Origen was the greatest of the Alexandrian theologians attempting to reconcile Christianity with Greek, (that is, Platonic) philosophy through speculative and allegorical interpretations of biblical texts. His adventurous doctrines, for instance the pre-existence of souls, aroused much subsequent controversy, and Origenism was finally condemned in 533 AD.

original sin. In traditional Christian teaching, the doctrine that the whole human race inherits, and is corrupted by, the sinfulness first brought into the world through the disobedience of Adam and Eve. Hence, since the Fall, human nature as such has been inherently sinful, a state from which it can be rescued only by divine grace. Many modern theologians interpret the doctrine, not as a historical account of the origin of human sinfulness, but rather as an expression of the insight that sin originates in human pride and self-will, rebelling against the authority of God.

Orphism. A modern term for two related but different phenomena of ancient Greek religion. **1.** A massive tradition of writing, beginning as early as the 7th century BC and supposedly inspired, if not composed, by the mythical singer Orpheus. **2.** The way of life expected of those initiated into the Mysteries of Eleusis. The importance of Orphism to us is the influence of its main ideas on *Pythagoras, *Empedocles, and *Plato. These included stories of creation, judgment and punishment in an afterlife, and reincarnation into other, often non-human, bodies. The conversion of Pythagoras seems to have been so complete that *Aristotle calls Orphic notions Pythagorean. In Plato, the wise "who hold that the body is a tomb" (*Gorgias* (493B), *Cratylus* (402B)) are Orphics. The notions of, but not the philosophical arguments for, pre-existence and immortality in *Meno* and *Phaedo* are traces of Orphism, as is the whole *myth of Er in *Republic*, Book X.

Ortega y Gasset, José (1883–1955). Spanish philosopher and essayist. Major works: *Meditaciones del Quijote* (1914), translated as *Meditations on Quixote* (1961), *El tema de nuestro tiempo* (1923), translated as *The Modern Theme* (1933), and *La rebelión de las masas* (1930), translated as *The Revolt of the Masses* (1931). He played a major part as a journalist, publisher, editor, and politician, as well as a philosopher, in the 20th-century regeneration of Spain's cultural and literary life. His theory of knowledge, which he called *perspectivism, was the view that the world can be interpreted by alternative systems of concepts, each unique and equally true. The only ultimate reality is each individual's life (a concept that he expressed as "I am I and my circumstances").

ostensive definition. *See* definition.

other minds. The problem whether and how anyone knows that any other organism is sentient. For, surely, there is no contradiction in suggesting that the behaviour and talk of others might in every way resemble mine though they were unconscious automata; while someone in a cataleptic trance might be to all appearance dead, yet conscious.

This problem should have been discovered by *Descartes when, after concluding that he was an incorporeal thinking substance (redefining 'thought' as all and only modes of self-consciousness) the *Discourse* proceeds to ask how to tell whether human bodies are inhabited by such thinking substances (see ghost in the machine). But Descartes seems forthwith to have forgotten his redefinition, which went against the grain of established verbal habits, for his "two most certain tests" refer to rationality rather than consciousness. In fact the problem gained wide attention only with the rise of various sorts of *behaviourism.

other-regarding. See self-regarding.

ought. See obligation.

ousia. (Greek for: substance.) The principal of *Aristotle's ten categories. It has sometimes been translated as 'reality'. The term also occurs in the context of Christian theological debate about the nature of Christ.

Owen, Robert (1771-1858). Welsh social reformer and advocate of cooperative settlements, influential in British social legislation through relentless campaigning against abuses of the early industrial system. The cotton factory he acquired at New Lanark became a model project. In *New View of Society* (1813) as well as in numerous articles, he argued for common ownership, but stressing a multiplicity of producer cooperatives rather than the state monopolies favoured by most later socialists. Against *Malthus he maintained that the increase in population would be offset by a greater increase in the productive capacity of the human race.

P

Paine, Thomas (1737-1809). English-born American revolutionary, political philosopher, author, and deist. He achieved fame with the publication of *Common Sense* (1776), an appeal for American independence and an exposition of the theory that government and society are distinct entities. Throughout the American Revolution he published the 'Crisis' pamphlets in its support. In reply to Burke's critical *Reflections on the Revolution in France* (1790) he published *The Rights of Man* (1791-2), giving a theoretical defence of democracy and republican principles. His attack on Christianity, *The Age of Reason* (1794, 1796), brought him a reputation for atheism although the work was intended as a defence of *deism.

Panaetius of Rhodes (185-09 BC). Philosopher, and head of the Stoa 129-09 BC. His writings are now lost. A friend of Scipio Aemilianus, Panaetius helped to make Stoic philosophy (see Stoicism) known and acceptable to Romans. Eclectic and sometimes heterodox in his teachings, he was best known for his ethics with their new, practical emphasis on the duties of ordinary men as against the perfections of the sage. His work *On what is appropriate* was the source for Books I and II of Cicero's highly influential *De Officiis*.

panpsychism. The theory that holds that the world is rendered more comprehensible on the assumption that every object is invested with a soul or mind. Like the related doctrines of *animal soul and *world soul, the theory is anti-materialist (see materialism) and historically rooted in post-Cartesian debates about whether only man can be said to possess a soul or mind. In various forms, panpsychical views are evident in the philosophy of *Leibniz and *Schopenhauer. The most notable modern proponent of the theory has been A.N.*Whitehead. *See also* hylozoism.

pantheism. The doctrine that the divine is all-inclusive and that man and Nature are not independent of God, but are modes or elements of his Being. Its precise significance—if such indeed there is—depends on the initial conceptions of God (and independence). But clearly any theology stressing God's infinity and omnipotence gives pantheism at least some plausibility. Although pantheistic tendencies appear in various religious and philosophical traditions, Christian *theism has always rejected it, finding its identification of Nature with God dangerously close to *atheism. Spinoza's doctrine of *Deus sive natura* (God or Nature) is usually regarded as the classic example of pantheism in Western philosophy (*see* Spinoza).

paradigm. In the philosophy of science, a central overall way of regarding phenomena, within which a scientist normally works. The paradigm may dictate what type of explanation will be found acceptable, but in periods of crisis a science may exchange paradigms. In its usual employment in the present context the term is both ambiguous and vague.

paradigm case argument. The argument that infers from the fact that a word is taught by reference to clear (paradigm) cases, the conclusion that examples of the thing referred to by the word must exist. This controversial argument has been deployed to attack sceptical contentions: those, for example, denying the reality of freewill or any knowledge of the existence of material things.

Thus it has been argued that we can learn the use of such phrases as 'We know for certain there are several chairs here' only by being confronted with circumstances in which such phrases truly apply. Since we *have* learned to use such phrases, we must have met situations in which we *are* entitled to be certain that such things exist.

paradox. A situation arising when, from a number of premises all generally accepted as true, a conclusion is reached by valid deductive argument that is either an outright *contradiction or conflicts with other generally held beliefs. Such a result is both perplexing and disturbing because it is not clear which of one's well entrenched beliefs should be rejected, while it is plain that in the interests of consistency some modification must be made (*see* consistent and inconsistent). Philosophers cannot claim exclusive rights on paradoxes; they crop up in other theoretical disciplines— relativity has its *clock paradox and mathematics the Skolem paradox (*see* Löwenheim-Skolem theorem). There is, however, a whole family of paradoxes, known as the self-referential paradoxes, which has been of particular concern to philosophers and logicians and some of which have played a crucial role in the historical development of the foundations of mathematics. One of the best known and oldest of these is the *liar paradox: Epimenides, a Cretan, claims 'All Cretans are liars'. Is he telling the truth or not? One or other must be the case, but if it is indeed the case that all Cretans other than Epimenides are liars, both cases lead to contradictions. *Russell's paradox is a logical paradox that had very serious repercussions in the theory of classes (*see* class) and thus also in the foundations of mathematics. Consider the class of all classes that do not belong to themselves. Does it belong to itself? Answering either 'Yes' or 'No' results in a contradiction. From this Russell drew the conclusion that no such class exists, but it is not easy to justify this conclusion. *See also* logical paradoxes; semantic paradoxes; Zeno's paradoxes.

parallelism. *See* psychophysical parallelism.

parapsychology. A term now replacing 'psychical research' as the name for the study of ESP, PK, and a miscellany of other putative phenomena not recognized by established scientific disciplines.

See extrasensory perception; psychokinesis.

Parmenides of Elea. Greek philosopher, who, if Plato's dialogue *Parmenides* is to be trusted, must have been born around 510 BC. Parmenides wrote a poem of which more is preserved than we have from any other of the *Presocratics. It is also more, in our sense, philosophical than anything earlier. One part, the 'Way of Truth', consists in a priori arguments about the nature of being. The other, the 'Way of Seeming', is an unreconstructible traditional cosmology in which not even its author believed. In the former, with its denials of the reality of time, plurality, and motion, Parmenides stands out as the first European philosophical metaphysician (*see* metaphysics).

partial ordering. *See* ordering relation.

particulars. *See* universals and particulars.

Pascal, Blaise (1623-62). French mathematician, physicist, and theologian. Acclaimed for work on hydrodynamics and the mathematical theory of probability, he experienced in 1654 a revelation calling him to religious studies. He became closely associated with the Jansenist *Port Royal group.

In the 18 *Lettres Provinciales* (1656-7), directed primarily against the Jesuits, Pascal examined the fundamental problems of human existence from psychological and theological points of view. His *Pensées*, which is a compilation made from his notes and issued in 1670, is a work of Christian apologetics, stating that the true function of reason is to bring man to God in order to attain the truth or supreme good to which his nature aspires.

Pascal's wager. An argument known chiefly from its formulation by *Pascal in his posthumous *Pensées*, but certainly developed earlier. Pascal starts by presenting our human predicament as a betting situation, in which each one of us has to stake his destiny upon some

world outlook. He then concedes to his possible opponent that we are, and cannot but remain, cosmically ignorant. There is no positive *natural theology, and we cannot rationally identify any putative system of religious revelation as the genuine article: "Reason can decide nothing here."

It is upon this agnostic assumption that Pascal proceeds to argue that sane and prudent persons must bet their lives on Roman Catholicism, labouring to persuade themselves of the truth of that system. If they do, and it turns out to be true, then they have won an eternity of bliss. If it turns out to be false, and death is after all annihilation, what has been lost? If instead they choose to make the best of what this world has to offer, then that, at best, is what they win; while, at worst, they suffer an eternity of torment. "And so," Pascal insists, "our contention is of infinite force, when there is the finite to stake in a game in which the chances of winning and of losing are equal and there is the infinite to gain" (Brunschvicg arrangement § 233).

The main but not the only fault in this argument is that Pascal assumes that there are only two alternative bets: become a Roman Catholic or not. But on his own basic premise of total ignorance, the set of conceivable alternative cosmic systems, all by the hypothesis equally probable, must be infinite. This is also true of the subset of those promising eternal bliss, and threatening eternal torment, respectively to reward and punish, an infinite range of different favoured or disfavoured ways of life. Since the basic idea of the wager had in any case been introduced into Christendom from Islam, it is perhaps curious that Pascal did not here think of at least that particular alternative bet.

Pascal's wager is unique among the famous arguments of natural theology in offering a motivating rather than an evidencing reason for belief (*see* reason). For Pascal is clearly trying to provide a prudential reason for self-persuasion rather than any sort of evidence to show that the recommended conclusions are actually true.

William *James in a famous essay on 'The Will to Believe' contended, following Pascal, that, in certain limited but specially important cases, our beliefs ought to be determined entirely by "our passional nature". He also stressed, using an electrical image, that certain options are for particular people at particular times, psychologically live or dead. But this important observation cannot plug the hole in Pascal's argument.

pathetic fallacy. The accepted name for the mistake—not strictly a *fallacy— of attributing to inanimate objects the feelings, dispositions, and reactions which could only characterize animate creatures, and in particular people. The expression appears to have been first used in a sense of this sort by John Ruskin in *Modern Painters* (1843-60).

Peano's postulates. Five postulates (or axioms) from which the rest of arithmetic can be developed. They were presented by Giuseppe Peano in 1889 (although Richard Dedekind had in fact published them previously in 1888) in order to free the concept of number from dependence upon mere intuition. They are:

(1) 0 is a number.
(2) The successor of any number is a number.
(3) No two numbers have the same successor.
(4) 0 is not the successor of any number.
(5) If P is a predicate true of 0, and if whenever P is true of a number n it is also true of the successor of n, then P is true of every number.

Peirce, Charles Sanders (1839-1914). American physicist and philosopher, founder of *pragmatism. He graduated from Harvard in 1859 and worked for the U.S. Coast and Geodetic Survey, devoting his leisure time to studying and occasionally teaching philosophy. His essays on logic, epistemology, and metaphysics were published posthumously in eight volumes: *Collected Papers* (1931-58).

Pragmatism as Peirce advanced it, was a philosophical method for establishing the meanings of concepts and beliefs, stating that one's idea of anything is the idea of its sensible effects distinguished according to their practical significance. True ideas are those to which responsible investigators would assent after thorough examination (*see also* fallibilism). In the essay *Fixation of Belief* Peirce points out the practical difference between belief and doubt: the former is action guiding, the latter stimulates enquiry in the struggle to attain belief. Disagreement over the definition of 'truth' advanced in William *James' work led Peirce to rename his own theory "pragmaticism".

Peirce was also a pioneer in the development of modern formal logic. Inspired by De Morgan's work, he extended the algebraic methods of Boole to the logic of relations, introducing the distinction between monadic, dyadic, and polyadic relations. He also presented the first treatment of the propositional calculus as a calculus of truth-values. His contributions to the philosophy of science include an improvement of earlier versions of the frequency theory of *probability, and the introduction of the idea of justifying *induction as the method which must succeed—if any method will—in the long run (*see* vindication).

Pelagianism. A heresy, propagated by the 5th-century British monk Pelagius. It denied original sin and held that man can, of his own freewill and without the intervention of God's grace, live sinless and attain eternal life. *See also* Augustine of Hippo, St.

perception. In an interpretation restricted to sense perception, a topic much discussed by philosophers. Their interest has been in the analysis of claims to perceive objects in the *external world —not only material things but also other perceivables such as shadows, flames, and rainbows. The main disputed question has been how far we have here a source or form of knowledge. The common-sense view that of course we do is challenged by the argument from illusion (*see* illusion, arguments from). This urges that, since we are always liable to make perceptual mistakes, and in fact often do, therefore we have no sufficient reason to accept perception as generally, or even ever, reliable. The *representative theory of perception and the more general *causal theory of perception both suppose that objects in the external world stimulate us into having (private) *sense data. But both theories then deny that we are ever directly aware of the (public) objects themselves (*see* veil of appearance). If this were right, and if in what we uninstructedly think of as perception we never do directly confront any public objects, then it must be impossible to know anything about, or even that there are, such objects, and hence to know that they are causing us to have sense data, some of which may or may not be faithful representations of their producers.

*Phenomenalism meets this radical difficulty with a comparably radical response: all talk about such putative public objects really is reducible to talk about our own actual or possible private sense data. Many other philosophers today defend what they think of as a sophisticated version of a position that opponents unflatteringly label *naive realism. The sophistication is to maintain that, when some public object causes a percipient to have an appropriate sense datum, then that percipient is perceiving, and hence is directly aware of, that object. Usually something is added about the danger of confounding a physiological account of the mechanisms of perception (in which sensory machinery appears to provide links in long causal chains) with a philosophical analysis (in which actual perception should be explicated as essentially immediate and direct).

perfection. *See* degrees of perfection argument.

perfection, principle of. A principle of the philosophy of Leibniz, stating that God creates the best of all possible worlds, that is, a world in which a maximum of perfection is achieved with a minimum of deficiency. *See also* Leibniz; theodicy.

performative. An utterance, such as 'I promise', which is itself the performance of an act (in this case, the act of promising) rather than a description of that act. J. L. *Austin, who introduced the term, seems not to have recognized that this insight was anticipated by *Hume, especially in his account in the *Treatise* of promising.

per genus et differentiam. (Latin for: by kind and difference.) A method of definition characteristic of Aristotelian logic. The traditional definition of man as 'the rational animal' places our *species, man, within the wider class or *genus, animals. It then distinguishes it from all the others as capable of rationality and, by the same token, irrationality also. The *fundamentum divisionis* is thus this capability, or the lack of it.

Peripatetic. A follower of Aristotle, the word deriving from restless practices in his *Lyceum.

Peripatos. Aristotle's *Lyceum.

perlocution. An utterance with perlocutionary effects. Effects that may (but need not) be caused *by* utterances (for example, embarrassment) are called their 'perlocutionary effects'. *See* J. L. Austin.

per se notum. (Latin for: known through itself.) A phrase favoured by St. Thomas *Aquinas for what he thought to be in some way self-evident.

person. A term that has had various technical and semitechnical applications in philosophy. *Boethius defined the Latin '*persona*' as "*naturae rationalis individua substantia*" (an individual substance of a rational kind) and the concept of rationality has recurred in subsequent accounts of 'person'. *Locke distinguished 'person' from 'man' calling the former "a forensic term" that applies "only to intelligent agents capable of a law, and happiness and misery" (*An Essay Concerning Human Understanding*, Book II, Chapter 27). The term has a particular importance in the moral philosophy of *Kant, who defines it in much the same way as Locke: "A *Person* is the subject whose actions are capable of *imputation*" (*Introduction to the Metaphysic of Morals*). Kant says that because persons are capable of imposing laws upon themselves they are worthy of *respect*.

The question of whether persons are essentially *mental* or *physical* entities has been much discussed (*see* personal identity). P. F. Strawson has suggested that 'person' is a "*logically primitive* concept such that *both* predicates ascribing states of consciousness *and* predicates ascribing corporeal characteristics are equally applicable to a single individual of that single type."

personal identity. The concept posing the philosophical problem of explaining what it means to say that this at this time is the same person as that at that time. *See* person; soul; survival and immortality.

personalism. The theory, largely of 20th-century American origin, that the person is ontologically fundamental, and that all philosophical enquiry should proceed in reference to the concept of person. Idealist in character, the theory is also generally theistic in regarding God as the primary manifestation of personality. *See also* idealism.

perspectivism. The view that the external world is to be interpreted through different alternative systems of concepts and beliefs and that there is no authoritative independent criterion for determining that one such system is more valid than another. Perspectivism occurs in many of the writings of *Nietzsche, but is best known from the work of *Ortega y Gasset. Extended into the field of language studies it poses problems that have interested *Quine

and other philosophers, regarding the possibility or impossibility of translating one language into another (*see* translation).

persuasive definition. *See* definition.

pessimism. *See* optimism and pessimism.

petitio principii. Latin for: *begging the question.

phenomenalism. An analysis of physical object propositions. It rejects the notion that there are forever inaccessible objects shrouded behind the *veil of appearance, by reducing all talk of things perceived or perceivable to talk about actual or possible perceptual experience. Thus J. S. *Mill defined material objects as "permanent possibilities of sensation"; when such an object is said to be perceived some of these possibilities are actualized. *Mach, many leading members of the *Vienna Circle, and the young A. J. *Ayer all defended versions of phenomenalism. The main objections are: (1) that there can be no intelligible talk about (private) *sense data except in so far as language users can first give this meaning by reference to (public) physical objects; and (2) that phenomenalism analyses what appear to be categorical propositions about usually impersonal, public, and independent objects in terms of mainly hypothetical contentions about the private experiences of persons.

phenomenology. In philosophy, the term referring to the method of enquiry developed by *Husserl, following his own teacher *Brentano. It is supposed to begin from a scrupulous inspection of one's own conscious, and particularly intellectual, processes. In this inspection all assumptions about the wider and external causes and consequences of these internal processes have to be excluded ('bracketed'). Although this sounds like a programme for a psychology of *introspection, Husserl insisted that it was an a priori investigation of the essences or meanings common to the thought of different minds. *See also* Heidegger; Merleau-Ponty.

phenomenon. Any object or occurrence perceived by the senses. **1.** (in Greek philosophy) Sensible appearance, contrasted with the real object apprehended by the intellect. **2.** (in *Kant) The object interpreted through categories, contrasted with *noumenon. *See also* category.

Philo (*c.*20 BC–*c.*50 AD). A leading figure of the Jewish community of Alexandria, who achieved a far-reaching synthesis between Greek and Jewish thought. His voluminous writings (more than 30 philosophical treatises survive in the original Greek, together with some Latin and Armenian translations of others) are our fullest guide to Hellenistic Jewish ideas, and also constitute an important historical source. They consist mainly of allegorical expositions of the Pentateuch, but they include some purely philosophical works. There are also two historical documents, chronicling anti-Jewish riots in Alexandria and a subsequent embassy to Rome which he led. His most important direct influence was on Greek Christian thinkers, beginning with *Clement of Alexandria and *Origen, but his aims and methods laid the basis for medieval Islamic, Jewish, and Latin Christian philosophy.

Philolaus of Croton. A follower of *Pythagoras, born in the mid 5th century BC. The 20 often substantial fragments attributed to Philolaus seem to be post-Aristotelian forgeries, but one source attributes to him embryological suggestions that may throw light on an early stage in the development of the Pythagorean cosmology. *See* Presocratics.

philosopher kings. In *Plato's *Republic*, genuine rulers and philosophers who, knowing the Platonic Forms or Ideas, thus become experts about ends and values. Plato argued that "unless philosophers rule as kings...or those who are now called kings and princes become genuine and adequate philosophers...

there will be no respite from evil...for humanity." The label is now widely applied to all elite groups claiming or exercising absolute power in the name of any shared *ideology that supposedly yields expertise in what their present or future subjects really need.

philosopher's stone. The hypothetical substance sought by alchemists (*see* alchemy) for converting base metals into gold. It appears in the alchemical literature under hundreds of different and fanciful names.

philosophes. 1. The designation of fashionable and influential thinkers of the *Enlightenment. **2.** In the *Encyclopédie*, one of the areas of the literary world (contrasted with *érudites* and *beaux esprits*): the field of wisdom distinguished from the fields of learning and pleasure. *See also* Encyclopedists.

Philosophical Radicals. Followers of *Bentham, themselves primarily theoreticians, who aimed at and achieved considerable practical influence. The group included James *Mill, who largely defined it, the economist and MP David Ricardo, the historian George Grote, the jurisprudent John *Austin, and in due course John Stuart *Mill. In the first three quarters of the 19th century the Philososphical Radicals were influential in much the same ways as the Fabian Society later, though in the former case the influence favoured economic and political liberalism. Their views should not be confused with *radical philosophy.

philosophy. Most of what might have appeared here as a general description of what philosophy is about will instead be found in the Preface. There are text articles on the various branches of philosophy: aesthetics, ethics, epistemology, logic, and metaphysics. Articles will also be found on the philosophies of education, history, language, law, mind, psychology, religion, science, and space and time, and on political and social philosophy.

phrastic *and* **neustic.** A distinction introduced by R. M. Hare. *Phrastic* refers to the common element that may exist between sentences in different moods. (Frege used 'sentence-radical' for the same concept.) Thus 'You are going to shut the door' (indicative) and 'Shut the door!' (imperative) have a common element expressible by the incomplete sentence (phrastic) 'your shutting the door in the near future'. This may be completed by adding a *neustic.* Thus, if to 'your shutting the door' I add 'Move', I indicate an imperative; if I add 'yes', I indicate an indicative. The device is used by Hare to explore logical relations between imperatives.

physicalism. The doctrine that all propositions asserting "matters of fact and real existence" can be formulated as statements about publicly observable physical objects and activities (*see* Hume's fork). This doctrine was first developed by leading members of the *Vienna Circle of logical positivists, and is now pressed by J. J. C. Smart and other hard spokesmen for the *identity theory of mind. *See also* Carnap.

physico-theological argument. One of the three terms of *Kant's tripartite classification of all possible attempts to prove the existence of God. The type includes among its tokens (*see* token) every attempt that takes as a premise any actual or supposed fact or facts about the Universe—as opposed to those two other kinds of attempts that start either from the mere fact that there is a Universe or from a mere concept of God. All the Five Ways of St. Thomas Aquinas, and not the fifth only, which is his version of an *argument to design, would accordingly have to be rated as specimens of physico-theological argument. *See also* cosmological argument; creation; degrees of perfection argument; First Cause; First Mover; natural theology; ontological argument.

Pico della Mirandola, Giovanni (1463–94). Italian philosopher, who had strong personal and scholarly links with the *Academy of Florence. His study of the *Kabbalah was the first serious work in this field by a Christian scholar. Although he was orthodox in religion, his proposed disputation on 900 theological and philosophical questions was banned by the Pope (1486). His oration on man, composed for that occasion, is an eloquent exposition of human responsibility and dignity.

PK. *See* psychokinesis.

Plato (*c.*428 –*c.*348 BC). Greek philosopher, born into an aristocratic Athenian family. Plato seems to have found his political ambitions frustrated, although no details are known of this or of other important features of Plato's life. He was closely associated with Socrates up to the latter's trial and execution, when Plato was 29 or 30. But it is not certain when Plato began to write dialogues in which Socrates usually figures as the central character. It may have been before Socrates' death or as late as twenty years after. Nor is it certain when, together with the mathematician Theaetetus, Plato established a school known as the Academy; Plato may have been in either his late thirties or middle fifties.

There are over two dozen dialogues that may be attributed with confidence to Plato. There is no certainty about the precise order in which they were written but they fall naturally into three groups, which are taken to represent early, middle, and late periods of development. Not all dialogues have a unanimously agreed place in this classification; the relocation of a single dialogue, such as the *Timaeus,* can have far-reaching implications for a scholar's view of Plato's development.

Most of the early dialogues are preoccupied with excellence of character (*aretē*) and its development. Socrates is often portrayed as seeking definitions of particular excellences: courage (in the *Laches*), soundness of mind (in the *Charmides*), piety (in the *Euthyphro*), or excellence in general (in the *Meno*).

Professing perplexity, Socrates goads another person into offering an account of an excellence, but refuses to be satisfied with examples, insisting on a general characterization that can be used to tell whether something is, indeed, an example of that excellence. When an account is offered Socrates presses the other party with questions requiring a 'yes' or 'no' answer, and by means of inferences drawn from the statements to which the other party is committed, Socrates drives him into a contradiction. Another definition may be tried, or occasionally the other party may be given a chance to change his answer to one of Socrates' questions. In either case another contradiction results and the dialogue eventually ends with the participants in the same state of perplexity as Socrates.

Plato has Socrates pursue more than definitions. Answers to questions about excellence (such as 'Can excellence be taught?' or 'Is righteousness the same thing as piety?') are also subjected to this treatment. But it is more than once suggested that one must first determine *what* an excellence is before one can say anything about it, or say whether a man or action exhibits that excellence.

Although the early dialogues do not commit themselves to any definitions, they do contain ethical doctrines. Where these are made explicit (as in the *Protagoras* and *Gorgias*), their paradoxical character is not played down. The kind of account that clearly attracts Plato, even when he has Socrates demolish it, is one that would make all excellence knowledge. For example, courage would be knowledge of what to fear. A man does not acquit himself bravely in battle because he is master over a natural disinclination to be killed or maimed, but because he knows it is worse, and he is therefore *more afraid*, to disgrace himself or to be captured and made a slave.

Closely related to this is Plato's early view of rational persuasion. To persuade a man to act in a certain way we frequently show him how acting in this way will realize (or failing to act will prevent the realization of) something he wants, something he would call 'good'. It is evident that all people seek after, and would call something (such as their own survival or advantage) 'good'; and that some people can be persuaded to change their minds about what they seek when shown it conflicts with something they want more, or would call 'better'. From this Plato advanced to the thesis that all men are really seeking after an ultimate good and act wrongly only because they are ignorant of what that good is.

But if all men, who do evil, want to do good and fail only because they do not know what is good, no wrongdoing can be voluntary. Furthermore, if all wrongdoing is the result of ignorance, there can be no man who knows what is good and lacks the strength of character to pursue it, so there is no *akrasia*, or *weakness of the will. Another paradoxical thesis is that the knowledge required for one excellence is the same as that required for any other. This results in what is known as "the unity of virtue", which means simply that the excellences are not separable; it is not possible to possess soundness of mind without also possessing courage and vice versa.

What Plato makes Socrates do in the early dialogues is as important as any doctrines that emerge. His procedure is probably based on a common debating game of the period known as eristic: one person defended a thesis against an opponent who tried to get him to agree to statements that contradicted the thesis. In the hands of the unscrupulous, victory could turn on fallacious arguments; some of these are displayed in the *Euthydemus*, where Socrates falls into the hands of two *sophists who have a bag of trick arguments.

Plato used the word 'eristic' abusively, contrasting eristic with a purified version of the activity which he called 'dialectic'. Often, however, the arguments put in Socrates' mouth are as fallacious as those used against him in the *Euthydemus*. This may be due to the circumstance that Plato had no very firm theoretical hold on the difference between valid and fallacious arguments. It was *Aristotle, a pupil and later a teacher in Plato's Academy, who founded logical theory by writing a handbook for students of dialectic. Plato's explicit complaint against practitioners of eristic is not that they argue fallaciously but that they argue over trivial matters for personal glory. Socrates is always made to disclaim any personal credit for his refutations and if his arguments seem at times frivolous, the object and conduct of his search is certainly not.

Nevertheless the method Plato portrays Socrates as employing is essentially negative. It is capable of exposing the inadequacies of a proposed definition of, or a thesis about, the excellences of character, but not of producing the sought for definition. This gap between method and objective opens Plato to the charge that dialectic, however seriously pursued, will only serve to undermine people's faith that there are standards of conduct to be sought. Plato's middle period may be seen as an attempt to close the gap and answer such a charge.

The middle period, however, is distinguished by more than a concern with this gap. Socrates is no longer made to inflict dialectical cross-examination on other people. Instead in long passages punctuated by agreement and encouragement from his interlocutors he expounds a system of doctrine. The change in style is strikingly illustrated by the difference between the first book of the *Republic* (probably drafted in the early period) and the other nine books. Changes in outlook which accompany the change of style may reflect a profound crisis in Plato's life, about which it is possible only to speculate.

The early dialogues do not, in contrast to those of the middle period, suggest that to acquire the knowledge that is needed for excellence of character, one must withdraw from this world, become indifferent to wealth or reputation, or learn to despise the pleasures of the

body and the information of the senses. Preoccupation with a realm apart from this world becomes in the middle period as much a source of excellence as the knowledge of what is to be found there. The *Phaedo* rejects as illogical the idea that true courage can arise from the fear of something else. Its source has to be disciplined indifference to the body's pleasures and pains.

Although a distinction between knowledge and belief appears in the early dialogues, it is not suggested there that the object of knowledge (what is known) is different sort of thing from the object of belief. The *Meno*, indeed, suggests quite the opposite, that a man can turn his true belief into knowledge by working out reasons for what he believes. But in *Republic* Book V it is argued that knowledge and belief are distinct capacities and have distinct objects. What is known *is* in the full sense of 'is' (is fully real) while what is believed, if correct, *is* but not in the full sense of 'is' (is only partly real).

To understand this peculiar way of speaking, consider a Socratic search for a definition of justice. What Socrates wants is a formula, 'XYZ', saying what justice is. This formula fails if there is any respect in which XYZ may fail to be just. If justice is said to be giving back to people what they loaned you, and there might be a case in which this would not be a just thing to do, then this formula is inadequate. For it to be adequate there must be no time, place, circumstance, or anything in relation to which XYZ may be said not to be just. If there is any respect in which XYZ may be said not to be just, we cannot say XYZ *is*, in the full sense, justice—it is not *really* or truly justice.

Socrates, as he is portrayed by Plato, is after more than a mere form of words. A statement is true or false in virtue of something that is called 'reality'. An important presupposition of Socrates' enterprise is that the formula he seeks is not correct by convention or decision, but is *true*. So there must be a reality that the definition is true in virtue of, and Socrates is seeking knowledge of this reality. The reality described by a true definition of justice is not one located in any particular place or time, it does not change, and it *is* in every respect (*is* fully) just. In the absence of any adequate description of this reality Plato refers to it as "the just itself" and writes of similar realities as Forms or Ideas.

The insistence that the objects of knowledge must be Forms is the result of an exaggeration of the requirement that what is known must be true, helped along by a Greek idiom that suggests that characteristics are substances. If what is known must be true without qualification (the exaggeration) then it must be possible to say it *is* without qualification, but one can only say this of Forms. No object of sensory experience can be described as just, beautiful, large, or heavy without qualification. Such things will always by unjust, ugly, small, or light in comparison with something else. Hence there can be no *knowledge* of the justice, beauty, size, or weight of sensory objects—at best only true belief.

This is the theory of Forms. It is Plato's attempt to work out what must be the case if the search for definitions is to succeed. It provides no answer; it only characterizes the objective of the search. How it might be possible actually to arrive at a definition is answered in one way by the doctrine of *reminiscence or recollection (anamnēsis)*. This first appears in an early dialogue, the *Meno*, where Plato suggests that we are born already in possession of knowledge of which we are not conscious but which we will readily recollect if carefully prompted. He has Socrates illustrate this by drawing the answer to a geometrical problem out of a slave boy who knows no geometry.

This takes place in two stages: in the first the slave is made aware of the problem and his inability to solve it; in the second he is supposedly led to find the answer for himself by a careful series of questions. The first stage is evidently

meant to correspond to and justify Socrates' practice of refuting the definitions he goads other people into offering. This does make them aware of a problem and of their inability to solve it. But no one, including Socrates, already has the answer and is able to guide us over the second stage. We may stumble on something that prompts our recollection of what we are already supposed to know, but we have no systematic way of finding such things.

No connection is made in the. *Meno* between recollection and Forms; this is done in the *Phaedo*. However, no mention of recollection is made in the *Republic*'s extensive discussion of a discipline called 'dialectic' which is supposed to study the forms. This discipline evidently has affinities to Socrates' practice in the early dialogues, since it is forbidden to those under 30 because youths too readily indulge in refutation for its own sake and are vulnerable to disillusionment from witnessing too many refutations. The difference seems to be that Plato thought he had hit on a systematic application of the early practice of dialectic. The system has something to do with laying down and testing hypotheses, but Plato goes on to picture the advance of dialectic up a ladder of hypotheses—at the top of which is a special Form, the Good—without leaving us any clear account of how to get from one rung of the ladder to the next.

One thing that is clear about the 'method of hypothesis' is that one can only be confident of the correctness of any account of a Form from the vantage point of the top of the ladder, after one has reached the Form of the Good. Since Socrates is not made to claim that he has completed the ascent, the account of justice (or rightness) offered in the *Republic* is put forward as tentative. The account of what makes a state just is given in terms of a model state that has three social classes, workers, soldiers, and rulers. Justice is said to be the performance by each class of its job and non-interference in the jobs of the other classes. Plato is able to give the same account for what it is that makes a man just (righteous) by first dividing the human soul into three parts that correspond to the social classes of his state: desire (workers), spirit (soldiers), and reason (rulers). A just (righteous) man is ruled by reason and not by desire since each of his parts is doing its job and not the job of another part.

The possibility that desire rather than reason may rule a man seems to open also the possibility that a man may know what is best and not be able to overcome a desire or fear that prevents him from doing what is best. This suggests, contrary to the early period, the possibility of weakness of will. However certain images used in the *Phaedrus* suggest that Plato would not have allowed that a man whose reason did not rule his desire really did know what was best.

The third period is marked by a new concern with questions that belong to what is now called philosophical logic; these include the structure of sentences, how complex expressions are related to simple ones, and how negation and falsity are possible (in the *Cratylus*, *Theaetetus*, and *Sophist*). Dialectic is characterized as the study of how Forms are related to (interwoven with) one another and is associated, if not identified with a new procedure of 'collection and division', which bears little relation to the practice of the early dialogues. Collection involves a synoptic survey of Forms including that to be defined, until one widely embracing Form is chosen and then divided and subdivided by the selection of differences—for example, art is divided into acquisitive and productive; acquisitive art into that which involves exchange and that which involves capture, etc.—until a satisfactory definition is reached (*Phaedrus*, *Philebus*, *Sophist*, *Statesman*).

It is not clear that the Forms of the third period are quite the same as those of the middle period, for the whole theory is subjected to a searching examination in the *Parmenides*. It is

hard to estimate Plato's own view of the criticisms raised there. The most famous, known as 'the third man argument' depends essentially on a motivation for the Forms, known as 'the one over many principle' which Plato mentions in only one other place. The one over many principle says that where a plurality of things is called by a single name, say 'man', there is an ideal (Form of) man apart from these, which is pre-eminently man and is that in virtue of which each member of the plurality is recognized as man. The 'third man' argues that the original plurality plus the ideal will form a new plurality which is called by a single word (all are 'men') and so there is a need for yet another ideal man for this plurality. This launches an infinite regress, for each ideal introduces the need for yet another ideal. (The *Parmenides* also suggests serious difficulties with the method of hypothesis and this may explain the shift of emphasis to collection and division.)

Plato does not offer to rebut the criticisms, nor does he tell us whether he regards the theory as in need of overhaul and if so with what effect. One interpretation holds that Plato abandoned the separation of the Forms, that is, he ceased to think of them as belonging to a world apart from the sensible world. It is clear that separation is what Aristotle, who was by this time Plato's junior colleague in the Academy, objected to most of all in the theory. This interpretation requires finding independent grounds for assigning the *Timaeus*, which endorses the full theory of separate Forms, to the middle rather than the final period. Even with this reassignment it is possible to read the third period as working within and for the theory of the middle period. Scholarly opinion is sharply divided on this issue.

Aristotle attributes a highly mathematicized account of the Forms to Plato's later years. This might have been Plato's response to difficulties he saw with the middle period theory. Apart from what may be hints in this direction in the

Philebus, Plato left no record of this alleged final version of the theory.

Platonism. As the philosophy deriving directly or indirectly from the work of Plato, Platonism can be seen as a commentary on complexities in Plato's own thought (*see also* Plato).

Plato's philosophy offers almost every obstacle to simple systematic exposition. He transmitted it to posterity principally through dialogues written over a period of 50 years, during which his thought developed considerably. Modern scholarship distinguishes between (1) the inclusive, aporetic dialogues of his early, so-called Socratic period, (2) the great works of his middle period like the *Phaedo* and the *Republic* with their positive metaphysical, psychological, and political doctrines, and (3) late writings like the *Parmenides* and the *Sophist*, in which these doctrines are subjected to radical reappraisal and modification. Even in his middle period, Plato's teachings tend to vary in detail and implications from one dialogue to another.

The central doctrine in this period, indeed the centre of Plato's whole work as a philosopher, is the theory of Forms or Ideas. These eternal transcendent realities directly apprehended by thought are contrasted with the transient contingent phenomena of our empirical existence. The Forms fulfil a number of barely compatible functions, appearing sometimes in the role of universals (*see* universals and particulars), sometimes as ideal standards, sometimes as the intelligible model or blueprint of the sensible world. Plato's theory of substantive Ideas has to account singlehanded for a variety of facts—ontological, epistemological, and ethical. It shows a variety of philosophical influences, Heraclitean, Pythagorean, Parmenidean, and Socratic; it also reveals, like Plato's work as a whole, two contrasting motives: on the one hand, a poetic, religious awareness of an unseen eternal world, dimly reflected in the phenomena around us, and, on the other, a mathematical urge to analyse reality into its ultimate units. Doctrines of such complexity do not lend themselves readily to systematic exposition, which Plato anyway distrusted. The dialogue, with its dramatic elements, its ironies, its recourse to mythical figurative language, was his chosen literary vehicle for teachings that he was not propounding as a definitive system.

But a system was precisely what philosophers in later antiquity, the Middle Ages, and the Renaissance sought and found in Plato's philosophy. To yield the necessary coherence and integration, the dialogues required a great deal of creative exegesis, a process that culminated in the long predominant Neoplatonic interpretation of Plato (*see* Neoplatonism). The greatest exponents of this interpretation were the Neoplatonist philosophers *Plotinus (205-70 AD) and *Proclus (*c*.419-85 AD); but its main features had appeared a century before Plotinus, and its origins go back to Plato's own lifetime. Its starting-point was Plato's contrast between eternal Ideas and the transient objects of sense, a contrast suggesting two lines of speculative enquiry. First, what is the connection, or is there anything to mediate, between intelligibles and sensibles, the worlds of Being and of Becoming? Second, is there any principle beyond the Ideas, or are they the ultimate reality?

Plato's *Timaeus* had presented the visible cosmos, in mythical language, as an artefact modelled after an ideal archetype by an ungrudging agent, the *Demiurge. One obvious intermediary between the visible world and its intelligible archetype was the soul, which can take cognizance of them both. In the Neoplatonic system, Soul emerged as a distinct *hypostasis or realm of reality, mediating between the sensible world and that of Ideas—or, rather, of *Nous* (Mind). The latter was a realm in which (on the Aristotelian principle that "what thinks and what is thought are the same") Ideas are fused with Intelligence and with the Demiurge, understood here as cosmic rationality.

On the second question, Plato had identified the supreme principles as "the One" and the "Indefinite Dyad", sources respectively of unity and plurality in the world. These interact to produce the Ideas. He had also referred to "the Good" as "beyond being in dignity and power" and this reference, combined with an interpretation of the *Parmenides* Part II as serious ontology (rather than just a dialectical exercise), led to the Neoplatonic view of the ultimate principle as a single ineffable 'One' or 'Good', with plurality appearing first at the stage of Mind. There are thus three 'hypostases' or realms of incorporeal reality: Soul, Mind, the One. The original dichotomy between intelligibles and sensibles turns into a hierarchy of Being, that can be depicted as a descending set of concentric circles around the One: these comprise Mind, Soul, and the corporeal world (we can say roughly 'the realm of Nature'), terminating in sheer blank matter.

For 1500 years, this was to be the standard Platonist view of the world. In the hierarachy, human beings are active on more than one level. By turning their purified attentions upwards and inwards, they can reach and live the divine intellectual life of Mind (Platonist writers speak here of "assimilation to God"). However the still higher "return to the One", an entity beyond intelligible Being, can only be a mystical, supra-intellectual union by love, of the kind first suggested by Plato in the *Symposium*. Its ideal of sublime spiritual eros was to remain one of Platonism's most potent attractions.

Against that, the political concerns that dominate Plato's two longest dialogues, the *Republic* and the *Laws*, received next to no attention from philosophers in the Platonist tradition (with the notable exceptions of the 10th-century Arab *al-Fārābī and the 15th-century Byzantine Gemistus Plethon). The Neoplatonic interpretation of Plato took shape over a long period of specu-lation and syncretism, during which his teachings came to be fused with Stoic, Aristotelian, and, above all, with Pythagorean elements. Some of the most important contributors to the Platonist tradition were in fact Neopythagoreans, like Moderatus of Gades (*c.*50–100 AD) who was ready to claim that Plato had stolen his main doctrines from Pythagoras. As early as the 1st century BC, Plato was seen as standing with Pythagoras in a tradition that was later extended to include such works as the *Corpus Hermeticum* (*see* hermeticism) and the *Chaldaean Oracles*. In the Renaissance, Plato's dialogues would be studied alongside the works of Orpheus, Hermes Trismegistus, the Pythagoreans, Plotinus, Proclus, Dionysius the pseudo-Areopagite, and others, as texts of "pious philosophy", the so-called *philosophia perennis* (perennial philosophy) alter-native to the bibical revelation. Such syncretism hardly made for historical clarity, but it did lead Christian Platon-ists like *Nicholas of Cusa, *Ficino, and Benjamin *Whichcote to an unusual broadmindedness in religious questions.

The historical development of Platon-ism falls into five main periods: (1) the Old Academy, (2) the Hellenistic Academy, (3) 'Ancient Neoplatonism', (4) the Middle Ages, and (5) the Renais-sance.

(1) Under Plato's first two successors, Speusippus (*c.*407-339 BC) and Xeno-crates (d. *c.*314 BC), the *Academy of Athens, which Plato had founded, continued the logical and metaphysical studies of his final period, which had taken a strongly mathematical turn. His greatest pupil, however, was *Aristotle, who founded his own school (*see* Peri-patetics). Aristotelian philosophy, des-pite its obvious debts to Plato, was long to rank as the principal rival to Platon-ism (*see* Aristotelianism).

(2) Under *Arcesilaus (*c.*316-242 BC), the Academy adopted a sceptical approach to philosophy, regarding such a procedure as the method of Socrates in Plato's early aporetic dialogues (*see* Carneades; Scepticism). Its 200 years of

scepticism were never entirely forgotten. Thanks to Cicero's *Academica* and St. Augustine's *Contra Academicos*, the "Academic" picture of Plato as essentially an unaffirmative, undogmatic thinker was known to the medieval West. It enjoyed a modest revival during the Renaissance, as an alternative to the dominant Neoplatonic interpretation. Traces of it can still be found in the emphasis by some modern scholars on the tentative, self-critical character of Plato's thought.

(3) During and after the 1st century BC, following the return of Antiochus to dogmatic philosophy (*see* Antiochus of Ascalon), a number of Plato's doctrines —above all, that of immaterial substance —were revived and fused with Stoic, Aristotelian, and Neopythagorean teachings. The outcome was the Neoplatonism of Plotinus. Characteristic features of Platonism in the intervening three centuries, sometimes called 'Middle Platonism', are the concept of Ideas as "thoughts in the mind of God", the moral ideal of "assimilation to God", and an elaborate doctrine of demons as intermediaries between the divine and the human. This stage of Platonist thinking had its widest influence indirectly, through the theology of the Alexandrians, notably *Philo Judaeus, Clement, and *Origen. With Plotinus, Platonism found its greatest philosopher after Plato himself; and the Plotinian system was to remain the basis of subsequent Platonist philosophy. Absorbed by St. *Augustine, it found its way into the mainstream of medieval Western thought. But there were other 'Neoplatonic' systems, notably that of Iamblichus and his successors, and the luxuriant metaphysical speculations of *Proclus were to exert considerable influence on medieval thinkers through works fathered onto *Dionysius the pseudo-Areopagite. The closure of the Academy by Justinian in 529 AD signalled the end of philosophical speculation in the ancient world, though scholarly work on Platonic and other philosophical subjects continued, not-

ably at Alexandria (*see* Alexandrian School).

(4) In the Middle Ages, the old Greco-Roman world found itself divided into three cultural areas: Arab, Byzantine, and the Latin West. The Arabs had translations of some Platonic dialogues (*Republic*, *Laws*, *Timaeus*) and of some Neoplatonic writings. But their interest was primarily in the sciences, genuine and occult. Here Platonism had nothing to rival the work of Aristotle, who first acquired his title "the philosopher" in the Arabic world. In Byzantium, Platonism survived the closure of the Academy, embedded as it was in the works of the Church Fathers. Plato's dialogues remained in the literary school curriculum. Active Platonist speculation resumed in the school of Michael Psellus (c.1018-79), author of a work *On the Operation of Demons*. A 15th-century dispute on the merits of Plato versus those of Aristotle moved to Italy, where it long continued.

Philosophy in the medieval West had Platonist beginnings. Almost all its sources were works of Platonist character: Chalcidius' translation of and commentary on the *Timaeus*, Macrobius' commentary on Cicero's *Somnium Scipionis*, Boethius' *Consolatio*, writings by Apuleius, and, more importantly, works by St. Augustine. (Aristotle was known simply through the *Vetus Organon*, which comprised the translations by Boethius of the *Categories* and the *De Interpretatione*, along with Porphyry's *Isagoge* or *Introduction*). In the 9th century, the ranks of Platonist works swelled with the translated works of Dionysius the pseudo-Areopagite, under the inspiration of John Scotus *Erigena. Further translations of Plato and Proclus appeared in the 12th and 13th centuries. But their influence was now nothing to that of the newly translated *Corpus Aristotelicum*. The systematic order and organization of Aristotle's works, with their developed terminology and methods of argument, suited them ideally to the scholastic aim of transforming Christian theology and the other disciplines into coherent systems arranged by topics. Aristotle's impact was overwhelming, with the result that the Platonist elements in some scholastic philosophies—and still more in the Augustinianism of popular and mystical theology—are easily overlooked.

(5) Reaction against scholasticism, by humanists from Petrarch onwards, took the form of praising Plato at the expense of Aristotle. A philological concern with the ancient texts, characteristic of *humanism, is what most distinguishes Renaissance from earlier Platonism. Translations of Plato, Plotinus, and Hermes Trismegistus into fluent Latin were published by Marsilio Ficino (1433-99), and the study of Greek revived in Western Europe. The characteristics of Renaissance Platonism emerge clearly when Ficino's philosophy is contrasted with that of his older contemporary Nicholas of Cusa (1401-64). For all its remarkable intimations of later cosmography, Nicholas of Cusa's thought was clearly a product of the medieval tradition, influenced preponderantly by Dionysius the pseudo-Areopagite. Ficino, ensconced in his Florentine Academy, was consciously reviving the splendours of antiquity, and continuing the "pious philosophy" of Plotinus, Plato, and their predecessors. He combined a recognizably Plotinian hierarchy of Being with a new emphasis on the immortality of the soul and a new ideal of spiritual love in which Platonic "eros" was fused with Augustinian "charity". His younger contemporary Giovanni *Pico della Mirandola (1463-94) was still more eclectic.

As "perennial philosophy" with a pedigree stretching back to Orpheus and Zoroaster (the occult, fantastic elements in the tradition being taken very seriously indeed), Renaissance Platonism flourished all through the 16th century, alongside Aristotelian and scholastic philosophy. Thanks to humanists like John Colet (1466-1519), *Erasmus (1469-1536), St. John Fisher (1469-1535), and St. Thomas More (1478-

1535), it came early to England, where it also had its final flowering in the work of the 17th-century *Cambridge Platonists. Benjamin Whichcote (1609-83), Henry More (1614-87), Ralph Cudworth (1617-88), and others could expound an attractive combination of vitalism in natural science, contemplative inwardness and high moral feeling in ethics, and broad tolerant reasonableness in religion, opposed alike to the philosophies of Hobbes and Descartes, to empiricism and Calvinism, and, in short, to all the tendencies dominant in 17th-century thought.

The Cambridge Platonists were an anachronism. By the date of Cudworth's death in 1688, Platonism in its Renaissance form had become untenable. The rise of modern science and scientific method had undermined the old Platonist and Aristotelian cosmologies; at the same time, a growing awareness, originally fostered by Protestant writers, of the historic Plato's distance from Plotinus and other luminaries of the "perennial philosophy", invalidated the whole Neoplatonic interpretation. (The view, now orthodox, that Plato himself had been neither a Neoplatonist nor a sceptic, and that he had indeed had positive doctrines that were not those of Plotinus, became standard in the 18th century. The first major philosopher to profess it was *Leibniz.) But without some Neoplatonic interpretation, Platonism was no longer a serious possibility as a philosophical creed; it could hardly base itself on a fundamentalist attitude to the dialogues, which Plato had clearly not meant to be holy writ.

The demise, however, of professed Platonist philosophy did not mean the end of Plato's influence, which has continued to reflect the variousness of his work. The mathematical approach of *Kepler and *Galileo to natural science had its Platonic and Neoplatonic inspirations. Plato's poetic sense of an eternal world reflected in ours has profoundly affected some imaginative literature, for example, the poetry of Spenser and Shelley. The connection between Platonic and Christian theology has been long and intimate, especially among theologians who had a predilection for natural human reason, such as the Cambridge Platonists or 19th-century Broad Church Anglicans.

In philosophy, Plato's influence has been yet more pervasive and hence hard to summarize. Almost every principle or ploy with affinities to something in the dialogues can be called 'Platonic'. Logicians who postulate the self-subsistent reality of universals or mathematicals are open to (and often happily acquiesce in) a charge of Platonism; politically, Plato has been seen, rightly or wrongly, as the patron of both revolutionary and traditional authoritarianism; and so forth. His influence has been more conspicuous in some places (for example, Whitehead's cosmology) than in others, but the truth is that every philosopher in the Western tradition has been exposed, directly or indirectly, to Plato's thought. It has always been, and will doubtless continue to be, a force to inspire philosophical discourse as well as aesthetic sensibility and religious awareness.

platonism. See mathematics, philosophy of.

plenitude, principle of. A phrase coined by A.O. *Lovejoy to describe the notion that all possibilites are realized in the world. The entire created Universe is conceived of as a continuum in which there are no gaps, no dislocations ("Nature makes no leaps"), and no unrealized potentialities. Compare chain of being.

plenum. Space totally filled with matter; the opposite of a vacuum. The concept featured in a number of cosmologies from the Stoics (see Stoicism) to *Descartes.

pleonotetic logic. See plurative logic.

Plotinus (c.205-70 AD). Neoplatonist philosopher. Born in Egypt, Plotinus studied at Alexandria. From 245 to 268, he taught at Rome. His writings, produced between 253 and 270, covering every major branch of philosophy except politics, were posthumously edited by his disciple Porphyry into six "groups of nine", the Enneads. Tentative in formulation, composed in a language elliptical and often very obscure, they expound unsystematically a highly systematic philosophy.

Its central doctrine is that of the three hypostases or realities. In ascending order of unity, realness, and value, these are Soul, Nous (or Mind), and an ineffable first principle which Plotinus, following Plato, calls "the One" or "the Good". The doctrine serves three purposes: expounding what Plato had "really" meant, describing certain metaphysical entities, and correlating these with certain levels of consciousness. According to this correlation, Soul corresponds to discursive thought, Mind to intuitive thought, and the One to highest mystical awareness. Reality, for Plotinus, can be visualized as a set of increasingly fragmented reflections, proceeding from the One to Mind and then Soul, before fading out into sheer blank matter. Everything that exists derives ultimately from the One and is therefore good; in value, however, it cannot be compared with the One and its separate existence is, from this point of view, a regrettable "audacity". Soul derives from Mind, and Mind from the One, by a process (logical rather than chronological) of emanation and reflection, of procession and reversion. Pouring forth spontaneously and formlessly as light from the sun, an hypostasis acquires its form only by turning back and contemplating its source—"contemplation", for Plotinus as for Aristotle, being to receive the form of the object contemplated; it thus becomes an image, albeit imperfect, of its parent hypostasis, absorbing vitality from it, and hence able to generate its own spontaneous reflections.

Mind, as the fragmented image of the One with its total Unity, is "thought-thinking-itself", a "unity-in-diversity" of intuition and all its objects, in which every idea is present in every other.

Soul, however, can only contemplate its objects in succession; it has to move from one to another, and its movement produces time, space, and the material world; all physical properties, even magnitude, are simply projections of Soul on undifferentiated matter. As the transcendent principle here of intelligent organization, Soul generates a quasi-hypostasis, Nature, or the immanent principle of life and growth. Nature, too, "contemplates"; but its contemplation is "dreamlike", absorbing little vitality from above; and its products are too feeble to generate any further reflections on the utter negativity of matter. Individual souls are manifestations of cosmic Soul, concentrations of it on particular bits of the physical world. Human beings are microcosms, active as we are on the levels of Nature, Soul, and transcendent Mind; what we become depends on the level to which we direct our consciousness. Our goal is to transcend ourselves, to return as far as possible to the One, through contemplation.

pluralism. The view that the world contains many kinds of existent, which in their uniqueness cannot be reduced to just one (*monism) or two (*dualism). It is usual to distinguish substantival pluralism (the doctrine that there are many substances) from attributive pluralism (the doctrine that there are many *kinds* of attribute). *Leibniz was a substantival pluralist, but, since Leibnizian monads were all of one kind (that is, souls), he was, in the attributive sense, a monist. The doctrine of *logical atomism as developed by *Russell is perhaps the most thoroughgoing pluralism in the history of philosophy.

plurality of forms. A doctrine that held that bodies possessed a number of forms —of plants, of elements, etc., the form of light being the highest of these and responsible for generating all the rest. It is associated with the writings of *Grosseteste and occurs in Augustinian philosophical circles, often in conjunction with the theory of *hylomorphism.

plurative logic. The little known field of the logic of majorities, also called pleonotetic logic: if, for instance, 'Most *A*s are *B*s' and 'Most *A*s are *C*s', then necessarily 'Some *B* is *C*'. It was Sir William *Hamilton who first argued that 'most' is a *quantifier on all fours with 'all', 'some', and 'no'.

pneuma. (Greek for: breath of life.) In Stoic and Epicurean philosophy, the fiery creative energy that is the vital force in man. Hence, in the New Testament, the pneuma is the spirit of man, contrasted with the *psyche, or soul.

pneumatology (*or* **pneumatics**). In the 17th and 18th centuries, a branch of metaphysics dealing with the theory and science of spiritual beings, which included God, the angels, and the human soul. During the 18th century the term was increasingly used to denote only the last of these, but there is also a current sense of pneumatology that applies only to the hierarchy of non-human spiritual beings.

Poincaré, Jules Henri (1854-1912). Mathematician, philosopher, and engineer. Poincaré is often labelled a conventionalist, because he argued that the fundamental axioms of different geometrical systems express neither a priori necessities nor contingent truths, and because he also detected important definitional elements in physics. But we must remember that Poincaré never doubted the existence of a universal natural order, which it is the business of science to uncover. In mathematical philosophy he was an intuitionist (*see* intuitionism), attacking in his later years the *logicism of *Russell and Peano.

polar concepts. Opposites such as immediacy and mediation, unity and plurality, ideal and real. The 'principle of polarity' advanced by M. R. Cohen states that members of such pairs are intelligible only in terms of contrast with each other.

political philosophy. What is in fact presented and discussed under this label often is not, and is still more rarely shown to be, a branch of philosophy as a non-normative conceptual enquiry. A course in political philosophy usually takes as its subject matter general justifications for the state and for either political institutions, and for particular actual and imagined ideal forms of these: it all tends to be the abstract politics of quarterlies rather than the concrete politics of the dailies. Besides the state, such other institutions as property, the family, the legal system, government and public administration, international relations, education, class structure, religion, and individual rights, duties, and obligations are discussed. In this environment questions of the sort that are elsewhere rated philosophical are few and somewhat far between.

Plato's *Republic* is the first surviving attempt to deal with these problems, and is still a standard text. The just state, in which everyone and everything fulfils its appropriate function, represents an ideal attainable, Plato suggests, only if kings study philosophy or philosophers become kings (see philosopher kings). ('Philosopher' is here implicitly defined as one who knows the Forms or Ideas and is thus able to know what justice, goodness, etc., really require.) This utopian vision was criticized by Plato's pupil Aristotle in his *Politics*, which proceeds to present a piecemeal and down-to-earth evaluation of contemporary constitutions and institutions. Nature herself, Aristotle insisted, has established the authority of rulers over ruled just as she has set masters over slaves, husbands over wives, and fathers over children. The best form of the state in practice must be a mixed and balanced constitution. These classic works of political philosophy set the terms of the subject for such Roman contributors as Cicero and Polybius.

Political philosophers of the Christian era, particularly St. *Augustine and St. Thomas *Aquinas, considered the place of the state and politics within a Chris-

tian view of history and the cosmos. The exciting issues were the contrast between the temporal political order and the hereafter, the divine right of kings to rule, and the relative jurisdictions of secular and religious authorities. These issues dominated the works of political philosophers between the late Roman Empire and the Renaissance.

Niccolò Machiavelli's influential works *Discorsi* (completed by 1517) and *Il Principe* (1512-13) recommend the virtues of the Roman republic: unity, discipline, glory, and freedom deriving from an institutional balance between nobility and common people. Christianity, Machiavelli argued, had fostered an other-worldly attitude foreign to classical ideals of citizenship. Machiavelli's attempt at a detached political science and his justification of the economical use of violence to achieve political ends distinguish his work from that of medieval theorists.

The problem of the individual and his rights is characteristic of modern political philosophy and divides it from the earlier classical and Christian traditions, which gave primacy to the requirements of the good state and its advantages for the community at large. It is in this new context that ideas of a social contract have appeal. But talk about a social contract has been employed by many very different thinkers for very different purposes, for instance, by *Hobbes, *Locke, and *Rousseau. The original notion of a social contract is that the members (or the ancestors of the members) of a political society somehow transfer specified rights to the sovereign authority so that other rights, which they retain, may be protected or so that other advantages may be gained. Abuse of power by the state, the question of just rebellion, and the extent of the individual's obligation to obey the state become central issues. Our participation in existing states, it is sometimes argued, constitutes tacit consent to an informal and unwritten social contract, so our obligations arise as if we had undertaken the contract explicitly. In some 20th-century works of political philosophy, such as John Rawls's influential *A Theory of Justice* (1972), the idea of a social contract as the basis of (social) justice has been revived.

Philosophical reactions against theories of the individual and his rights have taken historical, idealist, and Marxist forms. In the writings of Edmund *Burke, for example, custom and tradition within a particular political community take precedence in politics over any doctrine of what is natural or universal for man. He argues that theorizing cannot adequately take account of the infinite subtlety of social relationships and institutions as they have developed historically, and any attempt to introduce political change on such an allegedly rational basis will result in disaster. Similar views have been expressed since the 1960s in works of political philosophy by Michael Oakeshott.

Idealist philosophers take society to be more real and more fundamental than the individual: it simply makes no sense to talk to the individual as if he were somehow apart from political relationships and could bring them into existence at will. Idealists thus take social and political concepts as their starting point and reject what they see as unsound analytical methods of over-simplification and false abstraction. G. W. F. *Hegel in his *Philosophie des Rechts* (second edition, 1833) and T. H. *Green in his *Lectures on the Principles of Political Obligation* (published in Green's collected works 1885-8) have constructed political philosophies making the state and its claims in every way primary.

The views of *Marx and *Engels that history has hitherto consisted of class struggles, and that the state is essentially an instrument for the oppression of one class by another, have led to another sharply different philosophy of politics. In the Marxist view the proletarian revolution will put an end to class oppression and hence the state as we know it. The role of the party before and after the revolution, transitional insti-

tutions between contemporary and future communist societies, and the nature of communist society itself are some of the problems considered somewhat peremptorily by V I. *Lenin, Rosa Luxemburg, and Georg Lukács.

In the liberal tradition, philosophers such as J. S. *Mill have argued for the need to respect the rights of individuals in striking a balance between even the democratic state and its constituents. His *On Liberty* (1859) is the classic account.

While not denying the individual his rights, the political philosophy of elitism, propounded by Gaetano Mosca, Vilfredo Pareto, and Robert Michels, seeks to demonstrate that the nature of human social life is such that true democracy is impossible and that political decisions must always be in the hands of an elite. If we fail to recognize this truth and take the democratic ideal to an extreme, we put ourselves in peril of anarchy—no government at all.

Anarchism, as advocated, for example, by Mikhail Bakunin, takes the individual as sovereign and all authority as unjustified repression of his will. For anarchists the political problem of reconciling the individual and common interests by means of institutions and the threat of force is simply insoluble, and attempts to solve it are an outrage.

Linguistic philosophy has left its mark on contemporary political philosophers who have considered the definition and use of such characteristic political terms as 'freedom' or 'liberty', 'authority', 'power', 'rights', 'obligation', 'consent', 'democracy', and 'justice'. Sir Isaiah Berlin's *Four Essays on Liberty* (1969) and Steven Lukes's *Power* (1975) are two works of modern analytical political philosophy.

In recent years traditional non-linguistic political philosophy has been on the defensive against criticism that political science has in some way superseded it. Political science is said to be descriptive, that is, concerned with facts. Political philosophy is said to be normative, that is, concerned with values; about these individuals will always differ, much as they differ on matters of taste or personal preference. What, curiously, seems not to have been much said or pressed is that traditional political philosophy is remarkably unlike the disciplines that are usually taken to be other branches of philosophical enquiry.

polyadic. In logic, denoting a *predicate that requires the addition of more than one singular *term in order to make a well-formed sentence. '...hits...' and '...is between ... ...' are polyadic (or *n*-place). The former is two-place (or *dyadic), the latter three-place.

pons asinorum. (Latin for: bridge of asses.) **1.** (in mathematics) A humorous nickname for the fifth proposition of the first book in *Euclid, so-called on account of the difficulty experienced by the less intelligent in "getting over it". **2.** (in traditional logic) A method by which dull-witted would-be logicians can find their way confidently from the *major or *minor to the middle term of a *syllogism and work out their relations. Its formal title is '*inventio medii*' and its discovery is attributed to a 15th-century rector of Paris University, Peter Tartaretus.

Popper, Sir Karl Raimund (1902-). Philosopher of natural and social science who studied and taught in his native Vienna until the threat of Nazi occupation sent him abroad. He lectured in New Zealand and later in London before becoming Professor of Logic and Scientific Method at the London School of Economics (1949-69). He was knighted in 1965. Main philosophical works: *Logik der Forschung* (1935), translated as *The Logic of Scientific Discovery* (1959), *The Open Society and its Enemies* (1945), *The Poverty of Historicism* (1957), *Conjectures and Refutations* (1963), *Objective Knowledge* (1972).

Popper's first major contribution to philosophy was his novel solution to the problem of the demarcation of science. According to the time-honoured view,

science, properly so-called, is distinguished by its inductive method (*see* induction)—by its characteristic use of observation and experiment, as opposed to purely logical analysis, to establish its results. The great difficulty was that no run of favourable observational data, however long and unbroken, is logically sufficient to establish the truth of an unrestricted generalization. This led immediately to the disquieting but apparently inescapable conclusion that science (or at least the important part of it that deals in such generalizations) simply had to live by faith in some kind of *uniformity of nature, hard to define satifactorily, and seemingly impossible to prove without circularity.

Popper accepted that unrestricted generalizations could not be verified. But, he pointed out, they could be *falsified*. (While no amount of observation of black crows verifies the statement 'All crows are black', one—properly authenticated—observation of a white crow falsifies it.) And falsifiability, for Popper, is the hallmark of science. Science, in other words, characteristically puts itself at risk, commits itself, by implication at least, as to what is, or would be, observed under specific circumstances; and hence its theories are always liable to be discarded or modified if the observations fail to agree with its expectations. It follows that no scientific theory is ever conclusively verified, no matter how many tests it has survived. And this conclusion, Popper points out, accords very well with the history of science: even something as well attested and widely accepted as Newtonian physics has not proved permanently immune from revision.

Science can, of course, improve its theories, by transforming them into, or replacing them by, new theories, that pass all the tests that its earlier ones passed, and more as well. But it can never say finally, "Here at last is The Truth about Nature" (though the concept of truth still has an important role in stimulating and directing its efforts). When we speak of our scientific knowledge all we can mean is those bodies of theories that, thus far in history, have survived sustained and systematic attempts at falsification.

In the field of social and political philosophy, Popper is best known for his critique of historicism, particularly as exemplified by Plato, Hegel, and Marx. This is the doctrine that there are laws or principles of historical development, mastery of which would enable us to predict the future course of human history, much as the astronomer predicts eclipses. In Popper's view predictions are only possible for systems that are "well-isolated, stationary and recurrent" (*Conjectures and Refutations*, 1974 edition, p. 339) and this does not, and could not, hold of human society, where among the major factors determining development are our own decisions about how to respond to our situation. Thus, for example, the technology that has become such a powerful influence on contemporary society could not even in principle have been predicted a century ago. For Popper the choice and responsibility have to remain with individuals; we can never have sufficient grounds for saying, "Society must develop thus, whether its members want it so or not."

For Popper, in practical as in theoretical matters, we can never be certain we have the right answers. Hence his case for the widest possible freedom to criticize and experiment, for democracy as he understands it is a system under which rulers, whose attempted solutions to a society's problems no longer appear the most promising, can be replaced without violence. For him, the crucial question is not who should wield power, but how the misuse of power, in the interests of social or political dogma, as well as personal advantage, is to be prevented.

Porphyry (*c*.232-305 AD). Biblical critic, philosopher, and disciple and editor of *Plotinus. Apart from the *Life of Plotinus* and arrangement of his books, Porphyry's 77 works included the aphor-

istic metaphysical *Launching-points to the realm of Mind*, a moral address *To Marcella* his wife, the vegetarian *Abstention from Meat*, fifteen books *Against the Christians* (now lost), and various technical and philological works, as well as commentaries on Plato, Plotinus, Aristotle, and Theophrastus. The most notable of these commentaries was the highly influential *Introduction* (*Isagoge*) to Aristotle's *Categories*, subsequently translated into Latin by *Boethius. A polymath rather than an original philosopher, Porphyry exercised his greatest influence as a popularizer of Plotinus' thought in the Latin West.

Port Royal. Cistercian abbey, home of the Jansenist community in 17th-century France. The name was given to a system of logic developed by *Arnauld, Nicole, and *Pascal, which emphasized the need for careful definition of terms and concepts and laid the foundations of modern linguistic analysis. The first two produced the influential book *L'Art de Penser* (1662), usually known as the *Port Royal Logic*.

Posidonius of Apamea (*c*.135-51 BC). Stoic philosopher, historian, polymath. His works survive in fragments. The last major contributor to Stoic thinking, Posidonius combined philosophical with scientific interests more thoroughly than anyone since Theophrastus, producing important works on geometry, meteorology, geography, and history. His philosophy was *Stoicism generously laced with Platonic, Aristotelian, and other doctrines, the principal motive for such eclecticism being a desire to arrive at causes. Thus his best documented innovation was to reject as an inadequate explanation of the facts Chrysippus' view that our 'irrational' passions are essentially misjudgments by our reason, and to explain them, on an adaptation of Plato's tripartite psychology, as the natural function of nonrational forces in the soul. His philosophy of Nature stressed the unity of the Universe and the sympathy of its parts. Posidonius' influence on subsequent philosophy, while doubtless considerable, is unclear; it used to be overestimated and seen as the start of *Neoplatonism.

positive freedom, concept of. *See* liberty; Spinoza.

positivism. The name given to the philosophical position primarily developed by *Saint-Simon, and more explicitly and influentially by Auguste *Comte, in 19th-century France. Its ancestry can, however, be traced back at least as far as Francis *Bacon and the British empiricist school of the 17th and 18th centuries. The term 'positive' has here the sense of that which is given or laid down, that which has to be accepted as we find it and is not further explicable; the word is intended to convey a warning against the attempts of theology and metaphysics to go beyond the world given to observation in order to enquire into first causes and ultimate ends. All genuine human knowledge is contained within the boundaries of science, that is the systematic study of phenomena and the explication of the laws embodied therein. Philosophy may still perform a useful function in explaining the scope and methods of science, pointing out the more general principles underlying specific scientific findings, and exploring the implications of science for human life. But it must abandon the claim to have any means of attaining knowledge not available to science. Whatever questions cannot be answered by scientific methods we must be content to leave permanently unanswered.

Positivism in the 19th century was characterized by optimism about the benefits that the extension of scientific method could bring to humanity. Comte himself claimed to have pioneered a positive sociology; and it was hoped that the systematic study of human nature and human needs would provide, for the first time in history, a truly scientific basis for the reorganization of society. 'Science whence comes prediction; prediction whence comes action' summarized Comte's programme. He even tried to develop positivism into a religion or religion-substitute, and in several countries Positivist Societies were formed, in which worship of Humanity replaced the worship of God.

In Britain, Jeremy *Bentham, James *Mill and John Stuart *Mill, though they avoided the more extravagant claims of Comte, adopted essentially the positivistic standpoint; they shared the hostility to theology and metaphysics, the respect for science as the only source of genuine knowledge, and the programme of extending scientific method to the study of, and for the benefit of, all aspects of human life. There was, however, room for disagreement about the nature of science. J. S. Mill, in particular, rejected, from a more radically empirical standpoint, Comte's confidence in the ability of science to formulate laws based on observation, that were completely certain and immune from the danger of refutation by further experiment. Evolutionary theory was frequently linked with positivism, notably in the work of Herbert *Spencer, so that a major task of philosophy became the generalized study of the all-embracing evolutionary process.

The positivist programme has undoubtedly a perennial appeal as something hard-headed and common-sensical. But it must be remembered that the questions of the essential nature of science, and whether all our knowledge, properly so-called, could ever in principle be reduced to science, untainted by theology or metaphysics, are still matters of unresolved debate. *See also* empiricism; law, philosophy of; logical positivism; Popper.

possibility. *See* impossibility.

post hoc ergo propter hoc. (Latin for: after this therefore on account of this.) It is perhaps better Englished as 'the after-so-because fallacy'. For example, because food prices in Britain rose sharply after British entry into the European Economic Community it does not follow that entry was the or even a cause of the rise.

postulate. *See* axiom.

potentiality. *See* actuality and potentiality.

pour soi. *See* Sartre.

power set. The set of all subsets of a given set. It is called 'power set' because if a set A has n members, then the power set of A (symbolically $P(A)$) has 2^n members. For example, if $A = \{1, 2, 3\}$, then $P(A) = \{\emptyset, \{1\}, \{2\}, \{3\}, \{1,2\}, \{1,3\}\{2,3\}, A\}$

praedicabilia. Latin for: *predicables.

praedicamenta. (Latin for: *predicaments.) *See* categories.

pragmaticism. A term coined by C.S. *Peirce in 1905 to denote his own particular variety of *pragmatism, after the latter term had been appropriated and its scope widened by other philosophers.

pragmatics. One of the three traditional divisions of *semiotics. Pragmatics studies the purposes, effects, and implications of the actual use by a speaker of meaningful piece of language. *See also* speech act.

pragmatism. A label for a doctrine about meaning first made a philosophical term in 1878 by C. S. *Peirce. "Consider what effects, which might conceivably have practical bearings, we conceive the object of our conception to have. Then our conception of these effects is the whole of our conception of the object." The term was soon borrowed by William *James, F. C. S. *Schiller, and John *Dewey, who all in their different ways made pragmatism a theory of truth. Thus in his *Pragmatism* James said, "Ideas become true just so far as they help us to get into satisfactory relations with other parts of our experience." Peirce reacted by coining the substitute 'pragmaticism', a word too ugly to be purloined. *Russell assailed the pragmatist notion of truth as obscurantist. *See also* instrumentalism.

precognition. In *parapsychology, a word now having a particular reference to that kind of *extrasensory perception (ESP) in which guesses, dreams, hunches, etc., precede their fulfilments. One philosophical problem is that the phenomena are seen as themselves being, or warranting, foreknowledge; which is taken either to make the future events inevitable or to show that they always must have been (*see* freewill and determinism; inevitability; predestination; seafight). The other philosophical issue is that precognitive ESP is often construed as involving backwards causation: perhaps because it is thought of on the model of perception, the 'fulfilment' is taken to be a causally necessary condition of the 'anticipation' (*see* causal theory of perception). C. D. *Broad and others have argued that on this definition the concept must become incoherent: causes bring about their effects and what has already happened cannot later either be made to happen or made not to have happened.

predestination. The doctrine that everything that happens, including particularly the making of all choices, has been fixed in advance by God: "The first dawn of creation wrote what the last day of reckoning shall read." *See* creation; freewill and determinism; inevitability; predictability; theism.

predicables (*or* **praedicabilia**). A confused and confusing doctrine of the sorts of things that can be predicated of subjects. It originated with Aristotle and was prominent among the scholastics. Aristotle distinguished four predicables: (1) the definition or essence; (2) properties which though not essential nevertheless belong to the subject alone; (3) the genus; and (4) accidents that may possibly belong or not belong to the subject. Thus a circle is (1) a plane curve every point of which is equidistant from a given point; (2) such that the angle in the segment subtending a diameter is a right angle; (3) a plane curve; and (4) something that may have a diameter of four inches. *Porphyry, to whom, rather than to Aristotle, we owe the traditional doctrine, listed five predicables—genus, species, differentia, proprium, and accident—and his subject is an individual qua individual rather than an individual of a particular sort.

predicaments. An obsolescent synonym for 'categories', in the Aristotelian sense. *See* categories.

predicate. 1. (in scholastic and Aristotelian logic) The *term appearing in predicate position in a subject-predicate sentence; for example, 'man' in 'Socrates is a man'. It is that which is affirmed or denied of the subject. The same term may be the predicate of one sentence and the subject of another; for example, 'man' is the subject of 'Man is an animal'.
2. (in predicate calculus or predicate logic) An expression that, when attached to a singular term, gives an indicative sentence expressing a proposition about the object denoted by the singular term. For example, '…is tall' in 'Hugh is tall'. Sometimes the term 'predicate' is restricted to expressions that require the addition of just one singular term in order to yield a sentence. In this case 'predicate' stands in contrast to '*relational expression*'. Often, however, the use of 'predicate' is extended to cover any expression that may be obtained by omitting *one or more* singular terms from a sentence, in which case a distinction is drawn between *monadic*, or one-place predicates, and *polyadic*, or *n*-place predicates. For example, omitting 'David' and 'the king' from 'David killed the king' leaves the two-place predicate '…killed…'. These expressions are such that when their gaps are filled by singular terms, indicative sentences are formed; for example, 'The Pope is tall' and 'Brutus killed Caesar'. For this reason predicates are also sometimes called *sentential functions*—functions from singular terms to sentences (*see* function). In symbolizing predicates the gaps are marked by variables 'x', 'y', …, a distinct variable for each gap created by removal of a distinct term; the words 'is tall', 'killed', etc., are represented by upper case letters, say 'T' and 'K' respectively. The symbolic

representation of '…is tall' is then Tx and that of '…killed…' is Kxy. If 'h' abbreviates 'Hugh' the sentence formed by filling the gap in '… is tall' by 'Hugh' is then represented by Th.

predicate calculus. *See* calculus.

predication. The attribution of a *property to a subject.

predicative. *See* attributive.

predictability. The capability of being foretold. It means only and exactly what it says, and must therefore be distinguished from both *predestination and causal determinism (*see* freewill and determinism). Future happenings, and in particular future human actions, might be in practice predictable without our being required from this to infer either that their occurrence is ensured by the Creator, or that there are sufficient antecedent physical causes making them inevitable. *See* creation; inevitability.

prediction paradox. The paradox of propositions that are falsified by the utterance of the prediction they announce. The stock example is that of the unexpected examination: a schoolmaster announces that a surprise examination will be held within the next five days; and by definition, a 'surprise examination' here is one the time of which cannot be known until the morning of the day it is held. The paradox is that it seems that such an event can never take place, as the prediction is falsified by the definition when it is taken in conjunction with the announcement as formulated. If the examination were to be left until the fifth day, then clearly there would be no surprise. Next, that day having been ruled out, a parallel argument also rules out the fourth day; and then the third, the second, and the first.

pre-established harmony. *See* clocks, image of the two; Leibniz.

prejudice. Any belief, whether correct or incorrect, held without proper consideration of, or sometimes in defiance of, the evidence. A distinction must be made between this meaning and its use as a term of abuse for all strongly held, erroneous, or alien convictions. Judges instructing juries to consider carefully, and without prejudice, all and only the materials presented in court are not asking them to refuse to bring in convinced and decisive verdicts.

premise (*or* **premiss**). In any argument, one of the statements from which another statement (the conclusion) is deduced or of which the conclusion is presented as a consequence. These statements, from which the conclusion is claimed to follow, are the suppositions on which the conclusion rests.

prenex normal form. *See* normal form.

prescriptive definition. *See* definition.

prescriptivism. The view that the primary function of moral judgment is to prescribe courses of action. R. M. *Hare, who coined the term, holds that if a statement is prescriptive then (a) anyone who sincerely accepts it, and can act upon it, does so act, and (b) it cannot be entailed by a purely descriptive statement. *Compare* descriptivism.

Presocratics. All the Greek speculative thinkers about Nature as a whole before *Socrates. No complete work has survived, so their views have to be reconstructed as best may be from quoted fragments and other references in later writers. Much Presocratic material is not in any very strict sense philosophical. However, *Parmenides was without question a major philosophical meta-physician, while the paradoxes of *Zeno of Elea (*see* Zeno's paradoxes) constitute a perennially fascinating contribution of philosophical genius. *See also* Alcmaeon; Anaxagoras; Anaximander; Democritus; Diogenes of Apollonia; Empedocles; Eurytus; Heraclitus; Leucippus; Melissus; metaphysics; Philolaus; Pythagoras; Thales; Xenophanes.

presupposition. An assumption that involves either a necessary or a contingent truth. If p is logically presupposed by q then it is a necessary truth that to deny the assumption p while asserting q would be a contradiction. Presuppositions that do not satisfy this requirement involve a contingent truth.

Price, Richard (1723-91). A Welsh dissenting minister who in his *Review of the Principal Questions and Difficulties in Morals* (1758) took polite and friendly issue with the unbelieving *Hume. This work develops a deontological theory, seeing the concepts of right and obligation as fundamental to ethics, objective rather than humanly projected, and even in some sense a priori (*see* deontology). An address by Dr. Price was the occasion which provoked Burke's *Reflections on the Revolution in France* (1790), while other works made him one of the main targets for the *First Essay* of *Malthus.

Price, Henry Habberley (1899-). English philosopher, whose major work *Perception* (1932) presents a theory of knowledge of the external world. He agrees with *Russell in his belief that what we directly know are *sense data, but rejects both the causal and representative theories of *perception. Although he is often mistaken as a phenomenalist, Price rejects *phenomenalism (the view that material things are just sense data, or possibilities of sense data), holding that material things have causal powers beyond their abilities to cause sense impressions in us.

prima facie obligations. The label popularized by Sir David Ross for those authentic moral claims that may on occasion be overridden by other and stronger moral claims. Your *prima facie* (Latin for: on first appearance) obligation not to hurt someone might well be overridden by a stronger moral claim to tell him something which though painful he should know.

primary *and* **secondary qualities.** A distinction made first by *Democritus, revived by *Galileo, accepted by *Descartes and *Newton, and finding its classical formulation in *Locke's *Essay*. Primary qualities are those which things do actually have, secondary are only powers to produce experiences in us. Locke lists as primary "solidity, extension, figure [that is, shape], motion or rest, and number", while sounds, tastes, colours, and smells are all secondary. This division corresponds well with those between measurable and non-measurable characteristics, and those of which classical mechanics could and could not take account. *Berkeley argued that all sensible qualities, not only those which his predecessors had relegated as secondary, must be equally in the mind. *Hume took Newton's Lockean account of colour as a model, arguing that both values and the necessities of causes are in similar ways projections of our own reactions out onto a world which is iself value-free and without causal connections.

Prime Cause. See First Cause.

Prime Mover. See First Mover.

principium individuationis. Latin for: principle of *individuation.

privacy. See private language; privileged access.

private language. A language the terms of which are defined to refer to the private sensations of the user, and whose meanings can therefore be known only to him. The questions surrounding this concept are suggested in Locke's *Essay Concerning Human Understanding* (III-(i)1-2, (ii)1-5). *Wittgenstein argued in the *Philosophical Investigations* that a man could not have a logically private language. The problem hinges on whether there could be genuine rules of use for such expressions, or whether whatever seems right to the user will be right. Wittgenstein's remarks leave room for disagreement as to whether he was presenting an argument, and if so quite what it is and what its significance is for the philosophy of mind. See also privileged access.

privatio boni. (Latin for: privation of good.) See privation.

privation. The belief that evil is essentially negative—the lack or absence of good (*privatio boni*). This doctrine, sometimes employed in an attempt to ease the theists' problem of evil, finds its ultimate inspiration in Plato's conception of the Form or Idea of the Good which is at the same time the Form of the Real (see Plato).

privileged access. The particular relationship we have to the contents of our own consciousness, but that none of us has to the contents of anybody else's.

probabilism. 1. The doctrine particularly associated with scepticism, to the effect that no definite knowledge can be attained: opinions and actions should therefore be guided by probability. 2. In ethics and especially in Roman Catholic *casuistry, the practice of adopting the advice of one particular respected authority in situations in which there is no obviously correct course of action and authorities conflict with each other.

probability theory. The mathematical theory of probability enables us to calculate the probability of some kind of event given the probability of others. For instance, we can calculate the probability of a double six on two tosses of a dice if each side has a one in six probability of coming up, or the probability of a bridge hand containing fewer than two court cards, if each card has an equal chance of being chosen. The arithmetic of such combinations, investigated in the 17th century by *Pascal and Fermat, has developed into a general theory of measures on sets, which correspond to possible values of a random variable (see randomness). Its most familiar axiomatic treatment is due to the Russian mathematician Kolmogorov (1903-).

Philosophically the problems arise when we consider the application of the mathematical calculus. What is meant by calling an event, or proposition, or theory, probable? What kind of fact is claimed when something is judged probable, and what evidence justifies this kind of claim? Part of the difficulty is that sometimes the judgment is made when we have evidence from the repetition of a large number of trials, as with testing a dice for bias by tossing it, but sometimes the judgment is derived from calculation on the basis of probabilities supposedly known a priori. Yet it is uncomfortable to claim that the notion is just ambiguous, although some philosophers have been driven to do so.

The *classical theory of probability* was that probability judgments describe sets of so-called equipossible alternatives. The initial judgment of equipossibility, in the hands of writers such as James Bernoulli and *Laplace, would be made through using the principle of *indifference. This is not satisfactory as an account of the meaning of 'probable', since 'equipossibility' disguises a judgment of equal probability. Nor does it suggest a very comprehensive way of coming to know probability judgments; for although some investigations may proceed by initially assigning equal probability to various events, not all do. For example, the probability of a male Englishman being between five and six feet tall is judged simply from the empirically given distribution of heights in the population.

Impressed by such examples, many philosophers follow a *long run frequency theory of probability*, according to which the probability of a thing G having a property F is simply the long run frequency of Fs among Gs, that is, the limit towards which the proportion of Fs tends. According to von Mises, this limits probability judgments to classes for which there is such a limit and which satisfy other constraints making them into collectives (see collective). It makes it impossible to attach such a judgment to an individual event (such as my having a car accident), since any individual will fall into many different classes, in which the property has different limiting frequencies. But there is something extravagant about making probability into such a highly theoretical notion, both hard to know about and of no

immediate relevance to short run confidence in events. More subtle frequency theories, such as that of Braithwaite, see the link between frequency and probability not as definitional, but in terms of the existence of rules telling us when a body of data entitles us to accept or reject a particular probability judgment.

One influential modern approach, pioneered by F. P. *Ramsey and Bruno de Finetti, is content to safeguard the links between frequency and probability by *Bernoulli's theorem, and sees probability judgments as simply subjective expressions of confidence, subject not to empirical constraints, but only to a requirement of coherence. This prevents assignments such that if you bet on them you would lose whatever happens. The approach removes the sense that probabilities are there to be discovered, and it protects the close link between probability and practice. Its main problem is that the coherence constraint applies to a particular person at a particular time, and therefore allows anyone to change his mind, forming the most outlandish judgments, in the face of any evidence. There would be nothing irrational, on this approach, in holding that the probability of rain some time next year in New York is only one in six.

The probability of theories has been treated in terms of a logical relation between the theory and a class of evidence. J. M. *Keynes and C. D. *Broad, followed by *Carnap, Kneale, and others, have attempted to define the essential logical relation, but the enterprise comes up against the problems of *confirmation theory: it also shares the problem bedevilling the classical theory, that without an a priori input of probability judgments no final assessments ensue. It should, in conclusion, be noticed that, in one very common use, to say 'probably p' is certainly not to say anything either about evidence or about relative frequency, but only to assert p, guardedly. See also science, philosophy of; statistics.

problematic. A term in Aristotelian logic used to indicate the *mode or modality of a proposition. A problematic proposition is one that asserts that something is possible, for example, 'It is possible that it will rain'.

Proclus (c.410-85 AD). Pagan Neoplatonist philosopher, head of the *Academy of Athens (see Neoplatonism). He was author of *Platonic Theology*, the conciser *Elements of Theology*, commentaries on Plato's *Timaeus, Republic, Parmenides, Alcibiades I*, and *Cratylus*, as well as various scientific and literary works. The last major synthesizer of ancient Greek philosophy, Proclus had considerable influence, largely through *Dionysius the pseudo-Areopagite, on medieval thinking and still more on that of the Renaissance.

proof. 1. (in non-formal contexts) A proof (or *demonstration*) of a proposition *C* is a valid argument from true premises with *C* as conclusion. 2. (in a *formal system) A proof of *C* in the system *S* is a sequence $P_1 \ldots P_n$ of wffs of *S* such that $P_n = C$ and each P_i, $1 \le i \le n$, is either an axiom of *S* or there are $j_1 \ldots j_m < i$ such that P_i follows from $P_{j1} \ldots P_{jm}$ according to some rule of *inference of *S*.

proof theory. The syntactic study of formal systems that proceeds by examining the structure of the proofs that can be constructed within them. A *proof in a *formal system is a symbolic structure that can be characterized by referring only to the *syntax of the system. The nature of the structure is determined by the axioms and/or rules of inference of the system (see axiom; inference, rule of). As such structures, proofs themselves become objects that can be studied by mathematical techniques. In particular, because proofs in formal systems are finite structures, they can be studied using relatively weak, that is number-theoretic, finitistic, or constructive methods. This is in marked contrast to the strong, that is, infinitistic and non-constructive methods required by *model

theory (the semantic study of formal systems via their interpretations). For this reason, proof theory is preferred by many logicians working in the foundations of mathematics.

proper names. A particular class of referring expressions, such as 'London' or 'Benjamin Franklin'. To philosophers they have seemed problematic because it is unclear exactly how they related to the things in the world that they name and because it has been disputed that they do have a meaning or connotation (see denotation). J. S. *Mill claimed that proper names denote but have no connotation. It is, after all, notorious that in rendering a passage of, say, German into English, it is a mistake to try to translate a proper name or to look it up in a dictionary. But a description such as 'the inventor of bifocals' refers to some one man iff he *is* the inventor of bifocals; the meaning of the expression, that is, determines its reference. So what determines to which thing the expression 'Benjamin Franklin' refers if it *has* no meaning? In answer, a view typified by *Frege and *Russell holds that the meaning of a proper name must be the description or cluster of descriptions that speakers associate with the name. But as *Kripke and others have pointed out, someone might conceivably have done none of the things we in fact associate with his name. A third view claims that the reference of a name is fixed at some time, ostensively or by description, and its reference is determined subsequently not by meaning but causally, by passing the name from speaker to speaker. *See also* sense and reference.

property. 1. A characteristic. The applicability of the term is sometimes limited in two ways (a) with reference to the *indiscernibility of identicals, and (b) with reference to non-relational characteristics. To understand (a) contrast 'belonging to the buttercup family', which is true of (the same flower) aquilegia or columbine with 'being referred to here by a name derived from the Latin for dove' (which will make a true sentence only when the flower is being called 'columbine'). The latter is therefore not a property in this restricted sense. The point about (b) is that relational characteristics are sometimes discounted; for example, 'being taller' does not qualify, but 'being green' does. *See also* proprium. 2. Whatever can be thought or claimed to be owned, including immaterial things like copyright. Ownership includes the right to 'alienate' or dispose of property, but not necessarily its unrestricted use, as is the case with a weapon. What is property, and whose property it is, is a matter of law and ultimately, perhaps, of morals, not of brute natural fact.

The Church Fathers, seeking the origin, and justification, of property thought that is was instituted after the Fall as a result of the sin of covetousness. *Locke held that men have a natural right to property. *Hume justified property rights as making for social utility and harmony. In the 19th century the French socialist, Pierre-Joseph Proudhon (1809-65) equated property, in a famous slogan, with theft. *Marx, partly on the basis of a conjunction of his own economic theories with the traditional "labour theory of value" (according to which men had been thought entitled to the full produce of their labour), argued for the public ownership of the means of production, distribution, and exchange, and for the eventual distribution of all consumer goods according to the principle of need.

proposition. In philosophy, but not in business or sexual activity, a proposition is whatever can be asserted, denied, contended, maintained, assumed, supposed, implied, or presupposed. In other words, it is that which is expressed by a typical indicative sentence. The same proposition may be expressed by different sentences in the same language or by sentences of different langages; for example, 'I love you', 'You are loved by me', and 'Je t'adore' express the same proposition. The proposition that such and such is the case is symbolized as 'the proposition p', or simply 'p', and the argument that if both this and that then the other is correspondingly abbreviated as 'If both p and q then r'. The term 'proposition' with its more impersonal and logical flavour has completely replaced the older less impersonal and more psychological 'judgment'.

Starting from this account some logicians have raised questions about the ontological status of propositions, preferring to talk only of sentences and so to relate logical relations to a given language: in this treatment, the symbols 'p', 'q', 'r', etc., which occur in logical formulae are used as abbreviations of sentences, not propositions. Others have urged that some contentions of the same *grammatical form are not, from a logical point of view, truly propositions. In particular, it has been maintained that claims that something is wrong, and ought not to be done, though grammatically indicative, are logically imperative or even ejaculatory, and hence do not really express propositions. *See also* imperative.

propositional calculus. *See* calculus.

propositional function. A technical term due to *Russell, used to denote that for which a *predicate of predicate logic stands. An n-place predicate, when complemented by n singular terms, yields a sentence that expresses a *proposition about the objects denoted by those terms. The n-place propositional function for which the predicate stands is such that when applied to n objects, the result is a proposition concerning those objects. Just as two different sentences may express the same proposition, two different predicates may stand for the same propositional function.

Those who cast doubt on the status of propositions are equally dubious about propositional functions. When a sentence such as 'Aristotle was bald' is represented symbolically by 'Ba', where 'a' abbreviates 'Aristotle', it is not always clear whether 'B' abbreviates the particular predicate '…was bald' or whether 'B' stands for the general propositional function denoted by both '...was bald' and '...had very little hair on his head'.

proprium. (Latin for: a possession *or* characteristic.) **1.** (in medieval Aristotelianism) A characteristic peculiar to and dependent upon the *essence of a species, but not a necessary part of its essence. Aristotle contrasted, in a way that is not entirely clear, *proprium* with *accident. For instance, a *proprium* of dogs is tail-wagging, but the essential definition of a dog is not 'a tail-wagging animal'. **2.** *See* property.

Protagoras of Abdera (*c.*485–*c.*420 BC). Philosophically one of the most interesting of the Greek *sophists. Plato's early dialogue *Protagoras*, which handles the question of whether virtue can be taught, is probably an accurate representation of the sophist's views on the subject. In the dialogue Socrates is shown as expressing admiration for Protagoras' wisdom; Plato, while dissenting from Protagoras' scepticism, always treats his arguments with respect. Protagoras' most famous maxim, "Man is the measure of all things" (quoted in Plato's *Theaetetus*) was generally taken to express profound scepticism about the possibility of attaining a universally valid theory of knowledge.

protasis. *See* conditional.

protocol statements. (German: Protokollsätze). According to the *Vienna Circle, those basic statements that are immediately verifiable by experience, mutually independent logically, and perhaps also incorrigible. All everyday or scientific statements have either to be reduced, or at least justified and supported by reference, to these protocols. In some respects protocol statements resemble the atomic propositions postulated by *Wittgenstein. Prolonged arguments arose over how, or whether, any statement satisfies these conditions.

pseudo-Dionysius. *See* Dionysius the pseudo-Areopagite.

psyche. (Greek for: soul or mind.) The root found in innumerable English compound words such as 'psychology', 'psychosomatic', 'psychophysical', etc. *See* soul.

psychokinesis *or* **PK.** Movement by the mind or soul, a term introduced in *parapsychology to refer to the putative phenomenon in which a person moves some object without any physical contact with that object. An example would be making a dice fall into one particular alternative position by just willing that it do so. Many, perhaps most, parapsychologists outside the socialist bloc take for granted a Cartesian view of man, and hence think of the agent here not as the flesh and blood person but as an incorporeal mind or soul. The soul of *Descartes would, presumably, act upon its body by psychokinesis, which must also be God's mode of operation upon the material creation.

psychologism. The theory that psychology is the foundation of philosophy, and that *introspection is the primary method of philosophical enquiry. First propounded in the early 19th century by the German philosophers J.K.Fries and F.E.Beneke as an interpretation of philosophy in general, psychologism has since been particularly associated with a tendency in logic. J.S.*Mill's *System of Logic* (1843), for example, claims that all mathematical axioms and principles of logic are revealed by introspection. However, though there remain traces of psychologism in *Russell's work, contemporary logic is largely founded on the severe antipsychologism of logicians such as *Frege and *Carnap.

psychology, philosophy of. The study of the philosophical implications of psychology and psychological research.

Although what might be called speculative psychology was itself a branch of philosophy until the 19th century, it is the development of experimental psychology as a distinctively independent science, and its subsequent impact on 20th-century thought, that has given rise to a critical philosophy of psychology. For while the psychologist now largely concerns himself with the empirical investigation of mental functioning and behaviour, it is held to be a philosophical task to examine the peculiar concepts of psychology, and their and its presuppositions and implications. (The psychologist asks, 'What happens, and why?' The philosopher asks, 'So what?'.)

As an empirical rather than strictly philosophical study, psychology may be said to have its roots in the associationist theories of mind first introduced by Hume (see association of ideas) and later elaborated in the work of James Mill and John Stuart Mill. For on associationist theory, it seemed possible to define mental operations by attending to prevailing customs and habits in our practical experience of the world. However, Kant's critical reaction to Hume in particular, and to the general idea of an empirical psychology (which Kant regarded as mere anthropology), led to a determined interest, especially among German thinkers, in establishing a clear and secure scientific foundation for psychological research. As a result, a new, experimental approach to the mind began to gain favour, and, in 1879, Wilhelm Wundt was to provide a symbolic focus for the emerging science when he instituted the first psychological laboratory. At about the same time in England, the old associationist psychology was in decline, mainly as a result of the impact of Darwin's evolutionary theories of mental functioning. Moreover, a strong biological and genetic slant was developing through Francis Galton's work on the inheritance of psychological characteristics and G. F. Stout's approach in what was to be for many years the standard text in psychology, his *Manual of Psychology* (1898).

As the new science matured during the 20th century, a number of rival schools of psychology developed, and each seemed to propose a distinct theory of mind founded on experimental data. Philosophical attention was quickly drawn back to the subject from which it had only recently been separated, for the three dominant schools of psychology were not only proposing new theories of mind, but, in the process, questioning certain deep-lying philosophical precepts. The Gestalt theorists, for example, challenged the psychological atomism that, since Hume, had been the foundation of philosophy of mind in the empiricist tradition (see Gestalt); and Freud's work seemed to undermine a standard assumption about the conscious nature of mental functioning (see consciousness; Freud). But perhaps the most sweeping challenge occurred in the form of the behaviourists' objections to the conventional account of the *mind-body problem, and to the concepts of mind to which it had given rise (see behaviourism). Each of these psychological theories was to have considerable influence upon subsequent philosophical discussion of the mind. Indeed a great deal of contemporary philosophy of psychology remains concerned with the issues that are raised by these theories. See also mind, philosophy of.

psychophysical parallelism. The view that mental (psychical) and bodily (physical) events occur in separate but parallel sequences. Psychical events exist in a causal relationship with other psychical events, and, similarly, physical events with other physical events, but the physical and the mental do not interact one with the other (*compare* interactionism). One of the classical responses to the Cartesian formulation of the *mind-body problem, psychophysical parallelism is particularly associated with Leibniz, who postulated a perfect, divinely pre-established correlation between mental and physical, without any direct causal connection between the two (see also clocks, image of the two).

Ptolemaic system. The theory of the Alexandrian astronomer Claudius Ptolemaeus (c.90–168 AD), based on the works of *Plato and *Aristotle. It assumes that the earth is the fixed centre of the universe, surrounded by concentric spherical shells, seven of which are the paths of the moving heavenly bodies, the eighth and outermost accommodating the fixed stars.

puruṣa. (Sanskrit for: self, spirit.) In general, the principle of consciousness in man or the Universe. But its exact function is variously conceived in the different systems of *Indian philosophy.

Pyrrho of Elis (c.365–275 BC). Sceptical philosopher, generally regarded as the first systematic Sceptic, Scepticism and Pyrrhonism being virtually synonymous. Pyrrho appears to have believed that by "suspending judgment", by confining oneself to "phenomena" or "objects as they appear", and by "asserting nothing definite" as to how they really are, one can escape the perplexities of life and attain an "imperturbable peace of mind". To this end, he assembled arguments showing that things-in-themselves are "indistinguishable, imponderable and indeterminable". Pyrrho wrote nothing, but his views were promulgated in prose and verse by his disciple, Timon of Phlius (c.320–230 BC). *See also* Sextus Empiricus.

Pythagoras of Samos. Greek philosopher and mystic, said to have fled from his native island to escape the tyranny of Polycrates. He settled in Croton, a Greek colony in southern Italy, where he must have died towards the end of the 6th century BC. Yet already when *Plato was young, at the end of the 5th century, Pythagoras was a figure of mystery and legend. He seems to have been the founder of a religious sect as well as perhaps the most important speculative forefather of modern natural science—the guru of an ashram as much as the director of a research institute.

In the former capacity he taught a doctrine of the transmigration of souls and the consequent kinship of all living things. His brotherhood demanded many kinds of ritual purity; most notoriously, it is said, eating beans was taboo.

On the scientific side there is no reason to doubt the tradition that it was Pythagoras himself who discovered,

presumably by measuring the appropriate lengths of string on a monochord, that the chief musical intervals are expressible in simple numerical ratios between the first four integers. This apparently modest finding was the cue for the crucial Pythagorean insight, that the secret of understanding Nature lies somehow in mathematics. If numbers alone are sufficient to explain the "consonances", might not everything else be likewise expressible as a number or a proportion? And, furthermore, given the importance here of the first four integers, and given that their sum can be represented in a remarkable equilateral triangle of ten dots, perhaps this number ten, the decad, somehow "embraces the whole nature of number". This representation,

$$*$$
$$*\quad*$$
$$*\quad*\quad*$$
$$*\quad*\quad*\quad*$$

was known as the tetractys of the decad. Characteristically it became an object of religious veneration, and the most binding oath of the Pythagoreans began, "Nay, by him that gave to our generation the tetractys which contains the fount and root of eternal nature …'.

Pythagoras may well himself have discovered the theorem that still bears his name, and its corollary the incommensurability of the sides and the diagonal of the square. It is slightly less probable that he invented the doctrine of the *music (or harmony) of the spheres and discovered the identity of the Morning Star with the Evening Star.

Pythagoreanism. The philosophical teachings and way of life associated with *Pythagoras. His followers soon split into two groups: the 'Akousmatics' or 'Pythagorists', who treasured the mystical and ritual side of his teaching, and the 'Mathematicians', who developed his scientific interests. The latter strongly believed that the Universe is somehow essentially mathematical, and in particular arithmetical; indeed they seem even to have thought that it is constituted of numbers. For this notion Pythagoras' own discovery of the incommensurability of the diagonal and the sides of a square constituted a major difficulty, and the Pythagoreans' troubles were intensified by the criticisms of *Parmenides and *Zeno of Elea. The dual influence of Pythagoras as an immense but always shadowy figure has continued through the centuries. It is seen, in both its aspects, in the *Republic* of *Plato, and also, albeit at several removes, in both the infatuated numerology of Nostradamus and the scientific dialogues of *Galileo: "The book of nature is written in the language of mathematics." *See also* Neopythagoreanism.

Q

quadrivium. The four mathematical disciplines (astronomy, geometry, arithmetic, and music) that during the Middle Ages constituted the higher division of a university course in the seven liberal arts. The *trivium* (grammar, rhetoric, and logic) constituted the lower division. *See also* scholasticism.

quaestio. (Latin for: question.) One of the two principal forms of philosophical writing in the Middle Ages, originating in the practice of oral debate in the universities. *See* scholasticism.

qualities, primary *and* **secondary.** *See* primary and secondary qualities.

quantification theory. Predicate calculus. *See* calculus.

quantifier. A form of *operator introduced by *Frege. It indicates what was, in traditional logic, called the *quantity* of a statement, namely whether it is universal, as 'All bats are blind', or particular, as 'Some swans are black'. Frege treated 'All bats are blind' as equivalent to 'For any object x, if x is a bat, then x is blind'. This is now symbolically represented by (x) $(Bx \rightarrow Cx)$, where 'B' abbreviates 'is a

bat', 'C' abbreviates 'is blind', and '(x)' is the *universal quantifier*, which is read 'For any x' or 'For all x'. It is sometimes also written $(\forall x)$. (Frege's own symbolism was somewhat different and was never widely adopted.) A universal negative statement, such as 'No saints are sinners' is read as 'For any x, if x is a saint, then x is not a sinner' and would be formally represented by '$(x)(Sx \rightarrow -Tx)$', where 'S' abbreviates 'is a saint', and 'T' abbreviates 'is a sinner'. 'Some swans are black' is taken as having the force of 'There is at least one thing x which is a swan and is black'. This is symbolized as '$(\exists x)(Sx \ \& \ Bx)$' where '$S$' abbreviates 'is a swan', 'B' abbreviates 'is black', and '$(\exists x)$' is the *existential quantifier*, which is read 'There is at least one thing x such that'.

More generally, the universal and existential quantifiers are operators on predicates (*see* predicate) such that if $Px_1 \ldots x_n$ is an n-place predicate, $(x_i)Px_1 \ldots x_i \ldots x_n$ and $(\exists x_i)$ $Px_1..x_i..x_n$ are $(n$-1)-place predicates. If Px is a one-place predicate, $(x)Px$ and $(\exists x)Px$ are sentences, read 'For all x, Px' and 'There is an x such that Px', respectively. The application of these operators is sometimes called *quantification*. The logic treating of rules governing the use of quantifiers is sometimes called *quantification theory*, but more usually, predicate *calculus.

The truth or falsity of a quantified statement (that is, one containing a quantifier) cannot be assessed unless one knows what totality of objects is under discussion, or where the values of the variables may come from. For example, 'All five-year-olds go to school' may be true if one is just talking about English children, but false if one is talking more generally about European children. The class from which values of the individual variables are to be drawn is called the *domain of quantification* or the *universe of discourse*.

quantifier shift fallacy. The mistake of arguing from 'For all values of x there is some one (thing) y such that x bears F

to y'—symbolically, $(\forall x)(\exists y)(Fxy)$—directly to the conclusion that 'There is one y such that for all values of x, x bears F to y'—symbolically, $(\exists y)(\forall x)$ (Fxy). This would be the mistake of arguing from 'Every girl loves some boy (that is, some boy or other)', which might conceivably be true, to 'There is some (one particular) boy whom every girl loves', which is certainly false.

This fallacy is committed more than once in the *Five Ways. For instance, since "secondary movers do not move unless they are moved by a first mover", the conclusion is drawn that there must therefore be one single First Mover that moves them all, "and this all men call God." *See* quantifier; scope.

quantity. *See* quantifier.

quantum mechanics. A system of mechanics used to explain the behaviour of atoms, molecules, and elementary particles. In 1901 Planck suggested that energy must be radiated in discrete units or quanta. In 1913 Niels Bohr applied this theory to the structure of the atom; later his 'solar system' model of the atom was superseded by the formal equations of Heisenberg and Schrödinger. These yield the required predictions of the frequency and amplitude of radiation emitted by the atom. But one consequence, the *uncertainty principle, discovered by Heisenberg in 1927, is that the variables usually interpreted as specifying the position and the momentum of subatomic particles cannot both take definite values simultaneously. This places severe limits on the degree to which these particles or wave-packets can be interpreted as ordinary spatiotemporal objects. The problem thus becomes a locus of dispute between realist and formalist philosophies of science. In addition the conception of fundamental particles as more like disembodied waves than particles challenges a simple material view of the world. *See also* materialism; science, philosophy of.

quiddity. The real nature or logical essence of a thing. The term is derived from the Latin noun 'quidditas', translating the Greek for the 'that-which-it-is-to-be' of something. This word was common in scholastic arguments about essential differences between particular things. Later *Berkeley wrote of "The positive abstract idea of quiddity, entity, or existence". It is often found now in pejorative contexts suggesting wanton hairsplitting.

Quine, Willard Van Orman (1908-). American logician, Professor of Philosophy at Harvard. Quine's writings are on both formal logic and philosophy; they include *Mathematical Logic* (1940), *Word and Object* (1960), *Set Theory and its Logic* (1963), *Philosophy of Logic* (1970), *The Roots of Reference* (1973), and the collections of papers *From a Logical Point of View* (1953), *The Ways of Paradox* (1966), and *Ontological Relativity and other Essays* (1969).

Quine has been the most important follower of *Carnap and the most influential empiricist in recent American philosophy. His fame flowered with the publication of the paper 'Two Dogmas of Empiricism' in 1951. In it he argued that empiricism could not allow the analytic/synthetic distinction, nor make sense of the notion of equivalence of meaning essential to reductionist programmes like Carnap's. His own model for a scientific theory is that of an interconnected web, with no part immune to revision in the light of experience, and no experience forcing rejection of just one part. He believes in the light of this that single sentences have no meaning, and supported this view in *Word and Object* by the famous thesis of the 'indeterminacy of radical translation': the view that a sentence can always properly be regarded as meaning a multitude of different things. This hostility to meanings, propositions, and necessity has been the most discussed part of Quine's work, but he has made notable contributions to many subjects, particularly ontology and set theory. *See* *also* Duhem; meaning; modalities; translation.

quintessence. In Aristotelian physics, the pure fifth element (Latin: quinta essentia), believed to be the component of heavenly bodies. It was distinguished throughout the medieval period from earth, air, fire, and water (*see* four elements) but was believed to be latent in them. Alchemists (*see* alchemy), equating it with the *prima materia* or first matter, from which the rest of the world was made, attempted to distil it from the other elements.

R

racecourse (*or* **stadium**) **paradox.** *See* Zeno's paradoxes.

radical philosophy. A movement started in the 1970s, centring on a journal of the same name. The journal expresses concern that philosophy should be relevant, not trivial, and that more attention should be given to some continental movements and other relatively neglected areas. "The philosophers have only *interpreted* the world in various ways," Marx said in 1845, "the point, however, is to *change* it"(italics original). *Compare* Philosophical Radicals.

Ramsey, Frank Plumpton (1903-1930). Cambridge mathematician and philosopher. His main contributions to philosophy appear in the posthumously published *Foundations of Mathematics and other Logical Essays* (1931).

Among the interesting and influential ideas Ramsey produced in his brief academic career were proposals for meeting some of the difficulties besetting the attempted reduction of mathematics to logic in *Principia Mathematica* (*see* Russell; Whitehead), a discussion of probability as measurement of "partial belief", and an account of generalizations (of the form "All *X*s are *Y*") as *rules* for framing propositions about specific *X*s

rather than themselves genuine propositions having truth-values.

Ramsey sentence. The sentence generated, after the sentences of a scientific theory have been conjoined together, by replacing the theoretical terms with variables and existentially quantifying into the result (*see* quantifier). In plain terms the sentence reproduces the structure of the theory, and its empirical consequences, but removes the impression that we are dealing with understood theoretical items and properties.

randomness. The situation that arises when, in repetitions of a trial in which there is a known, fixed probability of a particular result, there is no rule for predicting that result that tends towards any different success rate. Thus, for example that if there is a 1 in 37 probability of the number 7 coming up on a roulette wheel, then there is no rule for predicting 7s which tends towards a success rate different from 1 in 37. The frequency theory of probability considers only repetitions of a set of conditions, where on each repetition only one result from a given set of possible results, can occur. The result is the value of the *random variable* for that trial. A probability will attach to a particular result only if, first, there is a relative frequency, or proportion of trials with that result, towards which the observed proportion in sequences of trials tends as the number of trials increases; and, second, only if there is no effective method of selecting trials on which the relative frequency of the result tends towards a different limit. This second requirement is that of randomness.

random variable. *See* randomness.

range. *See* function.

rational. 1. Opposed to irrational. 2. Opposed to non-rational or arational. Those who have spoken of man as the rational animal have of course been employing the word in the second sense, meaning capable of either rationality or irrationality, not trying to make it true by *definition that everyone in fact achieves the one rather than the other. *Compare* moral.

rationalism. 1. In a narrow sense, the doctrines of a group of philosophers of the 17th and 18th centuries, whose most important representatives are Descartes, Spinoza, and Leibniz. The characteristics of this kind of rationalism are: (a) the belief that it is possible to obtain by reason alone a knowledge of the nature of what exists; (b) the view that knowledge forms a single system, which (c) is deductive in character; (d) the belief that everything is explicable, that is, that everything can in principle be brought under the single system. 2. In a wider sense, the term used to refer to the views of philosophers who accept only (b) and (d), that is, the thesis that everything is explicable in terms of one system. In this sense Sartre, for example, has been called a rationalist. 3. In the most popular sense, the rejection of religious belief as being without rational foundation.

rational number. *See* number.

real definition. *See* definition.

realism. 1. (in scholastic philosophy) The view (contrasted with *nominalism) that universals (*see* universals and particulars) have a real substantial existence, independently of being thought. *Duns Scotus was the most able supporter of this position. 2. (in modern philosophy) Most commonly the view (contrasted with *idealism) that physical objects exist independently of being perceived. Thus understood, realism obviously reaffirms the standpoint of common sense, and it achieves the status of a philosophy only because a case against it has been seriously argued. But many thinkers have, on various grounds, been puzzled over how perceptions (or experiences of any sort) can yield knowledge of a mind-independent world; and some have concluded that such a world is unknowable or non-existent, and that what we call physical objects are in fact mind-dependent, that, as *Berkeley said, their being consists in being perceived.

Realists have replied, as in G. E. Moore's famous 'Refutation of Idealism', that idealists see themselves thus imprisoned with their own perceptions because they confuse, for example, the *act* of seeing a colour, which is necessarily mind-dependent, with its *object*, the colour itself, which is not; that to call physical objects arrangements of "ideas" or "impressions" is simply misusing language; or that any statement of idealism, fully explicated, can be seen to rest on realist assumptions. *See also* critical realism; science, philosophy of.

real number. *See* number.

reason. A word used in many, various, often vague senses, with complex and sometimes obscure connections one with another. In one most important usage, sometimes marked by an initial capital, reason is contrasted with such hypostatized internal or external rivals as *imagination, *experience, passion, or faith, and the main questions are their various proper fields and relations. These great issues are too often debated as if they concerned the powers and province of some superperson. Yet there is no access to any answers save through discovering what can and cannot be established by different forms of argument, and what actions may or may not be commended as reasonable. We have no independent road to acquaintance with the Goddess Reason.

Practical reason has since *Aristotle been distinguished from theoretical or discursive reason. By proclaiming, scandalously, that "Reason is, and ought only to be the slave of the passions" (*Treatise* III (iii) 3), *Hume in effect recommended a dramatized tautology. For he implicitly defined 'passion' to include every conceivable motive for action; while 'reason', in a complementary sense, covered only inert and neutral appreciation of what in fact is the case and what follows from what.

Three categories of reason are to be distinguished: (1) evidencing; (2) motivating; and (3) causally necessitating. A reason (1) for believing p is a item of evidence showing or tending to show that p is true. A reason (2) for doing something is a possible motive for that action. *Pascal's wager is unique in the battery of classical theist arguments in starting from the concession that (evidencing) "reason can decide nothing here", and proceeding then to deploy purely prudential grounds for self-persuasion. The reason (3) why the volcano erupted will be all the causes together necessitating that eruption.

recollection, argument from. See reminiscence, argument from.

recursive. A term in formal logic and mathematics, applied to definitions and functions. **1.** A recursive definition of a *function or *predicate defines it (1) explicitly as applied to the first term in a series and (2) for any successor term, via the predecessors of that term. Thus, a recursive definition of 'x is a descendant of y' would be: (1) 'x is a child of y', or (2) 'x is a descendant of a child of y'. **2.** (1) Functions definable from successor, constant, and projection functions, through composition of functions and recursive definition, are called *primitive recursive*; those definable from primitive recursive functions by the least value scheme are called *general recursive*. (2) Sets characterized by recursive functions are called recursive sets; they are *decidable.

redefinition, high and **low.** Two expressions introduced by Paul Edwards in 'Bertrand Russell's Doubts about Induction' (1949). A high redefinition increases, a low decreases, the qualifications to be demanded for admission to the class in question. See no-true-Scotsman move.

reductio ad absurdum. (Latin for: reduction to absurdity.) Refutation (see refute) by displaying absurd consequences following as a matter of (logical) *necessity.

reductionism (or **reductivism**). **1.** The belief that human behaviour can be reduced to or interpreted in terms of that of lower animals; and that, ultimately, can itself be reduced to the physical laws controlling the behaviour of inanimate matter. Pavlov with dogs, Skinner with rats, and Lorenz with greylag geese have all used lower animals to illustrate instinctive behavioural patterns than can, by analogy, be correlated with some aspects of human behaviour. **2.** More generally, any doctrine that claims to reduce the apparently more sophisticated and complex to the less so.

reduction sentence. A device introduced by *Carnap in order to solve the problem of scientific terms that resist explicit definition, such as those denoting dispositional properties. For example, 'soluble (in water)' might be defined this way: 'A substance is soluble iff, if it is placed in water then it dissolves' (formally: (x) $(Sx \leftrightarrow (Wx \rightarrow Dx))$, where Sx stands for 'x is soluble', Wx for 'x is placed in water', and Dx for 'x dissolves'). But if the conditional '$\rightarrow$' in the second clause is taken in the logical sense of material implication (see implication and entailment), it will be true if the antecedent is false, that is, if the substance is *not* placed in water. Hence the whole sentence will be true of a substance never placed in water (that is, any substance never placed in water will turn out to be soluble by this definition). Carnap proposed a *reduction* of the sense of such terms, in place of definability. Thus the sense of 'soluble (in water)' should be captured in the reduction sentence 'If a substance is placed in water, then it is soluble iff it dissolves' (formally: (x) $(Wx \rightarrow (Sx \leftrightarrow Dx))$. This does not explicitly define 'soluble (in water)'; it avoids the problem by giving conditions under which a thing is either soluble or not soluble.

redundancy theory. See truth and falsity.

referent. That to which a word refers. Cows are thus the referents of the word 'cows'.

reflexive. *See* relation.

refute. Strictly, not only to deny but also to provide sufficient reason for believing that what is denied is in fact false. If you say that somebody refuted something you thereby associate yourself with both parts of this claim, and must expect to be challenged to make good the more disputatious second. (In general usage the word is frequently employed as a mere synonym of 'deny'.)

Reid, Thomas (1710–96). Scottish philosopher. After a period in the Presbyterian ministry, he was appointed Regent of King's College, Aberdeen (1751) and then Professor of Moral Philosophy at Glasgow (1764). Main philosophical work: *Enquiry into the Human Mind on the Principles of Common Sense* (1764).

Reid is best known as the originator of the Scottish "common-sense" school of philosophy. He saw Hume's philosophy as bringing out the all-destroying scepticism inherent in the empiricist notion of ideas (that is, mind-dependent entities) as the immediate objects of our perception, memory, and thought. He developed an alternative epistemology which undertakes to defend the common-sense view that these faculties are essentially capable of giving us immediate contact with a mind-independent reality. *See also* common sense; empiricism; experience; sense data; veil of appearance.

reincarnation. *See* metempsychosis.

reism. The attempt to preserve an objectivity fof all kinds or intentional entities, exemplified in the philosophies or *Brentano and *Meinong (*see* intentionality). The objects of our desires, or beliefs, or hopes, may not actually exist. Yet the mere fact that they can be thus objects is thought nevertheless to give them some kind of objectivity. This view is also called 'concretism'.

relation. A *propositional function of two or more arguments. A relation symbol will thus be a two- or more place *predicate. For example, 'x is the father of y', 'x is between y and z' (two- and three-place predicates respectively) stand for relations. There may be more than one way of expressing a given relation. Thus, 'a is one of b's parents' and 'b is a's child' both assert that the relation of parent to child holds between a and b. Put more formally, '$Rx_1 \ldots x_n$' and '$Sx_1 \ldots x_n$' express the same relation if, for all $x_1 \ldots x_n$, '$Rx_1 \ldots x_n$' is true iff '$Sx_1 \ldots x_n$' is true. The *extension of a propositional function of one argument, say Px, is the class of all objects a for which 'Pa' is true. By analogy, the extension of a relation $Rx_1 \ldots x_n$ is the class of all sequences of objects $a_1 \ldots a_n$ for which '$Ra_1 \ldots a_n$' is true. If '$Ra_1 \ldots a_n$' is true, it does not follow that, for example, '$R\ a_n a_2 \ldots a_1$' is true (if a is b's father, b is certainly not a's father). Thus the order in which the terms $a_1 \ldots a_n$ are given is important. For this reason the extension of $Rx_1 \ldots x_n$ is represented by the class of all *ordered n-tuples $\langle a_1, \ldots, a_n \rangle$ such that '$Ra_1 \ldots a_n$' is true.

Most common are the two-place, or *dyadic*, relations. The logical properties of these relations have been studied extensively, as the validity of many arguments, particularly those in mathematics, depends on the properties of such relations. For example, $3/8 > 1/3$, $1/3 > 5/16$, therefore $3/8 > 5/16$. The most important of the properties are as follows. ('R' stands for a dyadic relation throughout.)

Transitivity: A relation R is *transitive* iff whenever Rab and Rbc, then Rac. For example, 'is taller than' is transitive because if a is taller than b, and b is taller than c, a is taller than c.

Symmetry: A relation R is *symmetric* iff whenever Rab then Rba. 'Is the same length as' is symmetric because if a is the same length as b, b will be the same length as a.

Asymmetry: A relation R is *asymmetric* iff whenever Rab it is not the case that Rba. Thus, 'is the father of' is asymmetric, since if a is the father of b, b is not the father of a.

Antisymmetry: A relation R is *antisymmetric* iff whenever Rab and Rba, a and *b* are identical. For example, 'is a number not less than' is antisymmetric, for if *a* is a number not less than *b*, and *b* is a number not less than *a*, *a* and *b* must be the same number.

Reflexivity: A relation *R* is *reflexive* iff for any object *a*, it is the case that *Raa*. Since any object weighs the same as itself, 'weighs the same as' is reflexive.

Irreflexivity: A relation *R* is *irreflexive* iff for no object *a* is *Raa* true. Since no object is heavier than itself, 'is heavier than' is irreflexive.

Connectedness: A relation *R* is *connected* over the class *C* of objects iff, whenever *a* and *b* belong to *C* and *a* and *b* are distinct, then either *Rab* or *Rba*. For example, 'is less than' is connected over the natural numbers, since for any two numbers *a* and *b* such that $a \neq b$, either *a* is less than *b* or *b* is less than *a*.

Two important kinds of relation can be defined in terms of these characteristics. *R* is an *equivalence relation iff *R* is reflexive, transitive, and symmetric. *R* is a *partial ordering* relation iff *R* is reflexive, antisymmetric, and transitive. *See also* ordering relation.

relational expression.   *See* predicate.

relations, internal and external. If an individual *X* has a property which is such that, by virtue of having that property, *X* necessarily has a relation *R* to a certain thing or things, then *R* is an *internal relation* of *X*. For example, if *X* is a wife, then the relation of being married to someone is an internal relation of *X*. But if *X* has a relation *R* to a certain thing or things, and there is no property of *X* such that, by virtue of having that property, *X* necessarily has this relation, then *R* is an *external relation* of *X*. For example, if *X* is a wife who is taller than her husband, then the relation of being taller than would, in this case, usually be regarded as an external relation of *X*. However, some Hegelians—and in particular the British idealists (*see* idealism)—have asserted that all relations are internal. Taken in conjunction with their view that what would normally be counted as one

individual has relations to absolutely all things, this implies that a truth about, say, Socrates is really a truth about the whole universe; for into the meaning of the term 'Socrates' there enter all Socrates' internal relations, and these are all his relations to everything.

relations of ideas.   *See* Hume's fork.

relativism.   There are many sorts of relativism, and many senses of 'relativism'. But all are best understood when seen as reactions—stimulated by advances in anthropology and the *sociology of knowledge—to the sort of fact noticed in *Aristotle's *Nicomachean Ethics*; "Fire burns both in Hellas and in Persia; but men's ideas of right and wrong vary from place to place" (v(vii)2) (*see* Herodotage). The relativist recognizes: first, the importance of the social environment in determining the content of beliefs both about what is and what ought to be the case; and, second, the possible diversity of such social environments. To be a relativist about value is to maintain that there are no universal standards of good and bad, right and wrong. One difficulty is to avoid saying that what is right is whatever actually is commended whenever and wherever anyone happens to be. For, whatever its other faults, the general maxim 'When in Rome do what the Romans say' expresses, not unbridled individualistic idiosyncrasy, but a specific and categorical universal standard. To be a relativist about fact is to maintain that there is no such thing as objective knowledge of realities independent of the knower. The parallel difficulty here is to eschew the inconsistent claim that the relativistic thesis is itself an item of objective knowledge. *See* idealism; subjectivism.

relativity.   A scientific principle, established in two parts by Albert *Einstein. The first part (1905), special relativity, refers to non-accelerated systems and has immense philosophical implications both in respect of the extent to which it upsets the classical notions of time and motion and more specifically because of its impact on the concept of simultaneity (*see also* space and time, philosophy of).

According to Newtonian mechanics, the velocity of a body B, travelling at a velocity v_B, will appear to an observer travelling with a body A, at velocity v_A, to be travelling at a velocity $v_{AB} = v_A - v_B$. This simple and apparently common-sensical view of relative velocities was upset by the Michelson-Morley experiment of 1887, which failed to find any difference between the velocity of light as measured in the direction of the earth's rotation and the velocity perpendicular to this direction.

Einstein's solution to this paradox relies on his realization that the velocity of light plays a dominant part in our view of the universe. More particularly, that it is absolute in the sense that it is not relative to anything, and especially that it is not relative to the velocity of the measurer. The simple Newtonian equation relating velocities is seen, in Einstein's theory, as only an approximation—valid at velocities that are small compared to the velocity of light. The relativistic relation is: $v_{AB} = (v_A - v_B) [1 - (v_A v_B / c^2)]^{-1}$, where c is the velocity of light. This equation can be used to establish the very simple relationship between mass (m) and energy (E): $E = mc^2$. The conversion of mass into energy in the atom bomb, in accordance with this law, was the first practical application of the special theory of relativity.

Its philosophical implications arise from its impact on our understanding of the nature of space and time. To an astronomer on earth, an event in his observatory may appear to be simultaneous with an event, observed through his telescope, on Jupiter. However, two consequences of special relativity are that information cannot travel faster than the speed of light and the velocity of light is the same for all frames of reference. Therefore the event in the observatory must have occurred 35 minutes *after* the event on Jupiter (the time taken for light to travel the 630 million km from Jupiter). But to an observer on Jupiter, the event on Jupiter would have appeared to have occurred 35 minutes *before* the event on earth. Before, after, and simultaneously are clearly relative terms: for observers in different frames of reference, 'now' has different meanings. This conclusion and its implications on time order and causality has exercised both physicists and philosophers for the last 70 years.

The second part of Einstein's theory (1915), general relativity, deals with relative motion between accelerated systems. It makes further extensive modifications to our concepts of space and time, treating them as a non-Euclidean continuum, "curved" by the presence of matter in such a way that gravitation appears as a consequence of the geometry of the universe.

Space and time are concepts that form part of the models we construct to represent the real world. But not all concepts have a counterpart in reality: atoms probably do, phlogiston certainly does not. Relativity has made us modify our concepts of space and time and with it our model of reality; it has also made us reconsider some of the underlying concepts of *epistemology itself.

religion, philosophy of. It is not always possible to draw a sharp dividing line between philosophizing about and simply explicating religious belief. We can, however, say at least that the philosophy of religion is not primarily concerned either to promote or to discourage such belief, or to add to our factual knowledge of religious history or psychology or the detailed differences between sects and traditions. Rather it is concerned to analyse the special roles played, and the special problems raised, by the characteristic comcepts and doctrines of religion within the whole structure and economy of human thought.

Thus a thinker may set himself to analyse the concept of religion itself, to bring out just what it is that distinguishes religion properly so-called from other beliefs and activities — from moral codes, for example, or customs, attempts at magic, and the beginnings of science or philosophy. Such analyses have yielded some brave attempts at a comprehensive definition, usually in terms of belief in, together with the worship and service of, some supreme or absolute Being. They have also yielded some valuable, even if partial, insights, like those expressed in Schleiermacher's dictum, "The essence of religion consists in the feeling of an absolute dependence", or Whitehead's "Religion is what the individual does with his own solitariness." It seems likely, however, that there is in fact no single feature or set of features belonging to all those, and only those, things which we should ordinarily call religions, but rather that they form what Wittgenstein called a "family", with a complex network of resemblances and interrelations—so that a satisfactory answer to the question "What is religion?" would be more like an encyclopedia than a one-sentence definition.

If so, then it can readily be understood how the topics and problems of the philosophy of religion may vary with the religious traditions most familiar and important to the thinkers concerned. Thus, in the Mosaic tradition (Judaism, Christianity, Islam), but not necessarily in all others, the primary philosophical concern has inevitably been with the concept of God, regarded as the single omnipotent and omniscient creator and controller of everything else that exists, and also as essentially personal, caring for and communicating with mankind. The most obvious topic for philosophy has been the validity or otherwise of arguments purporting to prove the existence of such a Being; and a vast literature about such arguments has accumulated over the centuries (see God, arguments for the existence of). But there are also questions, logically more fundamental, to be raised about whether this concept is internally coherent: whether any human conceptual and linguistic equipment could possibly be adequate for the description of God; or whether in this field we can do no more

than use metaphor and analogy to point towards something only very dimly seen or understood.

The Mosaic form of theism has given rise to other time-honoured philosophical questions: for example, about how the presence of evil in the world is to be reconciled with the idea of a benevolent and all-powerful creator; or the possibility of miracles, specific divine interventions in the order of nature, and the circumstances in which any occurrence could justifiably be called miraculous in this sense; or how the absolute and limitless nature of God can be reconciled with a measure of independence in his creation, and, in particular, with human freedom and responsibility.

There are further questions to be considered about how, and to what extent, human beings can gain knowledge of God. For example, especially among empirically minded thinkers who are sceptical about what can be achieved by metaphysical argument, there has been considerable interest in the phenomena of religious or mystical experience, alleged direct encounters with the divine. The concept of revelation is also of central importance in this connection, since there is an obvious case for saying that any genuine knowledge of God could not be the outcome of human research, but could only be God-given.

In recent times, philosophy of religion, like other branches of philosophy, has been much preoccupied with questions of language and meaning. *Logical positivism had a short way with religion. Granted that religion's basic teachings about God were not empirically verifiable, then they were devoid of factual meaning, and could at best be seen as misleadingly phrased expressions of emotional attitudes. More recently, however, largely under the influence of the later works of *Wittgenstein, religious discourse has come to be seen as a distinct *language game, or use of language, which neither has nor needs any justification outside itself. Whatever one may think of specific attempts to characterize this "game"—for example, as presenting not quasi-scientific theses about reality but pictures or images that guide our responses to it—this approach has at least had the merit of turning philosophical attention away from somewhat over-cultivated fields (the proofs of the existence of God, etc.) towards a fresh examination of what religious belief and discourse, in the lives of ordinary believers, are actually like.

reminiscence (*or* **recollection**), **argument from.** *Plato's argument that certain kinds of knowledge could not have been acquired in this life, but involve the recollection (Greek: *anamnēsis*) of a previous acquaintanceship with the Forms or Ideas. In *Meno* the knowledge is of geometry, particularly the conclusion of the theorem of *Pythagoras. In *Phaedo* it is knowledge of ideal concepts never adequately instantiated in the corporeal world of change, particularly perfect equality. *See also* innate ideas.

representationalism (*or* **representationism**). A generic term that broadly refers to theories of perception wherein the sensing mind is believed not to have direct acquaintance with its objects, but to apprehend them through the medium of ideas that are supposed to *represent* those objects. Descartes seems to have believed in this representative process, and it appears in almost all theories involving *sensa. It is always a problematic feature because any version of it calls for an explanation of this so-called representative relationship, whether it be causal or one of correspondence or similarity, and because it starts by laying down an obstacle to such explanation since it assumes initially that human minds do not apprehend objects directly. *See* causal theory of perception; perception; veil of appearance.

representative theory of perception. The view that is also known as *representationalism or representationism.

residues, method of. *See* Mill's methods.

resistentialism. A fictitious school of fashionable continental philosophy invented by Paul Jennings in 1948. This particular and popular invention is often wrongly included among the many similar contributions of Michael Frayn, consequent upon his undergraduate work in philosophy at Cambridge. *See* existentialism.

responsibility. The notion that a person is answerable for his actions and so is a proper subject for praise or blame. This can be so only when the act is within the agent's power ('up to him'); but philosophers disagree as to whether this implies an absolute, internal, 'contra-causal' freedom, or simply the absence of external constraint and other defeating conditions. Two principal conditions are normally necessary for responsibility: (1) that the agent knows what he is doing, and (2) that his desires and intentions play some role in the act (or omission). Awkward exceptions to this neat schema are cases where a person is blamed for unintentional acts (such as carelessness), or for the unintended consequences of his acts. *See also* law, philosophy of.

revealed theology. *See* natural theology.

Richard's paradox. A paradox presented by Jules Richard in 1905. It involves a diagonal argument (*see* diagonal procedure) concerning denoting phrases and what they denote and is thus considered to be one of the *semantic paradoxes. Some phrases of the English language denote real numbers between 0 and 1. Consider *all* such phrases which denote and imagine the numbers so denoted to be represented as non-terminating decimals in a table; for example,

$$0.01345\ldots$$
$$0.33333\ldots$$
$$0.49999\ldots$$

and so on.

Consider the denoting phrase 'the real number between 0 and 1 whose nth decimal place is 0 if the nth decimal place of the nth number in the table is 1, and whose nth decimal place is 1 otherwise'. The foregoing English phrase denotes a real number between 0 and 1, but paradoxically ensures that the number it denotes is not in the table, because it gives a procedure for constructing a number that is guaranteed to be different from any number in the table. (It is different in the 1st decimal place from the 1st number, in the 2nd place from the 2nd number … and so on.) But this is a number denoted by an English phrase; so it should be in the table.

rights. A person's privileges as a member of society, including 'liberties', such as the right to use the public highway, and 'claim-rights', such as the right to defence counsel. "To have a right", said Mill, "is to have something society ought to protect me in the possession of." The word 'ought' is important: the language of rights is inescapably normative (though the question of what rights actually are recognized in a particular society is straightforwardly factual). Mill considered rights to be grounded in general utility, but this seems radically confused: the function of assertions of rights (for example, to freedom of speech) seems to be precisely to *block* arguments for curtailment based on general expediency. A longstanding philosophical tradition asserts the existence of certain fundamental natural rights—a notion Bentham called "nonsense on stilts".

rigid designator. An expression that designates the same thing in every possible world. The phrase 'the 39th President of the U.S.' is a *designator* of Jimmy Carter, but it is not a *rigid designator* as he might not have won the 1976 election. However certain expressions necessarily designate the objects they do, for example 'the positive $\sqrt{4}$' designates the number two not only in this world but in every possible world, no matter how different. Many philosophers believe that *proper names are rigid designators.

romanticism. A broad movement of thought in philosophy, the arts, history, and political theory, at its height in Germany, England, and France towards the end of the 18th and in the earlier part of the 19th centuries. A reaction against the *rationalism and *empiricism of the period of the *Enlightenment, romanticism is best characterized by its idealist celebration of the self, by its respect for the transcendental, and by its conviction of the power of the imagination and of the supreme value of art.

Philosophically, the movement has its roots in *Kant's theories in respect of the relation of self to the phenomenal world and of the unknowability of the noumenal world. But the most direct manifestation of philosophical romanticism is to be found in the extreme transcendental idealism of *Schelling. Through *Coleridge, Schelling's views exercised a strong influence over the English romantic poets, *Wordsworth and *Shelley; in history and political theory, the work of Shelley's father-in-law William *Godwin was much admired by the romantics, who were also deeply interested in the ideas of the French Revolution. However, the arch-romantic is perhaps *Goethe, whose drama, *Faust*, still remains the clearest expression of romanticist feeling.

Rosenzweig, Franz (1886–1929). A pupil of *Cohen and close friend of *Buber (with whom he collaborated in a German translation of the Bible). Rosenzweig abandoned German idealism for a more existential philosophy involving a radical rethinking of the classical understanding of Judaism and Christianity. His major work, *Der Stern der Erlösung* (1921), is the last great monument of German Jewish philosophy, and has exercised a profound influence on subsequent Jewish philosophical thought.

Rosicrucianism. A movement for political reform and spiritual regeneration that originated in early 17th-century Germany. It centred on a fictitious religious society reputedly founded by a certain Christian Rosenkreuz in 1484. The philosophical content of its teachings is heavily coloured by alchemy, mysticism, and occultism.

Rousseau, Jean-Jacques (1712–78). Political and educational philosopher, born in Geneva. From 1741 he lived mainly in Paris, where he contributed to the *Encyclopédie* and became one of the chief spokesmen for *romanticism. Publication of *Émile* (1762), a treatise on education, and *Du contrat social* (1762), which was to become a bible for the Jacobins, brought official disfavour. He spent several years outside France, partly under the protection of Frederick the Great but also in England. There he was befriended by, but soon quarrelled with, Hume.

Rousseau's key political idea was the general will rather than the social contract. Political society was seen as involving the total voluntary subjection of every individual to the collective general will; this being both the sole source of legitimate sovereignty and something that cannot but be directed towards the common good. Obedience to this perhaps not easily discovered general will must be in everyone's individual interests, must indeed be what we all really and truly want. (Hence, if we are coerced in its name, we are being, in Rousseau's own chillingly paradoxical words, "forced to be free".)

This doctrine has and was bound to have an enormous appeal to all who see themselves as members of a party of the vanguard; knowing, and determined to enforce, the supreme collective will—of course, for the good of all. *See also* noble savage.

Royce, Josiah (1855–1916). American philosopher, professor at Harvard from 1892. Influenced by *Hegel, he developed his own philosophy of absolute *idealism in *Religious Aspects of Philosophy* (1885), in which he argued that to have a conception of an orderly continuous world it is necessary to assume that there is an "Absolute experience to which all facts are known and for which all facts are subject to universal law". In *The World and the Individual* (1900–01) he develops the notion of the "internal meaning" of an idea as the purpose which that idea fulfils and from which its cognitive or "external meaning" (reference) derives.

Russell, Bertrand Arthur William (1872–1970). British philosopher who studied mathematics and philosophy at Trinity College, Cambridge. He subsequently held a variety of university posts in Cambridge and elsewhere, interspersed with other pursuits, literary, educational, and political. From his long list of publications the following may be picked out as philosophically the most important: *The Philosophy of Leibniz* (1900), *The Principles of Mathematics* (1903), *Principia Mathematica* (with A.N. Whitehead, 3 volumes, 1910–13), *The Problems of Philosophy* (1912), *Our Knowledge of the External World* (1914), *The Analysis of Mind* (1921), *The Analysis of Matter* (1927), *An Enquiry into Meaning and Truth* (1940), *Human Knowledge: Its Scope and Limits* (1948), and *Logic and Knowledge* (a collection of some of his most important essays) (1956).

Russell's thought covered many topics and developed through many phases during his long career. It is widely accepted, however, that his most original and influential contributions to philosophy, at least to academic philosophy, belong, in the main, to his pre-1914 period. After having been attracted briefly to idealism, he reacted strongly towards first a thoroughgoing realism, the most notable expression of which was his *Principles of Mathematics*; here, on the basis of an equation of meaning and reference, we require real entities as referents for all the terms we can meaningfully use, including the distinctive vocabulary of mathematics, number, point, etc. The result however, is a picture of a world so rich in imperceptible real entities as to be somewhat disquieting to common sense; and

Russell soon adopted, like his mentor *Whitehead, the alternative of *logical constructions (the policy being to substitute, wherever possible, constructions out of known entities for inference to unknown ones).

The presentation of pure mathematics as a development from logic exemplifies this policy. According to Russell, "logic is the youth of mathematics and mathematics is the manhood of logic"; that is, starting from an irreducible minimum of logical concepts and axioms we can, by rigorously logical steps, derive therefrom, without allowing ourselves any additional equipment, the whole content of logic and mathematics as ordinarily understood. Thus, for example, if we discuss the arithmetical properties of a given number, we need not think of ourselves as discussing a given entity, a Platonic Form, as it were; we are simply talking about the properties of a certain class of classes of things, that is, the class of all classes similar to a given class, where similarity is defined in terms of one-to-one correspondence of members. The working out of the whole programme in *Principia Mathematica*, which occupied Russell and Whitehead for a decade, gave rise to some of Russell's most ingenious and controversial ideas, such as the *axiom of infinity and the theory of types (see types, theory of). How far the enterprise succeeded is open to argument—serious objections and rival theories have been advanced—but it remains a major landmark in the development of logic and the philosophy of mathematics.

Logical constructionism can be seen also in *Our Knowledge of the External World*, where Russell regards physical objects like chairs and tables as highly complex sets of the immediate data of experience (see sense data); this helps to solve some of the traditional problems of empiricism but gives rise to difficulties of its own about how we are to identify the sets in question. Again, in the *Analysis of Mind*, the mind is seen not as a Cartesian 'thinking substance' which receives these data but as the whole complex pattern of the data themselves. Hence arises a form of neutral *monism in which mind and matter emerge as different constructions out of (largely) the same basic components—which themselves cannot properly be classed as either mental or material.

Like many other 20th-century philosophers, Russell often approached the world through considerations of language. Once the real, as opposed to the apparent, structure of our statements is made explicit, we can discover, he thought, an isomorphism between this structure and that of the world. Thus, in his lectures on logical atomism (1918-19), he suggested that all statements, however complex, were truth-functions of atomic statements, which report minimal facts about the content of experience. (This theory he later found to need at least substantial modification.) Corresponding to such atomic statements are the atomic facts of experience, not further analysable, and mutually independent so that no one of them logically requires any other. Here we have a manifestation of the radical pluralism which, in one form or another, has been a persistent feature of Russell's thought.

Throughout his career Russell held that the existence of God and personal immortality are at best bare logical possibilities, and that no sufficient grounds for believing in either can be found in any feature of our experience. Indeed, he went much further than this in criticizing religious belief, not only as rationally indefensible but as a positive hindrance to human progress and well-being. In this, as in many other features of his thought, there is an obvious similarity to *Hume—except that Russell's mathematical and logical equipment was much more formidable.

Russell's paradox. An important paradox in *set theory. Some sets (classes or collection) are members of themselves and some are not. For instance, the set of horses is not a member of itself since it is a set and not a horse, whereas the set of non-horses is a member of itself. Is the set of all sets which are not members of themselves, a member of itself? If it is then it is not. If it is not then it is. The paradox, discovered by Bertrand Russell in 1901, had a profound influence on both the development of set theory and on our understanding of what sets are. Increasingly sets were conceived of as being determined by their members rather than determined by specifying conditions. See also types, theory of.

Ryle, Gilbert (1900–76). British philosopher who, except for war service and lecturing trips abroad, spent his entire working life in Oxford. He was first, from 1924, a Student of Christ Church, and then, from 1945, Waynflete Professor of Metaphysical Philosophy. His earliest philosophical publications treated the phenomenology of *Husserl and *Heidegger's *Sein und Zeit*, but shortly after *Wittgenstein's return to England and philosophy they became friends. From then on Ryle's philosophy was in a linguistic mode, his conversion being announced in a signpost article 'Systematically Misleading Expressions'(1932). The thesis was that a main part of philosophy must be "the detection of the sources in linguistic idioms of recurrent misconstructions and absurd theories".

Ryle's first book, *The Concept of Mind* (1949), consisted in a sustained and punishing bombardment of the Cartesian conception of man, characteristically labelled "the dogma of the *ghost in the machine". Ryle was, as he later agreed, trying to find how far he could push analytical behaviourism—the doctrine that psychological notions can be analysed in terms of actual or possible behaviour. Next came his Tarner Lectures on *Dilemmas* (1953): these were attempts to untie some knots produced when "theories, or, more generally,...lines of thought" get at apparently irreconcilable cross-purposes with one another. Later, came the mischievous yet suggestive developmental study *Plato's Progress* (1966). Finally, there were two substantial volumes of *Collected Papers* (1971), showing how

extensive and how various Ryle's contributions had been, both to independently creative philosophy and to the constructive history of ideas, especially with reference to Plato. What does not appear from the corpus of the writings is the unmeasurable extent of his face-to-face influence. *See also* categories; category mistake.

S

Saʻadya (ben Joseph) (882–942). *Gaon* (principal) of the rabbinic academy of Sura in Mesopotamia (from 928).

The first major Jewish philosopher of the Middle Ages, Saʻadya was also a halakhic (legal) writer, liturgical poet, pioneer of the study of Hebrew grammar, biblical exegete, and translator of the Bible into Arabic. His main philosophical work, *Kitāb al-Amānāt wa'l-Iʻtiqādāt* (Book of Beliefs and Opinions), essentially a work of Muʻtazilite *Kalām setting out rational proofs of religious doctrines, exerted a great influence on subsequent medieval Jewish philosophy.

Sadducism (*or* **Sadduceeism**). The beliefs of the Jewish sect of Sadducees, active around the time of Christ, particularly in so far as they concerned denial of the resurrection of the body and the existence of spirits. In post-Renaissance writings, the term came to be applied by opponents of materialistic unbelief (such as the *Cambridge Platonists) to the position of those who denied the existence of angels, ghosts, and other spiritual beings allegedly as a preliminary to denying the existence of God. *See also* Glanvill.

Saint-Simon Claude-Henri de Rouvroy, Comte de (1760–1825). One of the founding fathers of French and hence of world socialism. He joined enthusiastically in the French Revolution of 1789 before retiring from active politics to devote himself to writing. He was associated successively with both the historian Thierry and the positivist *Comte. Two key ideas were the need to ground political visions in historical and social science, and the conflict between *les industriels*, all the useful and productive people, and the parasites, the bureaucrats. He inspired many future captains of industry, who though not, in Marxist terms, working class were nevertheless, in his sense, *industriels*.

salva veritate. (Latin for: the truth being preserved.) A condition of synonymy, first formulated by *Leibniz. Expressions are synonymous (or may be said to have the same meaning) if they are mutually substitutable without altering the truth-value of the statement in which they occur. Thus, 'male parent' may be substituted, *salva veritate*, for 'father' in any sentence referring to a particular relationship between two individuals. There are, however, difficulties with this condition, notably contexts where it does not seem to be applicable (*see* extension and intension; identity; opacity and transparency).

Sāṃkhya. The most archaic of the systems of *Indian philosophy. Ideas typical of it can be traced as far back as the middle of the 1st millennium BC, and they dominate the speculation found in the *Mahābhārata* (which includes the *Bhagavadgītā*), the *Purāṇas*, and some of the *Upaniṣads*. The Sāṃkhya remained one of the leading schools of thought till about the 6th century AD and influenced most of Indian theology. The source-books of the *classical* system are the *Sāṃkhyakārikās* by Īśvarakṛṣṇa (before 500 AD) and the anonymous commentary *Yuktidīpikā* (*c.* 550 AD).

Unlike the older forms of the system, classical Sāṃkhya rejected any kind of monism. An eternal primal matter (*pradhāna*, prakṛti), consisting of three qualitatively different constituents (*guṇas*), differentiates itself periodically through the varying distribution of the *guṇas* into the multifarious world of phenomena. Its first development is a set of *buddhis* (the word variously translated as 'mind', 'perception', 'consciousness',

etc.), each of which evolves an *ahankāra* ('ego-awareness'), which in turn produces the sense-organs, the *manas* ('intellect'), and the five elements. Together they constitute man's psychosomatic frame. Totally distinct from this, there appear an infinite number of 'selves' or 'souls' (*puruṣa*). These are powerless and passive, while *prakṛti* or her evolutes are active; thus all forms of perception or consciousness are regarded here as materially conditioned.

This system of thought as a whole combines an approach which is typical of the *Vaiśeṣika (a quasi-scientific reduction of the vast variety of phenomena to basic types) with an interpretation of man's entanglement in, and liberation from, the cycle of rebirth. Thus the peculiarity of the sequence of differentiation is motivated by the interpretation of the process leading to (individual) liberation as the reversal of *prakṛti*'s (cosmic) evolution.

saṃsāra. (Sanskrit for: transmigration.) The doctrine, characteristic of all Indian religions, of an almost endless cycle of death and rebirth. *See also* karma; metempsychosis; mokṣa.

Santayana, George (1863–1952). Spanish-born American poet, novelist, and philosopher, student of William *James, and professor at Harvard. His lectures on the philosophy of history formed the foundation of *The Life of Reason* (1905–06), an interpretation of the role of reason in the manifold activities of the human spirit. In 1912 he returned to Europe. He spent his last years at a convent in Rome; he professed to be attached to Catholicism in its historical and aesthetic aspects, though "entirely divorced from faith".

Santayana's Platonist as well as materialist system of philosophy is set out in the comprehensive 4-volume *Realms of Being*, comprising *The Realm of Essence* (1927), *The Realm of Matter* (1930), *The Realm of Truth* (1938), and *The Realm of Spirit* (1940). The introduction to this work, *Scepticism and Animal Faith* (1923) formulates the basic necessary scepticism. All rational processes are expressions of animal compulsion to believe in certain things, such as the existence of matter. A grasp of essences explains and elucidates existence, enabling the mind to retain the character and identity of the changing data of experience.

Sartre, Jean-Paul (1905-). French philosopher and novelist. He studied at the Sorbonne and under *Husserl at Göttingen, and became, with *Heidegger, a leading exponent of atheistic *existentialism. At the end of World War II Sartre emerged as one of the leaders of left-wing Paris intellectuals; he was co-founder (with *Merleau-Ponty) and editor of the journal *Les Temps Modernes.* Sartre professed to be a Marxist even after his claim to have broken with the Communist party, maintaining that Marxism and existentialism are complementary in their critique of society and the aim to express in political liberty the freedom inherent in human nature.

The semi-autobiographical novel *La Nausée* (1938) and the essay *L'Existentialisme est un humanisme* (1946) express Sartre's fundamental concern with the nature of human existence and the freedom of the will. Man is nothing at birth, and is condemned to be free in his choices of action and doomed to bear the burden of responsibility. In the attempt to deny this and alleviate the anxiety it occasions, he behaves as if his life and choices were predetermined by the situations and social roles in which he finds himself (*see also* Angst; bad faith).

In his chief philosophical work *L'Être et le néant* (1943), Sartre investigates existence, the self, and the nature of imagination and of the emotions. Being is transphenomenal, that is, its character is not fully revealed in the totality of its manifestations. There is no concealed *noumenon, but everything which has being transcends the categories, descriptions, and designations through which it is knowable to man. Two types of being

are distinguished: that of *en-soi* ('in-itself') and *pour-soi* ('for-itself'). Being-in-itself roughly corresponds to the being of an inert object, complete and fixed, expressing no relationship either with itself or with anything outside itself. It is uncreated, without reason for being, and absolutely contingent. Being-for-itself—human being or consciousness—is fluid, characterized by lack of determinate structure, by openness towards the future, and by potency. Man's intuition of nothingness makes judgment possible: individual things, the alternatives of choice, are distinguished by their 'not-being' something else.

Sarvâstivâda. A school of Thēravāda *Buddhist philosophy. With its roots in the Abhidharma teachings of the last few centuries BC, it culminated in the Abhidharmakośa of Vasubandhu (400-480 AD). The tenets of Buddhist belief were given here a rationalistic, ruthlessly consistent formulation. Any idea of a soul, a person, or lasting substance was rejected, and the entire world of phenomena reduced to atomic factors (*dharmas*). These were envisaged as existing for precisely one moment, then to be replaced by similar ones. Thus complex phenomena like the (empirical) person are no more than sequences of momentary aggregates of form-, quality-, emotion-, mental-, etc, *dharmas* (*compare* logical atomism). A particular type of *dharma*, called *prāpti* (literally 'obtainment') was postulated to account (a) for the homomorphic continuity of these sequences, and (b) for the adherence of 'defilements' (ignorance, desire) to these sequences (transmigration). The archaic realism of the school assumed the reality of *all dharmas*, including those of the past and future; *sarvâsti* means 'everything is'. Nirvāṇa is defined as a *dharma* which, when attached to a particular sequence (the 'person') eliminates the *prāpti dharma*, thus giving rise to liberation, which is the cessation of this sequence.

A closely related school, the Sautrântika (founded by Kumāralāta, possibly in the 3rd century AD) went even further. The archaic realism of 'sarvâsti' was replaced by a nominalist position. The notion of *prāpti* is rejected, and also the conception of *nirvāṇa* as a *dharma*; liberation is pure nothing, the mere cessation of a *dharma* stream.

satisfaction. A technical term in formal *semantics; the condition in which an object, or sequence of objects, 'satisfies' a *predicate, that is, the predicate is true of that object, or sequence of objects. For example, Birmingham satisfies 'x is a large industrial city' because this expression is true of Birmingham. Put in another way, an object named by 'a' satisfies a one-place predicate 'Px' iff 'Pa' is a true sentence. A sequence, or *ordered n-tuple $\langle a_1,\ldots,a_n \rangle$ of objects satisfies the n-place predicate '$Px_1,\ldots,x_n$' iff '$Pa_1,\ldots,a_n$' is a true sentence. For example, the triple $\langle$ Russia, Alaska, the U.S.$\rangle$ satisfies 'x sold y to z' if the objects are assigned to the variable-marked places in the order given (*see* variable). The triple $\langle$ the U.S., Russia, Alaska$\rangle$ does not satisfy the expression as the objects of the triple are in the wrong order—the sentence, 'The U.S. sold Russia to Alaska', is not true. The relation that holds between an object, or sequence of objects, and a predicate iff that object, or sequence of objects, satisfies the predicate is called the *satisfaction relation*. Sometimes it is convenient to treat satisfaction as a relation between infinitely long sequences and expressions, which, of course, have only finitely many places to be filled. In this case conventions are established to make it clear which objects of the sequence to assign to which places, and the remainder of the sequence is ignored. Using the notion of satisfaction, Tarski was able to make important advances in semantic theory, in particular in his *truth theory. *See also* interpretation.

Sautrântika. *See* Sarvâstivāda.

Scepticism. In a general sense and with a small s, the philosophical attitude that maintains that sure knowledge of how

things really are may be sought, but cannot be found. (The Greek word *skepsis* meant 'seeking' and 'sceptic' is contrasted with 'dogmatic'.) Scepticism (with a capital S) is the name attached to a particular school of ancient Greek philosophy.

The classic arguments for scepticism— that our senses are unreliable and that the experts contradict one another— were old enough. Sceptical attitudes were expressed by various Presocratics, notably Xenophanes, and were developed by sophists like Gorgias and Protagoras. Methodical Scepticism, however, was principally a Hellenistic phenomenon; its three main representatives were *Pyrrho of Elis, the Academy from approximately 280 to 80 BC, and the school of *Aenesidemus.

Pyrrho appears to have produced something like a Hellenistic system of philosophy by organizing various arguments for "suspension of belief" into a basis for a whole attitude to life. Happiness, he said, depends upon considering the correct answers to three questions. "What are things really like?" Unknowable; that is, we can say nothing definite about them. "What should our attitude be towards them?" Non-committal. "What will we gain from this attitude?" Peace of mind.

The Hellenistic Academy had other objectives. In no longer teaching positive Platonism and in arguing, instead, against any given philosophical position, *Arcesilaus could claim to be following Socrates, whose philosophical role had been to refute error, rather than to impart knowledge. His principal "dogmatic" opponents were the Stoics with their claim that certain unmistakable sense impressions—"cataleptic phantasies" (*see* Stoicism)—are a criterion for truth. In the next century, *Carneades extended the Academic critique, attacking Stoic and other dogmas on our criterion for knowledge, on fate and causality, on the nature of the gods, on prudence and justice, and on the ends of human conduct. To counter the criticism commonly levelled at scepticism, that the absence of any certain criterion for knowledge must inhibit action, he claimed, at least for the sake of argument, that one impression, though not certain, may be clearer, more "persuasive" (Latin: *probabilis*), and as such more serviceable, than another, and that its persuasiveness increases when associated impressions and a closer inspection corroborate it.

Scepticism remained the doctrine of the Academy till about 80 BC when *Antiochus reverted to dogmatism. Soon afterwards, Aenesidemus established at Alexandria his own school of "authentic", hardline Pyrrhonism. Systematizing and working out in detail the ideas of earlier sceptics, he organized the grounds for disbelief into ten "tropes" or modes. His successor Agrippa (1st century AD) produced a system of five such "tropes". This sceptical tradition in philosophy developed links with the empirical school of medicine, the best-known representative of the alliance being *Sextus Empiricus.

Schelling, Friedrich Wilhelm Joseph von (1775-1854). German idealist philosopher. While Schelling's transcendental idealism stands in clear relation to the work of *Kant, *Fichte, and *Hegel, he is generally regarded as the principal philosopher of *romanticism. Through *Coleridge, Schelling's influence on the English romantics was considerable.

Schelling's major work, *The System of Transcendental Idealism* (1800), is primarily an attempt to elaborate upon and modify Kant's and Fichte's views of the relation of the self to the objective world. For Schelling, *consciousness itself is the only immediate object of knowledge, and knowledge of the objective world arises merely in the form of a limiting condition in the process by which consciousness becomes aware of itself. He goes on to argue that it is in art alone that the mind can become fully aware of itself, and that in this respect the condition of art is that to which true philosophical reflection should aspire.

schema. (*pl.* schemata) *See* inference, rule of.

Schiller, Ferdinand Canning Scott (1864-1937). British philosopher, who taught at Corpus Christi College, Oxford, and in Los Angeles. A supporter of William *James's pragmatic theory of truth, he opposed the rigid Hegelian absolutism espoused by *Bradley.

In his main work, *Humanism* (1903), Schiller declared himself a follower of *Protagoras, maintaining that truth and reality are man-made and denying that "there is an objective world given independently of us and constraining us to recognize it". He distinguished *humanism from *pragmatism by claiming that the former is of larger range, applicable not only to logic and also to ethics, aesthetics, metaphysics, and theology.

Schiller, Johann Christoph Friedrich (1759-1805). German philosopher, poet, and playwright. Although Schiller finally abandoned philosophy, his contributions to *aesthetics remain of considerable interest. Stimulated by *Kant's theories, Schiller sought to elaborate the view that aesthetic experience constitutes an important focus of attention in philosophical accounts of human nature. His view that there is an aesthetic or 'play' impulse was later taken up by others as a central theme in aesthetics, but Schiller had in mind an even wider context. In his major work, *Letters on the Aesthetic Education of Mankind* (1794-5), he argued that an education that acknowledges the interests of the aesthetic impulse, as well as the claims of reason and the senses, is critical for our moral and social development.

Schlick, Moritz (1882-1936). Professor of Philosophy of the Inductive Sciences, Vienna (1922-36), who came to this from the study of physics. He was a founding member of the *Vienna Circle. His extensive writings include *Allgemeine Erkenntnislehre* (1918), *Fragen der Ethik* (1930), translated as *The*

Problems of Ethics (1939), and *Gesammelte Aufsätze 1926-36* (1938).

Like other logical positivists, Schlick saw philosophy as essentially concerned with meanings, and struggled with the problems of finding a satisfactory formulation of the verificationist theory of meaning (*see* logical positivism; verification). Traditional philosophical doctrines were to be exposed as neither true nor false but meaningless, since they were neither analytical (like pure mathematics), nor in principle testable by experience (like natural science). His main problems were over the status of the doctrine that these are the sole conditions of meaningfulness, the kind of testability in question, and the analysis of experience in such a way as to preserve *intersubjectivity.

scholasticism. The kind of philosophy practised in the schools of the medieval universities. The roots of the term stretch back to the Greek word for 'leisure', since it was recognized from antiquity that for the contemplation of the ultimate reasons for things, leisure is an essential condition. The adjective 'scholastic' is also applied to medieval theology. Although no clear distinction was made between philosophy and theology in the Middle Ages, Aquinas did suggest that the one operated with premises supplied by nature and the other on the basis of revelation.

Although 'scholasticism' is now generally applied to the central phase of Western Latin medieval thought, neither its Greco-Roman antecedents nor its Arabic and Jewish concomitants should be ignored. Typical of scholasticism's heterogeneous antecedents is the work of the Italian *Boethius (*c.*480-524 AD), who produced an influential commentary on an *Introduction* (the *Isagoge*) to Aristotle's *Categories*, which had been written by the Syrian Neoplatonist *Porphyry. This commentary, together with Boethius' own commentaries on Aristotle's *De Interpretatione* and *Categories*, constituted the chief basis of the 12th-century Old Logic (*Logica*

Vetus); in combination with the works of late Latin grammarians, such as Priscian and Donatus, it stirred highly significant developments in the theory of meaning. Of these developments, the controversy concerning universals was but one early symptom (*see* Abelard; Anselm).

The controversy over universals was shaped by Porphyry's organization into a systematic form of the vocabulary of chapters 4, 5, and 8 of Book 1 of Aristotle's *Topics*. This system took the headings of Aristotle's *Categories* to designate "most general sorts" (*genera generalissima*); beneath each of these one could distinguish relatively broad sorts (*genera*) whose sub-classes (*species*) would embrace their individual members. '*Man* is a species' and '*Animal* is a genus' are examples of the sentence forms whose semantic complexities generated the controversy. When, slightly later, Aristotle's *Sophistical Refutations* became available in Latin, it confirmed this linguistic bent and in due course gave rise to the ingenious medieval doctrine of *suppositio*, which attempted to characterize the varieties of word-object relations.

Prior to the assimilation in the 13th century of the full *corpus* of Aristotle's works, studies were largely based on the work of Boethius. When not carried out for their own sakes (as they already often were), they were exploited for the purpose of theological clarification along the lines laid down in the work *On Christian Doctrine* of St. *Augustine of Hippo (354-430 AD). The *Sentences* of Peter Lombard (*c.* 1100-1160), a systematic collection of authoritative opinions, became the basis on which for centuries newly fledged masters (*see* Aquinas; Duns Scotus) would exercise their skill in commentary.

The respect for authority, and the consequent need to reconcile discordant authorities, can be seen as one of the main impulses behind medieval philosophy. But perhaps the prime driving force was the perennial conflict between faith and reason. Faith was represented by

Christianity, the Bible, and St. Augustine; reason by logic and Aristotle. Scholasticism had its heyday in the 12th and 13th centuries, the two centuries in which the bulk of Aristotle's works were first translated and then slowly assimilated by the Latin West. In fact the history of scholastic philosophy can be seen as the history of the Church's confrontation with and assimilation of Aristotle (see Aristotelianism).

Before the 12th century only two works of Aristotle—the *Categories* and *De Interpretatione*—were known to Western scholars. In the early 12th century a new interest in logic emerged, principally in the works of Peter Abelard, whose passion for logic and whose critical spirit make him one of the founders of scholasticism. In particular, his provocative *Sic et Non*, juxtaposing passages in the Bible that contradict each other, provided a challenge that theologians felt bound to meet. Moreover, they could only meet it by using the same logic that Abelard had used so devastatingly to embarrass them; this created the uneasy relationship between reason and faith that characterizes scholasticism. Reason always presented an actual or potential threat to faith, yet at the same time reason had to be used to explain and defend faith.

The often heterodox notions accompanying the incursion into the Latin West of Arabic Aristotelianism generated tensions that became topics of debate in the new universities and among the orders of friars, notably the Franciscans and Dominicans. Doctrines of this nature included the eternity of the world and man's participation in a unitary world-intellect. In 1277 the Bishop of Paris condemned 219 such 'Averroist' (see Averroës) propositions, and excommunicated all who persisted in maintaining any of them. This condemnation is an index of these conflicts, which Aquinas and Scotus laboured in their diverse fashions to resolve. Scotus, for instance, continued the move away from the evaluation of human beings on the basis of their intellectual accomplishments (a

view inherited from Plato and Aristotle) towards the doctrine that being a complete human being hinges upon correct intentions and affections. As Augustine had long before realized and as a whole stream of medieval Augustinians had continued to maintain, only thus could one make sense of the high esteem placed on non-intellectual figures and doctrines within the Judaeo-Christian tradition.

Almost all branches of linguistics, logic, and philosophy were developed by the scholastics. Not only metaphysics, but also epistemology, philosophy of mind, ethics, political thought, and theory of law, as well as the various branches of so-called natural philosophy (especially optics and mechanics), flourished in the nurturing environment of linguistic and logical consciousness. At the same time, and no matter how daring or remote the speculations, or how quaint the illustrations, the persistent Aristotelian background encouraged a basic empiricism. Thus, everyone respected an appeal to how things are actually found to be by all human beings at all times and in all places. This foundation was not to be undermined by the speculations of special people in special places using instruments whose data were subject to controversial or hypothetical interpretations. Although this attitude is inimical to science as we now know it, it had the philosophical advantage of discouraging the rift between ordinary men and philosophers that is so characteristic of modern philosophy. Again, a view of propositions as concrete individual occurrents could lead a 14th-century Dominican, Robert Holkot, to defend the thesis that God can know more (or less) than he knows, on the basis that n equiform inscriptions of a truth yield n propositions and so n more things for God to know, and n less to know if they are erased.

This acute interest in philosophy, combined with an educational system originally based on the *trivium* (grammar, rhetoric, and logic (or dialectic)) meant that the nature of language, meaning, fallacy, and inference has rarely been so thoroughly studied. Presentday linguistics has its counterpart in the copious works of the so-called speculative grammarians. Similarly, there can be few modern logical theories (propositional and functional calculus, quantification and type theories, theory of deduction, modalities, paradoxes, etc.) that are not also foreshadowed. However, owing to lack of adequate notation and to dependence on manuscript copying by ignorant scribes, the material became altogether unmanageable. It was only under pressure from the Renaissance classicist pedants that it later became simplified into such versions as the influential 17th-century *Logic* of *Port Royal.

In view of Aristotelian insistence on the varieties of methods and standards of certitude appropriate to diverse subject matters, a scholastic discourse on method would have been out of place. Nevertheless the philosophical context did give rise to certain general casts of argument. Chief among these is the *quaestio* (question), which sprang from the practice of oral disputation in the universities. These debates became highly formal and stylized. The presiding master—a Master of Arts—would raise a question "*Utrum...*" ("Whether..."). One student would argue for one answer, another for the opposite answer, and then the master would break in and answer the question himself and resolve all the contradictory arguments set up by the students.

Characteristically the arguments for and against would be based on appropriate quotations from authorities, such as Boethius, Aristotle, St. Augustine, or the Bible. The master's resolution would depend on his drawing distinctions in the meaning of words,so that one authority could be seen to be quite in accord with another, so long as it was understood that they were using their key terms in different senses. Hence the scholastic adage: "Where there is a contradiction draw a distinction."

This is the bald outline of that sort of dispute (*quaestio disputata*) that would have taken place between masters and students only and would have been cast into detailed logical form at many points. However, the open disputes (*quaestiones quodlibetales*) were intellectual sports of such importance that, to enable everyone to attend, university business was suspended on the few days of the year on which they took place. Questions could be raised by anyone (*a quolibet*), including outsiders, on any subject whatsoever (*de quolibet*). So challenging and unpredictable were the objections the defending master had to face, that some found it an ordeal that they did not care to undertake.

It was from this practice of oral debate that the stereotyped literary form of the *quaestio* arose. The *quaestio*, in which opposing authorities are paraded and then reconciled, predominates in medieval academic writing. The great syntheses —such as the *Summa Theologiae* and the *Summa contra Gentiles* of Aquinas —are basically a chain of *quaestiones*: one is resolved and leads on to another, until the whole field is systematically covered and all possible questions are asked and answered. The resulting answer can be seen as a great unified system. (Hence, paradoxically, it also comes about that most of the early objections to Aquinas' doctrines are contained within his own works.)

Another characteristic literary product of the Middle Ages was the commentary on an authoritative text. In philosophy this came to mean primarily the works of Aristotle; the number of such surviving medieval commentaries is truly vast. In fact virtually the whole of medieval philosophical and theological literature is cast in the form of either commentary or *quaestio*—the one expounding authorities and the other reconciling them.

For a Western Latin scholar of the 13th and 14th centuries, therefore, intellectual life could prove to be fairly strenuous. He was further dogged by the difficulties and uncertainties of translation (some of Aristotle's works being translated from Greek into Syriac, Syriac into Arabic, and Arabic into Latin), by the comparative slowness and inaccuracy of copyists, by the physical insecurities of transmission and storage of documents, and by the lack of punctuation, uniform spelling, and cross references in the endless columns of crabbed manuscripts, with their often varied conventions for the contraction of written word forms. Add to these impediments, the Spartan discomfort of working conditions, the inadequate diet, and the fact that most of the great figures, were, by modern standards, marathon walkers (being required by the rules of their organizations to travel on foot) and it becomes clear that scholasticism was far from being the easeful aristocratic pursuit that the etymological origins of its name might seem to imply.

Since the Renaissance, scholasticism has had a bad reputation. The humanists (see humanism), rediscovering pagan literature and cultivating Ciceronian prose for its own sake, attacked both the barbarous style and the arid subject matter of the "schoolmen". The offending characteristics of scholasticism, the humanists thought, were lack of literary grace, abstract subject matter, futile logic-chopping, and excessive reliance on authority. To this day it is often said and widely, but falsely, believed that all scholastic philosophical debate turned upon the great question of how many angels could be accommodated upon a pinhead.

In recent years, however, there has been an increasing realization among non-Roman Catholic philosophers that there is a deal of very good philosophy to be found in the writings of the great scholastics, and that this contribution can be and should be treated in exactly the same way as that of any other classical writers: it is neither to be dismissed unheard as if it were disingenuous official propaganda of ideological hacks, nor to be accepted with uncritical servility as the revelation of some privileged Master. For instance, not to take account of medieval discussions of

the problem of the *seafight —a problem set by Aristotle's *De Interpretatione* —is quite simply bigoted and purblind. The great need is for interpreters, who are both good medievalists and good philosophers, who will make this contribution more available to an ever more secular world.

Schopenhauer, Arthur (1788-1860). German post-Kantian philosopher. Schopenhauer's philosophical reputation has never been assured, either in his lifetime or in more recent thought, partly through his severe opposition to the prevailing and, in his view, corrupting *Hegelianism of his time, and partly through his truculent attitude to academic philosophy in general. Yet there is some truth in his own belief that, of all the post-Kantians, he provided the most lucid and penetrating development of Kant's philosophy (see Kant).

Schopenhauer's earliest work was *Über die vierfache Wurzel des Satzes vom zureichenden Grunde* (On the Fourfold Root of the Principle of Sufficient Reason) (1813), a Kantian delimitation of the kinds of reasons legitimate in philosophical explanation of why anything is as it is. His major contribution was *Die Welt als Wille und Vorstellung* (The World as Will and Idea (or Representation)) published in 1818 and again, in a considerably amplified edition, in 1844. Later work was largely an application of his ideas in the field of moral philosophy.

The essence of Schopenhauer's theory, which relates to Kant's division of the phenomenal and noumenal worlds, is that there are two aspects of the self: the self as it appears phenomenally as an object of perception and the self as it is in itself (see Ding-an-Sich), noumenally, as a manifestation of will. The distinction is fruitful in several ways: for instance, in its anti-dualistic conception of man as a single entity viewed under the aspects either of body or of will; and—an idea which was to stimulate Freud—in its pessimistic emphasis upon the distorting and covert forces of the will. In this latter respect, a focal point of Schopenhauer's attention was art, conceived as the sole arena of human endeavour in which man may escape subjection to the will in free aesthetic contemplation.

Schopenhauer wrote elegantly, in a style notably free of jargon and obscurity, and it was as an essayist, in his collection *Parerga und Paralipomena* (1851), that he first commanded wide attention. He subsequently attracted such figures as Tolstoy, Conrad, Proust, Mann, and Freud. It remains true, if regrettable, that Schopenhauer is still more often read for his cultivated aphoristic writings than for his metaphysics.

science, philosophy of. Organized empirical science provides the most impressive result of human rationality and is one of the best accredited candidates for *knowledge. The philosophy of science seeks to show wherein this rationality lies; what is distinctive about its explanations and theoretical constructions; what marks it off from guesswork and pseudo-science and makes its predictions and technologies worthy of confidence; above all whether its theories can be taken to reveal the truth about a hidden objective reality.

Science does not consist merely in making timid generalizations from wide collections of data, for the scientist's selection of data is dictated by some theoretical interest, and his results are not simply inductive extrapolations, but rather explanations, models, and theories. *Induction is just one part of the process, although one whose justification is necessary to the confidence placed in scientific prediction. Another part, emphasized by *Popper, is the creation of bold, predictive theory, that may then be rigorously subjected to test: on this view the rationality of the scientist (as opposed to the pseudo-scientist) is his eagerness to seek out such tests and abide by a negative result. Popper is able to use this falsifiability criterion to dismiss various world-views (Marxism, psychoanalysis) as unscientific, but it has been pointed out that the standards

he sets may not be met even by more respectable sciences. In any case it remains obscure why rationality, so construed, should lead to reliable prediction or further discovery of the truth.

*Logical positivism needs above all to reconcile its verification theory of meaning with the intelligibility of the theoretical concepts of science. *Carnap, *Hempel, and others sought to do this by a specification, for each sentence of a theory, of the experimental conditions issuing in its confirmation or refutation: these conditions would constitute the operational or real meaning of the concepts (*see also* phenomenalism). One criticism of this programme (by *Quine) is that it ignores the holistic nature of theory, whereby individual assertions only face experience through their links with other aspects of theory, making a one-to-one correlation of each claim with a set of experimental observations impossible. According to the extreme formalism of *Duhem, whereby a theory is regarded as an uninterpreted device for obtaining new predictions from old observations, this would not matter, but to anyone regarding theories as yielding explanations and knowledge it raises in an acute form the problem of meaning.

The cumulative character of scientific theory, whereby new theories not only take over the observations that led to the old, but also try to preserve as much of the old theory as possible, is characteristic of successful sciences. It suggests realism about theories: they describe real states and structures of nature, and succeed each other as successive approximations to the full truth. It also puts a stumbling-block in front of less sober accounts according to which a change of theory merely represents the substitution of one self-contained set of concepts for another—a process only marginally subject to empirical control and in which there is nothing that could be described as progress or increase in knowledge (Kuhn, Feyerabend). Realism can also claim that this cumulative character supports it against instrumentalism which, like formalism, sees the value of theories as exhausted by their pragmatic virtues. Realism will often see different theories (for example, wave and particle theories of light) as conflicting, while instrumentalism may be happy to see them as complementary recipes for getting results. Anti-realist conclusions are also suggested by the 'underdetermination thesis' of Duhem, which asserts that many different theories could always equally well account for any possible totality of evidence. This fact, as we have seen, would be congenial to an instrumentalist, but a realist shrinks from its obvious sceptical implications.

Realism is probably under most pressure when the scientific theory makes it impossible to 'understand what is going on', that is, to regard the structures revealed in terms of antecedently intelligible models and mechanisms. *Action at a distance, electromagnetic radiation, subatomic particles, and many other theoretical constructs, have all provoked this complaint: the best realist retort is to follow *Hume by maintaining that it is an illusion to suppose that we understand familiar macroscopic interaction any better. But this still leaves the problem of the very meaning of such constructs in an unsatisfactory state. This may be regarded as part of the general difficulty with meaning. For, ever since *Kant, epistemologists have found similar problems in our understanding of very ordinary 'empirical' properties, such as spatial shape and solidity. In the light of such difficulties the very distinction between observational and theoretical properties becomes suspect.

In addition to these comprehensive issues, philosophers of science devote themselves to problems arising from particular concepts involved in statistics, measurement, teleology (the explanation of events in terms of their purpose or end), causal explanation, the relations between different sciences, the conditions under which one science reduces to

another, and the specific concepts of individual sciences.

scientia media. (Latin for: mediate knowledge.) A phrase coined by Luis de Molina (1535-1600) to describe the special knowledge that it is supposed that God has of hypothetical future contingents (*futuribilia*). These could in certain circumstances come into existence and are conceived of as being neither mere possibility nor actual future occurrence. This attempt to harmonize God's foreknowledge with human freewill is still acceptable to many Roman Catholic theologians (see freewill and determinism).

scientism. 1. The belief that the human sciences require no methods other than those of the natural. 2. In a more general sense, practices that pretend to be, but are not, science. In both cases the term is employed only by opponents.

scientology. The doctrine of a Church founded in 1953 in the U.S. by L. Ron Hubbard. Disingenuously investigated and mildly obstructed by public authorities in several normally liberal countries it has almost no connection with science or even *scientism.

scope. Of a logical *operator, the shortest *propositional function in which it occurs. Thus in $(y)-(Fy \to (\exists x)(Rxy \& Gx))$, the scope of '-' is $-(Fy \to (\exists x)(Rxy \& Gx))$ whereas that of '&' is $(Rxy \& Gx)$. The scope of the *quantifier '(y)' is the whole formula, whereas the scope of '$(\exists x)$' is $(\exists x)(Rxy \& Gx)$. In this case '&' is said to occur *within the scope of* '-', or '-' is said to have a *wider scope* than '&', and similarly '$(\exists x)$' occurs within the scope of '(y)'.

Brackets are used in the formalization of sentences to indicate the scope of the various operators. It is important that the relative scopes of the operators be clearly demarcated, for otherwise ambiguities result. Such ambiguities are often present in ordinary language where the determination of scope is often left to the context in which the sentence is used. Thus, for example, 'I will go to the university and play tennis if it is not raining' could be taken to mean either that I will go to the university anyway, and will play tennis if it is not raining (taking 'if' to occur within the scope of 'and'), or to mean that I will only go to the university to play tennis, if it is not raining (taking 'and' to occur within the scope of 'if'). The difference between these would be indicated formally as the difference between '$p \& (-q \to r)$' and '$-q \to (p \& r)$'. 'Everyone was killed by someone' is ambiguous between 'There is one person who killed all people (including himself)' and 'Everyone was killed by a person, but not necessarily by the same person in each case'. Formally this would be the difference between '$(\exists x) (y) Kxy$' and '$(y) (\exists x) Kxy$'. Such ambiguities are called *scope ambiguities. See also* quantifier shift fallacy.

Scotism. The philosophy of *Duns Scotus and his followers.

Scotus. See Duns Scotus.

seafight. The problem set by *Aristotle in *De Interpretatione* IX. Since it is clearly necessary that either there will be a seafight tomorrow or there will not, surely whichever in fact happens must happen necessarily and inevitably (*see* inevitability)? The first crux is to sort out the nature and position of the necessities involved. Certainly the disjunction $p \lor -p$ is logically necessary. But it does not follow either that either p or $-p$ is itself logically necessary, or that, if either of these is a contingent proposition about a future occurrence, that occurrence will happen inevitably. The second crux is what came to be called the problem of future contingents, contingent propositions about the future. If such propositions are true, must it follow that what they assert will happen inevitably? And, if it does, can we avoid *fatalism by maintaining that such future contingents are neither true nor false but indeterminate? Others urge: that the 'is' in 'It is true that this will happen' is timeless; that 'This will inevitably occur' simply does not follow

from 'This will occur'; and that both the first two heroic alternative solutions are wildly paradoxical. The problem was much discussed in the Middle Ages, and is the subject of *William of Ockham's *Treatise on Predestination, God's Foreknowledge, and Future Contingents.*

secondary causes. Ordinary, everyday causes 'within the *Universe' seen in relation to and in contrast with the *First Cause. If everything at all times is the immediate work of God, that still leaves us able and needing to find and explore a causal order within the Universe. Indeed the theoretical commitment to say that everything is the work of the First Cause leaves it as possible as it is practically necessary to insist that this is caused by that, and the other by something else again. From the late 1600s onwards, secularizing thinkers in many different fields began, while slyly allowing that everything is of course ultimately to be traced to the will of the First Cause, to pretend to a humbler concern to uncover also the secondary causes through which the divine purposes are effective. The growth and spread of the Christian Church, for instance, can be allowed to be the gracious work of a self-revealing God, while, simultaneously, a more or less completely secular account is given of the secondary causes of a this-worldly, and often quite sordid, historical phenomenon.

secondary qualities. *See* primary and secondary qualities.

secundum quid. (Latin for: in a qualified sense.) The abbreviation for both *a dicto secundum quid ad dictum simpliciter* and *a dicto simpliciter ad dictum secundum quid. See* converse fallacy of the accident.

self. 1. An obsolescent technical term for a person, but a person thought of as incorporeal and essentially conscious. Sometimes the self is simply identified with Plato's concept of *soul. In contrast, *Descartes, arguing in the *Discourse* that the 'I' of his 'I think, therefore I am' is essentially a thinking substance, would thus be said to be presenting a substance theory of the self. *Hume, on the other hand, contending in the *Treatise* that nothing is experienced save loose and separate "perceptions of the mind", attempts a serial account. Most contemporary philosophers would bypass the whole issue, urging that experiences can only be identified as the experiences of flesh-and-blood people. **2.** Synonym for 'ego' as when Hume denies that we are ever "intimately conscious of what we call our SELF". *See also* survival and immortality.

self-contradiction. The affirmation by the same person of two propositions that are in *contradiction, or *contradictory, one to the other. What that person has thus said is *self-contradictory.*

self-contradictory. *See* self-contradiction.

self-deception. A state resembling but distinguishable from that of ignorance or of false belief, and consisting in a motivated blindness to facts that are in some way or for some reason undesirable or unacceptable to the individual concerned. Self-deception has been much discussed by philosophers. Cases are generally determined on grounds of the availability of correct information and the degree of effort that the individual might reasonably be expected to make to establish the facts, or the failure to raise relevant questions for fear of unacceptable answers. It is psychologically explained as the unconscious distortion of the appreciation of a state of affairs to satisfy the individual's own motives. *See also* bad faith.

self-regarding. A term applied by J.S. *Mill to actions that affect only the agent, to be contrasted with not self-regarding (or other-regarding) actions. In *On Liberty* Mill held that the only sphere in which outside coercion or interference with the individual (by the law, the government, etc.) was permissible was with respect to other-regarding actions, that is, in order to prevent an individual from harming others. An individual's liberty should never be constrained with respect to self-regarding actions.

semantic paradoxes. Usually distinguished from the *logical paradoxes in that they arise from the use of semantic notions such as truth and reference. Sentences that exhibit them are often variations on the *liar paradox, for example, 'This statement is false'. If that sentence is true then what it says of itself must be true—namely that it is false; but if it is false then what it says must be false, so it must be true. The work of *Tarski and others in attempting to analyse or avoid these paradoxes has resulted in making the semantic notions involved extremely precise logically, and has blurred the original distinction between the semantic and logical paradoxes. *See* paradox.

semantics. 1. (in general) The study of signs and their relations to what they signify. 'Semiosis' and 'semiotics' are also used in this sense. **2.** (in formal or mathematical logic) The *interpretation of formal languages. **3.** (in philosophy of language) The attempt to find truth definitions for natural languages (*see* truth definition).

semiotics. 1. The theory of signs; also called 'semiology'. It is traditionally divided into three parts: syntactics, the study of grammar; semantics, the study of meaning; and pragmatics, the study of the actual purposes and effects of meaningful utterances. **2.** More generally, the study of all patterned communication systems.

Seneca, Lucius Annaeus (4 BC-65 AD). Roman statesman, Stoic, and man of letters. Seneca's extant works include a satire, nine tragedies, ten moral essays or *dialogi* (*On Anger, On Peace of Mind,* etc.), an incompletely preserved *On Clemency,* the casuistic *On Benefits,* in seven books, *Natural Questions,* originally in eight books, and 124 *Moral Epistles to Lucilius* (his most successful work). Seneca's Stoicism was eclectic.

His philosophical works, written in a glittering "pointed" prose, are deliberately untechnical and unsystematic. Like other Roman Stoics (*see* Epictetus; Marcus Aurelius), Seneca saw philosophy as a matter primarily of moral edification, of curing the soul, and he wrote less to expound than to persuade.

sensa. A wide term covering all the locutions used in the perennial attempts to differentiate, from what publicly exists and is actually perceived, that which is *merely* felt, and the feeling of which does not, of itself, imply that anything either exists or has any specifiable qualities. Thus sensa tend to be regarded as private and individual experiences rather than public objects. Since the origin of Western philosophy with the ancient Greeks there has been the recurrent suspicion that material things are not directly the objects of perception, and terms have been sought to enable whatever directly *is* that object to be mentioned in discussion. *Locke wrote of "ideas of sense" which might be simple or complex. *Berkeley wrote of "ideas ... imprinted on the senses" and considered also ideas which were actually not, but *might* be, in principle imprinted on the senses. This notion of a possible-but-not-actual "sensible quality" has been used to explain what is meant by an unobserved thing's continuing to exist although it is not perceived. Most of *Hume's 'impressions' were another form of sensa. So are 'representations'. More recently, derivations from the root word 'sense' have been made (perceptual sensations and *sense data are sensa) and other terms (for example, 'percepts' and 'qualia') have been used. The choice of words for theorizing about *perception is not arbitrary, however, and the neologisms in this field have been intended either to free the writer from unwanted assumptions (for example, that we experience sensa because material objects *cause* us to do so) or to give him a fresh edge of meaning (for example, that the sensa he is thinking about do

not exist in the way material objects do, or do not have duration, or have atomic or extended identities).

sensation. 1. Ordinarily, having such feelings as cold, pressure, thirst, itches, or pains. 2. Technically, mental entities of a kind private to their owner. They are also caused to exist, for example, by light waves or sound waves stimulating his eyes or ears, and are affected by the condition of these, and of the whole nervous system attendant upon them. Sensations therefore may be not only visual or auditory, but olfactory, tactile, or kinaesthetic. Kant used the concept (German: *empfindung*) to refer to the modification of a conscious subject by the presence of some object.

The extent of a sensation has caused some puzzlement. It has been thought that just as matter could be analysed into indivisible atoms, so there were basic sensations each corresponding to a particular nerve cell. *Gestalt psychologists, on the contrary, have contended that our sensory awareness is of complete wholes, not quasi-atomic elements into which these might be analysed. In the present century philosophers have been dissatisfied with the broadness of the concept of sensation and have preferred to use the terminology of sense datum (*see* sense data) or sense content in their theories, thus excluding non-sensory sensations.

sensationalism (*or* **sensationism**). The theory, associated chiefly with *Mach, that sensations are the ultimate and real components of the world. There is no justification for regarding them as signs of anything other than themselves. Anything knowable can be discovered through sensory experience and analysis, though it is permissible and necessary for science to infer from similarities in behaviour and reports that people experience similar sensations.

Sensations are logically prior to objects: the latter are analysable into, or can be "constructed" out of sensations, but the reverse operation is impossible. There is no real distinction between the subject matters of different branches of science, since the so-called facts they investigate are the relations between observable sensations. *See also* Berkeley; monism; phenomenalism.

sense *and* **reference.** Now the standard translations of Frege's *Sinn* and *Bedeutung*. Frege distinguished sense and reference for singular terms in order to explain how identity statements could be informative. Such statements cannot express a relation between objects because, trivially, every object is identical to itself and nothing else. The two singular terms, 'the Morning Star' and 'the Evening Star', have distinct modes of presenting (that is, senses for) one and the same object; the terms are then said to have the same reference (that is, the planet Venus). Frege intended the distinction to apply to all singular terms including proper names and would not have recognized Russell's *logically proper names which were supposed to have a reference but not sense. The distinction also applied to predicate terms, which Frege called 'concept expressions', and to relation terms. *See also* denote.

sense data. What are given immediately to us through sight, touch, hearing, smelling, and tasting. The claim to have had or be having a sense datum carries no implication that the claimant has been or is in perceptual contact with anything. The singular, 'sense datum', is mistakenly believed to have been introduced by Russell or Moore c.1910, but was in fact used earlier by Josiah Royce (1887) and William James (1890), and possibly by others earlier still. Although used by "sense datum theorists", the expression was "meant to be a neutral term", the use of which "does not imply the acceptance of any particular theory" (H. H. Price, *Perception*, p.19).

sense experience. That portion of a living agent's history that is derived from reception of stimuli through the five senses; or, a single or identifiable and unified body of such stimuli. This feature of life raises several philosophical questions. In receiving such stimuli, is an agent absorbing or responding to the activities and qualities of physical objects existing in a material world "outside" himself? Do such objects, if any, cause him to have the sense impressions he does have? Can these impressions in any way provide clues to the nature of supposed external bodies? What gives a single sense experience its singularity as distinct from the plurality of a compound one? These questions may be summed up as: What knowledge, and about what, can be gained from sense experience? *See also* perception.

sensibilia. (*sing.* sensibile) A term for a kind of *sense data that might be thought to exist unsensed. At one time Russell used the word for this purpose; sensibilia (literally, what are able to be sensed) were "...objects which have the same metaphysical and physical status as sense data without necessarily being data to any mind." He was considering the theory that a physical object is a family of sense data, and found this difficult to sustain if sense data did not exist unsensed. The phenomenalist alternative (*see* phenomenalism) to assuming that there actually are sensibilia is to insist that we should think only and non-committally of what sense data would or might be had in certain circumstances.

sensible world. The world as we have access to it in *sense experience. According to *Kant our "theoretical", in contrast to "practical", knowledge is limited to the realm of sense experience. Kant apparently thought that the true nature of the world external to the sensing agent was not accessible to beings limited in their sentient existence to the sensible world, or world of "phenomena" (*see* phenomenon). Kant held that we cannot know about "things-in-themselves", but only about the ways in which they *appear* under the *a priori forms of reason, for example the temporal and spatial dimensions that we impose on our sense experience in order to make it intelligible.

sensor. 1. An organ of sense in a living thing, that receives stimuli. 2. A whole organism that is, among other things, capable of receiving stimuli.

sensorium. (*pl.* sensoria)(Latin for: thing of sensing.) The term used by Newton and his contemporaries to refer to the seat in the brain of sensation and perception.

sentences. *See* statements and sentences.

sentential function. *See* predicate.

sentential operator. *See* operator.

set. A set is a collection of objects known as the members or elements of the set. The set, *A*, consisting, say, of objects *a*, *b*, and *c* is conventionally written as $\{a, b, c\}$. *a* is a member of *A* is written as $a \in A$. Sets themselves are objects and so there can be sets of sets, and sets of sets of sets, etc. The basic property of sets is that two sets are identical iff they have the same members (the condition of extensionality). Sets were conceived of as either being 'built' from their members or as being defined by a condition. For instance in the latter conception, the condition 'is red' defines the set of red things. However, as *Russell's paradox indicates, not every condition defines a set. *See also* class.

set theory. The field pioneered by *Cantor from 1874 to 1897 and further developed by *Russell and Zermelo. The original motivation that led to the formulation of set theory derived from problems arising out of investigations into certain types of infinite sets of real numbers and the recognition of a need for a theory of the infinite. Russell later showed that most of received mathematics is deducible in set theory. The discovery of *Burali-Forti's paradox and *Cantor's paradox called into question the 'size' and existence of certain sets, and *Russell's paradox showed that the unrestricted conception of sets as being determined by all predicates (conditions) was inconsistent. Russell's response was to develop an axiomatized (set) theory

in which sets were viewed as being arranged in a hierarchy of types. Types were assigned to any set such that each of its members was of a lower type. Zermelo's axiomatization of set theory restricted the existence of sets determined by a predicate to just those sets whose members were members of a given set and satisfied the predicate. It is then necessary to add further axioms governing set existence to ensure the deduction of mathematics.

One of these, the axiom of *choice, has occasioned controversy. Loosely, it states that for any set *X* the members of which are all non-empty sets with no members in common, there exists a way of selecting (choice function) exactly one member of each member of *X*. Another problem, first formulated by Cantor, is whether the cardinal number associated with the set of real numbers is the least cardinal greater than the cardinal number associated with the set of natural numbers (*see* number). Paul Cohen has done recent work in these areas.

Sextus Empiricus (2nd century AD). Physician and sceptic philosopher. Sextus' surviving works are *Outlines of Pyrrhonism*, in three books, and *Adversus Mathematicos* (Against the Professors), a refutation of dogmatism, in eleven books. Of these last, Books I-VI concern the liberal arts (grammar, rhetoric, geometry, arithmetic, astronomy, and music), while Books VII-XI (sometimes called *Against the Dogmatists*) deal with the three branches of philosophy: logic (VII, VIII), physics (IX, X), and ethics (XI). Prolix and unoriginal as they are, these works are our fullest source for ancient *scepticism, and they had an enormous influence in the decades following the first printing in 1569 of complete Latin translations.

Shaftesbury, Anthony Ashley Cooper, third Earl of (1671-1713). British essayist and moral philosopher. Shaftesbury's education was directed by *Locke, and Locke's influence was to be evident in many of his writings, collected in the three-volume work, *Characteristics of Men, Manners, Opinions, Times* (1711). While his stylish essays were addressed to a wide variety of cultural and philosophical topics, Shaftesbury is principally credited with the anti-Hobbist view that man is naturally moral in respect of an inherent affection for virtue. The idea of such affection, construed as the idea of an inner moral sense, was later developed in the moral philosophy of Francis *Hutcheson. *Compare* Hobbes.

Shelley, Percy Bysshe (1792–1822). English romantic poet. Shelley's prose writings are informed by philosophical ideas drawn from Plato, Spinoza, and Berkeley, and he was particularly influenced by the transcendental idealism of F.W.J. von *Schelling. In early, atheist writings, Shelley argues that religious doctrines are metaphorically rather than philosophically true, and that the idea of God is best expressed as the symbol of a *world soul. In *A Defence of Poetry* (1821), this view becomes central to Shelley's consideration of the relation of poetry to religion. *See also* romanticism.

Sidgwick, Henry (1838–1900). English philosopher, who studied and taught at Cambridge for most of his life, being Fellow of Trinity (1859–69) and Knightsbridge Professor of Moral Philosophy (1883–1900). Among extensive writings on many topics, *The Methods of Ethics* (1874) is philosophically the most important. Sidgwick's moral philosophy has been described as *utilitarianism on an intuitional basis (*see* intuitionism). The obligation to promote the general happiness is intelligible only if regarded as a fundamental moral intuition, but specific moral rules can then be justified, in utilitarian fashion, as ways of fulfilling this obligation—and, in general, common-sense morality is thus justifiable. To reconcile individual self-interest and morality would require a *theism that Sidgwick regarded as "natural" but rationally indefensible.

sign *and* **symbol.** No satisfactory general definitions exist for these terms, although candidates have been presented. Thus, *Peirce suggested 'a sign stands for something else'. But although spots are a sign of measles they do not 'stand for' measles. 'Ideational' accounts ('a sign summons up an idea') and 'behavioural' accounts ('a sign disposes us to act as if the thing signified were present') also raise difficulties. General definitions being unhelpful, it is more productive to list and compare various uses of the term 'sign'. One difference that emerges is between natural signs (clouds as a sign of rain) and non-natural (sometimes called 'conventional') signs such as words. (A cloud is a sign of rain only if rain follows; but a red flag can mean (signify) 'danger', even if hoisted by mistake.) Non-natural signs, including words, are often called 'symbols'. This use of 'symbol' should be kept distinct from other uses; as when the meaningless marks of a *formal language are called 'symbols'; or when a literary creation, such as *Moby Dick*, is called symbolic; or when we contrast using words with employing symbolism.

simple enumeration. An inductive method. If this A and that A and the other A are all φ, and these are all the As which you are acquainted with, then it is an *induction by simple enumeration to conclude that all As are φ.

simple ordering. *See* ordering relation.

sin. Strictly, a theological term, meaning offence against God. What is a sin, therefore, may or may not violate this-worldly moral standards.

singular term. *See* term.

Sinn. (German for: sense.) In the philosophical logic of *Frege, the term contrasted with *Bedeutung* (reference). *See* sense and reference.

Skolem paradox. *See* Löwenheim-Skolem theorem.

Smith, Adam (1723–90). Scottish political economist and philosopher. He studied moral philosophy under *Hutcheson in Glasgow, where he subsequently lectured on logic and ethics. His lectures were published in Theory of the Moral Sentiments (1759).

The Wealth of Nations (1776) set out a comprehensive moral and social programme, based on the study of market forces and expounding the economic philosophy of "the obvious and simple system of natural liberty". General welfare depends on allowing the individual to promote his own interest freely "as long as he does not violate the laws of justice"; in this way "he frequently promotes [the interest] of the society more effectually than when he really intends to promote it." In all this Smith was making much of the key sociological notion, common to all the Scottish founding fathers of social science, of the unintended consequences of intended action.

social Darwinism. The belief that the development and structure of human societies can be explained in terms of the evolutionary forces that shape non-human biology, and particularly in terms of "the survival of the fittest". Herbert *Spencer, an early proponent, was in fact a social Darwinist before *Darwin. The prospect of some normative social application of the notion of natural selection attracted people as diverse as *Marx, Hitler, and Theodore Roosevelt. The central objection to any such application is that it seems to construe what is supposed to be an inexorable descriptive law of nature as if it could be at the same time and by the same token morally or politically mandatory. See also laws of nature; naturalistic fallacy.

social philosophy. An expression afflicted with the same vagueness and ambiguity as besets the word 'philosophy' itself, as well as with other troubles of its own. Originally it was applied to any general and comprehensive vision of how society is or ought to be. It is in this sense that many works that librarians would not classify as philosophy—works such as Adam Smith's The Wealth of

Nations (1776) or the Communist Manifesto (1848) by *Marx and *Engels—can be said to express (very different) social philosophies. More recently the same expression has come to be used like 'political philosophy', 'moral philosophy', 'metaphysics', and 'epistemology', to mark out an area within philosophy as an academic discipline. In this understanding social philosophy is usually taken to include almost everything in the philosophy of the social sciences, as well as a great deal of what it would be equally correct to label as either moral philosophy (see ethics) or *political philosophy.

Three of the central questions of the philosophy of the social sciences, and hence of social philosophy, are as follows. First, are there and could there be any laws of nature in this area; or is the necessity of such laws incompatible with a possibility of alternatives essential to the idea of human conduct? Second, how far, if at all, can sciences of man and society be objective and value-free (see Weber)? Third, is the explanation of the behaviour of human groups reducible to the explanation of the conduct of their component individuals; or does it have to refer to notions and entities that are irreducibly social or collective?

One paradigm case of social philosophy which is not at the same time philosophy of social science is the widespread discussion of the attempt made by John Rawls to explicate and articulate a concept of (social) *justice in his A Theory of Justice (1972). Another is the examination of the notions of individual and collective rights and responsibilities. This poses such questions as: 'Exactly who is responsible for war crimes, and how far?'; 'Must policies of "affirmative action" and "positive discrimination" in favour of members of formerly disadvantaged sexual or racial groups violate the rights of members of other sexual or racial groups, and be in themselves sexist or racist?'; and 'What is a right anyway, and how, if at all, are any rights to be identified as genuinely existing?'.

sociology of knowledge. A misnamed discipline, which is in fact devoted to discovering the social causes of people having whatever beliefs they do have, without prejudice to the quite different question of whether they have, or there are, sufficient grounds to warrant rating these beliefs as knowledge. Sociologists have in practice concentrated upon precisely those areas of belief in which they have themselves been most disinclined to award the diploma title 'knowledge'—religious belief, for instance, and other people's ideologies (*see* ideology). Partly for this reason, some people have more or less openly assumed that to produce a sociological explanation of the holding of a belief is *ipso facto* to discredit it—an assumption that must require of its misguided clients a fight to the last ditch against any sociology of sociology! *See* epistemics; epistemology; knowledge.

Socrates (*c*.470-399 BC). Greek philosopher, who was born and lived in Athens. He wrote no philosophical treatises but his influence on the development of philosophy was so strong that all philosophy before him has come to be known as 'Presocratic'. This influence was exerted through his younger associates, among whom the most famous and brilliant was *Plato. It is clear that Socrates had a compelling personality which attracted aristocratic young men and made him welcome in prominent Athenian circles. He remained on the fringe of public affairs, which probably accounts for his surviving many years of political turmoil in Athens. However, when he was over 70 he was convicted by the Athenian Assembly of impiety and corrupting youth, and sentenced to die by drinking hemlock. Plato's *Phaedo* contains a vivid portrayal of Socrates' last hours up to the time the sentence was carried out. As with all the dramatic accounts of Socrates—whether by Plato, Xenophon, or Aristophanes—it is impossible to separate fact from embellishment. Plato's account of the effects of hemlock do not agree with other sources and few scholars would nowadays claim the theory of Forms, prominent in the *Phaedo*, was invented by Socrates. It is common to assign the method and doctrines of Plato's early period to Socrates. But while the influence of Socrates must be strongest on this period, it is unlikely Plato *ever* acted purely as his master's stenographer.

Socratic fallacy. The mistake, characteristic of the Socrates of *Plato's earlier dialogues, of arguing that no one knows anything about *X*s, or even that any *X*s truly are *X*s, unless he can provide a *definition of the word '*X*'. The label was introduced by P. T. Geach, following Wittgenstein. This fallacy generates two paradoxes: first, many with every apparent claim to know what *X* is really cannot; second, no one could test any disputed definition of '*X*' against known instances of *X*hood.

Socratic method. The dialectical method supposedly employed by the historical Socrates, and displayed in *Plato's earlier dialogues. The crux is that the teacher should by patient questioning bring the pupil to recognize some true conclusion, without the teacher's telling the pupil that that conclusion is true. In *Meno*, for instance, Meno's slave is supposed to be induced to remember the conclusion of the theorem of *Pythagoras without his ever having been taught it either on this occasion or previously (*see* reminiscence, argument from). Tutors who have attempted to follow Socratic method will have been made aware of the importance of the fact that Plato was able to script the answers as well as the questions.

Socratic paradox. *See* Socratic fallacy.

solipsism. The theory that I am the sole existent. To be a solipsist I must hold that I alone exist independently, and that what I ordinarily call the outside world exists only as an object or content of my consciousness. This doctrine, though doubtless psychologically very difficult, if not impossible, to hold, is philosophically interesting in that many thinkers have thought it necessary to attempt refutations, or even to admit that, however bizarre, it is strictly irrefutable. Once we concede (following Descartes, Locke, and many others) that the immediate objects of sense experience are mind-dependent (ideas, impressions, *sense data, etc.), it is indeed questionable whether we can argue validly to the existence or nature of a mind-independent external world. Modern critics have, however, challenged this initial premise as misuse of terms; similarly objections have been raised against the use of 'I' which eliminates its normal contrasts. And Wittgenstein's *private language argument, if valid, in effect makes solipsism incompatible with our having a language to express it (see Wittgenstein). See also other minds; Reid; veil of appearance.

some. Traditionally in logic, at least one and perhaps as many as all but one. See quantifier.

sophists. Purveyors, usually professional and itinerant, of enlightenment and higher education, widely influential in Greece around 400 BC. The Greek word *sophistes* originally meant "expert"; it could apply to anyone possessing, or capable of imparting, expertise in virtually any subject; and some 5th century sophists, notably Hippias of Elis, had very wide interests. But the expertise principally demanded of them was the so-called political art of public communication by oratory and argument. Hence sophistic enlightenment tended to be a matter of rhetoric combined with the over-confident use of a primitive and often fallacious logic— the sophistries that brought the sophists into a lasting disrepute. Their principal achievement was to encourage independent thought in the Greek world by clarifying its moral attitudes and assumptions.

The sophists were very heterogeneous; no generalization can cover them all.

The two most eminent were *Protagoras of Abdera, with his subjectivist thesis that "man is the measure of all things", and Gorgias of Leontini, who made important contributions to rhetorical and aesthetic theory. The most influential doctrine associated with the sophists was the antithesis of Nature and Convention as moral authorities. It had numerous applications. Most commonly, the variations of law and Convention would be contrasted with Nature's eternal universally binding morality, itself identified with some sort of hedonism (as by Antiphon) or "the right of the stronger" (as by Callicles in Plato's *Gorgias* and Thrasymachus in the *Republic*). The contrast was to provide a basis for Cynic critiques of society (see Cynics), eventually finding a certain resolution in the Stoic concept of "natural law".

Sorel, Georges (1847-1922). French philosopher and social theorist, influenced by Nietzsche, Marx, and Bergson; a proponent of revolutionary *syndicalism and opponent of liberalism. Some of his ideas became the foundation of Italian fascism and were later reflected in the tenets of German national socialism.

Refléxions sur la violence (1908) sets out the doctrine of direct action, emphasizing the creative role of violence in history. Mediation and compromise were rejected as characteristic of the decadent (and liberal) bourgeoisie. The 'social myth' (an irrational means of directing the people towards expressing their aspirations) serves to bring about collective action. (True) socialism could be achieved only through violent revolution led by a disciplined and educated proletariat.

sorites. An argument with any number of premises and terms that otherwise satisfy the criteria for syllogisms, and can be set out as a series of syllogisms each of whose conclusions forms one premise of the succeeding syllogism. See syllogism.

soul. In one sense, the principle of life, defined as what makes living things alive. The Greek word for 'alive', like the equivalent Latin word '*animatus*' and its English derivative 'animate', is etymologically the same as 'ensouled'; this is the ancient connection between the ideas of soul and of life. *Plato, presumably following Socrates, both identified the soul with the person who reasons, decides, and acts, and assumed that this person or soul is not the familiar creature of flesh and blood but rather the incorporeal occupant and director of, even the prisoner in, that corporeal being. The separate Greek word translated 'soul' or 'mind' later becomes the English 'psyche', which is also the root in our 'psychology', 'psychosomatic', 'psychophysical', etc.

Having made this move, for which there were anticipations both in popular religion and earlier philosophy (*see* Orphism; Pythagoreanism), Plato, without apparently noticing the gulf between these two different interpretations of the word 'soul', proceeded to contend: first, that souls, like common-sense persons, are substances (*see* substance); and, second, for various reasons—including the fact that it is the principle of life—that the soul must be immortal. The later technical term 'substance' is here defined as something that can significantly be said to have a separate existence: like a dog, or the face of a Cheshire Cat, but unlike that dog's temper, or the grin on the Cheshire Cat's face. If souls are not in this sense substances, then it makes no sense at all to suggest that they might survive the dissolution of their bodies. Thus, given *Aristotle's account of the soul (in *De Anima*)—that it is simply the form of organization of a living body—it must be just nonsensical to suggest that this might survive the death and dissolution of its body.

Again, it is partly in terms of the same distinction that we have to understand another crucial contrast. When the soul is said to be what makes living things alive, this claim can be construed in two fundamentally different ways, which are often confused. In one, the key word 'makes' indicates the criterion in accordance with which things are to be said to be either alive or not alive. In the other it is causal, and the suggestion is that it is the presence and activity of a substantial soul which is responsible for bringing about all the various phenomena of life. Neither the soul nor the mind can serve as a term in the causal explanation of anything unless it is interpreted as the word for a substance. If 'having a soul' is defined as equivalent to 'being alive', or 'having a first class mind' as being able to perform at that level, then the soul or mind cannot be said to produce the phenomena; and to say that this has a soul or that has a first class mind is just another slightly more picturesque way of expressing (and therefore cannot explain) the facts that this is alive or that that displays high academic ability. (You cannot explain why it is the case that *p* simply by reiterating that *p*!) If, on the other hand, 'having a soul' or 'having a first class mind' are understood as referring to the possession and presence of entities that, although presumably incorporeal, are nevertheless in the present sense substantial, then it does at least make sense both to say that these entities might survive the dissolution of the bodies to which they are temporarily attached and to suggest that various important phenomena are to be attributed to their activity. *See also* survival and immortality.

space and time, philosophy of. The philosophy of space and time is more intimately connected with the nature of physical theory than any other branch of philosophy. Among the more philosophical questions are: whether it is proper to treat space and time as real things (as, in the words of *Newton, "the places as well of themselves as of all other things"); whether it is possible that there should exist empty space or eventless time; whether our conception of our world as spatially and temporally extended beyond us is a function of an a priori scheme we impose on reality rather than of reality itself (Kant); whether it is proper to think in terms of time flowing, or of the present existence of past events; and whether the asymmetry between past and future is logically inviolate (so that, say, time travel is logically impossible) or only contingently so. Among the problems that arise more urgently when we consider physical theory are: what is involved by way of observation and what by way of convention when we measure spatial extension and temporal duration; what sense it makes to talk of space as having a given topology (shape) or even, as *non-Euclidean geometry may have it, a finite size; what are the implications of the two theories of relativity for the relationship between space and time.

The main opposition is between champions of *absolute* and *relational* theories. An absolutist takes Newton's metaphor of the container seriously. He regards space or time as real things, containers of infinite extension or duration within which the whole succession of natural events in the world has a definite position (but in which they could have had another, had the whole process started earlier or in a different place). Similarly, things may really be at rest or really moving, and this will not simply be a matter of their relations to other objects changing. The first thoroughgoing relationist opposition to this came from *Leibniz: in his metaphysics absolute space vanishes, partly because reality—being composed of non-extended mental items—is not spatial at all. Similarly in *Kant the interpretation of our experience as that of a spatially extended world is an act of the mind: things-in-themselves have no spatial properties. Less strenuous relationists try to preserve the reality of space (or time) by interpreting propositions about them as asserting nothing but relations among ordinary material things: the container is not logically distinct from the things it is said to contain. The obvious obstacle here is that the relations involved are *sui generis*—spatial and temporal—so that

the gain is unclear. One intriguing focus for this dispute is Kant's problem of the incongruous counterparts: if we imagine a universe containing just one hand and nothing else then it *must* be either a left hand or a right hand (they cannot superimpose upon each other) even although all the relations of things, for example, of the palm to the index finger, would be the same in either case (*see* enantiomorphs).

The application of a geometry to space became problematic when it was found that mathematically space could be regarded as not the infinite box of Euclidean geometry, but finite and spherical, or, for instance, the shape of an American doughnut (toroidal). Can we really make sense of such suggestions? Or must they remain formalisms that are maintained only because of a decision to take something that is really curved as our standard of a straight line (the path of light, or the direction of gravitational force)? The classic proof that it is intelligible to conceive space as non-Euclidean is by Hans Reichenbach (1891–1953), who also insists on the conventionality ultimately involved in choosing any one geometry with which to interpret the regularities of our observation. In this he is following the conventionalist tradition of *Poincaré, who urged the parallel point for time: "Time should be so defined that the equations of mechanics may be as simple as possible." The equality of two time intervals is not intrinsic, but only relative to whichever clock is chosen to define (not measure) regular duration.

These worries about the measurement of duration culminated in the work of *Einstein. Philosophically, the fundamental shift in the special theory of relativity is the view that a judgment of simultaneity of two events corresponds to no unique physical reality. It would do if it were possible to synchronize clocks that are apart spatially, but it is not possible to do this without making assumptions about the speed of light. When these assumptions are made, events simultaneous relative to one observer are not so relative to one in motion with respect to him. This consequence is clearly congenial to the idealist tradition of seeing time as a subjectively imposed ordering. But the precise implications of Einstein's work are still controversial, particularly when in the general theory the geometry of space-time seems to play the part of a real fact, with explanatory properties.

Perhaps the most puzzling of the pure philosophical problems about time is that of its 'passage'. It is almost irresistible to think either in terms of its flowing or of our moving through it. But if so, we seem to imply that it could flow faster or slower—but then with respect to what? This problem demands a full understanding of the asymmetry between past and future; what has sometimes been called the nature of time's arrow. In this century attempts have been made—for example, by Reichenbach and Adolf Grünbaum (1923-)—at theories that see the asymmetry as fundamentally dependent on asymmetrical causal relations among events, thereby reversing the more natural idea, which is that causal relations are themselves subject to an independent temporal ordering. *See also* causation; relativity.

species. *See* genus.

specious present. The least temporal interval such that two modifications of experience, separated by that interval, may nevertheless seem to the subject to be co-present in his consciousness.

speech acts. Acts performed when words are uttered. J. L. *Austin claimed that the complex act of uttering words involves various simple component acts. There is, first, the *locutionary* act (saying words). This involves a *phonetic* act (making noises), a *phatic* act (using grammar) and a *rhetic* act (using meaningful words). Next there is the *illocutionary* act (act done *in* uttering words, for example, promising or stating). Finally there is the *perlocutionary* act *by* which we cause effects, for example, embarrassment, in other people by our words. Austin and others have believed that the study of speech acts may clarify problems about meaning, reference, and so on.

Spencer, Herbert (1820-1903). British philosopher. He had a varied career in teaching, engineering, and journalism, before settling down to develop, before Darwin's *Origin of Species*, his own central idea of evolution. Of a series of volumes on many aspects of philosophy and science, *First Principles* (1862) and *Principles of Ethics* (6 parts, 1879-93) are philosophically the most important.

For Spencer, philosophy is distinguished by its complete generality; unlike other sciences, it claims that its characteristic theories are true of everything. But only in the case of evolutionary theory is this claim empirically defensible, and Spencer set himself to show how his principle of evolution, of progress from "an indefinite incoherent homogeneity to a definite coherent heterogeneity", is exemplified throughout Nature (though significantly he has least to say about its inorganic side) and in the individual, social, and even moral life of humanity. *See also* social Darwinism.

Spengler, Oswald (1880-1936). German philosopher of history. Main work: *Der Untergang des Abendlandes* (2 volumes, 1918, 1922). Rejecting traditional unilinear accounts of historical development, Spengler portrayed the human past as being fundamentally the story of self-contained 'cultures' that conformed to quasi-biological patterns of growth and decay. He also committed himself to a thoroughgoing relativism: every system of thought or value, being culturally determined, was necessarily devoid of universal validity.

Spinoza, Benedictus (*also* Baruch) de (1632-77). Rationalist philosopher of Jewish extraction, who was born in Amsterdam and spent his working life in Holland. His family had fled from Portugal to escape Catholic persecution, but even in relatively tolerant Holland his own views excited hostility. He was expelled from the Jewish community in 1656 for heresy; later, his *Tractatus Theologico-Politicus* (Treatise on Theology and Politics) (1670), was attacked by Christian theologians because of its radical views about the Bible, and was banned in 1674. Because of such attacks Spinoza's major work, the *Ethics* (Latin title: *Ethica Ordine Geometrico Demonstrata*), did not appear until 1677, after his death.

Spinoza's philosophy, which is expressed in an elaborate and highly personal vocabulary, is notoriously difficult. However, much light is thrown on it if it is regarded as the expression of a certain view about the Nature and scope of explanation. Like Descartes (whose views he had studied carefully, but critically) Spinoza believed that explanation is in essence deductive. This view can be related to what was in the 17th century a new science—the science of mathematical physics. Scientists such as Descartes and Galileo explained the nature and activity of bodies by concentrating on their measurable aspects. Universal laws were stated in quantitative terms, and the behaviour of individual bodies or classes of bodies was shown to follow logically from these laws. Spinoza, like Descartes, saw this as just one application of a method that could be applied to everything that human beings are capable of knowing. All genuine explanation was deductive in nature; everything that we really understand can be shown to follow with logical necessity from a few basic truths or axioms of a very general kind. These axioms were not conjectures, but were known to be true, in that they could not logically be denied. The task of the philosopher was to state these axioms and develop their logical consequences in the areas that concerned him. Spinoza's main interests lay in the field of moral philosophy, and in his *Ethics* he presented his views about the nature of the good in the form of the geometry of Euclid, the most perfect deductive system known to him.

In order to give a deductive proof of propositions about what is good for human beings, Spinoza had to establish truths about the nature of such beings, and these truths in turn had to be derived from others that are still more fundamental. So Spinoza begins his *Ethics* with an account of what, for him, is the most fundamental being—an absolutely infinite Being, whose existence cannot logically be denied. Spinoza calls this infinite being by the name of 'God', but this God is very different from the God of theism. For Spinoza's God is not a personal, creative agent, separate from the Universe that he creates. What Spinoza thinks about the nature of God, and the relations between God and things, is to be found in his doctrine of substance, attribute, and finite modes. In the *Ethics*, Spinoza begins with substance and proceeds to the finite modes by way of the attributes, but for expository purposes it is convenient to reverse this order. Finite modes are particular things, where 'thing' has a wide sense, so that it covers not only physical things, but also the minds of individuals. Spinoza's use of the term 'mode' to refer to particular things is an example of what would now be called 'conceptual revision'. Descartes had said that minds and bodies are substances—mental and physical substances respectively. Spinoza argued that this way of talking is misleading, in that it suggests that particular things have an independence that they do not really have. Take, for example, a physical thing such as Descartes' body. This is really a complex entity (in Spinoza's language, an 'individual') consisting of certain corpuscles in certain relations, and it lasts just as long as these corpuscles preserve these relations. These corpuscles, however, are not atoms. Although Spinoza admired the Greek atomists, he would have said that they were wrong in supposing the existence of a large number of corporeal substances. The ultimate units of physics are really modes of matter, differentiated simply by motion and rest. To call them 'modes' is to say that they cannot really be separated from matter, any more than, say, the cubical shape of a body can be separated from the body itself. Similarly, the ultimate entities with which the philosophy of mind deals—Spinoza calls them 'ideas'—are modes; more specifically, they are modes of thought.

In place of the term 'matter', Spinoza normally uses the term 'extension', but it is important to realize that for Spinoza, extension is not something abstract. It is *that which* is extended, just as 'thought' for Spinoza is that which thinks. Now, although thought and extension have modes, they are not themselves substances. If they were, they would be entirely independent of each other, and it would be impossible to explain why, given such and such a state of X's body, there is (and indeed must be) such and such a state of X's mind. This was something that Descartes had failed to explain; but, Spinoza would add, Descartes' insistence on the absolute distinction between mind and matter was not wholly mistaken. Mind is not body, nor is body mind. Moreover, in giving a causal explanation of physical events, we must state our explanations in purely physical terms; a physical event is never caused by a mental event. Similarly, a mental event is never caused by a physical event. It seems, then, that mind and matter are distinct, and yet intimately related. Spinoza argues that the problem is to be solved by viewing mind and matter, not as distinct substances, but as different 'attributes' of one and the same infinite substance. A physical event and the corresponding mental event—say, the puncturing of X's skin and X's feeling of pain—are modes of one and the same substance, expressed through the different attributes of extension and thought. The infinite substance, to which the attributes must be ascribed, is God. All things, then, are in a sense 'in' God, and for this reason Spinoza's philosophy is often called a *pantheism. In his own time, Spinoza was often called an 'atheist'; and indeed, if by 'atheism' one means the denial of the existence of a personal God, then Spinoza was an atheist. He could, however, defend his use of the term 'God' to refer to an impersonal being. He could point out that the term 'God' was commonly used in philosophy to refer to the ultimate ground or explanation of all things; and (he might say) his God is just that.

The nature of the substance-attribute relation in Spinoza has been the subject of much controversy. He does not seem to want to say that the attributes are ways in which a substance that is neither extended nor thinking appears to us; substance is really extended and really thinks. Nor, again, is 'substance' merely a collective name for mind and matter. If it were, the necessary connection between mental and physical events would remain unexplained. None of this, however, explains what the substance-attribute relation is. Pressed by a correspondent to explain this relation, Spinoza once (Letter No. 9, March 1663) compared the way in which the same individual is sometimes referred to by different names. What is said truly of Jacob is, and must be, true of Israel also; not because there is some inexplicable correspondence between two individual substances, but bcause 'Jacob' and 'Israel' are different names for the same individual. This corresponds roughly to a modern view, according to which one should speak, not of 'mind' and 'matter' as separate entities, but of a 'mental language' and a 'physical language' as providing different and independent ways of describing the same events.

What has been said so far has concerned Spinoza's views about the nature of explanation. To give a rounded account of his philosophy, it is necessary to sketch his views about the scope of explanation, and the way in which he faces the consequences of these views. Spinoza holds that everything is explicable; of everything that exists or happens, we can in principle say why it exists or happens. Given Spinoza's views about the nature of explanation, it follows that everything *must* exist or happen as it does. In Spinoza's language, "Everything is determined by the necessity of the divine nature" (*Ethics*, Part I, prop. 29). Or, in less metaphysical terms, "Everything is determined by universal laws of nature to exist and act in a certain and determinate way" (*Tractatus Theologico-Politicus*, chap. 4). This led Spinoza to deny the existence of freewill (*see* freewill and determinism). Whenever a person makes a decision, his decision is determined; that is, it is necessitated.

It may seem from this that Spinoza's philosophy can have no place for the concept of freedom, but this is not so. Spinoza says that an agent is free, not in so far as his acts are undetermined—there are no such acts—but in so far as they are self-determined (*Ethics*, Part I, definition 7). It is in this sense that God is free. Spinoza's God does not have the freedom that is ascribed to the God of theism—that of an agent who can make a choice other than the one that he actually makes. Whatever Spinoza's God does follows necessarily from the nature of God. On the other hand, it follows from the nature of God *alone*—there is nothing outside God which could, as it were, force God's hand—and so Spinoza can ascribe freedom to God. It might be thought that *only* God can be free, in that only the infinite being can be self-determined. Spinoza, however, ascribes freedom to some (though not all) human beings. In each individual, Spinoza declares, there is an endeavour (*conatus*) to persevere in its own being as far as it can, that is, to resist forces that are external and hostile to it. In the case of human beings, such forces include the emotions that Spinoza calls 'passions'. In so far as a man overcomes these and follows the life of reason, he preserves his real being and so can be called 'free'. The idea that freedom consists in the mastery of the passions through the life of reason is an important one in the history of ethics, and is sometimes called *the concept of positive freedom*. Another important strand of Spinoza's ethical thought is to be found in his idea of freedom. In calling the rational man the free man, Spinoza does not imply that his ideal of humanity is the 'cold intellectual'. The free man has emotions, but they are emotions that spring from the whole man and not (as the passions do) from just a part. Spinoza's ideal of humanity, then, is not a fragmented or stunted individual; he is the integral human being, the whole man.

spirit. A word commonly used to translate the Hegelian term *Geist* (also translated as 'mind'). According to Hegel, spirit differs from nature in that spirit is an 'I'; in Hegel's language, spirit has being 'for itself' (*Encyclopaedia*, par. 381, Addition). Hegel recognizes three types of spirit: subjective, objective, and absolute. The philosophy of *subjective spirit* studies the individual in abstraction from his social relations, and discusses such topics as consciousness, memory, thought, and will—topics that are covered by what is commonly called 'the philosophy of mind'. The philosophy of *objective spirit* deals with a man's relations to his fellow men; the fundamental concept here is that of 'right' (*Recht*), a term having both a legal and a moral sense. This part of Hegel's philosophy includes his ethics and his political theory. The highest stage of spirit is *absolute spirit*, whose three parts are art, religion, and philosophy. According to Hegel, the study of absolute spirit has to do with spirit as 'infinite', by which he means, not spirit as something boundless, but as having returned to itself from self-estrangement. This is to say that, at this stage of thought, one recognizes that subjective and objective are one; in other words, one has grasped a basic principle of Hegel's idealism. *See also* Hegel.

square of opposition. In medieval texts, a diagram summarizing the logical relations between the four categorical propositions each having the same subject and *predicate terms (*see* syllogism). These propositions are traditionally represented by A, E, I, O.

When the propositions involved are formalized within contemporary, predicate logic, it appears that these relationships were not all correctly stated. This

square of opposition

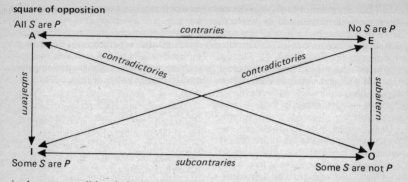

is because traditional logic operated under the assumption that for each term used there is, or has been, at least one thing to which that term applies. The corresponding assumption is not made for predicates in contemporary logic; there may be nothing to which a given predicate can be correctly applied. If it is allowed that there may be no things which are S, then of the relations indicated on the diagram only those of *contradiction continue to hold.

The term 'square of opposition' is also sometimes extended to cover any set of four propositions between which there are the 'oppositions' or logical relationships indicated on the diagram. Such propositions may, for example, be constructed using any two terms A and B (such as 'black' and 'white') for which 'c is A' and 'c is B' are contraries but not contradictories. 'c is not A' and 'c is not B' will then be subcontraries. *See also* contradictory; contrary; subcontraries.

stadium (*or* **racecourse**) **paradox.** *See* Zeno's paradoxes.

Stagirite, the. Aristotle, so called after his birthplace, Stagira.

statements *and* **sentences.** Many recent philosophers have accepted "statements" as the least unsatisfactory one word answer to the question "What is it that we call true or false?" This contrasts with ordinary usage, which tends to reserve the term for important, carefully worded pronouncements, and applies it

to the setting-out of a problem or proposal, which has no truth-value, as well as to an assertion of (purported) fact, which has. A more serious difficulty is that "statement" can mean either the-act-of-stating or what-is-stated; while the latter seems clearly better fitted to bear a truth-value, it creates problems over whether what-is-stated must be accepted as some kind of entity—and if so what kind—independent of the act-of-stating and the words used therein.

Sentences, while they can be variously assessed, for example as good or bad English, are not in themselves true or false, though sometimes loosely spoken of as such. They have meanings but not truth-values. Thus even a sentence which, so far as grammatical structure is concerned, *can* be used to make a statement, can also be used for other purposes, like story-telling or providing an example in a lesson, where no question of truth or falsity arises. Statement-making is simply one among the many uses of such sentences.

statistics. The science of handling information about classes of things, or populations, where each member is associated with one of a set of possible properties or outcomes. A statistical hypothesis will describe the class by assigning a probability to each outcome (or in the case of a continuous property, such as height, to an outcome falling in any defined range). An outcome may be regarded as the value of a random variable (*see* randomness), and the hypothesis gives the variable a distribution. Some distributions are well known: the bell-shaped normal distribution describing the probability of the various proportions of heads in sequences of tosses of a coin, or the Poisson distribution assigning a probability to a square having 0, 1, 2… peas on it if one scatters peas across a chessboard. Various distributions, such as the X^2, test the likelihood of given results if a particular statistical hypothesis is assumed.

Philosophical interest attaches to the meaning of the probability statements arrived at (*see* probability theory); to the inductive assumptions involved in supposing that a process generating a class of events is describable in terms of fixed probabilities (*see* induction); and to the logic of acceptance or rejection of statistical hypotheses by the evidence of frequency or outcome in given finite samples. This evidence never strictly falsifies or proves a statistical hypothesis. Controversy has centred on whether it ever licenses the rejection of a statistical hypothesis in isolation, as maintained by the followers of R. A. Fisher, or only licenses its rejection in favour of some other hypothesis having a better fit with the observed frequencies, as held by the followers of Neyman and Pearson. *See also* distribution; likelihood; randomness.

stipulative definition. *See* definition.

Stoa. *See* Stoicism.

stochastic. Denoting a physical process that gives rise to a class of events within which a characteristic has a definite probability; that is, a random variable (*see* randomness) takes on a defined *distribution.

stochastic process. A process whose development is probabilistic, that is whose stages are determined by the values of one or more random variables (*see* randomness). The classic example is the varying length of a queue, which has a probability of members arriving or leaving within a given time interval.

Stoicism. A philosophy named after the *Stoa Poikile*, a hall in Athens where it was first promulgated around 300 BC by *Zeno of Citium. Stoicism, especially in its definitive formulation by *Chrysippus (280-07 BC), was rigorously systematic. Its logic, ethics, and physics were united by a pervasive concept, deriving ultimately from *Heraclitus, of *logos. For the Stoics, the principles of rational discourse studied in logic reflect the processes of cosmic Reason studied by natural philosophy (Nature and Reason—like Fate, Providence, and God—all refer in fact to the same agency), while a "life consistent with Nature" and with Reason is the goal of human existence.

Physics. The Stoics were materialists, denying full existence to anything without body. They also believed that the world is a living intelligent Being. Thus they analysed the ultimate principles of reality as passive unqualified matter and a rational active cause, namely God. But these are abstractions. Matter in fact is never completely without qualities; it breaks down into earth, water, air, and fire—elements qualified as dry, wet, cold, and hot respectively and capable of turning into each other. (Hence the doctrine of cosmic conflagration, the periodic absorption by fire of the other grosser elements.) Equally, God can only act upon matter through the material vehicle of "artistic fire" or "intelligent *pneuma*", a mixture of air and fire. The *pneuma* permeates the whole cosmos, a finite continuum of matter set in an infinite void. Highly active, it "totally interpenetrates" other inert matter, and so differentiates things. Individual objects are no more than local dispositions of the material continuum; what marks off one from another and holds it together is a "tensional motion" of the *pneuma* in it to and back from its surface. The name *pneuma* which gives inorganic structures their cohesion becomes, when present in other ratios, *physis* or the power of growth in plants and soul in animals. In human adults, it achieves its purest and fieriest temper as *logos*. What in animals is soul is reason in human beings; our so-called irrational impulses or passions are not devoid of reason, but rather malfunctionings of it. Impulses in fact are formed in the same way as judgments; both entail "assent" to an "impression" (*phantasia*) of something which is or should be. Impressions made on the mind through the senses by external objects are, further, the basis of knowledge, our criterion for truth being the *cataleptic* (apprehending) *phantasia*, (an impression of X such that it could only derive from X), which, when grasped, entails grasp of its object (*compare* Descartes). Our general concepts and hence our knowledge are built up, directly or indirectly, from such impressions. Human reason with its powers of knowledge, thought, and decision is the same substance as cosmic Reason which, in the guise of Fate, Necessity, or Providence, is the active cause of all that occurs; and they operate by the same rules. Thus effects follow their causes, internal and external, with the inevitability of conclusions following premises in a valid syllogism. Our freedom is one simply of spontaneity: we can wish or not wish to act as we act, but we cannot act otherwise. "Fate draws the willing, drags the recusant"; and the Stoics maintained, with manfully "stoic" optimism, that all things occur, when viewed from a cosmic perspective, for the best.

Logic. 'Physical', or metaphysical, doctrines had their effect on Stoic logic, a subject including grammar as well as formal reasoning. (The Stoics in fact pioneered various linguistic studies.) Thus the belief that bodies alone are fully real led to an important distinction between significant utterance (the spoken words 'Dion walks'), its material reference (Dion himself) and its meaning, an incorporeal *lekton* or "thing said" (the statement about Dion). Only if it refers to particular individuals can a proposition be wholly true, and the Stoic syllogism is concerned primarily with relating propositions that do so; its basic form is "If p, then q. But p. Therefore q."

Ethics. Stoic morality was rigorously naturalistic. Our supreme good is "to live consistently with Nature", which means "consistently with Reason" or "virtuously". The Stoic gradation of values and actions rested on zoological theory. Every animal is born with an instinctive *oikeiosis* (affection) for itself, which makes it seek things—like food, shelter, a mate—that "accord with its nature", and ensure its preservation. For human beings too, with our further endowment of reason, such activities are "appropriate". Health, wealth, and, since we are social animals, the good of our community are all "according to nature", and it is proper for us to seek them. Reason, however, enables us to determine "appropriate actions" with ever-increasing accuracy and consistency, till ideally we reach the point of discerning something incomparably more precious than "things according to Nature", and that is the sheer concord and rationality of Nature's prescriptions. Once discerned, this preempts our affection; to act in harmony with it, whether or not our actions are successful, is virtue; and "virtue on its own is enough for blessedness." The Stoics drew the sharpest, most paradoxical distinctions between moral worth which alone is good and things according to Nature which are merely preferable, between right action based on full moral knowledge and merely appropriate action, between the seldom if ever occurring wise man and the foolish remainder of mankind. These paradoxes, along with the condemnation of all passion as essentially a misjudgment of good and evil, were the most controversial features of Stoic ethics.

The 'Old Stoa' of Zeno and his successors down to Antipater (d. 129 BC) is commonly distinguished from the more eclectic 'Middle' Stoa of *Panaetius and *Posidonius, as well as from the Late or Roman Stoa with its increasing concentration on the well-being of the soul (*see* Epictetus; Marcus Aurelius; Seneca).

Stratonician presumption. The claim that it is up to anyone wanting to postulate a God (or any other initiating or sustaining principle outside and beyond the *Universe) to show sufficient reason for so doing. Why cannot the Universe's existence and fundamental characteristics be themselves the ultimates of explanation? The *Five Ways of St. Thomas *Aquinas are deployed to meet and, hopefully, to defeat two objections, one of which is in effect a statement of this presumption. The name refers to Strato of Lampsacus.

Strato of Lampsacus (d. 269 BC). Head of the *Lyceum after Aristotle's successor Theophrastus, from about 286 BC. Strato wrote extensively and his revision of Aristotle's physics, eliminating the *teleology, influenced Hero and other Alexandrians. He thus cleared the way for what Bayle and after him Hume were to call 'the Stratonician atheism'. This was the view that the *Universe is ultimate and self-sustaining and there is no call to appeal to some divine explanatory principle outside it. See First Cause; First Mover.

straw man. A position, not in fact held by an opponent in an argument, which is invented and assailed in preference to attending to his actual stance. The adoption of this disreputable evasive tactic must suggest that the actual position is more defensible.

Strawson, Peter Frederick (1919-). British philosopher, Waynflete Professor of Metaphysical Philosophy at Oxford (1968-).

A leading advocate of 'ordinary language philosophy', he argues in the article 'On Referring' (*Mind*, 1950) and again in his book *Introduction to Logical Theory* (1952) that some sentences, though meaningful, make no assertion and thus have no truth-value (*compare* descriptions, theory of); the use of a sentence in a specific context cannot be disregarded in analysis. In the book he also examines the relationship between ordinary language and formal logic,

holding that the complexity of the former is very inadequately represented by the latter. Strawson points out that since inductive arguments are by definition reasonable, the method requires no further justification (*see* induction).

Individuals (1959) (subtitled *An Essay in Descriptive Metaphysics*) examines the structure of thought about the world and posits material objects as the 'basic particulars' in relation to which all (including non-spatiotemporal) objects are identifiable.

stream of consciousness. A phrase coined by the psychologist William *James as a characterization of the mind, that is, that it is a process of continuous thought. It can be seen as an attempt to find a middle way between two previous opposing concepts of the mind: the Cartesian (that mind is a special and unknown kind of mental substance), and the Humean (that it is nothing but a bundle of sensations). "The traditional psychology," James once wrote, "talks like one who should say a river consists of nothing but pailsful, spoonsful, quartpotsful, bowlsful, and other moulded forms of water. Even were the pails and pots all actually standing in the stream, still between them the free water would continue to flow. It is just this free water of consciousness that psychologists resolutely overlook."

strict implication. See implication and entailment.

structuralism. A method of approach, rather than a distinct philosophy, that has application in both linguistics and the social sciences. **1.** (in linguistics) The theory that language is best described in terms of its irreducible structural units in morphology, phonology, etc. See structure, deep and surface. **2.** (in the social sciences) The view that the key to the understanding of observed phenomena lies in the underlying structures and systems of social organization. See Lévi-Strauss.

structure, deep and surface. Terms occurring in Chomsky's analysis of grammar. This analysis supposes that speakers possess rules for combining various grammatical elements, such as verbs, tense signs, and nouns, into sequences. These initially unidiomatic strings (the deep, underlying structure) are then converted into vernacular speech by *transformation rules. They thus take on the surface structures of everyday speech. Ambiguous surface structures, for example, 'Flying planes can be dangerous', may have two different structures underlying them. Again, two surface structures may have one underlying structure: 'John hit Bill' and 'Bill was hit by John' are optional variations in idiomatic English of one underlying structure. Furthermore, whereas 'John was persuaded by Bill to ski' superficially takes 'John' as subject, its deep structure shows 'Bill' to be the 'real' subject. Other philosophers have stressed that that element in language that Chomsky calls surface grammar may be misleading and a temptation to philosophical error; they include *Russell ('On Denoting'), *Wittgenstein (*passim*), and *Ryle ('Systematically Misleading Expressions').

Sturm und Drang. (German for: storm and stress.) A German literary movement of the late 18th century, which can be seen as the earliest phase of German *romanticism. Its characteristic themes were the exaltation of nature and an opposition to the rationalism of the *Enlightenment. The major figures of the movement were the young *Goethe and J. C. F. *Schiller, and it was influenced by *Herder's philosophy of art.

subaltern. A statement *q* is a subaltern of the statement *p* iff *q* is true whenever *p* is true and *p* is false whenever *q* is false. For example, 'Some swans are black' is a subaltern of 'All swans are black'. *Subalternation* is a term used in scholastic logic for the relation that is now more often called logical implication (*see* implication and entailment). See also square of opposition.

subconscious. A mental state or process occurring just below the level of awareness. In psychoanalytic terms, it occurs between the *unconscious and the conscious. *See* Freud.

subcontraries. A pair of statements that can be simultaneously true but which cannot be simultaneously false. For example, 'Some rats are brown' and 'Some rats are not brown' are subcontraries. *See also* square of opposition.

subject. *See* predicate; term.

subjective idealism. *See* idealism.

subjectivism *and* **objectivism.** Two meta-ethical views (*see* ethics) that can be discussed together, since any argument in favour of one is usually an argument against the other and vice versa.

Subjectivism. In its simplest form, the position held by someone who believes that all moral attitudes are merely a matter of personal taste. 'Eating people is wrong', for example, and its contradictory become not true or false but simply expressions of the dietary preferences of the speaker. Fortunately, since people raised in the same society will have received a similar moral education their tastes will usually coincide. But this should not blind us to the fact that, if we encounter someone who does not share our tastes, then there is no form of proof by which we can demonstrate his error.

Simple subjectivism is so naive that it is unlikely to be held by anyone in its pure form. Typically the subjectivist will develop his position in one of two ways. (1) He may say that morality is not dependent on individual taste but on the natural desires of mankind taken as a whole. It is a contingent and not a necessary fact that men have the desires they do, so that given a change in human preferences morality could change. But as a matter of fact, men do value certain things more than others and morality is an expression of these collective tastes. Thus '*X* is good' becomes 'All, or most, men desire *X*'. The problem with this analysis is that it rules out as literally meaningless any attempt to alter majority belief by moral argument. (2) Alternatively, the subjectivist may continue to rely on the individual, in the sense of ultimately regarding human desire as the source of moral value, but allow greater scope for rational argument in maintaining that moral judgments must be supported by evidence and are as open to logical appraisal as any other judgment. This would mean for instance that the moral judgment of 'X is good' would mean 'X has certain qualities, a, b, c, and I approve of anything with those qualities". Unlike (1) this leaves room for argument. He who maintains 'X is good' can be challenged by showing that X does not include one or any of the qualities, a, b, c, or by showing that he does not always accept the principle that anything which is a, b, c, is necessarily good, since here is Y with all those qualities and he disapproves of, or dislikes Y.

Objectivism. The belief that there are certain moral truths that would remain true whatever anyone or everyone thought or desired. For instance, 'No one should ever deliberately inflict pain on another simply to take pleasure in his suffering' might be thought of as a plausible example. Even in a world of sadists who all rejected it, the contention remains true, just as '5 + 7 = 12' remains correct even if there is no one left to count. The problem for the objectivist is to determine the status of moral truths and the method by which they can be established. If we accept that such judgments are not reports of what is but only relate to what ought to be (see naturalistic fallacy) then they cannot be proved by any facts about the nature of the world. Nor can they be analytic, since this would involve lack of action-guiding content; 'One ought always to do the right thing' is plainly true in virtue of the words involved but it is unhelpful as a practical guide to action (see analytic and synthetic). At this point the objectivist may talk of 'self-evident truths', but can he deny the

subjectivist's claim that self-evidence is in the mind of the beholder? If not, what is left of the claim that some moral judgments are true? The subjectivist may well feel that all that remains is that there are some moral judgments with which he would wish to associate himself. To hold a moral opinion is, he suggests, not to know something to be true but to have preferences regarding human activity. See also relativism.

sublime, the. 1. That which is beyond all comparison (that is, absolutely) great, either mathematically in terms of limitless magnitude, or dynamically in terms of limitless power. This is the standard meaning, derived from *Kant. 2. The term used to designate natural objects that inspire a kind of awed terror through sheer immensity.

In the 18th century, it was common to consider aesthetic experience under the paired concepts of the beautiful and the sublime. The sublime was held to be satisfying either, as for Edmund *Burke, in virtue of the pleasurable nature of the terror that it arouses, or, as for Kant, in virtue of its intimation of a capacity of the mind to apprehend the limitless or indeterminable.

subsistence. A mode of *being distinguished by *Meinong and others from the three-dimensional, full-colour existence of objects existing in space and time. Subsistence is thought of as a monochrome and insubstantial analogue possessed by universals, numbers, and the difference between red and green. Others would allow subsistence to the fictional and the imaginary also.

substance. A term with several interrelated senses. 1. One definition of substance makes use of the logical notions of subject and *predicate; regarded in this way, S is a substance if S is a subject of predicates, but cannot be predicated in turn of any other subject. This concept of substance can be traced back to Aristotle (Categories 2a12), and plays an important part in the philosophy of Leibniz.

2. A substance of the kind just described is also said (for example by Aristotle, *Categories* 2a13) to be that which does not exist in a subject, where something is understood to 'exist in' a subject if it cannot exist separately from it (Aristotle, *Categories* 1a24-5). In this sense, then, a substance may be said to be that which has an independent existence. Philosophers disagree about *what* has independent existence; for example, Aristotle said that a particular man is a substance, whereas Spinoza would say that only God has a truly independent existence.

3. One and the same substance (in senses 1 and 2) can have predicates that are contrary to each other, provided that these predicates are not simultaneous (*compare* Aristotle, *Categories* 4a10); that is, a substance which has the predicate *P* at one time may have the predicate not-*P* at another. Viewed in this way, a substance is regarded as that which remains the same through change. This concept of substance, which involves a reference to time, is defended by Kant in the *Critique of Pure Reason*.

4. The Greek word that is translated as 'substance' (*ousia*) can also be rendered as 'essence', and some philosophers view the substance of a thing as what it really is, as opposed to the way in which it appears. This sense of 'substance' is related to sense 3, in that the essence is regarded as remaining the same, whereas the appearances change. Locke (who also uses the term 'substance' in sense 2) is among the philosophers who regard the substance of a thing as what it really is.

substrate (*or* **substratum**). That which bears properties. For example, the subject of any change between a pair of opposites, such as the material without which heat cannot itself change into cold, is a substrate.

Subtle Doctor. The traditional scholastic nickname for *Duns Scotus.

sufficient condition. *See* necessary and sufficient conditions.

sufficient reason, principle of. A principle of *Leibniz, stating that for every fact there is a reason why it is so and not otherwise. This reason takes the form of an a priori proof founded on the nature of the subject and predicate terms used in stating the fact. Leibniz used the principle freely; to prove, for example, that there could not be two identical atoms (for there would be no reason for one to be in one place and the other somewhere else, rather than vice versa) or that the world did not begin at a moment in time (for there would be no reason for it to have begun at one moment rather than another).

sui generis. (Latin for: of its (or his or her) own kind.) Of a thing believed to be unique, and not a member of a class with other fellow members. God is often said to be *sui generis*.

summum bonum. (Latin for: the greatest good.) The concept, introduced into ethical discourse by *Aristotle, of the greatest good that is sought by all men. The Latin phrase was put into currency among moral philosophers by the writings of *Cicero. There has, naturally, been considerable disagreement as to what, if anything, may be correctly so called.

supervenient characteristics. Properties or qualities that depend on some other property or quality.

suppositio. In medieval logic, the thing or things for which a noun or substantive stands. For non-substantives, for example, adjectives or verbs, there was a corresponding *copulatio*. A variety of types of *suppositio* was distinguished. Thus *suppositio simplex* meant the class concept to which a common noun refers, for example, 'man' in 'Man is an animal'.

surface structure. *See* structure, deep and surface.

survival *and* **immortality.** All doctrines here should be seen as rival responses to familiar, undeniable, and undenied realities; that, first, in the understanding in which after some disaster we distinguish the dead from survivors, it is logically impossible to survive death; and that, second, in the same understanding, and discounting certain miraculous exceptions, all men are mortal (*see* miracle). Among claims that some or all do nevertheless survive death, perhaps for ever, we have to distinguish two fundamentally different sorts. One, which most consider the only genuine article, is distinguished by a crucial implication: if such a claim is true about a person, then that person has to expect to continue to have *experience after death. The other employs the words 'immortality', and more rarely 'survival', while disclaiming all such personal implications. A classical example is Aristotle's notoriously difficult doctrine of the immortality of the intellect; belief in personal survival, and still more personal immortality, was for him a textbook illustration of the preposterous.

The first obstacle for the champion of personal survival to get around or over —and with personal immortality too it is the first step which counts—is the fact of death and dissolution. Three routes may be attempted, with possibilities of combining elements from more than one.

The first way, not favoured by any philosopher of repute, maintains that people really are their astral bodies, real bodies albeit not presently detectable by any normal means, which at death detach themselves from the ordinary mortal body. For obvious reasons this is how film-makers usually represent survival. The problem is to specify positive content for the adjective 'astral' without thereby making the whole hypothesis demonstrably false.

The second way, appealing first to religious revelation rather than philosophical argument, accepts both that our corporeality is essential and that death involves our dissolution, but maintains that dead people will in due course be reconstituted by an act of sheer Omnipotence. Thus the *Koran* warns confidently mortalist unbelievers: "Do they not see that Allah, who has created the heavens and the earth, has power to create their like? Their fate is preordained beyond all doubt" (The Night Journey). The objection here is that such new creations would indeed be only "their like"; replicas, that is, not the unbelievers themselves. Mixing elements from two ways, and defending the similar Christian doctrine, *Aquinas could reply that the continuity between this life and the next, and hence *personal identity, would be maintained by the surviving disembodied soul. For the soul in the synthesizing Aquinas is sufficiently Platonic to be a substance while still sufficiently Aristotelian to be, without body, not a person.

The third, and among philosophers by far the most popular way, is Platonic-Cartesian. This argues that the person, or at least the essential person, is an incorporeal substance. It has to be a *substance, meaning something which can significantly be said to exist separately, since it could make no sense to suggest that anything like the Aristotelian *soul, as the form of organization of the living body, might survive the dissolution of that body. It has to be incorporeal, since how else could it escape unnoticed and unnoticeable? "How shall we bury you?" Crito asks in Plato's *Phaedo* (§115C), and Socrates replies with a gentle laugh, "However you please, if you can catch me and I do not get away from you."

Here there are still enormous difficulties to overcome before we have an evidently coherent hypothesis to test. Can these putative incorporeal substances be identified and individuated? Can we, that is to say, give a positive account of such a substance, explaining how one is in principle to be distinguished from another existing at the same time, or identified with itself at another time? That these are hard questions is seen by considering the difficulties with the problem of personal identity encountered by Locke, Hume, and others who take people to be incorporeal or not essentially corporeal. And that assumption itself is countered by Wittgenstein's insistence that almost everything to be said about people in some ways presupposes our corporeality: "The human body is the best picture of the human soul" (*Philosophical Investigations*, II (iv)).

syllogism. As defined by Aristotle, the founder of the traditional formal *logic, a 'discourse in which, certain things being stated, something other than what is stated follows of necessity from their being so'. Although this definition theoretically comprehends every kind of valid *deduction, Aristotle himself, and almost all his successors for over two millennia, in practice confined their attention very largely, if not quite exclusively, to syllogisms linking propositions that can be expressed in a categorical subject-predicate form. There are traditionally considered to be four forms that such categorical propositions can take. If S and P are terms, the categorical propositions with S as subject are 'All S are P', 'No S are P', 'Some S are P', and 'Some S are not P'. The simplest, atomic syllogism consists in three propositions of which the first two, the premises, are supposed to entail the third, the conclusion. If the argument is indeed valid, it is so in virtue of the fact that it would not be possible to assert the premises and to deny the conclusion without thereby contradicting oneself. Where the three propositions are categorical it is said to be a *categorical syllogism*. The propositions of a categorical syllogism must between them employ exactly three terms, each term appearing twice, as, for example, in 'All men are mortal, and no gods are mortal, therefore no men are gods.' The arrangement of the terms in the premises determines the *figure* of the syllogism. The four possibilities are set out in the diagram. The term M, which appears in both premises but not in the conclusion, is called the *middle term* (or *medium*) of the syllogism.

The restriction of attention to categorical syllogisms precluded, in particular, any adequate treatment of arguments involving propositions that

1	M – P		2	P – M
	S – M			S – M
	S – P			S – P

3	M – P		4	P – M
	M – S			M – S
	S – P			S – P

state some relation between two or more terms: the very simple relational proposition 'Calgary is south of Edmonton', for instance, cannot without gross violence be represented as attributing a predicate peculiar to either of these two cities.

Inferences can be divided into *immediate*, on the one hand, and *mediate* or syllogistic on the other. To move from 'That is a husband' to 'That is a man' is an immediate inference because the conclusion is drawn from a single premise. To argue from 'All men are mortal' to 'No men are gods' requires a middle term, in this case the term 'mortal'.

symmetric. *See* relation.

symptom. In the later work of *Wittgenstein, a type of evidence contrasted with a *criterion. X is a symptom of Y, if X and Y are independently identifiable but the empirical (inductively established) correlation between them is such that the presence of X can be used as evidence for that of Y.

syncategorematic. In traditional logic, denoting a word that cannot stand on its own, but must be joined to a *categorematic term in order to enter a categorical proposition, for example, 'all', 'and', and 'some'. In modern logic the sense has been extended to apply to any symbol that has no independent meaning. Some words that seem grammatically categorematic are often classed as syncategorematic, for example, *attributive adjectives such as 'large' or 'good'. These, unlike 'red' or 'is a man' do not have independent meaning. Something can simply be red, but cannot simply be large; it must always be (understood as) large-for-a-φ or large-relative-to-something else. That is, something may be large for a flea but small for an insect, large relative to this but small relative to that.

syncretism. The blending of inharmonious elements. Philosophical movements that exhibit syncretist characteristics include efforts by 16th-century philosophers to reconcile the theories of Plato and Aristotle, and Neoplatonic attempts to systematize and unify all known significant world religions on the basis of discernible resemblances between their various deities.

synderesis (*or* **synteresis**). In *Aquinas and other scholastic writers, the innate intellectual quality that enables every man to intuit the general and basic principles of practical moral reasoning. It is equated with St. Jerome's *scintilla conscientiae* (spark of conscience) and derives from a late Greek word meaning 'careful guarding' or 'preservation'.

syndicalism. Anticapitalist doctrine rooted in anarchist and antiparliamentarian tendencies among French trade union leaders in the late 19th century, and developed in the writing of *Sorel. Differing from traditional socialism, it considered the state to be an inherently oppressive and inefficient bureaucratic system, and advocated its replacement by organized production units (*syndicats*) linked by a general centre (*bourse*) for estimating economic capacities and necessities, and coordinating production. The solidarity arising from employment within such units would override divergences in religious or political opinions.

synonym. One of two or more words with the same meaning; for example 'donation' is synonymous with 'gift'. *See* antonym; homonym.

syntax. 1. (of a natural language) The system of rules governing the grammatical construction of sentences of the language. 2. (of a *formal language) A specification of the vocabulary (or list of symbols) of the language together with the rules (*formation rules) for the construction of allowable combinations of the items in the vocabulary. *See also* proof theory; wff.

synthesis. *See* Hegel.

synthetic. *See* analytic and synthetic.

systematic ambiguity. *See* ambiguity.

system of logic. Any set of axioms and/or rules of inference governing some or all of the logical operators. The formal validity (*see* validity and truth) of an argument containing those logical operators can be checked by reference to such a system. If C can be derived from $P_1 \ldots P_n$ by employing only rules of inference and/or axioms of the system, then the argument '$P_1 \& \ldots \& P_n$, therefore C' is formally valid (in that system). *See also* axiom; inference, rule of; logic; operator.

T

tabula rasa. (Latin for: a blank tablet.) A phrase used by *Locke to describe the state of the human mind at birth. His contention was that innate a priori knowledge is a fiction and that only experience can furnish the mind with ideas. *See also* empiricism; experience; innate ideas.

tao. (Chinese for: the Way.) *See* Chinese philosophy; Confucianism; Neo-Confucianism; Taoism.

Taoism. (Chinese *tao chia*: the school of the Way) Chinese philosophy at least as ancient as *Confucianism, although the two earliest and most important Taoist works, the *Lao-tzu* (also known as *Tao te ching*, The Way and its Power) and the *Chuang-tzu* (Master Chuang), were not compiled until *c.*300 BC. The former, attributed to the legendary figure of Lao-tzu (literally, the old master), is a poetic celebration of the Way (*tao*) of the primordial forces of nature, and a description of how the sage identifies himself with them in his conduct. So great is the influence of the power (*te*) of the Way operating through him that the people of his state spontaneously accept him as ruler over their community, content to lead a primitive existence in harmonious innocence. The book advocates a return to natural simplicity and detachment from worldly pursuits. Conventional moral, political, and social standards are discarded because they are based on value judgments and only lead men to undertake activities that alienate them from nature and endanger their lives. On the other hand feminine receptivity and humility, and negative qualities such as weakness, emptiness, uselessness, and passivity (*wu wei*) are extolled. (Taoism's veneration of female, particularly maternal, characteristics has led to speculation that it may have originated in an earlier matriarchal society.) For the adept who cultivates these Taoist virtues the immediate goal is physical survival, the 'long life' which is the central preoccupation of the Taoist; various yoga-like and even alchemical techniques were also directed towards this end. The adept achieves it through recapturing the instinctive unity with nature that man has lost in developing an artificial culture. Ultimately the sage attains to a spiritual equanimity that transcends considerations of physical survival, yet mysteriously guarantees immunity from physical as well as metaphysical harm.

These themes are more fully developed in the *Chuang-tzu* (*c*.315 BC). Through rational argument, interspersed with anecdotes and parables, it challenges all conventional wisdom on its own terms, and explores the mysterious laws that operate in the great organic process of which man is but a part. Unlike the almost Machiavellian *Lao-tzu*, the *Chuang-tzu* is not addressed to any potential ruler: rejecting all government, its concern is with the enlightenment of the individual and his transcendental enjoyment of an absolutely free existence.

Tarski, Alfred (1902-). Polish-American mathematician and logician, who has produced highly influential work in pure mathematics (especially *set theory and *algebra) and in mathematical logic (especially *metamathematics). His greatest significance for philosophy has been his pioneering work in *semantics, his method of systematically formalizing the relations between expressions and the objects that they denote, and his definition of the concept of truth for formal logical languages. This last was presented in *Der Wahrheitsbegriff in den Formalisierten Sprachen* (1935) (translated as *The Concept of Truth in Formalized Languages*, in *Logic, Semantics and Metamathematics* (1956)). Tarski himself was unsure about the possibility of applying his truth definition to natural languages, but many philosophers of language have found it fruitful to use a Tarski-type theory of truth as a basis for a theory of *meaning. *See* correspondence theory of truth; truth definition; truth theory.

tautology. A term that has acquired a specialized use in logic, signifying a *truth-functional compound that is true for all possible assignments of truth-values to its component propositions (*see* truth-value). The *truth-table for a tautology thus contains only *T*s in the final column entered. For example

(p	$\lor$	q)	$\lor$	-	p
T	T	T	T	F	T
T	T	F	T	F	T
F	T	T	T	T	F
F	F	F	T	T	F
(0)	(1)	(0)	(2)	(1)	(0)

is a tautology since it is true no matter what the actual truth-values of p and q. For this reason one can say that a tautology is an empty, or vacuous, proposition, that says nothing about how things are in the world, since its truth-value is independent of the way things are. It is a logical and not a factual truth; true because of the logical nature of the operators used to construct it rather than because things are in the world as they are said to be in the statement. *See also* validity and truth.

te. (Chinese for: power, efficacy.) A term implying active moral excellence. *See* Taoism.

Teilhard de Chardin, Pierre (1881-1955). French Jesuit, geologist, palaeontologist, and philosopher. He lectured in pure science at the Jesuit College in Cairo, and from 1918 was professor of geology at the Institut Catholique in Paris. Palaeontological research in China and central Asia earned him academic distinction. But, because his findings conflicted with religious doctrines, he was forbidden to teach and his works were only published posthumously.

La Phénomène humain (written 1938-40) and *Le Milieu divin* (1957) present two basic principles in the evolution of organic matter: nonfinality and complexification. These explain why *homo sapiens* is unique in resisting division into further species. Both works include transcendental speculations to prove God's existence.

teleological argument. *See* argument from (or to) design.

teleology. **1.** A doctrine that everything in the world has been designed by God to be of service to man. *See also* argument from design.
2. The theory or study of purposiveness in nature: characteristically, certain phenomena seem to be best explained not by means of prior causes, but *ends* or aims, intentions or purposes. Teleological explanation seems typical of living or organic things—plants, animals, people. Thus an animal's behaviour is sometimes best described in terms of its goal (food seeking, for example); a chess player's activity can be understood in terms of his purpose—to win.
*Kant, in his *Kritik der Urteilskraft* (*Critique of Judgment*), wrote extensively on teleological judgments. The subject has been much discussed recently in the philosophy of science, especially in connection with biology and psycho-

logy, and there have been many attempts to show how teleological explanations do not, as they appear to, explain present events by future ones.

telepathy. *See* extrasensory perception; precognition.

term. **1.** (in Aristotelian logic) According to Aristotle, who introduced the device of symbolizing arguments in order to exhibit their forms, a term is that 'into which the proposition is resolved, that is both the predicate and that of which it is predicated, "being" or "not being" being added.' Here it is assumed that the proposition is simple and merely asserts (or denies) that something (the predicate) applies to something else (the subject), as in 'Socrates is a man', where 'Socrates' and 'man' are the terms (*termini*) of the proposition predicating 'man' of 'Socrates'. Letters, *A*, *B*, *C*, etc., are then introduced to stand for terms, so that a proposition such as 'Man is an animal' is represented by, or given the form, '*A* is *B*'. From this definition, which talks only of terms in a given proposition, there is derived a non-relative notion of a term as any expression that may stand as the subject or predicate in an assertoric proposition (but that may also appear in, for example, subordinate clauses of complex propositions). As so defined, terms may be either singular or general. A *singular term*, such as 'Socrates' or 'this book' can occur only as the subject of a proposition, never as the predicate, whereas a *general term*, such as 'man', being applicable to many individuals may occur either as subject, as in 'Man is rational', or as predicate, as in 'Socrates is a man'.
2. (in predicate calculus or predicate logic) Where a distinction in kind is drawn between subjects and predicates, so that no expression can be seen as functioning logically as subject in one sentence and predicate in another, 'term' always means singular term, that is any expression denoting a particular object or person. This includes not only *proper names, like 'Mount Everest' or 'Plato',

but also a *definite description such as 'the capital of Poland' and 'the positive square root of four'.

tertiary qualities. *See* consequential characteristics.

Thales of Miletus. The first Greek enquirer into the nature of things as a whole. The only firm date we have in Thales' life is 585 BC, the year of the eclipse which, presumably drawing on the work of Babylonian astronomers, he predicted. Good stories are told of his impracticality, but also of his making a commercial killing by cornering oil-presses in advance of a heavy olive crop. His attempt to provide a rationalistic, as opposed to a mythopoeic, account of the phenomenal world seems to have been based on the belief that water is somehow the first principle of nature. This was probably derived from Egyptian or Babylonian cosmogonic myths (*see* cosmogony).

Theaetetus (*c*.414–*c*.369 BC). Greek mathematician, who joined with *Plato in founding the *Academy of Athens and whose work was later used by *Euclid. Plato's dialogue *Theaetetus* is devoted to the question of the definition of 'knowledge'.

theism. Belief in God, where God is understood to be the single omnipotent and omniscient creator of everything else that exists. He is regarded as a Being distinct from his creation though manifesting himself through it, and also essentially personal, caring for and communicating with mankind, and infinitely worthy of human worship and obedience. Theism is thus clearly a central element in the whole Judaeo-Christian religious tradition.

The philosophical problems it raises are, in the first place, those of maintaining the various elements of this conception of deity in a coherent unity. For example, there is the problem of doing justice to the limitless nature of God without falling either into pantheism, or denial of human freedom, or the belief that all concepts borrowed from the finite world—including that of personality —are hopelessly inadequate and misleading if applied to God. On the other hand, there is the difficulty of doing justice to the independence of creation, without thinking of God simply as a First Cause, who after the initial creative act leaves the world entirely to the operation of the laws of nature. Furthermore, there is the problem of reconciling the benevolence and omnipotence of the creator with the presence of evil in creation. And, of course, even if the conception proves internally coherent, there is the question of our grounds for claiming that anything actually exists corresponding to it. *Compare* deism; pantheism.

thema. (*pl.* themata) *See* inference, rule of.

theodicy. Attempts "to justify the ways of God to men" by solving the problem that evil presents to the theist. The word derives from the title of the *Theodicy* of *Leibniz. Given that a perfect and omnipotent Being must have created "the best of all possible worlds", how can one reconcile this with both the visible facts of this world and traditional beliefs about a next? "The work most worthy of the wisdom of ... God involves ... the eternal damnation of the majority of men."

Theophrastus (*c*.370–*c*.288 BC). Polymath and Peripatetic philosopher; pupil, collaborator, and successor of Aristotle as head of the *Lyceum. Theophrastus' surviving works include the taxonomic *Researches into Plants*, *Causes of Plants* (on plant physiology), a doxographical survey *On Sense-Perception* (from the lost *Opinions of the Natural Philosophers*), ten short essays on scientific subjects, and (his most popular work) the *Characters*, 30 sketches depicting, for literary rather than ethical purposes, various types of vice, folly, and impropriety. Empirically minded, a researcher more than a philosopher, Theophrastus continued Aristotle's work, modifying some of its more speculative aspects.

theorem. **1.** (of an axiomatic theory.) A statement that can be proved from the axioms; that is, one that occurs as the conclusion of a valid deduction in which only axioms of the theory appear as premises. *See* axiom. **2.** (of a *natural deduction system) A statement that can be proved; that is, that occurs as the conclusion of an argument constructed according to the rules of the system and for which there are no premises.

theory-laden. Denoting a concept, term, or statement that refers to, and can only be understood in the light of, a particular theory. For example, the phrase 'collective unconscious' makes sense only in the context of Jungian psychology.

theosophy. An esoteric trend in religious thought. Initiates strive towards mystical insight into God's nature. The original Greek term, found in *Porphyry and *Proclus, signified wisdom about God. Theosophical speculation characterized numerous religious movements (*see also* Boehme), but the word is now particularly associated with the Theosophical Society, founded in 1875 by Helena Blavatsky (1831-91). Modern theosophical doctrines are a blend of Hindu and Neoplatonic elements. *Compare* anthroposophy.

thesis. *See* Hegel.

thing-in-itself. *See* Ding-an-sich.

thinking. The mental activity of (a) theoretical contemplation directed towards some object with a view to reaching a propositional conclusion; or (b) practical deliberation directed towards some object with a view to reaching a decision to act.
   Historically, there has been a wide variety of theories about what occurs in the process of thinking. For Descartes and Locke, the process involves bringing concepts or ideas before the mind; for Berkeley and Hume, the process constitutes a sequential series of ideas or images in the mind; for Hobbes, in an early version of a favoured modern view,

the process is an activity that employs verbal images in a form of inner speech. However, against this tendency to regard thinking as an essentially inner and conscious activity, *Ryle and the behaviourists have argued that some states that may be described as thoughtful, contemplative, or deliberative are no more than dispositions to behave intelligently, dispositions which the agent may or may not articulate in words (*see* behaviourism).
   In contemporary philosophy, there are three main areas of concern with respect to the concept of thinking: (a) the conceptual and linguistically based nature of thought (the relation of thinking to the way in which objects are conceived and enter into the language); (b) the intentionality of thought (the way in which thought is necessarily directed towards an object); and (c) the intensionality, or non-extensionality, of thought (the implications of the fact that a thought *t* about an object *o* implies nothing in respect either of the existence of *o* or the truth or falsity of *t*).

third man argument. *See* Plato.

Thomism. The philosophy of St. Thomas *Aquinas and his intellectual disciples. *See also* Neo-Thomism.

Thoreau, Henry David (1817-62). American writer, poet, and transcendentalist philosopher, friend and associate of *Emerson. His writings were primarily concerned with the possibilities of human culture within a natural environment. *Walden* (1854) affirms his faith in the "unquestionable ability of man to elevate his life by conscious endeavour".

time. *See* space and time, philosophy of.

time-lag argument. An argument casting doubt on the reliability of our perception of real physical objects. It was formulated most succinctly by Russell in *Human Knowledge* (p. 204): "...though you see the sun now, the physical object to be inferred from your seeing existed eight minutes ago; if, in the intervening minutes, the sun had gone out, you would still be seeing exactly what you are seeing. We cannot, therefore, identify the physical sun with what we see."

time's arrow. *See* space and time, philosophy of.

Timon of Phlius (*c.*320–230 BC). Sophist and pupil of *Pyrrho of Elis, whom he greatly admired. His *Silloi* (Lampoons) now surviving only as fragments, ridicule philosophers, including Plato, Aristotle, and Arcesilaus.

token. Any particular specimen of any general class. All these specimens may be described as the several tokens of that single *type*. If, for instance, you commit a fallacy of some recognized and labelled sort, then your particular argument is one token of that general fallacy type.

token-reflexive. Denoting a word or expression of which it is necessary to know first who is speaking or writing it, and when or where, in order to know to what particulars reference is being made. All personal pronouns, for instance, are token-reflexive since to know to whom 'you' or 'I' refer we have to know who is speaking or writing to whom. 'Yesterday', 'today', and 'tomorrow', and all tensed verbs are also token-reflexive since their temporal reference is a function of the occasion of utterance.

topic-neutral. A term describing concepts that are neutral for any particular subject matter. *Ryle introduced this (rather unclear) notion in attempting to give an account of *logical constants. Examples of topic-neutral expressions would be words like 'all', 'and', 'not', etc. Ryle's view was that it is purely arbitrary as to which particular topic-neutral concepts are chosen to be the logical constants (and that it would be just as reasonable to choose others). Most logicians, however, hold that while there may be different notions applicable to different logical systems, some of the concepts that we choose to represent as

logical constants, for example negation, are fundamental to any logical system.

trademark argument. *See* ontological argument.

transcendent. Beyond experience. The word is often used by theists (*see* theism) to describe the way in which God supposedly exists beyond and independent of the created world. *Compare* immanent.

transcendental argument. An argument that answers the question: of a proposition known to be true, what conditions must be fulfilled for transcendental knowledge to be possible? *Kant called all knowledge transcendental "which is occupied not so much with objects as with our mode of cognition of objects, so far as this is possible a priori" (*Critique of Pure Reason* B25, A11–12). A transcendental argument will then make clear what the precise meaning is of the proposition which is known to be true. For example, Kant takes it for granted that we know that the propositions of Euclidean geometry are true, but argues that this is only possible if space is the form of outer sense, that is, that the mind itself determines the spatial characteristics of the objects it perceives.

transcendentalism. 1. Kant's philosophy of the transcendental, and hence any theory asserting the dependence of the world of experience on the activities of reason. 2. A mode of thought that emphasizes the intuitive and supersensuous. 3. A form of religious mysticism. 4. The particular doctrine adopted by a movement in New England under the leadership of *Emerson and his associates, influenced by Platonism and German idealism and reacting against dogmatic rationalism.

transcendental number. *See* number.

transcendentals. A term used by medieval philosophers to signify predicates that transcend the Aristotelian categories. Subsequently applied by *Kant to that which transcends, or goes beyond the correct application of, his list of categories, and hence of that which cannot be an aspect of possible experience. *See also* categories.

transfinite induction. *See* induction; least number principle.

transformation rules. The instructions governing the transformation of one *wff in a *formal language into another.

transitive. *See* relation.

translation. A concept that has posed two distinct types of problem for philosophers. One type arises when we reflect on the ways in which language is intimately involved with our whole conceptual scheme or way of regarding the world. This reflection can give rise to various claims about the direction of this involvement, the most famous being the "Sapir-Whorf" hypothesis, named after the linguists Benjamin Lee Whorf and Edward Sapir. This urges that a conceptualization of the world is entirely a function of the language of a community. Different languages may in that case be entirely incapable of inter-translation. Similar conclusions may be supported by Wittgenstein's stress on the connection between linguistic activity and a "way of life".

The more abstract problem concerns the evidence for a scheme of translation: *Quine has argued that there can never be a unique translation of a sentence of one language into one of another, not because of different thinking by their speakers, but because the empirical evidence for one scheme of translation could always be reinterpreted in favour of another. He uses this thesis, of the "indeterminacy of radical translation", to cast doubt on whether there is a fact of the matter about what a sentence means, and hence whether there is a fact of the matter about whether one sentence means the same as another.

transmigration. *See* metempsychosis.

transparency. *See* opacity and transparency.

triad. *See* Hegel.

triple. *See* ordered *n*-tuple.

trivium. *See* quadrivium.

truth *and* **falsity.** "What is truth? said jesting Pilate; and would not stay for an answer" (Francis Bacon, *Essays*, 'Of Truth'). Pilate's example could profitably be followed now, for the 'problem of truth' has been extensively discussed by recent philosophers, stimulated, perhaps, by the flights of fancy of the 19th-century idealists. Philosophers prior to this might well have agreed that no more need be said than the *Shorter Oxford English Dictionary*'s definition of 'truth': "conformity with facts, agreement with reality".

This definition encapsulates the common-sense theory of truth, *the correspondence theory*, which claims that a statement is true if it corresponds to the facts (*see also* correspondence theory of truth).

But various other theories have been advocated. The absolute idealists put forward a *coherence theory* of truth, in which the only absolute truth is 'the whole'—anything less than that can only aspire to degrees of truth. William *James argued for a *pragmatic theory* of truth, according to which the problem of truth is one of welfare economics, for a true assertion is one that proves the best for us in the long run. *Tarski attempted to avoid problems of self-reference (*see* semantic paradoxes) by claiming that 'truth' can only be defined in a metalanguage.

In the *Tractatus Logico-Philosophicus*, *Wittgenstein developed a theory of truth that combined elements of both a correspondence and a coherence theory. Basic statements, concerning, as it were, the atoms of knowledge and experience, directly corresponded to reality. From them, other more complex statements were derived, the truth of which depended on their consistency or coherence with the constituent basic statements. So far as the basic statements were concerned, Wittgenstein thought of the relationship between truth and reality as the same as that between a picture and what it represents.

F. P. *Ramsey thought he had dissolved the problem of truth by pointing out that 'p' and 'p is true' mean the same thing, and therefore that 'is true' is redundant (hence, the *redundancy theory*). *Strawson has developed this idea further, while J. L. *Austin has defended a version of the correspondence theory. *Compare* validity and truth.

truth conditions. *See* interpretation.

truth definition. A formal characterization of the set of true sentences of a language which is already used meaningfully—a characterization which is derived from an *interpretation of the language. Any interpretation affords a way of describing the set of true sentences of a language. But if it is to count as a truth definition, an interpretation has to satisfy the constraint that it assigns the value 'true' to all those sentences which are already, intuitively, regarded as true, and to no others. Tarski expressed this constraint by saying that we want to assign 'true' to the sentence 'Snow is white', iff snow *is* white. In general, 'p' is true iff p. This last formula expresses the condition that any adequate truth definition must satisfy, and is called by Tarski, "the material adequacy condition". (It is also known as 'convention T'). It should not be confused with a truth definition, although a trivial definition of truth for a language could be derived from an interpretation which is given by saying 'Assign to a sentence the value 'true' iff it is true'. A non-trivial definition of truth might involve assigning objects to names and *satisfaction conditions to the predicates of the language and allowing a recursive procedure (*see* interpretation) to determine the values of all the sentences of the language. It is not at all trivial that such an interpretation should satisfy the material adequacy condition.

truth-functional. 1. (of a *connective) Describing a connective when the *truth-value of any statement formed using it is determined in a systematic way by the truth-values of the connected statements. For example, for any statements p and q, 'p and q' is true when both p and q are true, but false otherwise. The logical connectives 'and', 'or', 'if...then...', and 'if and only if (iff)' are, in most logic texts, treated as *truth-functional connectives*.

2. (of a compound) Describing a compound or complex statement whose truth-values are determined by the truth-values of its component statements; every statement formed by use of truth-functional connectives is thus a *truth-functional compound*.

3. (of an *operator) Describing an expression which can be added to one or more statements to yield a further statement whose truth-value is systematically dependent on the truth-value(s) of the original statement(s). 'And' is thus a two-place *truth-functional operator*. If it is held that for any proposition p, not-p is true if p is false and false if p is true, then 'not' is being taken to be a one-place truth-functional operator. By contrast, 'He believes that...' is a one-place operator which is not truth-functional, since the truth-value of 'He believes that there is life on Mars' is not determined by the truth-value of 'There is life on Mars'; one may have both true and false beliefs. To each truth-functional operator there is a corresponding *truth-function*, that is a *function taking truth-values (those of the statement(s) to which the operator is added) as arguments, and whose value is again a truth-value (that of the statement resulting from the application of the operator). Each such function may be defined by displaying its *truth-table, and conversely, each truth-table can be treated as defining a truth-function. Notationally distinct operators may each determine the same truth-function, in which case they are said to be *truth-functionally equivalent*. This is the case with 'and' and 'but', since 'p but q' can

be true only if both p and q are true and is false otherwise.

truth is always in the middle. A demonstrably false maxim, yet perennially appealing to those who like to see themselves as balanced and moderate judges. If this maxim were true, then the truth must lie at B midway between A and C; but then it is also and incompatibly at the midpoints between B and A and B and C.

truth-table. A device, sometimes also known as a *matrix*, for exhibiting the conditions under which a *truth-functional compound is true or false. A truth-table may thus be used to define a truth-functional connective or operator by exhibiting the truth-function to which it corresponds, but it may also be used for testing the validity of arguments (*see* validity and truth). The idea of a truth-table is that each row represents a possible combination of truth-values for the component propositions of the compound, and that there be sufficient rows to cover all possible combinations. Thus, assuming that every statement must be either true or false (*see also* bivalence), there are only two possibilities to consider for a compound formed by application of a one-place operator, such as 'not':

$$-p$$
$$\text{F T}$$
$$\text{T F}$$

That is, p may either be true or false; if it is true $-p$ is false and if it is false, $-p$ is true. Where the compound contains just two distinct component propositions there will be four possibilities, and hence four rows to the truth-table. In general n distinct components generate 2^n possible combinations of truth-values for those components so that the truth-table must have 2^n rows.

To ensure that all these possibilities are actually covered, a systematic procedure for writing down the rows of the table must be adopted. On each row the truth-value taken by the compound is then indicated, this being written under the operator, if there is just one, or

under the main *connective if more than one appears in the compound. The truth-table for 'p *or q' is

$$p \lor q$$
$$\text{T T T}$$
$$\text{T T F}$$
$$\text{F T T}$$
$$\text{F F F}$$

This indicates that 'p or q' is false only when both p and q are false. Where the compound contains more than one truth-functional operator, the table is worked out in stages. Take, for example $-(p \lor q) \lor (p \& q)$. Consider the situation in which p is true and q is false. Substituting 'T' for 'p' and 'F' for 'q' in the compound then gives $-(T \lor F) \lor (T \& F)$. In this case the truth-table definitions of '$\&$' and '$\lor$' show that '$p \lor q$' will have the value T and '$p \& q$' will have the value F, so that $-(T \lor F) \lor (T \& F)$ reduces to $-T \lor F$. Since the negation of a true proposition must be false this further reduces to $F \lor F$, which, from the truth-table for '$\lor$', can be seen to take the value F. This calculation can be represented in tabular form by

$$p\ q \mid -(p \lor q) \lor (p \& q)$$
$$\overline{\hspace{0.5cm}} \hspace{-0.5cm} $$
$$\text{T F} \mid \text{F T T\ \ F\ \ F\ \ T F F}$$

where the truth-value of the whole compound, when p is true and q is false, appears under the main connective, '$\lor$'. This process is then repeated for each possible combination of truth-values of the compound's component propositions.

It is evident that, given the truth-table definition of each logical connective, truth-tables for compounds of any degree of logical complexity can be constructed purely mechanically (a computer could be programmed to produce them). *See also* truth-value.

truth theory. Any account of how, given truth conditions (*see* interpretation) for the semantic elements of a language, the truth-values of the sentences of the language are to be determined. Tarski's theory of truth (*see* Tarski) uses truth-tables together with an account, based on the notion of *satisfaction, of how the values of quantified sentences are to be determined. (For a brief description of this, see interpretation). Tarski's theory is sometimes referred to as 'Tarski's definition of truth'. It defines truth in the sense that it describes in general how truth-values are to be assigned to the sentences of languages with a certain kind of structure. This sense of definition of truth should not be confused with a *truth definition for a particular language.

truth-value. A technical term introduced by *Frege, who saw a strong analogy between concepts or predicates and mathematical functions. Consequently he thought of sentences (expressions in which a *predicate is applied to an object) as standing for, or denoting, a value in the same way that 3^2 denotes 9, the value of the function x^2 for $x = 3$. When a statement is, or is evaluated as true, it is said to have the truth-value True (indicated by T) and when it is false is is said to have the truth-value False (indicated by F). Although True and False are the most commonly considered truth-values, they are not necessarily the only possible ones; to maintain that they are is to uphold the principle of *bivalence. It might be that a statement is evaluated or assessed as merely probable, with possibly some numerical assignment of its degree of probability, in which case this numerical value could be treated as a truth-value.

two clocks. See clocks, image of the two.

two-place operation. See operation.

two-place predicate. See dyadic.

two-way interactionism. See interactionism.

type. See token.

types, theory of. Russell's attempt to deal with the problem of self-reference. He produced two versions of the theory—the simple and the ramified. The problem itself is famously illustrated by the assertion of Epimenides the Cretan, "All Cretans are always liars" (see liar paradox).

Russell became interested in the problem in his attempted definition of numbers in terms of classes. He encountered paradoxes generated by the notion of a class of classes, which includes itself as a member. Not all classes are members of themselves. But is the class of all classes which are not members of themselves a member of itself or not? Whichever answer we choose, we are led into contradiction (See Russell's paradox).

Russell's solution to the paradox was to say that self-referring statements are without meaning, and in particular, to speak of "all statements" is meaningless. Instead, we must speak of sets of statements that form a genuine totality. A statement refering to other statements must, Russell says, be of a different type from, a higher order than, the statements it is about. So we must say that the class of all first order classes which are not members of themselves is a second order class, and hence it will be "obvious nonsense" to say of a class either that it is or that it isn't a member of itself. Thus the paradox disappears.

U

uncertainty principle. A law of physics, first stated in 1927 by Werner Heisenberg (1901-76), that has profoundly affected quantum theory (see quantum mechanics) and the theory of *causation. It states that the position and momentum of a particle cannot both be known without uncertainty because the process of establishing either must affect the other. If Δp is the uncertainty in position and Δq that of momentum, then $\Delta p.\Delta q = h/4\pi$, where h is the Planck Constant.

Because h is very small, the effect is only apparent on the subatomic scale; for tangible objects, involving millions of atoms, the statistics of large numbers obscures the uncertainties. However, for an electron, say, travelling at a known velocity, its position at a particular instant can only be expressed in terms of a probability. This implies an uncertainty in both its identity and destiny. How, then, can two consecutive observations of the same particle be distinguished from observations of two different particles? If a particle cannot be identified without uncertainty, how can one say what will happen to it in future? And if identity and destiny are in doubt how can one know whether the law of cause and effect is obeyed?

unconscious. 1. The ground of all existence, combining the spiritual principle of nature, will, and reason. The notion was developed by K. R. E. von Hartmann (1842-1906) in *Die Philosophie des Unbewussten* (1869), synthesizing the theories of *Schelling, *Schopenhauer, and *Hegel. The misery of existence is explained by the suffering of the unconscious from the constant strife between will and reason; it can be alleviated only by conscious reason gaining ascendancy over blind impulse, until the final liberation of the unconscious at the end of physical life.
2. A source of influences on behaviour, accounting for the fact that not all purposive action is consciously directed. In Freud's theory, it is the container of memories of experiences that are repressed in personal consciousness, as a consequence of habits, developed from childhood, of denying impulses that might occasion (parental) disapproval. Such repressed impulses persist as unconscious wishes and often adversely influence personality development (*see* Freud). *Jung distinguished between the personal and the collective unconscious; the latter contains 'archetypes' or symbols respresenting inherited ways of responding to particular types of experience. Man's basic drive is towards self-realization; freedom is attainable through assimilation of the unconscious by consciousness.

undistributed. *See* distributed.

undistributed middle, fallacy of the. An argument in which the proposed conclusion is invalidly attained because one of the premises needs to be and is not a *distributed assertion. Suppose you argue, given that 'Every member of the Labour Party is a socialist', and given that 'He is a socialist', then 'He is a member of the Labour Party'. The middle term in this invalid *syllogism is 'socialist', but to reach the proposed conclusion validly by this sort of route it would be necessary to have as a premise a distributed assertion about socialists: 'All socialists are members of the Labour Party'.

uniformity of nature. A principle used (for example, by J. S. *Mill) in attempts to justify *induction in particular and science in general. It is usually expressed as 'the future will resemble the past', which is taken to mean that what has happened once will happen again, if circumstances are sufficiently similar. However, to be a principle on which induction can be rested, the uniformity of nature must not itself rely on inductive justification. Mill claimed that the principle was confirmed by all our experience. This seems either false (the future often surprises us), or can only be warranted by: (a) filling out the phrase 'similar circumstances' so that the principle is at least made true in the past, and (b) an inductive inference from past 'futures' to future 'futures'—that is, a claim that the uniformity of nature will continue to hold.

unit class. A class with only one member.

Universal Doctor. The traditional scholastic nickname for *Albertus Magnus.

universalizability. The principle that, while individual moral judgments may be particular, they will always imply a universal judgment. Although this term was coined by the English moral philosopher, R. M. Hare (1919-), it refers to a view of morality that has been widespread since at least the time of *Kant (*see also* categorical imperative). The proposition 'Smith ought to keep his promise', while referring to a particular person on a specific occasion, will entail, in the opinion of the universalist, the universal proposition that 'Anyone in like circumstances to Smith ought to keep his promise'. This may be contrasted with, for instance, a prediction about Smith's behaviour: 'Smith will keep his promise' in no way implies that 'Anyone in like circumstances to Smith will keep his promise'. Although universalizability may not be found in moral utterances alone it is seen as one of their distinguishing features. The importance of this logical feature of morality is its use in moral arguments, since if we admit that particular moral judgments are linked to universal rules we are prevented from making arbitrary decisions in respect of given individuals.

universal quantifier. A logical *operator, often written as ∀. See quantifier.

universals and **particulars.** Things are particulars and their qualities are universals. So a universal is the property predicated of all the individuals of a certain sort or class. Redness is a universal, predicated of all red objects. Universals have been claimed by some philosophers to have an existence distinct from the particular things instantiating the property. For *Plato and Platonists, the observed world is only a reflection of the real world, consisting for Plato of the Forms, which are something like universals.

Other philosophers have claimed that universals have "mental existence". It is by comparison of an object with the appropriate universal that we are able to attribute the appropriate property to the object. Thus we are able to say, for example, that a car is red by comparing the colour of the car with our mental conception of redness. For the idealists, only universals have "real" existence, and particular objects become mere collections of universals. On the other hand nominalists make the claim that objects having the same quality have nothing in common but their name.

D. F. Pears, in an influential article ('Universals' in Logic and Language, second series, edited by A. G. N. Flew), has argued that theories of universals have failed because they have assumed that there is a general answer to the question, 'Why are we able to name things as we do?'. The answer 'A thing is called by a particular name because it instantiates a certain universal' looks imposing, but turns out to be vapidly circular. Pears' conclusion is that any attempted comprehensive explanation of naming is necessarily circular. See also idealism; nominalism; realism.

Universe and **universe.** Two senses of this word are usefully distinguished by the presence or absence of the initial capital. **1.** 'Universe' is defined as including everything there is, with the exception of the creator God, if such there be. See also argument to design; cosmological argument; creation; First Cause; First Mover. **2.** A universe may be a part only of that total Universe: the Andromeda nebula has thus sometimes been said to constitute 'an island universe'. In this second sense philosophers sometimes speak of different universes of discourse: that, for instance, of physics as opposed to that of art criticism.

universe of discourse. A system of concepts and entities related to a particular topic or area of interest, within which certain terms and expressions acquire their own meaning or significance. For instance, 'Bellerophon rode on Pegasus' is recognizable as a true statement within the universe of discourse of students of mythology. But it has no place in the communication of historians or zoologists. See also interpretation.

univocal. Having only one meaning. Compare equivocal; equivocate.

Unmoved Mover. See First Mover.

use of words. See mention and use of words.

utilitarianism. Probably the most famous normative ethical doctrine (see ethics) in the English-speaking tradition of moral philosophy, designed to explain why some actions are right and some wrong. Although it had precursors throughout philosophical history, and although it is still accepted by many moral philosophers today, its heyday was undoubtedly from the late 18th century through to the last quarter of the 19th. Its three classical exponents were Jeremy *Bentham, John Stuart *Mill and Henry *Sidgwick.

In its original formulation, utilitarianism was very simple, perhaps deceptively so. J. S. Mill wrote "The creed which accepts as the foundation of morals, Utility or the Greatest Happiness Principle, holds that actions are right in proportion as they tend to promote happiness, wrong as they tend to produce the reverse of happiness. By happiness is intended pleasure and the absence of pain; by unhappiness, pain, and the privation of pleasure." Thus actions are judged by their consequences and the amount of pleasure all concerned derive from those consequences; the aim is the greatest happiness of the greatest number.

In recent years the theory has been subdivided into two variants. *Act utilitarianism* is the simpler, being the view that each individual action taken should be assessed on the results it alone produces, so that if the question, for example, is one of paying a debt or giving to charity one must try to estimate the gains in terms of happiness to be made by either act on that particular occasion. *Rule utilitarianism* is not concerned to assess individual acts but considers the utility of a rule for action types, for example, 'Everyone should pay their debts.' The idea is to do whatever would be prescribed by the optimum set of rules even if on the occasion concerned less total happiness would result. Thus where the act utilitarian asks, "What will be the outcome of my doing that?" the rule utilitarian's question would be, "What if everyone did that?".

There are three most obvious criti-cisms of utilitarianism: (1) the practical difficulty of its application—how can we accurately assess the amounts of happiness likely to be yielded by either individual action tokens or general rules?; (2) its unfairness—the majority happiness may best be served by the sacrifice of some innocent party or by some manifestly unjust institution like slavery; and (3) its one-sidedness in that morality is analysed entirely through actions and their consequences, never through motives or intentions.

utility, principle of. The *greatest happiness principle. *See also* utilitarianism.

utopianism. The beliefs of those con-cerned to establish not just a better but a perfect society. The term, usually employed by opponents who believe such aspirations to be unrealistic, is derived from the imaginary ideal state depicted in Sir Thomas More's *Utopia* (1516). Other works in the same genre are Plato's *Republic*, Tommaso Campanella's *La Città del Sole* (1602), Francis Bacon's *New Atlantis* (1624), and William Morris' *News from Nowhere* (1890). Utopias appear in our century to have been replaced by nightmares, such as Aldous Huxley's *Brave New World* (1931) and George Orwell's *1984* (1948). *Marx liked to compare his own supposedly scientific socialism with earlier utopian socialism. Sir Karl *Popper too has a favourite contrast between wholesale utopian and piece-meal reformist social engineering with Marxism-Leninism as his paradigm case of the former.

Uttara Mīmāṃsā. The system of Indian philosophy usually known as *Vedânta.

V

vacuous. In logic, describing the status of sentences that are true *because* their subject terms have no *denotation or *because* their antecedents are false. For example, a conditional (if P then Q) is true if its consequent (Q) is true or if its antecedent (P) is false. So 'If pigs can fly then the earth is flat' is vacuously true. Universal statements ('All Fs are G') are also interpreted as conditionals ('If anything is F then it is G': formally $(\forall x)$ $Fx \supset Gx$), and so if their subject term has no denotation they too will be vacuously true. For example, 'All dragons are wingless' is considered to have the *logical form 'If anything is a dragon then it is wingless', and is true *because* there are no dragons. Terms are sometimes said to *occur vacuously* in a sentence; that is, when they occur in such a way that, if they were to be replaced by any other grammatically similar term the truth-value of the sentence would be unaltered. In the sentence 'Everything is either square or not square', 'square' occurs vacuously.

vagueness. The existence of indefiniteness in the meaning of a word, expression, or statement, in as much as it is thought to be in some relevant respect imprecise in its implications. One stock example is the term 'bald'. A man can properly be said to be bald while still retaining some hair; there is no precise and determinate point in the process of depilation at which the victim must first be said to be bald. In the gnomic words of Wittgenstein: "To remove vagueness is to outline the penumbra of a shadow. The line is there after we have drawn it, and not before." *Compare* ambiguity.

Vaiśeṣika. One of the systems of *Indian philosophy, and the most important precipitate of the ancient philosophies of nature, older layers of which go well back into the 1st millennium BC. The system as such was outlined in Kaṇāda's *Vaiśeṣikasūtras* (date unknown) and developed in Praśastapāda's *Padârthadharmasangraha* (*c.*575 AD) at the end of the creative period. In its oldest form, it assumed four eternal elements (earth, water, fire, air) and an infinite number of functionally defined, eternal souls (*jīvas*) which account for perception, organic growth, will, etc., in material bodies. A second stage in the development (shared by *Nyāya, *Jain philosophy, and *Mīmāṃsā) was marked by an atomistic theory. The four elements are now defined as consisting of infinite eternal and unchangeable atoms. The totality of the cosmic processes is explained by applying laws of mechanics to the interactions between elementary atoms and *jīvas*, suggesting a purely mechanistic conception. Another feature was then introduced, the theory of the six categories: substance (*dravya*), quality (*guṇa*), action (*karma*), commonness (*sāmānya*), difference (*viśeṣa*), and inherence (*samavāya*, as, for example, of quality in a substance). The mechanistic theory about the atoms and *jīvas* is now reformulated in terms of the categories (for instance, the psychological processes are described as *qualities* of the *jīvas*). Eventually the system was drawn into the discussion of transmigration and liberation, without however anyone being able to say more about the state of liberation than that in it the *jīva* finds complete rest, like a fire whose fuel is exhausted.

valid *and* **invalid.** Terms that may be applied to arguments or to patterns or forms of argument. Arguments may be assessed as valid or invalid, whereas statements, the components of arguments, are assessed for truth or falsity. Logicians are interested primarily in the validity or invalidity of arguments and not in the actual truth or falsity of their premises and conclusions. An argument is *valid* when it is impossible for its premises to be true and its conclusion false; it is *invalid* otherwise. An argument may thus be valid even though it has a false premise, and conversely, all the premises and even the conclusion of an invalid argument may be true. Thus, 'If pigs had wings, they could fly. Pigs do have wings. Therefore pigs can fly' although logically impeccable, will not convince us that pigs can fly. But neither should one find the argument 'If this substance is salt, it will dissolve in water. It has dissolved in water, so it must be salt' convincing, even though its conclusion might be true. The premises give one insufficient grounds for believing the conclusion; if the substance had been sugar it would also have dissolved in water.

Having defined validity as above one must still seek to answer the question 'How does one determine whether an argument is or is not valid?'. To put it another way, 'How does one decide that it is impossible for the conclusion to be false when the premises are true?'. This is a non-trivial question and one that does not always have an answer. There is no guarantee that for any given argument one will be able to reach a decision as to its validity in a finite number of steps. It is, however, one of the aims of logical systems to provide criteria for making this decision, and they do so by determining which patterns of argument or which rules of *inference, if followed, will always lead to the construction of valid arguments. For this reason one may say that they are concerned with *formal validity*—that which derives from the mode or form of argument used and which is independent of its subject matter.

An argument is said to be *formally valid* iff, it is an instance of a valid form of argument, where a form of argument is valid when all its instances are valid. Thus a first step in the determination of the formal validity of an argument is to see it as an instance of a general form or pattern of argument (*see also* logical constants; logical form). A single argument may be seen as an instance of more than one form, depending on how it is analysed and on how much detail is included in its symbolic representation. For example, the foregoing argument concerning winged pigs could be seen to take the form 'If p, then q. p. Therefore q.' but it might also be seen as an instance of the more complex form 'If all Ps are W, then all Ps are F. All Ps are W. Therefore, all Ps are F.' In this case the simpler pattern is sufficient to reveal the formal validity of the argument whereas if 'All men are mortal. Socrates

is a man. Therefore Socrates is mortal.' is assigned the form 'p. q. Therefore r.', its formal validity will not be apparent; it becomes apparent only when the additional complexity is represented as in 'All Ms are P. s is M. Therefore, s is P.'

validity *and* **truth.** Validity, a term applicable to arguments, is defined by reference to the possible truth-values of the component sentences of arguments. If the argument '$P_1 \ldots P_n$, therefore C' is valid, it must be impossible for C to be false when $P_1 \ldots P_n$ are *all* true. This will be the case iff the material *conditional statement '$P_1 \& \ldots \& \supset C$' is always true. If $P_1 \ldots P_n, C$ are all *truth-functional compounds, to say that '$P_1 \& \ldots \& P_n \supset C$' is always true is to say that it is a *tautology. Working out the *truth-table for '$P_1 \& \ldots \& P_n \supset C$' provides a mechanical procedure for determining whether this conditional is or is not a tautology, and thus also provides an *effective procedure for deciding that an argument that has a logical form involving truth-functional compounds is indeed valid. If '$P_1 \& \ldots \& P_n \supset C$' is revealed, by its truth-table, to be a *contradiction, no argument having the form '$P_1 \ldots P_n$, therefore C' can be valid. If it is shown to be neither a tautology nor a contradiction, the form '$P_1 \ldots P_n$, therefore C' is not valid, but some arguments which are instances of that form but which are also instances of a more complex form of argument may be formally valid.

Thus, while showing that '$P_1 \& \ldots \& P_n \supset C$' is not a tautology does demonstrate that '$P_1 \ldots P_n$, therefore C' is not a valid form of argument, it does not necessarily show that every argument having this form is invalid. For arguments whose sentences involve *logical constants which are not truth-functional operators there is no such automatic procedure for determining their formal validity. In this case a form of argument '$P_1 \ldots P_n$, therefore C' is said to be logically valid iff there is no *interpretation of the formal language to which

$P_1 \ldots P_n$, and C belong in which C is false and $P_1 \ldots P_n$ are all true. It is the purpose of *semantics to characterize the possible interpretations of a language and so it is by reference to semantic theory that the validity of some forms may be decided, but a decision in a finite number of steps is not necessarily possible. (The proof that it is not necessarily possible for first order predicate logic with relation symbols is due to A. Church (1903-) and is known as *Church's theorem.) The invalidity of a form of argument may be shown by producing an interpretation of the formal language in which its premises are all true and its conclusion is false. Such an interpretation provides a *counter-example to the claim that the form in question is valid.

Valla, Lorenzo (1405-57). Italian humanist of the Renaissance, who exposed the historical fiction of the Donation of Constantine, a bulwark of papal pretensions to secular sovereignty. In philosophy Valla wrote a very sympathetic treatment of the ethics of *Epicurus, and a *Dialogue on Freewill.* This argued that, while God's foreknowledge (personified as Apollo) is no threat to human autonomy, God's power (Zeus) may be. That problem, perhaps prudently, Valla forebore to pursue.

valuation. See interpretation.

value. A theory of value is a theory about what things in the world are good, desirable, and important. Such theories aim at answering a practical rather than a purely theoretical question since to conclude that a state of affairs is good is to have a reason for acting so as to bring it about or, if it exists already, to maintain it.

Within the context of moral philosophy the central problem is the relation between the moral rightness of certain actions, for example, telling the truth and the non-moral value of certain states, for example, happiness. For the teleologist actions are right if and only if they are means to some admitted non-moral good whereas for the deontologist they

are valuable in themselves (see deontology; teleology). In more general terms this is the question of whether or not morality requires an external justification.

The other traditional problem of value concerns the relation of those things supposed to have an extrinsic value and those of intrinsic worth. X has extrinsic value if it is a means to, or in some way contributes to, Y. Y has intrinsic value if it is good, worth pursuing in itself, without reference to some other entity. Thus exercise is good as a means to health (has extrinsic value), whereas health is good in itself (intrinsic). Obviously it is easier to show that a thing has extrinsic value since that it is a means to a given end is empirically verifiable. However X cannot be good, even extrinsically, unless Y to which it leads is good in an absolute sense. Hence any theory of value must propose some things that are good in themselves or at least a method for assessing the claims of any candidate.

value-freedom. The ideal, recommended by Max *Weber, that social scientists should eschew value-judgments about people and institutions within their fields of study. This aim is certainly hard, perhaps impossible, to realize completely. However, it was never intended to preclude attention to the valuations made by the people being studied, or choice of one subject of study rather than another, or judgments about the strength of evidence for this or that; it is, therefore, not discredited by pointing to the inescapability of these three things. See Hume's law; naturalistic fallacy.

variable. Originally a symbol introduced as a place-holder for an expression of some specified kind. Variables were first widely used in equations in algebra and co-ordinate geometry as a means of defining functions. Thus the equation $y = x^2$ gives y as a function of x; when the variable 'x' is replaced by a numeral, a corresponding numerical value for y can be determined.

Variables have come to be used extensively in logic. For example, *propositional variables*, usually '*p*', '*q*', '*r*', are used in representing the possible forms of complex propositions, such as '$p \rightarrow (q \lor r)$'. *Individual variables*, usually '*x*', '*y*', '*z*', are used to indicate places for names of objects in expressions for functions, whether propositional or mathematical, as in '*x* is the brother of *y*'. These examples of *free occurrences* of variables, that is, occurrences of variables where they can be replaced by particular expressions of the appropriate kind. For example, in '*x* burns, and *y* fiddles', both *x* and *y* are *free variables*. If both are replaced by names we have a sentence such as 'Rome burns, and Nero fiddles'. However, when a *quantifier is applied to a *predicate, giving, for example, (*x*) (*x* burns, and *y* fiddles), the variable '*x*', occurring once in the quantifier and once in the predicate, becomes a *bound variable* and one that can no longer be replaced by a name, although *y* remains a free variable and can be replaced by 'Nero' to give (*x*) (*x* burns, and Nero fiddles), or 'Everything burns, and Nero fiddles'. If a further quantifier is added, to give, say, (∃*y*) (*x*) (*x* burns, and *y* fiddles), then there are no longer any free variables in the expression which is now a sentence rather than a predicate.

The quantifiers, although the most commonly encountered, are not the only variable-binding operators. Another example is the description (or iota) operator (ɿ*x*) which can be applied to a one-place predicate *Px* to give a singular term, thus for example, (ɿ*x*) (*x* is queen of England), read 'the *x* such that *x* is queen of England', is a term denoting Elizabeth Windsor, in which '*x*' cannot be replaced by a name.

Veblen, Thorstein (1857-1929). American economist and sociologist who taught at Chicago, Stanford, and Missouri. Main works: *The Theory of the Leisure Class* (1899), *The Instinct of Workmanship and the State of the Industrial Arts* (1914), and *An Inquiry into the Nature of Peace and the Terms of its Perpetuation* (1917). A vigorous social critic with a utilitarian bias, Veblen attacked the organization of contemporary industrial society as wasteful, competitive, and encouraging "conspicuous consumption".

Vedânta. Traditionally, one of the six systems of *Indian philosophy, but in fact an umbrella term denoting a great variety of schools. The teachings of the *Upanisads* provide a common ground of scriptural authority. This tradition of thought postulates one ultimate principle (called *brahman*) which underlies the world of phenomena and can be realized in meditational trance. Bādarāyaṇa's *Brahmasūtras* (possibly 4th/5th century AD) are the earliest extant attempt to systematize Upaniṣadic teachings, and they became the textual basis for all further developments in the Vedânta. While the cosmos is seen here as a real transformation (*pariṇāma*) of *brahman*, the liberation of the individual soul is regarded as a monistic merger into *brahman*. Gauḍapāda (in his *kārikās* on the Māṇḍūkya-*Upaniṣad*, c.7th century AD) utilized conceptions typical of Mahāyāna Buddhism (*see* Madhyamaka; Vijñānavāda) and interpreted the world of phenomena as a purely illusory imposition (*vivarta*) upon the universal consciousness (= *brahman*). This interpretation found its classic expression in Śankara's commentary on the *Brahmasūtras* (between 650 and 750 AD). He postulated two levels of reality, an empirical and an ultimate. The world of phenomena is explained as the effect of (universal) 'ignorance' (*avidyā*) upon pure consciousness (*brahman*) and individuality as the effect of (individual) ignorance upon the self (*ātman*), which in essence is identical with *brahman*. The distinction of a universal and an individual ignorance avoids a total idealist *solipsism (by explaining social agreement on facts), and permits one to demarcate, as a third level of reality, personal error (mistaking a rope for a snake) and dreams, as distinct from the second level constituted by public experiences. From the ultimate point of view, *brahman* is the sole existent and *avidyā* cannot possess separate existence; thus its relationship with *brahman* is styled *advaita*, that is, 'non-dual'. The discussion of the precise relationship of *brahman* with ignorance (or, increasingly common, with *māyā* 'illusion') gave rise to a number of different schools within the *advaita* Vedānta. Padmapāda (*c*.8th century), author of the *Pañcapādikā*, and Vācaspati Miśra (*c*.850 AD), author of the *Bhāmatī*, may be singled out as the founders of two such schools.

The Vedânta tradition contains a second, *theistic*, stream. The *Bhagavadgītā* (*c*.3rd century BC) had already suggested a combination of Upaniṣadic ideas with the concept of a *personal* absolute. Stimulated by Śankara's system, Rāmānuja (12th century AD), in his commentaries on the *Brahmasūtras* and the *Bhagavadgītā*, suggested a fundamentally realistic interpretation, while maintaining the unity of being by suggesting that matter and spirit constitute, as it were, the body of the personal absolute, *brahman*, which is identified with the god of popular religion, Viṣṇu. Between the 13th and 16th centuries AD, further systems in which *brahman* is envisaged as Viṣṇu (in others also as Śiva), were formulated by theologians like Madhva, Nīmbarka, Vallabha, Caitanya's disciples, Meykaṇṭañ, Umāpati, and Aruḷnanti, along similar, although increasingly religious and mythological, lines.

veil of appearance. *Sense data viewed as interposing between the experiencer and the external world. Since the revival in the late 1500s of the classical Greek Scepticism most people with what *Hume was to call "the slightest philosophy" have taken it that all of which we are or can be immediately aware is our own private experience. The sensory elements in this experience are thus viewed as standing forever between us and the *external world (if such, indeed, there be). The rising opposition to this once established view describes sense

data so conceived as the veil of appearance.

Venn diagram. A pictorial representation of logical statements, useful for clarifying and checking logical arguments. In 1880 the English logician John Venn presented a method, using circles, that greatly improved on previous attempts (for example, by Leonhard Euler) to use similar logic diagrams for syllogisms. The terms of the *syllogism are seen as classes represented by closed curves or circles, with the members of a class as the set of points within the circle. A syllogism is represented as intersecting circles: shading a compartment indicates no members, an *x* in compartment shows that it has at least one member, and an *x* on the border of compartments indicates that at least one of the compartments has members. Thus, the syllogism, 'All *A* is *B*. Some *C* is *A*. Therefore some *C* is *B*.' is represented by the diagrams (1), (2), and (3) below. (1) illustrates the first premise; that part of *A* that lies outside *B* is empty. (2) illustrates the second premise; the intersection of *C* and *A* is not empty, so there is an *x* on the border of two compartments in the overlap of *C* and *A*. (3) shows that, when *A* is shaded, the *x* shifts to the only remaining compartment it can go to, and is now inside *C* and *B*. Thus some *C* is *B* and the conclusion of the syllogism is valid.

verbal definition. *See* definition.

veridical. Telling the truth. *Compare* falsidical.

verifiability. The condition of admitting verification. Verification is any procedure carried out to determine whether a statement is true or false. A statement which might be shown to be true is said to be in principle verifiable. Some sorts of statements that are thus in principle verifiable could not be shown to be false (are not *falsifiable*). We may believe that the statement 'There are, or once were, unicorns' is false, but in fact we cannot show it to be so. For some unexplored corner of the world might

Venn diagrams

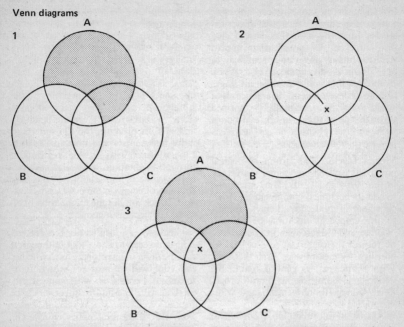

yet yield a unicorn or the unmistakable fossil of one. But while existence claims can be verified but never conclusively falsified, claims of a universal form, 'All crows are black', could not be verified but can be falsified (once a non-black crow has been discovered). Because science aims at making such universally quantified statements, *Popper claimed that the interesting notion was not verifiability, as the logical positivists (*see* logical positivism) had assumed, but falsifiability. He also repudiated the positivist use of verifiability as a criterion of meaningfulness, and offered falsifiability as a criterion for distinguishing science from non-science—not as a rival criterion of general meaningfulness.

verification (*or* **verifiability**) **principle.** The criterion of meaningfulness applied by the logical positivists to any proposition. *See* logical positivism.

vicious circle principle. An explanation of certain logical paradoxes discussed in Russell's theory of types. A vicious circle is generated whenever it is supposed that "a collection of objects may contain members which can only be defined by means of the collection as a whole". For instance, in employing the concept of classes of objects, one cannot—without reaching paradoxical results—pass to a higher order concept of classes which are themselves composed of various classes of objects (*see* types, theory of).

Vico, Giambattista (1668–1744). Italian philosopher of history. He was professor of rhetoric at the University of Naples (1699–1741). Main work: *Scienza nuova* (3rd edition, 1744).

Despite his reputation as the propounder of a cyclical theory of history, Vico's chief claim to fame rests upon his original conception of the presuppositions and methods of historical enquiry. He held that, because the "world of nations" had been made by men, it was open to modes of understanding quite distinct from those available in the investigation of the physical universe; thus a deep divide separated historical studies from the natural sciences. Vico also attacked the notion that human nature remains invariant from age to age. Radical divergences of outlook manifested themselves at different stages of human development, divergences that could only be imaginatively grasped through the critical interpretation of such cultural phenomena as language, law, myth, and ritual.

Vienna Circle. The group of logical positivists centred on Vienna University in the 1920s and 1930s. They attempted to add the technical equipment and logical rigour of modern mathematical logic to the empirical tradition of *Hume, *Comte, and *Mach, with its characteristic respect for empirical science and its hostility to metaphysics and theology. With Schlick as its central figure, the Circle included at various times Carnap, Feigl, Gödel, Hahn, Neurath, and Waismann.

At first an informal club, from 1929 it became more organized, with its own manifesto, journal (*Erkenntnis*), and series of publications and congresses. Its considerable influence, especially on English-language philosophy, persisted long after the Circle itself dissolved in the late 1930s. *See also* logical positivism.

Vijñānavāda. A school of Mahāyāna *Buddhist philosophy. On the basis of ideas expressed in Mahāyāna religious works (particularly the *Lankâvatārasūtra*) and by Sāramati (*c*.250 AD, author of the *Ratnagotravibhāga*), an idealist system was developed by Maitreya (*c*.300 AD, author of the *Abhisamayâlankāra* and *Mahāyānasūtrâlankāra*), Asanga (*c*.4th century AD, author of *Mahāyanasangraha*), and Vasubandhu (*c*.4th century AD, author of two *Vijñaptimātrasiddhis*) and in the anonymous compilation *Yogâcārabhūmisśāstram*. Intense contemplation on an object had shown that it was possible to conjure up a mental image of it which appeared as 'real' as the original, and combining this insight with the teaching about the 'emptiness' of all phenomena (*see* Madhyamaka), the Vijñānavāda postulated that both the objects of the external world and the perceiving subjects are merely the illusory projections of universal Consciousness (*vijñāna*, also *tathatā* 'thusness'). Although in essence pure, it also functions as the storehouse (*ālaya*) for latent 'impressions' (*vāsanās*) which are the result of, and in turn produce, the illusion of an individual subject and objective reality. Liberation consists in the realization, through meditation (*yogâcāra*, an alternative name of the school), of the pure *thusness* of being or universal Consciousness, which implies the elimination of all subject/object distinction.

vindication. A justification of *induction that seeks to show that, although it may be quite indeterminate as to whether induction will work or not, it is rational to use it because it will work if any method will. The future universe may be regular or chaotic. If it is regular, induction will be the best policy. If chaotic, no method will be applicable so the user of induction will be no worse off than anyone else. *Compare* Pascal's wager.

vitalism. An often elusive doctrine, ultimately inspired by *Aristotle, which holds that the phenomenon of life cannot be fully explained in purely material terms, but that it is something nonmaterial in living organisms that differentiates them from inanimate bodies. For some vitalists, but not Aristotle himself, these vital elements are entities that could significantly be said to survive the dissolution of their organisms (*see* soul; survival and immortality). Following the considerable advances in biological science in the 19th century, vitalists (sometimes referred to as neo-vitalists) such as the biologist-philosopher Hans Driesch (1867–1941) opposed the doctrine of *mechanism which claimed that activities (for example, growth and reproduction) that characterize all living things can be accounted for in terms of physico-chemical processes. According to Driesch, such activities were due to entelechies (see entelechy) defined as autonomous, mindlike, non-spatial entities that exercise control over the course of organic processes. See also Bergson.

void. In Pythagorean cosmogony, the factor in the Universe by means of which units could be separated and distinguished. The notion was denied by *Parmenides, who held that it rested on the assumption of a "not-being". The atomists, in an attempted synthesis of the two views, admitted that "not-being" could not be said to exist. But they claimed that although "that which is" is an absolute *plenum, it is not indivisible but a conglomerate of an infinite number of particles moving in a void.

In later philosophies the question resolved into a distinction between matter and space. Aristotle suggested a definition of void as "place bereft of body". Descartes, in an argument similar to those of the early Greeks, considered the idea of empty space absurd. The subject of *absolute space became the focus of a famous controversy between Leibniz and Newton.

volition. An act of will preceding a physical movement. What is the difference between my arm going up and my raising my arm? The traditional answer is that in the second case the physical movement was preceded by a prior volitional act. This theory comes under fire in Ryle's *Concept of Mind*; among his objections is that, if a volition is a voluntary mental act, and if voluntary acts must originate in volition, then each volition itself must presumably issue from a prior volition, and that from another, and so on, ad infinitum.

Voltaire (pen-name of François Marie Arouet) (1694-1778). French essayist, dramatist, historian, and philosopher, who became one of the major figures of the *Enlightenment. He was elected to the French Academy in 1764 but his writings also involved him in law suits, and he suffered periods of exile and imprisonment. Main philosophical works: *Lettres philosophiques* (1734),

Candide (1759), *Dictionnaire philosophique* (1764).

Between 1726 and 1729 Voltaire visited England, and was strongly influenced both by the philosophical empiricism of *Locke and by liberal English political institutions. This shows in *Letters Concerning the English Nation* (1733), of which his *Lettres philosophiques* was the expanded French version. The work contributed to the rise of liberal thought on the Continent. His largest philosophical work, the *Dictionnaire philosophique*, presented his views on metaphysics, religion, politics, and ethics. Though a deist rather than an atheist, Voltaire was anti-Christian and strongly critical of the clergy. He deplored the despotism of the king and the privileges of the nobility, and recommended the elevation of the merchant classes, fair taxation, and generous support of the arts and sciences. In his satirical novel *Candide* he attacked the philosophical optimism of *Leibniz (which was expressed in the notion that God must have created 'the best of all possible worlds'), insisting that that world includes evil. Deeply concerned with the improvement of the human condition, Voltaire's writings are a call for positive action.

voluntarism. 1. A certain sort of metaphysics (of which Schopenhauer's is typical), that holds that the true nature of reality is will. **2.** In controversies about the nature of history, a theory that attaches too much weight to the human will as a factor in history, and too little to 'objective', that is economic, factors. Marxists often accuse other Marxists of 'voluntarism' of this kind.

voting paradox. A paradox that illustrates a fatal flaw in the attempt to determine the "collective preference" of a community by means of a simple majority voting system. Suppose a vote shows (1) a majority preference for policy X over policy Y and (2) a preference for policy Y over policy Z. It might seem to follow that the community has a preference for policy X over policy Z. But, paradoxically, it need not at all follow from (1) and (2) that the majority prefer policy X to policy Z. Consider an electorate of three citizens, where A prefers X to Y and Y to Z; B prefers Y to Z and Z to X; and C prefers Z to X and X and X to Y. Here conditions (1) and (2) are satisfied, but the majority prefer policy Z to policy X.

W

Waismann,   Friedrich (1896-1959). Viennese-born philosopher. A prominent member of the *Vienna Circle*, he later taught in Cambridge and Oxford. Main philosophical works: *An Introduction to Mathematical Thinking* (first published in German (1936), English translation 1951), *The Principles of Linguistic Philosophy* (1965), and *How I See Philosophy* (1968), a collection of his most important papers.

Waismann defended *conventionalism in mathematics, basing it on human choice of conventions rather than on independently necessary truths. He argued also that our linguistic conventions influence our view of reality; and that the *open texture of our concepts rules out strict *verifiability by observation, even of empirical statements.

weakness of the will. The state of mind an agent is said to be in when he performs an intentional action that goes against his better judgment. That is, it is in his power (or he at least thinks it is) to do action x or action y, and he thinks it would be better to do x, but he intentionally does y. This is also known as incontinence or acrasia. Philosophers from Plato onwards have been interested in this as a problem in morality—what leads a rational man to perform an action he believes to be wrong? But incontinence is also seen as a troublesome paradox for the analysis of intention as a whole, for it is usually assumed that an agent intentionally performs some action x rather than action y only

if he wants to do x more than he wants to do y; and furthermore, that if he thinks, all things considered, that it would be better to do x than y, then he *wants* to do x more than he wants to do y. Incontinent actions would, then, appear to be impossible.

Weber, Max (1864-1920). Influential German sociologist, who argued that explanation in social science and history cannot be of a crude physical or economic kind. In *Die Protestantische Ethik und der Geist des Kapitalismus* (1904-05) (translated in 1930 as *The Protestant Ethic and the Spirit of Capitalism*), he contended that a purely economic or technological analysis could not account for the development of capitalism, but that religious and ethical ideas were of crucial importance, especially Calvinism's rigorous ascetic morality and emphasis upon predestination to salvation or damnation. In his sociological works, such as *Gesammelte Aufsätze zur Wissenschaftslehre* (1922) (English translation, *On the Methodology of the Social Sciences* (1949)), he argued that studies of social phenomena differ from pure science in that they involve conscious human agents who themselves attach sense or meaning to their actions. Thus social scientists need the concept (and practice) of *verstehen*, that is understanding, empathy, or intuition, in order to describe and explain.

well-formed formula. (*pl.* well-formed formulae) See wff.

well ordering. See ordering relation.

Weltanschauung. (German for: world outlook.) Any general view of the Universe and man's relationship to it. Usually the term is applied to a philosophy affecting the practical (as opposed to purely theoretical) attitudes and beliefs of its adherents.

wertfreiheit. German for: *value-freedom.

wff. The standard abbreviation for 'well-formed formula'. It is understood that such a formula will be a sequence of symbols from a *formal language and that to say that it is a well-formed formula is to say that is has been constructed according to the *formation rules of that language. These rules are recursive in nature, that is, they specify which are the sequences of symbols that constitute the simplest (or *atomic*) wffs. They then say what are the permissible ways of forming new wffs from one already given. Such a rule would, for example, take the form 'If '*A*' and '*B*' are wffs, then '*A & B*' is a wff'. By this means a potentially infinite class of expressions is defined by a finite set of rules. Although the definition of a wff is given in purely formal 'syntactical' terms, the wffs of a language are intended to be those expressions that can be interpreted as expressing propositions or propositional functions. Thus a *closed wff* is one that does not contain any free variables (*see* variable) and corresponds to a sentence. An *open wff* contains one or more free variables and thus corresponds to a *predicate.

Whichcote, Benjamin (1609-83). English philosopher and theologian, who, though he published nothing in his lifetime, was the spiritual leader of the *Cambridge Platonists. His sermons (published in selection, 1698) and *Aphorisms* (1703) express a concern with a practical and ethical religion, based on the naturalness and reasonableness of man's aspirations to love and imitate the divine. There is no conflict between reason and faith because it is God who has endowed man with the ability to reason. Hence Whichcote's fondness for the biblical saying, "The spirit of man is the candle of the Lord", and his generally hopeful view of man's capabilities.

Whitehead, Alfred North (1861-1947). British mathematician and philosopher, who, after a full academic career as a mathematician, first in Cambridge (Fellow of Trinity College, 1884-1910), and later in London (Professor of Applied Mathematics, 1914-24), moved to Harvard and a chair of philosophy

(1924-37). Main works of philosophical interest: *Principia Mathematica* (in collaboration with Bertrand *Russell, 3 volumes, 1910-13), *Principles of Natural Knowledge* (1919), *The Concept of Nature* (1920), *Science and the Modern World* (1925), *Process and Reality* (1929), *Adventures of Ideas* (1933).

Whitehead's philosophy is best seen as rooted in the British empirical tradition. In the works (often regarded as his best) on the philosophy of nature, such as the *Principles of Natural Knowledge* and *Concept of Nature*, he developed rigorously the notion of nature as nothing more than that which is observed in perception through the senses. He attacked the "bifurcation of nature" into apparent nature (the world of immediate experience characterized by colour, sound, etc.) and causal nature (the world as science supposedly tells us it is, that is, the world of particles in motion which does not itself really possess colour or sound but somehow gives rise to our perceptions of them). For Whitehead, natural science had to be simply an account of the content of perception, not a speculation about the causes. Influenced by relativity theory, he analysed that content as a four-dimensional structure of overlapping events; he devoted much space and ingenuity to showing how concepts used in mathematics and physics, those of point, line, instant, etc., which are not directly given in experience, can be defined in terms of things which are, that is, simply as certain sets of events, contained within each other "like nests of Chinese boxes", and converging to a certain ideal simplicity of character.

The later works present an all-embracing view of reality in which, very roughly, each of its basic elements, each "actual entity", is essentially a process of self-development, or self-creation, by selection and rearrangement of the material provided by its background— on the completion of which it in its turn becomes material for the self-creations of the next generation of actual entities. The obvious analogy is with the life cycle of plants and other organisms—hence the title 'philosophy of organism'. With a characteristic effort of generalization, Whitehead here proposes to apply concepts which originate in the study of organisms to the interpretation of everything from physics to human psychology. How far he succeeds is, of course, open to question, but the overall result is one of the most formidable attempts in the present century to characterize the concrete reality of the world, rather than the convenient abstractions of everyday discourse.

William of Ockham (c.1285-1349). English Franciscan. Main works: *Commentary on the Sentences*, commentaries on Aristotle's logical writings and on the *Physics*, *Summa Logicae*, *Quodlibeta Septem* (all before 1327), political writings (1333-47), minor logical treatises (1342-8). He studied and taught at Oxford until called to Avignon on charges of heresy (1324). In 1327 he fled in the emperor's service to Munich. He is famous for his two anti-realist theories of universals (*see* universals and particulars). One was of *ficta*, a concept drawn from Aureolus, that is of entities with only intensional being. He later rejected this in favour of Walter Chatton's identification of universals with the acts of understanding themselves. His account of the modes of *suppositio* in terms of descent to singular propositions stimulated 14th-century extensional logic. *See also* Ockham's razor.

Wisdom, Arthur John Terence Dibben (1904-). British analytical philosopher, not to be confused with his cousin J. O. Wisdom. Educated at Cambridge, Wisdom was deeply influenced by *Wittgenstein. In an early series of articles, 'Logical Constructions', which appeared in *Mind* in 1931-3, Wisdom argued a version of the *logical atomism of Russell and Wittgenstein, holding that certain entities (for example, material objects) are no more than logical constructions out of more fundamental elements (for example, sense impres-

sions), and that statements about the former may be translated into statements about the latter. Later works such as *Philosophy and Psychoanalysis* (1953) and *Paradox and Discovery* (1965) are centrally concerned with Wittgensteinian views about the nature of philosophical analysis.

Wittgenstein, Ludwig (1889-1951). Viennese-born philosopher, who studied engineering before going to Cambridge (1912-13) to work under Russell's tuition. After serving in the Austrian army in World War I, he abandoned philosophy for a decade, before being persuaded to return to Cambridge in 1929, first as a research fellow at Trinity College, later as Professor of Philosophy (1939-47). Out of a mass of philosophical writings the *Tractatus Logico-Philosophicus* (1921, English translation 1922) was the only book to appear in his lifetime. Of the posthumous publications the most important are *Philosophical Investigations* (1953), *Remarks on the Foundations of Mathematics* (1956), *The Blue and Brown Books* (1958), *Philosophische Bemerkungen* (1964), *Zettel* (1967), *Philosophische Grammatik* (1969), and *On Certainty* (1969).

Throughout his career, despite the differences between its earlier and later phases, Wittgenstein had an abiding preoccupation with the scope and limits of language, and, in particular, with the consequences for the philosopher of the fact that he is, perforce, a user of a common language, and bound by its limits. In the *Tractatus* he is concerned primarily with language as a representing medium, a means of conveying how things are in the world; he attempts to set out in the most general terms what *must* be true of the world and of language to make such representation possible. The world, or reality, here is simply that which is represented; to equate it, as has sometimes been done, with the sum of our sense data is to write a particular value into Wittgenstein's quite general formulae. There seems to be little reason in principle why, say, a materialist as such should find the *Tractatus* unacceptable. The world, we are told, is the totality of facts, the existence of certain situations, or states of affairs. Facts can be more or less complex, but the theoretical limit of analysis—in practice, it would seem, unattainable—would be atomic facts, which cannot be analysed into simpler facts, and which are mutually independent (that is, the existence of one never logically requires, or excludes, the existence of any other).

The linguistic counterparts of these are atomic propositions which relate to atomic facts as (purported) 'pictures' thereof. The basic conditions of being a picture in this sense are a one-to-one correspondence of elements between picture and thing pictured and a common structure or 'logical form'. (Compare the way in which, in a naturalistic painting of a landscape, we might have dabs of colour, corresponding to the elements distinguished in the landscape, arranged in a way reflecting the arrangement of those elements.) According to Wittgenstein, *all* our propositions consist of such pictures. Admittedly, because of the telescoping and short-cuts of ordinary discourse, most of them do not appear to meet the conditions mentioned. But, in Wittgenstein's view, if they were fully analysed they would emerge as sets of his atomic propositions which do meet them; all propositions are truth-functions of atomic propositions, in the sense that their truth-values are fully determined by the truth-values of their constituent atomic propositions.

One feature that recommended the picture theory to Wittgenstein was the fact that it seemed to account for the versatility of language; once its initial conventions have been established, we can then construct and understand an indefinite range of propositions (see *Tractatus*, 4.026 ff), without the need to introduce any further conventions. He is said to have been impressed by a newspaper report of how, in a law court, model cars had been used to represent the vehicles in a road accident; once it had been established that, say, the red

model was to represent the defendant's car, the black the plaintiff's, etc., an indefinite range of juxtapositions could be introduced without more ado. And it struck Wittgenstein that this, essentially, was how propositions functioned. Certainly it would seem that to account for this versatility of language, we must admit at some point some non-conventional relation between language and the world. But it is much more doubtful whether Wittgenstein's "logical form", which shows itself as common to the proposition and the corresponding state of affairs, is the appropriate relation.

Much of the *Tractatus* is taken up with the apparent exceptions to the picture-theory. These are things that we should ordinarily want to call propositions, but which are not, or do not seem to be, reducible to pictures in the required sense. There are for example, the tautologies of logic and the equations of mathematics, which do not tell us anything about how things are in the world, but do serve to explicate something about our equipment for representing it. Then there are the propositions of the *Tractatus* itself. Wittgenstein here takes the heroic course of admitting that he himself is trying to *say* what can only be *shown*, to stand outside language and the world and describe the relationship between them, instead of simply using his language to talk about states of affairs within the world. Hence what he says is strictly 'nonsensical'. But it may still be illuminating nonsense, in the sense that Wittgenstein's analogies with pictures and musical scores, his comments on logic, etc., may help the reader towards an insight into how language actually functions, and hence arm him against the temptation to misuse it.

For a time Wittgenstein thought that, in the *Tractatus*, he had done all that, as a philosopher, he could do; hence his abandonment of philosophy for other pursuits. Under a variety of influences, however, he came to see the *Tractatus* account of language as, at least, seriously over-simplified in contrast to "...the multiplicity of the tools in language and of the ways they are used…" (*Philosophical Investigations*, I.23). And in his later work the approach is no longer 'Despite all appearances to the contrary this *has* to be the case', but rather 'Let us look and see what *is* the case, what language-users actually do with their language'. Language is now seen as essentially a social instrument, or range of instruments, being continuously developed by society to serve an indefinite variety of purposes, and interacting with all other aspects of the life of that society.

The 'picture' analogy gives place to the 'tool' and 'game' analogies; language is compared to a bag of carpenter's tools, each with its own particular function and technique of use, or with a range of games (tennis, cricket, golf, etc.) each with its own equipment, its own rules, its own criteria of success and failure. And, of course, new tools and new games can be added indefinitely, given the need and the inventiveness. To understand, and assess, any given use of language we have to know what game is being played, and what its rules and objectives are. A linguistic move, like a move on the sports field or at the card-table, is to be seen as a move *within* a particular game, and can only be judged permissible or impermissible, a success or a failure, accordingly. There are no all-embracing criteria of assessment to which we can appeal.

Philosophers have been traditionally inclined to look for simplicity and uniformity where none exist, and hence to ignore the important differences in function between such superficially similar sentences as 'He has a good mind' and 'He has a big head', or 'I have a pain' and 'I have a pound', or 'God made the world' and 'John made the table'. The attempt to assimilate one function of language to another, or to treat one as a paradigm to which others must conform, is, for Wittgenstein, the source of many of our time-honoured philosophical problems. Philosophy (that is, bad philosophy) is what happens when 'language goes on holiday', when it is taken away from its everyday functions. Good (that is, Wittgensteinian) philosophy is, to vary the metaphor, a 'therapy', a process not of offering a new solution to, say, the problems of 'mind-body relations' or 'other minds' as traditionally posed, but of patiently 'assembling reminders' of how a term like 'mind' actually functions in the language-game which is its original home. The aim is to bring out the misunderstandings that give rise to the problems in the first place.

Language, as we have seen, is for Wittgenstein essentially social. In his famous attack on the idea of a 'private language', he tried to show that it would be impossible for anyone to develop such a language, one which it is, in principle, impossible to teach to anyone else. If, for example, someone tried to invent names for his various sensations, so as to keep a record of their occurrence in his private diary, there would be no criterion for distinguishing between the case where he kept his rules for the correct use of these, and the case where he merely *seemed* to keep them—as there always is, in principle, with any use of our ordinary public language. And where such a criterion is impossible, then, according to Wittgenstein, there are no genuine rules at all, and hence no genuine language. If he is right about this—the point has been much debated—then there are important philosophical consequences. The more extreme forms of scepticism, which call in question the existence of anything or anyone independent of one's own mind, are ruled out by the mere fact of the existence of a language in which to formulate them; and, if we think out the implications of there being a whole society of language-users, we are taken a long way back towards a common-sense view of the world.

Wittgenstein devoted a lot of his attention in the later works to examining the workings of our 'public' language for talking about our 'mental' lives, our thoughts, feelings, etc. The range and subtlety of his analyses make summary virtually impossible, but, roughly, we may say that he develops a view distinct from either mind-body dualism or behaviourism. Thus, for example, we do not learn to identify sensations of pain independently of certain patterns of physical reactions (pain-behaviour) and then discover inductively a correlation between the two. But neither is the pain identified *with* the pain-behaviour. Rather, it is identified *by means of* it, so that the behaviour provides logically sufficient grounds for saying that someone is in pain. And hence the idea that other people's pains (desires, thoughts, etc.) are simply inferences from their overt behaviour by analogy with one's own case, and philosophical worries about the weakness of such inferences, arise simply from misunderstanding about the particular way in which mental language functions and the criteria for its correct use.

The success of Wittgenstein's various applications of his therapeutic view to philosophy, is, of course, open to argument and it would be unwise to turn it into a dogma. But treated simply as a policy, a line of approach to be explored in relation to specific philosophical problems, it has undeniably proved extremely fruitful in many contexts, and has been one of the most influential contributions to philosophy, at least in the English-speaking world, in the present century.

Wolff, Christian (1679-1754). German rationalist philosopher and follower of *Leibniz. Of Wolff's many works, the most notable is *Philosophia Prima Sive Ontologia*(1729), an account of Leibniz's ontology. Wolff achieved a reputation for his highly systematic approach to philosophy rather than for any great originality of mind. His primary tenets were that philosophy is strictly the study of essence, not existence, and that all maxims and assumptions are derivable from the Leibnizian principles of sufficient reason and identity.

In Germany, an influential school grew up around Wolff's philosophy, and, though it did not long survive his death, the chief amongst his followers, A.G. *Baumgarten, had some philosophical impact on Kant.

Wordsworth, William (1770-1850). English romantic poet. As a young man, Wordsworth was drawn to the revolutionary ideals in France, and, like his romantic contemporaries, to the radical political theory of *Godwin. From 1795, however, he came under the influence of *Coleridge, who encouraged him in the ambition of becoming a major philosophical poet. With Coleridge, Wordsworth published the *Lyrical Ballads*, to which he contributed the famous preface of 1800, arguing the view that poetry should ground itself in the primary and simple feelings of the common man. From about that time, Wordsworth was engaged on what were to be his epic philosophical poems, *The Recluse* (published only as an extract, 'The Excursion', in 1814), and *The Prelude* (published posthumously in 1850, with the subtitle 'Growth of a Poet's Mind'). These works, while they embody no systematic philosophical views, illustrate Wordsworth's deep *transcendentalism and *pantheism, particularly in respect of the *sublime in nature. *See also* romanticism.

world soul. An analogue, in the world as a whole, of the human soul or mind. Anti-materialist (*compare* materialism) in conception, the idea is founded on the view that the world is productive of life and animation, and can therefore be regarded as itself animate. *See also* animal soul; panpsychism; Shelley.

X

Xenophanes of Colophon (*c.*570-475 BC). Ionian philosopher who appears to have lived after the Persian conquest of his native land as a wandering refugee. His poems attacked the immorality and the anthropomorphism of the established

Homeric religion: "If cattle and horses...had hands...horses would draw the forms of the gods like horses, and cattle like cattle...". This anthropologically oriented negative criticism was linked with a very vague and negatively conceived monotheism. Observations of fossils led him to conjecture that the whole earth had suffered successive inundations. Some methodological fragments have caught the admiration of such successors as Sir Karl *Popper: for example, the statements that "The gods have not revealed all things to men from the beginning, but by seeking men find out better in time", and that our certain knowledge is of exposed error, the rest being at best probable, "opined as resembling the truth". See also Presocratics.

Y

yin yang. Concepts that have permeated Chinese thought since the Warring States period (403-221 BC), when they were incorporated into the cosmology of the so-called Yin Yang school. However, they almost certainly originated in the popular culture of earlier times. These concepts figure prominently in Taoist writings, and also occupy an important place in *Neo-Confucianism, though they are not mentioned by Confucius or Mencius. They are conceived as being the two great opposite but complementary forces at work in the cosmos, and are the basic elements constituting the ch'i (matter-energy) of which man and all phenomena are formed. Yin is the supreme feminine power, characterized by darkness, cold, and passivity, and yang, its masculine counterpart, is representative of brightness, warmth, and activity. Their cosmic influence is codified in the hexagrams of the I-ching (Book of Changes), and in man their equilibrium governs moral and physical health.

Yoga. 1. One of the systems of *Indian philosophy. The old school was closely related to the *Sāṃkhya, but specialized in the cultivation and interpretation of the meditational exercises of yoga. Its teaching was first systematized in the Yogasūtras attributed to Patañjali (possibly 4th or 5th century AD) and the philosophical implications of the sūtras were discussed by Vyāsa (possibly 500 AD) in his commentary. Rather artificially the Yoga has been treated as an independent system; it differs from the Sāṃkhya only in so far as within a common metaphysical framework the emphasis is on meditational (not on rational) insights, and one puruṣa (individual soul) is postulated who was never entangled in the cycle of rebirths, but who otherwise serves no other purpose than as a possible topic of meditation for the unliberated puruṣas. 2. See hatha-yoga.

Yogâcāra. See Vijñānavāda.

Z

Zeno of Citium (c.334-262 BC). Founder of *Stoicism. This Zeno's writings are lost. Born in Cyprus, he studied in Athens before setting up his own school in about 300 BC. The Stoic system of philosophy, though greatly elaborated by *Chrysippus, was essentially Zeno's creation, but the contributions of the two men are not easily distinguished.

Zeno of Elea (born c.490 BC). A pupil of *Parmenides. Zeno's genius is seen in the famous paradoxes, offered as reductions to absurdity of the 'hypotheses' of plurality and motion. His main opponents, the Pythagoreans (see Pythogoreanism), had contended that everything is composed of spatially extended units, and had also been inclined to confuse these with the points of geometry. The four arguments against motion—Achilles and the tortoise, stadium, flying arrow, and moving rows—constitute a supremely elegant set of pairs equally effective against both the contrary assumptions that space and time are and are not infinitely divisible. *See also* Presocratics.

Zeno's paradoxes. The genius of Zeno of Elea was displayed in developing two sets of arguments designed to discredit opponents of *Parmenides of Elea, in particular the Pythagoreans. First, there were about 40 putative refutations of plurality, of which only two survive (*see* millet seed paradox). These are enough to show that Zeno's special target in a general defence of the Parmenidean One was the Pythagoreans' notion that the Universe is somehow composed of spatially extended units, units which they seem to have confused with the points of geometry. Second, there were the four perennially fascinating arguments against motion. Either space and time are infinitely divisible, in which case motion is continuous and smooth-flowing, or else there are indivisible minima, in which case motion is fundamentally cinematographic, proceeding ultimately in tiny jerks. The stadium (or racecourse) and the Achilles attack the first alternative, the flying arrow and the moving rows (or blocks) the second.

(1) In the stadium paradox (also known as the dichotomy paradox) Zeno argues that it is impossible to complete the course. Before you reach the far end, you must reach the halfway point. Before you reach that, you must reach the halfway point to it. And so on indefinitely. If space is infinitely divisible any finite distance must, allegedly, consist in an infinite number of points; and it is, it is also said, impossible to reach the end of an infinite series of operations in a finite time.

(2) If Achilles gives a tortoise a handicap he can never overtake. For when Achilles reaches where the tortoise starts, then the tortoise will have moved on. When Achilles gets there, then the tortoise will have got a little further. And so on, indefinitely.

(3) Objects at rest occupy a space equal to their own dimensions. An arrow in flight at any moment occupies a space equal to its dimensions. Therefore an arrow in flight is at rest.

(4) Solid bodies of the same size moving at the same speed pass each other in opposite directions and another similar mass which is at rest. Presumably, these bodies are of the supposed minimum size and those in motion pass those at rest in the minimum unit of time. But then those in motion must pass each other in less than that putative minimum period.